A LITERARY HISTORY OF ENGLAND

A LITERARY HISTORY OF ENGLAND

—VOLUME I—

The Middle Ages (to 1500)

KEMP MALONE
Johns Hopkins University
ALBERT C. BAUGH
University of Pennsylvania

—VOLUME II—

The Renaissance (1500–1660)

TUCKER BROOKE

MATTHIAS A. SHAABER
University of Pennsylvania

—VOLUME III—

The Restoration and Eighteenth Century (1660–1789)

GEORGE SHERBURN

DONALD F. BOND
The University of Chicago

—VOLUME IV—

The Nineteenth Century and After (1789–1939)

SAMUEL C. CHEW

RICHARD D. ALTICK
The Ohio State University

A LITERARY HISTORY OF ENGLAND

Second Edition

Edited by Albert C. Baugh

————————VOLUME I————————

THE

MIDDLE AGES

The Old English Period (to 1100)
KEMP MALONE

&

The Middle English Period (1100–1500)
ALBERT C. BAUGH

APPLETON-CENTURY-CROFTS
EDUCATIONAL DIVISION
New York   MEREDITH CORPORATION

Preface to the First Edition

The purpose of the work of which the present volume forms a part is to provide a comprehensive history of the literature of England, an account that is at once scholarly and readable, capable of meeting the needs of mature students and of appealing to cultivated readers generally. While the literature of England is commonly thought of as literature in English, it is not likely that any one will quarrel with the fact that some mention is made of writings in Latin and French during the medieval period, at a time when these languages served as vernaculars for certain classes. The Latin writings of the Renaissance and later periods, however, have been omitted for lack of space. Nor will any one object to the inclusion of Scottish and Irish writers who do not belong geographically to England. Custom sufficiently sanctions including them. The original plan brought the history to an end with the year 1939 (the outbreak of the Second World War); but delay in publication caused by the war has permitted reference to a few events of a date subsequent to 1939.

The extent of English literature is so great that no one can hope to read more than a fraction of it, and the accumulated scholarship—biographical, critical, and historical—by which writers and their works, and the forms and movements and periods of English literature have been interpreted, is so vast that no single scholar can control it. A literary history of England by one author, a history that is comprehensive and authoritative over the whole field, is next to impossible. Hence, the plan of the present work. A general harmony of treatment among the five contributors, rather than rigid uniformity of plan, has seemed desirable, and there is quite properly some difference of emphasis in different sections. Thus, there is more of strictly philological matter in the section on Old English literature, and more of political, economic, and social history in the treatment of the Nineteenth Century and After. It is hoped that the approach to the different sections will seem to be that best suited to the literature concerned.

Since it is expected that those who read this history or consult it will wish for further acquaintance with the writings and authors discussed, it has been a part of the plan to draw attention, by the generous use of footnotes, to standard editions, to significant biographical and critical works, and to the most important books and articles in which the reader may pursue further the matters that interest him. A few references to very recent publications have been added in proof in an effort to record the present state of scholarly and critical opinion.

It is a pleasure for the authors of the present volume to record their special obligations. Professor Arthur G. Brodeur has read most of the Old English section. The late Professor Clarence G. Child and Professor MacEdward Leach read the Middle English portion, Dr. Hope Emily Allen the chapters on the Ancrene Riwle and Richard Rolle, Professor William Roach the chapters on Arthurian romance. To these scholars the authors express their warm sense of appreciation.

K. M.

A. C. B.

NOTE TO SECOND EDITION

The reception of the *Literary History of England* has been so gratifying as to call for a number of successive printings, and these have permitted minor corrections to be made. The present edition has a further aim—to bring the book in line with the most recent scholarship. Small changes have been made in the plates wherever possible, but most of the additions, factual and bibliographical, are recorded in a Supplement. The text, Supplement, and Index are correlated by means of several typographical devices. Explanations of these devices appear on each part-title page as well as at the beginning of the Supplement and the Index.

The editor regrets that the authors of Books II, III, and IV did not live to carry out the revisions of those books, but their places have been ably taken by the scholars whose names appear with theirs in the list of collaborators. It has been the desire of the editor, as well as of those who have joined him, that each of these books should remain essentially as the original author wrote it, and we believe that other scholars would concur. Any new points of view, it is hoped, are adequately represented in the Supplement.

A. C. B.

Contents

List of Abbreviations

AJP	American Journal of Philology
Archiv	Archiv für das Studium der neueren Sprachen und Literaturen
ARS	Augustan Reprint Society
CBEL	Cambridge Bibliography of English Literature (4v, Cambridge, 1941)
CFMA	Les Classiques français du moyen âge
CHEL	Cambridge History of English Literature (14v, 1907–17)
CL	Comparative Literature
E&S	Essays and Studies by Members of the English Association
EETS	Early English Text Society, Original Series
EETSES	Early English Text Society, Extra Series
EHR	English Historical Review
EIC	Essays in Criticism
ELH	*ELH*, A Journal of English Literary History
ELN	English Language Notes
EML Series	English Men of Letters Series
ES	English Studies
ESt	Englische Studien
GR	Germanic Review
HLQ	Huntington Library Quarterly
Hist. Litt.	Histoire littéraire de la France (38v, 1733–1941, in progress)
JAAC	Journal of Aesthetics and Art Criticism
JEGP	Journal of English and Germanic Philology
JHI	Journal of the History of Ideas
KSJ	Keats-Shelley Journal
LTLS	(London) Times Literary Supplement
MA	Medium Ævum
MLN	Modern Language Notes
MLQ	Modern Language Quarterly
MLR	Modern Language Review
MP	Modern Philology
MS	(Toronto) Medieval Studies
N&Q	Notes and Queries
NCF	Nineteenth-Century Fiction
PMLA	Publications of the Modern Language Association of America

PQ	Philological Quarterly
REL	Review of English Literature
RES	Review of English Studies
RLC	Revue de littérature comparée
RR	Romanic Review
SAB	Shakespeare Association Bulletin
SATF	Societé des anciens textes français
SEL	Studies in English Literature, 1500–1900 (Rice Univ.)
SF&R	Scholars' Facsimiles and Reprints
ShS	Shakespeare Survey
SP	Studies in Philology
SQ	Shakespeare Quarterly
SRen	Studies in the Renaissance
STS	Scottish Text Society
UTQ	University of Toronto Quarterly
VP	Victorian Poetry
VS	Victorian Studies

BOOK I
The Middle Ages

⤜⤐⤐⤏

PART I
The Old English Period
(to 1100)

I[1]

Folk, State, and Speech

England and the English, state and folk,[2] are not old as historians reckon time. Tacitus set down the English name, it is true, as early as A.D. 98, but the Anglii of the *Germania* [3] were only a Germanic tribe of the Jutland peninsula, politically independent but culturally *part* of a nationality, not yet a nationality in their own right. They won cultural independence and national status by migration. In the fifth and sixth centuries of our era the Angles, like many another Germanic tribe of that day, gave up their old seats and sought land and loot within the bounds of the Roman Empire. If Bede is right, the whole tribe left home in this migration, and parts of at least two neighboring tribes, the Saxons and the Jutes, took ship in the same move.[4] All three tribes settled anew in the Roman province of Britannia, the eastern half of which they overran, from the Channel to the Firth of Forth. The western half held out longer against them, though without help from Rome, who had withdrawn her legions from Britannia one after another until, early in the fifth century, the land was left stripped of troops. Not until the ninth century did Cornwall yield to English arms, and further north the Welsh kept their freedom, more or less, until 1282, over 200 years after the English lost theirs at Hastings. But by the end of the sixth century most of the geographical area now known as England had fallen into the hands of

Migration to Britain

[1] Bibliography: A. H. Heusinkveld and E. J. Bashe, *A Bibliographical Guide to Old English,* Univ. of Iowa Humanistic Studies, iv, 5 (Iowa City, 1931); see also the Old English section (1. 51-110) of the *CBEL,* and W. L. Renwick and H. Orton, *The Beginnings of English Literature to Skelton* (1940), pp. 133-252. Literary history: recent works are E. E. Wardale's *Chapters on Old English Literature* (1935) and C. W. Kennedy's *The Earliest English Poetry* (1943); an older work, S. A. Brooke's *English Literature from the Beginning to the Norman Conquest* (1898). The best treatment remains A. Brandl's *Englische Literatur,* in H. Paul's *Grundriss der germ. Philologie,* 2ed., II. Band, I. Abteilung, VI. Abschnitt (Strassburg, 1908), a work which, in spite of its title, deals almost wholly with Old English; also issued separately under the title *Geschichte der altenglischen Literatur.* Poetic texts: the corpus of Old English poetry was first edited by C. W. M. Grein, under the title *Bibliothek der ags. Poesie;* R. P. Wülcker's rev. ed. of this (1883-1898) is still standard; it is cited sometimes as Grein-Wülcker, sometimes as Wülcker or Wülker; a new collection in six volumes, *The Anglo-Saxon Poetic Records,* edited by G. P. Krapp and E. V. K. Dobbie, begun in 1932, was completed in 1953; we cite it as Krapp-Dobbie. Prose texts: the corpus of Old English prose still wants collecting, though a number of texts have been published in the *Bibl. der ags. Prosa,* the Early English *Text Society* series, and elsewhere.

[2] Political history: F. M. Stenton, *Anglo-Saxon England* (Oxford, 1943); see also R. G. Collingwood and J. N. L. Myres, *Roman Britain and the English Settlements* (Oxford, 1936); R. H. Hodgkin, *A History of the Anglo-Saxons* [to A.D. 900] (2v, Oxford, 1935); Charles Oman, *England before the Norman Conquest* (1910).

[3] Cap. 40; cf. K. Malone, *Namn och Bygd.* XXII (1934). 26-51.

[4] *Hist. Eccl.* I. 15. The *j* of *Jutes* (from Bede's *Iutae*) is in origin a blunder, by confusion of *ı* and *j*. A better form would be *Iuts* or *Euts,* but these forms are current among the learned only.

the Germanic tribesmen, and these, whatever their tribe, had begun to think of themselves as members of a larger unit, a new nationality which went by the English name. The old tribal name *Angl(i)i* in its extended or generic sense, denoting the Germanic inhabitants of Britain irrespective of tribe, first appears in the writings of Pope Gregory the Great (d. 604).[5] The rise of this national name marks the beginnings of English national (as distinct from tribal) feeling.

New Units

By this time, indeed, the tribes no longer existed as such. When the Roman mission which Gregory had sent out reached England in the year 597, the missionaries did not find any tribal organizations of Angles, Saxons, and Jutes; they found a number of kingdoms, each autonomous but those south of the Humber drawn together, loosely enough, through their recognition of the *imperium* or overlordship of the reigning king of Kent. Earlier holders of such a personal imperium had been a king of Sussex and a king of Wessex, and later holders would be kings of various realms north and south of the Humber, until in the ninth century King Egbert would win it permanently for the royal house of Wessex.[6] We know nothing of the political connections of the various Germanic settlements in Britain before the rise of the first imperium, but we have little reason to think that any tribal organization, as such, outlived the migration from Germany. It seems altogether likely that the settlements started their respective careers as mutually independent political units, and that the tribal affiliations of given migrants or groups of migrants had little practical importance even at the time of migration, and soon became a matter of antiquarian and sentimental interest only.[7] No tribal loyalties, therefore, stood in the way of the English nationalism which, by virtue of geographical and cultural community, early came into being. On the religious side, moreover, this nationalism was fostered, not hindered, by the conversion to Christianity in the seventh century: the Roman missionaries organized a Church of England, not separate churches of Kent, Wessex, and the like, and in the year 664, at the synod of Whitby, the Romanizers, led by Wilfrid of York, won the field over their Irish rivals, ensuring thereby the religious unification of all England in a single Church.[8]

Rise of the Unified State

On the political side, it is true, English nationalism could hardly win much ground so long as the various kingdoms kept their autonomy, subject only to the shifting imperium of one or another of the many royal houses. But this particularistic system of government broke down for good and all in the ninth and tenth centuries. In the ninth Egbert set up and Alfred

[5] The Pope presumably had the term, directly or indirectly, from the English themselves. Certainly *Saxones* was the generic term current among the insular Celts, and on the Continent, in and before Gregory's day, and in setting this old and familiar term aside in favor of *Angli,* Gregory must have been trying to conform to English usage (which with good reason might be held authoritative here). The Pope's example was followed by Gregory of Tours and other writers of the seventh and eighth centuries.

[6] Bede, *op. cit.,* II. 5; see also *OE Annals* under A.D. 827. With the *imperium* went the title *Bretwalda* "ruler of Britain."

[7] Cf. J. N. L. Myres, in *Roman Britain and the English Settlements,* pp. 347-348.

[8] See S. J. Crawford, *Anglo-Saxon Influence on Western Christendom* (Oxford, 1933), pp. 48-49; cf. J. L. G. Meissner, *Celtic Church in England after the Synod of Whitby* (1929).

clinched the overlordship of the kings of Wessex, while in the tenth these kings took for title *Rex Anglorum* "King of the English." The other royal houses died out or lost their kingly rank and function; Alfred's followers on the throne won back the Danelaw; the former English and Danish kingdoms in Britain became mere provinces of a kingdom of England; in sum, an English nation replaced the old imperium. The political nationalism which grew up hand in hand with the new nation found focus, naturally enough, in the person of the king, and to this day English patriotism has not lost its association with the crown. But this is not the place to tell the tale of English nationalism in the tenth and eleventh centuries.[9] It will be enough to mention one of its many fruits, the "King's English" or standard written speech which had grown current all over England by the end of the tenth century. In this form of Old English nearly all the vernacular writings of the period were set down, and the scribes, in copying older writings, usually made them conform to the new standard of speech, though they might let an old spelling, here and there, go unchanged.

England, with its national king (descendant of Alfred, the national hero), its national Church (founded by a papal mission and in communion with Rome), its national speech (the King's English), and its old and rich national literature, stood unique in the Europe of the year 1000. No other modern European state reached full nationhood so early. And yet this English nationhood did not come too soon. Indeed, if it had not been reached early it might not have been reached at all, for the eleventh was a century of political disaster. The state succumbed to foreign foes, and for more than 200 years of French rule the only weapon left to the English was the strong nationalism handed down to them from the golden days of the past. But for this nationalism, the English language in particular would hardly have survived as such, though it might have lingered on for centuries in the form of mutually unintelligible peasant dialects, and with the triumph of French speech England would have become a cultural if not political province of France, doomed to a fate not unlike that which in later times actually befell Ireland at English hands. The nationalism which saved England from such a fate owed much of its strength, of course, to the rich literary culture of the centuries before Hastings, a culture marked from the beginning by free use of the mother tongue (alongside Latin) as a medium of expression. To this mother tongue, and to the literature of which it was the vehicle, let us now turn.[10]

English history (as distinguished from prehistory) begins in the year 597. *The* The Roman and Irish missionaries taught the English to make those written *Mother* records from which the historians glean their knowledge of early England. *Tongue*

[9] The tale is told by R. W. Chambers, *EETS*, 186 (1932). lxi-lxxx. See also Chambers, *Man's Unconquerable Mind* (1939), pp. 70-87. Chambers fails to point out that Old English nationalism was summed up and given official expression in the legal formula *an Christendom and an cynedom æfre on ðeode* "one Church and one state always in the land." See F. Liebermann, *Gesetze der Angelsachsen*, 1 (1903). 385.

[10] A standard guide to the language of the period is the *Old English Grammar* of J. and E. M. Wright (3ed., Oxford, 1925).

and the particular records written in the vernacular give us our earliest documentation of the mother tongue. Then as now this tongue went by the
Related English name.[11] Its nearest kinsman was the speech of the Frisians. Closely
Tongues kindred tongues, too, were Saxon and Franconian (or Frankish), the two
main dialects of Low German.[12] The dialects of High German, and those
of Scandinavian, had features which made their kinship to English less close.
English was akin to all these neighboring tongues, and to Gothic, in virtue
of common descent from Germanic, a language which we know chiefly
through its offspring, as it had split up into dialects at a date so early that the
records of it in its original or primitive state are few. Germanic in turn was
an offshoot of Indo-European, a hypothetical tongue which we know only
through the many languages which are descended from it. To the Indo-
European family of languages belonged, not only English and the other children of Germanic, but also Latin (with its offspring, the Romance languages),
Greek, the various Celtic and Slavic languages, Persian, Sanskrit (with other
languages of India), Armenian, Albanian, Lithuanian, Latvian, etc.[13] Here,
however, the kinship is so remote that it is overshadowed by a connection
Latin of another kind: a fellowship, so to speak. Latin, for instance, is only re-
motely linked to English by common descent from Indo-European, but it is
closely linked to English by common participation in European life. The
fellowship between English and Latin, it must be added, has always been
one-sided; Latin has done the giving, English the taking, and this because
Latin, the language of the Church and the vehicle of classical culture, had
much to give and found little if anything that it needed to take.[14]

That English has many words taken from Latin is a fact familiar to
everyone. Such words began coming in even before the migration to Britain
(e.g., *street* and *cook*), and they have kept coming in ever since. Less familiar, perhaps, are the so-called semantic borrowings: native words with
meanings taken from Latin. Two examples will have to serve: *gōd-spell*

---

[11] Throughout historical times the adj. *English* (used in the absolute construction) has been
the regular name for the language spoken by the Germanic inhabitants of Britain. From the
seventeenth century onward, the adj. *Anglo-Saxon* (a learned coinage of modern times) has
had more or less currency as a synonym of *English*; among scholars it was commonly used to
denote the earliest forms of English, but this meaning has never become familiar to the general
public, and most scholars now call the language in all stages by the name which it has always
had among those who spoke it: namely, *English*. See K. Malone, *RES*, v (1929). 173-185.
When qualification by period is thought needful, a suitable qualifying term may be prefixed.
See K. Malone, *English Journal*, College Edition, xix (1930). 639-651. The usual division by
periods gives *Old English* (beginnings to 1100), *Middle English* (1100 to 1500), and *Modern
English* (1500 to present day). Linguistically speaking, this division is not accurate, but all
divisions in the nature of the case are more or less arbitrary.
[12] The chief modern representatives of the Franconian dialect of Low German are Dutch
and Flemish.
[13] The traditional classification here followed is figurative (for a language is no plant or
animal and neither begets nor brings forth offspring). Classification in biological terms, moreover, like any other way of ordering phenomena, stresses some features at the cost of others.
If, however, we bear all this in mind, we may accept the linguistic family tree as a legitimate
device, serving a useful purpose.
[14] Here we must distinguish between classical and medieval Latin. The former took nothing
from English; the latter (more precisely, that variety of medieval Latin current in England)
became more or less colored, in time, by its English setting.

(modern *gospel*), literally "good news," is a translation of Latin *evangelium* (itself taken from Greek), and its meaning is restricted accordingly; *þing* (modern *thing*) originally had in common with Latin *res* the meaning "(legal) dispute, lawsuit," whereupon, in virtue of the equation thus set up, other meanings of *res* came to be given to the Old English word, including the meaning most common today.[15] But the fellowship with Latin affected English idiom and style as well as vocabulary; thus, the Latin *mundo uti* "live" reappears in the *worolde brucan* of *Beowulf*.

The fellowship of English with French began much later (toward the *French* end of the Old English period), but has proved just as lasting, and French comes next to Latin in the list of foreign tongues that have set their mark on English speech. The only other important medieval fellowship was that with Danish (as it was then called) or Scandinavian (as we call it now). *Danish* Here matters were complicated by the kinship of the two tongues. Both Danish and English went back to Germanic, and often one could not tell whether a given word was native English or of Viking importation, so much alike were the two languages. The Scandinavian origin of many of our most familiar words, however, can be proved by earmarks of one kind or another (e.g., *sky* and *take*). The fellowship with Danish, beginning in the ninth century, was at its height in the tenth and eleventh; after that it lessened, and though it never died out it has played only a small part in modern times.

Fellowship with foreign tongues is no peculiarity of English; all languages have connections of this kind, though some are more friendly than others. Such fellowships markedly affect the stock of words (including formative prefixes and suffixes), but as a rule leave almost or altogether unchanged the sounds and inflexions. Their effect on syntax, idiom, and style is hard to assess with precision. In the Old World of medieval times, four great linguistic cultural empires flourished side by side: Latin, Arabic, Sanskrit, and Chinese.[16] The languages of western Europe (whether Celtic, Germanic or Romanic) gave their allegiance to Latin, and English yielded with the rest,[17] but the Latinizing forces did not reach the height of their power in English until the Middle Ages were dead and gone. The medieval Englishman, meekly though he bowed before imperial speech, clung stubbornly to his linguistic heritage.

So much for externals. What of the mother tongue in its own right? Texts written partly or wholly in English (including glosses) have come down to us from the seventh century onward, and by the eleventh their number has greatly grown. From them we learn that the language was not uniform throughout the country but fell into dialects. Our records show *Dialects* four main dialects: one northern, commonly called Northumbrian; one midland, known as Mercian; and two southern, Kentish and West Saxon. The

---

[15] These and other examples may be found in S. Kroesch's paper, "Semantic Borrowing in Old English," *Studies ... in honor of Frederick Klaeber* (Minneapolis, 1929), pp. 50-72.
[16] Greek had a medieval empire too, but it was a mere shadow of its Hellenistic self.
[17] Of all the western tongues, Icelandic alone held out against Latinization.

last of these is abundantly represented in the texts; it served as a basis for standard Old English speech. The other dialects are recorded rather meagerly, but the texts we have are enough to give us some idea of the dialectal distinctions. Other dialects than these presumably existed, but for want of texts we know little or nothing about them. The Old English dialects, unlike their descendants, the dialects of modern times, had undergone no great differentiation, and their respective speakers understood each other with ease. The Old English standardization of speech came about, not from any linguistic need but as a by-product and symbol of national unity: the King's English won for itself a prestige that proved overwhelming.

The Place of Old English

We shall not undertake to give in this history a detailed or even a systematic description of Old English speech. We shall do no more than mark, as best we can, where Old English stands on the road from Germanic times to the twentieth century. Here the classical or standard speech of A.D. 1000 will serve as our basis of comparison, and we shall compare this stage of Old English with primitive Germanic on the one hand and current English on the other. With our terms so defined, the temporal place of Old English is midway between Germanic and the speech of today. But mere lapse of time means little, since the tempo of change varies markedly down the years. Let us look at a few particulars each for itself. And first the matter of differentiation.

Independence

In the year 100, Germanic was already split up into dialects, but these dialects had not yet grown far apart, and the unity of the language was still unbroken. More precisely, the Anglo-Frisian or proto-English dialect had no independent existence, but was merely a regional form of Germanic. By the year 1000 a revolutionary change had taken place. English had become a language in its own right, fully developed and self-sufficient; in the process it had grown so unlike its Continental kinsmen that their respective speakers could not understand each other. No comparable change took place after the year 1000; since that date the language has simply kept the independence which it earlier won. In other words, the differentiation of English from the other Germanic tongues, a process which has been going on without a break for some 1500 years, was of the utmost importance in its early stages, but became relatively unimportant after English won its independence and established itself as a going concern. In the matter of differentiation, then, the fundamental changes took place in the first, not in the second of our two periods—before, not after A.D. 1000.

Simplified Forms

Next we take up the simplification of the inflexional system. Germanic was a highly inflected speech; Germanic and Latin were at about the same stage or level of inflexional complexity. Modern English, on the other hand, has a rather simple inflexional system and relies largely on word order and particles, devices not unknown to Germanic but less important than they are today in expressing syntactical relationships. How far had simplification gone by the year 1000? Among the nouns it had gone pretty far, though grammatical gender did not break down until Middle English times.[18] Among the adjectives, simplification went more slowly: the elaborate double system of adjectival inflexion characteristic of Germanic and kept to this day in German was kept in Old English too, and was not wholly given up until the fifteenth century. Much the same may be said of the demonstratives: *that* in Old English still had twelve forms as against the three current today (*the, that, those*),[19] and *this* still had ten forms as against the two of today (*this, these*). In the inflexion of the personal pronouns, however, the beginnings of the modern three-case system appear as early as the text of *Beowulf*, where we find the datives *me, þe, him* used now and then as accusatives; thus, *him* thrice occurs in accusative constructions (lines 963, 2377, 2828). This use led later to the loss of the personal (and interrogative) accusative forms, the old dative forms doing duty for both cases.[20] The Germanic system of verb inflexion also underwent marked simplification in Old English.[21]

This loss or reduction of many inflexional endings did not occur as a *Stress* strictly inflexional change, but made part of a change much wider in scope, and phonetic rather than inflexional in kind. English shared with the other Germanic tongues a system of pronunciation by which the first syllable of a word was stressed at the expense of the other syllables;[22] these, by progressive weakening, underwent reduction or were lost. Most of the many monosyllabic words in Old English go back to Germanic words of two or more syllables, and most of the dissyllabic words go back to Germanic polysyllables. The tendency to reduce or get rid of the unstressed syllables set in more than once in Old English times; thus, the so-called Middle English leveling of the inflexional endings actually took place in the tenth century, though traditional spelling kept the old distinctions in the texts (more or

[18] Nearly all Old English nouns belonged to one of three declensions: *a*-stems, *ō*-stems and *n*-stems. In the plural all these had a three-case system of inflexion: one form for the nom. and acc., one for the gen. and one for the dat. (Modern English has a two-case system: one form for nom. dat. acc., another for gen.). In the singular, the *a*-stems had a three-case inflexion parallel to that of the plural. (Modern English likewise has a two-case system parallel to that of the plural). The other two declensions, however, had a two-case inflexion of the singular: one form marked the nom., the other the oblique case. (The neuter *n*-stem nouns had a different two-case system: one form for the nom. acc., the other for gen. dat.). Moreover, by the year 1000 the distinction between nom. and oblique had been lost in the singular of *ō*-stems, and tended to be lost in the singular of *n*-stems. The consequent inability of speakers to make case distinctions in these declensions may have had something to do with the Middle English tendency to give *a*-stem inflexion to the *ō*-stem and *n*-stem nouns. At any rate, this tendency existed and was carried through (to the incidental destruction of grammatical gender), and the modern inflexion of nouns is only a somewhat simplified form of the old *a*-stem inflexion. Other Germanic declensions, of which only remnants or traces appear in Old English, were *i*-stems, *u*-stems, *s*-stems, *r*-stems, *þ*-stems, *nd*-stems, and monosyllabic consonant stems.

[19] But the indeclinable definite article *the* occurs in Old English times (notably in annal 963 of the Laud text of the *Annals*).

[20] But the neut. acc. forms *hit* and *hwæt* were kept, and did duty for the dat. as well.

[21] Thus, the passive was lost, except for the form *hatte*; the dual was lost; the three persons were no longer distinguished except in the indicative singular, and even here only in the present tense (in the preterit the second person had a distinctive form, but the first and third persons were identical).

[22] But the inseparable preverbs did not take the stress (e.g., *be* in *becuman* "become"), and the prefixes *be-, for-,* and *ge-,* whether used as preverbs or not, usually lost whatever accent they may once have had (e.g., *forbod* "prohibition").

less) for 200 years thereafter. Nor did the year 1000 mark the end of such changes; the tendency has kept up to this day. It goes with our emphatic or dynamic style of utterance, a style which strengthens the strong and weakens the weak to gain its characteristic effects. The rhythm of English speech has always been apt for emphasis, but has lent itself less readily to indifference. In the quietest of conversations the points still come too strong for a really smooth flow; the dynamic style natural to the language makes itself felt in spite of everything. Perhaps the likewise hoary English taste for litotes has had the function of neutralizing the emphasis with which even an understatement must be uttered. And the quiet low voice which the English take such pains to cultivate may have a like function. In Old English verse the dynamic quality of ordinary speech rhythm was sharpened by alliteration and reinforced by an ictus which (unlike that of Latin verse) never did violence to the natural stress pattern. In effect the verse rhythm was a heightened prose rhythm; by virtue of this heightening, the words of the poet gained in strength and worth.

*Stock of
Words*

Finally we come to the development of the English vocabulary. Germanic was a speech well suited to those who spoke it, but its stock of words fell woefully short of meeting the needs of a civilized people. Many new scientific, technical, and learned terms had to be coined by the English after their conversion to Christianity and their adoption of that civilization which the missionaries brought up from the south. Indeed, the change from barbarism to civilization had marked effects on every aspect of English life, and names had to be found for all the new things that kept pouring in. The English rose magnificently to the occasion. They gave new meanings to old words, and made new words by the thousand. A good many Latin words were taken over bodily, but most of the new words were coinages, minted from the native wordstock whether inspired by Latin models or of native inspiration.[23] This creative linguistic activity made English an instrument of culture equal to the needs of the time. By the year 1000, this newcomer could measure swords with Latin in every department of expression, and was incomparably superior to the French speech that came in with William of Normandy.[24] But the shift from English to French in cloister

[23] On the Old English wordstock, see A. C. Baugh, *History of the English Language* (1935), pp. 75-80 and 101-110. Note also Professor O. Vocadlo's characterization of Old English: "The language of Wessex as it was developed by Alfred and his followers was certainly the most refined and cultured speech among all early Teutonic dialects. . . . with its rich vocabulary, which conformed to a Latin pattern in the formation of native abstract words and was a fit tool even for the subtleties of philosophical and theological thought, [it] was no doubt the only fully developed vernacular language in Europe: the only medieval language which at an early period developed a remarkable nomenclature of science, religion and philosophy out of its own resources" (*Studies in English by Members of the English Seminar of the Charles University*, Prague, 1933, p. 62).

[24] Sir James Murray, in *The Evolution of English Lexicography* (1900), p. 14, puts the matter thus: "In literary culture the Normans were as far behind the people whom they conquered as the Romans were when they made themselves masters of Greece." Not until the twelfth century did the development of French into a literary language get well under way. In other important aspects of culture, too, the English were ahead of the Normans. As R. W. Chambers points out, in his *Continuity of English Prose* (1932), "the Norman conquerors were amazed at the wealth of precious things they found in England—a land which in that respect,

and hall brought about a great cultural decline among the hapless English, and when their speech at last rose again in the world it had been stripped of much of its cultural freight and now turned to Latin or French for words that it would never have needed if only it could have kept its own. By turning to foreign stores the language built up anew its lessened word stock, but at heavy cost. From that day to this it has gone the easy way, borrowing from others instead of doing its own creative work, until its muscles have become flabby for want of exercise, while the enormous and ever increasing mass of foreign matter taken into its system has given it a chronic case of linguistic indigestion.

In sum, the English language became a vehicle of civilization in Old *Summary* English times, but during the twelfth and thirteenth centuries, the great medieval centuries, it lost rather than gained cultural ground, and its remarkable recovery in the fourteenth and succeeding centuries took place in such a way that permanent damage was done. Thanks to this recovery, English has kept its function as a vehicle of civilization, but in so doing it was merely holding fast to an Old English inheritance. Today we carry on, but we owe our cultural tradition to the pathfinding work of the men of oldest England.

---

they said, surpassed Gaul many times over. England reminded them of what they had heard of the riches of Byzantium or the East. A Greek or a Saracen would have been astonished, said William of Poitiers, at the artistic treasures of England" (p. lxx). Again, "English jewellery, metal-work, tapestry and carving were famed throughout Western Europe. English illumination was unrivalled, . . . Even in stone-carving, those who are competent to judge speak of the superiority of the native English carver over his Norman supplanter" (*ibid.,* p. lxxvii). The verdict of one of "those who are competent to judge" reads thus: "in the minor arts the Norman conquest was little short of a catastrophe, blotting out alike a good tradition and an accomplished execution, and setting in its place a semi-barbaric art which attempted little and did that little ill" (A. W. Clapham, *English Romanesque Architecture before the Conquest* [1930], p. 77). See also M. Schapiro, *Gazette des Beaux-Arts,* VI Series, XXIII (1943). 146.

II

Anglo-Latin Writings

Composition in a foreign tongue has always been something of a *tour de force*. Few people ever master a language not their own, and writings done in an alien speech rarely rise above the level of school exercises. Now and then some genius transcends these limitations, but, even so, his work usually remains an aesthetic curiosity, of little consequence in the literary scheme of things. The Anglo-Latin writings [1] which we shall now take up make no exception to the general rule. They have their importance in the history of English culture, but they cannot be reckoned triumphs of literary art.

The custom of composing in Latin came to England with the missionaries of the Church, and the English converts (more precisely, those of them in training for holy orders) learned to read and write Latin as part of their professional education. Christianity, though Jewish in origin, had grown up in the Hellenistic world, and Greek accordingly became the language of the early Church. In the course of the third century, however, this linguistic unity was lost: Greek, kept in the east, yielded to Latin in the west as the masses there gradually gave up their native tongues and took the idiom of their Roman rulers. Into this *lingua franca* of the west St. Jerome translated the Bible; in this common speech his contemporary St. Augustine of Hippo [2] and other Church fathers wrote. By A.D. 597, when the conversion of the English began, a rich Christian literature in the Latin tongue had come into being. The Church made this literature accessible to the converts, along with secular and pagan literature in the same tongue. [3]

We know very little about the state of Latin learning among the English before the synod of Whitby. [4] After that synod (one of the great turning-

---

[1] The most convenient bibliography of Anglo-Latin writings for students of English literature is the section called "Writings in Latin" of the *CBEL* (1. 98-110). But the Anglo-Latin part of this section (it includes Celto-Latin writings as well) is incomplete and badly organized. By inadvertence F. J. E. Raby's *History of Secular Latin Poetry in the Middle Ages* (Oxford, 1934) is not listed in this section, though it is duly listed later (1. 281). It will here be cited as "Raby 1934," and the same author's *History of Christian-Latin Poetry* . . . (Oxford, 1927) will be cited as "Raby 1927."

[2] Jerome died in A.D. 420; Augustine, in A.D. 430.

[3] Some indication of the particular works current in early England may be had from the study of J. D. A. Ogilvy, *Books Known to Anglo-Latin Writers from Aldhelm to Alcuin* (Cambridge, Mass., 1936). We have no like study of vernacular writers, though learned sources for many Old English writings have been suggested, as will appear below, *passim*.

[4] See above, p. 4. From the witness of Bede (*Hist. Eccl.,* III. 3, 27) and from investigations into the sources of Anglo-Latin and vernacular writings, it looks as if the instruction which the Irish gave to their English pupils went beyond the elementary stage. We have no reason to credit the Roman mission, however, with anything more than elementary instruction in reading, writing, and singing.

points in English history) the reigning pope sent Theodore of Tarsus to *First*
England to serve as Archbishop of Canterbury and to make as fruitful as *Period*
possible the victory of the Romanizers at Whitby. With Theodore went
his fellow-monk, Abbot Hadrian, as chief helper in the work. Both were
men of learning, at home in Latin and Greek. They set up at Canterbury
a monastic school which worked wonders. Within a generation England
became the chief seat of scholarship in western Europe, and that golden
age of the English Church began through which the English people made
the greatest of all their contributions to civilization. During this momentous
period England led the world and set the course of history as she was not
to do again until modern times.[5]

The great service which the scholarship of the golden age rendered to us
and to all men was the preservation and transmission of classical culture.
This culture, long in decline, seemed doomed in its ancient western seats,
where barbarization proceeded apace. Luckily it found, first in Ireland and
then in England, a haven of refuge. Here Christianity soon won the hearts
of the heathen, and with the new faith came Mediterranean civilization, of
which the Church had made herself the bearer. In particular, monasticism
flourished, and the monks learned to read and copy the books that kept the
past alive. Further than this most of the monks did not go, but some took
the next step and composed works of their own in the Latin tongue. The
first Englishman of note to do this was Aldhelm; with him we begin our
brief survey of Anglo-Latin writings.

Aldhelm or Ealdhelm (d. 709) [6] was a man of Wessex, a kinsman of the *Aldhelm*
West Saxon king. He began his studies under the Irish scholar Maeldub,
but got most of his training at Canterbury under Theodore and Hadrian.
He gained a remarkable command of Latin, and learned some Greek besides, and even a little Hebrew. His duties as monk, as abbot of Malmesbury,
and finally as bishop of Sherborne did not keep him from doing a substantial amount of writing. He is said to have composed in English as well
as Latin, but his vernacular compositions have not come down to us; presumably they were thought of as trifles, unworthy of written record. For the
same reason only scraps have survived of Aldhelm's rhythmical Latin verse;
i.e., verse done in isosyllabic lines.[7] Nearly all we have of his poetry is in
hexameters, and belongs to the classical quantitative tradition.

[5] See S. J. Crawford, *Anglo-Saxon Influence on Western Civilization 600-800* (Oxford,
1933). See also W. Wattenbach, *Deutschlands Geschichtsquellen im Mittelalter* (3ed., Berlin,
1873), I. 102; L. von Ranke, *Sämmtliche Werke* 3ed., xxxvii (Leipzig, 1907). 11-13; K. Malone,
JHI, I (1940). 292-293; J. W. H. Atkins, *English Literary Criticism, the Medieval Phase*
(Cambridge, 1943), p. 38. The student would do well to read, besides, the chapter on the
golden age in R. H. Hodgkin's *History of the Anglo-Saxons* (Oxford, 1935). The latest study
of these matters is that of W. Levinson, *England and the Continent in the Eighth Century*
(Oxford, 1946).

[6] R. Ehwald, *Aldhelmi Opera* (Berolini, 1919; *Mon. Germ. Hist., Auct. Antiq.*, xv).

[7] See Ehwald, *ed. cit.*, pp. 520-521, where the items are brought together. Ehwald also
includes in his edition (pp. 523-537) five *Carmina Rhythmica* by pupils of Aldhelm: four by
Æthilwald, one by a pupil whose name is not known. For a discussion of these poems see
Raby 1927, pp. 144-145 and Raby 1934, I. 172-174. Rhythmical verse must be kept apart
from accentual verse, of which it was a forerunner. A truly accentual Latin versification
developed too late in the Middle Ages to come within the scope of this chapter.

Aldhelm's major poem is _De Virginitate_ (2904 lines), a versification of a prose treatise of his which bears the same name. He also wrote a number of short _Carmina Ecclesiastica_ (428 lines in all), and 100 versified riddles, done on the model of the 100 _Enigmata_ of Symphosius,[8] but departing from these in various ways.[9] Aldhelm incorporated his riddles into the learned prose treatise which he wrote on versification, a treatise which took the form of a letter to King Ealdfrith of Northumbria, whence its title _Epistola ad Acircium_.[10] In it Aldhelm set forth in some detail the principles of metrics as he understood them, with many examples drawn indiscriminately from classical and postclassical writings, sacred and profane. A few other letters of Aldhelm's also survive.

Aldhelm wrote Latin well, by the standards of his own time. His taste for rare words, involved expression, and stylistic display reflects that of the age, and should not be held against him personally.[11] He had great gifts, but his education proved too much for them. Overawed by the postclassical literary culture which his teachers hammered into him, he took it as he found it and made it his own, without thought of criticism. What else could be expected of a man who was but one remove from barbarism? His writings won the admiration of many (e.g., Bede), and later writers were more or less influenced by him, especially in the composition of Latin and vernacular riddles.[12] The cultural developments in northern England, however, proved more important for Anglo-Latin letters; to these developments let us now proceed.

Benedict
Biscop

Benedict Biscop (628-690), a Northumbrian monk of noble birth, happened to be in Rome, on the second of his five journeys to the Continent, when the Pope made Theodore Archbishop of Canterbury. At the Pope's request, Biscop accompanied Theodore to England, and helped him start his work there, serving two years as abbot of the monastery at Canterbury. After his return to his native Northumbria, Biscop founded at Wearmouth a Benedictine monastery on the Roman model; a few years later he estab-

---

[8] For the text of Symphosius see R. T. Ohl, _The Enigmas of Symphosius_ (Philadelphia, 1928). The editor prints the Latin text and an English translation on opposite pages. In his Introduction (pp. 20-23) he sketches briefly the influence of Symphosius on Anglo-Latin writers.

[9] Thus, the riddles of Symphosius are all the same length (three lines), whereas those of Aldhelm vary greatly in length. Aldhelm's riddles were edited by J. H. Pitman, _Yale Studies in English_, LXVII (1925). The editor gives an English translation in blank verse, and in his introduction discusses Aldhelm's style and influence.

[10] Ehwald, _ed. cit._, pp. 33-204. For an explanation of the curious name _Acircius_, see Ehwald, p. 61.

[11] That this taste was no peculiarity of Celto-Latin writers seems clear. Certainly Aldhelm's training at Canterbury did not teach him the error of his ways. Cf. J. W. H. Atkins, _op. cit._, pp. 41-42.

[12] This influence went with that of Symphosius; see the discussions of Ohl and Pitman mentioned above. Besides the riddles of Aldhelm, we have 40 Latin riddles by Tætwine (d. 734), to which his contemporary Hwætberht or Eusebius added 60 in order to bring the total to the conventional century. Wynfrith or Boniface (d. 755) and Alcuin (d. 804) also wrote riddles; the former must be reckoned a disciple of Aldhelm. On the riddles associated with Bede, see F. Tupper, "Riddles of the Bede Tradition," _MP_, II (1905). 561-572. For a study of wider scope see E. von Erhardt-Siebold, _Die lateinischen Rätsel der Angelsachsen_ (Heidelberg, 1925); the author notes that "the Latin riddles give . . . a picture of an amazingly developed culture in Old England. They . . . bear witness, further, to the amazing amount of reading done by their clerical authors" (pp. 3-4).

lished a sister monastery at Jarrow. These foundations soon became centers of learning unequaled in western Europe. For them, in repeated journeys to Rome, Biscop brought together a library adequate to the needs of scholarship. In his own teaching he applied the lessons he had learned at Canterbury and elsewhere, and his successor, Abbot Ceolfrid, kept up the good work. Under these two masters Bede, "the teacher of all the Middle Ages," [13] and many other Englishmen got a training comparable to that given by Theodore and Hadrian at Canterbury. The English golden age reached its height in the double monastery of Wearmouth-Jarrow.

The Venerable Bede (673-735), the greatest of Biscop's pupils and the *Bede* chief Anglo-Latin writer of the golden age, entered the monastic school at Jarrow when he was seven years old, and spent the rest of his life in this monastery, becoming a deacon at 19, a priest at 30; he performed the regular duties of a Benedictine monk up to his last illness. His writings are too many to be listed here; [14] they include grammatical and critical handbooks like *De Metrica Arte,* scientific treatises like *De Ratione Temporum,* commentaries on various books of the Bible (canonical and apocryphal), homilies, saints' lives, and verse. Many of his books had a wide circulation in medieval Europe and held their own for centuries as the authoritative treatments of their respective subjects. At present, however, Bede's fame rests chiefly on a work of his latter years, the *Historia Ecclesiastica Gentis Anglorum* ("Church History of the English People").[15] This work is our primary source of information about the most momentous period in English history: the period of change from barbarism to civilization. In other words, Bede is not only first among English historians in point of time; he is also first in importance.

The story of the great change found in Bede a worthy teller. The merits of Bede as a historian have often been pointed out and need not be dwelt upon here. In assessing his merits as a writer we must bear in mind that he was first of all the scholar, not the literary artist. He undertook the labor of composition to set forth historical truth, not to provide aesthetic delight. But it remains a pleasure to read the *History*. Bede wrote Latin with the

[13] W. Wattenbach, *loc. cit.*

[14] Bede lists nearly all of them himself at the end of the *Hist. Eccl.* Editions: J. A. Giles, *Works of Venerable Bede* (12v, 1843-1845); J. P. Migne, *Ven. Bedae Opera Omnia* (Paris, 1850-1851), in *Patrologiae Cursus Completus* (Sec. Ser.), xc-xcv (but Vol. xcv is only partly devoted to Bede); *Expositio Actuum Apostolorum et Retractatio,* ed. M. L. W. Laistner (Cambridge, Mass., 1940). See also M. L. W. Laistner, *A Hand-List of Bede Manuscripts* (Ithaca, N. Y., 1943), reviewed by N. Ker, *MA,* XIII (1944). 36-40; and C. W. Jones, *Bedae Pseudepigrapha* (Ithaca, N. Y., 1939). See also R. W. Chambers, "Bede," in *Proc. Brit. Acad.,* XXII (1936). 129-156. For a discussion of Bede's grammatical and critical writings, see J. W. H. Atkins, *op. cit.,* pp. 43-51. For a discussion of his Latin poetry, see Raby 1927, pp. 146-149 and Raby 1934, I. 174-175. The only vernacular poem of Bede's that has come down to us, the *Death Song,* is taken up below, p. 44.

[15] Ed. C. Plummer, *Bedae Opera Historica* (Oxford, 1896), and J. E. King, *Baedae Opera Historica* (Loeb Classical Library, 1930). Both these editions also give the *Vita Beatorum Abbatum* (the lives of the abbots of the double monastery at Wearmouth-Jarrow), the letter to Archbishop Egbert, and Cuthbert's letter on the death of Bede. The Loeb edition gives Latin text and English translation on opposite pages. Another translation: Everyman's Library No. 479, with an admirable introductory essay by Vida D. Scudder. Concordance: P. F. Jones, *A Concordance to the Hist. Eccl. of Bede* (Cambridge, Mass., 1929).

competence to be expected of a gifted man whose life had been spent in speaking, reading, writing, and teaching that tongue. His Latin style was no miracle, *pace* Hodgkin.[16] It lacks the showiness of Aldhelm's style because Bede, unlike Aldhelm, did not care for show. The style, in its strength and simplicity, reflects the man.

Bede included in his *History,* alongside the events commonly reckoned historical, many miracles, visions, and other matters which strike the modern reader as unhistorical enough. Here we must allow for the credulity of the age and, in particular, for the influence of Pope Gregory's *Dialogues.* Yet even here Bede makes every effort to be accurate. He admits wonders only after he has investigated them and found them well authenticated. His standards of verification are not ours, of course. If today a victim of snakebite were to drink down some scrapings of Irish books and get well, we should not conclude that the scrapings had worked the cure. But Bede in accepting this conclusion not only echoed the medical science of his day; he also paid tribute to the sanctity and miracle-working power of the sister island. Certainly no Irishman could outdo Bede in reverence for Ireland. He realized to the full, Romanizer though he was, how much the English owed to their Irish teachers, and he showed himself deeply grateful and appreciative.

Most of the unhistorical matter in Bede's *History* belongs to legend in the technical sense; that is, to hagiography. Besides the incipient or abbreviated saints' lives scattered through the work, Bede wrote saints' lives as such, notably two lives of St. Cuthbert, the shorter in hexameters, the longer in prose.[17] Bede's contemporaries Felix and Eddi also wrote saints' lives,[18] and thenceforth this kind of biography flourished in England as elsewhere in Christendom.[19] Secular biography is exemplified in Bishop Asser's *Life of King Alfred,*[20] but many centuries were to pass before this genre really began to flourish.[21]

One of Bede's pupils, Egbert, became Archbishop of York and there set up a cathedral school which in time eclipsed Wearmouth-Jarrow as a center

---

[16] *Op. cit.* 1. 354.

[17] Here Bede was presumably imitating the fifth-century poet Sedulius, who balanced his *Carmen Paschale* with a prose *Opus Paschale.* Compare Aldhelm's two versions of *De Virginitate,* likewise inspired by the example of Sedulius.

[18] For Felix, see below, p. 75. Edition of Eddi: B. Colgrave, *The Life of Bishop Wilfrid, by Eddius Stephanus:* text, translation, and notes (Cambridge, 1927). As early as 713 some monk of Whitby (name unknown) had written a life of Gregory the Great; it was edited in 1904 by (Cardinal) F. A. Gasquet.

[19] Other hagiographies of the golden age: Æthelwulf, *Carmen de Abbatibus Cellae Suae,* in T. Arnold's edition (*Rolls Ser.,* 75) of Simeon of Durham's *Hist. Eccl. Dunhelmensis* (1882), Appendix 1. 265-294; Alcuin, *De Pontificibus et Sanctis Ecclesiae Eboracensis Carmen,* in Wattenbach and Duemmler, *Monumenta Alcuiniana* (Berlin, 1873), pp. 80-131, and in J. Raine, *The Historians of the Church of York and its Archbishops* (*Rolls Ser.,* 71), 1. 349-398; Alcuin, *Vita Sancti Willibrordi* (prose and verse), in Wattenbach and Duemmler, *ed. cit.,* pp. 35-79, and in Migne, *Patr. Lat.,* c1. 694-724; Willibald, *Vita Bonifatii,* in *Mon. Germ. Hist., Scriptorum,* 11. 331-353 (translation by G. W. Robinson, Cambridge, Mass., 1916); the anonymous *Vita Alchuini Abbatis* in Wattenbach and Duemmler, *ed. cit.,* pp. 1-34.

[20] Ed. W. H. Stevenson, *Asser's Life of King Alfred* (Oxford, 1904). Translations: by A. S. Cook (Boston, 1906); by L. C. Jane (1924).

[21] The first autobiography by an Englishman is the *Vita ... Willibaldi ...* in T. Tobler, *Descriptiones Terrae Sanctae ...* (Leipzig, 1874), pp. 1-55. Willibald died in A.D. 786.

of learning. Of the Englishmen trained at York the greatest was |Alcuin| *Alcuin*
(735-804).[22] The writings of Alcuin have no great literary worth, it is true,
but the man himself remains one of the most important figures in the
cultural history of the West. He owes his importance to the part he played
in the revival of learning which took place under Charles the Great: the
so-called Carolingian Renaissance. Thanks to this revival, the culture of
classical antiquity did not die out in western Europe but was transmitted
to later generations and became the foundation upon which modern civilization was built. But Charles could not set the revival going out of the
resources of his own empire, where only remnants of classical culture survived. He had to turn to Italy, to Ireland, and above all to England for
teachers and cultural leadership generally. And for captain of his little
troop of scholars he chose Alcuin, who reformed and built up the court
school of Charles on the model of the cathedral school at York, and had
a hand in founding other centers of learning, notably the one at Tours,
where he served as abbot. The success of the Carolingian Renaissance was
largely due to Alcuin's able leadership. But no revival of learning would
have been possible, even so, had not the great reform of the Gallican and
German churches, earlier in the eighth century, prepared the way. This
reform was the work of Boniface, another Englishman. To Alcuin and
Boniface, then, we of the West owe so much that they will always remain
major figures in the history of our culture.[23]

While English missionaries and scholars were busy bringing civilization *Second*
back to the Continent. Viking raids were laying low the cultural centers of *Period*
England. During the ninth century the destruction went so far that, in
King Alfred's words,[24] whereas

men from abroad used to seek wisdom and learning here in this country, ...
now, if we were to have such wisdom and learning, we could get them only
from outside. So utterly had book-learning fallen away in England that there
were very few, this side the Humber, who knew how to interpret their [Latin]
service-books in English, or even how to translate from Latin into English a
written message; and I think there were not many beyond the Humber.

The good King made great efforts to revive the learning of the golden age,
but not until the latter part of the tenth century did Latin scholarship
again begin to flourish in England. At that time, under the leadership of
the three bishops Dunstan, Æthelwold, and Oswald, backed by King Edgar,

22 Ed. J. P. Migne, *Alcuini Opera Omnia* (Paris, 1863), in *Patrologia Cursus Completus*
(Ser. Lat. Prior), Vols. c and ci; [W.] Wattenbach and [E.] Duemmler, *Monumenta
Alcuiniana* (Berlin, 1873), sixth volume of P. Iaffe's *Bibl. Rerum Germ.* See also *Mon. Germ.
Hist.*, for poems and letters: poems in *Poetae Latini Aevi Carolini*, i and iv; letters in *Epistolarum*,
iv. See A. F. West, *Alcuin and the Rise of the Christian Schools* (1892); C. J. B. Gaskoin,
Alcuin: His Life and his Work (1904); R. B. Page, *The Letters of Alcuin* (1909). W. S.
Howell, *The Rhetoric of Alcuin and Charlemagne*: introduction, text, translation, and notes
(Princeton, 1941). On the verse see Raby 1927, pp. 159-162 and Raby 1934, I. 178-187, and
for criticism J. W. H. Atkins, *op. cit.*, pp. 51-58.

23 For a brief discussion see Raby 1927, pp. 154-158; see also Atkins, *op. cit.*, p. 61. For
fuller treatment see S. J. Crawford, *op. cit.*, and W. Levinson, *op. cit.*

24 From the Preface of his translation of Gregory's *Cura Pastoralis*.

a monastic reform took place which brought about, among other things, a marked renewal of scholarly activity.[25] The learning of late Old English times, however, was chiefly concentrated in the south and west: at Glastonbury, Winchester, Canterbury, Worcester, and other centers. Monasticism in the north had been so thoroughly uprooted by the Danes that in spite of the efforts of Archbishop Oswald of York it did not come back into its own until the twelfth century.

In this second period of learned activity the Anglo-Latin writings seem to have been chiefly in prose. Frithegoda of Canterbury and Wulfstan of Winchester wrote verse, it is true,[26] but, apart from their compositions, little except prose has come down to us. The prose writings of the period follow the pattern laid down in the golden age, though not without variation. Hagiography continues to flourish.[27] Historical writing proper is represented by the *Chronica* of the ealdorman Ethelwerd [28] and the *Historia Novorum in Anglia* of Eadmer.[29] We also find translations from English into Latin, foreshadowings of the decline in vernacular letters which lay ahead.[30] The most active field, however, came to be that of monastic education and discipline. Here Æthelwold led the way with his *De Consuetudine Monachorum,* but his pupil Ælfric, best known for vernacular writings, composed the fundamental schoolbooks needed for teaching Latin to the oblates. These books, the *Grammar,* the *Glossary,* and the *Colloquy,*[31] gave to the masters in the monastic schoolrooms admirable tools. The *Colloquy* in particular is so good that even today we have nothing better to offer to would-be learners of a foreign tongue. Nothing of comparable merit can be found among the schoolbooks current at this time on the Continent.

[25] Consult D. Knowles, *The Monastic Order in England: A History of its Development* ... *943-1216* (Cambridge, 1940); J. A. Robinson, *The Times of St. Dunstan* (Oxford, 1923). See also F. Tupper, *MLN*, VIII (1893). 344-367.

[26] See Raby 1927, pp. 152-153. Bibliography in *CBEL*, I. 107.

[27] Hagiographies of the second period: B.'s life of Dunstan, in W. Stubbs, *Memorials of St. Dunstan; Rolls Ser.,* 63 (1874), pp. 3-52 (but Stubbs thinks that B. was a Continental Saxon, not an Englishman); Osbern's life of Dunstan, in Stubbs, *ed. cit.,* pp. 69-161; Eadmer's life of Dunstan, in Stubbs, *ed. cit.,* pp. 162-249; Ælfric's life of Æthelwold, in J. Stevenson's edition (*Rolls Ser.,* 2) of the *Chronicon Monasterii de Abingdon,* II (1858). 253-266; Wulfstan of Winchester's life of Æthelwold (prose with appended verses), in Migne, *Patr. Lat.,* CXXXVII. 79-114; Frithegoda of Canterbury's life of Wilfrid (verse), in Raine, *ed. cit.,* I. 105-159; Eadmer's life of Wilfrid, in Raine, *ed. cit.,* I. 161-226; the anonymous life of Oswald, in Raine, *ed. cit.,* I. 399-475; Eadmer's life of Oswald, in Raine, *ed. cit.,* II. 1-59; Eadmer's life of Anselm, in M. Rule's edition (*Rolls Ser.,* 81) of Eadmer's *Historia Novorum* (1884), pp. 303-440; the anonymous life of Edward the Confessor, ed. H. R. Luard (1858; *Rolls Ser.,* 3), pp. 387-435.

[28] *Monumenta Historica Britannica* (1848), pp. 499-521. As Ethelwerd was a layman, one would not expect him to write good Latin; the thing to wonder at is his ability to write Latin at all. So far as we know, western Europe possessed no other Latin-writing layman of royal blood *c.* 1000.

[29] Ed. M. Rule, *ed. cit.,* pp. 1-302. Eadmer's work is well done, but does not live up to its title; it amounts to a life of Anselm, told by a devoted follower of his.

[30] Thus, we have a translation into Latin of the *Old English Annals.* Colman's life of Bishop Wulfstan of Worcester was written in English but survives only in a Latin translation (by William of Malmesbury). See R. W. Chambers, *EETS,* 186 (1932), pp. lxxxiii-iv.

[31] Ed. J. Zupitza, *Ælfrics Grammatik und Glossar* (Berlin, 1880); W. H. Stevenson, *Early Scholastic Colloquies* (Oxford, 1929), pp. 74-102 (Stevenson's book includes other Anglo-Latin colloquies as well); G. N. Garmonsway, *Ælfric's Colloquy* (1931).

Ælfric's other Latin works, though written with characteristic competence, have less cultural importance.[32]

If the golden age is marked by a fusion of cultures, the period with which we are now dealing shows an ever growing predominance of the Mediterranean over the native component in the fusion-product. By the eleventh century English monastic life had come to differ little from that of western Europe in general. The medieval world was fast becoming a cultural unit, dominated by a Church international in outlook and centralized in administration. To this trend of things the Church of England, by her devotion to the Papacy and her missionary efforts in behalf of papal supremacy, had made the decisive contribution, through Wilfrid, Boniface, and a host of other workers in the field. In the cataclysm which was about to sweep the English nation into foreign bondage, one element of the national life stood firm: Anglo-Latin letters. The literature of learning held its own, and even made forward strides, because its linguistic medium and scholarly pattern were already international.

[32] Bibliography in *CBEL*, 1. 91-92.

III

The Old Tradition:[1] Poetic Form

*Speakings
and
Writings*

Few things of man's begetting outlast for long the times that give them birth, and works of literary art share the fate of the rest. The loss is the heavier when (as in Old English) much of the artistic activity takes the shape of *speakings;* that is, literary compositions designed for oral rendition (sung or said) and as a rule not circulated in written form.[2] No speakings, of course, could come down to us unless they happened to get recorded, and even then the chances would be all against their survival, for most of the old manuscripts perished long ago, victims of the years.[3] One might therefore reasonably expect to find the Old English literary records (or what is left of them) made up chiefly of *writings;* that is, compositions designed for circulation in written form. And when the records are studied, this expectation is more than fulfilled; indeed, the student may seek long before he finds any speakings at all. The few that survive are our oldest literary heirlooms, for the literary art of the English (as of the other Germanic peoples) before their conversion to Christianity found expression in speakings only.

Runes

The English of heathen times knew how to write, it is true. They brought with them from the Continent a *futhark* or runic alphabet of twenty-four letters, and to this in the course of time they added several new signs of their own. But the runes were epigraphic characters, and their use was therefore limited to inscriptions, cut or hammered out on hard surfaces (e.g., the pommel of a sword, the sides of a monumental stone, the top or sides of a box). This kind of writing is obviously not well suited to the recording of literary compositions, which (unless very short) need more space than a runemaster would be likely to find available. Moreover, even if a suitable

---

[1] The chief work on the Germanic literary tradition is A. Heusler's *Die Altgermanische Dichtung* (Berlin, n.d. but copyright 1926). For the Germanic background in general, J. Hoops's *Reallexikon der germanischen Altertumskunde* (4v, Strassburg, 1911-1919) is useful.

[2] Speakings are also known as "oral literature," a subject treated at length by H. M. and N. K. Chadwick, *The Growth of Literature.* The actual and hypothetical speakings of Old English are discussed in Vol. 1 of this work (Cambridge, 1932). The authors, however, take for speakings many compositions which others interpret as writings.

[3] Only eight Old English MSS with much vernacular poetry in them have survived. These are the Corpus MS, more precisely MS CCCC 201, at Corpus Christi College, Cambridge (whence the abbreviation CCCC); the so-called Paris Psalter, or MS Fonds Latin 8824 of the Bibliothèque National in Paris; the Vercelli Book, or Codex cxvii of the cathedral chapter library at Vercelli in northern Italy; the Exeter Book, preserved in the library of Exeter Cathedral; MS Junius 11 (often called the Cædmon MS) at the Bodleian Library, Oxford; and three MSS in the Cotton collection at the British Museum: Vitellius A xv (2nd MS, the Nowell or *Beowulf* codex), Otho A vi (the Boethius MS), and Tiberius B 1. Nearly all these MSS, moreover, have come down in a more or less damaged or mutilated state.

hard surface could be found, it would hardly be used to put a poem on unless there were some very special reason for making such a record. Be it added that runemasters were few and far between, and presumably drew good pay for cutting an inscription; in other words, epigraphic writing was expensive. The poets, for their part, would naturally be interested in making their compositions known to the public (i.e., in uttering them, or having them uttered, before audiences), not in making records of them which few would see and fewer could read. Certainly no English poems of heathen times have come down to us in the form of runic inscriptions, and we have no reason to think that such poems were ever so recorded in English (though Scandinavian cases of the kind are known).

With the introduction of Christianity a great change took place. The missionaries brought parchment, pen and ink, and the custom of writing literary compositions down. They also brought the Roman alphabet.[4] The *The* English futhark, epigraphic though it was in origin and history, might *Roman* perfectly well have been used for writing with pen and ink on parchment, *Alphabet* but the foreign missionaries and their English pupils associated the Roman alphabet with this kind of writing and used it, not only in copying Latin texts, but also in making English texts. Yet the old runes were not given up for centuries. They were kept alongside the new letters, and the coexistence of two kinds of writing naturally led to overlapping. On the one hand, letters might be used in inscriptions; on the other, runes might be used in manuscripts. The two runes *thorn* and *wynn,* indeed, were added to the alphabet, as symbols for sounds wanting in postclassical Latin but common in English. And the new practice of recording literary compositions had its effect on native epigraphy: thus, the *Dream of the Rood* won epigraphic as well as manuscript record.[5]

In Old English times the Church monopolized the production of manu- *MSS* scripts. A layman might know how to read; he might even be an author (like King Alfred). But it would hardly occur to him to undertake the work of a scribe, any more than it would occur to the ordinary reader or author of today to undertake the work of a printer. The making of manuscripts was in the hands of the Church because the art or craft of writing on parchment with pen and ink was part of the professional equipment of the well-trained cleric, and of him alone. And the monopoly was strengthened by the workings of supply and demand. The Church made manuscripts chiefly though not wholly for her own use; the readers of the day were mostly clerics. Old English literature as we have it (not as it was) therefore reflects the tastes and professional interests of the clergy; from the MSS we get a one-sided picture of the literary art of those days. Poems that the

[4] Most of the Old English MSS were written in the so-called insular hand, a minuscule script developed by the Irish out of half-uncial and brought to England by Irish missionaries in the seventh century. Toward the end of the Old English period the insular hand lost favor, and the so-called Caroline minuscule script, already dominant on the Continent, became fashionable in England as well.

[5] Runes were used for some alliterative verses inscribed on the Franks Casket (eighth century?). Text in Krapp-Dobbie, VI. 116.

clerics for any reason disliked or disapproved of did not get recorded, unless they happened to strike the fancy of some nonconformist scribe or anthologist who had the courage of his heterodoxy. Moreover, since little space was available, items thought of as trivial or as less important stood little chance of inclusion in a MS miscellany. Few things in lighter vein could be expected to come down to us under such conditions, and in fact the tone of the extant literary monuments is prevailingly serious and edifying.

Authors   Departures from the normal pattern we owe, no doubt, to the likes and dislikes of individual makers or takers of MSS. In many cases pride of authorship may have played a part; certainly a clerical author had ways of getting his compositions written down, even if he did not write them down himself, and the bulk of what we have was presumably composed as well as written down by clerics. A few compositions seem wholly secular, and two of them (*Wife's Lament* and *Eadwacer*) purport to be by women. But even here we cannot be certain of lay authorship; in every period of English literature clergymen have composed works secular enough in tone and spirit, and a male author might perfectly well make a woman his mouthpiece. The case is otherwise when the composition is definitely heathen (rather than secular); here clerical authorship must be ruled out. Unluckily no compositions of this kind, on the literary level, have come down to us, except a few spells (or charms), and most of these, in their recorded form, show more or less of a Christian coloring. On the other hand, we cannot safely presume clerical authorship of every work religious in tone or subject. Cædmon was a farmhand (Hild made him a monk *after* God had made him a poet), and other religious pieces besides his may well have been composed by men who had never taken holy orders or monastic vows. Our uncertainties are the greater since in most cases we do not know so much as the name of the author of a given work, and even if we happen to know the author's name we may be little the wiser; thus, our knowledge of the poet Cynewulf is limited to what we can glean from his poems. This want of biographical information, however, need not disturb us overmuch. Literary art in Old English times was highly traditional, and the personal history of the author did not come out in his compositions so markedly as it does in times when originality rather than mastery of a conventional mode wins the prizes.

Old English writings might be in prose or verse; speakings were restricted to verse, in early times at least.[6] We set the prose aside for the time being. The verse, writings and speakings alike, was regularly composed in the alliterative measure that had come down to the English from their Germanic forefathers. Before taking up the poetic kinds (or genres) cul-

[6] It seems unlikely that the English of heathen times cultivated the prose speaking or anecdote as a literary art-form; certainly we have no evidence of the existence of such an art-form then, though it may have developed in later times. See C. E. Wright, *The Cultivation of Saga in Anglo-Saxon England* (Cambridge, 1939), and K. Malone, *English Studies*, xxiii (1931). 110-112.

tivated in this measure, it will be needful to consider the measure itself, and the style that went with it.

Old Germanic verse makes many problems for the prosodist, and none of the methods of scansion proposed need be taken as definitive.[7] Here we shall deal briefly with the main points. The rhythm of the verse grew naturally out of the prose rhythm (as we saw above), by a process of metrical heightening and lowering. A metrically heightened syllable is called a *lift* (German *hebung*); a metrically lowered syllable, a *drop* (German *senkung*). Only a syllable that took or might take a main stress in the prose rhythm was subject to metrical heightening; in the same way, only a syllable that lacked or might lack stress in the prose rhythm was subject to metrical lowering. We do not know just how the metrical heightening and lowering were brought about, but time as well as stress played a part, and such verse as was sung or chanted necessarily made use of pitch patterns different from those of ordinary speech. The metrical heightening might be reinforced by alliteration[8] or rime, giving a *major* lift. A lift not so reinforced is a *minor* lift. The basic metrical unit was the short verse, made up of a varying number of syllables, at least one of which was a lift. Usually the short verse had two lifts. Such a verse might stand alone or in series. We illustrate with a passage from a legal text, *Hit Becwæð:*[9]

Short Verse and Line

ne plot ne ploh,	nor plot nor plowland,
ne turf ne toft,	nor sod nor site,
ne furh ne fotmæl,	nor furrow nor foot-length,
ne land ne læse,	nor tillage nor pasturage,
ne fersc ne mersc,	nor fresh [water] nor marsh,
ne ruh ne rum,	nor rough [land] nor open [land],
wudes ne feldes,	of wood nor of field,
landes ne strandes,	of land nor of strand,
wealtes ne wæteres.	of wold nor of water.

Here we have nine short verses in series. The first six verses make a group, and the last three verses make another group; grouping by twos (giving long verses or *lines*) does not occur in this passage. The verses are not linked one to another by alliteration; each verse is a closed system so far as alliteration goes. Six verses have alliteration, two have rime, and one dispenses with both these aids.

Passages like that from *Hit Becwæð* were exceptional in Old English.

---

[7] A recent study: J. C. Pope, *The Rhythm of Beowulf* (1942). Earlier studies: E. Sievers, *Altgermanische Metrik* (1893); A. Heusler, *Deutsche Versgeschichte* I (1925). See also K. Malone, *ELH*, VIII (1941). 74-80.

[8] Two syllables are said to alliterate if each begins with the same sound. But in Old English verse only lifts were included in an alliterative pattern. Morover, the consonant combination *sk* (*sc*) for alliterative purposes was reckoned a single sound, and alliterated with itself only; similarly with the combinations *st* and *sp*. On the other hand, all vowels and dipthongs, for alliterative purposes, were reckoned the same sound.

[9] F. Liebermann, *Die Gesetze der Angelsachsen*, I (1903). 400. The text was also printed by F. Grendon, *Jour. of Amer. Folk-Lore*, XXII (1909). 179-180. The title *Hit Becwæð* "[he] bequeathed it" comes from the first two words of the text; compare *Habeas Corpus* and the like.

Ordinarily the short verses were grouped by twos, and a given verse occurred as the *on-verse* (first half) or the *off-verse* (second half) of a line. Here alliteration could not be dispensed with, for the line was an alliterative unit. A short verse included in a line is commonly called a *half-line*. A good example of an Old English line of poetry is *Beowulf*, 1725,

> hu mihtig God   manna cynne
> how mighty God to mankind.

Here *hu mihtig God* is the on-verse, *manna cynne* the off-verse. The two halves of the line are bound together by alliteration: the stave (i.e., the alliterating sound) is *m*. The line has four lifts, two in each half; two of the lifts are major, two are minor. The second and third lifts have no drop between them, but they have a pause between them which separates them more sharply than a drop could do. A more unusual (though not rare) type is *Beowulf*, 2987,

Lifts

> heard swyrd hilted, ond his helm somod
> hard sword hilted, and his helm besides.

Here the two halves are doubly bound by alliteration: *heard, hilted* and *helm* are linked by the *h*-stave, *swyrd* and *somod* by the *s*-stave. There are five lifts: three in the on-verse, two in the off-verse. The first three lifts are juxtaposed, and so are the last two. All the lifts are major. Yet a third type is *Beowulf*, 2995,

> landes ond locenra beaga;   ne ðorfte him ða lean oðwitan
> of land and linked rings;   he needed not to blame him for those rewards.

Here we have six lifts, three in each half-line. Three lifts are major, three minor. Each lift is accompanied by one or more drops. Many other varieties occur, but the fundamental features of the line remain the same.

Sievers, Heusler, Pope

It is easier to determine the lift-pattern of a line than to divide its half-lines into feet (or measures). Here it is customary to distinguish between the half-lines of normal length (as in *Beowulf*, 1725) and so-called swollen or abnormally long half-lines (as in *Beowulf*, 2995). According to Sievers, a normal half-line had two feet; a swollen half-line, three feet. According to Heusler and Pope, however, each half-line, whether normal or swollen, had two feet. Heusler recognized only one kind of foot: this began with a main stress and included also a subordinate stress. Sievers, however, recognized four kinds of feet. To these he gave no names, but we shall call them classes 1, 2, 3, and 4. In class 1 (e.g., *drýhten* "lord") the stress came at the beginning; in class 2 (e.g., *begóng* "circuit") the stress came at the end; in class 3 (e.g., *féa* "few") the foot was monosyllabic; in class 4 (e.g., *wél-þùngen* "excellent") the foot was polysyllabic, with initial main stress and medial or final subordinate stress.[10] Both Heusler and Sievers began

---

[10] Here the acute accent marks main stress; the grave, subordinate stress. Sievers did not include in his system a polysyllabic foot with initial or medial subordinate stress and final main stress: e.g., *fùl arǽd* "quite inexorable" (*Wanderer* 5).

the half-line, on occasion, with an *onset* of one or more syllables reckoned as anacrusis: a kind of running start that belonged indeed to the half-line but made no part of the podic pattern. For Heusler this pattern was the same in every foot: two beats to the measure, whatever the number of syllables in the foot. The first or stronger beat coincided with the main stress of the prose rhythm. The second or weaker beat coincided with the subordinate stress of the prose rhythm, if such a stress occurred; otherwise, the weaker beat fell on an unstressed syllable, or on a pause (metrically a rest) in the prose rhythm, and served to heighten the syllable or the rest as the case might be. We illustrate Heusler's system of scansion with the on-verse of *Beowulf*, 1173:

> beo wið Geatas glæd   be kind to the Geatas.

Here *beo wið* made the onset, *Geatas* the first foot, and *glæd* the second foot. The stronger beats fell on the alliterating syllables. The weaker beat of the first foot fell on the ending of *Geatas;* that of the second foot, on the rest after *glæd*. For Sievers the half-lines fell into five types. In type *A*, both feet were of class 1; in type *B*, both were of class 2; in type *C*, the first was of class 2, the second was of class 1; in type *D*, the first was of class 3, the second was of class 4; in type *E*, the first was of class 4, the second was of class 3. Examples of these types follow, all taken from on-verses of *Beowulf*. The onset is set off by double diagonals; the feet are divided by single diagonals.

A 1987 hu // lómp eow on / láde	how went it with you on the road?
B 1939 þæt hit scéa / denmǽl	that it the damascened sword
C 1192 him was fúl / bóren	the cup was borne to him
D 2705 for // wrát / Wédra hèlm	The Weders' lord cut through
E 1160 gléomànnes / gýd	the gleeman's song.

Pope's system of scansion may be described as a modification of Heusler's. According to Pope, each half-line had two feet, sung or chanted in 4/8 time (normal verse) or 4/4 time (swollen verse). The first foot of a half-line might be heavy or light. The second foot was regularly heavy. The light foot of Pope answers to the onset of Heusler; its lifts (one main and one subordinate) were both weak, and were excluded from the alliterative pattern of the line. We illustrate with *Beowulf*, 264a:

> gebàd wíntra wòrn   he lived many years.

Here *gebad* makes the first foot, *wintra worn* the second. The first foot is light; it begins with a rest beat which takes the main stress. The second foot is heavy; it has *two* major lifts.

The systems of Sievers, Heusler, and Pope are outlined here for the information of the reader, but the student will do well enough in reading if he follows the natural rhythm of the lines, with due heed given to the lift-patterns and in particular to those syllables which the poets by alliteration and rime marked for heightening.

We have already seen that the short verse, the basic metrical unit, usually occurred by twos—that is, in *lines,* the two parts of which were linked by alliteration. Old English verse in all periods was almost exclusively *linear* (that is, made up of lines). In the oldest linear verse the end-stopped style prevailed: every line ended with a syntactical pause and every sentence made either a line or a couplet (i.e., a two-line unit). This pre-classical style of composition was kept, almost intact, in the mnemonic parts or thulas (i.e., metrical name-lists) of *Widsith,* where one sentence runs to six lines but all the others make either a single line or a couplet each. The *Leiden Riddle* likewise was done (though with less strictness) in the old style, and many one-line and two-line units occur in the spells. Otherwise, only relics of the pre-classical style may be found in the monuments.[11] Formulas like *Beowulf,* 456,

> Hroðgar maþelode, helm Scyldinga
> Hrothgar spoke, the helm of the Scyldings,

seem to reflect such a style, and other one- or two-line formulas occur in the laws and elsewhere. One might have expected to find end-stopping used a good deal in the gnomic verses, but here the clerical writers have given us the traditional material in remodeled form.[12] A few pieces of gnomic wisdom, however, have come down to us in lines or couplets. *Exeter Gnomics,* 158,

> licgende beam læsest groweð
> a fallen tree grows least

may serve to illustrate the one-line gnomic, while *Age mec,* 117-118,

> biþ þæt selast þonne mon him sylf ne mæg
> wyrd onwendan þæt he þon wel þolige
>
> that is best, when one himself cannot
> amend his fate, that he then put up with it

exemplifies the two-line gnomic. Somewhat similar in style is the linear formula of consolation used six times in *Deor.* Such formulas, nevertheless, regularly appear in a setting dominated by the run-on style of linear composition. In general, a plurilinear unit of classical Old English poetry was held together, not by uniformities of rhythmical or alliterative pattern, nor yet by uniformities of grouping (i.e., strophic structure), but by the use of run-on lines.

Yet the classical style grew out of the older, end-stopped style of composition, and kept what could be kept of the earlier technic. In the matter of plurilinear units the poverty of the old style was marked: only the two-line unit or couplet existed. The richness of the classical style in plurilinear units is no less marked: we find many such units of three, four, five, six, or

---

[11] The *Riming Poem* relies on rime rather than syntax to mark its three quatrains, 21 couplets and 33 single lines as separate and distinct units, and can hardly be taken as a survival or revival of the old end-stopped style of composition.

[12] See A. Heusler, *Zeitschrift des Vereins für Volkskunde,* XXVI (1916). 52.

seven lines; indeed, there was no limit to the number of lines permissible in making such a unit. This great change was brought about with the least possible disturbance to the old order. We illustrate with *Beowulf*, 639–641:

> Ðam wife þa word wel licodon,
> gilpcwide Geates. Eode goldhroden
> freolicu folccwen to hire frean sittan.

> To that woman those words were pleasing,
> the proud speech of the Geat. She went, gold-adorned,
> the noble folk-queen, to sit by her lord.

Here we have a three-line unit, made up of two sentences, each a line and a half long. Sentences of this length were forbidden to the oldest poets, but it would have been easy for them to say the same thing in two one-line sentences, as follows:

> Ðam wife þa word wel licodon.
> Folccwen eode to hire frean sittan.

These lines bring out, besides, the starkness of the old style. It may well have been a wish to make this style less bare which led to the expansion of the sentences beyond the linear limits; if so, the new plurilinear units were a mere by-product of a process set going for reasons unconnected with plurilinear structure.

In this connection we distinguish two kinds of run-on line. In the first, *Run-On* the sentence goes on to the next line without a syntactical pause; in the *Style* second, it goes on with a syntactical pause. The second kind of run-on line has obviously kept something of the old end-stopped style, and presumably grew out of the linear sentence. We further distinguish three stages in the development of the run-on style. The early stage is exemplified in the amnemonic parts of *Widsith* (the mnemonic parts, as we have seen, exemplify the end-stopped style). Here the plurilinear units vary in number of lines, but this variation is held within comparatively narrow limits: no unit longer than nine lines occurs. All the natural divisions of the poem end with a line; not one ends with an on-verse (i.e., in the middle of a line). Single lines and couplets make a respectable proportion of the whole. Most of the run-on lines are of the second kind mentioned above; that is, they end with a syntactical pause, though not with a full stop. *Beowulf* may serve to illustrate the middle stage of the run-on style. Here some of the plurilinear units are of great length; their length may be so great, indeed, that they no longer can be felt as units and include diverse matters. Single lines and couplets are infrequent. The fits (or cantos, as some prefer to call them) all end with a line, but some of the natural divisions end with an on-verse: thus, the Finn and Ingeld episodes, and one of the speeches.[13] Six of the speeches begin with an off-verse. *Judith* exemplifies the late stage of the run-on style. Here one can hardly speak of plurilinear units at

---

[13] Line 389. But here the text seems to be defective.

all, or indeed of clean-cut units of any kind, apart from the fits. If we follow the punctuation of Wülcker, only 11 of the 350 lines end with a full stop, and three of these mark the end of a fit. Since the sentences usually begin and end in the middle of a line, the syntactical and alliterative patterns rarely coincide at any point, and the matter is presented *en masse,* so to speak. The verses give the effect of a never-ending flow, but this continuous effect is gained at a heavy structural cost.[14]

Variation   So far as one can tell, the technic of adornment or elaboration was essentially the same in pre-classical and classical poetry. The starkness of the pre-classical style went naturally with its end-stopped lines, which left little room for ornamentation, but any room left did not fail to be used. Sheer adornment, it is true, may have been wanting in the oldest poetry: equivalents and attributives may have been put in, first of all, for the sake of the additional information which they gave. But if this was their origin, their original function soon became secondary. The use of equivalents for poetical purposes is technically known as *variation.* We illustrate, first, with a few linear formulas. In *Beowulf,* 3076,

> Wiglaf maðelode, Wihstanes sunu,

the on-verse gives us needful information: namely, that the next passage is to be a speech by Wiglaf. The off-verse may be said to give us further information about the speaker, but since this same information had been given to us earlier (in line 2602) the chief function of the off-verse is hardly informative but rather poetic or (if you will) stylistic. More precisely, since we know already that Wiglaf is Wihstan's son, the off-verse serves primarily to repeat the subject in variant form, and, technically speaking, *Wihstanes sunu* is a variation of *Wiglaf.* The repetition includes the predicate as well (for *maðelode* is to be understood after *Wihstanes sunu*), but not in variant form; not formally, indeed, at all. We may therefore put the line into modern English as follows:

> Wiglaf spoke, the son of Wihstan [spoke].

It will be seen that the variation, though appositive on the face of it, is felt rather as a repetition that involves the sentence as a whole. The term *apposition* therefore does not adequately describe the device, and the use of a special term *variation* seems quite in order. In *Widsith,* 1,

> Widsið maðolade, wordhord onleac,

the off-verse repeats the predicate (not the subject) in variant form, and we may put the line into current speech as follows:

> Widsith spoke, [he] unlocked the word-hoard.

Here the variation can hardly be said to give us any further information, and its function is strictly poetic or stylistic.

---

14 In this history a poem in the run-on style the stage of which is not specified may be presumed to belong to the middle stage. See, further, K. Malone, *RES,* xix (1943). 201-204.

In both the examples which we have considered, the variation may be called *inner,* since it varies something already expressed in the same sentence. In *Beowulf,* 360,

> Wulfgar maðelode to his winedrihtne,

we have a case of *outer* variation: *his winedrihtne* "his lord" varies something already expressed, indeed, but not in the same sentence; we know only from the context who Wulfgar's lord is. In outer variation no parallelism of grammatical construction is to be expected as between the variation and the thing varied. Even in inner variation, indeed, such parallelism need not be thoroughgoing. In *Beowulf,* 1458,

> þæt wæs an, foran, ealdgestreona,

the adverb *foran* varies the adjective *an,* and the line means "that was unique, [that was] to the fore, among old treasures." In *Beowulf,* 2377-2378,

> hwæðre he him on folce freondlarum heold,
> estum, mid are, oð ðæt he yldra wearð,

"but he backed him up, in the tribe, with friendly teachings, [he backed him up] with kindnesses, [he backed him up] with help, until he grew older," the prepositional phrase *mid are* varies the simple case-forms *freondlarum* and *estum.* Here the variants, though loosely synonymous, are not identical in meaning (a state of things often found in the technic of variation). But more nearly synonymous variants may differ in grammatical construction. Thus, in *Andreas,* 1074b-1076,

> him seo wen gelah,
> syððan mid corðre carcernes duru
> eorre æscberend opene fundon,

"that expectation played them false when the company, the angry spearmen, found the doors of the prison open," the prepositional phrase *mid corðre* varies the nominative plural *æscberend* (here we have also a case in which the variation precedes the thing varied). Such variations in *mid* (or in the simple dative) presumably arose out of ordinary accompaniment: *A with B* was another way of saying *A and B.* When a variation happened to be almost or altogether identical in meaning with the thing varied the machinery of accompaniment might still be used, even though in such cases this machinery perforce lost its proper meaning and became a mere form of words.

Stereotypes of another kind were the *kennings,* a characteristic feature of *Kennings* Old Germanic poetical diction. These arose as variations, but in many cases became so familiar that they could be used without previous mention of the thing varied. A kenning may be described as a two-member (or two-term) circumlocution for an ordinary noun: such a circumlocution might take the form of a compound, like *hronrad* "sea" (literally "riding-place of the whale"), or of a phrase, like *fugles wynn* "feather" (literally "bird's joy").[15] Alongside the kenning we find the *heiti,* a one-term sub-stitute for an ordinary noun: e.g., *ash* or *wood* in the sense "spear" (the weapon-name being varied in terms of material, like *iron* for "sword"). The heiti differed from the kenning in that it was simplex, not composital or phrasal, but it resembled the kenning in that it arose as a variation. In their use of kenning and heiti the English poets showed a characteristic classical restraint. These stylistic features did not have in England the luxuriant growth that they had in Iceland (whence come their names). One may note in passing that the circumlocutions for verbs, like *grundwong ofgyfan* "die" (literally "give up the earth"), were markedly fewer in number than those for nouns, and did not give rise to a technical term parallel to *kenning.*[16]

Poetic adornment might also take attributive form. The adjective in such a phrase as *fealu flod* "fallow flood" is not without descriptive value and presumably came into use, as part of the phrase, because it had descriptive value, but it early became a standing or conventional poetic epithet by virtue of frequent use in such phrases. Many standing expressions like *fealu flod* may be found in Old English poetry. Thus, a *þeoden* "prince" is commonly and conventionally illustrious: he is a *mære þeoden.* The device is not limited to poetry, of course, but the poets made much use of it and not a few expressions of the kind belong definitely to poetic diction.

Poetical Diction

In general it may be noted that the vocabulary and phraseology of poetry differed greatly from that of prose. Words and phrases may be marked as poetical by occurrence, dialectal form, or both. Thus, the word *mece* "sword" is doubly marked: it does not occur in prose (apart from glosses) and its dialectal form is Anglian (i.e., Northumbrian or Mercian).[17] Poetic diction, though out of fashion at the moment, is still with us, and the phenomenon, as such, hardly needs explanation here. The Anglian dialectal forms are another matter. Nearly all the Old English poetry extant has come down to us in West Saxon versions. In these versions, however, Anglian forms often occur, and some words, like *mece,* never take the West Saxon form which one would expect in a West Saxon setting. This feature, characteristic of so many Old English poetical texts, is commonly explained on the theory that the poems were first composed and recorded in an Anglian dialect, and that the scribes who made the West Saxon versions sometimes copied an Anglian dialectal form mechanically instead of substituting the equivalent West Saxon forms. Fixed forms like *mece* are explicable on the theory that the Anglian dialects held a certain prestige in metrical composition, and that the fixed forms served to give poetic flavor, for a West Saxon audience at least.

As in any traditional period, so in Old English times poetic effects could

---

[15] A modern parallel: *Monty's moonshine* "artificial daylight."

[16] Sometimes *kenning* is applied to verbal as well as to nominal circumlocutions. The most detailed study of Old English kennings is that of Hertha Marquardt, *Die altenglischen Kenningar* (Halle, 1938); see also K. Malone, *MLN,* LV (1940). 73-74.

[17] The corresponding West Saxon dialectal form *mæce* occurs, be it noted, in the prose compound *mæcefisc* "mullet."

be had, more or less mechanically, by using words and turns of phrase not customary in prose but familiar to the poet's audience as part of the stylistic tradition of poetry. Such words and turns of phrase need not be labeled archaic; certainly they were very much alive in the mouths of the poets and in the ears of their hearers.[18] A given poet was reckoned worthy if he handled with skill the stuff of which, by convention, poems must be made. This stuff was not merely stylistic, however; matter as well as manner was prescribed. And that brings us to another part of our subject.[19]

---

[18] For want of evidence we cannot tell (in most cases) whether a given word or turn of phrase had earlier been used in prose, though now restricted to poetry.

[19] Many stylistic features must here be left out, for want of space. Thus, we include no discussion of familiar rhetorical devices like litotes or understatement. For further discussion, see especially A. C. Bartlett, *The Larger Rhetorical Patterns in Anglo-Saxon Poetry* (1935) and the pioneer paper by J. Kail, "Ueber die parallelstellen in der angelsächsischen Poesie," published in *Anglia*, XII (1889). 21-40. The most important recent article on the subject is that of L. D. Benson, *PMLA*, LXXXI (1966). 334-341. On the oral-formulaic theory in general, see H. L. Rogers, *English Studies*, XLVII (1966). 89-102.

IV

The Old Tradition: Popular Poetry

The oldest Germanic verses extant are two metrical lists of names, recorded in works of the first and second centuries of our era. Such a metrical
Thulas   list is technically known as a *thula*.[1] Tacitus in his *Germania* (A.D. 98) gives us a two-line thula the names of which appear, of course, in Latinized form.[2] This thula has for us a special interest for another reason: it is our first record of the English name. The thula reads thus:

> Reudi*n*gi, Auiones, Anglii, Varini,
> Eudoses, Suardones, *U*nithones.

A like thula, giving our earliest record of the Saxon name, is set down in the *Geography* of Claudius Ptolemy (*c.* A.D. 150):[3]

> Saxones, Sigulones, Sabalingii, Cobandi,
> Chali, Phunusii, Charudes.

In both cases the alliteration shows that we have to do with verse, and verse of this kind is well evidenced, later on, in vernacular sources. Thus, the pedigree of King Cynric of the West Saxons is given metrical form in the following thula:[4]

> Cynric [wæs] Cerdicing, Cerdic Elesing,
> Elesa Esling, Esla Gewising,
> Gewis Wiging, Wig Freawining,
> Freawine Friðugaring, Friðugar Bronding,
> Brond Bældæging, Bældæg Wodening.

The King's descent from Woden could be told in correct verses all the better for being fictitious—the names were chosen to fit the alliterative rules. More elaborate are the three thulas of the sixth century incorporated in *Widsith*. The first of these (lines 18-33 of the poem) falls into two parts: a five-couplet unit and a six-line unit. The first couplet may serve to show the structure and subject-matter of this thula:[5]

---

[1] The term comes from Iceland, where the genre flourished. The metrical name-lists of *Widsith* were first called thulas by Heusler and Ranisch, *Eddica Minora* (1903), p. lxxxix.

[2] Cap. 40. For a full discussion of the passage, see K. Malone, *Namn och Bygd*, XXII (1934). 26-51. For the Latin text, see p. 317 of the standard edition of the *Germania*, that of R. P. Robinson (1935).

[3] II, 11, 7. See K. Malone, *Namn och Bygd*, XXII (1934). 30-31.

[4] *OE Annals*, ed. Earle-Plummer (1892), pp. 16 (A.D. 552), 20 (A.D. 597). See also R. W. Chambers, *Beowulf, An Introduction* (2ed., 1932), pp. 316-317. The suffix *ing*, used 10 times here, means "son of."

[5] *Widsith*, ed. K. Malone (1936), pp. 67-68; see also pp. 12-20.

Ætla weold Hunum, Eormanric Gotum,
Becca Baningum, Burgendum Gifica

Attila ruled the Huns, Ermanric the Goths,
Becca the Banings, Gifica the Burgundians.

The first thula is a list of kings; each king (30 are listed) is identified in terms of the tribe he rules. The second thula, as we have it, consists of twenty lines (57-64, 68-69, 75, 79-87): ten single lines and five couplets. Its first two lines (a couplet) sufficiently indicate its pattern:

Ic wæs mid Hunum ond mid Hreðgotum,
mid Sweom ond mid Geatum ond mid Suþdenum

I was with the Huns and with the Hreth-Goths,
with the Swedes and with the Geats and with the South-Danes.

This thula is a list of tribes (54 are listed), given in terms of the personal experiences of the speaker. The third thula as it stands is made up of nine lines (112-118, 123-124), of which the first reads

Hehcan sohte ic ond Beadecan ond Herelingas
I sought out Hehca and Beadeca and the Herelings.

This thula gives us a list of 28 men (presumably heroes); as in the second thula, they are listed in terms of the personal experiences of the speaker.

Such terms are to be taken as no more than a part of the mnemonic machinery. In general, thula composition seems to have had a highly practical purpose: that of making it easier to remember the names listed. It follows that the names in the lists were thought worth remembering, and in fact the mnemonic material given in the thulas is weighty matter. It meant much to a West Saxon king that he trace his descent from Gewis, the eponym of the tribe, and from Woden, the chief god of the tribe. We have reason to think that his political hold would have been strengthened likewise by belief that he had Wig and Freawine for ancestors, and we may presume that some of the other names in his genealogy were meaningful to our forefathers even though they are only names to us. In sum, the thula which gave Cynric's genealogy was a political poem of the first importance. The upstart West Saxon dynasty gained thereby in rank and worth: thenceforth its kings could face as equals the kings of the ancient Mercian house.[6] The importance of the thulas of *Widsith* lay elsewhere. The first thula embodied historical, the second ethnological lore; the third seems devoted to figures of story rather than (or more than) history. And many names in all three presumably brought to mind in the hearer things that we miss, or know little of. The artistic worth of a list has always lain in the associations which its names evoke. Every name is an allusion for those who know it, and a series of names makes a series of allusions. The names gathered in the thulas of *Widsith* stand for a world now long for-

---

[6] Compare the Chadwicks, *op. cit.*, p. 271, note 2.

gotten, the Germanic world of the migration period. Much of that world still lived in the England of the *Widsith* poet, and the old thulas had then a rich allusiveness which we see but darkly and know but in part.

Runic Poem

Beside the thulas we set the *Runic Poem,* another example of mnemonic verse.[7] Its practical value for would-be runemasters is comparable to that of ABC poems for learners of the alphabet. The runes were learned by name, and in a fixed order. The name of the rune gave one the clue to its phonetic value, and its place in the sequence gave one the clue to other values which need not be gone into here. It seems altogether likely that the runes from the first were learned by means of a poem in which each rune-name began a section, though in the original poem the sections may have been quite brief—possibly no more than a short verse each. From this original poem the three runic poems extant were presumably descended. For the Norwegian and Icelandic runic poems we refer the reader to the edition of Dickins. The English poem is much more elaborate than the other two. We illustrate with the first section, devoted to the first rune:

> Feoh byþ frofur fira gehwylcum;
> sceal ðeah manna gehwylc miclun hyt dælan
> gif he wile for drihtne domes hleotan.

> Valuables are a joy to every man;
> yet every man must needs be openhanded with them
> if he is minded to win favor with the Lord.

Feoh is the name of the *f*-rune, and accordingly begins the section and sets the stave for the first line of the section. Moreover, the section has *feoh* for its theme. This theme is treated in a manner reminiscent of the riddles. We can turn the section into a riddle, indeed, by putting *ic eom* for *feoh byþ:*

> I am a joy to every man;
> yet every man must needs be openhanded with me
> if he is minded to win favor with the Lord.

The poem is 94 lines long. It consists of 29 sections, devoted to as many runes: 19 three-liners, seven four-liners, two two-liners, one five-liner (the last section). The section quoted above is representative of the whole, though the run-on style is much more pronounced in some of the other sections. The two-liners make up in length of line for shortness in number of lines. The *Runic Poem,* like the thulas, started as a speaking, but in its present form it is better classified as a writing. Its literary elaboration may well have taken place under the influence of the riddles, of which more anon. If so, the poem as it stands hardly antedates the eighth century and may be much later. The eleventh-century MS Cotton Otho B x in which the poem came down was lost by fire in 1731, and for our text we must rely on Hickes.[8]

---

[7] The best ed. is that of B. Dickins, *Runic and Heroic Poems* (Cambridge, 1915).
[8] G. Hickes, *Linguarum Veterum Septentrionalium Thesaurus* (Oxford, 1705), I. 135.

Another notable piece of mnemonic verse, the Old English *Menologium* Meno-
or calendar poem,[9] is recorded in the eleventh-century MS Cotton Tiberius logium
B I. This MS is commonly localized at Abingdon, but there are indications
that the menologist himself lived in Kent; note, for instance, the poet's special knowledge of the Canterbury minster (line 105). The poem is 231
lines long. It is written in standard Old English (i.e., West Saxon) of the
later period, and the poet seems to have flourished *c.* A.D. 1000. At the end
of the poem we are told what practical purpose it is meant to serve: "now
ye can find the feast days of the saints that one is duty bound to keep in this
kingdom (i.e., England) nowadays." For sources the menologist presumably
used church calendars and the like. The want of English saints in the
poem [10] indicates that one was not then duty bound to keep their days; the
older saints were more important. But the poet gives much that he need
not have included: the four seasons and the English names of ten of the
twelve months, with striking poetical descriptions of nature attached.[11]
We think it possible that in making his poetical calendar he drew not only
on Latin sources but also on a now lost native mnemonic poem of popular
character, a poem in which the months and seasons (but not the saints'
days) were named and characterized by descriptions not unlike those of
the *Menologium*.[12] This possibility must serve as our excuse for considering
the Old English calendar poem in the present chapter. In any case the
menologist was no mere clerk, learned in Church Latin only. He was
steeped in classical Old English poetry, as his style and choice of words
reveal. Yet another example of mnemonic verse, Cynewulf's *Fates of the
Apostles,* will be taken up with the other works of that poet.

The English of old, unlike their Continental contemporaries, made legal *Legal*
records in the mother tongue as well as in Latin. The laws of King Æðel- *Verse*
birht of Kent were set down in English as early as A.D. 602 or 603, and this
king's example was widely followed by English rulers of later times.
Many charters, wills, and other legal documents in the vernacular have Hit
come down to us as well.[13] One of these, *Hit Becwæð,* is metrical through- Becwæð

[9] Ed. R. Imelmann (Berlin, 1902); Krapp-Dobbie, VI. 49-55. See also H. Henel, "Ein
altenglisches Prosa-Menologium," in (Förster's) *Beiträge zur englischen Philologie,* XXVI (1934).
71-91. The work which Henel here edits is obviously a prose companion-piece to our poem,
though it cannot be reckoned literary and therefore will not be taken up in our chapter on
Old English literary prose.

[10] One English saint (Cuthbert) appears in the prose Menologium; see Henel, p. 71.

[11] The months are not named (whether in English or Latin) in the prose Menologium,
though the seasons are duly named (in English).

[12] The seasons in Old English: *winter, lencten, sumor, hærfest.* The months: earlier and
later *iula* (Dec. and Jan.), *sol* month (Feb.), *hlyda* (Mar.), *easter* month (Apr.), *þrymilce*
(May), earlier and later *liþa* (June and July), *weod* month (Aug.), *halig* month (Sept.),
winterfylleð (Oct.), *blot* month (Nov.). The menologist gave only the Latin names of January
and July, but the English names can readily be inferred from those of December and June.

[13] The best English editions of the laws are those of F. L. Attenborough, *The Laws of
the Earliest English Kings, edited and translated* (Cambridge, 1922), and A. J. Robertson,
The Laws of the Kings of England from Edmund to Henry I, edited and translated (Cambridge, 1925). A more complete edition is that of F. Liebermann, *Die Gesetze der Angelsachsen*
(3v, Halle, 1903-1916). Most of the charters and wills may be found in the volumes of A. J.
Robertson (*Anglo-Saxon Charters,* Cambridge, 1939) and D. Whitelock (*Anglo-Saxon Wills,*
Cambridge, 1930); these may be supplemented by A. C. Napier and W. H. Stevenson, *Craw-*

out.[14] It falls into 46 short verses, nine of which were quoted above (p. 23). The text gives us the answer of a nameless landowner to some plaintiff who had laid claim to the defendant's land. It is addressed, not to any court but to the plaintiff, who is told his claim has no merit and is urged to drop the suit. More precisely, the defendant says: (Sec. 1) that the previous owner, now dead, had a clear title; (Sec. 2) that he, the defendant, got it from the previous owner; (Sec. 3) that he, the defendant, would never give it up to the plaintiff; (Sec. 4) that he would keep it all his life, just as the previous owner had done without challenge to his ownership. The fifth and last section reads:

> Do swa ic lære:
> beo ðe be þinum and læt me be minum;
> ne gyrne ic þines,
> ne læðes ne landes,
> ne sace ne socne,
> ne ðu mines ne ðærft, ne mynte ic ðe nan ðing.

Do as I say: keep to thine and leave me to mine; I crave nothing of thine, neither ground nor land, neither sake nor soke; neither hast thou need of mine, nor have I aught in mind for thee.

The text is one of A.D. 1000 or thereabouts. For the historian of literature its chief interest is metrical; note in particular the author's use of rime instead of alliteration to bind together the two halves of the line *beo ðe . . . minum,* a use familiar in Middle English but rare in Old English alliterative poetry. As a piece of self-expression, too, the poem is worthy of note. The author speaks vigorously and to the point and makes his case come alive.

Many other legal texts are metrical in spots. Short verses, alone or in series, are scattered here and there through the prose, and sometimes one comes upon a line or even a series of lines. Thus, the author of *Gerefa* brings his treatise to a metrical end: [15]

> Fela sceal to holdan hames gerefan
> and to gemetfæstan manna hyrde.
> Ic gecende be ðam ðe ic cuðe;
> se ðe bet cunne, gecyðe his mare.

Many things are required of a loyal overseer
and dependable director of men.
I have set forth [the subject] as best I could;
Let him who knows [it] better make more of it known.

---

ford *Collection of Early Charters and Documents* (Oxford, 1895), and F. E. Harmer, *Select English Historical Documents of the Ninth and Tenth Centuries* (Cambridge, 1914). The earlier collections of Thorpe, Kemble, and Birch are also still useful, though they must be used with caution.

[14] See also Heusler, *Altgerm. Dichtung,* p. 66. For a contrary view, see Liebermann, III. 236.

[15] Liebermann, I. 455.

The following passage from *Rectitudines* may also be quoted: [16]

> Laga sceal on leode luflice leornian,
> lof se ðe on lande sylf nele leosan.

> The laws of the realm he must lovingly learn
> who is unwilling to lose his good name in the land.

In the *Gerefa* passage the third line has only three lifts and the fourth follows an alliterative pattern quite unusual though probably old,[17] while in the *Rectitudines* passage the alliteration foreshadows Middle English and ignores classical Old English practice. Such irregularities are common in the linear verse of legal texts. By its end-stopping too this verse is marked as non-classical; here it harks back to earlier times. The short verses usually have a two-beat pattern. Examples: *ægðer ge dæde ge dihtes* "both in act *Tags* and in aim" (with alliteration); *æt ræde ne æt dæde* "by rede nor by deed" (with rime). As the examples indicate, we have to do with traditional formulas of one kind or another. Such tags are still common in legal phraseology, though the modern tags more often than not are without alliteration or rime, and consequently are not thought of as verse. Want of rime and alliteration in an Old English tag does not mean, of course, that the tag is unmetrical; it means that we cannot be sure of the tag's metrical character unless the context points to metrical treatment. The stock of verse formulas varied more or less down the centuries; some old formulas went out, and others came in. Thus the tag *ne sace ne socne* in *Hit Becwæð* is late. Metrically speaking, nevertheless, it is of a piece with prehistoric English formulas, and its introduction cannot be looked upon as a metrical innovation. Setting their age aside, we classify the formulas in terms of the relationship between the members. This relationship may be of sound or sense. In terms of sound, the two members of a typical formula may be free (e.g., *ne gyrne ic þines*) or bound by rime (e.g., *landes ne strandes*) or alliteration (e.g., *ne plot ne ploh*). Again, they may be symmetrical (e.g., *ne turf ne toft*) or asymmetrical (e.g., *ne furh ne fotmæl*). A symmetrical formula may be simple (e.g., *ne ruh ne rum*) or compound (e.g., *on ceapstowe oððe cyricware* "at marketplace or churchmeeting"). The members of a compound formula may be linked by a common first element (e.g., *oferseah and oferhyrde* "oversaw and overheard") or second element (e.g., *on scipfyrde, on landfyrde* "in ship-army, in land-army"); here the relationship is one of both sound and sense. The same holds of complete identity (e.g., *hand on hand* "hand in hand") and partial identity in asymmetrical formulas (e.g., *ne cyse ne cyslyb* "nor cheese nor cheese-rennet"). So also in cognate constructions (e.g., *to ræde gerædan* "advisably advise, wisely decide"). Meaningful relationships may be of contrast (e.g., *ær oððe æfter* "before or after") or of likeness (e.g., *healdan and wealdan* "hold and

---

[16] Liebermann, I. 452. Other single or double lines will be found in *I Cnut*, 2 and 25 (Lieb., I. 280 and 304); *II Cnut*, 38 (Lieb., I. 338); *X Æðelred*, Prol. I (Lieb., I. 269); *Excom.*, 2 (Lieb. I. 438); *Geþyncðo*, 3 (Lieb. I. 456); etc.

[17] See K. Malone, *Beiblatt zur Anglia*, XLVIII (1937). 351-352.

rule") or of mere association (e.g., *manige menn* "many men"). Other classifications might be made (have been made, indeed),[18] but these will serve well enough to bring out the characteristic features of the short verses.

The metrical formulas here taken up belonged, for the most part, to everyday Old English speech, which made more use of short verses, and had a greater awareness of the metrical side of speech, than is the case in current English. If these short verses may be counted by the hundred in legal writings, the reason is not far to seek: everybody uses stereotyped expressions but the legal mind has a particular fondness for them. It was above all in legal texts, then, that these fragments of popular metrical speech found place and held out against the literary verse and prose which imposed itself nearly everywhere else.[19] Yet in a few spells and sayings likewise the popular verse-form managed to keep a precarious foothold.

Spells and Sayings

Versified wisdom, like versified tags and name-lists, is old in English; older than the language, indeed. But it had to pay for the privilege of written record. The clerics who wrote down what we have of it made fewer changes, interestingly enough, in the spells than in the sayings. They presumably feared that a spell would not work unless they kept the old wording, while they knew a saying would hold good whatever the wording.

We begin with the supernatural or magical wisdom of the spells (or charms). In Grendon's collection,[20] thirteen are wholly or partly in English verse. Of these, two (A 21 and 22) are obviously variants of the same spell. We thus have twelve spells to consider. Two survive in MSS of the tenth century;[21] nine are recorded in MSS of the eleventh century;[22] one, written in a hand of *c.* 1100, occurs in a MS of the tenth century.[23] We have no way of knowing who made these spells, when or where they took shape,

---

[18] Liebermann, II. 77-78. See also D. Bethurum, *MLR*, xxvii (1932). 263-279.

[19] See below, p. 101, for the rhythmical prose of Ælfric.

[20] F. Grendon, "The Anglo-Saxon Charms," *Jour. of Amer. Folk-Lore*, xxii (1909). 105-237. Item A 15 II of the collection is not a spell but the legal poem *Hit Becwæð*, which we took up above.

[21] From BM MS Regius 12 D xvii we have *Wið Wæterælfadle* "against waterelf sickness" (Grendon, B 5, p. 194; Krapp-Dobbie, vi. 124-125). From BM MS Harley 584 we have *Wið Cynnel* "against scrofula" (Grendon, A 9, p. 170; see also F. P. Magoun, Jr., *Arkiv för nordisk Filologi,* lx [1945]. 98-106).

[22] From BM MS Cotton Caligula A vii we have *Æcerbot* "acre-boot, field-remedy" (Grendon, A 13, pp. 172-176; Krapp-Dobbie, vi. 116-118). From BM MS Harley 585 we have: (1) *Wið Færstice* "against a sudden stitch in the side" (Grendon, A 1, pp. 164-166; Krapp-Dobbie, vi. 122-123), here called *Stice*; (2) *Wið Dweorh* "against a dwarf" (Grendon, A 2, p. 166; Krapp-Dobbie, vi. 121-122); (3) *Wið Ceapes Lyre* "against loss of cattle" (Grendon, A 22, p. 184; Krapp-Dobbie, vi. 123), here called *Lyre* when distinguished from its variant *Þeofend* but otherwise called *Bethlem;* (4) *Nigon Wyrta Galdor* "nine wort spell" (Grendon, B 4, pp. 190-194; Krapp-Dobbie, vi. 119-121), here called *Wyrta;* (5) *Wið Lætbyrde* "against slow birth" (Grendon, E 1, pp. 206-208; Krapp-Dobbie, vi. 123-124), here called *Lætbyrd*. From the Corpus Christi College Cambridge MS 41 we have: (1) *Wið Ymbe* "against a swarm of bees" (Grendon, A 4, p. 168; Krapp-Dobbie, vi. 125); (2) *Siðgaldor* "hap spell" (Grendon, A 14, pp. 176-178; Krapp-Dobbie, vi. 126-128); (3) *Wið Feos Nimunge* "against cattle theft" (Grendon, A 16, pp. 180-182; Krapp-Dobbie, vi. 125-126), here called *Garmund;* (4) *Wið Ceapes Þeofende* "against cattle theft" (Grendon, A 21, p. 184; Krapp-Dobbie, vi. 126), here called *Þeofend* when distinguished from its variant *Lyre* but otherwise called *Bethlem*.

[23] *Wið Wennum* "against wens" (Grendon, A 3, p. 166; Krapp-Dobbie, vi. 128), BM MS Regius 4 A xiv. This spell will here be called *Wenne*.

and how (if at all) the originals differed from the texts we have, apart from the ordinary linguistic changes down the years. We do not even know whether our texts were drawn from oral or written sources, though their ultimate source was presumably oral tradition. Strictly Christian spells like *Bethlem* may go back to a heathen original, but we need not make this presumption, since such spells might perfectly well have come into being in Christian times. Heathen elements in the spells are presumably old. Christian elements may reflect substitutions or additions. Much of the matter cannot be tied to religious belief, and is better classified as pseudo-science. In this history we take up the spells as examples of literary art, and leave to others the manifold non-literary problems which a student of spells must face.[24]

Our spells make a literary group of their own, not only in subject-matter but also in versification and style. They reflect a tradition independent of classical Old English poetry, but allied to legal verse and to pre-classical end-stopped linear verse.[25] Nearly all our twelve spells include prose as well as verse. In the verse parts a line may be followed by a short verse, a short verse by a line. Alliteration may be heaped up, or may be wanting. A line may be made up wholly, or almost wholly, of lifts. The three-lift verse, too, is in use here: a verse-pattern longer than the short verse but shorter than the line. A poem may show much greater variety in line pattern than would be possible in classical poetry. Run-on lines are rare. The familiar classical device of variation is avoided. We find, instead, repetition, and serial effects not unlike those achieved in the thulas of *Widsith* or in certain passages of *Beowulf* (e.g., lines 1392 ff., 1763 ff.). The *epitheton ornans* and other commonplaces of the classical style are likewise rare in the spells. These vary much in literary merit, but they all have freshness and go. We will look at a few of them.

The 13-line spell *Wenne* is marked by humor and lightness of touch. We quote in modernized form the first four and the last three lines: *Wenne*

> Wen, wen, wen-chicken,
> here thou shalt not build nor have any homestead,
> but thou shalt [go] north from here, to the near-by hill.
> There thou hast a wretch of a brother. . . .
>
> Do thou become as small as a linseed grain,
> and much smaller, like a handworm's hipbone,
> and become so small that thou become nothing at all.

Note the humorous shift of stress in *chicken,* a shift which makes the word rime with *wen.* The thrice repeated *become* is also of stylistic interest. But the reader can make his own commentary.

---

[24] There is a useful study by F. P. Magoun, Jr., *Archiv,* CLXXI (1937). 17-35, with bibliography; see also L. K. Shook, *MLN,* LV (1940). 139-140.

[25] Traces of strophic arrangement have been found by I. Lindquist (*Galdrar,* Göteborgs Högskolas Årsskrift, XXIX [1923]), and F. P. Magoun, Jr. (*ESt,* LXXII [1937]. 1-6).

Bethlem

The two variants of *Bethlem* have some importance for the textual critic, and are therefore given here (the same translation will serve for both):

Lyre

Bæðleem hatte seo buruh,
Þe Crist on acænned wæs.
Seo is gemærsod geond ealne middangeard.
Swa þyos dæd for monnum mære gewurþe.

Þeofend

Bethlem hattæ seo burh ðe Crist on geboren wes.
Seo is gemærsod ofer ealne middangeard.
Swa ðeos dæd wyrþe for monnum mære.

Bethlehem is called the town that Christ was born in.
It has become famous the world over.
So may this deed become famous in men's sight.

Lyre gives us the better text, but the two non-classical verses with which it began displeased somebody, and he made them into one line by putting *geboren* for *acænned*. Evidently a Christian spell could not always hold its own against the classical tradition.

Garmund

The following passage from *Garmund* is quoted for its metrical and stylistic features:

Garmund, godes ðegen,
find þæt feoh and fere þæt feoh
and hafa þæt feoh and heald þæt feoh
and fere ham þæt feoh

Garmund, God's thane,
find the cattle and bring the cattle
and have the cattle and hold the cattle
and bring home the cattle.

Here the alliteration, the two three-lift verses, and the repetitions are worthy of special note. The appeal to Garmund was addressed, one may suspect, to Godmund in heathen times.

Lætbyrd

The verses of *Lætbyrd* have power and poetry beyond expectation. We find space for a couplet only. A woman unable to feed her newborn child takes "part of her own child's caul," wraps it in black wool, and sells it to chapmen, saying:

I sell it, may ye sell it,
this black wool and seed of this sorrow.

Siðgaldor

The four long spells are *Siðgaldor* (40 lines), *Æcerbot* (38 lines of verse and much prose), *Wyrta* (63 lines of verse, followed by a short prose passage), and *Stice* (27 lines of verse, preceded and followed by a few words of prose). Of these, the first seems wholly Christian; in style as well as matter it stands closer to classical religious poetry than do the other spells. Among other things it gives us lists of biblical worthies, a feature reminiscent of the thulas. Except for a few lines it has little artistic merit. *Æcerbot* is Christian for the most part, but has passages (often quoted) that almost certainly go back to heathen times. Thus, the line *eorðan ic bidde and upheofon* "I pray to earth and to high heaven" has a strongly Christian context but nevertheless is unmistakably heathen. The famous line,

Æcerbot

> Erce, Erce, Erce, eorþan modor,

whatever it means, surely appeals to mother earth, and the noble, hymn-like passage,

> Hal wes þu, folde, fira modor,
> beo þu growende on godes fæþme,
> fodre gefylled firum to nytte,

> Hale be thou, earth, mother of men,
> be thou with growing things in God's embrace,
> filled with food for the good of men,

takes us back to agricultural fertility rites, solemn ceremonies of immemorial antiquity.

Wyrta names nine worts or plants that have virtue against poisons (particularly snake-bite), aches and pains, infections, and demons.[26] We are told that these nine worts counteract as many devils, poisons and infections, but no list of nine devils is given. We do get a list of nine kinds of poison, followed by another list of six kinds of swelling or blister:

Wyrta

> Now these nine worts are potent . . .

> against the red poison, against the runl [27] poison,
> against the white poison, against the blue poison,
> against the yellow poison, against the green poison,
> against the dark poison, against the blue poison,
> against the brown poison, against the purple poison;

> against worm-swelling, against water-swelling,
> against thorn-swelling, against thistle-swelling,
> against ice-swelling, against poison-swelling.

Next comes a passage devoted to the cardinal points:

> if any poison come flying from the east
> or any come from the north
> or any from the west over the people.

Nothing harmful was expected from the south, it would seem. The passages quoted show the serial effects characteristic of the literary art of the spells, an art marked by repetition and parallelism. The versification, too,

---

[26] On the names of the worts, see H. Meroney, *MLN*, LIX (1944). 157-160.
[27] The meaning of *runl* is unknown, but it seems to be a color word.

with its mixture of line and short verse, is interesting. Running water also has virtue, against snake-bite at least, and a couplet is added accordingly:

> Ic ana wat ea rinnende
> and þa nygon nædran behealdað.

> I alone know running water
> and that [i.e., running water] nine adders look to.[28]

The boast befits our learned spellman, but boasting is a conventional feature of spells as of epics. The best known passage in this spell, however, has yet to be quoted:

> A snake came creeping, tried to slit a man open.
> Then Woden took nine glory-rods;
> then he struck the adder, so that it burst into nine.

This narrative or "epic" passage, done in the pre-classical end-stopped style, is a precious relic of English heathendom; unluckily we do not know the Woden myth which it summarizes.

Stice

Wyrta has come down to us markedly imperfect; perhaps the disorder was there from the start. *Stice,* however, is well built as it stands. First come some directions, in prose. Then we get a pseudo-scientific explanation of the stitch: spear-casts made by evil spirits (female, it would seem) cause these sudden pains, and the magic weapon must be drawn out of you before you can get relief. This explanation is given in highly poetical dress: the women, loud and bold, have ridden over the hill, overland; you must protect yourself to stave off this attack. Here the spellman inserts, for the first time, the oft-repeated curative formula,

> ut, lytel spere, gif her inne sie !
> out, little spear, if thou be in here,

which also serves as a kind of refrain, marking the end of the passage. But your shield fails you: the magic dart pierced you

> when the mighty women drew up their forces
> and [when] they hurled yelling spears.

The spellman now comes to help you. He promises to fight the evil spirits with weapons of his own:

> Six smiths sat,
> murderous spears they made;
> out, spear, not in, spear!

> If there be in here a bit of iron,
> the work of a witch, away it shall melt!

The incantation then proceeds in serial form (compare that quoted above from *Wyrta*). The whole makes a little masterpiece of its kind.

[28] The second line of this couplet agrees in alliterative pattern with the last line of *Gerefa* (see above, p. 36).

So much for the spells. We go on to the sayings. The term *sayings* is *Gnomic* here taken to mean versified words of stock everyday wisdom: short, pithy, *Verse* homespun generalizations about the common concerns of life, whether proverbial, descriptive, or moralizing. The sayings that won record in Old English times are found (1) imbedded here and there in a number of texts, and (2) brought together in gnomic poems. Four such poems are extant. Three of them are recorded in the Exeter Book, a MS of *c.* 980; [29] they go by the collective name *Exeter Gnomics* (206 lines in all, as usually reckoned), and are distinguished by the letters *A, B, C.* The fourth, set down in the eleventh-century MS Cotton Tiberius B 1, is called *Cotton Gnomics* (66 lines).[30] The imbedded sayings must first, of course, be winnowed out. Here the author or compiler of the text may help us. Thus, the compiler of the (Latin) laws attributed to Edward the Confessor quotes

> Bugge spere of side oððe bere
> buy spear from side or bear

as a proverbial expression current among the English.[31] In the same way, a nameless correspondent of St. Boniface (the great English missionary of the eighth century) calls the following couplet *saxonicum verbum:*

> Oft daedlata dome foreldit,
> sigisitha gahuem; suuyltit thi ana.[32]
>
> Oft a sluggard puts off decision,
> Lets all his chances slip; so he dies alone.

More commonly, however, no such help is forthcoming, and we must go by internal evidence alone. A gnomic passage once found, we need to know besides (if possible) whether the generalization was original with the author or common literary property. The latter is normally to be presumed, in virtue of the traditional and conventionalized character of Old English literary art. And sometimes we have special reasons for coming to this conclusion. Thus, *Beowulf,* 1384b-1385,

> selre bið æghwæm
> þæt he his freond wrece þonne he fela murne
>
> it is better for every man
> to avenge his friend than to mourn [over him] much,

[29] Facsimile edition: *The Exeter Book of Old English Poetry* (London, 1933). Printed edition with Old English text and modern English rendering: Part I, by I. Gollancz (*EETS,* 104); Part II, by W. S. Mackie (*EETS,* 194).

[30] The four gnomic poems are best studied in the edition of Blanche C. Williams, *Gnomic Poetry in Anglo-Saxon* (New York, 1914). Here, too, Miss Williams gives a thorough treatment of the imbedded sayings.

[31] Liebermann, *ed. cit.,* I. 638-639. The popular character of this saying is reflected in its metrical form; note the rime *spere—bere* and the irregular alliteration. The saying seems to mean "pay wergeld or take the consequences," though the reference may equally well be to Danegeld or to tribute generally.

[32] H. Sweet, *Oldest English Texts,* p. 152. The couplet (which we may name *Verbum*) is obviously early, and keeps something of the old end-stopped style, but has a classical and even bookish ring; note in particular the use of variation. We reckon it a writing, not a speaking.

fits Old Germanic morality but clashes with Christian morality. It seems unlikely, then, that the pious poet himself gave birth to this generalization; the chances are that he was quoting a stock piece of popular wisdom, handed down from heathen times.[33]

In studying the four gnomic poems we have to consider not only the individual sayings which these poems embody but also the poems as such. These are primarily compilations of traditional sententious wisdom, but the clerical compilers have more or less remodeled their material to make it fit the classical run-on linear style (though now and then they fail to do this and the older versification stands out). Sometimes, too, we find a single saying expanded or developed at some length, and not a few passages are homiletic or reflective rather than gnomic in character. Christian piety has made its way into the gnomic matter besides, and the poems as a whole give us a remarkable mixture of old and new. While the nature of the material makes a clean-cut structural pattern impossible, most of the sayings fall, more or less loosely, into groups, and certain passages are built up systematically enough. The sayings are so little organized in the Cotton Gnomics that the old term "gnomic verses" seems appropriate; the gnomic monuments of the Exeter Book, however, are properly poems rather than mere collections of verses.[34]

Bede's Death Song

Markedly different from all these is that famous piece of pious wisdom, the so-called *Death Song* of the Venerable Bede (d. 735), preserved to us by having been quoted in the *Epistola Cuthberti de Obitu Bedae*.[35] The modern rendering which follows is based on the text of the *Epistola* found in MS St. Gall 254 (ninth century): [36]

> Before the needful journey [i.e., death] no one becomes
> wiser in thought than he needs to be
> to think over, ere his going hence,
> what of good or evil about his spirit,
> after his day of death, may be decided.

This five-line poem of a single sentence evidently belongs to the classical, not the pre-classical style of composition. The thought as it stands is Christian, and Bede had Doomsday in mind. Yet the point of view needs but a slight shift to give us words that would befit Bede's heathen forefathers, who prized above all else that good name after death which may be had by living worthily, and not otherwise. An old ideal of conduct here held its own by taking new shape.

[33] For the sake of completeness we mention here two metrical proverbs, recorded in the BM MSS Cotton Faustina A. x and Regius 2 B. v. One proverb comes to two lines, the other to one line of verse. They are based on Latin originals. Texts in Krapp-Dobbie, vi. 109.

[34] For a study of the structure of one of these poems, see K. Malone, *MA*, xii (1943). 65-67.

[35] The standard study of Cuthbert's letter is that of E. V. K. Dobbie, *Columbia Univ. Stud. in English and Compar. Lit.*, cxxviii. (1937). 49-129.

[36] The *Death Song* has been edited by A. H. Smith, *Three Northumbrian Poems* (1933), but this edition needs a few corrections in the light of Dobbie's study.

V

The Old Tradition: Courtly Poetry

So far, we have dealt with verse that reflects the traditional lore of oldest *Scop or* England. Such verse was popular in that it belonged to the people as a *Gleeman* whole. We come now to verse more personal in character and more limited in aim. At an early date Germanic kings began to keep professional poets, with functions not wholly unlike those of the poet laureate or official poet of later times. Among the English a court poet was called a *scop* or *gleeman*.[1] We are lucky enough to have in *Widsith* an early English poem on the Widsith scop.[2] From this poem (named after its hero) we learn something of the career and the repertory of an ideal gleeman, creature of a seventh-century poet's fancy.[3] The poem consists of a prologue (9 lines), a speech by Widsith (125 lines), and an epilogue (9 lines). The speech is built up round three old thulas and a thula-fragment (47 lines in all; see above, p. 32), which the author puts in his hero's mouth; to these are added 78 lines of the author's own composition.[4] Structurally the speech falls into five parts: an introduction, three fits or main divisions, and a conclusion. Each fit comprises (1) a thula and (2) passages added by the author.[5] The thulas were put in Widsith's mouth to bring out his knowledge of history, ethnology, and heroic story. Several of the added passages serve the same purpose. Other passages bring out the hero's professional experience and first-hand information (as do the second and third thulas); more particularly, they emphasize his success in his chosen calling. Thus, we are told of his professional performances:

> When Scilling and I, with sure voice, as one,
> made music, sang before our mighty lord,
> the sound of harp and song rang out;
> then many a man, mindful of splendor,
> those who well could know, with words spoke and said
> that they never heard a nobler song. (lines 103-8)

---

[1] See L. F. Anderson, *The Anglo-Saxon Scop* (Toronto, 1903).

[2] Recent edition: K. Malone, *Widsith* (1936). See also Lascelles Abercrombie, "*Widsith* as Art," *Sewanee Rev.*, XLVI (1938). 124-128. The edition of R. W. Chambers (*Widsith*, Cambridge, 1912) will always remain the best presentation of nineteenth-century Continental Widsithian scholarship. This scholarship is now largely out of date, because of the great advances made during the present century in our understanding of the poem; for crucial particulars, see K. Malone, *JEGP*, XXXVIII (1939). 226-228, XLIII (1944). 451, and XLV (1946). 147-152. But Chambers' book still has more than historical interest.

[3] For recent speculations about the author of *Widsith*, see especially W. H. French, *PMLA*, LX (1945). 623-630.

[4] Or 74, if lines 14-17 be rejected, as they commonly are.

[5] For a fuller analysis, see K. Malone, *ELH*, V (1938). 49-66.

Even the critics thought highly of Widsith's art! From this passage we learn, incidentally, that the scop sang his poems to the accompaniment of the harp. Whether Scilling was Widsith's harpist or a fellow scop (in which case the performance was a duet) we cannot tell; it has even been conjectured, indeed, that Scilling was the name of Widsith's harp.[6] The author makes it clear that his hero was composer as well as performer (though he would hardly have understood the distinction we make between these offices). Widsith sings in mead-hall about his own experiences (lines 54-56), and he composes and sings a poem in praise of his patroness, Queen Ealhhild (lines 99-102). We may safely presume that an actual scop would do as much for the kings who made him welcome at their courts and gave him gifts. The relationship between a scop and his royal patron comes out in the epilogue of our poem: [7]

> As gleemen go, guided by fortune,
> as they pass from place to place among men,
> their wants they tell, speak the word of thanks,
> south or north find someone always
> full of song-lore, free in giving,
> who is fain to heighten his favor with the worthy,
> do noble deeds, till his day is ended,
> life and light together; below he wins praise,
> he leaves under heaven a lasting fame. (lines 135-43)

The word of thanks is to be taken as a poem in honor of the prince, whose fame could hardly have been expected to last unless celebrated in song; poetry was then the only historical record. We conclude that the scop had the important function of immortalizing his patron by singing his praises. These poems of praise, handed down by word of mouth, and making part of the repertory of many a gleeman, were meant to keep the prince's name and deeds alive in the minds of men forever.

But the scop had another function, older and even more important: that of entertainer. In *Beowulf* we get descriptions of the entertainment. From these we gather that a gleeman's performance was short, and made part of a celebration which included amusements of other kinds. Thus, the royal scop sang one morning out of doors, in an interval between horse-races (864-918); the day before, he had sung at a feast in the hall (489-498). A given song might deal with contemporaries (witness the gleeman who celebrated, the morning after the deed, Beowulf's triumph over Grendel), or it might deal with figures of the past. But always, so far as we know, its theme was high and its tone earnest. The entertainment which the scop had to offer made demands on the audience; it could not be enjoyed without keen participation in thought and feeling; there was little about it restful

---

[6] W. J. Sedgefield, *MLR*, xxvi (1931). 75. In humbler circles the performer played his own accompaniment, as we learn from Bede's story of Cædmon.

[7] The metrical translations of *Widsith* 103-108 and 135-143 are taken, by permission, from K. Malone, *Ten Old English Poems* (Baltimore: Johns Hopkins Press, 1941).

or relaxing. The scop held his hearers because he and they were at one: schooled and bound in the traditions of a poetry that gave voice to their deepest loyalties and highest resolves. The theme that moved them most was the theme of sacrifice, dominant in the old poems and strong in the life which these poems reflected and glorified. King and dright [8] made a com- *King and* pany of warriors held together by the bond of sacrificial friendship. The *Dright* king shared his goods with the dright and took them into his very house- hold; the dright shielded him with their bodies on the field of battle, and if he fell they fought on, to victory or death, deeming it base to give ground or flee when their lord lay slain. The famous speech of Byrhtwold in *Maldon* tells us more than pages of exposition could: [9]

> Thought shall be the harder, heart the keener,
> mood shall be the more, as our might lessens.
> Here lies our earl, all hewn to earth,
> the good one, on the ground. He will regret it always,
> the one who thinks to turn from this war-play now.
> My life has been long. Leave I will not,
> but beside my lord I will sink to earth,
> I am minded to die by the man so dear. (lines 312-19)

But the theme of sacrifice need not take the form which it takes in *Maldon*. And other themes might be used, as we have seen. Whatever the theme, the old poems had strength in them to stir the heart and steel the mood. The scop sang of heroes and called his hearers to the heroic life. He held out no false hopes: heroism leads to hardship, wounds, and death. But though all must go down in defeat at last, the fight is worth making: the hero may hope for a good name among men. The value set upon the esteem of others, and in particular upon fame, marks this philosophy social and secular (heathen is hardly the word). The gleemen who taught it in song were upholding the traditional morality of the English people, a way of life known to us from the pages of Tacitus. The entertainment that the scops gave was *ei blot for lyst*.[10] The old poems, and the new ones composed in the same spirit, kept alive for hundreds of years after the conversion to Christianity the old customs, conventions, and ideals of conduct. In so doing they did not stand alone, of course; many other things in English life made for conservatism. But they had a great and worthy part to play in the preservation of the nobler features of our Germanic heritage. It must not be thought, however, that the scops were conservators and nothing more. It was they who made the important stylistic shift from pre-classical to classical; the clerics who produced most of the classical poetry extant simply carried on and elaborated a style the basic features of which had already been set by the scops. Moreover, the personal themes which the scops favored,

[8] Comitatus, body of retainers.
[9] From K. Malone, *Ten Old English Poems* (Baltimore: Johns Hopkins Press, 1941), by permission.
[10] "Not merely for pleasure," the old motto of the Royal Theatre in Copenhagen.

courtly though their setting and heroic though their appeal, opened the way to the lyricism of *Wife's Lament* and *Eadwacer*.

Deor

Only one poem definitely attributed to a specific scop has come down to us. This poem, commonly called *Deor* after its reputed author, is recorded in the Exeter Book.[11] The *terminus ad quem* of its composition is therefore A.D. 980 or thereabouts; a *terminus a quo* will be set below. The poem belongs to the first stage of the run-on style. It is 42 lines long, and falls into seven sections of varying length. The sections are all mutually independent; each is complete in itself and could perfectly well stand as a separate poem, without change. Nevertheless the seven sections make a well-knit whole, as we shall see. We quote the last section, where the reputed author speaks in the first person:

> That I will say, of myself to speak,
> That the Heodenings had me a while for scop,
> the king held me dear; Deor they called me.
> For many winters my master was kind,
> my hap was high, till Heorrenda now,
> a good man in song, was given the land
> that my lord before had lent to me.
> That now is gone; this too will go. (lines 35-42)

The last line is the so-called formula of consolation. It tells us (1) that the misfortune set forth in the other lines of the section has now been overcome or outlived, no matter how; and (2) that the misfortune, whatever it may be, of the present moment will pass likewise. The moral is: bear your troubles in patience; they cannot last forever. In the section quoted, the author mentions a misfortune of his own; in the first five sections, he mentions as many pieces of adversity that befell others; each section gives us a new victim (or victims), but ends with the same formula of consolation. The various misfortunes taken up were drawn from Germanic story. This parallelism in theme, source, and treatment links the sections and gives unity to the poem.

The sixth section, however, goes its own way. It reads,[12]

> The man that is wretched sits bereft of gladness,
> his soul darkens, it seems to him
> the number of his hardships is never-ending;
> he can bethink him, then, that through this world
> God in his wisdom gives and withholds;
> to many a man he metes out honor,
> fame and fortune; their fill, to some, of woes. (lines 28-34)

11 The only separate edition is that of K. Malone (1933). See also K. Malone, *Acta Phil. Scand.*, IX (1934). 76-84, *English Studies*, XIX (1937). 193-199, and *MP*, XL (1942). 1-18; L. Whitbread, *MLN*, LV (1940). 204-207, LVII (1943). 367-369, LXII (1947). 15-20.

12 The metrical translations of *Deor* 28-34 and 35-42 are taken, by permission, from K. Malone, *Ten Old English Poems* (Baltimore: Johns Hopkins Press, 1941).

This poetry is timeless and nameless. The victim of misfortune stands for mankind in general, and his troubles are left unspecified. The consolation offered has a correspondingly generalized character. We are told (1) that woe, like weal, comes from God, who knows what is best for us, and (2) that our troubles are of this world (and therefore sure to come to an end). The marked differences between this section and the others have led many to reject it as interpolated. But it sums up admirably the theme of the poem and seems appropriate enough as a concluding passage. We incline to the opinion that it was composed for that purpose. If so, the section with which the poem now ends is best taken as an afterthought on the part of the poet. Certainly it differs from the first five sections in that it is no allusion but a plain summary account of the particular misfortune with which it deals.

Deor bears no likeness to the poems of praise that we hear about in *Beowulf* and *Widsith,* and cannot be reckoned typical of the gleeman's art. The last section comes under the head of personal experience, however, and verses dealing with such experiences are credited to Widsith, as we have seen. The theme of *Deor,* then, does not lie outside a scop's traditional range, though the treatment shows marked originality and the poem therefore makes difficulties for historians of literature, who can find no pigeonhole into which it will fit. If the reputed author actually composed the poem, the date of composition could hardly be set later than the sixth century, and only one section of his poem (the last) has survived: a sixth-century poet could not have composed the general section with its Christian coloring, nor yet the first five sections, which belong to a later stage of English poetic tradition, a stage marked by the use of German sources (compare *Waldere* and *Genesis B*). Most recent commentators have been unwilling to take the consequences of a sixth-century dating, and therefore make the scop Deor into a literary fiction, or, if historical, into a mere mouthpiece of the poet, not the poet himself.[13] The problems involved are too formidable for discussion here. It will be enough to say that *Deor* as it stands cannot plausibly be dated earlier than the ninth century and may have been composed as late as the tenth.

Another poem composed by a scop is that to which scholars have given the name *The Fight at Finn's Borough,*[14] or *Finn* for short. Only a fragment of this poem has survived: 46 lines and 2 half-lines. If the whole came to about 300 lines,[15] then we have somewhat less than a sixth of the text; if the poem was longer, the part we have is proportionately smaller. Our fragmentary text of uncertain date is known to us only from the faulty

Finn

---

[13] R. Imelmann, *Forschungen zur ae. Poesie* (1920), pp. 254-257, contends that the *Deor* poet was familiar with the ninth eclogue of Virgil and gave himself a pen-name in imitation of Virgil.

[14] The text of Hickes reads *Finnsburuh* (one word), but this can hardly be right; see F. P. Magoun, Jr., *Zeitschrift für deutsches Altertum,* LXXVII (1940). 65-66. The poem is included in most editions of *Beowulf* by way of appendix. B. Dickins also includes it in his *Runic and Heroic Poems* (Cambridge, 1915).

[15] For this bold and doubtful conjecture, see F. Klaeber, *Beowulf* (3ed., 1936), p. 236.

transcription of Hickes; [16] the manuscript leaf from which he took it has vanished. A poem which dealt with the same events (possibly the very poem of which we have a fragment) was known to the *Beowulf* poet, who calls it a "gleeman's song" (1160a). The author of *Beowulf* does not give us the text of this song, in whole or in part, but from his own treatment of the theme (1063-1159a) we learn something of the events on which the song was based. In style the Finn episode of *Beowulf* is consonant (for obvious artistic reasons) with the poem of which it makes a part, and differs correspondingly from the Finn fragment, which belongs to the early stage of the run-on style (see above, p. 27). Episode and fragment are not directly comparable in plot, since they deal with different stages of the action. It is customary to reconstruct the plot of the old tale by putting fragment and episode together. Unluckily the beginning of the action nowhere survives, and can be reconstructed only by conjecture. In the following summary of the plot, the conjectural items are bracketed:

King Hnæf of the Danes, with 60 followers, is in Frisia, [on a visit to] his sister Hildeburh, wife of King Finn of the Frisians. [Trouble arises between hosts and guests. The Danes take possession of a hall at Finn's seat, possibly Finn's own hall, and make ready to defend themselves. A Danish sentry (or wakeful warrior) rouses King Hnæf before dawn to report that he sees a light outside and to ask what it means.] Hnæf replies that an attack upon the hall is about to begin. He rouses his men and they take their appointed places to await the onslaught. The Danes hold the doors of the hall without loss to themselves for five days. *Here the fragment ends and the episode begins.* The Danes go over to the offensive [presumably in a sortie] but lose heavily, being reduced to a *wealaf* "remnant of disaster"; King Hnæf himself falls in the struggle. The Frisians too have had severe losses, including Finn's own son. The fight is a stalemate and Hengest, the spokesman for the *wealaf* and its informal leader, comes to terms with Finn. The Danes swear allegiance to Finn and are guaranteed the same rights and privileges that Finn's other followers have. In particular, anyone who taunts them for following their lord's slayer is to be put to the sword. The bodies of the fallen on both sides are then burned with appropriate rites. Life at Finn's court on the new basis continues the winter through. With spring, travel by sea again becomes possible, and Hengest is eager to go but his thoughts are not so much on the voyage itself as on the vengeance he would like to wreak on the "children of the Eotens" [i.e., the Frisians]. Eventually Guthlaf and Oslaf [presumably with the rest of the *wealaf*] get away by sea [to Denmark] and whet their compatriots at home against Finn. A Danish fleet-army attacks and slays Finn at his stronghold and bears off much booty to the ships. Queen Hildeburh goes back to her native land with the Danish victors. We are not told what became of Hengest.

This is not the place to discuss the many problems of fragment and episode.[17] We limit ourselves to the literary treatment of the theme. Both

[16] G. Hickes, *Ling. Vett. Sept. Thesaurus* . . .(1705). I; 192-193.

[17] For recent discussions, see K. Malone, *ELH,* x (1943). 257-284; *MA,* xiii (1944). 88-91; *RES,* xxi (1945). 126-127; and *MP,* xliii (1945). 83-85, together with the references to other studies there given.

fights are mentioned in the episode, but obviously the interest of the *Beowulf* poet centered, not in the fighting but in the tragic situation of Hildeburh and Hengest during the period between the two battles. The hapless queen makes a pathetic figure; husband and brother wage war against each other, and son and brother fall, fighting on opposite sides. Hers is a woman's tragedy; she can do nothing to keep her nearest and dearest from killing each other. The poet lays stress on her sorrow and her innocence. She did not deserve the fate that befell her.

The tragedy of Hengest (and of the *wealaf* [18] as a whole, for whom he stands) strikes deeper. The Danes not only made terms with their lord's slayer; they actually entered that slayer's service, became his men. This debarred them from carrying out their last and most solemn obligation to Hnæf: that of avenging his death. Indeed, they were now honor-bound to defend Finn against attack. The poet pictures Hengest in a kind of mental rebellion against his unhappy fate. He is eager to see the last of Frisia, but above all he yearns to wreak that vengeance on the Frisians which he cannot honorably wreak. We are told nothing more about him, and we need not speculate on his further activities. The tragedy of the *wealaf* as a whole, however, seems to have been resolved by the voyage of Guthlaf and Oslaf to Denmark. Though the Danes in Finn's service could not honorably turn upon him themselves, they could incite their fellow Danes to do so; such was the legalistic ethics prevalent in those days among the Germanic tribesmen. Whether Finn let the *wealaf* go that summer or whether they took advantage of an opportunity to desert, we have no means of knowing. In any case Guthlaf and Oslaf could hardly have made the voyage to Denmark without a crew, and the *wealaf* was the only crew available.

What of the gleeman's song on which the episode is based? Did its author see eye to eye with the *Beowulf* poet? Here we must go by the fragment. From this it would seem that the scop did not dwell on the early events and was hurrying on to something else. Hnæf's answer when he saw the light outside,[19]

> Here day dawns not, here a dragon flies not,
> and here the horns of this hall burn not,
> but here they bear forward, birds of prey croak,
> the greycoat yells, the gory spear shouts,
> shield answers shaft. Now shines this moon,
> wandering, on the earth; now woe-deeds arise,
> that will bring to a head this hatred between peoples.
> But waken now, warriors mine,
> take up your shields, think only of fighting,
> join battle in front, be bold-hearted (lines 3-12),

[18] Danish survivors.
[19] The metrical rendering of lines 3-12 of the *Finn* fragment is taken, by permission, from K. Malone, *Ten Old English Poems* (Baltimore: Johns Hopkins Press, 1941).

the manning of the doors (13-17), the challenge and reply with which the fight begins (18-27), are done with breadth and leisure, but then the tempo changes. The fight between challenger and defender, though elaborately introduced, is not reported in detail; the scop finds it enough to tell us that Garulf, the challenger (Finn's man), lost his life, and even this information is not given separately, but is incorporated in a brief description of the sounds and sights that go with battle (28-36). The course of the fight for five days is then disposed of in six lines (37-42) taken up chiefly with praise of Hnæf's following. The tempo slows again with the last lines of the fragment (43-48), which report, in indirect discourse, a dialogue between Hnæf and a wounded Dane. We surmise that the crisis of the battle is at hand, but here the fragment breaks off. The *Beowulf* episode makes clear the further course of the struggle. The Danes took the offensive after their long and successful defensive stand. The object of their sortie may have been to win through to the shore and take ship for home, or perhaps they had run short of water and needed a fresh supply. Whatever their reason for sallying forth, the sortie cost them dear: their king and many others fell and the company of sixty was reduced to a mere *wealaf* of, say, twenty or thirty men. As total destruction loomed before them, one of the retainers, Hengest by name, took command, not by inherited right but as a born leader who rose to the emergency. Under his leadership the Danes rallied, fought Finn to a standstill, and regained the shelter of the hall, where they held out against all the forces Finn could bring to the attack. In all likelihood the major part of the old lay was devoted to this stirring, heroic struggle, with Hengest as hero. The expression "Hengest himself" in line 17 of the fragment points to the centrality of this character in the poem, and his actual centrality in the *Beowulf* episode completes the demonstration. But we have no reason to think that the fighting proper was played down in the lay as it is in *Beowulf*. On the contrary, the lay first of all told the story of the battle, though of course the scop's interest was not in military tactics but in heroic deeds.

Hengest's heroism, however real, was far from ideal, as the *Beowulf* episode shows. The greatness of the man was marred by a tragic flaw. He and his fellows of the *wealaf,* rather than throw away their lives round the dead body of Hnæf, as the code prescribed, chose to live on, and even to enter the service of their lord's slayer. Why should a scop celebrate such a man in song? One may surmise that the lay of Hengest was first composed and sung by a scop in service at the Kentish court. If the Hengest of story was the man who began the English settlement of Britain (and many scholars have been of this opinion),[20] the scops of the kings of Kent might be expected to sing his virtues and to overlook or minimize his faults. And it is not without weight that the hero Hengest appears in English but not in Continental story.

[20] See especially E. Björkman, *Studien über die Eigennamen im Beowulf* (Halle, 1920), pp. 60-61.

The famous English scholar Alcuin in a letter of the year 797 (No. 124 *Lost* in Duemmler's edition) [21] bears incidental witness to the existence of a song *Songs* about Ingeld, the unfortunate king of the Heathobards mentioned in *Beowulf* and *Widsith*. This king sacrificed honor, love, and life itself in a fruitless attempt to avenge a defeat which the Danes had inflicted upon his tribe.[22] From allusions in extant literature and elsewhere we may infer with certainty that many other songs composed by scops were once current in England, though their texts have not come down to us. Sometimes the allusions give us a good idea of the events celebrated in an old poem, but often we must go to Iceland or Denmark or Germany for the story, and often we search in vain for further information. It would be interesting and worth while to make a list of songs once sung by English gleemen, but now lost. We find it safer, however, to list some of the heroes that were celebrated in these lost songs. In so doing, we begin with the Goths. The Gothic heroes fall into three groups: early, middle, and late. The early heroes are those mentioned as such by Jordanes, the sixth-century historian of the Goths, who tells us [23] that their deeds were celebrated in song. Three of these heroes, Emerca, Fridla, and Wudga (Widia), find place in *Widsith;* presumably they became known to the English through the scops. We add King Eastgota and his son Unwen to the early group; they are later in date than the ancient heroes in Jordanes' list, but lived too early (third century) to be put with the middle group, and the *Widsith* poet associates them with Emerca and Fridla. The chief hero of the middle group, and of the Goths in general, is King Ermanric, who figures largely in *Widsith,* and is mentioned in *Beowulf* and *Deor*. He flourished in the fourth century. To the middle group also belong Wulfhere and Wyrmhere, mentioned in *Widsith* as leaders of the Vistula Goths in their warfare against the Huns; these heroes presumably flourished *c.* A.D. 400. The case of Hama makes difficulties; in *Widsith* he goes with the early hero Wudga, while in *Beowulf* he goes with Ermanric. In all likelihood *Widsith* gives us the older tradition here, while the *Beowulf* allusion reflects the beginning of a process carried through in later times, a process whereby the gigantic figure of Ermanric drew various Gothic heroes into his circle, irrespective of chronology.[24]

---

[21] *Monumenta Germaniae Historica . . . Epistolarum,* IV (Berolini, 1895). 183. The passage may be translated thus: "The words of God are to be read at a corporate priestly meal. There it is proper to hear a reader, not a harper; sermons of the fathers, not songs of the heathen. What [has] Ingeld [to do] with Christ? Narrow is the house: and it cannot hold both. The heavenly king will not have to do with so-called kings, heathen and damned, because that king reigns in heaven, world without end, while the heathen one, damned, laments in hell. . . ." See also No. 21, *ed. cit.,* p. 59: audiantur in domibus vestris legentes, non ludentes in platea "readers in your houses, not players in the street are to be heard."

[22] The tale of Ingeld is the subject of a *Beowulf* episode (lines 2014-2069a) and a *Widsith* passage (lines 47-49). See K. Malone, *MP,* XXVII (1930). 257-276; *Anglia,* LXIII (1939). 105-112; *GR,* XIV (1939). 235-257; *ELH,* VII (1940). 39-44; *JEGP,* XXXIX (1940). 76-92; and *Essays and Studies in Honor of Carleton Brown* (1940), pp. 1-22.

[23] *Getica,* cap. v.

[24] Monograph: C. Brady, *The Legends of Ermanaric* (Berkeley, 1943); reviewed by K. Malone, *MLN,* LIX (1944). 183-188 and *JEGP,* XLIII (1944). 449-453; by P. W. Souers, *Speculum,* XX (1945). 502-507.

The only Gothic hero of the late period is Theodric, the conqueror of Italy; he is mentioned in *Waldere*.[25]

Three Burgundian heroes are mentioned in *Widsith*: Gifica, Guðhere and Gislhere. The fall of Guðhere in battle against the Huns may well have been the subject of an English song. The Frankish hero Sigemund, son of Wæls, together with Sigemund's nephew Fitela, was celebrated in song by a scop, according to the *Beowulf* poet, who gives us (lines 874-897) some idea of the deeds celebrated. But Sigemund's famous son Sigfrid or Sigurd seems to have been unknown to the English, and the tale of the Wælsings was not combined with that of the Burgundians as it was in the Icelandic *Völsungasaga* and the German *Nibelungenlied*. The Frankish king Theodric, eldest son of Clovis, appears twice in *Widsith* and his rule over the Mærings (the Visigoths of Auvergne?) is mentioned in *Deor*. He answers to the Hugdietrich of German story.[26] The Langobards held a high place in English song, if we may judge by *Widsith*, where no less than six Langobardish heroes appear: the ancient kings Ægelmund and Hun(d)gar, of whom a tale is told by Paulus Diaconus, the historian of the Langobards;[27] another ancient king Sceafa; two later kings, Eadwine and Ælfwine, the Audoin and Alboin of the historians; and a king or kemp Elsa otherwise unknown. Hagena, King of the Rugians, appears in *Widsith* 21, where he is coupled with a certain Henden, King of the Glomman. The line may well be an allusion to the Hild story, in which father and lover fight about the lady.[28] Wada, King of the Hælsings, was still sung in Chaucer's day, and his inclusion in *Widsith* indicates that the scops sang him too. Many Scandinavian heroes, besides, figured in English song. We learn of them chiefly in *Beowulf*, the major Old English poetic monument. Only one English hero found much favor with the scops, it would seem, but they made amends by composing two songs in his honor. King Offa, who ruled the English in Sleswick, before their migration to Britain, won fame both as a fighter and as a wife-tamer. His fight is told of in *Widsith* (38-44); his marriage, in *Beowulf* (1933-1962). At the opposite extreme from Offa stands King Attila of the Huns, the only non-Germanic hero whom the scops celebrated in song. We end our list with Weland the smith, the only mythological character included (unless Wada and Sceafa are mythical, as some scholars think).[29]

The heroes listed have much in common. First of all, their nationality is Germanic; even Attila may be looked upon as Germanic by adoption. For

---

[25] If the Beadeca of *Widsith* is rightly identified with King Totila, we have another Gothic hero of the latest or Italian period.

[26] See K. Malone, in *Acta Phil. Scand.*, IX (1934). 76-84, and *ESt*, LXXIII (1939). 180-184.

[27] The tale answers, in part, to the "Helgakviður" of the *Elder Edda*; see K. Malone, *Amer. Jour. Philology*, XLVII (1926). 319-346, and *MLQ*, I (1940). 39-42.

[28] For the various versions of this and other tales referred to here, see M. G. Clarke, *Sidelights on Teutonic History in the Migration Period* (Cambridge, 1911).

[29] Many other names might be added (e.g., those of eponyms and others from the royal genealogies), but we have given enough to serve the purposes of this history.

many centuries the English had enjoyed political independence, but culturally they still belonged to a commonwealth of nations, the Germania of their Continental forefathers. Within that commonwealth they were at home, and felt the Goth, the Swede, the Langobard alike to be cultural fellow-countrymen. Secondly, the heroes all flourished in a period thought of as heroic in some special or exclusive sense, though without definition. This period ended with Ælfwine, the Langobardish conqueror of Italy. When it began we cannot say with precision. The heroic period answers roughly to the great migration of the Germanic tribes in the third, fourth, fifth, and sixth centuries, a migration which overthrew the Roman Empire in the west and ushered in the Middle Ages. For the Romans and the Romanized peoples of western Europe this period was one of disaster; for the Germanic tribes it was a period of glorious achievement, a heroic age indeed. Thirdly, the heroes all fought their way to glory: their reputation was based on prowess in battle. A king might win martial fame, it is true, by good leadership or good luck in warfare, but personal courage remained the chief virtue of every hero, be he king or kemp. Along with courage a king must have generosity; his dright, loyalty to him. The two virtues went together: a niggardly king could not win or keep loyal followers, and faithless followers could not expect generous gifts from their lord. The king gained riches through inheritance and war; he gave land, weapons, and other valuables away in order to build up a large and loyal body of followers, by whose help he could win new victories and fill or swell his hoard. A dright was recruited from the whole Germanic world; the fame of a generous and victorious king would draw to his court many a *wrecca* "adventurer" from many a tribe. The king's fellow-tribesmen nevertheless made the backbone of his following. Fourthly, the heroes nearly always belonged to the upper classes of society; they could and did boast of distinguished fathers and forefathers. The society in which they lived, however, aristocratic though it was, had hardly begun that differentiation of classes so marked in the modern world: high and low thought and acted much alike; they had much the same cultural background, viz., that of the peasant. One may compare the peasant culture reflected in the *Iliad* and the *Odyssey,* a way of life simple and dignified, with much form and ceremony upon occasion, but with many freedoms (e.g., boasting) that good manners now forbid.

Much more might be said about these heroes and the songs in which their heroic deeds found record, but we must go on to the tenth century, when nameless followers of the tradition of the scops composed two poems of praise which posterity has found worthy of admiration. These poems deal with contemporary events, not with events of the heroic age, and so far as we can tell they give us accurate historical information. They illustrate, therefore, a feature not always found in works of literary art, but characteristic of the tradition which the scops set going: the poet as historian.

Brunanburg   Under the year 937 in the *Old English Annals* is recorded a poem of 73
lines in praise of King Athelstan of England and his brother Edmund.[30]
The occasion for the poem was a battle which the brothers fought and won
"at Bruna's borough (stronghold)," against an invading force of Scots and
Vikings, led by Kings Constantine and Anlaf. The poet, after praising the
brothers and telling of their foes' losses on the field of battle, goes on to
praise the English army: [31]

> The West-Saxons
> pressed on in force all the day long,
> pushed ahead after the hostile army,
> hewed the fleeing down from behind fiercely,
> with mill-sharp swords. The Mercians withheld
> the hard handplay no whit from a man
> of those that with Anlaf came over the waves,
> by ship invaded our shores from abroad,
> warriors doomed to die in warplay. . . . (lines 20-28)

He continues with the flight of Constantine and Anlaf, told with relish
and elaborated with passages of exultation. The last section (lines 57-73)
falls into three parts: (1) the triumphant homecoming of the brothers; (2)
the fate of the bodies of the slain; and (3) the following historical comment:

> So vast a slaughter
> of men never yet was made before this
> on this island of ours with the edge of the sword
> (if we take for true what is told us in books
> or by the old and wise), since from the east hither
> the Angles and Saxons came up, to these shores,
> over broad waters sought Britain out,
> the keen warsmiths, overcame the Welshmen,
> the worshipful kemps, and won the land. (lines 65-73)

The poem is done with high technical skill. The transitions in particular
show the poet's mastery of his medium. Noteworthy, too, is a nationalism
which goes beyond loyalty to the king's person or to the reigning dynasty.
The reference to books, alongside oral tradition, marks the poet a clerk
rather than a scop and his poem a writing rather than a speaking.[32] The
verses belong, however, to the tradition of the scops in matter and manner.
Like the scops, the author is not concerned to describe the course of the
battle in any detail; he has made a poem of praise which happens to be a
battlepiece as well because victory served as an occasion for praise. If this
poem falls short of greatness, brilliant though the poet's performance, its

[30] The best edition of *Brunanburg* is that of A. Campbell (1938).
[31] The metrical translations from *Brunanburg* here quoted are taken, by permission, from
K. Malone, *Ten Old English Poems* (Baltimore: Johns Hopkins Press, 1941).
[32] Reference to sources is of course a conventional feature, in writings and speakings alike.

occasion must take the blame, in part at least. Defeat, not victory, found the old poets at their best.[33]

Such a defeat was the battle of Maldon, and the poem so named rises   Maldon
magnificently to the tragic occasion. The battle was fought in the year 991
at the estuary of the Blackwater (or Panta) in Essex near Maldon. The
hero of the poem is Byrhtnoth, Earl of Essex, leader of the English fyrd
(militia); the poet does not name the leaders of the Viking invaders. The
text of the poem, preserved in the Oxford MS Rawlinson B 203 (eighteenth
century),[34] has come down to us incomplete: it wants both beginning and
end. The beginning presumably told of the arrival of the Viking fleet and
the measures for defense taken by the Earl. We have no way of knowing
what form the end took; possibly the author left his work unfinished. It
seems unlikely that any great proportion of the poem has been lost: the
324½ lines that survive give us the meat of the matter. *Maldon* (like *Brunanburg*) was presumably composed shortly after the event which it com-
memorates: the fall of Byrhtnoth and his dright in battle against the Danes
at Maldon. The later differs from the earlier poem markedly—much more
than the difference in theme would lead one to expect. We illustrate with
the transitions. The *Maldon* poet leans heavily on the connective *þa* "then."
In *Brunanburg* this connective does not occur (unless line 53 gives us an
instance); the earlier poet does his structural dovetailing so deftly that he
must shun a crude device like *þa*—it would spoil the finished effect he aims
at. But such deftness would defeat the purpose of the later poet, who is
telling a tragic tale with high simplicity; he gains his effects the better for
his loose composition.[35] The action of *Maldon* divides naturally into two
parts: the course of the battle before (1-184) and after (185-325) the fall
of Byrhtnoth. Another two-fold division, equally natural, is that made in
terms of the hero's generalship; here the turning-point comes at line 96,
when the Earl has made the mistake of withdrawing the holders of the

[33] No less than 13 other poems, occasional in theme, were included in the. *Old English
Annals*. Seven of these deal with events of the tenth century; six, with events of the eleventh.
Some of them resemble *Brunanburg* in that they are panegyrics, done in correct classical verse.
They lack the brilliance and fervor of *Brunanburg*, however, and their shortness gives them
something of an annalistic character. The other poems incorporated in the *Annals* have a
certain interest because of their departure from the classical tradition in style and technic; one
notes in particular the growing use of rime and the growing freedom in alliteration (e.g., *st*
need not be an alliterative unit). Their artistic worth is negligible. Some of the 13 poems were
presumably composed or quoted by the annalists themselves (more precisely, by the original
compilers of the annalistic material sent round to the monasteries); others seem to be
interpolations, or insertions made by readers. Note K. Jost's demonstration (*Anglia*, XLVII
[1923]. 105-123) that two of the poems were composed by Archbishop Wulfstan of York.
Such compositions led to the metrical chronicles of Middle English times.

[34] Cotton Otho A XII, the old MS in which *Maldon* found record, was badly burned in the fire
of 1731; only fragments remain. Luckily J. Elphinston had copied the poem several years
earlier. His copy, now in the Rawlinson collection at Oxford, has served directly or indirectly,
as the basis for all editions of the poem. The latest and best separate edition of *Maldon*, that
of E. V. Gordon (London, 1937), is based directly on Elphinston's transcript.

[35] The same striving for naturalness comes out in the *Maldon* poet's preference for the early
stage of the run-on style, and in his departures from the rigorously classical versification and
technic favored by the *Brunanburg* poet. The freedoms found in *Maldon*, be it added, mark no
breakdown of the classical tradition; they exemplify, rather, normal and proper variation within
that tradition.

ford and letting the Vikings cross the river. The two schemes of division may be combined into a threefold scheme: first the English have the upper hand (1-95); after Byrhtnoth's mistake in generalship but before his fall, the issue of the battle hangs in the balance (96-184); after his fall the English lose the day (185-325). The hero's fatal error grew out of his martial spirit, to which the foe cunningly and successfully appealed. Here lies the tragic flaw which made possible the catastrophe. But it was the flight of the cowardly Godric, mounted on the hero's horse, that precipitated and ensured defeat for the English. Others followed his example (many misled by his mount into thinking it was the Earl himself that fled) and the faithful retainers who stood their ground were left in hopeless case. To their stand lines 202-325 are devoted, over a third of the poem. But this proportion should not mislead us. The thane who dies fighting to the last by his lord's body makes a noble figure, a figure that the scops loved to draw, but he is not a hero in his own right. His devotion typifies that of the dright as a whole, and serves to exalt the lord who won such loyalty. Earl Byrhtnoth is the hero of *Maldon*. But the poet does more than glorify a hero. He glorifies the institution: the relationship of lord and dright that gives rise to the heroism which he celebrates. The poem belongs to the tradition of the scops, and most of it might be put back into heathen times with little or no change in word or thought. Only one truly Christian passage occurs, the prayer of the dying hero:

> I thank thee, O God, Governor of peoples,
> for all the blessings that on earth were mine.
> Now, mild Master, I most have need
> that thou grant to my ghost the grace of heaven,
> that my soul have leave to seek thee out,
> depart in peace, pass into thy keeping,
> Prince of angels. I pray it of thee
> that the fiends of hell afflict her not.[36] (lines 173-80)

These moving words befit the hero, who, as we know from history, was a man of deep Christian piety. He and the cleric who composed the poem in his praise held warfare righteous if in a good cause, and what better cause could be found than defense of church and state, hearth and home against heathen invaders? Our poet upheld and glorified the heroic traditions of his forefathers with a clear conscience; he felt no conflict (in Byrhtnoth's case, at least) between these traditions and Christianity.

The heroic point of view, and the stylistic conventions that go with it, are manifest in the poet's account of the fighting. The battle in *Maldon*, like the battles in the *Iliad*, takes the form of single combats between champions; the common soldiers are ignored. Over a fourth of the poem is made up of speeches. Contrast *Brunanburg*, where neither single combats nor

---

[36] Taken, by permission, from K. Malone, *Ten Old English Poems* (Baltimore: Johns Hopkins Press, 1941).

speeches occur. Both poems are properly described as poems of praise, but they evidently represent different species of this genus. *Maldon* bears some likeness to the epic, *Brunanburg* to the panegyric of the ancients. The differences, however, are too great to admit of southern inspiration in either case. We must presume, rather, a differentiation within the tradition of the scops.

VI

Religious Poetry: Cædmon and His School

English religious poetry begins with a sharpness unusual in the history of literature. An elderly illiterate farmhand of Yorkshire, Cædmon by name, who had never learned how to make verses and would flee for shame when, at entertainments, his turn came to sing, suddenly began to compose poems of a kind hitherto not known in English: religious narrative verse on themes drawn from Holy Writ. The story of Cædmon is told in Bede; [1] it is so familiar that we need not tell it again here. Cædmon served as lay brother and, later, as monk in a monastery at Strenæshalc (Whitby?) under the abbess Hild; his literary activity thus falls between the years 657 and 680 (Hild's term as abbess). Bede gives a Latin paraphrase of Cædmon's first poem, the so-called *Hymn,* and texts of the poem in a dialect of the Northumbrian English native to the poet have come down to us in MSS of Bede's work. The following translation into modern speech is based on the Moore MS text, printed in A. H. Smith's edition: [2]

Hymn

> Now [we] shall praise the heaven-realm's Keeper,
> God's might and his mood-thought,
> the work of the glory-Father, as he of each wonder,
> the eternal Lord, the beginning ordained.
> He first made to the children of men
> heaven for roof, the holy Creator.
> Then the middle-yard mankind's Keeper,
> the eternal Lord, afterwards created
> for men, the earth, the Ruler almighty.

This poem obviously belongs to the early stage of the classical run-on style (see above, p. 27); every line but the eighth ends with a pause, and every sentence ends with a line. The poet made use of a fully developed system of variation. He adapted the technic of the scops to his own purposes neatly enough: royal epithets like *ruler, lord, keeper* became epithets for God by qualification with *almighty, eternal, mankind's* and *heaven-realm's.* To speak more generally, Cædmon took God for his theme and sounded his praises much as a scop would sound the praises of his royal patron. And just as the scop celebrated the heroic deeds of the prince he served (or of that

[1] *Hist. Eccl.* IV. xxiv.
[2] *Three Northumbrian Poems* (1933), pp. 38, 40. But the editor's punctuation might be improved. For the history of the text, see E. V. K. Dobbie, *Columbia Univ. Stud. in English and Comp. Lit.,* No 128 (1937), pp. 10-48.

prince's forefathers), so Cædmon celebrated the glorious works of the prince _he_ served: namely, God. As Bede informs us,

he sang about the creation of the world, and the origin of mankind, and the whole tale of Genesis; about the exodus of Israel from Egypt and entry into the Promised Land; about many other tales of Holy Writ; about the incarnation, passion, resurrection and ascension into heaven of the Lord; about the coming of the Holy Ghost and the work (doctrina) of the apostles. He made many songs, too, about the terror of doomsday to come and the horror of hell-fire but the sweetness of the kingdom of heaven; but also many others about divine benefits and judgments.

Thereby the pious poet provided the body of monks with entertainment suitable for the monastic refectory, though modeled after the worldly entertainment with which the scops had long regaled the body of retainers in the royal beer-hall.[3] Like the scops again, Cædmon could not read or write, and learned by word of mouth the stories he put into verse. But his poems, in virtue of their matter, were deemed highly edifying, and scribes took them down from the first. The poems of Cædmon make a bridge between speakings and writings: they were composed as speakings, but at once became writings too.

We cannot point to any particular source of Cædmon's _Hymn,_ other than divine inspiration and Christian tradition.[4] There exists, however, in the Bodleian library at Oxford, a famous MS called Junius 11 and made up of verse obviously based, for the most part, on Holy Writ.[5] This verse was long attributed to Cædmon, although nowadays it is customary to put the poems of the Junius MS under the head "school of Cædmon"—a label which denies their Cædmonian authorship. We take up these and related poems here. The MS as it stands is divided into two books: the first given over to verse dealing with Old Testament story; the second, to verse about Christ and Satan. According to Gollancz (p. xviii).

Junius MS

The writing of Book I belongs to the last quarter of the tenth or the early years of the eleventh century. No long interval divided the writing of Book II from that of the earlier portion.

Book I was done by one scribe, who had no hand in the copying of Book II, carried out by three scribes "less than a generation"[6] later. Many leaves have been lost from Book I, which therefore has come down to us markedly incomplete; in Book II no such losses took place. Book I is profusely il-

---

[3] But worldly poems composed by scops were still being sung in refectories long after Cædmon's day, as we learn from Alcuin's letter (see above, p. 53). The performer of such a song might be a scop turned monk, or a scop who was spending the night at a monastery. We do not know to what extent (if at all) court poets, or others who followed the courtly tradition, gave performances for the general public (at markets and like places).

[4] But see Sir Israel Gollancz, facsimile ed. _Cædmon MS_ (Oxford, 1927), pp. lxi-lxii.

[5] Edition of MS: see Krapp-Dobbie I. Editions of individual poems: F. Holthausen, _Die ältere Genesis_ (Heidelberg, 1914); B. J. Timmer, _The Later Genesis_ (Oxford, 1948); F. A. Blackburn, _Exodus and Daniel_ (Boston, 1907); M. D. Clubb, _Christ and Satan_ (New Haven, 1925). See also Clubb, _MLN,_ XLIII (1928). 304-306.

[6] Clubb, _ed. cit.,_ p. xii.

lustrated, though the artists did not finish their work, leaving many pages blank; Book II is written solid except for the lower half of two pages. We set the second book aside for the moment. The MS text of the first book is divided into 55 fits. With fit 42 the tale shifts from Genesis to Exodus; with fit 50, from Exodus to Daniel. Modern philologists accordingly divide the book into three independent poems. *Genesis,* the first of these, is by far the longest; it comes to 2936 lines.

Genesis

The poem opens with a few lines in praise of God, lines which lead naturally to a short passage in which is depicted the happy lot of the angels in heaven. Next we are told of the discontent and rebellion of Satan and his crew, God's wrath, the creation of hell to house the rebels, their overthrow and expulsion from heaven, and God's design to make the world as a means of filling with "better people" (95) the space left empty in heaven by the transfer of the wicked angels to their new abode.

The better people were presumably the souls of the blessed, the elect of the seed of Adam (as yet uncreated). The world was to be made as a breeding-place for these. Pope Gregory the Great gave a like interpretation to the story of the fall of the angels, and our poet doubtless got his ideas on the subject, directly or indirectly, from Gregory's writings. With line 103 the story of the world and man begins, a story based on the biblical narrative; more specifically, the poet's source was St. Jerome's Latin translation of the Scriptures, commonly called the Vulgate. This the poet follows faithfully from its beginning to Gen. 22:13; here the poem breaks off. We do not know whether it was left unfinished or once had a continuation now lost.

Genesis A and B

Through loss of MS leaves our text has gaps in several places. Lines 235-851 do not belong to the poem at all, but make a great interpolation taken from a later poem on the same subject; this poem was an English version of a Low German (more precisely, an Old Saxon) original. We therefore distinguish between the *Earlier Genesis* or *Genesis A* (lines 1-234 and 852-2936) and the *Later Genesis* or *Genesis B* (lines 235-851). Of the later poem only that part survives which was interpolated into *Genesis A;* of its original, three fragments survive, one of which answers to lines 790-817a of the interpolation. The beginning of *Genesis B* is lost, but the interpolated verses from it dealt with the temptation and fall of Adam and Eve: Gen. 2:16-17 and 3:1-7. Into this story the German author had inserted an account of the fall of the angels, and our text therefore gives us two versions of this event: the rather short and simple version at the beginning of *Genesis A,* and the long, striking version in *Genesis B*. Of the two Genesis poems, the later has great poetic power; indeed, the speech of Satan to the fallen angels bears comparison with *Paradise Lost* in vigor if not in finish. The poet of *Genesis A* outdid his German fellow in craftsmanship but lacked his genius, and the poem is hardly what one would expect of Cædmon. It is worthy of particular note that Bede's list of Cædmon's poems begins, not with the fall of the Angels, but with the creation of the world. From Bede's list and discussion one gathers, further, that Cædmon's poems, like those of the scops, were many and short, not few and long. By its shortness the *Hymn,* Cædmon's authorship of which is certain, lends support to this interpretation of Bede's words. Moreover, the *Hymn* belongs to the early, *Genesis A* to the middle stage of the run-on style. We conclude that Cædmon hardly composed the latter poem, though its author may well have been inspired by Cædmon's songs to undertake a metrical paraphrase of Genesis which would differ from Cædmon's work by reproducing the sacred text in detail. Such a reproduction would of necessity make a long poem, and long poems of this kind would win favor among the clerics, at the expense of short poems, because of their completeness—little or nothing said in Holy Writ, however trivial or by the way, was left out. Again, though both short and long poems were composed for didactic entertainment in refectory, the long poems presumably followed the pattern traditional for monastic meals: they were meant to be read aloud, not sung to the accompaniment of the harp. Certainly the middle and late stages of the run-on style do not go well with musical performance. Ecclesiastical authority might be expected to favor poems for reading, as against poems that were performed after the secular courtly fashion; the latter, though not worldly in theme, had at least a touch of worldliness in performance. It was the practice of reading aloud, we may add, which made possible the rapid development of the run-on style in Old English poetry, freeing the poet as it did from the limitations imposed by musical performance. And the taste for long poems, aroused by the metrical paraphrasts and nourished by study of the *Æneid,* led to extended treatment of secular themes like those of *Beowulf* and *Waldere.*

With Bradley [7] we think that the author of *Genesis A* was a clerk who, as he wrote, had before him a copy of the Vulgate. But he had other sources besides. Gollancz has noted (p. lvii) that

in the poet's treatment of *Genesis* generally, one can trace the use of commentaries and legendary additions, as for example, the story that the raven sent out from the ark perched upon the floating bodies of the dead and so did not return,

and we saw above that the poet began with the fall of the angels, a story which he did not find in Genesis. Moreover, he drew freely from the tradition of the scops, not indeed for matter but for stylistic motifs and devices, and phraseology in general. Thus, the battles of Genesis are described after the manner of the scops. We quote the following passage by way of illustration:

---

[7] *Collected Papers of Henry Bradley* (Oxford, 1928), p. 248. In *DNB,* VIII. 200, Bradley put the matter thus: "a servile paraphrase of the biblical text can only have proceeded from a writer who was able to read his Latin Bible; to a poet who, like Cædmon, had to depend on his recollection of extemporised oral translation, such a performance would have been absolutely impossible."

> There was hard play there,
> exchange of deadly spears, great roar of battle,
> loud war clamor. With hands they drew,
> the heroes, from sheaths the ringed swords,
> the strong-edged [swords]. There it was easy to find
> booty for the fighter who had not had
> enough of combat. (lines 1989-95)

Typical here is the description of the victor: the one who wins booty (i.e., the battle) is the one who is not willing to stop fighting. Dogged does it— such was the spirit of the English then, even as now. The earlier *Genesis,* whether by Cædmon or not, is commonly reckoned a product of the Northumbrian school of poets which Cædmon brought into being, and is commonly dated *c.* 700. The later *Genesis* cannot be earlier than its German original, a poem of the ninth century, and cannot be later than the Junius MS. We know nothing of the translator.

Exodus
The second poem of Book 1 is known as *Exodus;* it has no name in the MS. It is 591 lines long by the reckoning of Blackburn, who in his edition rightly followed the pointing of the MS; earlier editors printed the poem in 589 lines.

We divide the text into the following parts: an introductory period on the Mosaic law (1-7); an epitome of the career of Moses (8-29); a sketch of events in Egypt that led up to the departure of the Hebrews (30-55); the march of the Hebrews to the Red Sea (56-134); the Egyptian pursuit and the rearguard set by the terrified Hebrews (135-246); the passage of the Red Sea and the destruction of the Egyptian army (247-515); conclusion (516-591).[8]

A digressive or episodic passage of more than 80 lines (362-446) on Noah and Abraham follows the description (310-353a) of the order of march of the Hebrew tribes; a short passage (353b-361) on the common ancestry of the tribes serves to tie the digression, loosely enough, to the main story. Through loss of MS leaves the text has two serious gaps: one between lines 141 and 142 and one (fit 48) between lines 446 and 447. The poet's theme is not Exodus as a whole but the passage of the Red Sea by the Israelites, or, better, the heroic leadership of Moses in this passage. Noteworthy are lines 208 ff., in which the despair of the fugitives at the approach of the Egyptian host changes to courage when Moses bids them "make up their minds to perform deeds of valor" (218b). Unluckily the battle-scene (fit 48) is lost. The poet gives much space to speech-making by his hero; the speeches are reported now in direct, now in indirect discourse. In general, the poet follows English heroic tradition: Moses answers to a Germanic king and the picked fighters of the Hebrews answer to a Germanic dright. For his story the poet relies chiefly on chapter 14 of Exodus. A few verses elsewhere in Exodus are used too, and some use is made of other books of Moses, notably Genesis. But the author goes much further afield. Modern

[8] The conclusion makes problems too involved for discussion here; see Gollancz, pp. lxxv-lxxix, whose conjectural rearrangement of the lines cannot surmount the obstacle of *swa* 549.

investigators have emphasized his learning and his originality, as reflected in style and in sundry details of the text.[9] The freedom with which he treated his main source finds extreme illustration in lines 447-515, based on a single Bible verse: Exod. 14:28. The half-line *flod blod gewod* "blood filled the flood" (463b) reveals a fondness for striking metrical effects. Now and again the poet's wording seems fanciful or even strained, as when he calls the Hebrews seamen (333) because they were crossing the Red Sea (on foot). But it would be a mistake to reckon the poem precious; [10] it departs somewhat from the classical mean characteristic of most Old English poetry, but remains traditional on the whole. The difficulties which the text makes come chiefly from its faulty transmission, and for this the poet cannot rightly be blamed. Date and authorship are unsolved problems. Gollancz was so impressed by the poet's learned preciosity (as he took it) that he suggested authorship "if not by Aldhelm, then by one of his school, and certainly by a kindred spirit" (p. lxix), but he admitted that the text bore marks of Anglian origin. The scanty evidence points to a Northumbrian clerk of the Age of Bede, when learning was at its height in Old England. Since the poem belongs to the middle stage of the run-on style, it can hardly have been composed earlier than *c.* 700.

The third and last poem of Book 1 is that called *Daniel*. It has no title   Daniel
in the MS. By Blackburn's count it comes to 764 lines; earlier editors wrongly made two lines of line 224.

Author or scribe divided the text into six fits. The first of these falls into two parts: an introduction, on Hebrew history down to the war with Nebuchadnezzar (1-41a); and the story of that war, with its consequence, the Babylonian captivity of the Jews, to which is added an account of the three Hebrew children, Hananiah, Mishael, and Azariah, with their training for Nebuchadnezzar's service (41b-103). The second part of the fit is based on the first chapter of Daniel, much of which, however, the poet leaves out; in particular, he fails to mention Daniel. The next fit likewise falls into two parts: it begins with a condensed paraphrase (104-167) of Daniel 2, in which we learn of Nebuchadnezzar's first dream (about the image) and Daniel's success with it after the Chaldean wise men had failed; then comes a versification of Dan. 3:1-18, the story of the golden image which the king sets up and which the three Hebrew children refuse to worship, though the king threatens to cast them into a fiery furnace (168-223). Through loss of a MS leaf the poet's paraphrase of Dan. 3:2-6 is wanting here. The third fit falls into three parts: first, a paraphrase of Dan. 3:19-27, telling how the king carried out his threat and how an angel came down into the furnace and saved the children (224-278); next, the apocryphal prayer of Azariah (279-332); last, a repetition of the rescue story, the angel's coming being represented

---

9 Obviously he knew his way about in a monastic library, with its Latin classics, Church fathers, martyrologies, commentaries and miscellanies. In particular, he has been credited with knowledge of Avitus, Sedulius, Jerome, Josephus, Augustine, Bede, and Ealdhelm. The following studies are worth listing: L. L. Schücking, *Untersuchungen*, etc. (Heidelberg, 1915); S. Moore, *MP*, IX (1911). 83-108; J. W. Bright, *MLN*, XXVII (1912). 13-19 and 97-103; R. Imelmann, *Forschungen* etc. (Berlin, 1920).

10 Imelmann, *op. cit.*, pp. 390-408, gives a needful corrective for the extravagances of Schücking and his followers.

as in answer to Azariah's prayer (333-361). The fourth fit too falls into three parts: it begins with the apocryphal Song of the Three Youths in praise of God (362-408), continues with a paraphrase of Dan. 3:24-29, in which the story of the angel is told a third time (409-485), and ends with a passage of transition to the next fit (486-494). The fifth fit versifies Daniel 4, telling of Nebuchadnezzar's second dream (about the tree) and Daniel's interpretation (495-674). The last fit versifies Daniel 5, on Belshazzar's feast (675-764); through loss of a MS leaf the end of this fit is missing. The poet seems not to have versified the story of Daniel in the Lions' Den (Daniel, 6).

Daniel
A *and* B

The second and third parts of the third fit make an interpolation into our poem. We therefore distinguish *Daniel A* (1-278 and 362-764) and *Daniel B* (279-361). The former poem belongs to the early stage of the run-on style. This may mean that it was composed early, but its author may have lived later and used the older style simply because he preferred it. The poem is no masterpiece, but shows good workmanship; the transitions especially are well done. The old link between fits three and four is lost, replaced by the interpolation. The repetitious treatment of the angel in *Daniel A* makes problems too knotty for this history. The poet does not follow his source slavishly; he leaves much out, and sometimes puts things in, as when he has Nebuchadnezzar wake up from a drunken sleep (116). He expands freely when he likes, and even includes a lyric piece: the Song of the Three Youths. His source here was not the Vulgate, but a canticle the Latin text of which is preserved in the so-called *Vespasian Psalter*.[11] We have no evidence, however, that the poet's English version of the Song once existed free of its setting in *Daniel A*. The Song does not fall into five-line stanzas, as some have maintained. *Daniel A* presumably goes back to early Northumbria (*c.* 700?).

Azariah

The interpolator took *Daniel B* from a poem which the philologists call *Azariah*.[12] A copy of this poem has come down to us in the Exeter Book. More precisely, the compiler of that MS miscellany included part of a poem on the third chapter of *Daniel,* presumably the part he liked best; certainly he left out the beginning, for his text begins, abruptly enough, with the introduction to the prayer of Azariah. The part preserved in the Exeter Book comes to 191 lines. Of these, lines 28-29 make what is left of a defective passage that answers to *Daniel,* 307-312; the missing words were recorded on the lost part of folio 53.

The poem as we have it consists of the introduction to the prayer of Azariah (1-4), the prayer (5-48), the rescue by the angel (49-67a), the introduction to the Song of the Three Youths (67b-72), the Song (73-161a), the outcry of the heathen at the miracle (161b-165), the report of the miracle, made to Nebuchadnezzar by his *eorl* (166-179a), and the king's reaction: he went to see the miracle

[11] H. Sweet, *Oldest English Texts* (EETS, 83). pp. 414-415. The canticle was drawn from the Roman Breviary.

[12] Ed. W. Schmidt, *Bonner Beiträge,* xxiii (1907). 40-48. See also editions of the Exeter Book. The latest of these is Krapp-Dobbie, iii.

with his own eyes and then told the youths to come to him, whereupon they left the furnace in triumph (179b-191).

Daniel B is so like *Azariah*, 1-72 that we cannot speak of two poems but must reckon the two texts mere variants of the same original. The likenesses of *Daniel A* to the corresponding parts of *Azariah* need another explanation. The evidence indicates that the *Azariah* poet had before him, not only the Vulgate text but also a copy of *Daniel A*. This copy he drew upon freely at the beginning of the Song of the Three Youths, but less and less as he proceeded; in making his version of the Song he followed the Canticle text but took the Vulgate text into account as well. He expanded his sources with reflective and devotional matter much more freely than did the *Daniel* poet. We reckon the report of the *eorl* to Nebuchadnezzar a piece of conventional English heroic machinery; it may have been suggested by the speech of the counselor in *Daniel A* (416 ff.), but bears little likeness to that speech. Azariah belongs to the middle stage of the run-on style. It was composed later than *Daniel A,* and earlier than the time of compilation of the Exeter Book. Its author followed in the tradition set going by Cædmon, and may well have been a Northumbrian clerk, but of this we cannot be sure. If he was Northumbrian, his poem can hardly have been composed later than *c.* 875.

Another poem based on Old Testament story is *Judith;* it has come down Judith to us in the Nowell codex, BM Cotton Vitellius A xv, 2d MS (late tenth century).[13] The poet had for source the Vulgate text of the apocryphal book of Judith. Unluckily only the last part of the poem survives: 348 lines and 2 half-lines, making a little more than three fits. If we go (as we must) by the MS numbering, the complete poem made at least 12 fits; the fragment we have begins toward the end of the ninth fit, and versifies Judith 12:10 to 16:1. We cannot tell whether the poet stopped here or composed a thirteenth fit, answering to the canticle of thanksgiving in Judith, 16. If such a fit 13 ever existed, it has been lost.

The tenth fit (15-121) deals with the feast at which Holofernes became drunk and with his death at the hands of Judith. The eleventh fit (122-235) deals with the return of Judith and her maid to Bethulia, bringing the head of Holofernes; the joyous welcome Judith got from the Hebrews; her speech exhorting them to go forth to battle; and their attack upon the Assyrian host. The twelfth fit (236-350) deals with the hesitation of the Assyrians, though under attack, to wake Holofernes; their terror and flight when at last one of them ventured into the general's tent and found his headless body; the slaughter the Hebrews made and the booty they took; finally the spoils awarded to Judith and the praise she gave to God.

The poem belongs to the last stage of the run-on style (see above, p. 27). Its author shows himself a master of his medium. Indeed, he has produced a *tour de force*. In spite of the many swollen lines (nearly a fifth of the

---

[13] This codex, better known as the *Beowulf* MS, is now available in facsimile: *Early English MSS in Facsimile* xii (Copenhagen, 1963), ed. K. Malone.

whole), the long periods, the frequent variations and descriptive details, we find the tempo swift, the action sharp and straightforward. An elaborate and sophisticated style, made for epic breadth and leisure, is here seized upon and forced to yield effects akin to those of the scops, though without that singing quality which the gleeman's older and simpler art had kept. The heroic tone of *Judith* goes without saying. The battle scenes have rightly been praised, but owe less to the poet than to tradition. The scene of drunken revelry (15 ff.), however, stands unmatched in Old English. The poet has not hesitated to depart from his source when his art is served thereby. His fondness for rime is worthy of note. We take him to have been an Angle (Mercian) of the tenth century, though Saxon authorship is possible.

Christ
and Satan

The second book of the Junius MS is given over to some 733 lines of verse, a poem which Grein aptly called *Christ and Satan;* it has no name in the MS.

The text is divided into 12 fits. The first of these begins with a brief account of Creation (attributed to the Son) and the fall of the angels (1-33); then come a lament by Satan (34-50), a reproachful reply by his crew (51-64), and a homiletic passage (65-74). Satan's second lament makes the second fit (75-125). The third fit gives us two more laments of Satan: the third (126-159) and the fourth (160-189). The fourth fit is a short homily inspired by the fate of the fallen angels (190-224). With the next fit (225-255) Satan begins a fifth lament, which he finishes in the first part (256-279) of the sixth fit. The rest of this fit (280-315) and the whole of the seventh (316-365) make a kind of homily on the sorrows of hell and the joys of heaven. The eighth fit repeats in résumé the story of the fall of the angels (366-379a) and begins the story of Christ's harrowing of hell (379b-442). This story is finished in the ninth fit (443-469), which ends with Christ's speech to the souls he has rescued from hell and taken up to heaven (470-513); in this speech Christ tells of the creation and fall of man, of his resolve to save man, and of his incarnation and earthly life. The tenth fit is devoted to the Resurrection (514-557). The eleventh fit tells of the Ascension, Pentecost, the fate of Judas, and Christ's kingdom in heaven, to which men too may come (558-597). The twelfth fit goes on to Doomsday (598-643), gives yet another reminder of the joys of the saved (644-664), and adds an account of Christ's temptation in the wilderness (665-710); the fit ends with Satan's return to hell and to the curses of his followers after his failure to tempt Christ (711-733).

This poem makes many problems which cannot be taken up here.[14] Apart from the faulty transmission of the text, we must reckon with a scheme of presentation anything but straightforward. The sequence, chronological in the main, does great violence to chronology on occasions. Thus, the temptation of Christ comes at the end of the poem, and the fall of man is not spoken of until long after the event (410-421 and 481-488). In telling the story of Christ from Creation to Doomsday, the poet plays action down and situation up. His interest lies, not in the narrative but in the punishments and rewards of the life to come, and he pictures these over and over, using

---

14 See the discussions in the editions of Clubb and Gollancz cited above (p. 61).

all the devices at his command, and constantly hammering home the moral: we should follow Christ, not Satan. The laments put in Satan's own mouth make clear in dramatic fashion the folly of choosing such leadership as his. The Satan of this poem is not the defiant and indomitable leader of *Genesis B*, but a leader broken by defeat, who must swallow the curses of his own dright. The fate of Satan and his crew serves as the supreme object-lesson by which mankind may take warning. On the positive side, Christ's rejection of Satan's lordship in the temptation scene serves as the supreme example which all men should follow when faced with the temptations of earthly life. This scene therefore makes a fitting end for the poem, and we cannot accept the view of Gollancz that the poet after finishing his poem tacked the temptation on by way of afterthought. No immediate sources have been found for this remarkable work. The author drew on Christian tradition, as known to him from the Bible and elsewhere. He handled his material with a freedom which suggests that he wrote without having any books before him; he seems to have relied on his memory of the events and to have given rein to his fancy. His verses have power and vividness, but too much should not be made of their originality: the poet combines lyric, dramatic, and epic in typical Old English fashion. We reckon the poem Anglian in origin, and of the ninth century, but we do not set even so loose a date as this with confidence. We agree with all recent authorities that Cædmon did not compose *Christ and Satan*. The clerk who made the poem belonged to Cædmon's school, but learned from another school as well: that of Cynewulf. The work of this school will be considered in the next chapter.

VII

Religious Poetry: Cynewulf and His School

Nearly all Old English poetry is anonymous. One poet, however, had a habit of signing his verses, and from these signatures we know his name: Cynewulf.[1] His motive was not vainglory but (as he himself explains) hope that those who liked his poems would name him in their prayers. The signatures took the form of runes, woven in the verses towards the end but not at the very end of a given poem. From them we learn that the poet spelt his name indifferently *Cynewulf* and *Cynwulf*. Since he did not use the spelling *Cyniwulf* we infer that he lived after weak medial *i* had become *e*. The date of this sound-shift varies with the dialect. Other linguistic evidence, however, marks Cynewulf an Angle, and only the Northumbrian and Mercian dialects need be considered. Northumbrian weak *i* was kept until the middle of the ninth century, while Mercian variants with *e* appear early in that century, and this *e* may go back to the last years of the eighth. The earliest possible time for Cynewulf, then, is the last quarter of the eighth century, and the ninth makes a safer date. Of the man we know nothing except what we glean from his work. We have four poems of his: a list, a sermon, and two legends (i.e., saints' lives). We take them in the order given.

The Fates of the Apostles

The Fates of the Apostles is a poem of 122 lines, recorded in the Vercelli Book[2] (late tenth century). It falls into two parts: the list proper, in which are named the places or countries where the twelve apostles taught and died (1-87); and the poet's signature with accompanying verses (88-122). Unlike the *Menologium,* our poem does not include the feast-days of the twelve, but we need not infer with Krapp (p. xxxii) that "the motive which inspired its composition was, therefore, purely literary and devotional." A certain learned, antiquarian spirit also enters in, and such a list, though without dates, obviously had practical (didactic) worth besides. No single source answers precisely to lines 1-87, and such a source will hardly be found: Cynewulf starts by telling us he "gleaned far and wide" how the apostles "made their virtue known," and one naturally infers that the poet made a compilation drawn from various sources. Name-forms like *Petrus*

---

[1] See S. K. Das, *Cynewulf and the Cynewulf Canon* (Calcutta, 1942); K. Jansen, *Die Cynewulf-Forschung* (Bonn, 1908); K. Sisam, "Cynewulf and his Poetry," *Proc. Brit. Acad.,* XVIII (1932). 303-331. The texts are edited by A. S. Cook, *The Christ of Cynewulf* (Boston, 1900), and *The OE Elene . . .* (New Haven, 1919); W. Strunk, *The Juliana of Cynewulf* (Boston, 1904); G. P. Krapp, *Andreas and the Fates of the Apostles* (Boston, 1906). On the so-called *Christ* see especially Brother Aug. Philip, *PMLA,* LV (1940). 903-909.

[2] Facsimile edition by Max Förster (Rome, 1913); printed verse texts in Krapp-Dobbie, II.

and *Paulus* point to Latin sources, and like lists in Latin have been pointed out by Krapp and by Sisam. The poem has a so-called epic opening consonant with the worth of the theme. The following passage is representative:

> Certain ones in Rome,
> bold ones and brave, gave up their lives
> through Nero's cruel cunning,
> Peter and Paul; that apostleship
> is widely honored among the nations. (lines 11-15)

The personal part of the poem (88-122) makes more than a fourth of the whole. The disproportion springs from the author's eagerness to win the prayers of others, an eagerness which drives him to repeat, after the runic passage, the request for prayers which he had already made before that passage. Art here yields to soul's need! Otherwise the poem is marked by good craftsmanship. The riming half-line *nearwe searwe* (13b) is worthy of note.

The Ascension (otherwise known as *Christ B*) is a poem of 427 lines Ascension recorded in the Exeter Book. The poem is divided into five fits. These we analyze as follows:

I. Exhortation to an "illustrious man" (the poet's patron?) to make every effort to understand why the angels at the nativity did not appear in white robes (1-10a); the contrast here between nativity and ascension (10b-19a); the throng [before the ascension] in Bethany (19b-34); Christ's farewell to his followers (35-51); the ascension and the song of the angels (52-66); the two angels appear to the disciples and explain the event (67-77).

II. The parting words of the angels to the disciples (78-87); Christ assumes his seat in heaven amid rejoicing on high (88-93); the disciples return to Jerusalem and await Pentecost as Christ had bidden before he ascended (94-107); white-robed angels (i.e. splendor) befit Christ's return to his throne above (108-118); song of angels, celebrating Christ's harrowing of hell and return to heaven with the redeemed souls (119-146); lyric passage (with rime) on the plan of salvation and man's need to choose between good and evil (147-160).

III. Man should thank God for his gifts, the greatest of which is the hope of salvation, held out at the ascension (161-187); Christ's earthly life, from nativity to ascension, made our salvation possible (188-193); of this Job sang, using the figure of a bird [Job 28:7], but the Jews could not understand (194-219); Christ divides gifts among men; no one gets all spiritual wisdom, for fear of pride harming him (220-246).

IV. God by gifts honors his creatures, whose worth reflects God himself, our sun (247-258); the Church is likened to the moon; after the ascension she shone forth over the earth (259-264a); through the gift of the Holy Ghost [at Pentecost] the Church was enabled to withstand the persecutions which began after the ascension (264b-272); the six leaps of Christ (conception, nativity, crucifixion, burial, descent into hell, ascent into heaven), referred to by Solomon [Song 2:8] (273-304); so ought we to leap from strength to strength until we reach heaven through holy works; to that end we must choose the good and reject the evil; God will help us against devils; we must keep watch all our lives and pray to God, our benefactor, to whom be praise and glory for ever (305-339).

V. If God helps us, we need not fear devils (340-343a); Doomsday is near, when we shall be judged by our deeds (343b-346a); Christ's first coming was in humility [the angels did not appear in white robes]; his second coming will be in judicial sternness, and many will be punished (346b-357); runic passage (the poet's signature) on Doomsday (358-368a); the destruction of the world by fire (368b-375); be mindful of the soul's need now, before it is too late (376-384); the terrors of Doomsday (385-410); life is like a voyage, and heaven is like a port made ready for us by Christ when he ascended (411-427).

In this poem Cynewulf versified the conclusion of Gregory the Great's sermon on the ascension (the 29th of his gospel homilies).[3] Lines 220-246 owe much to another source, presumably an English poem not unlike the extant *Gifts of Men* (see below, p. 83). The Bible and other works seem to have been used more or less besides. The poet treated his matter with freedom and artistic skill, though of course his thought is derivative and traditional enough. This versified sermon must be reckoned successful. In structure it is governed by its chief source.

Juliana   *Juliana* is a poem of the Exeter Book. It comes to 731 lines as we have it, but through loss of MS leaves two passages are wanting: one before folio 70 (between lines 288 and 289), the other before folio 74 (between lines 558 and 559). The poem is made up of seven fits. These may be outlined as follows:

I. Under the Roman emperor Maximian (A.D. 305-311), persecutor of the Christians, there lived in Nicomedia a pagan official named Heliseus [Eleusius], who fell in love with the young and beautiful Christian virgin Juliana; she wished to keep her virginity, but her pagan father Africanus betrothed her to Heliseus; she refused to marry him unless he turned Christian; he protested to her father, who expostulated with her (1-104).

II. Juliana replied, holding her ground; Africanus argued further with her but could not move her; he turned her over to Heliseus for judgment; her betrothed, after pleading with her in vain, had her stripped and scourged; he then urged apostasy upon her with threats; she defied him and his false gods (105-224).

III. Heliseus had Juliana hanged on a tree by the hair and beaten for six hours; he then threw her into prison; a devil visited her there in angel form, to persuade her to yield; at her prayer a voice from heaven revealed the tempter's identity and gave orders that she seize the fiend and not let him go until he had confessed all; she obeyed and thereby forced the wretch to reveal the secrets of deviltry (225-344).

IV. The fiend continues his confessions (345-453).

V. He concludes; at his entreaty Juliana lets him go back to hell (454-558).

VI. An angel saved Juliana from the fire into which her persecutor had thrown

---

[3] For the Latin text see Migne, *Patrologia Latina*, LXXVI. 1218.

her; she was then put into a vat of boiling lead but took no hurt; 75 pagans were killed by the lead as it splashed; the judge then ordered that her head be cut off (559-606).

VII. Juliana's martyrdom; her persecutor's death by drowning; Juliana's burial and the honors paid to her then and now; personal ending, with runic signature and plea for prayers in the poet's usual style (607-731).

It is worthy of note that beheading (i.e., a normal form of execution) killed the saint, whereas the various (unhistorical) tortures left her unharmed. The poet had for source a Latin prose life of St. Juliana not substantially different from that printed in the Bollandist *Acta Sanctorum* under the martyr's feast-day, February 16. He followed his source in the main, but left out certain objectionable features of the lady's conduct, and used phraseology drawn from English heroic tradition. His departures from his source show a critical eye; his own verses, a practised hand. *Juliana* is not prentice work, as some scholars seem inclined to think. In particular, we do not blame the poet for keeping the miraculous instruction by which his heroine holds the devil fast in her clutches, grotesque though the scene to the modern reader. The poem's weakness lies elsewhere: it is hack work, verse done to order (or so we make bold to conjecture).

The author did better with the legend of St. Helen (mother of Con- Elene stantine) and the true Cross. *Elene* is a poem of the Vercelli Book. It comes to 1321 lines. The MS text is marked for division into 15 fits. We summarize these as follows:

I-II. Constantine wins a battle by the sign of the cross, revealed to him in a dream, and becomes a Christian (1-193).

III. He learns Christian lore, especially the story of Calvary, and sends his mother Elene to seek the burial-place of the cross on which Christ died. Elene makes her way to Jerusalem by sea and land (194-275).

IV-VIII. Elene and the Jews; by keeping one of them, Judas, in a pit, without food, she finally makes him agree to help find the burial-place (276-708).

IX. Judas is led to Calvary but, not knowing just where the Cross is buried, prays to God for a sign (709-802).

X. God makes the sign; Judas digs in the spot indicated and finds three crosses 20 feet down; they are brought to Elene, and the true Cross is identified by another miracle: it brings a dead man back to life (803-894).

XI. War of words between Satan and Judas (895-967).

XII. Constantine rejoices when messengers from Elene bring the news; he orders a church built on the spot where the Cross was found; Elene sees to this; Judas is baptized (968-1043).

XIII. Judas is made bishop of Jerusalem; his name is changed to Cyriacus; Elene longs for the nails by which Christ was fastened to the Cross; Judas prays to God for a sign, God answers the prayer, and the nails are found; the people rejoice and Elene thanks God (1044-1147).

XIV. Elene seeks advice about the nails; a wise man suggests that they be made into a bit for Constantine's horse. Elene gives treasure to Cyriacus before leaving for Rome; she urges regular observance of the day (May 3) when the Holy Rood was found; the poet calls down blessings upon those mindful of this festival (1148-1236).

XV. In a rimed passage the poet tells of his art; in a runic passage he signs his name; he ends with a passage on Doomsday (1237-1321).

This legend differs from the usual saint's life in that the interest attaches to a deed not linked with the saint's death. The Latin text which lay before Cynewulf as he wrote has not come down to us. If Carleton Brown is right,[4] it was of Irish origin; certainly it differed in some details from any extant version of the legend. The name-form *Cyriacus* (instead of *Quiriacus*) indicates that Cynewulf's immediate source stood close to the Greek original: no unexpected feature of an early Irish Latin text. In regular Old English fashion, Cynewulf took much from native heroic set pieces: e.g., the admirable but conventional descriptions of voyage and battle, heroic names and all.[5] His own contribution looms larger in the less poetical parts; he told his tale clearly and simply, as Old English poets go. Here he doubtless owed something to his Latin source (the suggestion is Sisam's), though he was far from modeling his style on that of Latin prose. The *inventio sanctae crucis* ends with line 1236, and the riming and runic passages of the last fit are commonly taken to be autobiographical, along with the runic signatures in the other poems. Sisam is probably right in taking 1259 f. to mean that the poet had a patron, and it seems plausible to infer from 1237 f. that Cynewulf was old when he composed *Elene,* though this age, coupled with divine inspiration (1251), reminds one of Cædmon and may have been put in by way of imitation of Bede's familiar story. Otherwise, we learn that the poet felt himself a sinner, in need of prayers, when his thoughts turned to doomsday: information accurate enough, no doubt, but too vague to help us much. The various runic passages make formidable problems which we cannot deal with here.[6]

The work of Cynewulf marks a new stage in the history of English religious poetry. This had begun with paraphrases of biblical story. It now went on to themes more pointedly didactic. Cynewulf himself versified exemplary deeds of saints and a sermon on the ascension. We do not know whether he took the lead in departing from Cædmon's themes, or whether he was following someone else.[7] In any case, the school which goes by his

---

[4] *ESt,* XL (1909), 1-29. See also F. Holthausen, *Zeitschrift für deutsche Philologie,* XXXVII (1905). 1-19, with the references there given.

[5] The poet's Francan, Hugas, Hreðgotan, and Hunas did not actually fight in the ranks of Maxentius at the Milvian bridge, where Constantine by tradition had his vision of the cross.

[6] See Sisam's discussion and R. W. V. Elliott, *English Studies,* XXXIV (1953). 49-57.

[7] The author of *The Dream of the Rood* probably lived before Cynewulf, but this poem is a thing apart.

name greatly widened the scope of vernacular verse. We have looked at
Cynewulf's own poems. We now take up the poems of others on kindred
themes.

The English hermit St. Guthlac early became the subject of a Latin
life by Felix, a monk of Croyland.[8] This life served as source for an English prose life of the saint. Two English verse lives have likewise come
down to us; they are known as *Guthlac A* and *B*,[9] and are recorded to- Guthlac
gether in the Exeter Book. One passage in *A* (between lines 368 and 369)
and the last few lines of *B* have been lost by mutilation of the MS. *A*
comes to 818 lines, divided into eight fits; *B*, to 561 lines, divided into seven
fits. In each poem the first fit makes a kind of prologue. In *B* this prologue
is devoted to the story of Adam and Eve; Guthlac is introduced toward the
end of the fit. In *A* the prologue begins with the bliss of heaven, and goes
on to the problem of how to attain this bliss: some of the ways of leading
one's life on earth are considered, and finally the poem comes to the hermit's
way. Guthlac is not introduced until the second fit. In both poems Guthlac
is plagued by devils, but is sustained by forces of good and dies in the odor
of sanctity. Grein wrongly attached the first 29 lines of *A* to the preceding
poem about doomsday, which ends with a passage on the life eternal. *B*
seems to be based chiefly on the Latin life. It has been attributed to Cynewulf on stylistic grounds, but since his signature is wanting we find it
safer to attribute the poem to some Anglian who belonged to the same
school. *A* is commonly reckoned earlier; its author owed little if anything
to Felix, but relied on oral tradition, though making use of literary sources
in giving literary form to this tradition.

Yet another legend, known to scholars as *Andreas*, has come down to us Andreas
in the Vercelli Book.[10] Its 1722 lines of verse are divided into 15 fits. The
poem tells how St. Andrew at God's bidding rescued St. Matthew from the
cannibal Mermedonians, and, after suffering much at their hands through
the machinations of Satan, called forth upon them a miraculous flood which
made them see the error of their ways. When they had taken for theirs the
true faith, Andrew left them, but God bade him turn back and stay with
the converts a week longer. He then went away for good, to their great
grief. The poem ends with a choral song in praise of God, put in the
mouths of the erstwhile cannibals. The poet had for source a Latin version
(of which two fragments survive) of the Greek apocryphal *Acts of Andrew
and Matthew*. He treats his source with a freedom for which he apologizes
in a well-known passage (1478-1489a): his paraphrase is selective rather than
inclusive. The verses make lively reading. They may lack polish, but they
have vigor to spare. Like most Old English religious poets, the author leans

---

[8] Text printed by P. Gonser, *Anglistische Forschungen*, xxvii (1909).

[9] Good texts will be found in editions of the Exeter Book. For a discussion, see G. H.
Gerould, *MLN*, xxxii (1917). 77-89.

[10] Ed. G. P. Krapp, *Andreas and the Fates of the Apostles* (Boston, 1906). A prose life of
St. Andrew also existed, ed. J. W. Bright, in his *Anglo-Saxon Reader* (4ed., 1917), pp. 113-128.
For the Latin source-material, see F. Blatt, *Die lateinischen Bearbeitungen der Acta Andreae et
Matthiae* (Giessen, 1930).

hard on heroic tradition for the phraseology of poetic elaboration, and for purple passages in general. The epic opening,

> What! we have learned of the twelve under the stars
> in days of yore, heroes rich in glory,
> thanes of the Lord. Their might did not fail
> in warfaring, when banners clashed,
> after they scattered as the Lord himself,
> high king of the heavens, had set their portion.
> Those were famous men the earth over,
> brave folk-leaders and bold in fight,
> doughty warriors, when shield and hand
> on the field of battle defended helmet, . . .

is not unlike that of *Beowulf,* though it would be wrong to presume borrowing: both poets drew from a common stock of heroic formulas. The military metaphor need not disturb us more here than in "Onward Christian Soldiers," or Eph. 6:10-17.

Phoenix   From legend we go to fable. Mediterranean (originally Eastern) lore about beasts and birds early made its way to England, where the poets, like their sources, put it to allegorical and didactic use. *Phoenix* is the most notable composition of this kind in Old English. The poem is recorded in the Exeter Book. It has 677 lines, divided into eight fits.[11]

The first fit pictures an earthly paradise in the east. The second describes the life of a fabulous bird, the phoenix, in this paradise, and tells of its flight to Syria, every 1000 years, to renew its youth. The process of renewal (by fire) is explained in the third fit. In the fourth we get a description of the new bird, risen from the old bird's ashes; then comes an account of the departure of the phoenix for its old home. With the fifth fit the bird returns to its paradise, and the author begins (381) an allegorical treatment of the fable: the phoenix is likened (1) to the elect of Adam's seed, and (2) to Christ. This comparison, together with pertinent digressions (such as the story of Adam and Eve), takes up the rest of the poem to lines 661b-666, which make a conventional ending in praise of God (compare *Andreas* 1718-1722) but are followed by a second ending, in macaronic verse, on the rewards of the good in the life to come.

Lines 1-380 are based on the *De Ave Phoenice* of Lactantius (*fl. c.* 300).[12] The allegorical comparisons, etc., were drawn from various learned sources; in part, from the author's fancy. The verse, though rising to no heights, is competently done and makes pleasant reading. The poet was evidently a clerk and presumably an Angle; he lived in Cynewulf's day or thereabouts. Earlier scholars had more precise views, but the old datings go beyond our scanty evidence. As Sisam remarks in another connection,[13]

11 Ed. A. S. Cook, *Elene, Phoenix and Physiologus* (New Haven, 1919). For the eleventh-century *Phoenix,* see F. Kluge, *ESt,* VIII (1885). 474-479, and Cook, *ed. cit.,* pp. 128-131.

12 O. F. Emerson compares the Latin and English poems in *RES,* II (1926). 18-31.

13 *Proc. Brit. Acad.,* XVIII (1932). 307. See also R. Imelmann, *Forschungen zur ae. Poesie* (1920), p. 239.

Elaborate linguistic and metrical tests have been applied to establish the chronological order of Old English poems. Because these tests leave out of account differences of authorship, of locality, of subject, and of textual tradition, the detailed results, whether of relative order or of absolute date, are little better than guess-work hampered by statistics.

Unnatural natural history is further represented by a poem called *Bestiary* or *Physiologus*,[14] recorded in the Exeter Book. The name, which does not appear in the MS, is that of the poet's source. The poem, 179 lines long, falls into three fits, but most of the third fit is wanting, through loss of a MS leaf at some stage in the transmission of the text. The three fits are devoted respectively to panther, whale, and partridge; these have been thought to stand for the creatures of land, sea, and air. In the first fit (1-74), after an introductory passage on the lower animals in general, the panther's looks and ways are described and given allegorical interpretation: the beast itself is likened to Christ; its foe the dragon, to Satan. The whale (75-163) does not get so good a character; it is credited with passing for an island to entice unwary sailors, who "land" only to drown when the creature dives. Another trick of the whale's when hungry is to send forth a sweet scent from its open mouth, thereby luring its prey into its very jaws, which it then shuts upon them. In the allegory the whale stands for the devil and his crew of tempters; the whale's mouth for hell. The poet's treatment of the partridge (164-179) cannot be made out from the text as it stands, because of the loss of so many lines. The verses end with a passage (175-179) which seems to be of general application, like the introductory passage (1-8a) already mentioned. We thus have reason to think the poem complete, except for the lacuna in the third fit. The author presumably did not try to paraphrase the whole of his source, but restricted himself to three of the creatures considered in the pseudo-scientific book from which he drew. His poem might well have been written by the author of *Phoenix*. Whether it was or not, it belongs to the same period and reflects a like taste. In later times we find fuller and more elaborate treatment of unnatural natural history; see below, p. 161.

The Bestiary

[14] Ed. A. S. Cook, *ed. cit.*

VIII

Religious Poetry: Poems on Various Themes

Dream
of the
Rood

Old English religious poetry was not confined to biblical paraphrase, homily, legend, and allegory. Many other types are found. We take up first the dream or vision, exemplified in the *Dream of the Rood* (i.e., dream about the Cross), a 156-line poem of the Vercelli Book. Fragments of an older version have come down to us as a runic inscription on the great stone cross at Ruthwell in Dumfriesshire, Scotland. In the following, the two versions will be called *R* (Ruthwell) and *V* (Vercelli). The most recent editors of the *Rood*[1] date *R* early in the eighth, *V* late in the ninth century.[2] In any case, *R* belongs to the classical period of Old English poetry. Unluckily, little of it is left, and all editions of the *Rood* have been based on *V*. The poem is in the first person throughout.

It falls into three parts: the opening words of the dreamer (1-27), the words spoken by the Rood (28-121), and the words of the dreamer after the dream is over (122-156). The speaker begins with his dream, in which he saw the True Cross and it spoke to him, telling him its history from the time when it was a tree growing in the woods to the time when, centuries after it bore Christ on Calvary, it was found [by St. Helen, who is not named] and made an object of worship (28-94). The Rood goes on to urge the dreamer to promote its cult (95-121); here the practical point and purpose of the dream comes out. With the Rood's speech the dream presumably ends, though the dreamer's waking is passed over. The dreamer now explains how his dream about the Rood has changed his life; ever since, he has devoted himself to the cult of the True Cross, and hopes to win a heavenly home thereby. The poem ends with a short passage about Christ (144b-156): "may the Lord be a friend to me, he who. . . ." In this passage Christ's passion, death, harrowing of hell, and ascension are touched upon. This ending takes the place of the lines in praise of God with which so many devotional poems end.

The *Rood* is one of the glories of Old English literature; indeed, of English literature as a whole. The introductory words of the dreamer could hardly be bettered, and the story of the Cross on Calvary has overwhelming poetic power and beauty. We quote a few lines:[3]

[1] B. Dickins and A. S. C. Ross (1934). For further references, see the bibliography in their edition. See also the monograph of H. Bütow, *Das ae. "Traumgesicht vom Kreuz"* (Heidelberg, 1935).
[2] If the southern coast of Strathclyde continued to be held by the English after the Battle of Nechtansmere (685), an English inscription might well have been cut at Ruthwell as late as the eighth century. C. L. Wrenn, in *Trans. Philological Soc.* for 1943, pp. 19-22, dates *R* at the end of the eighth century.
[3] Taken, by permission, from K. Malone, *Ten Old English Poems* (Baltimore: Johns Hopkins Press, 1941).

It was many years ago—I remember it still—
that I was felled, afar, at the forest edge,
borne off from my roots. Evil men took me; . . .
When I saw the ends of the earth shaking
I dared not bow or break, against
the word of God. All at once I might
have struck his foes down, but I stood fast there. . . .
I quaked when he clasped me, but I could not bow to earth,
nor fall to the ground; it was my fate to stand.
As a rood I was raised; I bore my Ruler up,
the King of the skies; I could not bow down.
They pierced me with dark nails; the places are on me still,
the wicked wounds are open. Not one of them dared I harm.
They railed at us both. I was all running with blood,
as he gave up the ghost, with gore from his side.
A heavy burden I bore on that hill,
My lot was hard. . . . (lines 28-30, 35-38, 42-51)

Modern readers like the first 77 lines best, but the poem makes an organic whole, and the later passages on the cult of the Rood were essential to the poet's purpose. The final passage begins in the middle of a line, but otherwise the poem belongs to the early stage of the run-on style. Its author was a Northumbrian, as the dialect of *R* reveals. The story of Cædmon may have inspired him to choose the vision form. If, as Dickins and Ross suggest (p. 19), "the occasion for the revision of the poem was the gift of a piece of the True Cross to Alfred in 885," we may owe version *V* to a West Saxon reviser. We cannot be sure of this, however; we cannot be sure, indeed, that *V* represents any substantial revision or expansion of *R*. No definite source of the poem has been found, though various influences have been pointed out,[4] and it seems likely that the *Rood,* in both conception and execution, belongs to the short list of original Old English religious poems.

The poems which we shall next consider are not readily classified except by subject. First we take *The Advent* (or *Nativity;* also known as *Christ A*), a poem recorded in the Exeter Book.[5] Its beginning is lost; what we have left comes to 439 lines, divided into five fits. The last of these fits is devoted, in part, to praise of the Trinity, but the rest of the poem is given over to the theme of Advent: that season of the Christian year so named, not the nativity proper. The season is marked by joyful expectancy, and the poet has caught this expectant mood. The note of wonder, too, is sounded again and again. Much of the text is best described as hymn-like. Hortatory and expository passages also occur, as well as two dialogues: one between Mary and dwellers in Jerusalem, the other between Mary and Joseph. The latter opens in a way reminiscent of secular heroic poetry, but this poem owes

Advent

---

[4] See especially M. Schlauch, *Essays and Studies in Honor of Carleton Brown* (1940), pp. 23-34.
[5] Ed. A. S. Cook, *The Christ of Cynewulf* (Boston, 1900). A more accurate text is that of Krapp-Dobbie, III.

less than most to the tradition of the scops; in style it marks a stage at which religious verse had reached maturity and independence. The poem is based, in large part, on antiphons of the Breviary. The dialogue between Joseph and Mary on the Conception goes back, ultimately, to Matt. 2:18-25; its immediate source has not been found. The poet is sometimes too medieval for the modern stomach, as when he likens Mary to a door, the key to which God alone holds and uses, but most of the poem makes good reading still. The anonymous author in all likelihood was an Angle of the ninth century. The ascription of this poem to Cynewulf rests on no evidence worthy of the name.

Harrowing
of Hell

The Harrowing of Hell is a poem of the Exeter Book.[6] It comes to 137 lines, though a hole in the MS has done some damage to the text. The poem opens with the visit of the Marys to Christ's tomb on Easter morning, but soon (23b) shifts to hell, where John the Baptist serves as spokesman for the souls held there until the harrowing. John makes a short speech (26-32) before the harrowing; he predicts the coming of Christ. After the harrowing has begun, we are told who await release:

> Adam and Abraham, Isaac and Jacob,
> many a bold leader, Moses and David,
> Isaiah and Zachariah,
> many patriarchs and a throng of heroes too,
> the company of prophets, a host of women,
> many virgins, a countless multitude of folk. (lines 44-49)

When John sees Christ enter he makes a second speech. This falls into two parts: first, words of thanks to Christ, followed by apostrophes to Gabriel, Mary, Jerusalem, and Jordan (59-106); secondly, a prayer to Christ, asking that he have mercy upon the captives in hell and that he baptize them (107-134). At this point a scribe seems to have skipped an uncertain number of lines; the extant text continues with three lines (135-137) obviously spoken, not by John but by somebody else who is supporting John's plea that the captives be baptized. Here the poem breaks off. The lost conclusion presumably told of the baptism of the captives and their triumphant translation to heaven. Lines 1-23a are based on the biblical account of the resurrection. The rest of the poem goes back to the second part of the apocryphal gospel of Nicodemus, but this can hardly be called a source in any strict sense, as our text differs markedly from it in detail. The poem is anonymous and the date of its composition is uncertain.

Doomsday
Poems

Three poems on Doomsday have come down to us from Old English times. We distinguish them as *A, B, C.*[7] The first, *Doomsday A,* is recorded in the eleventh-century MS 201, Corpus Christi College, Cambridge. The

6 Dissertations: J. H. Kirkland (1885), J. Cramer (1896); the latter's also published as an article in *Anglia,* xix (1897). 137-174. Text in Cramer; also in editions of Exeter Book.

7 See G. Grau, [Morsbach's] *Studien zur englischen Philologie,* xxxi (1908). Editions: *A,* Hans Löhe, *Be Domes Dæge* (*Bonner Beiträge,* xxii, 1907); *B,* not separately edited, but included in editions of the Exeter Book; *C,* not separately edited, but included in A. S. Cook, *The Christ of Cynewulf* (Boston, 1900).

poet for the most part follows closely his Latin original, a poem *De Die Judicii* attributed to Bede. The greater length of the English version (308 lines for the 157 of the Latin) reflects in a few passages some expansion of the source but more commonly a mere effort to reproduce in full the thoughts there expressed. The English version seems to have been done in the tenth century. Its author used standard West Saxon speech, though a few Anglian forms occur. We cannot name or plausibly localize the poet, but can say that he made an effective English version of the Latin poem. *Doomsday B* is a poem of 119 lines, recorded in the Exeter Book. The scribe marked two fits, lines 1-80 making the first, lines 81-119 the second. The anonymous author drew on Christian tradition, as handed down in Latin poems, prose treatises, etc.[8] His verses show good workmanship, for the most part, but no great poetic gift. They were hardly composed earlier than the ninth century, and later composition is possible enough. *Doomsday C* (also known as *Christ C*) is likewise a poem of the Exeter Book. It makes a text 798 lines long, and divided into seven fits. Various connections and parallels have been pointed out;[9] as a whole, *C*, like *B*, rests on Christian tradition, not on a single source. The poet takes up the resurrection of the dead, their assembly for judgment, the destruction of the world, the second coming of Christ, the separation of the souls into two groups (sheep and goats), the words of Christ to each group, the punishments of hell and the rewards of heaven, together with much homiletic matter and many details which need not be listed here. In developing his theme the poet does not follow a rigorous order, and the poem gives us a combination, familiar in Old English, of narrative, description, reflection, exhortation and rhapsody. The verses show a practised and skilful hand; they include eloquent and beautiful passages, but nothing that deserves the name great. Swollen verses appear not infrequently. We know nothing of the poem's authorship; the old attribution to Cynewulf lacks evidential basis. The time of composition cannot be set with precision, but the poem is neither early nor late.

Closely linked in theme to the Doomsday poems is *Soul and Body*, a poem in which wicked and righteous souls speak to their respective (dead) bodies.[10] The poem falls naturally into two fits: in the first (lines 1-129) the wicked soul speaks; in the second (130-169), the righteous. The first fit has come down to us in two MSS: Vercelli and Exeter. The two texts differ more or less in wording and even in number of lines. *V* comes to 126 lines, *E* to 121; putting them together, we reach our total of 129. The second fit appears in Vercelli only, where through loss of one or more MS leaves it breaks off in the middle of a sentence. The poem begins with a prologue

Soul and Body

---

[8] For an attempt to specify the sources more narrowly see Grau, pp. 176-180. The homiletic tone of the poem is worthy of note.

[9] See Cook, ed., pp. 170-225 and Grau, pp. 48-83. See also R. Willard, *PMLA*, XLII (1927). 314-330.

[10] Ed. Wülker, II. 92-107. A recent discussion of the body and soul theme is that of E. K. Heningham, *An Early Latin Debate of the Body and Soul* (1939). The same author discusses the relationship between the Old English poem and the Middle English material in *PMLA*, LV (1940). 291-307.

of eight lines about soul and body in general. Then we are told (9-14) of the approach of the wicked soul: the poet thus sets the scene for the action of the first fit, though he confuses matters somewhat by explaining here (instead of in the prologue) that a soul must visit its dead body weekly for 300 years. Lines 15-16 announce the wicked soul as speaker, and the speech itself takes up lines 17-103. In the speech the soul reproaches its body for the damnation which will be its lot on Doomsday. In lines 104-109 we are told of the soul's return to hell uncomforted: the body cannot speak, or help the soul in any way, now that it is dead; the soul's reproaches have come too late. Next we learn in detail (110-127a) what happens to a dead body, and the fit ends with two generalizations: the body is destined to be food for worms, and every wise man is mindful of that. The second fit of course has no prologue. It begins with the approach of the righteous soul (130-134). The souls of the righteous are then announced as speakers (135-137) and the beginning of their speech follows (138-169): they give the body as much praise as the wicked soul gave it blame. Unluckily the rest of the speech (and poem) is lost. In spite of inconsistencies and rough spots (some of which may safely be attributed to faulty transmission) the poet does what he set out to do: he brings home with power the lesson that life on earth, vain in itself, has the grim function of determining our lot in the life to come. We do not know where, when, or by whom the poem was made. Its theme is one old and familiar in medieval literature, though the righteous soul rarely figures in such compositions.[11]

In Middle English the soul and body theme also occurs in dialogue form: the soul blames the body and the body replies in kind (see below, p. 162). The dialogue, a literary genre handed down from antiquity, was much used in Old and Middle English alike for didactic purposes. We take up here the two Old English metrical dialogues between Solomon and Saturn.[12] Both are recorded in the tenth-century MS 422, CCCC, pp. 1-6 (first poem) and 13-26 (second poem). The first 93 lines of the first poem are also recorded, in a hand of c. 1100, on the margins of pp. 196-198 of MS 41, CCCC. Through loss of leaves and other damage the text of MS 422 is markedly defective; that of MS 41 is late, fragmentary, and poor. The poems come to 169 and 336 lines respectively, as we have them, but the first poem may be incomplete, while four serious lacunae mar the second poem. The poems seem to have different authors. The first poem may well have been composed somewhat later than the second; both probably belong to the ninth century, though the tenth remains a possibility. The scanty evidence indicates that the authors were Angles. The first poem, though a dialogue in form, comes close to being a monologue in fact; Solomon does nearly all

Solomon
and
Saturn

---

[11] Two late and fragmentary versions (at Worcester and Oxford respectively) of an address of soul to body have been edited by R. Buchholz, in *Erlanger Beiträge*, VI (1890). The Oxford fragment of 25 lines is better known under the title *The Grave*. For a different interpretation of the Oxford fragment, see L. Dudley, *MP*, XI (1914). 429-442.

[12] Ed. R. J. Menner, *The Poetical Dialogues of Solomon and Saturn* (*MLA Monograph*, XIII, 1941). By way of appendix Menner also prints a fragment of a prose dialogue. See also K. Sisam, *MA*, XIII (1944). 28-36.

the talking. His subject is the Lord's Prayer, the virtues of which, as a whole and letter by letter (or rune by rune), he explains in detail, with much use of highly figurative speech. These virtues are magical: the author evidently conceived of the Latin text of this prayer as a kind of spell. His poem has little artistic worth. The author of the second poem moved on a higher level. He made a true dialogue, in which Saturn and Solomon discuss matters of weight. Saturn personifies heathen wisdom (eastern and northern alike); Solomon, Christian (and Jewish) wisdom. Their dialogue is a contest, won, of course, by the representative of Christianity. The whole makes a worthy example of reflective religious poetry. Witness the following passage:

> A little while the leaves are green;
> then, afterwards, they fade, they fall to earth,
> and rot away; they turn to dust. (lines 136-8)

The immediate Latin sources on which the authors drew have not come down to us. These sources belonged to Oriental rather than to Roman Christian tradition, it would seem, and Irish transmission has been suggested.[13]

We go on to eleven somewhat shorter didactic or reflective poems, more *Eleven* or less religious in tone or inspiration. The compiler of the Exeter Book *Shorter* included in his poetic miscellany a number of such poems. Five of them *Poems* make a sequence in the MS: *Wanderer* (115 lines), *Gifts of Men* (113), *A Father's Teachings* (94), *Seafarer* (124), and *Overmood* (84). Another sequence consists of three gnomic poems (already considered; see above, p. 43), and *Fates of Men* (98 lines), *Wonders of Creation* (102) and *Riming Poem* (87). We include here the fragmentary *Admonition* as well, on the strength of lines 3-7, which agree strikingly with *Wanderer,* 11-18.[14] We add from the Vercelli Book the fragment *Falseness of Men* (47 lines) and from MS 201, CCCC, the exhortation to godly life commonly called *Lar* (80 lines).[15]

Of these poems, *Wanderer* and *Riming Poem* are least marked by Wanderer specific reference to God and the Faith. It would be wrong, however, to *and* infer that their Christianity served only for garnish. Both poets made their Riming central theme the vanity of worldly achievement; more particularly, the Poem inevitable end which awaits lord and dright. For both poets the grace of God was the only gleam of hope in the life of men on earth. They differed, it is true, in method of presentation. The wanderer begins in the depths; only by retrospect does he give us glimpses of his earlier success and happiness. The riming poet, on the contrary, starts with birth and ends with

---

[13] Like most contests of wisdom, the dialogue includes diverse matters, such as riddles, out-of-the-way lore, etc. See Menner's admirable discussion, *ed. cit.,* and his papers in *JEGP,* xxxvii (1938). 332-354 and *Studies . . . in Honor of F. Klaeber* (Minneapolis, 1929), pp. 240-253.

[14] The rest of this 20-line fragment seems to be based on the Nicene Creed. We call attention, besides, to the nine-line poem on almsgiving and the eight-line poem on the size of Pharaoh's army. All these poems may be found in editions of the Exeter Book.

[15] Renamed *An Exhortation to Christian Living* in Krapp-Dobbie, VI. 67.

death and the grave; he traces point by point the curve, first rising, then falling, of a distinguished earthly career,[16] and he follows this scheme so strictly that his poem has a certain stiffness, while *Wanderer* flows free by virtue of its looser structure.

Riming Poem got its name from the fact that its half-lines are systematically bound together into lines by rime as well as by alliteration. Now and then its author, like many other Old English poets, uses rime for ornamental rather than structural purposes. Neither the structural nor the ornamental riming helps much in dating or localizing the poem. The events set forth are given autobiographical form, but the poet's career, though it has a courtly setting, is highly generalized: so much so, indeed, that the speaker loses his individuality and becomes a mere representative of mankind. Much less abstract is the art of the *Wanderer* poet, who puts most of his verses in the mouth of a kemp (the wanderer) made homeless by the death of his lord.[17] Here, too, the characters are nameless and the events happen in no particular spot and at no particular time. The wanderer may be described as an old soldier turned sage. His dearly bought wisdom takes two main forms: (1) gnomic sayings, and (2) reflections on the transitory nature of all earthly things. The reflections at times amount to lamentations, but the poem is no elegy. The following passage is characteristic:[18]

> The tried kemp must grasp how ghastly it will be
> when the weal of this world stands waste wholly,
> as now in many a spot through this middle earth
> the wind-blown walls stand waste, befrosted,
> the abodes of men lie buried in snow,
> the wine-halls are dust in the wind, the rulers
> dead, stripped of glee; the dright all fell,
> by the wall the proud sought shield.... (lines 73-80)

Seafarer

Seafarer purports to give the poet's own experiences but is representative if not indeed symbolic in meaning. The author describes vividly his hardships at sea; he explains but vaguely why he would set out anew:

> Deep goes the mood that drives my soul
> to fare from home, that, far away,
> I may find the stead where strangers dwell....
> So, now, my soul soars from my bosom,
> the mood of my mind moves with the sea-flood,
> over the home of the whale, high flies and wide
> to the ends of the earth; after, back to me
> comes the lonely flier, lustful and greedy,
> whets me to the whale-way, whelms me with his bidding
> over deep waters. Dearer, then, to me

[16] Compare the so-called sermon of Hrothgar in *Beowulf*, 1724-1768.
[17] For a recent study of *Wanderer* see B. F. Huppé, *JEGP*, XLII (1943). 516-538.
[18] The quotations from *Wanderer* and *Seafarer* are taken, by permission, from K. Malone, *Ten Old English Poems* (Baltimore, 1941).

the boons of the Lord than this life that is dead
in a land that passes; I believe no whit
that earthly weal is everlasting. (lines 36-38, 58-67)

Lines 64-67, however, give us a hint that the speaker thought the soft life
of a landsman incompatible with heavenly bliss; in ascetic mood he chose,
instead, the hard life of a seaman.[19] The call of the sea in this poem has
nothing in common with the romantic glamor of modern feeling; it is a
call to suffering, toil, privation. Only by denying oneself here can one win
salvation hereafter. Seafaring thus represents and symbolizes the sterner
side of the Christian way of life. After this autobiographical section, the
poet gives us conventional reflections about death, fame and God. Of particular interest is the chronological primitivism implicit in lines 80 ff. *Riming
Poem, Wanderer,* and *Seafarer* are compositions of unusual poetic power and
beauty. We cannot name their authors, and we do not know just when
or where these authors lived. The other eight poems named above have less
interest for the modern reader, and we shall leave them without discussion
here.

The Psalter held so important a place in Christian devotions that one
might expect to find an Old English metrical version of the whole body of
psalms. Such a version in fact once existed, but it has not come down to us
intact. Fragments of it were included in a Benedictine service-book of the
eleventh century,[20] and Psalms 51 to 150 were recorded in the so-called
Paris Psalter, an eleventh-century MS which survives in a mutilated state.[21]
The author of the metrical psalms[22] departed widely from classical versification; so much so, indeed, that we must take him to have been indifferent
to classical poetic tradition (or perhaps even ignorant of that tradition).
His verses may reflect a development of the popular pre-classical style as
independent of the classical movement as is the versification of the spells.
In any case, we have no right to measure these verses by classical standards
and stigmatize them as irregular. Their metrical peculiarities give us no
evidence of value in setting time or place of composition. The translation
is not without literary merit.

      The Paris Psalter

An independent metrical version of *Psalm 50 (51)* in the Kentish dialect
is recorded in the tenth-century MS Cotton Vespasian D 6. The paraphrast
begins with a prologue about David, Nathan, Uriah, and Bathsheba (1-25).
The psalm proper (31-145) is preceded by an introduction (26-30) and followed by a conclusion (146-153) announcing David as speaker of the psalm
and emphasizing his penitence. Then comes an epilogue (154-157) in the
form of a prayer. The whole makes a neatly rounded work of art, some-

      The Kentish Psalm

---

[19] For a somewhat different interpretation see O. S. Anderson, *The Seafarer* (Lund, 1937).
See also S. B. Liljegren, *Studia Neophilologica,* XIV (1942). 145-159.

[20] See E. Feiler, *Das Benediktiner-Offizium* (Heidelberg, 1901). The text of the fragments
is in Krapp-Dobbie, VI. 80-86.

[21] Text in Krapp-Dobbie, V. 3-150.

[22] Aldhelm, according to the late Eduard Sievers; see *Exeter Book of Old English Poetry*
(1933), p. 2, n. 3. The attribution will have weight with those who accept Sievers' *Schall-
analyse.*

thing more than a translation. Another poem in the Kentish dialect, a 43-line hymn in praise of God, is set down in the same MS.[23] Both these Kentish texts are sprinkled with West Saxon forms. Both poems are best given a tenth-century dating.

Pater-
nosters

Metrical versions of the Lord's Prayer, the Gloria Patri, and the Apostles' Creed were composed in Old English. Three such versions of the Lord's Prayer have survived; we call them the Exeter, Junius, and Corpus Paternosters, from the MSS in which they are recorded. The *Exeter Paternoster* (Exeter Book) comes to 11 lines; the *Junius* (Bodleian, Junius 121), to 36 lines; the *Corpus* (CCCC 201), to 123 lines.[24] In the longer versions, each clause of the prayer obviously inspired a passage of verse. A like expansion of the Latin text marks the *Junius Gloria Patri* of 57 lines (Bodleian, Junius 121, and CCCC 201) and the *Junius Apostles' Creed* of 58 lines (Junius 121).[25] The three-line *Cotton Gloria Patri* (Cotton Titus D xxvii) shows no expansion.[26]

We end our survey of Old English religious poetry with five items of some interest for one reason or another. The *Macaronic Poem* (CCCC 201),[27] also known as *Call* (or *Summons*) *to Prayer,* is 31 lines long. Its interest for us lies in its macaronic form: each on-verse is in English, each off-verse in Latin (but two off-verses are wanting). The *Cotton Prayer* of 79 lines [28] is commonly divided into three, on grounds which we think insufficient. The *Exeter Prayer* of 118 lines,[29] also called *Age Mec* from its first two words, goes beyond the precative form as it proceeds and becomes a kind of complaint; it ends, however, on a note of resignation, expressed in words of aphoristic wisdom (quoted above, p. 26). The mixture of genres does not keep the poem from having power and artistic distinction.

Thureth

A poem hard to classify is *Thureth*,[30] in which a *halgungboc* "dedication book" makes an 11-line speech, informing the reader that a certain Thureth had had it made in gratitude to God and in God's honor. One may compare King Alfred's metrical prologue to the *Pastoral Care,* and inscriptions like those on the Brussels cross (*rod is min nama* "rood is my name") and the Alfred Jewel (*Ælfred mec heht gewyrcan* "Alfred had me made"). The

Stanzaic
Poem

Stanzaic Poem [31] on fasting is of interest because it is the only Old English poem divided into regular stanzas. It is made up of 26 eight-line stanzas, one six-line stanza (the fourth), one nine-line stanza (the fifteenth), and

[23] The two Kentish poems are in Krapp-Dobbie, VI. 87-94.
[24] Texts in Krapp-Dobbie, III. 223-224 (Exeter), VI. 77-78 (Junius), VI. 70-74 (Corpus).
[25] Texts in Krapp-Dobbie, VI. 74-77 (Gloria), 78-80 (Creed).
[26] Text in Krapp-Dobbie, VI. 94.
[27] Text in Krapp-Dobbie, VI. 69-70.
[28] Cotton Julius A 2; the first 15 lines are also in Lambeth Palace Library MS 427. Text in Krapp-Dobbie, VI. 94-96.
[29] Exeter Book. Text in Krapp-Dobbie, III. 215-218.
[30] MS Cotton Claud. A III (eleventh century). Text in Krapp-Dobbie, VI. 97; see also A. S. Napier, *Trans. Philol. Soc.* for 1903-1906, p. 299.
[31] British Museum Add. MS 43703 (Nowell's sixteenth-century copy of the now fragmentary MS Cotton Otho B XI). Text in Krapp-Dobbie, VI. 98-104.

one incomplete stanza at the end, where the poem breaks off in the middle of line 230. Each stanza makes a unit of thought and ends with a full stop. The poem is an exhortation to the faithful to keep the fasts prescribed by the Church, especially Ember days and Lent. It was presumably composed in the tenth century.

IX

Secular Poetry

The triumph of Christianity in England had literary effects which went beyond the composition of vernacular religious poems. The new faith, and the southern culture which came to the English with that faith, brought about great changes in the treatment of secular themes as well, and led to the use of themes not characteristic of the old native tradition. Such a theme **Durham** is the *encomium urbis* exemplified in the *Durham Poem*,[1] a 20-line fragment **Poem** in praise of the city of Durham. The fragment as we have it belongs to the early twelfth century, in all likelihood, but it may represent a revision of the earlier composition referred to in line 19 of the text.[2] The verses have little merit, but are worthy of mention as the only surviving Old English example of a type of poem familiar in classical antiquity.

Ruin A contrasting theme, which we may call *de excidio urbis* (or *arcis*), is exemplified in *Ruin*,[3] a poem of the Exeter Book. The poem is commonly printed in 48 or 49 lines; we cannot be sure of the number because of the defective state of folio 124. The loss of many words of the text makes interpretation harder, too, of course. The poet describes the decay and destruction of a city (or stronghold), and contrasts its present desolation with its presumable splendor in the past. This theme has obvious kinship to that of *Wanderer*, 73-105, and a Latin poem of the sixth century, the *De Excidio Thoringiae* of Venantius Fortunatus, begins in much the same vein.[4] The *Ruin* poet's mention of hot baths has led many to identify with Bath the ruin described,[5] but since the poem is of the nameless timeless kind we doubt that its author had in mind one site only: the ruin which he made his subject was (we think) a creation of his own, though in describing it he drew on his knowledge of actual ruins. His poem departs from the usual Old English pattern in that the reader or hearer must himself supply the obvious moral: all earthly things perish. But possibly the lost passage at the end was a moralizing one. We reckon the poem secular: Wyrd, not God,

---

[1] MS: Camb. Univ. Lib. H. i. 27. Printed text and study: M. Schlauch, *JEGP*, XL (1941). 14-28.

[2] Line 20 in the text as printed in Krapp-Dobbie, VI. 27, where line 10 is divided into two lines.

[3] See C. A. Hotchner, *Wessex and Old English Poetry* . . . (1939); for criticism of this unconvincing dissertation see Joan Blomfield, *MA*, IX (1940). 114-116 and S. J. Herben, *MLN*, LIX (1944). 72-74. The text is in N. Kershaw, *Anglo-Saxon and Norse Poems* (Cambridge, 1922).

[4] So first A. Brandl, *Archiv*, CXXXIX (1919). 84.

[5] Identification with Hadrian's Wall has been proposed by S. J. Herben; see *MLN*, LIV (1939). 37-39.

brought the ruin about (contrast *Wanderer,* 85). It does not follow, however, that the poet was a heathen. We believe that his Wyrd answers to
the Fate of classical antiquity and that in attributing the destruction to
Fate he was conforming to some classical literary model. We do not know
when or where the poet flourished, but we do know from his poem that he
had poetic power.

Of much interest are the 95 metrical riddles of the Exeter Book.[6] Through *Riddles*
loss of leaves and other damage to the MS the text of many of these riddles
is defective. Most of the editors combine the 68th and 69th riddles, but in
the MS they are clearly distinguished. On the other hand, the 2nd and 3rd
riddles make one in the MS. The Exeter scribe recorded two versions of
the 30th riddle, while the 35th riddle survives also in a Northumbrian
version elsewhere recorded.[7] The riddles vary in length from one line (No.
69) to over 100 lines (No. 40). In general they must be reckoned literary
(not popular) compositions; they are done in the classical Old English
poetic style. Two are translations of extant Latin originals: No. 35 translates
Aldhelm's 33rd riddle, *Lorica;* No. 40, his 100th, *Creatura.* Several more go
back, with varying degrees of probability, to Latin riddles in the collection
that goes by the name of Symphosius.[8] Many others may well have been
based on specific Latin sources; certainly the composition of Latin riddles
in verse had a vogue among English clerics in the seventh and eighth centuries, though most of these riddles have not come down to us.[9] Not a few
of the Old English riddles have poetic worth. We call attention to Lascelles
Abercrombie's happy modernization of the eighth riddle.[10] Other riddles
give us examples of the *double entente* (No. 44), and one even incorporates
a joke (No. 42). A certain dry humor marks the lines on the bookworm
(No. 47):

> A moth ate words. To me that seemed
> an odd happening, when I found it out,
> that the crawling thing swallowed up the speech of a man,
> a thief in darkness [ate] noble discourse
> and its strong support [i.e., parchment]. The thieving guest
> was none the wiser for swallowing those words.

Here (as in other cases) the riddle form was stretched to include something merely paradoxical, and even this only by identification of the ink-
marks with the words they symbolize. Many of the riddles are in the first
person, the speaker being the solution personified. The collection was formerly begun (as still in Tupper's edition) with the poem of 19 lines now

---

[6] One of these, the 90th, is in Latin. Ed. F. Tupper, *The Riddles of the Exeter Book* (Boston,
1910); A. J. Wyatt, *Old English Riddles* (Boston, 1912).

[7] In Leiden Univ. MS Voss 106; ed. A. H. Smith, *Three Northumbrian Poems* (1933).

[8] See above, p. 14.

[9] See above, p. 14. For discussion of other riddles see especially *MLR,* xxxi (1936). 545-547;
Neophilologus, iv (1919). 258-262, xiii (1928). 293-296, xxvi (1941). 228-231, xxvii (1942).
220, xxix (1945), 126-127; xxxi (1947). 65-68; *Studia Neophologica,* xiv (1942), 67-70;
MLN, liv (1939). 259-262; *MA,* xv (1946). 48-54.

[10] *Poems* (1930), p. 16.

known as *Eadwacer*. The so-called 60th riddle in all likelihood does not belong to the collection either, but makes the first section of the poem known as *Lover's* or *Husband's Message*. We know nothing of the authorship of the riddles, though they were presumably composed by clerics. We give the collection an eighth century dating, but not with certainty.

Love Poems

Three love poems have come down to us in the Exeter Book: the poems *Eadwacer* and *Lover's Message* mentioned above, and a poem of 53 lines called *Wife's Lament* or *Complaint*.[11] Two of these, *Eadwacer* and *Wife's Lament*, purport to be by women. *Eadwacer* is one of the most obscure poems in the English language. We make no attempt to interpret it, but quote two passages remarkable for their power and beauty: [12]

> I waited for my wanderer, my Wulf, hoping and fearing:
> when it was rainy weather and I sat wretched, weeping;
> when the doughty man drew me into his arms—
> it was heaven, yes, but hateful too.

> Wulf, my Wulf, waiting for thee
> hath left me sick, so seldom hast thou come;
> a starving mood, no stint of meat. (lines 9-15)

The Wife's Lament

The *Wife's Lament* likewise makes trouble for the interpreter, though here the difficulties are far less serious.[13] The poem is in the first person throughout. The speaker is a woman who has lost her husband's favor and has been forced, by him, to live alone, in a cheerless wooded spot. She applies several uncomplimentary epithets to the house she lives in: *herh-eard* "heathenish abode," *eorð-scræf* "hole in the ground, tomb, hovel," *eorð-sele* "hut." Such terms of denunciation need not be taken too literally. Her unhappiness finds expression in the following passage (among others):

> Fallen is this house: I am filled with yearning.
> The dales are dim, the downs [i.e., hills] are high,
> the bitter yards with briars are grown,
> the seats are sorrowful. I am sick at heart,
> he is so far from me. There are friends on earth,
> lovers living that lie together,
> while I, early and all alone,
> walk under the oak tree, wander through these halls. (lines 29-36)

She tries to console herself by reflecting that

> it is the way of a young man to be woeful in mood,
> hard in his heart's thought, ... (lines 42-3)

[11] See R. Imelmann, *Forschungen zur ae. Poesie* (Berlin, 1920), pp. 1-314. The author includes also *Wanderer* and *Seafarer* in this investigation.

[12] The quotations from *Eadwacer* and *Wife's Lament* are taken, by permission, from K. Malone, *Ten Old English Poems* (Baltimore: Johns Hopkins Press, 1941).

[13] Ed. N. Kershaw, in *Anglo-Saxon and Norse Poems* (Cambridge, 1922).

and by drawing a picture of such a man (her husband) himself alone and in misery, but she finds this picture not so consoling after all, and ends with the dismal saying,

> hard is the lot
> of one that longs for [one's] love in vain. (lines 52-3)

The lyricism of *Eadwacer* and the *Wife's Lament,* wholly secular though it be, has little in common with the personal poetry of native tradition, the poetry of the scops, and one is tempted to look to classical antiquity for models. Here Virgil's story of Dido comes at once to mind, while the pages of Ovid give us other analogues.[14] We cannot take these classical tales for sources, but they may well have suggested a like literary treatment of native tales otherwise unknown to us. Imelmann sets the years 781-830 as the period within which these poems were composed.

The *Lover's Message* makes other difficulties.[15] The MS text falls into four clearly marked sections: of these the first (17 lines) and the third (13 lines) are intact; the second (11 to 13 lines) and the fourth (28 or 29 lines) are defective, because of a great hole in folio 123. The first section is usually but (we think) wrongly taken to be a separate poem, the so-called 60th riddle. In form, the *Lover's Message* is a speech, made by a stick of wood upon which a lover had cut (presumably in runes) a message to his lady. The stick explains how the man with his knife made it into a messenger, and then addresses the lady directly in that capacity (line 14), with mention of its journey to her from overseas, and with many pleas in the lover's be-half. The lady's answer is not given, but from the tone of the speaker we may infer that she said yes. The speech ends with a runic passage not alto-gether clear. The riddle (No. 30, second version) which immediately pre-cedes *Lover's Message* in the MS likewise has a wooden object for speaker and speeches by inanimate objects are characteristic of the riddles, as we have seen. We remember, too, that a piece of wood (the Cross) made a speech in *Dream of the Rood.* Our poet seems to have taken this device and used it in his own way, with striking effect. His suitor gives us a fore-taste, not so much of medieval as of modern love-poetry. The go-between, the emphasis on privacy, and the deferential tone remind one, it is true, of the later *service des dames,* while the setting is courtly enough, but the man proposes, and intends, marriage, not seduction, and he is the lady's equal, not her servant. The plain implication that the lady can do as she likes, even to the point of making a journey overseas to join her lover, gives to the poem a curiously modern touch. This touch would be removed, of course, if we took the lovers for man and wife, but the lover's pleas would then lose all point. The poem shows much literary merit, in spite of its mutila-

The Lover's Message

---

[14] See Imelmann, pp. 188-307, and H. Reuschel, Paul u. Braune's *Beiträge zur Geschichte der deutschen Sprache u. Lit.,* LXII (1938). 132-142.

[15] Also known as the *Husband's Message.* Ed. N. Kershaw, in *Anglo-Saxon and Norse Poems* (Cambridge, 1922).

tion. It was composed not later than *c.* 950. We know nothing of its author or of his sources.

A different kind of plea is that made by the scribe who copied the last part of the text of the Old English translation of Bede's *History* recorded in CCCC 41, a MS commonly dated *c.* 1030. At the end of this text the copyist added a 10-line poem of his own, a plea to readers of rank, urging his claims to patronage.[16] This versified advertisement for patrons he made as conspicuous as possible by writing every other line in red ink. Incidentally his verses show that he expected noble readers. We know of no other nation of western Europe which, in the first half of the eleventh century, could boast of a reading public that included laymen of noble rank.

A 17-line fragment of a poem in honor of Aldhelm (the famous English prelate and scholar) has come down in the tenth-century MS 326, CCCC. This poem is written in a curious mixture of English, Latin, and Greek not unsuited to its subject: Aldhelm had a weakness for showing off his learning. The anonymous poet probably wrote in Canterbury at a date not much earlier than that of the MS. The mixture of tongues in his poem reminds one of the charters, and differs from macaronic verse.[17]

The metrical writings of King Alfred will be taken up along with the prose in which they are imbedded.

Beowulf

The influence of southern culture on English secular poetry has shown itself chiefly, so far, in the choice and treatment of subject-matter, but two of the heroic poems that survive show marked influence in other ways as well. One of these poems, *Waldere*,[18] has come down in a state so fragmentary that we must set it aside for the moment. The other, however, *Beowulf*,[19] with its 3182 lines, gives us a broader basis for judgment. This famous poem, the chief literary monument of the Old English period, is the fourth article in the Nowell codex (see above, p. 67). The MS text is divided into a prologue and 43 fits. We look first at the theme of the poem. For this the poet turned to the heroic age of the Germanic peoples; more precisely, to heroes of the fifth and sixth centuries. And he chose for his setting Scandinavia, that motherland (or *vagina nationum*, as Jordanes puts it) from which so many Germanic tribes, the English among them, had gone forth down the years.[20] The poem thus celebrated, not contemporary deeds of heroism, but events of a past already remote, already glorified by a tradition centuries old. This tradition in its beginnings made part of the cultural baggage which the Germanic settlers in Britain brought with

---

[16] Text in Krapp-Dobbie, VI. 113.

[17] Text in Krapp-Dobbie, VI. 97-98.

[18] Ed. F. Norman (1933). See also *MA*, x (1941). 155-158.

[19] Facsimile ed.: J. Zupitza, *EETS*, 77 (London, 1882). Best printed editions: in English, F. Klaeber (Boston, 1922; 3ed. 1936); in German, E. von Schaubert (Paderborn, 1940), also referred to as 15th ed. of Heyne-Schücking's *Beowulf*. Most comprehensive study: R. W. Chambers, *Beowulf, An Introduction* ... (Cambridge, 1921; 2ed. 1932). See also W. W. Lawrence, *Beowulf and Epic Tradition* (Cambridge, Mass., 1928) and H. Schneider, *Das germanische Epos* (Tübingen, 1936). A good recent verse translation is that of C. W. Kennedy (Princeton, 1940).

[20] See K. Malone, in *Namn och Bygd*, XXII (1934). 41, 51.

them from Sleswick. It had taken a shape specifically English by the eighth
century, when in all likelihood *Beowulf* was composed.[21] In drawing from
it, the poet followed his own needs, not modern taste; too many critics
have scolded him for this.[22] The action of the poem falls into two main
parts. In part one, the hero Beowulf, then young, goes from his homeland
to Heorot, the hall of King Hrothgar of the Danes, in order to cleanse it
of Grendel, a troll who for years had haunted it at night; he overcomes
Grendel singlehanded and afterwards slays Grendel's mother, who sought
to avenge her son. In part two, the hero, now grown old, goes out to defend
his own kingdom of Geatland against the ravages of a dragon; with the
help of a faithful young kinsman he kills the dragon but himself falls in
the fight. These idealized folk-tales are not told in isolation, or for their
own sakes; they make part of an elaborate complex of fact and fable, matters of pith and moment, involving the fortunes of three Scandinavian
kingdoms, those of the Geats, the Danes, and the Swedes, over a period of
several generations. The poet has painted a vast canvas. And in glorifying
his hero he has not forgotten to glorify as well the heathen Germanic
courtly culture of which that hero was the flower. He gives us a spiritual-
ized picture of the Germanic heroic age, an age the memory of which the
English of the poet's day cherished as their very own. We believe that
Beowulf was meant to serve a purpose not unlike that which the *Æneid* of
Virgil served: each poem exalted a past which by tradition or fiction belonged to the cultural heritage of the poet's nation. In each poem, moreover,
this exaltation of the past took place under the influence of a foreign culture: pagan Greece in the *Æneid,* Christian Rome in *Beowulf.* The English
poet accordingly pictures a society heathen and heroic, but strongly colored
by Christian ideals of thought and deed. In particular, the hero is made as
Christ-like as the setting would permit: highminded and gentle, he fights
chiefly against monstrous embodiments of the forces of evil, and in the
end lays down his life for his people. But the Christianity known to the
poet had itself been strongly colored by the culture of classical antiquity.
Latin was the language of the Church in Old England, and Roman poets
were read and studied by learned clerics like the author of *Beowulf.* We
believe that the English poet knew the *Æneid* and was influenced by it in
designing and composing his own poem.[23] Alongside this influence, which
made for epic breadth and leisure, we put the influence of English religious
poems like *Genesis,* likewise marked by length and fullness in their narrative art. The *Beowulf* poet certainly showed originality when, in celebrating
a secular hero of the Germanic past, he did not compose a song after
the manner traditional to the scops (who before him had monopolized

21 A recent discussion of the date of *Beowulf* is that of D. Whitelock, *The Audience of Beowulf*
(Oxford, 1951). pp. 22-29. See also H. M. Flasdieck, *Anglia,* LXIX (1950). 169-171.
22 See J. R. R. Tolkien, *Proc. Brit. Acad.* XXII (1936). 245-285 and K. Malone, *RES,*
XVII (1941). 129-138. See also J. R. Hulbert, *MP,* XLIV (1946). 65-75.
23 See T. B. Haber, *A Comparative Study of the* Beowulf *and the* Æneid (Princeton, 1931).
See also A. Brandl, *Archiv,* CLXXI (1937). 165-173.

such themes), but used, instead, an elaborate, sophisticated narrative form reminiscent of the *Æneid*. In doing so, however, he was only carrying into the secular field a process of amplification and complication which, as we have seen, had already set in among the composers of English religious verse.

More striking is the originality of *Beowulf* in structure. The two main parts balance each other admirably, exemplifying and contrasting as they do the heroic life in youth and age. By treating in full two chapters only of Beowulf's career, the poet makes his tale marvelously simple, at bottom. The elaboration, which Grundtvig has aptly likened to the multitudinous embellishments of a Gothic cathedral, not only lends richness and variety to the action, but also makes the hero and his deeds part of the age in which he and they are set. Since the scene is laid in Scandinavia, most of the allusions and episodes deal with Scandinavian history and story, but other quarters of Germania are brought into the picture as well. Eormenric and Hama stand for the east. The allusions to the fall of Hygelac, and the Finn and Ingeld episodes, serve to link north and west. The association of Sigemund with Heremod, and the (rather artificial) connection of both with Beowulf himself, have a like function, while Offa, the representative of the Angles (the poet's own tribe), though introduced by a *tour de force,* well symbolizes the unity of ancient Germania: in after years both English and Danes claimed him for their own. In these and other ways the poet rises above mere story-telling; he brings before us a whole world, the heroic age of his forefathers and ours. But the greatness of *Beowulf* lies largely if not chiefly in its wording, and here the poet is no innovator; he is rather the master of a traditional style, a mode already old in his day. In the words of M. B. Ruud,[24] *Beowulf* has

a magnificence of language which leaves critic and translator helpless. Indeed, if the poem has a weakness as a work of art, it lies in this all-pervasive artistry. *Beowulf* seldom pierces one with a stab of eloquence straight from a heart on fire—as lesser poems do, even *Maldon*; it carries one along on a great golden stream of poetic rhetoric. ... It is a great literary tradition at its finest flowering. ... *Beowulf* may not be one of the half-dozen great poems of the world—I confess I do not know—but for sheer *style,* there are not many works to be put above it.

Waldere

With *Beowulf* we take the two *Waldere* fragments (of 32 and 31 lines respectively). These are recorded on two pieces of vellum, all that is left of an English MS of the late tenth century (167b, Royal library, Copenhagen). The verses are done in a style so broad and leisurely that they presumably made part of a long poem (one of 1000 lines or more, perhaps) [25] in which was celebrated the fight between the hero Waldere and a band of Burgundians led by King Guthere. This fight is known to us from other

[24] *MLQ*, II (1941). 138-139.
[25] For a different view, see F. P. Magoun, *MLN*, LIX (1944). 498-499.

sources, notably the tenth-century Latin poem *Waltharius*,[26] from which we learn that it was a fight of one against twelve, not counting the spectator Hagena (though he too was finally drawn in). In *Waldere* as in *Beowulf* the theme is secular, the treatment involved and sophisticated, bookish rather than popular. Both poems, moreover, celebrate events of the Germanic heroic age. The fragments are long enough to reveal that *Waldere* lacks the greatness of *Beowulf*. Its clerical composer, however, had considerable skill in versification, and though he used a German source he was steeped in traditional English poetry sacred and profane. In losing *Waldere* we lost a good poem and a stirring tale.

[26] For an earlier date, see K. Strecker, in *Deutsches Archiv für Geschichte des Mittelalters,* IV (1941). 355-381. Ed. K. Strecker, *Ekkehards Waltharius* (Berlin, 1924). Translated by H. M. Smyser and F. P. Magoun, Jr., in *Connecticut College Monograph No. 1* (Baltimore, 1941), pp. 111-145.

X

Literary Prose

*Prose
as an
Art Form*

All compositions in verse may be reckoned examples (by intention, at least) of literary art. This does not hold for prose compositions. In Old English times, even as now, prose was the normal form of non-literary speech and writing, and of the prose works left to us from the period we limit ourselves to those more or less literary in character. The literary prose of Old English is made up, for the most part, of translations or paraphrases of Latin writings. The English did not cultivate prose as an art form until they became acquainted with Latin literature, which gave them both sources and models for prose works of art. These sources and models, chiefly compositions of Christians though they were, had maintained the traditional great prose genres: history, philosophy, and oratory. In addition, minor genres like the epistle were represented. Everywhere, however, new wine had been poured into the old bottles. Thus, the oration appeared as a sermon. It was this Christianized classical tradition which the Roman missionaries brought to England and which the converts and their sons carried on in Latin and English. Throughout Old English times literary prose remained learned and clerical; for the people, verse continued to be the only natural medium of literary art.

*King
Alfred*

In spite of what we have just said, English literary prose owes its start to an unlearned layman. In the seventh and eighth centuries, the golden age of Old English literary culture, the prose writers composed in Latin only, so far as we know,[1] and it was left for King Alfred (849-899) to promote and, finally, himself to undertake composition in English when, in the last two decades of the ninth century, he tried to build up anew that flourishing civilization which the Danish invasions had brought to wrack and ruin. The writings of Alfred and his men must not be thought of as works of art; whatever literary merit they have is a by-product only. They were written as part of an educational program. Alfred hit upon the simple but revolutionary idea of using the mother tongue rather than Latin as the basic medium of instruction, both in the schools and in adult education.

---

[1] Except for Bede's incomplete translation of the Fourth Gospel, unhappily lost. An Old English *Martyrology* which antedates King Alfred should also be mentioned; ed. G. Herzfeld, *EETS*, 116 (1900). The editor dates the work *c.* 850 and localizes it in Lincolnshire. F. Liebermann, *Archiv,* cv (1900). 87, gives reasons for localization at Lichfield. The treatise on Kentish and other English saints published by Liebermann under the title *Die Heiligen Englands* (Hanover, 1889) seems to be little more than a ninth-century list, later extended by combination with another (non-Kentish) list. The treatise thus comes under the head of mnemonic prose. In its final form it is to be dated *c.* 1030.

Unluckily no English schoolbooks or works of reference existed. The King therefore with characteristic energy set out to fill the gap. He began with the history of the nation. We have no contemporary evidence of his part in compiling the Old English *Annals* (the so-called *Chronicles*) [2] or in preparing the Old English version of Bede's ecclesiastical history,[3] but we may reasonably presume (though we cannot prove) that he had something to do with both these undertakings; certainly the earliest extant form of each goes back to the time of Alfred's literary activity, and each was traditionally associated with Alfred.[4] We are better informed about the Old English versions of two works by Pope Gregory the Great: the *Dialogues* [5] and the *Pastoral Care*.[6] The former was translated for Alfred by his friend Bishop Wærferth of Worcester; the latter Alfred himself turned into English with the help of four scholars whom he names in his preface. Here ends what may be called the earlier period of Alfred's literary career. The later period begins with his translation of the world history of Orosius.[7] Next comes Alfred's major work, from the literary point of view: his translation of the treatise of Boethius on the consolation of philosophy.[8] Toward the end of his life he composed his *Blostman* ("Blossoms"), culled chiefly from the Soliloquies of St. Augustine.[9] The twelfth-century historian William of Malmesbury tells us that Alfred began but did not live to finish a translation of the Psalter,[10] and it has been conjectured that William is referring to the incomplete prose translation (Psalms, 1-50) recorded in the Paris Psalter; unluckily the MS itself throws no light on the identity of the translator.[11] Asser, the biographer of Alfred, tells in some detail, under the year 887, of yet another work: a Handbook which the King in that year began to compile. It seems in fact to have been a commonplace book. Possibly some of the passages entered in this book found place in the *Blostman;* the book as such has not survived.[12]

Gregory

[2] Ed. C. Plummer, *Two of the Saxon Chronicles* [A_1 and E] *Parallel, with Supplementary Extracts from the Others* (2v., Oxford, 1892-1899); H. A. Rositzke, *C* text (1940, in Förster's *Beiträge zur englischen Philologie*, xxxiv); E. Classen and F. E. Harmer, *D* text (Manchester, 1926); A. H. Smith, *The Parker Chronicle* (1935); trans. G. N. Garmonsway (1953).

[3] Ed. T. Miller, *EETS*, 95-96 and 110-111; J. Schipper, *Bibl. der ags. Prosa*, IV. See also F. Klaeber, *Anglia*, xxv (1902). 257-315; xxvii (1904). 243-282, 399-435.

[4] According to Gaimar's *Estorie des Engles* (twelfth century), lines 3451ff., Alfred had an English book written, consisting of events and laws, etc.; the reference is evidently to some MS (like the Parker) in which the annals are followed by legal texts. We have two Old English references to Alfred as translator of Bede: (1) in an eleventh-century MS of the Old English translation Alfred is named as translator; (2) Ælfric in his homily on Gregory the Great speaks of Alfred as translator.

[5] Ed. H. Hecht, *Bibl. der ags. Prosa*, v. See also P. N. U. Harting, *Neophilologus*, xxii (1937). 281-302.

[6] Ed. H. Sweet, *EETS*, 45 (Part II) and 50 (Part I).

[7] Ed. H. Sweet, *EETS*, 79 (Part I: Old English text and Latin original). The second part has never come out.

[8] Ed. W. J. Sedgefield (Oxford, 1899).

[9] Ed. H. L. Hargrove, *Yale Studies in English*, xiii; W. Endter, *Bibl. der ags. Prosa*, xi.

[10] *De Gestis Regum Anglorum*, II. iv (sec. 123).

[11] Ed. J. W. Bright and R. L. Ramsay, *The West Saxon Psalms* (Boston, 1907); see also J. H. G. Grattan, *MLR*, iv (1909). 185-189.

[12] An English translation of Æsop's fables is attributed to Alfred by Marie de France in the epilogue of her *Esope* or *Fables* (twelfth century), and Miss Helen Chefneux in her study

Asser

Asser, who wrote in 893, might have been expected to mention any books that Alfred had written or inspired up to that date. He actually mentions only Wærferth's translation of Gregory's *Dialogues,* but some version of the *Annals* must have been known to him, since in his biography he in-

Bede

cludes much annalistic matter up to the year 887. From Asser's silence we are bound to infer that the *Pastoral Care,* and of course all the works of Alfred's later period, were written after 893. The Bede, too, was presumably finished after 893, though quite possibly begun much earlier. It is best described as a revision of the original, made to fit the work into Alfred's educational program. Much was left out, condensed or summarized, while other parts were translated literally, to the sacrifice of English idiom now and again. In boldness of excision the translator reminds one of Alfred, but his literal renderings are less reminiscent of the King, who worked by para-phrase despite a few Latinisms. The other two translations of the earlier

Dialogues,
Pastoral
Care

period, those from Gregory, show less literalness, but greater fidelity to the texts, since they omit little and add little. Wærferth might be expected to understand his text better than Alfred understood his, but in fact the King does better than the bishop, thanks, no doubt, to the help he got. The works of the later period are marked by great boldness in the treatment of the text. Alfred felt free not only to omit but also to insert almost at will. Thus, the

Orosius

geographical chapter in Orosius struck him (rightly enough) as deficient when it came to Germany and Scandinavia. He therefore interpolated the famous account of the voyages of Ohthere and Wulfstan, together with a long and valuable section on Germanic and Slavic tribal geography in the ninth century.[13] In all his writings the King was concerned, not so much to reproduce his originals faithfully as to produce books good for his sub-jects and simple enough for them to understand. Through these books he hoped to give them an education at once practical and liberal. The history of the English nation and of the world, the principles of philosophy and the principles and practice of Christianity, such was the reading-matter to be pondered by English youths and men engaged in learning how to read and write their mother tongue. And in the *Dialogues* of Gregory he even provided edifying escape literature: stories of the wonders and miracles wrought by God and by saintly men of old.[14]

Alfred did his paraphrases in prose. To the *Pastoral Care,* however, he added two passages in verse: one of 16 lines at the beginning (between preface and table of contents) and one of 30 lines at the end. Moreover,

---

of the fables depicted on the Bayeux Tapestry (*Romania,* LX [1934]. 1-35, 153-194) makes it seem likely that the designer(s) of the tapestry drew on this lost English version of Æsop. For the so-called *Proverbs of Alfred* see below, p. 152.

[13] The latest discussion of King Alfred as geographer is that of R. Ekblom, *Studia Neophilo-logica,* XIV (1942). 115-144; reviewed by F. Klaeber, *ibid.,* XV. 337-338. See also A. S. C. Ross, *The Terfinnas and Beormas of Ohthere* (Leeds, 1940), and K. Malone, *Speculum,* V (1930). 139-167 and VIII (1933). 67-78.

[14] Bede's *History* is largely made up of like stories, of course. Alfred himself wrote a brief preface for Wærferth's translation of the *Dialogues,* and the translator added a preface of his own: 27 lines of verse in which he sings the King's praises.

after he had finished his prose rendering of Boethius, he made a verse rendering of most of the metrical parts of this work.[15] For the metres of Boethius, then, we have two Alfredian versions, one in prose and one in *Boethius* verse. The verse rendering depends on the prose, not directly on the Latin metres, and there are indications that when Alfred did the verses his prose rendering had been finished and set aside long enough to grow cold in his mind. Alfred was not a man trained in literary composition, and neither his prose nor his verse merits much praise as such. At times he rose above himself and gave us prose passages worthy of a skilled craftsman, but these passages are the exception, not the rule. His accomplishment stands out more clearly when we consider his work in the large. Though he began to write late in life, and had no tradition of English literary prose to feed on, he managed to overcome many of the ills that beset the beginner, and, in hours snatched from his manifold duties as head of the state and father of his people, he was able to produce a body of writings impressive in quantity, expressive of his personality, and readable enough. Moreover, in his later period, at least, he showed a remarkable independence of his originals. Most important of all, he gave prestige to prose composition in English, and thereby opened the way to the cultivation of important literary genres hitherto neglected.

In the year 891 some compiler, probably a cleric in King Alfred's service, *The* finished a set of annals devoted chiefly to the history of the English from *Old* their settlement in Britain to the year of compilation, though not without *English* record of other events in Britain and elsewhere (the earliest event recorded *Annals* is Julius Caesar's invasion of Britain). The compiler used various sources, such as earlier annalistic matter, genealogies, Bede's *History,* and oral reports. A number of copies of his text seem to have got into circulation; in all likelihood King Alfred had them made and distributed among his bishops (or abbots), with instructions to keep them up to date.[16] Certainly his educational program would require some such distribution, and we know that he so distributed the *Pastoral Care.* None of these original copies of the *Annals* survive, but the seven extant versions all descend in one way or another from the compilation of 891. As time went on, entries were added in various MSS by successive annalists. The A_1 text (CCCC 173) was carried down to 1070; the A_2 text (Otho B xi), to 1001; the *B* text (Tib. A vi), to 977; the *C* text (Tib. B i), to 1086; the *D* text (Tib. B iv), to 1079; the *E* text (Laud 636), to 1154; the *F* text (Dom. A viii), to 1058. The *Annals* thus record contemporary events of the ninth, tenth, eleventh, and twelfth centuries, besides the earlier events which the original compiler set down from various sources. For the historian of England these *Annals* are obviously of the first importance. Here we are concerned with them as literature. One goes to annalistic writing with no high expectations; the form

---

[15] Preserved in MS Cotton Otho A vi.

[16] Continuations, compiled at some center (presumably Winchester), seem to have been sent out from time to time; but the matter is too intricate for treatment here. The *Old English Annals* are often called less accurately the *Anglo-Saxon Chronicle.*

does not lend itself well to artistic effects. The early annals in particular give us, for the most part, mere lists of events, not narrative accounts, and the annalist for 755, who tried his hand at narration, did a bungling job, though he had a stirring story to tell (that of Cynewulf, Cyneheard, and Osric).[17] The narrative passages grow better in the ninth-century annals; the writers usually express themselves clearly and simply enough, and show some skill in avoiding the monotony so often found in annalistic writing. With the death (in 924) of King Edward the Elder, however, the *Annals* begin to languish, and they do not regain their Alfredian vigor and fullness until the reign of King Æthelred the Redeless (979-1016), when a truly literary historical prose emerges and maintains itself to the end of the Old English period. Evidently a traditional craftsmanship had begun to take shape in the midst of political disaster. Moreover, expertness in prose composition was not peculiar to the later annalists; it marks other writings of the period as well. If Old English poetry flowered in the late seventh and eighth centuries, Old English prose flowered in the late tenth and eleventh. We therefore reckon classical, not the early prose of Alfred and his men, but the late prose of the annalists and of other writers taken up below.[18]

Æthelwold   We have seen that the politically glorious tenth century was marked by a decline in English prose, while Æthelred's calamitous reign and the triumph of the Danes in the eleventh century did not keep English prose from reaching heights of achievement worthy of the name classical. Alfred had laid the foundations on which the classical Old English prose writers built, but it was the monastic reform movement of the tenth century, led in England by Dunstan, Æthelwold, and Oswald,[19] which produced and cherished the builders. Æthelwold himself set going the second or classical period of Old English prose with a translation of the *Rule of St. Benedict*[20] which he made about 960.[21] The extant copies of this work all go back to a text made for nuns, but the original text presumably was made for monks weak in Latin. In a historical appendix, found in one MS only,[22] Æthelwold explains that the translation owed its existence to King Edgar's initiative, and it seems evident that the King in having it made was following the example set by his great-grandfather. Æthelwold goes on to apologize for the translation, which he thought of as a concession to weakness (strict disciplinarian that he was), but the Alfredian tradition proved strong enough to overcome whatever scruples he may have had. Indeed, he did his work in the spirit of Alfred: his version of the *Rule* is a paraphrase, not a literal rendering, and

[17] See F. P. Magoun, *Anglia*, LVII (1933). 361-376, and C. L. Wrenn, *History*, xxv (1940). 208-215.

[18] See C. L. Wrenn, *Trans. Phil. Soc.* for 1933, pp. 65-88.

[19] Dunstan, Archbishop of Canterbury (d. 988); Æthelwold, Bishop of Winchester (d. 984); Oswald, Bishop of Worcester and Archbishop of York (d. 992).

[20] Ed. A. Schröer, *Bibl. der ags. Prosa*, II.

[21] Schröer, p. xviii. But F. Tupper, *MLN*, VIII (1893). 350, dates the translation about 970.

[22] Cotton Faustina A x. Old English text and modern rendering in T. O. Cockayne, *Leechdoms*, etc., III. 432-444. The appendix may have been composed by 970, though Liebermann, *Archiv*, CVIII (1902). 375-377, dates it after the death of Edgar in 975.

shows everywhere his concern to make things clear and simple for the reader. The smoothness and general competence of Æthelwold's English may reflect, more or less indirectly, the schooling he got under Dunstan at Glastonbury; certainly he was a man schooled and trained, not a self-taught writer like Alfred.

We come now to the leading prose writer of the period: Ælfric [23] *Ælfric* (c. 955-c. 1020), sometime pupil of Æthelwold at Winchester and lifelong disciple of his old master. Ælfric's many writings include homilies, pastoral letters, lives of saints, versions of books of the Bible, learned works of various kinds—a whole library to meet practical needs of the Church in his day. We pass over his *Grammar* and *Glossary*, with their pendant the *Colloquy*, in spite of their great cultural interest,[24] and begin with the 120 sermons, in three series of 40 sermons each, which he wrote between the years 990 and 998 [25] while a monk at Winchester or Cernel. The first and second series go by the name *Homiliae Catholicae;* the third series is called *Passiones Sanctorum*. These serial titles, however, cannot be taken strictly; saints' lives are included among the homilies, and homilies among the saints' lives. Each sermon was written for use on a suitable day of the Church year; thus, the sermon on Gregory was to be preached on March 12 (the day of that saint). Through his vernacular sermons Ælfric sought to make things easier for the preachers, who could use the discourses which he provided, without having to wrestle with the Latin originals, the meaning of which, in spots at least, those weak in Latin might find it hard to fathom. For sources Ælfric drew on the abundant stock of sermons and other religious writings available in Latin; he made particular use of Gregory, Bede, and Augustine. He treated his sources with great freedom, adapting the material to the needs of English pastor and flock. All three series are marked by good construction and clear, happy expression; as W. P. Ker has said, Ælfric is "the great master of prose in all its forms." [26] The series differ somewhat in style. In the first, alliteration is used now and then to heighten the effect; in the second, this device is used more freely; in the third, many passages are written in a rhythmic alliterative prose which some scholars have wrongly taken for verse and even printed as such. Ælfric in his rhythmical effects was following a fashion of his time, found in Latin prose and carried over into vernacular composition.[27] We note also, as we proceed from series to series, a shift of balance: the story looms larger, the mor-

23 See C. L. White, *Ælfric, . . .* (*Yale Studies in English*, ii). Ed. *Bibl. der ags. Prosa*, i (Grein), iii (Assmann), ix (Fehr), x (Crawford); *EETS*, 76, 82, 94, 114 (Skeat), 160 (Crawford), 213 (Henel). For other editions see *CBEL*, i. 89-92. Miss Dorothy Whitelock, in *MLR*, xxxviii (1943). 122-124, points out the inadequacy of the evidence for the date of Ælfric's death.

24 Ed. J. Zupitza, *Ælfrics Grammatik und Glossar* (Berlin, 1880); G. N. Garmonsway, *Ælfric's Colloquy* (1939). These works may have grown out of his experiences as teacher of oblates at the monastery of Cernel in Dorsetshire (987-989). See above, p. 18.

25 The first series was finished in 990 or 991; the second, in 992; the third, between 993 and 998. See K. Sisam, *RES*, vii (1931). 16-18, viii (1932). 55, 67-68.

26 *English Literature, Medieval*, p. 55.

27 G. H. Gerould, *MP*, xxii (1925). 353-366. Cf. also A. Cordier, *L'Allitération latine* (Paris, 1939).

alizing commentary smaller. The saints' lives in particular [28] tend to become tales of wonder not unlike the legends of Middle English times.

Alongside the three series of sermons we set, as a fourth major work of Ælfric, the so-called *Heptateuch*, an English version of the first seven books of the Bible. This version seems to have been made in several stages. Genesis was translated in 997 or 998, at the instance of the ealdorman Æthelweard, to whom its epistolary preface is addressed. For the same nobleman, and presumably at about the same time (if not earlier), Ælfric turned Joshua into English. The exact times and occasions of composition cannot be given for the other books of the *Heptateuch*, but the whole was hardly complete by 1005, when Ælfric became Abbot of Eynsham in Oxfordshire. The seventh book, Judges, was not included in the B text (MS Claudius B iv), and though included in the L text (MS Bodley Laud Misc. 509) it is there set off from the rest by a blank page; presumably Judges was first composed as an independent work, or as a fellow of the homilies on other books of the Bible: Kings and Maccabees, incorporated into the third series of sermons; Job, used in the second series; Judith; and Esther. The whole Bible was summarized by Ælfric in a treatise (really two treatises) on the Old and New Testaments written for a certain Sigwerd, and this treatise has been taken for an introduction to the *Heptateuch*, though its place in the MS (Bodley Laud Misc. 509) does not support the theory. Introduction or no, the treatise was composed later than the *Heptateuch* proper; not earlier than 1006, not later than 1012. If we compare Ælfric's *Heptateuch* with the original we find it a volume of selections; large parts of the scriptural text are omitted. This holds least for Genesis, though even here omissions may be noted. In general, Ælfric left out things which he thought unsuitable for an English layman. Incidentally he thereby made his version more readable. Whatever he chose to translate he reproduced faithfully, with due regard to English idiom. He made much use of alliteration and rhythm here as elsewhere. For the latter part of Genesis, and perhaps for Exodus and Leviticus as well, Ælfric had before him an English translation made by somebody else; this translation he seems to have incorporated (in somewhat revised form) into his own version. His procedure here is indicative of the man: he saw no reason to work out a fresh version when one already existed which with a little patching could be made to serve. His sermons meant more to him. Here he was capable of discarding earlier work of his own for the sake of giving more adequate treatment to a theme. Thus, the *Hexameron*, a homily on the Creation, treats more fully a theme which he had already used in the *Catholic Homilies*, and the MS evidence suggests that Ælfric wrote the *Hexameron* to take the place of this earlier creation sermon.[29]

In general, Ælfric's literary activities grew out of practical needs or de-

[28] On their form, see D. Bethurum, *SP*, xxix (1932). 515-533.

[29] The name *Hexameron* was traditional; Ælfric presumably got it from Bede. The six parts implied answer to the six days of Creation but Ælfric gives us much not mentioned in the Bible; his chief extra-biblical source was Bede.

mands; here he followed the tradition of Alfred, whose writings he knew. Sometimes Ælfric himself took the initiative in meeting such needs. In other cases he wrote to order: thus, bishops would commission him to prepare pastoral letters for use in their dioceses, and patrons (as we saw above) would ask him for English renderings or summaries of Holy Writ. Whatever the circumstances, his work shows a high level of competence, and often rises to æsthetic heights in its kind. Ælfric's artistic achievement, however, should not make us lose sight of the didactic purpose and effect which, for him, alone gave point to the labor of composition. The things he wrote proved, in fact, so well adapted to the needs of pastoral and monastic instruction that they withstood the cultural collapse brought on by the Norman Conquest, and kept alive till better days the tradition of English devotional prose.

The chief literary contemporary of Ælfric was his superior and friend *Wulfstan* Wulfstan,[30] Bishop of London (996-1002), Bishop of Worcester (1002-1016), and Archbishop of York (1002-1023). He died in 1023. He is best known as a homilist. Indeed his literary fame rests mainly on a single homily composed in the troublous year 1014: the eschatological *Sermo Lupi ad Anglos.*[31] He begins conventionally enough with the statement that "this world is in haste, and it draws nigh to the end." In other words, Doomsday is almost upon us. The evils of the time drive the preacher to his fateful conclusion, evils which he proceeds to particularize in vigorous speech. The English by their sinful ways have called down these evils upon themselves, and unless they repent and turn from wickedness to righteousness they will have every reason to quake before the judgment which is at hand. This powerful and timely sermon, thundered from the pulpit by Wulfstan himself or by some other clerical orator, might well have brought an eleventh-century congregation to sackcloth and ashes. Even today, after more than 900 years, its fiery periods stir the heart. The sermons of Ælfric were written to instruct; those of Wulfstan, to move; both homilists in the process produced works of art unmatched in their respective kinds. Wulfstan has aptly been compared to an Old Testament prophet; certainly he speaks with prophetic eloquence and zeal. The canon of his works remains a problem.[32]

The *Blickling Homilies*,[33] a batch of 19 sermons in a MS of *c.* 970 and *Blickling* named (by modern scholars) after the former home of the MS, antedate the *and* homilies of Ælfric and Wulfstan. Their literary merit is small, and we need *Vercelli* do no more than mention them here. The 23 prose pieces of the Vercelli *Homilies* Book, a collection made *c.* 1000 if not earlier, are mostly homilies,[34] but include a fragmentary life of St Guthlac.[35]

[30] See A. [S.] Napier, *Wulfstan* (Berlin, 1883); D. Bethurum, *PMLA*, LVII (1942). 916-929.
[31] The best edition is that of D. Whitelock (1939).
[32] But see K. Jost, *Anglia*, LVI (1932). 265-315.
[33] Ed. R. Morris, *EETS*, 58, 63, 73. See also A. E. H. Swaen, *Neophilologus*, xxv (1940). 264-272, and R. Willard, *Univ. of Texas . . . Studies in English*, 1940, pp. 5-28.
[34] Ed. (first half only) M. Förster, *Bibl. der ags. Prosa*, XII.
[35] A fuller text of the prose *Guthlac* is recorded in MS Cotton Vesp. D XXI. Edition, based on both texts, by P. Gonser, *Anglistische Forschungen*, XXVII (Heidelberg, 1909).

A number of other homilies and legends have come down to us, singly and in groups. Some of them still await publication.[36] We do not treat them in this history, but pass on to the gospel translations and other prose works. *Gospels* The West Saxon version of the four gospels [37] is commonly dated *c.* 1000. The translation, idiomatic but faithful to the Vulgate text, bears comparison with the Authorized Version of 1611 in literary quality.[38] The so-called Lindisfarne and Rushworth gospels are only glosses, and do not concern us here. The same may be said of the many glossed texts of the Latin Psalter. Such works as the penitentials attributed to Archbishop Egbert of York [39] likewise have little or no literary interest; they are essentially (ecclesiastical) legal texts. The many legal documents of Old English times have already been looked at (above, pp. 35-38) for the metrical bits which they incorporate. We omit from this history any consideration of legal prose. The *Handbook* of Byrhtferth,[40] and other works of interest to the historian of science,[41] we likewise omit. The translation of that famous medieval collection of proverbs known as the *Distichs of Cato* [42] may be worthy of mention. The most notable piece of late secular prose, however, is the Old *Apollonius* English version of the Apollonius of Tyre story.[43] This romance of classical antiquity, deservedly popular in the Middle Ages, found an English translator even though it served for entertainment pure and simple. Unluckily only a fragment of the translation has survived. Its author shows considerable skill in that difficult art; his version reads well and gives us some idea of what the English literature of entertainment might have become but for the Norman Conquest. Of less interest are two secular prose pieces recorded in the Nowell codex: [44] the Old English version of *Alexander's Letter to Aristotle,* and a piece known as *Wonders of the East.* Both these pieces, along with *Apollonius* and many a saint's legend, show a taste for Oriental wonders and adventures, a taste which the crusades were destined to whet.

Summary During the late tenth and eleventh centuries, the classical period of Old English prose, many writers were active and much good prose was written. Homiletic prose in particular reached heights of achievement comparable to the masterpieces of modern times. Historical prose, too, flourished, and

[36] On the unpublished homilies of MS CCCC 41, see R. Willard, in Förster's *Beiträge zur englischen Philologie*, xxx (1935). 2.

[37] Ed. J. W. Bright (4v, 1904-1906). On the Vulgate text used by the translator, see H. Glunz, in Förster's *Beiträge*, ix (1928) and *Kölner anglistische Arbeiten*, xii (1930).

[38] Here may be mentioned the Old F⌐glish version of the apocryphal gospel of Nicodemus. Text and discussion by W. H. Hulme in *PMLA*, xiii (1898). 471-515 and *MP*, i (1904). 579-614. Ed. E. J. Crawford (Edinburgh, 1927).

[39] Editions: *Poenitentiale* by J. Raith (1933); *Confessionale* by R. Spindler (1934).

[40] Ed. S. J. Crawford, *EETS*, 177 (1929). See also H. Henel, *JEGP*, xli (1942). 427-443, and *Speculum*, xviii (1943). 288-302.

[41] Many texts may be found in O. Cockayne's *Leechdoms, Wort-Cunning, and Starcraft* (3v, Rolls Series, 1864-1866); see also G. Leonhardi, *Bibl. der ags. Prosa*, vi (1905), and H. Henel, *EETS*, 213 (1942).

[42] Ed. J. Nehab, *Der altenglische Cato* (Berlin, 1879). See also G. Schleich, *Anglia*, iii (1880). 383-396.

[43] Ed. J. Zupitza, *Archiv*, xcvii (1896). 17-34. See also P. Goepp, *ELH*, v (1938). 150-172.

[44] Ed. S. Rypins, *EETS*, 161 (1924).

a beginning was made with scientific prose. Moreover, prose writers even ventured into the realm of fiction, territory hitherto monopolized by verse. Had this rapid development kept up, the twelfth and thirteenth centuries might have been as glorious in English literature as they actually were in Icelandic. But William of Normandy won at Hastings. King Alfred, the noblest Englishman of them all, had laid out the garden of English prose. Ælfric and his fellows brought it to high cultivation, and extended it with new plantings full of promise. The Normans laid it waste, and slew its keepers.[45]

[45] A. Brandl sums up the matter thus (*Grundriss,* p. 1133): "In the last phase of Old English culture, creative power was still active in the most diverse fields. In poetry the rise of rime was opening the way to a flowering of song. In prose, a homiletic style of singular force and vigor had grown up, and at the same time story telling made its way in a fullness comparable to the period of the crusades. In science, meager though the achievement, the zeal of the students was worthy of praise, while not only a great man [Ælfric?] but also an organization extending over the whole country provided for popular education. It was no tired, late autumnal culture but a field freshly sown with many promising seeds upon which fell the foreign rule of the Normans like the snows of winter." Less authoritative but of particular interest to Americans is the judgment of Ralph Waldo Emerson (*English Traits* [Boston, 1903], pp. 60-61): ". . . Twenty thousand thieves landed at Hastings. These founders of the House of Lords were greedy and ferocious dragoons, sons of greedy and ferocious pirates. They were all alike, they took everything they could carry, they burned, harried, violated, tortured and killed, until everything English was brought to the verge of ruin. . . ."

BOOK I
The Middle Ages

⌒∽∙∽⌒

PART II
The Middle English Period
(1100-1500)

Guide to reference marks

Throughout the text of this book, a point • set beside a page number indicates that references to new critical material will be found under an identical paragraph/page number (set in **boldface**) in the BIBLIOGRAPHICAL SUPPLEMENT.

In the Index, a number preceded by an **S** indicates a paragraph/page number in the BIBLIOGRAPHICAL SUPPLEMENT.

I

General Characteristics of the Period

The Middle English period may be defined chronologically as the period *The Period* from 1100 to 1500. Some scholars prefer to date the beginning from 1150, *Defined* and, so far as literature in English is concerned, there is much to be said for this view. It is not merely because little or nothing in English has come down to us from the first half of the century and what has, such as the *Old English Annals (Anglo-Saxon Chronicle)* carried on at Peterborough until 1154, is better thought of as a continuation of what went before, but because the changes in the Old English language, especially the wearing away of inflections, and the reflection of these changes in the orthography reach a point about 1150 which justifies our setting at this date the boundary between Old and Middle English. When we consider, however, that English literature is rightly to be thought of as the literature written in England,[1] reflecting English life and thought, whether it is written in English or in French or Latin, we may with equal justice begin our present survey with the opening of the twelfth century. The adoption of 1500 as a closing date has only the convenience of a round number to recommend it. However, most of fifteenth-century literature belongs indisputably to the Middle English tradition, and those developments at the end of the century which look forward to the Renaissance of the next are not of a revolutionary character and may be considered as faint stirrings of the new spirit helping to remind us of the complexity characteristic of any period, rightly considered, of literary history.[2]

[1] From the latter part of the fourteenth century on we must include the work of certain Scottish writers.

[2] The most valuable tool for the study of Middle English texts is John E. Wells, *A Manual of the Writings in Middle English, 1050-1400* (New Haven, 1916), with periodic supplements, now nine in number. Vol. 1 of the *CBEL* covers this period. Briefer bibliographical guides are W. L. Renwick and Harold Orton, *The Beginnings of English Literature to Skelton—1509* (1940), and Roger S. Loomis, *Intro. to Medieval Literature, chiefly in England: Reading List and Bibl.* (1939). Indispensable is Carleton Brown's *Register of Middle English Religious and Didactic Verse* (2v, 1916-20; *Bibliographical Soc.*). The second volume, revised and enlarged to include the secular verse, by Carleton Brown and Rossell H. Robbins, has been issued as *An Index of Middle English Verse* (1943; *Index Soc.*). Valuable bibliographical material is presented in Josiah C. Russell, *Dictionary of Writers of Thirteenth Century England* (1936; *Bull. Inst. of Hist. Research*, Special Suppl. No. 3). Additions appear from time to time in the *Bulletin*. Important older works are Thomas Tanner, *Bibliotheca Britannico-Hibernica* (1748), John Pits, *Relationum Historicarum de Rebus Anglicis* (Paris, 1619), John Bale, *Illustrium Majoris Britanniae Scriptorum . . . Summarium* (Ipswich, 1548; enlarged ed., Basle, 1557-9), Bale's *Index Britanniae Scriptorum*, ed. R. L. Poole and Mary Bateson (Oxford, 1902), John Leland, *Commentarii de Scriptoribus Britannicis* (2v, Oxford, 1709), and Thomas Wright, *Biographia Britannica Literaria*, Vol. II: *Anglo-Norman Period* (1846). — The Middle English period receives extensive treatment in Bernard Ten Brink, *Gesch. der englischen Literatur* (2ed., 2v, 1899-1912; English trans., 3v, 1883-96), suggestive but now somewhat antiquated. The

The
Norman
Conquest

In this period of four hundred years the dominant factor which changed the whole course of Middle English literature, as of English history during the same period, was the Norman Conquest. In 1066 William, the Duke of Normandy and one of the world's great figures, claimed the English throne as the next of kin to Edward the Confessor. He supported his claim by invading England with an army of Norman and French soldiers led by adventurers, ambitious nobles, and the younger sons of many important French families, conquered his rival, Harold, at the Battle of Hastings, and was crowned king. It required four years to stamp out opposition and win complete recognition, four years filled with ruthless campaigns in which he all but wiped out the English nobility. His Norman and French supporters who had made the conquest possible were rewarded with the lands and titles of the English nobles. The result was a new aristocracy in England, an aristocracy almost wholly French. Normans and French filled all important positions in both Church and State. Foreign in nationality and temperament, in tradition and association, they added a new element to the English nation and brought new qualities of mind and character to merge

---

discussion in J. J. Jusserand, *Histoire littéraire du peuple anglais* (2ed., 2v, 1896-1904) is along more general lines. The English trans. has the title *A Literary History of the English People* (2ed., 3v, 1906-9). Still of importance is A. Brandl, "Mittelenglische Literatur" in H. Paul, *Grundriss der germanischen Philologie*, Bd. II, Abt. 1 (1893), pp. 609-718. Wm. H. Schofield's *English Literature from the Norman Conquest to Chaucer* (1906) is readable and well known. There are useful but uneven chapters in the *CHEL* and bibliographies in the *CBEL*. C. S. Baldwin, *Three Medieval Centuries of Literature in England, 1100-1400* (Boston, 1932), P. G. Thomas, *English Literature before Chaucer* (1924), and R. M. Wilson, *Early Middle English Literature* [to 1300] (1939) may be noted. The last best represents the present status of scholarship. Hans Hecht and L. L. Schücking, *Die englische Literatur im Mittelalter* (1927) is slight. W. F. Ker's *English Literature: Medieval* (n.d.) in its brief compass is richly suggestive. Remarkable for its time was Thomas Warton's *History of English Poetry* (1774-81), best consulted in the edition of W. C. Hazlitt (4v, 1871). — For the Old French background the student should consult Gaston Paris's classic, *La Littérature française au moyen âge* (4ed., 1909) or the *Esquisse* translated as *Medieval French Literature* (1903); Karl Voretzsch, *Intro. to the Study of Old French Literature* (1931, from the third German ed.); Urban T. Holmes, *History of Old French Literature . . . to 1300* (2ed, Chapel Hill, 1937); G. Gröber, "Französische Literatur" in Gröber's *Grundriss der romanischen Philologie*, Bd. II, Abt. 1 (1902), pp. 433-1247; and the monumental *Histoire littéraire de la France* (39v, 1733-1950, in progress). On the Latin literature of the Middle Ages see the references at the end of ch. v. — For the historical background the reader may consult H. W. C. Davis, *England under the Normans and Angevins* (1905), Kenneth H. Vickers, *England in the Later Middle Ages* (1913), George B. Adams, *The History of England from the Norman Conquest to the Death of John (1066-1216)* (1905), T. F. Tout, *The History of England from the Accession of Henry III to the Death of Edward III (1216-1377)* (1905), and C. Oman, *The History of England from the Accession of Richard II to the Death of Richard III (1377-1485)* (1906). Charles Gross, *The Sources and Literature of English History . . . to about 1485* (2ed., 1915) is invaluable. On English life in the Middle Ages the following are of interest: *Medieval England*, ed. H. W. C. Davis (Oxford, 1924); A. Abram, *English Life and Manners in the Later Middle Ages* (1913); L. F. Salzman, *English Life in the Middle Ages* (Oxford, 1926); and the first two volumes of H. D. Traill's *Social England* (rev. ed., 1901-4). For a more general view of the Middle Ages see G. G. Coulton, *Medieval Panorama* (1938); *The Legacy of the Middle Ages*, ed. C. G. Crump and E. F. Jacob (Oxford, 1926); Karl Vossler, *Medieval Culture*, trans. W. C. Lawton (2v, 1929), with an extensive bibliography by J. E. Spingarn; Henry Osborn Taylor, *The Medieval Mind* (2v, 1911); Henry Adams, *Mont-Saint-Michel and Chartres* (1904); and, for the fullest treatment and widest scope, *The Cambridge Medieval History* (8v, Cambridge, 1911-36). Further references may be found in Louis J. Paetow, *A Guide to the Study of Medieval History* (rev. ed., 1931).

in time with those of the Anglo-Saxon. The practical and enterprising qualities of the Norman, and the French instinct for symmetry and order became part of the English race, and as characteristics of the race were reflected in English literature.

A more immediate consequence of the Norman Conquest was the introduction of French into England as the normal language of the governing class. The new nobility knew no English, and it is unlikely that they made much effort to become acquainted with it. The tradition that William the Conqueror made an unsuccessful attempt to learn the language is not too well founded. On the other hand there is abundant evidence that for at least two hundred years the nobility everywhere used French. We must remember that the conquerors came to England to enrich themselves, not to identify themselves with a people and a national culture which they regarded, with some justice, as less sophisticated than their own. They retained political and property interests in France which required frequent and extended sojourns there. Residence in England was not a matter of choice but of political necessity and financial expediency. Even the small percentage of the English nobles who acknowledged William's claim and retained their estates and titles soon learned French as the language of the class with which their own interests were most closely identified and with which they were mostly associated. The English language naturally continued to be spoken by the mass of the people, but it was the language of the uncultivated. England was thus in the unhappy linguistic situation of a house divided against itself. As to some extent in Belgium today, two languages were in use side by side, one by the upper class, economically and socially, the other by the common people. *The French Language in England*

How long such a situation would have continued if events had not occurred to bring about a change no one can say. Probably in time the weight of numbers would have told and English would once more have become the language of the whole country. But in 1204 England lost Normandy and an important political condition favorable to the maintenance of French in England came to an end. From this date we note the growing tendency for nobles with land in both France and England to divide their possessions geographically among their children and for members of a family to reach a similar agreement among themselves. Finally in 1244 decrees of the King of France and the King of England made it illegal for any one to hold lands in both countries. It is significant that the influx of French words into the English vocabulary assumes really large proportions in the period following 1250, a pretty clear indication that English is coming to be spoken by those accustomed to the use of French. The half century from 1250 to 1300 is the period during which the transition from French to English as the language of the nobility was occurring. By the beginning of the fourteenth century English is for all practical purposes universal. The author of a romance, writing not later than 1325, remarks that everybody now knows *Recovery of English*

English and many a noble can speak no French. From this time on a knowledge of French in England is merely a fashionable accomplishment or a cultural asset.[3]

Periods of Middle English Literature

The linguistic situation here described had an important effect upon the production of literature in the native tongue and determined in no small measure the character of that which was produced at different stages of the Middle English period. It would be wrong to suppose that the Norman Conquest caused a sharp cleavage, cutting off suddenly native production. Rather it altered the course of the native tradition, forced it for a time to run under ground, narrowed the stream. This will be apparent if we examine Middle English literature as a whole, for we will find that it falls into certain well-marked periods.[4] There is first the period running to 1250, the period during which English was the language of only the lower classes. It would be useless to look in it for romances and other types popular at the court. These were being produced in French, the language of the class to which poets looked for patronage. Since writing in English was bound to be without material rewards to the writer, we must look to the clergy for most of what was intended for the common people. It is not surprising, therefore, to find English writings at this date predominantly religious, representing the efforts of those in the Church to instruct the people in Bible story and in the ways of right living. The *Ormulum* (see p. 158) is a typical work of the first period—the Period of Religious Record.[5] When the upper classes begin to adopt English we get a much more varied literature in the native language. The object of English writings becomes entertainment as well as edification. Our earliest romances in English, for example, belong with one exception to the second half of the thirteenth century, and the hundred years from 1250 to 1350 are known as the Period of Religious and Secular Literature. When after 1350 English is once more secure as the language of both the court and the people and there has been sufficient time for the tentative and experimental efforts that seem to precede major literary periods, we reach the high point in Middle English literature. The fifty years from 1350 to 1400, in which Chaucer, Wyclif, Langland, and the *Pearl* poet, not to mention significant but less spectacular figures, appeared, has been called the Period of Great Individual Writers. The remaining hundred years, the fifteenth century, are for a time dominated by the influence of Chaucer and towards the end look forward to the developments which make the sixteenth century one of great literary renaissance. This century may be thought of as the Imitative or Transition Period.

---

[3] For a full treatment of the relation between French and English in England after the Norman Conquest see the present writer's *History of the English Language* (rev. ed., 1957), chs. V and VI.

[4] These chronological divisions were first suggested by Brandl in his *Mittelenglische Literatur*, noted on p. 110.

[5] The name is meant to suggest that classification is necessarily based on what was recorded in writing and therefore survived. There was doubtless much popular literature—song, ballad, story—which lived only on the lips of the people and the wandering minstrel and which therefore has not come down to us. Cf. p. 209.

The effect on literature of the Norman Conquest as we have so far *Effects of* described it is largely indirect, the consequence of the fact that a new ruling *Norman* class, alien in speech, came into being, interrupting the normal literary de- *Conquest* velopment and temporarily forcing English prose and poetry into the back- *on* ground. But the new influence was not merely negative or entirely bad. *Literature* The Norman conquerors and those who later came in their train brought to England much that was new and stimulating and valuable. They brought with them their Continental tastes and the literature on which those tastes had been formed. French literature in the twelfth century had burst suddenly into flower and was enjoying one of its great periods. It was the leading literature of Europe, rich and varied in theme, polite and urbane in spirit, easy and confident in performance. This literature circulated as freely at the English court as in France. In time it furnished a large body of new material for English poets and gave them new models and standards for imitation and emulation. The new wealth of the Norman nobles attracted French minstrels and poets to the English court and insured liberal rewards for their effort to provide solace or pleasing edification (cf. pp. 135 ff.). The policy of the Conqueror of filling English churches and monasteries with learned Norman bishops and abbots—men like Lanfranc and Gilbert Crispin —however detrimental it was to pastoral needs, gave a needed stimulus to English intellectual life. The close political connection with France, at first through Normandy and later through extensive English possessions in Anjou, Maine, Aquitaine, and Guienne, put an end to any sense of isolation that may have existed and brought England into the stream of Continental thought and culture. The English language was enriched with thousands of French words, becoming a more cosmopolitan and supple medium of literary expression, and the old Teutonic alliterative verse was largely replaced by the French syllabic line, standard all over Europe. We should look upon the Norman Conquest as bringing about the early merging of two great literary traditions, the Teutonic tradition which early England shared with other northern nations and the Romance tradition with its main source in France.

English literature in the period following the Conquest is in three lan- *Literature* guages—Latin, French, and English. Latin, as already in Old English times, *in Three* was not only the language of learning but the vernacular of the learned, *Languages* and the character of such twelfth-century works as Walter Map's *De Nugis Curialium* and Geoffrey of Monmouth's *Historia* attests its use outside the narrower field of scholarship. In French a large body of poetry was written in England or for English patronage and constituted for over two hundred years the literary entertainment of the English court. It is natural for us to take greater interest in the literature written in our own mother tongue and to trace its course as a separate stream. But whatever was written in England, expressing English thought and reflecting English social and intellectual conditions, is rightly to be considered a part of the national literature. For more than half of our period it is possible to distinguish between what was written for the aristocratic class and what was intended for the people merely by the language in which it is written. Even after English had regained its position at court numerous works avow their author's intention of writing for "lewd men," that is, the ignorant. Seldom outside of the Middle Ages is literature quite so class conscious. A great part of Middle English literature, for whatever class intended, must be recognized as derivative, secondary, and imitative. English writers eagerly adopted the themes and fashions of French literature, offering hospitality to the *Song of Roland* and showing a nice impartiality towards heroes of the French national epic. All through the thirteenth and much of the fourteenth centuries the literature of England was constantly indebted to French originals and followed French example. We are here, as always, speaking of what has been preserved. Popular poetry, which must have existed even though it has not come down to us, was surely thoroughly English. But of the productions that took written form a large number derive directly or ultimately from France. Even a British legend like that of King Arthur reached English romance not directly from the Celts but through the French romances of Chrétien de Troyes and his successors. The general character of Middle English literature will be imperfectly apprehended unless we recognize its tri-lingual form, its class distinctions, and its great indebtedness to French sources and models.

Some Character- istics of Medieval Literature
There are other general features of Middle English literature which should be noted, but these are characteristic of all medieval literature. One is what might be called its impersonality. In the first place a great deal of Middle English literature is anonymous. We don't know the names of those who wrote it. It is partly that people were more interested in the poem than in the poet, just as we admire the Lincoln Memorial and marvel at the Empire State Building without making an effort to learn who were the architects. The medieval author was at a disadvantage compared with popular writers today in having no publisher interested in keeping his name before the public. Again, the reproduction of books by hand tended to give them in time a communal character. A text was exposed both to unconscious alteration and conscious change. The medieval scribe was as likely as not to assume the rôle of editor or adapter, so that different manuscripts of a work often differ greatly from one another. Except in the case of a few works of well-known writers a medieval production was subject to the whims of successive generations of scribes. A third consideration tending to give an effect of impersonality to literature was the differing attitude of the Middle Ages towards originality. Originality was not a major requirement of medieval authors. Story material in particular was looked upon as common property and the notion that one could claim property rights in ideas is seldom encountered. To have based one's work on an old and therefore authoritative source was a virtue which led Geoffrey of Monmouth and even greater writers to claim such a source when none existed. It is not surprising that such an attitude raised translation to the level of original

creation.[6] The reader must be prepared for a less personal quality in medieval than in modern literature and to find that the original author of a work is often, for us, without a local habitation or a name.

Certain other characteristics distinguish medieval literature as a whole, and in some cases the literature between 1100 and 1500 from that of either earlier or later periods. One such characteristic results from the presence of women in the audience. We have only to notice the difference between *Beowulf* and *Sir Gawain and the Green Knight* to realize the change that takes place in narrative poetry when it passes from the mead-hall to the castle. *Beowulf* is heroic, *Sir Gawain* courtly in tone. In the second place, one is constantly aware in medieval literature of the all-important place of the Church in medieval life. It is often said that men and women looked upon this life mainly as a means to the next. Certainly they lived in much more fear of Hell and its torments and were vitally concerned with the problem of salvation for their souls. Religious writings are, therefore, a large and significant part of medieval literature, not off to one side as in our day, but in the main stream. They bulk large because religion overtopped the common affairs of life as the cathedral dominated the surrounding country. Thirdly, even where religion is not directly concerned, a moral purpose is frequently discernible in literature, openly avowed or tacitly implied as the justification for its existence. John of Salisbury in his *Policraticus* says that all writings serve a practical purpose and this purpose is to convey useful knowledge and promote virtue.[7] In the Middle Ages the literature of knowledge and the literature of power, to use De Quincey's distinction, are often close together if not much the same thing. Lyric poetry passes easily from ecstasy to warning, and in narrative the will to delight is often partner with the will to teach. Finally, it should be noted that much of literature until near the end of the Middle Ages was meant to be listened to rather than read. Until we approach the fifteenth century, literacy was not widespread even among the upper classes and books were expensive. Most people were dependent upon song and recitation, upon the minstrel and the poet reading his work, for their literary recreation. As a result, verse is the normal medium for most forms of literature. Much that would now be written in prose— history, popular instruction, moralizing—was put into verse as the form more easily carried in the memory and more pleasant to listen to.

It remains but to say a word in this chapter about the quality of medieval literature as art. And we must admit at once that judged by modern standards much of medieval literature, Continental as well as English, is infra-literary.[8] This does not mean that there are no great works of the imagination in the Middle Ages. There are some, but poems like the *Divine Comedy* are rare in any age. To admit that most works written between the Fall of Rome and the Renaissance do not claim a place among the

Artistic Quality of Medieval Literature

---

[6] Deschamps addresses a complimentary poem to Chaucer as "grand translateur."
[7] Book VII, chs. 9-11.
[8] The word is F. J. Mather's: cf. *The Bookman* (N. Y.), xxv (1907). 617-619.

world's greatest books is not to deny real interest and importance to the period. To the true humanist every effort of the race to express itself is of interest. The child is father of the man, and in medieval literature there is much of the simplicity of the child. Beauty is not to be denied on the grounds of immaturity, and simplicity itself is not without charm. With Gaston Paris we may recognize that it is not always for us to judge and to prove but to know and to understand. Medieval writing lacks the immediate appeal of the contemporaneous. The human mind grasps more easily the productions of its own day. There are fewer obstacles to understanding. Differences of language and custom will always limit the enjoyment of early literature to the cultivated few. But acquaintance with the past brings understanding, and understanding begets sympathy, appreciation, pleasure. One is privileged in this modern world to waive aside the literature of the Middle Ages, to reason that with life so short and art so long to learn, it is better to snatch the pleasure within easy reach, but such a one will not see later literature in historical perspective and he will miss a body of writings which, sympathetically approached, will be found to contain much of interest, and, as Rossetti observed, "beauties of a kind which can never again exist in art."

II

The Survival of the Native Tradition (1100-1250)

The state of England on the eve of the Norman Conquest is a question *Literary* on which opinion is divided. The older view, that the "history of the Anglo- *Conditions* Saxon from the time of King Alfred to the Norman Conquest is little else *at the* than the history of disorganization, degeneracy, and decay," [1] has been *Conquest* sharply challenged.[2] No doubt there was political and social slackness, but there was also heroism at Senlac. England was in a transition stage and Old English literature was likewise in transition. We can hardly expect new *Beowulfs* in the eleventh century. The heroic age was past; we do not find new *Iliads* in the Age of Pericles. Old English writers were turning to new themes such as Apollonius and Alexander,[3] themes which they were getting from the Continent and treating in the Continental manner. There is, of course, no way of telling what English literature would have become if it had been allowed to pursue its own course, but its normal development was interrupted by the Conquest. The Normans were not hostile to the native tradition. The decay of literary activity is suffiently explained by the destructive effects of four years of ruthless war, the rapid displacement of English bishops and English abbots in the monasteries, the eviction of the English language and English culture from the place they should have occupied in the national life, and the complete indifference of the new rulers to books in a language which they did not understand. Writing in the native tongue was paralyzed, but, as we shall see, it was not dead.

One indication that interest in the older literature did not die with the *Old* Conquest is the fact that Old English manuscripts continued to be copied. *English* Two of the six MSS of the West Saxons Gospels belong to the twelfth cen- *Survivals* tury and we have twelfth-century copies of King Alfred's *Boethius,* the *Distichs of Cato,* the *Gospel of Nicodemus,* numerous homilies of Ælfric and others, to mention only a few. Another indication is the fact that the *Old English Annals* were kept up for nearly a hundred years. One manuscript, now lost, was continued in the south of England until 1121 when it was borrowed by Peterborough, possibly to replace a copy destroyed by fire in 1116, and not only copied but carried on there until 1154. Finally there is

[1] T. Duffus Hardy, *Descriptive Catalogue of Materials Relating to the History of Great Britain* (3v in 4, 1862-71), II. p. xi. The view was echoed by Gaston Paris, *La Poésie du moyen âge* (Paris, 1885-95), II. 46-7.
[2] Cf. *CHEL,* I. 166; R. R. Darlington, "The Last Phase of Anglo-Saxon History," *History,* XXII (1937). 1-13; R. M. Wilson, *Early Middle English Literature* (1939), pp. 3-22; and above, p. 105.
[3] See above (p. 104) for *Apollonius of Tyre, The Wonders of the East,* etc.

a good bit of evidence that ballads and poems on historical and legendary themes were still being sung in the time of William of Malmesbury (c. 1125) and Henry of Huntington (d. 1155). The latter includes translations into Latin of a number of such songs, and William of Malmesbury tells many stories of Athelstan and Edgar and Queen Gunhilda which he says he has learned from *cantilenae* and *nostro adhuc seculo etiam in triviis cantitata*. There were legends of Offa,[4] of Wade, several times alluded to[5] but now known only in Latin epitomes such as Walter Map gives in his *De Nugis Curialium* (cf. p. 146), and of Hereward, the last of which is preserved in a Latin form based, as the author tells us, on an English original. While we must be careful not to attribute literary form to every popular story that has found its way into the chronicles, the lost literature of the period following the Norman Conquest was evidently considerable.[6]

Continuity with the Past

Continuity with the past is likewise evident in some of the earliest texts in Middle English. It can perhaps best be seen in certain miscellaneous collections of religious material. These are made up mostly of prose pieces of varying character and length, rather loosely classified as homilies. Two such collections, the *Lambeth*[7] and *Trinity Homilies*,[8] occur in MSS written around 1200 and on linguistic grounds are thought to have been copied in London.[9] But from mistakes which the scribe makes in the Lambeth MS it is apparent that he was working over older originals and there are indications that his originals were in a dialect further to the south and west. Two of the homilies and part of a third are from Ælfric. The Trinity collection does not betray its dependence upon an older source by mistakes of the scribe, but five of its pieces are also found in the Lambeth MS and the collection is presumably based in like manner on older material. A third group, the *Bodley Homilies*,[10] is almost wholly made up of pieces from Ælfric's homilies and *Lives of Saints,* and from Wulfstan and other Old English homilists, while the fourth collection, the *Vespasian Homilies*,[11] seems to be a commonplace book of extracts and adaptations, mainly from Ælfric. There is much that is interesting from the point of view of legend and popular belief in these homiletic texts—pieces on the Eight Vices, the

[4] The Latin text of the *Lives of the Two Offas* is printed in R. W. Chambers, *Beowulf: An Introduction* (2ed., Cambridge, 1932), pp. 217-243.
[5] Cf. Chaucer, *Merchant's Tale*, E. 1424.
[6] Cf. R. W. Chambers, "The Lost Literature of Medieval England," *Library*, n.s. v (1925). 293-321; R. M. Wilson, "Lost Literature in Old and Middle English, *Leeds Studies in English and Kindred Languages*, II (1933). 14-37; "More Lost Literature in Old and Middle English," *ibid.*, v (1936). 1-49; "More Lost Literature," *ibid.*, VI (1937). 30-49; C. E. Wright, *The Cultivation of Saga in Anglo-Saxon England* (Edinburgh, 1940).
[7] Richard Morris, *Old English Homilies,* First Series (1867-8; EETS, 29 and 34), pp. 1-189.
[8] Richard Morris, *Old English Homilies,* Second Series (1873; EETS, 53).
[9] See H. C. Wyld, "South-Eastern and South-East Midland Dialects in Middle English," *E&S*, VI (1920). 112-145.
[10] Partially edited in A. O. Belfour, *Twelfth Century Homilies in MS Bodley 343* (1909; EETS, 137), and A. S. Napier, *History of the Holy Rood-tree* (1894; EETS, 103).
[11] Rubie D-N. Warner, *Early English Homilies from the Twelfth Century MS Vesp. D. xiv* (1917; EETS, 152). These are not to be confused with the four Kentish homilies in the Cotton MS Vesp. A. XXII. The sources have been fully worked out by Max Förster, "Der Inhalt der altenglischen Handschrift Vespasianus D. XIV," *ESt,* LIV (1920). 46-68.

Eight Virtues, the Seven Holy Sleepers, the Gospel of Nicodemus, the History of the Holy Rood Tree, Signs before Judgment, etc.—but we are interested in them here for the evidence they furnish of the continuity of English prose,[12] a continuity unbroken by the Norman Conquest. Such continuity in verse is less well attested, but appears to some extent in the *Worcester Fragments,* containing among other things an early form of the Body and Soul theme, and the fragment of twenty-five lines of alliterative verse known as *The Grave.*[13] Both of these are conceivably Old English pieces in a twelfth-century form.

In the search for the beginnings of Middle English verse a few short pieces assume importance on account of their age. The earliest, if we disregard the *Curse of Urse,*[14] is *Cnut's Song.* In Book II of the *Liber Eliensis,* which is to be dated between 1108 and 1131, we are told that King Cnut, accompanied by Queen Emma and important men of his kingdom, on one occasion making his way by boat to Ely to celebrate the Feast of the Purification, heard the music of the abbey service floating across the water and ordered the boatmen to pull him nearer the church while he drank in the melody. And "he himself expressing with his own lips the joy in his heart, composed a song in English in these words, the beginning of which runs thus":

> Merie sungen ðe muneches binnin Ely
> Ða Cnut ching reu ðer by.
> Roweð, cnites, noer the land
> And here we þes muneches sæng.[15]

The historian tells us that these and the verses that followed were sung even down to his own day publicly in groups (*in choris*) and that the story of their origin was preserved in popular tradition. The passage sounds like an expression of local pride in which an Ely monk called to mind an incident treasured in the monastery. A second local incident is somewhat obscurely represented in the *Here Prophecy,* five lines of verse (*c.* 1191) refer-

Cnut's Song

[12] See the important essay of R. W. Chambers, *On the Continuity of English Prose from Alfred to More and His School* (Oxford, 1932), originally printed in *EETS,* 186.

[13] The Worcester fragments of the *Body and Soul* and the *The Grave* (Bodl. MS 343) are printed in R. Buchholz, *Die Fragmente der Reden der Seele an den Leichnam,* in *Erlanger Beiträge,* VI (Erlangen, 1890). Cf. Louise Dudley, "The Grave," *MP,* XI (1914). 429-442, and Eleanor K. Heningham, "Old English Precursors of *The Worcester Fragments,*" *PMLA,* LV (1940). 291-307.

[14] In the conquest of the west by the Conqueror, Gloucester and Worcester were put under the sheriff Urse of Abetot, who built a castle encroaching on the lands of the monks of Worcester. The monks appealed to the Archbishop, who came and uttered a malediction against the offender, the beginning of which is quoted by William of Malmesbury:

> Hattest þu [art thou called] Urs?
> Have þu Godes kurs.

Unfortunately he gives the rest only in Latin.

[15] Merrily sang the monks within Ely
When Cnut the king rowed thereby.
Row, knights, nearer the land
And let us hear the song of the monks.

ring apparently to a place in Northamptonshire.[16] But the most interesting from a literary point of view are three little poems known as *St. Godric's*

St. Godric   *Hymns*.[17] St. Godric, who died in 1170 at the somewhat mature age of a hundred and five, was born in Norfolk and after a career as a peddler, a merchant and ship-owner, and a pilgrim to Rome, Jerusalem, and other holy places, finally settled down as a hermit near Durham. In certain more or less contemporary lives of the saint are preserved the three short poems attributed to him, addressed to the Virgin and to St. Nicholas. His *Hymn to the Virgin* may be quoted for its artless charm and simple piety:

Sainte Marie, Virgine,
Moder Jesu Cristes Nazarene,
Onfo, scild, help þin Godric,   Receive, shield . . . bring him gloriously
Onfang, bring hehlic wið þe in Godes ric.   with thee in God's kingdom.

Sainte Marie, Cristes bur,   bower
Maidenes clenhad, moderes flur,   maiden's purity, flower of mothers
Dilie mine sinne, rixe in min mod,   wipe out . . . rule
Bring me to winne wið self God.   joy

The words fit the liturgical chant to which they are set in the manuscript.[18] *St. Godric's Hymns* are slight in themselves, but they are our earliest examples of the Middle English lyric.

Poema   The keynote of English poetry, and indeed of English prose, in the second
Morale   half of the twelfth century is struck early in one of the most important and spirited poems of this period, the *Poema Morale* [19] or the *Moral Ode* (*c.* 1170). In some four hundred lines of vigorous seven-stress verse the poet preaches a sermon on the theme, repent before it is too late. His method is suggestive of popular evangelism. He speaks first of his own misspent life and then paints the terrors of Doomsday, the torments of Hell, and the joys of Heaven. The beginning is somewhat disjointed and incoherent, but when the preacher in him begins to speak, the style becomes vivid, straightforward, and eloquent. There is a surprising note of cynicism in the opening lines. Whoever trusts too much in wife or child instead of thinking of himself is in danger of missing salvation. He will soon enough be forgotten by his friends and relatives. Such a mood, however, early gives way before the earnestness with which the author tries to make his points. The rich think to find safety in wall and ditch, but he who sends his treasure to Heaven need have no fear of fire or thief. Each man may purchase Heaven with what he has, the poor man with his penny as surely as the rich with his

---

[16] See discussion by W. W. Skeat and John W. Hales in *Academy*, xxx (1886). 189-190, 380-381.

[17] Edited by J. Zupitza, "Cantus Beati Godrici," *ESt*, xi (1888), 401-432. See also J. W. Rankin, "The Hymns of St. Godric," *PMLA*, xxxviii (1923). 699-711, and Irene P. McKeehan, "The First Biography of an English Poet," *Univ. of Colorado Studies*, Ser. B i (1941). 223-231.

[18] A facsimile of one MS is reproduced as a frontispiece to Saintsbury's *History of English Prosody*, Vol. i (1906).

[19] Hans Marcus, *Das Frühmittelenglische "Poema Morale," kritisch herausgegeben . . .* (Leipzig, 1934; *Palaestra*, No. 194).

pound. In the final doom a man's good works will all be known just as the devils have all his misdeeds written down. Repent now! When Death is at the door it is too late to cry for mercy. There is no virtue in hating evil when you can't do evil any more. All the terrors of Hell which the Middle Ages knew from the *Visio Pauli* are described in contrast with the joy which the blessed experience in God's presence. The wicked are enumerated in detail—those who made vows to God and didn't keep them, who led their lives in war and strife, who lied, cheated, persecuted poor men, etc., etc. The poet closes with an exhortation to choose the narrow and difficult road, the road which few follow. The poem is addressed to "simple men and poor" and must stand—as an illustration of matter and purpose—for a number of other twelfth-century pieces which we shall have to mention more briefly.

Similar in theme is a poem of 354 lines that has been named *Sinners, Beware*.[20] It lays the same emphasis on repentance and enforces its plea with a description of the pains of Hell and a warning against the Seven Deadly Sins, directed at various classes from covetous monks and mercenary priests to rich men and proud women. It recalls the horrors of the grave, where the body shall be eaten by worms, and pictures the Judgment Day when the cries of those who would not confess their sins to the priest are contrasted with the happy lot of those whom Christ recognizes as his friends who fed the hungry and clothed the poor. The poem is conventional—all too conventional—in theme, and unfortunately not distinguished in treatment. But it is remarkable in being written in the six-line stanza *aabaab* later often found in the romance and shows how far French verse patterns had penetrated into the English verse tradition by the end of the twelfth century. More flexible and easy is the style of the *Paternoster*,[21] an exposition of the Lord's Prayer in 305 four-stress lines riming in pairs. It is found among the *Lambeth Homilies* (cf. p. 118) and is obviously an intrusion among these prose pieces. But it is homiletic in spirit, explaining the meaning and purpose of each petition, and bidding "Goodmen, listen to me." *Sinners, Beware*

Distinct echoes of the *Poema Morale* are found in a group of poems belonging apparently shortly after the turn of the century and associated in two manuscripts.[22] They are unusually interesting, treating familiar themes in a lively and fresh spirit, in verse that shows considerable metrical skill. Most of them run from fifty to a hundred lines in length. *Long Life* serves warning that though we may expect to live long, Death "lurks in our shoes" and strikes suddenly. *An Orison of Our Lady* is a charming expression of devotion to the Virgin, who brought light where Eve brought night. This world will pass away. I have been a fool too long, says the poet. I will mend my ways. Lady, punish me in this life or let me live to correct my *Other Religious Pieces*

---

[20] *EETS*, XLIX. 72-83.

[21] *EETS*, XXIX. 55-71.

[22] Cotton Caligula A. ix and Jesus Coll. Oxford 29. In both MSS they occur together and are copied in the same order. The Cotton MS is dated before 1250. They are edited in R. Morris, *An Old English Miscellany* (EETS, 49), pp. 156-191.

faults. I am sorry for my sins. Mercy, Lady! *Doomsday,* which follows immediately in both MSS, seems to be by the same author. When I think of Doomsday, the poet reflects, full sore I am adread. Fire will consume everything. When angels blow their trumpets the rich who wore fine clothes and rode on palfreys will sing welaway. Christ will speak sweet words to the righteous, but will banish the wicked to Hell. Let us pray our Lady, sweetest of all things, to ask Heaven's King to save us for her sake. The same thought runs through the somewhat longer poem *Death* (264 lines). Hear of one thing, it begins, ye that wear scarlet and pall and sit on your bench: no man can escape death. At the latemost day our bliss is turned to nought. No tongue can tell the pains of Hell. At death the body is sewed in a clout. Then saith the soul with sorry cheer, "Away, thou wretched, foul body,"—and so for the greater part of the poem the soul berates the body with the familiar taunts and accusations of *The Debate between the Body and the Soul.* Finally, in *A Little Sooth Sermon,* there is a deal of plain speaking:

> Herkneþ alle gode men
> and stylle sitteþ a-dun,
> And ich ou wile tellen   you
> a lutel soþ sermun.

Adam brought us all to grief. He went to Hell. There also will go all back-biters, robbers, thieves, and lechers, and dwell there forever. So will false chapmen, bakers, and brewers, who hold the gallon down low and fill it with froth. All priests' wives shall be damned and those proud young men and women who run to each other in church and market place and speak of clandestine love. They take no thought of Mass and Matins; their pater-noster is at home. Robin will take Gill to the ale house, sit and talk and pay for her ale, and she will go with him in the evening shamelessly. But the poet concludes as suddenly as he began, with an appeal to his hearers to forsake their sins. There is something refreshing about the poems in this little group, something that helps us to understand better the secular verse, such as the *Brut* and *The Owl and the Nightingale,* that was occasionally being written at about the same date.

A Good Orison of Our Lady

    More varied in theme are a few scattered pieces that deserve to be singled out from the body of religious verse that constitutes the most characteristic expression of the poetic impulse before 1250. *A Good Orison of Our Lady* [23] is the work of a poet of the West Midlands writing either, as some think, at the end of the twelfth century or more probably at the beginning of the thirteenth. In it he professes with quiet simplicity his devotion to the Virgin and prays for her protection. He will sing his *lofsong* to her by day and by night. Angels delight to honor her. All who surround her are crowned with golden crowns and Heaven is bright with her presence. He laments his many sins, but says in extenuation that he forsook all that was dear

[23] *EETS,* xxxiv. 191-199.

to him and gave himself wholly to her. In the closing lines he voices the hope that "all my friends may be the better today that I have sung to thee this English lay," and he prays "that thou bring the monk to joy that made this song of thee." It is a "song" in the Old English manner. The long lines at the opening, with their irregular flow and alliteration, suggest chanting to the accompaniment of a harp, but though the movement recalls the four-beat rhythm of Old English verse, the alliteration becomes sporadic and the effect of which we are finally most conscious is that of couplets bound together by end-rime. As the monk has here set his love on the Virgin, so in Thomas of Hales' *Love Rune*,[24] a poem of 210 lines written *Thomas* a generation later, a "maid of Christ" is urged to choose as her lover the *of Hales'* Heavenly Bridegroom. Worldly lovers pass: where are Paris and Helen, *Love* Amadas, Idoine, Tristan, Iseult? Christ surpasses them all in beauty and *Rune* riches; even Henry, King of England, is his vassal. His gift to his bride is virginity, most precious of gems. The poet, in fulfilling the maid's request, sends her his poem open and unsealed, with the suggestion that she learn it and sing it and hope that Christ will make her his bride. *The Passion of Our Lord* [25] is an example of the longer, narrative poem, strongly suggestive of the secular romance. In a short prologue the poet says that his tale is not of Charlemagne and his twelve peers but of Christ's passion, which is not a fiction. Its seven-stress lines break into fours and threes with a certain jog-trot swing, but the movement is rapid and the narrative anything but pedestrian with its homely touches, realistic details, and frequent resort to direct discourse. Toward the middle of the century a short poem called *When Holy Church Is under Foot*,[26] with its blaming of simony for the evil state of the Church, shows English verse turned to the frank criticism of contemporary conditions.

The Katherine Group

Up to this point all the writings which we have spoken of, except for several collections of homilies, have been in verse. In some ways the prose of the period is even more remarkable. It consists, in the first place, of five closely related pieces known from the title of one of them as the Katherine Group. They are lives of three women saints—St. Katherine, St. Margaret, and St. Juliana—and two religious treatises, *Hali Meidenhad* and *Sawles Warde*. And in the second place there is that extraordinary work, the *Ancrene Riwle*, closely associated with these but so distinctive as to deserve consideration by itself. It is impossible to assign precise dates to any of them, but general opinion places them either toward the end of the twelfth century or early in the thirteenth.

---

[24] Thomas of Hales was a Franciscan. The Franciscans came to England in 1224. The poem was probably written fairly early in the reign of Henry III (1216-1272); he is most likely the King Henry twice mentioned in it. It is printed in *EETS*, XLIX. 93-99.

[25] *EETS*, XLIX. 37-57 (706 lines).

[26] *EETS*, XLIV. 89; on the date cf. C. G. Child, *Papers in Honor. . . . of Charles Frederick Johnson* (Hartford, 1928), p. 101n.

The legends and treatises composing the Katherine Group in all cases but one have as their primary aim the exaltation of virginity. They were al! written in the West Midlands, the evidence of dialect pointing to Hereford shire. There are resemblances between some of them that suggest the pos, sibility of common authorship for part of the group. And finally, they are associated in MS tradition: all five occur together in one MS, four appeal as a group in another, and three are copied in close proximity in a third. None of them is ever found separately.

All three of the saints' legends tell a story of heroic resistance and ultimate martyrdom in the heroine's determination to preserve her maidenhood.

St. Katherine [27] may be taken as typical. In ancient Alexandria the holy maiden Katherine one day chides the Emperor for his sacrifices to false gods. Thinking to overcome her scruples by reason, he sends for fifty of his finest scholars. But she overcomes them and they confess themselves power-less before the argument of one supported by the true God. The Emperor has them all burnt and they die the happy death of martyrs. He next tries flattery on Katherine, and the promise of worldly honors. But she replies that nothing "can turn me from the love of my beloved, in whom I believe. He has wedded himself to my virgin state with the ring of true belief ... He is my life and my love, ... my wealth and my joy; nor do I desire any-thing else." After this she is stripped and beaten and thrown into prison, where she remains for twelve days without food. During this time she is visited by the Queen and the captain of the guard. Both are converted and the captain in turn converts the two hundred knights in his company. Tor-tures are prepared—four wheels fitted with spikes, turning two by two in opposite directions. At the prayer of the saint God shatters the wheels, killing full four thousand "of that accursed folk" as they stood round about. "There one might have heard the heathen hounds yell and cry and scream on every side, the Christians laugh." The Queen addresses her husband: "Wretched man that thou art, wherefore wilt thou wrestle with the world's ruler? What madness maketh thee, thou bitter baleful beast, to war against Him who created thee and all earthly things? ..." For this affectionate out-burst she is tortured and put to death. The captain of the guard suffers a like fate. Katherine is finally beheaded, and miracles accompany her burial.

It has been necessary to recount the story at some length in order to con-vey an idea of the subject matter and tone of these legends. *St. Margaret* [28] is very similar in story and treatment although Margaret, unlike Katherine, does not court martyrdom. Her struggles are to escape marriage, but she undergoes like torture and suffers the same end. There is the same intem-perate language. She rails at her intended husband: "Thou workest the works of thy father, the wicked one, the fiend of Hell. But, thou heathen hound, the High Healer is my help; and if he have granted to thee my body to tear, he will, thou hateful reeve, rid my soul out of thy hands and

[27] E. Einenkel, *The Life of Saint Katherine* (1884; EETS, 80).
[28] Frances M. Mack, *Seinte Marherete* (1934; EETS, 193).

carry it to Heaven." In prison she is swallowed by a dragon, but she has made the sign of the cross, which causes the dragon to burst asunder, and the maiden steps forth unharmed. She is visited by a black devil, but she cows him and beats him and sets her foot upon his rough neck until he cries, "Lady, loose thy foot off my neck!" The differences between the two lives are accounted for by difference of source, but the resemblances are in features and in details that do not occur in the Latin legends which lie behind the English texts. *St. Katherine* and *St. Margaret* are either by the same author or *St. Margaret* was written by some one who knew the *St. Katherine* well.[29]

St. Juliana [30] is also a story of resistance to marriage. There are many marks of resemblance to both of the legends previously mentioned, but the tone is somewhat more restrained and the little touches that unite the *St. Katherine* and the *St. Margaret* are not so apparent here. **St. Juliana**

Hali Meidenhad [31] is an extended glorification of virginity in contrast with the baseness and grievous annoyances of marriage. Vehemence and strong conviction make up for the absence of a logical plan. There is little or no progression, but a single idea runs through the whole treatise—that virginity is in every way preferable to marriage. The idea is supported by the constant recurrence of two arguments: virginity is the state most pleasing to God, and marriage is not the happy lot that most people expect to find it. It is particularly in the latter argument that the author is at his best. "Ask even queens, and countesses, and proud ladies about their life. If they acknowledge the truth I will have them for witness that they lick honey off thorns." His picture of fleshly intercourse is so vivid that it shocked his first editor into Latin, for his rendering. It is a sorry picture that he paints of married life—quarrels between husband and wife, the pains of childbirth, the trials of the mother. When she comes in she hears the child scream, sees the cat at the flitch and the hound at the hide; her cake is burning on the hearth and the calf sucks all the milk; the crock spills into the fire and the churl scolds. In the light of such pictures of the married woman's life it is with good reason that the author urges the real or imaginary maiden for whom he writes to choose single blessedness and to think of Christ as her husband. In its wealth of homely illustration, its fondness for the proverbial phrase, and its sustained interest *Hali Meidenhad* is strongly suggestive of the *Ancrene Riwle,* but the uncompromising attitude towards marriage makes one hesitate to attribute it to the same author. **Hali Meidenhad**

---

[29] E. Einenkel, "Über den Verfasser der neuangelsächsischen Legende von Katharina," *Anglia,* v (1882). 91-123, argues that the *St. Katharine* was written first, that the other two legends were by a different author who used the *St. Katharine,* and that *Hali Meidenhad* was written after the *St. Margaret* by still a third author.

[30] S.T.R.O. d'Ardenne, *An Edition of þe Liflade ant te Passiun of Seint Iuliene* (Liége, 1936; *Bibl. de la Faculté de Philos. et Lettres de l'Université de Liége,* LXIV); also O. Cockayne and E. Brock, *The Life of St. Juliana* (1872; EETS, 51). For Cynewulf's treatment of the theme see above, p. 72.

[31] A. F. Colborn, *Hali Meiðhad* (Copenhagen, 1940); also O. Cockayne, *Hali Meidenhad* (1866; EETS. 18). new edition by F. J. Furnivall (1922).

Sawles
Warde

The homily called *Sawles Warde*[32] ("The Safeguarding of Soul"), although found in all three MSS with which the Katherine Group is identified, stands somewhat apart in theme and style. It makes only incidental mention of virginity. It is an elaborate allegory of the house, symbolizing the body, whose master is Wit and whose mistress is Will. The precious treasure of this house is the soul, guarded by the four cardinal virtues. Most of the treatise is made up of the discourse of two visitors—Fear, the messenger of death, and Love of Life, messenger of mirth. One describes at length the pains of Hell, the other the joys of Heaven. It is an adaptation of a treatise of Hugh of St. Victor called *De Anima*.

Prose or
Verse?

The prose style of the legends in the Katherine Group and of *Hali Meidenhad* is marked by the frequent use of alliteration, and the rhythm of the sentences is such that it can sometimes be read (with much forcing of the accent) as a kind of verse, which has been compared to that of the Old High German poet Otfrid in his *Krist*.[33] But it is a mistake to think of these pieces as anything but prose.

Promi-
nence
of the
Southwest

It is important to point out that such literary activity in English before 1250 as is surveyed in this chapter is practically confined to the west and south of England. There are also reasons for assigning to the west the *Ancrene Riwle*, which is the subject of the next chapter. Later we shall have occasion to speak of the *Ormulum*, which belongs to the northeast Midlands, the Essex *Vices and Virtues,* and the *Proverbs of Alfred,* which seems to have originated near the southern border of the East Midlands.[34] But of the works so far considered practically all appear to have been written in the West Midlands or within the limits of the late West Saxon kingdom. Two small collections of Kentish sermons[35] lie outside the area, but the rest all belong on the evidence of dialect to the west and south. Were it not for the fact that English was still being written in Essex and Kent and London (*Lambeth* and *Trinity Homilies*) we should be led to believe that a literary tradition in English lived on only where French influence was less felt. As it is, we must attribute its other than sporadic survival to the strength of the Old English culture in the districts which had least felt the devastating effects of the Scandinavian invasions and which had been most directly under the rule of Alfred and his successors.

[32] Edited by R. M. Wilson (Leeds, 1938); also in *EETS,* xxxiv. 245-267.

[33] Cf. Einenkel, *op. cit.;* opposed by Schipper, *History of English Versification* (1910), and others.

[34] All of these belong to the twelfth or the beginning of the thirteenth century, and are thus contemporary with the literature here under consideration.

[35] That in MS Vesp. A. xxii has been mentioned in footnote 11, above. The other, consisting of five short expositions in MS Laud 471, is of little interest except that the texts are translations of French originals, which accompany them in the MS, and show a considerable French element in the vocabulary, a fact which throws an interesting sidelight on the extent to which French words were understood by English listeners at the beginning of the thirteenth century.

III

The Ancrene Riwle

The *Ancrene Riwle* [1] ("Rule for Anchoresses") is the most remarkable prose work in English literature between King Alfred and Malory. To every new reader it comes as a complete surprise that anything with so unpromising a title should have so much interest and charm. Its appeal is not in its subject, since this has lost much of its significance in a materialistic and often skeptical world. But the freshness of its treatment and the personality of its author which shines through every page remain undimmed after the lapse of seven centuries. In two hundred pages of modern print this anonymous treatise offers a complete guide to, and a warm justification of, the anchoress's life. It is carefully planned throughout its eight distinctions or books. Book one is devoted entirely to religious observances and devotional exercises. Then follow books on the five senses as guardians of the heart, the advantages of a life of retirement from the world, the temptations fleshly and spiritual which must be resisted, confession, penitence, and the love of Christ. The eighth and last book gives specific advice on domestic matters—food, clothing, attendants, and a variety of small but important and interesting points.

One circumstance that lends an attractive personal quality to the treatise is the fact that it was not written for an unknown or imaginary audience but was composed at the request of three young women who had apparently long been known to the author. They were sisters in the literal sense of the word. He says, "There is much talk of you, how gentle women you are; for your goodness and nobleness of mind beloved of many; and sisters of one father and of one mother, having in the bloom of your youth, forsaken all the pleasures of the world and become anchoresses." Not only were they young when they entered upon their life of seclusion, but they were still young at the time the book was written, as the general tone implies. The phrase "gentle women," moreover, is no mere allusion to mildness of manner. They were almost certainly connected with a family of some social position and wealth. "I know not any anchoress that with more abundance, or more honor, hath all that is necessary to her than ye three have; our

Composed for Three Sisters

Their Social Position

---

[1] The only edition at present is that of James Morton, *The Ancren Riwle* (1853) in the Camden Society, Vol. LVII, which contains a translation on opposite pages. The translation can be had separately in the *King's Classics* (now the *Medieval Library*) under the somewhat misleading title *The Nun's Rule* (1905). A new edition of all the MSS is in preparation for the *EETS* by a group of scholars. In this series two volumes have appeared: *The Latin Text of the Ancrene Riwle*, ed. Charlotte D'Evelyn (1944; *EETS*, 216), and *The French Text of the Ancrene Riwle*, ed. J. A. Herbert (1944; *EETS*, 219). In the present book the spelling *Ancrene Riwle*, adopted by the *EETS*, is used.

Lord be thanked for it. For ye take no thought for food or clothing, neither for yourself nor for your maidens. Each of you hath from one friend all that she requireth; nor need that maiden seek either bread, or that which is eaten with bread, further than at his hall." They were permitted two servants. Their education suggests that of the upper class. The author quotes Latin at the very beginning without translation, although in general his practice is to translate or paraphrase his Latin citations, and the young women are advised to read either in French or English. Always the author seems anxious not to overtax their endurance and he urges them strongly not to take any vows: "for, whoso undertaketh any thing, and promises to God to do it as his command, binds herself thereto, and sinneth mortally in breaking it, if she break it wilfully and intentionally. If, however, she does not vow it, she may, nevertheless, do it, and leave it off when she will...." It is as though he realized the possibility that they might not be able to endure the life they had entered upon.[2] Although such advice is not unknown to other treatises of the kind, all this is consonant with the avowal that his rules are not intended "for any but you alone." Such a purpose is not inconsistent with a realization that his book might come into the hands of others and therefore with his speaking occasionally as though he had a wider audience in mind.

Versions in English, Latin, and French

That his treatise attained to this wider circulation is evident from the number of surviving MSS[3] and from the fact that there were versions in Latin and French as well as English.[4] A question has naturally arisen as to the language in which it was originally composed. We may be sure that it was not Latin. The Latin version contains numerous mistakes which are demonstrably due to misinterpreting the English. In the case of the French the evidence of translation is less obvious but is quite decisive.[5] Moreover, manuscripts of the English text were in the late thirteenth and the fourteenth century in the possession of religious houses with strong aristocratic connections, in which French was certainly the more familiar language and which would have preferred a French version if one had been obtainable.[6] It was not unsuitable to private individuals, for it is in many ways an admirable treatise on morals and a universal guide to piety. It is for this reason

[2] It should be remembered, however, that St. Bernard had written in the same vein concerning vows.

[3] Counting complete and fragmentary texts and including adaptations, there are seventeen MSS now known: eleven in English, four in Latin, two in French.

[4] A growing list of quotations and echoes from it is further evidence of its distribution.

[5] G. C. Macaulay, "The Ancren Riwle," *MLR*, ix (1914). 63-78; 145-160; 324-331; 463-474, an article which contains much useful matter, argues for the priority of the French version. His views were partially answered by Dorothy M. E. Dymes, "The Original Language of the *Ancren Riwle*," *E&S*, ix (1924). 31-49.

[6] The earliest MS of the French text dates from the end of the thirteenth or the beginning of the fourteenth century. The translation was probably made at about this time. On the French text in the Trinity MS see the paper of Miss Hope Emily Allen in *Essays and Studies in Honor of Carleton Brown* (1940), pp. 182-219. On the early ownership of the English MSS the researches of Miss Allen will throw much light. As yet her results are only partially available in her communication to the *LTLS*, Feb. 8, 1936, supplementing her discussion in *MLR*, xxviii (1933). 485-487.

that it was so easily adapted later to the needs of men and the conditions of monastic life.

What is it that distinguishes this book from other devotional treatises and *The* justifies the high position which it occupies in early English literature? It *Author's* is in the final analysis the personality of the author and the extent to which *Personality* that personality colors all his writing. His qualities of mind and temperament are as attractive to us as they must have been to the three young women for whom he wrote. There is, for example, his independence and remarkable freedom from the conventional attitudes of the ordinary religious writer of the Middle Ages. This independence is shown from the very beginning of his book where he replies to a rather orthodox question— "What rule should the three sisters follow?"—in a very unorthodox way. He tells them that the external rule that they follow is a very minor matter compared with the inward rule which imposes on them genuine piety and obedience to the dictates of their conscience. "All may," he says, "and ought to observe one rule concerning purity of heart, that is, a clean unstained conscience... But all men cannot, nor need they, nor ought they to keep the outward rule in the same unvaried manner.... The external rule ... ordains fasting, watching, enduring cold, wearing haircloth, and such other hardships as the flesh of many can bear and many cannot. Wherefore, this rule may be changed and varied according to every one's state and circumstances. For some are strong, some are weak, and may very well be excused, and please God with less; some are learned, some are not, and must work the more, and say their prayers at the stated hours in a different manner; some are old and ill-favored, of whom there is less fear; some are young and lively, and have need to be more on their guard. Every anchoress must, therefore, observe the outward rule according to the advice of her confessor, and do obediently whatever he enjoins and commands her, who knows her state and strength. He may modify the outward rule, as prudence may direct, and as he sees that the inward rule may thus be best kept." In like manner he says, "If any ignorant person ask you of what order you are, as ye tell me some do, who strain at the gnat and swallow the fly, answer and say that ye are of the order of Saint James." This is a very novel solution of their problem, for of course there was no order of St. James, but St. James, as he says, defined pure religion as visiting and assisting widows and fatherless children and keeping oneself pure and unstained from the world. "Herein is religion, and not in the wide hood, nor in the black, nor in the white, nor in the gray cowl." This is hardly a position which many in the Middle Ages would have dared to take and this independent attitude runs all through the book.

Equally refreshing is a certain boldness of speech. His reference to the *His* anchoress who is old and ill-favored and who is therefore less likely to be *Candor* tempted will be recalled in the passage already quoted. There are many such instances of candor. He tells his spiritual sisters that they shall take communion only fifteen times a year because "men esteem a thing as less dainty when they have it often." In advising them to spend some of their time in reading, he says, "Often, dear sisters, ye ought to pray less, that ye may read more. Reading is good prayer. Reading teacheth how, and for what, we ought to pray." He is sometimes blunt. In recommending silence he contrasts Eve's willingness to carry on a conversation with the Devil with Mary's modest demeanor at the Annunciation, and he concludes, "Do you, my dear sisters, imitate Our Lady, and not the cackling Eve." He shows a wholesome disrespect for the Devil, calls him "the old ape" and elsewhere says "he is such an old fool." Perhaps the most striking instances of his readiness to say what comes to mind are his allusions to clerical lapses concerning which reticence was more commonly the order of the day—that is, where we do not have to do with the avowed satirist or reformer. In treating of confession he directs the anchoress to be specific as to the person with whom she committed a sin. "Sir, it was with such a man; and then name him—a monk, a priest, or clerk, and of such an order, a married man, an innocent creature, a woman." There is something startling about the order which he adopts in this enumeration. At confession, he says, "let there be a third person present. . . . Some unhappy creature, when she said that she was at confession, has confessed herself strangely." He can even become ironical on occasion about his professional brethren. "Bathsheba, by unclothing herself in David's sight, caused him to sin with her, though he was so holy a king and God's prophet: and now, a feeble man comes forward and esteems himself highly if he have a wide hood and a close cope, and would see young anchoresses, and must needs look, as if he were of stone, how their fairness pleases him, who have not their complexion sunburnt, and saith that they may look confidently upon holy men, yea, especially such as he is, because of his wide sleeves." We cannot help being drawn to a man who is so free from restraint and whose honesty gives him the courage to be so outspoken.

Descriptive and Narrative Gifts   The author's knowledge of human nature is not the least of his qualifications for writing such a book as he has written, and it results in a number of excursions which anticipate the "characters" of Nicholas Breton and of Overbury.

The greedy glutton is the devil's purveyor; for he always haunts the cellar or the kitchen. His heart is in the dishes; all his thought is of the tablecloth; his life is in the tun, his soul in the pitcher. He cometh into the presence of his Lord besmutted and besmeared, with a dish in one hand, and a bowl in the other. He talks much incoherently, and staggereth like a drunken man who seemeth about to fall, looks at his great belly, and the devil laughs till he bursts.

His description of flatterers and his picture of the backbiter are masterly and have often been quoted. Perhaps less familiar is his vignette of the ways of the seducer:

No seduction is so perfidious as that which is in a plaintive strain; as if one spoke thus: "I would rather suffer death, than indulge an impure thought with regard to you; but had I sworn it, I could not help loving you; and yet I am grieved that you know it. But yet forgive me that I have told you of it; and, though I should go mad, thou shalt never after this know how it is with me." And she forgives him, because he speaks thus fair, and then they talk of other matters. But 'the eye is ever towards the sheltering wood, wherein is that I love.' The heart is ever upon what was said before; and still, when he is gone, she often revolves such words in her thoughts, when she ought to attend diligently to something else. He afterwards seeketh an opportunity to break his promise, and swears that necessity forces him to do it; and thus the evil grows, the longer the worse; for no enmity is so bad as false friendship. An enemy who seems a friend is of all traitors the most treacherous.

In a similar vein is his description of how the newly-wed husband breaks in a wife—in the medieval fashion—but there is not space for all the delightful passages in a work from which there is so much one could quote.

No analysis of the qualities which stand out in the *Ancrene Riwle* and *His* make it so attractive would be adequate which did not lay particular stress *Style* on the incidental features of its style—its proverbial quality, its bestiary allusions, its familiar illustrations from everyday life, its homespun metaphors, its humor. The author is very fond of proverbial wisdom. "Thus often, as is said, of little waxeth mickle"; "the dog enters gladly where he finds an open door"; "the cock is brave on his own dunghill." He has a rich fund of animal lore which he uses to point his moral—the pelican who pierces her own breast, the eagle who "deposits in his nest a precious stone which is called agate" and which keeps off poisonous things, the thievish fox and his cunning. Perhaps his most attractive illustrations are drawn from his own observation of the life about him. "Reflect again thus: that if a child stumble against any thing, or hurt himself, men beat the thing that he hurteth himself upon, and the child is well pleased, and forgetteth all his hurt, and stoppeth his tears." In another place he says, "Our Lord, when He suffereth us to be tempted, playeth with us, as the mother with her young darling: she flies from him, and hides herself, and lets him sit alone, and look anxiously around, and call Dame! dame! and weep a while, and then leapeth forth laughing, with outspread arms, and embraceth and kisseth him, and wipeth his eyes." If all his illustrations cannot have this same kind of charm, they nevertheless have the appeal of homely and familiar things. "A small patch may greatly disfigure a whole garment." "Our Lord doth to us as men do to a bad debtor; he accepteth less than we owe him, and yet is well satisfied." "When greedy dogs stand before the board, is there not need of a rod?" "A man ties a knot upon his belt, that he may be reminded of anything." Sometimes his figures have the simple beauty of the Bible: "All who are in heaven shall be as swift as man's thought now is, and as the sunbeam that darts from east to west, and as the eye openeth and shutteth." He has a beautiful symbol for the Crucifixion: "The true sun in the morning-tide ascended up on the high cross for the purpose of diffusing the warm rays of his love over all." But with all the high seriousness that is never absent from his purpose, he can be whimsical on occasion, as when he remarks that confession erases sin and gives the Devil less writing to do! And we could not miss the dry humor of a man who, in an earnest warning against the temptations of the flesh, can say, "The old woman spoke very truly, when with a single straw all her house caught fire, that 'much cometh of little.' "

Book VIII   The section which seems to have been least regarded in the Middle Ages— it is sometimes missing in the MSS—is the eighth book. But to the modern reader it often has the greatest appeal. It is the book in which the author gathers together his instructions covering the sisters' physical needs. It is here that we catch a glimpse of the actual life of the anchoress. As we would expect, he shows here the same moderation and the same liberal attitude in matters of food and dress as he displays on spiritual issues, but he touches on many details and these not only give the book its completeness but are the chief reason that it interests so much the modern reader. The little things are often the most interesting. "Wear no iron, nor haircloth, nor hedgehog-skins; ... do not with holly nor with briars cause yourselves to bleed without leave of your confessor." "In summer ye are at liberty to go and sit barefoot." "Ye shall eat no flesh nor lard except in great sickness ... and accustom yourselves to little drink. Nevertheless, dear sisters, your meat and your drink have seemed to me less than I would have it. Fast no day upon bread and water, except ye have leave. There are anchoresses who make their meals with friends outside the convent. That is too much friend-ship, because, of all orders, then is it most ungenial, and most contrary to the order of the anchoress, who is quite dead to the world. We have often heard it said that dead men speak with living men; but that they eat with living men, I have never yet found." The anchoress must not make purses to give her friends, or become a schoolmistress. She must not keep cattle. "For then she must think of the cow's fodder, and of the herdsman's hire, flatter the hayward, defend herself when her cattle is shut up in the pinfold, and moreover pay the damage. Christ knoweth, it is an odious thing when people in the town complain of anchoresses' cattle." The behavior of the servants is considered at some length. They should not "munch fruit or anything else between meals." The one who goes out on errands, "let her be very plain, or of sufficient age." No matter in this section is too small for his notice, and for this we can only rejoice.

Identity of the Three Sisters   We may now ask when and by whom this remarkable book was written. And the answer is not easy. Our earliest manuscripts of the work were written when the first quarter of the thirteenth century was already past— 1230 is a rough approximation to their date. But they are not the original; they are copies in some cases two or more removes from the author's auto-graph. How long before was the original written?

In 1918 Miss Hope Emily Allen, in an article of great importance,[7] directed attention to the granting, sometime between 1127 and 1134, of

---

[7] Hope Emily Allen, "The Origin of the *Ancren Riwle*," PMLA, xxxiii (1918). 474-546. See also the same author's "On the Author of the *Ancren Riwle*," PMLA, xliv (1929). 635-680.

Kilburn priory as a hermitage to "tribus puellis, Emmae, videlicet, et Gunildae et Cristinae"—i.e., to three unmarried women named Emma, Gunhilda, and Christina—by the abbot and convent of Westminster. Kilburn priory was in Hampstead, then about five miles outside of London and now a part of greater London. A later tradition at Westminster tells us that the beneficiaries of the grant had been maids-in-waiting (*domicellae camerae*) of Queen Maud, wife of Henry I. Many of the circumstances of the three sisters in the *Ancrene Riwle* fit the facts which can be learned about the Kilburn foundation. In a subsequent paper [8] Miss Allen proposed to identify the Emma, Gunhilda, and Christina of the Kilburn grant with three daughters of a certain Deorman, who gave lands, with the consent of their brother Ordgar, to Westminster abbey on condition that they should enjoy the full "society" of the church. The grant is allowed in a royal writ of Henry I. Their names are not mentioned in the writ and their identity with the recluses rests merely upon what Miss Allen calls "the extreme rarity of medieval trios of devout. women."

If the double hypothesis here suggested should prove to be true, it would *Miss* clear up a number of questions. It would, of course, identify the three *Allen's* sisters for whom the *Ancrene Riwle* was written. The Deormans were a *Hypo-* prominent and aristocratic Anglo-Saxon or Anglo-Danish family. The Kil- *thesis: Its* burn recluses have English or Scandinavian names. If they were Deorman's *Importance* daughters and were also the sisters of the *Ancrene Riwle* we could under- stand why this work, composed for women of gentle or noble blood, should have been written in English at a time when the language of the English court was French. And it would strongly suggest that the author was Godwin, hermit of Kilburn, who was the master in charge of the Kilburn recluses.

It must be admitted, however, that the acceptance of this very attractive *Certain* hypothesis presents certain difficulties. It would compel us to date the *Difficulties* *Ancrene Riwle* not later than *c.* 1140, and this is rather early. Certain parts of Book VI seem to be based upon the *Sententiae Exceptae* of Geoffrey of Auxerre, a work which must apparently be dated after 1153.[9] If so, it is hard to see how the three sisters of the *Ancrene Riwle* could have been treated as still young at a date subsequent to this, if they had once been in attendance upon Queen Maud, who died in 1118. A second objection is the fact that the earliest associations of the *Ancrene Riwle* are with the west. Practically all the earliest MSS are in the West Midland dialect and several of them have been convincingly assigned to Hereford and Worcestershire, the district with which the Katherine Group is associated on similar linguis- tic grounds. When we consider the close association, in theme, manuscript

---

8 "The Three Daughters of Deorman," *PMLA*, L (1935). 899-902.

9 R. W. Chambers, "Recent Research upon the *Ancren Riwle*," *RES*, I (1925). 4-23. Beatrice White, "The Date of the *Ancrene Riwle*," *MLR*, XL (1945). 206-207, argues that the reference in Book VII to Christ nailed to the Cross with one foot on top of the other suggests a date not earlier than 1200, and Morton W. Bloomfield believes that the treatment of the Deadly Sins can hardly be earlier than the beginning of the thirteenth century (*The Seven Deadly Sins*, East Lansing, 1952, p. 148).

tradition,[10] and allusion,[11] of the *Ancrene Riwle* with the Katherine Group one feels that any evidence that would place its composition in the neighborhood of London, or indeed, anywhere but in the west, and at a date far removed from 1200, must be very clear. The origin of the *Ancrene Riwle* is admittedly still an open question.[12]

The Author

We are accordingly thrown back upon the text itself for our knowledge of the author. From what has already been said and from many other indications scattered through his work, it is apparent that he was a man of maturity, both in judgment and in years. His position was such as to put him beyond the fear of criticism or rebuke. He was probably no obscure priest. He was a man of sound common sense, moderate and reasonable, never extreme in his views or fanatical. His only obsession seems to have been his abhorrence and fear of sensual indulgence. He was completely candid and free from any trace of hypocrisy. Without being of the world, he was not remote from it or ignorant of its ways. Above all, he was a kindly, benevolent spirit, one in whom a genuinely large nature was united with a becoming modesty and true simplicity of soul.[13]

[10] All three MSS in which the pieces composing the Katherine Group are found also contain the *Ancrene Riwle*.

[11] The *Ancrene Riwle* alludes to "the devil Ruffin, Belial's brother, in our English book of St. Margaret," and one can hardly doubt that this is the *St. Margaret* of the Katherine Group. The statement "Concerning those joys [of Heaven] ye have something written in another place" looks like a reference to *Sawles Warde,* another text of the Katherine Group although this cannot be proved.

[12] No one is more open-minded about it than Miss Allen. A good bit of discussion has grown out of her original paper. In addition to the articles cited in the preceding notes, a few further references may be given. Vincent McNabb, "The Authorship of the *Ancren Riwle,"* *MLR,* xi (1916). 1-8; "Further Light on the *Ancren Riwle,"* *MLR,* xv (1920). 406-409; H. E. Allen, "The *Ancren Riwle* and Kilburn Priory," *MLR,* xvi (1921). 316-322; G. G. Coulton, "The Authorship of *Ancren Riwle,"* *MLR,* xvii (1922). 66-69; H. E. Allen, "On the Author of the *Ancren Riwle,"* *PMLA,* xliv (1929). 635-680; J. R. R. Tolkien, "Ancrene Wisse and Hali Meiðhad," *E&S,* xiv (1929). 104-126. Father McNabb's later articles have not added anything of significance to his previous arguments.

[13] Four pieces of impassioned prose are found individually in MSS containing the *Ancrene Riwle.* The finest of them, *The Wooing of Our Lord,* is in a MS which contains some of the Katherine Group as well. It is a lyrical address to Christ in terms of passionate endearment, and may have been written by a woman. Cf. E. Einenkel, "Eine englische Schriftstellerin aus dem Anfange des 12. Jahrhunderts," *Anglia,* v (1882). 265-282, whose dating of the text is hardly consonant with his opinion that it was written by one of the anchoresses of the *Ancrene Riwle.* Two of the other pieces, *An Orison of Our Lord* and *A Lovesong of Our Lord,* express similar emotions. All contain at times phrases echoing now the *Ancrene Riwle,* now *Hali Meidenhad* and *St. Margaret.* The fourth piece, *A Lovesong of Our Lady.* addresses the Virgin in terms of equal affection. All four are printed in *EETS.* 34.

IV

Anglo-Norman Literature[1]

In an age when the song and recitation of the minstrel were the almost *French* universal entertainment of the upper classes at meals and in the evening *Literature* and indeed at all times when they could not find their recreation out of *in England* doors, literature was well-nigh indispensable. Since, as we have already seen, the language of the higher classes for more than two hundred years after the Norman Conquest was either wholly or mainly French, any literature that would be intelligible to them would have to be in that language. Naturally the whole body of French literature was at their disposal, but a nation seldom remains for any length of time solely dependent upon foreign sources even for its pleasure. It is not surprising, therefore, to find early in the twelfth century French poets in England, attracted no doubt by an aristocracy freely spending its newly acquired wealth. During the twelfth and thirteenth centuries much that is important in Old French literature was written in England. The dialect in which it was written is known as Anglo-Norman, and this body of writings as Anglo-Norman literature.

Patronage is the life blood of court poets. Where there is generous pa- *Courtly* tronage there is sure to be literature. The Conqueror himself is said to have *Patrons* been indifferent to poets; he may well have been completely occupied with the practical matters of conquest and administration. His successor, William Rufus, was without soul or intellect. But with the accession in the year 1100 of Henry I, the Conqueror's youngest son, literary activity at the court makes its appearance. It is probably not so much the result of his own encouragement—the nickname Beauclerc, which he enjoyed, seems not to have been wholly deserved—as of the fact that he was twice married, both times to women of literary tastes. His first wife Matilda (Queen Maud), though English born, seems to have cultivated French poetry with enthusiasm. The poet Guy of Amiens was her almoner. "Her generosity becoming universally known," says William of Malmesbury, "crowds of scholars, equally famed for verse and for singing, came over." Adelaide

[1] For a readable and admirably clear survey of the more important writings in Anglo-Norman see E. Walberg, *Quelques aspects de la littérature anglo-normande* (Paris, 1936); for a comprehensive list of Anglo-Norman texts, with bibliographical annotations, J. Vising, *Anglo-Norman Language & Literature* (London, 1923); and for a suggestive analysis of the Norman character, Gaston Paris, *La Littérature normande avant l'annexion* (Paris, 1899). Those who wish to savor the more important Anglo-Norman texts mentioned in this chapter will often find selections in Paget Toynbee, *Specimens of Old French* (Oxford, 1892), P. Studer and E. Waters, *Historical French Reader* (Oxford, 1924), and in the *Chrestomathies* of Bartsch, Constans, etc. The publications of the *Anglo-Norman Text Society* (since 1939) are making available a number of longer texts.

of Louvain, Henry's second wife, whom he married in 1121, is even better known as a patron. She had a poet named David who composed a rimed history of her husband's achievements, which is lost. We know of it through Gaimar, who boasts that he knew more tales than David ever knew or than Adelaide had in books. For her Philippe de Thaün wrote his *Bestiaire* (*infra*) and Benedeit his *Voyage de St. Brendan* (p. 139). Nor were Henry's queens the only patrons of letters at his court. Gaimar's *Estorie des Engles* is dedicated to "Custance la gentil," wife of Ralph Fitz Gilbert, while Samson de Nanteuil translated the *Proverbs of Solomon* into French verse for Adelaide de Condé. During the troubled years of Stephen's reign and his contest with Matilda poetry seems to have suffered a decline, although during this period Robert, Earl of Gloucester, the natural son of Henry I and one of the greatest patrons of letters in England, was generous in his encouragement of scholars and literary men. With the accession of Henry II and his queen, the famous Eleanor of Aquitaine, the English court became a veritable center of scholarly and literary activity. Henry II's own amazing energy was not confined to judicial reform and administrative reorganization, for which history remembers him, but extended over a wide range of intellectual interests. More than a score of books bear dedications to him, from Adelard of Bath's treatise *On the Astrolabe* to the *Lais* of Marie de France.[2] Eleanor is frequently mentioned in the verses of the troubadours and it was to her that Wace presented his *Roman de Brut*. It was under such auspices that Anglo-Norman literature had its beginnings. Its continuation in the century that follows was made possible by similar encouragement and support from the aristocratic classes.

Character of Anglo-Norman Literature

The Norman temperament was essentially practical. Neither romantic sentiment, nor mysticism, nor lyric cry have much part in the literature of Normandy or Norman England. But curiosity, it would seem, needed constantly to be gratified, and themes of a religious or moral nature are very numerous and imply a wide appeal. Viewed as a whole, Anglo-Norman literature is prevailingly moral and edifying, and relatively poor in works frankly romantic and fictional. This is well illustrated in the poems of the earliest Anglo-Norman poet known to us, Philippe de Thaün. His first work was a *Comput* (before 1120), a verse treatise on the calendar and the ways of determining the movable festivals of the Church, to which he added certain symbolical interpretations. His *Bestiary* is a type of poem about which we shall have more to say later, in which highly fanciful characteristics of animals are made the basis of a rather forced moral. He

Philippe de Thaün

[2] C. H. Haskins, "Henry II as a Patron of Literature," *Essays in Medieval History presented to Thomas Frederick Tout* (Manchester, 1925), pp. 71-77. On the reign of Henry II as an age of literary activity see William Stubbs, "Learning and Literature at the Court of Henry II," *Seventeen Lectures on Medieval and Modern History* (3ed., Oxford, 1900), chs. vi and vii, and on the general subject of patronage, Karl J. Holzknecht, *Literary Patronage in the Middle Ages* (Philadelphia, 1923). See also Josiah C. Russell, "The English Court as an Intellectual Center (1199-1227)," in *Three Short Studies* (Colorado Springs, 1927; *Colorado College Pub.*, Gen. Ser. No. 148), pp. 60-69. For Custance la gentil and her husband see Alex. Bell, "Gaimar's Patron: Raul le fiz Gilebert," *N&Q*, 12 Ser., viii. 104.

composed also a *Lapidary*, if not several, dealing with the characteristics and virtues of precious stones.[3] There are numerous other lapidaries in Anglo-Norman,[4] all of which go back to an eleventh-century Latin poem called *De Gemmis*, by Marbode, Bishop of Rennes, which enjoyed an immense vogue throughout the Middle Ages. Of similar didactic aim are the *Distichs of Cato*, translated into Anglo-Norman no less than three times, and a rather uninspired poem of 3000 lines called *La Petite Philosophie*,[5] a compendium of geography and cosmography.

There is a grain of truth in the statement that an uninteresting biography has never been written, and the English court seems early to have been attracted by this type of narrative. The lost poem of David on the achievements of Henry I has already been mentioned. Although Henry II at times initiated literary work, we may be quite sure he did not order the *Vie de Saint Thomas le Martyr*,[6] which was written shortly after the murder, by Garnier (more properly Guernes), a clerk of Pont-Sainte-Maxence, who came to England in 1174 expressly to collect his material on the spot and finish his poem. About 1170 Denis Piramus composed *La Vie Seint Edmund le Rei* in more than 4000 lines of eight-syllable verse.[7] At the time he was probably a monk of Bury St. Edmunds, though his earlier life had been spent, as he tells us, amidst the follies of the court, where he had written "serventeis, chanceunettes, rimes, saluz entre les drues e les drus." In the thirteenth century, at a date now generally thought to be about 1250 or shortly thereafter a life of the famous archbishop was written, apparently by no less a person than the celebrated chronicler Matthew Paris.[8] At approximately the same time (*c.* 1245) Henry of Avranches wrote *La Estorie de Seint Aedward le Rei* in 4680 lines and dedicated it to the Queen, for which (and a life of St. George) he received £10 from the Exchequer.[9] The most remarkable of Anglo-Norman biographies is the anonymous *Histoire de Guillaume le Maréchal*,[10] the celebrated Earl of Pembroke, running to some 19,000 lines. It was written at the command of the Earl's son and is not only important for its historical accuracy but is remarkable for its lifelike picture and vivid narrative.

Religious and Secular Biography

[3] Philippe de Thaün's poems may be read in E. Mall, *Li Cumpoz Philipe de Thaün* (Strassburg, 1873), E. Walberg, *Le Bestiaire de Philippe de Thaün* (Lund, 1900), and Studer and Evans (as below), pp. 201-259.

[4] Paul Studer and Joan Evans, *Anglo-Norman Lapidaries* (Paris, 1924).

[5] Wm. H. Trethewey, *La Petite Philosophie, An Anglo-Norman Poem of the Thirteenth Century* (Oxford, 1939; *Anglo-Norman Text Soc.*, No. 1).

[6] Ed. E. Walberg (Lund, 1922; and again, 1936, in *CFMA*, 77). For another Anglo-Norman life of Becket see *La Vie de Thomas Becket par Beneit, poème anglo-normand du xiie siècle*, ed. Börje Schlyter (Lund, 1941; *Études Romanes de Lund*, iv).

[7] The best edition is that of Hilding Kjellman (Göteborg, 1935).

[8] A. T. Baker, "La Vie de Saint Edmond . . . ", *Romania*, lv (1929). 332-381. It was dedicated to Isabelle of Arundel. The MS in which the life is found, the property of the Duke of Portland at Walbeck Abbey, contains thirteen Anglo-French saints' lives. For list, with the places where they have been printed, see A. T. Baker in *Romania*, lxvi (1940). 49n.

[9] Cf. J. C. Russell, *MP*, xxviii (1931). 267. The text is in H. R. Luard, *Lives of Edward the Confessor* (London, 1858; Rolls Series). For Henry of Avranches see below, p. 149.

[10] Ed. Paul Meyer in the *Société de l'histoire de France* (3v, Paris, 1891-1901); see also Meyer's discussion in *Romania*, xi (1882). 22-74. On the subject of the poem see Sidney Painter, *William Marshall* (Baltimore, 1933).

Historical Themes

It was in works of history that Anglo-Norman writers scored their greatest success, surpassing in both Latin and French the productions on the Continent at the same period. It is not difficult to understand the popularity of historical subjects at the English court. The conquerors had secured control of a new country, and pride in their achievement stimulated a natural desire to know more about the land over which they had become the rulers. Perhaps they also enjoyed the feeling that this land had had as illustrious a past as that of the kings of France and that their own record was worthy of regard. At any rate it is the history of England and of Normandy, not of Europe or antiquity, that they were interested in. About 1150 Geoffrey Gaimar, attached in some way to Ralph Fitz Gilbert of Lincolnshire, wrote for "dame Custance," his wife, a verse chronicle in two parts. The first was an *Histoire des Bretons,* that is, of the Celts in Britain, and was a working over in French of Geoffrey of Monmouth's *Historia Regum Britanniae* (see below, p. 168). It is now lost and we know about it only from the opening lines of the second part. This was the *Estorie des Engles.*[11] It consists of some 6500 lines and except for about 800 lines at the beginning, which tell the story of Havelok, later to be made the subject of an admirable English romance, it is a history of the English based on the *Old English Annals* with a few added episodes. Gaimar is not a gifted writer. His narrative, except on rather rare occasions, does not rise above the factual and commonplace. When he can escape from the impediments of fact and tell a story, as in the Havelok and one or two other episodes, interest is better sustained. But he betrays no marks of individuality, shows no prejudices, enthusiasms, or opinions. He treats conqueror and conquered alike, so that we cannot tell whether he was of Norman or Saxon descent. Most serious of all, he lacks the imaginative eye for vivid detail which his contemporary Wace has, and his work was valued only when it presented material not otherwise available in French. This is doubtless the reason that in all manuscripts Gaimar's first part is replaced by Wace's *Roman de Brut,* which covered the same ground.[12] There were several other adaptations of Geoffrey

Gaimar

[11] Ed. T. D. Hardy and C. T. Martin (2v, 1888-89; Rolls Ser.). For the Havelok episode see Alex. Bell, *Le Lai d'Haveloc and Gaimar's Haveloc Episode* (Manchester, 1925; *Pub. Univ. Manchester, French Ser.,* IV). On Gaimar cf. Alex. Bell, "Maistre Geffrei Gaimar," *MA,* VII (1938). 184-198.

[12] The *Roman de Brut,* since it occupies a place in the development of the Arthurian legend, will be touched on in chapter VIII, below. Wace was a Norman, who spent his early life at Caen and his last years as a prebendary of Bayeux; he does not belong, strictly speaking, to Anglo-Norman literature. But his *Roman de Brut,* on the testimony of Layamon, was presented to Queen Eleanor, and his second long poem, the *Roman de Rou,* a history of the dukes of Normandy, was begun about 1160 under the patronage of Henry II. Unfortunately he was not allowed to finish this undertaking; for some reason Henry replaced him, after he had written more than 11,000 lines, by a Maistre Beneeit, whom some identify with Benoît de Sainte-More. In addition to the two long poems just mentioned he wrote lives in verse of St. Nicholas, St. George, and St. Margaret, and a poem of 1804 lines on *La Conception Nostre Dame.* The last named enjoyed considerable popularity and found its way eventually into the *Cursor Mundi.* Wace is thought to have died shortly after 1174, at the age of seventy or more. The *Roman de Rou* is edited by H. Andresen (2v, Heilbronn, 1877-79). The latest edition of the *Vie de saint Nicholas* is that of E. Ronsjö (Lund, 1942; *Études romanes de Lund,* v). For the *Sainte Marguerite* see the edition of Eliz. A. Francis (Paris, 1932; *CFMA,* 71). The *Saint George* and the *Conception* are in V. Luzarche, *La Vie de la Vierge Marie* (Tours, 1859).

of Monmouth in Anglo-Norman which need not be mentioned. Of more importance is the fact that recent events were recorded in the same manner as the older history. In 1173 Henry's sons, supported by the Scottish king, revolted against their father. The following year Henry's forces took the Scottish king prisoner in Northumberland and put an end to the revolt. The events of this campaign were witnessed by Jordan Fantosme, who had been a pupil in Paris of the celebrated Gilbert de la Porée and was later secretary to Henry of Blois, Bishop of Winchester. His *Chronicle* of 2000 lines gives an account, full of picturesque detail, of the events of this campaign. Slightly later (*c.* 1225) we have an anonymous account, written in retrospect, of Henry II's conquest of Ireland. As late as the fourteeenth century verse history is still occasionally written in French, although such matter is now more commonly in prose. Peter Langtoft's *Chronicle* [13] covers the period from the destruction of Troy to 1307 in 10,000 lines, and was early translated into English by Robert of Brunne (cf. p. 204).

The body of Anglo-Norman religious literature of every sort is very large. *Religious* Mention has been made above of Samson de Nanteuil's translation into *Subjects* nearly 12,000 lines of verse of the *Proverbs of Solomon* (*c.* 1140). Early in the twelfth century the Psalter was twice turned into French, as were other parts of the Bible later in the century. At the end of the century a poet named Chardry versified the legends of *Barlaam and Josaphat* and the *Seven Sleepers,* and debated various moral questions in the *Petit Plet,* the three making a total of more than 6500 lines.[14] A great number of saints' lives appeared throughout the twelfth and thirteenth centuries. We have mentioned for their biographical interest those of Edward the Confessor, Thomas à Becket, and Edmund, Archbishop of Canterbury. Similar in character but of special interest is the *Voyage of St. Brendan* [15] *(1121)* by an unknown Benedeit, mentioned above as one of the works dedicated to Queen Adelaide. It tells the story, first found in the Latin *Navigatio Sancti Brendani,* of an Irish abbot named Brendan and some monks who accompany him on a quest in search of the other world. In the course of their seven-year journey they witness many marvels and are eventually rewarded by a vision of paradise. It is notable as the first introduction into popular literature in England of the Celtic spirit of the marvelous.[16] In the first half of the thirteenth century, the celebrated Bishop of Lincoln, Robert Grosseteste (d. 1253), wrote *Grosseteste* an allegorical poem which he called *Le Château d'Amour.*[17] It ranges all

[13] Edited by Thomas Wright (1866-68) for the Rolls Series.

[14] All three were edited by John Koch in the *Altfranzösische Bibliothek,* Vol. 1 (Heilbronn, 1879). Josophat, the son of a Hindu king, is converted to Christianity by the hermit Barlaam. The *Seven Sleepers* is the story of seven youths who slept for 362 years and awoke in the reign of Theodosius.

[15] E. G. R. Waters, *The Anglo-Norman Voyage of St. Brendan by Benedeit* (Oxford, 1928).

[16] Cf. Walberg, *Quelques aspects,* p. 90.

[17] Edited by J. Murray (Paris, 1918). For two Middle English translations see *EETS,* 98, pp. 355-394 and 407-442, and for the former of these the earlier editions of R. F. Weymouth (1864; *Philol. Soc.*) and J. O. Halliwell (1849). On the allegory of the castle in medieval literature see Roberta D. Cornelius, *The Figurative Castle* (Bryn Mawr, 1930).

the way from a debate of the Four Daughters of God,[18] after which Christ descends from Heaven into a castle which is the body of the Virgin Mary, to a discussion of the attributes of Christ and His final judgment of the world, distributing to each according to his deserts the joys of Heaven and the pains of Hell.

Several works of great length and encyclopedic character, dating from the middle of the thirteenth century, are still unedited. Robert of Gretham's *Miroir* or *Les Évangiles des Domnées*[19] (more than 20,000 lines) translates the Sunday gospels with explanations of their meaning. The same author seems to have written a second long poem called the *Corset,* a compendium of popular theology. The poems are dedicated to an unidentified Alain and his wife, to whom Robert served as chaplain. Of similar scope is the *Lumière as Lais*[20] (14,000 lines) of Peter of Peckham, adapted in part from the *Elucidarium* of Honorius of Autun (or Augustodunensis), and the *Manual des Péchés*[21] (11,000 lines) by William of Wadington (?), which was translated into English in Robert of Brunne's *Handlyng Synne* (cf. p. 204). Around the turn of the fourteenth century Nicole Bozon, a Franciscan, composed a miscellaneous collection of *Contes Moralisés*[22] and wrote a number of other works in both prose and verse, not all of which have been identified.[23]

Although religious literature and works intended to convey useful knowledge constitute the largest part of Anglo-Norman literature, there is also a fair number of pieces in which no other end is contemplated than entertainment. These are, as is to be expected, mostly romances, although some

Robert of Gretham

Peter of Peckham

Anglo-Norman Romances

---

[18] The standard treatment of the allegory is Hope Traver, *The Four Daughters of God* (Philadelphia, 1907).

[19] Unpublished, but there are considerable extracts in Marion Y. H. Aitken, *Étude sur le Miroir ou les Évangiles des domnées de Robert de Gretham* (Paris, 1922).

[20] This has not been printed; in one MS it is dated 1267. For an account of the author, MSS, sources, etc., see M. Dominica Legge, "Pierre de Peckham and His *Lumiere as Lais*," *MLR*, xxiv (1929). 37-47; 153-171. Peckham (the name occurs also as Peccham and Feccham) is the author also of a *Vie de Saint Richard*, written *c.* 1270 for the Countess of Arundel (ed. A. T. Baker, *Revue des langues romanes*, liii (1910). 245-396), and *Le Secré de Secrez* (2383 lines), written sometime after the *Lumière as Lais*. It is edited by Oliver A. Beckerlegge (Oxford, 1944; *Anglo-Norman Text Soc.*, No. 5). The latter is a version of the *Secreta Secretorum*, of which there were three in Anglo-Norman and several in Continental French. For English versions see below, pp. 296 and 302 (*Dicts and Sayings of the Philosophers*).

[21] This has been printed in somewhat incomplete form by F. J. Furnivall in his edition of the *Handlyng Synne* (1901-3; *EETS*, 119 and 123). See E. J. Arnould, *Le Manuel de Péchés: Étude de littérature religieuse anglo-normande* (xiiie *siècle*) (Paris, 1940), and D. W. Robertson, Jr., "The *Manuel de Péchés* and an English Episcopal Decree," *MLN*, lx (1945). 439-447.

[22] Edited by L. T. Smith and P. Meyer for the *Société des anciens textes français* (1889). For the fullest treatment of Bozon see *Hist. Litt.*, xxxvi. 400-424, which should be supplemented by Sister M. Amelia, "Nicholas Bozon," *Speculum*, xv (1940). 444-453, and the important Introduction to Johan Vising, *Deux poèmes de Nicholas Bozon* (Göteborg, 1919). Vising has also edited *La Plainte d'Amour* (Göteborg, 1905-7), probably by Bozon. A. C. Thorn has edited *Les Proverbes de bon enseignement* (Lund, 1921; *Lunds Univ. Årsskrift*, N.F., Avd. 1, Bd. 17, Nr. 4; another text, from the Vernon MS, is in *EETS*, 117, pp. 522-553) and Mary R. Learned has edited "Saints' Lives Attributed to Nicholas Bozon," *Franciscan Stud.*, xxv (1944). 79-88, 171-178, 267-271.

[23] It should be mentioned here that the religious drama is represented by the twelfth-century Anglo-Norman *Adam* (see p. 276), a *Resurrection* of the early thirteenth century (ed. Jean G. Wright for *CFMA* in 1931), and a recently discovered text (see T. A. Jenkins and J. M. Manly, "La Seinte Resureccion," Oxford, 1943; *Anglo-Norman Text Soc.*, iv).

fabliaux and an occasional satirical piece like *Le Jongleur d'Ely* give us a welcome glimpse of the English court in its lighter moments. Mention has been made above of the nearly 800 lines devoted to the story of Havelok the Dane at the beginning of Gaimar's *Estorie des Engles*. The same story in slightly longer form is told separately as a lay by an anonymous poet writing about 1130-40. It shows us the interest which the ruling class took in whatever was thought to concern the earlier history of the island, whether English, Danish, or Celtic. Among several other Anglo-Norman lays, *Amis and Amiloun* enjoyed perhaps the greatest popularity in the Middle Ages as a story of friendship put to a very great test. It should be remembered that the supreme author of such short romantic poems, Marie de France, lived at the English court and translated another of her works, a collection of fables, from English, as she herself tells us. The earliest and most famous and in some ways the best of the longer French romances written in England is the *Tristan* of Thomas, composed about 1170. It is one of the two earliest representatives of the lost French romance from which all subsequent treatments of the Tristan and Iseult story in literature descend. Sometime before the end of the century another Anglo-Frenchman, Robert de Boron,[24] wrote at least two romances on Arthurian themes, *Joseph d'Arimathie* or the *Estoire du Graal*, which in the four thousand lines that are preserved tells the story of the origin of the Holy Grail, and *Merlin*, of which only 400 lines have come down to us. About 1180 another poet named Thomas, who cannot be identified with the author of the *Tristan*, told the story of *Horn*, better known to modern readers in the English romance *King Horn* (cf. p. 175). Two long romances on pseudo-classical themes are the work of Hugh of Rutland. One, *Ipomedon* (*c.* 1185), resembles the story of Guy of Warwick in the hero's efforts to prove himself worthy of the lady he loves. The other, *Protheselaus* (*c.* 1190), relates the quarrel of two brothers, sons of Ipomedon, and their subsequent reconciliation. Each of these romances is more than 10,000 lines long. Of similar length and approximately the same date is Thomas of Kent's *Roman de Toute Chevalerie*, a story of Alexander the Great, while the longest of all the Anglo-Norman romances, the anonymous *Waldef* (22,000 lines) of the end of the twelfth century, relates the tragic struggle of an English king to regain his throne, and the avenging of his death by his sons.[25] Both the *Roman de Toute Chevalerie* and the *Waldef* still remain in manuscript. A romance of *Fouke Fitz Warin* in verse exists only in a later prose redaction.[26] It would seem that the writing of romances in French died out in England with the spread of English to the upper classes in the thirteenth century. Two, however, were produced in the first half of the century on subjects which were destined to enjoy

[24] There are those who believe that he was not an Englishman. See the discussion of W. A. Nitze in the *Manly Anniversary Studies* (Chicago, 1923), pp. 300-314. For a more acceptable position see the same author's "The Home of Robert de Boron," *MP*, XL (1942). 113-116.
[25] The Latin *Waldef* has been edited by R. Imelmann, *Johannes Bramis' Historia Regis Waldei* (Bonn, 1912; *Bonner Studien*, IV).
[26] The prose version is edited by Louis Brandin (Paris, 1930; *CFMA*, 63).

the greatest popularity when they were later treated in English—*Gui de Warewic* and *Boeve de Haumtone*. Some others probably once existed but are now lost, such as a *Richard Cœur de Lion* which is several times referred to in the English romance of that name.[27]

Anglo-Norman literature had passed its crest by about 1250,[28] although in diminishing amounts works in French continued to be written in England until the end of the fourteenth century. Even John Gower, who holds a modest but respectable place in English poetry, could write as late as 1376 one of his long poems, the *Mirour de l'Omme* (30,000 lines), in French.[29] Slightly more than four hundred texts, ranging from short lyrics to pieces of staggering length, are known today and testify to the place which French once held in the culture of the English upper classes.

[27] The romances mentioned in this paragraph will be found in the following editions: E. Kölbing, *Amis and Amiloun* (Heilbronn, 1884); J. Bédier, *Le Roman de Tristan par Thomas* (2v, Paris, 1903-5; *SATF*); for an English translation see R. S. Loomis, *The Romance of Tristram and Ysolt by Thomas of Britain* (1931); W. A. Nitze, *Robert de Boron: Le Roman de l'Estoire dou Graal* (Paris, 1927; *CFMA*, 57), containing also the fragment of the *Merlin*; earlier edition by F. Michel (Bordeaux, 1841); R. Brede and E. M. Stengel, *Das anglonormannische Lied vom wackern Ritter Horn* (Marburg, 1883; *Ausgaben und Abhandlungen*, VIII); E. Kölbing and E. Koschwitz, *Ipomedon* (Breslau, 1889); F. Kluckow, *Hue de Rotelande: Protheselaus* (Göttingen, 1924); A. Ewert, *Gui de Warewic* (2v, Paris, 1932-3; *CFMA*, 74-75; A. Stimming, *Der anglonormannische Boeve de Haumtone* (Halle, 1899).

[28] Walter of Bibbesworth, the author of two whimsical poems, is the author of a famous *Traité* (1240-50) written to teach French to the children of Dionysia de Munchensy. On the poems (now BM Add. MS 46919, formerly Phillipps MS 8336) see Miss Legge's *Anglo-Norman Literature*, pp. 348-9, on the *Traité* Alexander Bell, "Notes on Walter de Bibbesworth's Treatise," *PQ*, XLI (1962). 361-372, and Albert C. Baugh, "The Date of Walter of Bibbesworth's Traité," *Festschrift für Walther Fischer* (Heidelberg, 1959), pp. 21-33.

[29] A list of books owned by Richard II contains mostly romances in French. Cf. Edith Rickert, "King Richard II's Books," *Library*, n. s. XIII (1932). 144-147.

V

Early Latin Writers

In any age up to the Renaissance, the Latin literature of Europe is the *A* measure of its intellectual life. In a day when all books which made a pre- *Measure of* tense to learning were written in Latin, such books are a barometer record- *Intellectual* ing by their number and importance the advances, the retrogressions, or *Life* the periods of hesitation in European civilization. But while Latin is the language of learning, not all books written in it are necessarily learned. Learned men have their moments of leisure. All through the Middle Ages important positions in the government and at court were filled by bishops and clerks trained for the church, men whose progress through the schools or the university had by a process of natural selection marked them as possessed of the intellectual grasp and learning needed in dealing with the problems of government and the State. Such men, though churchmen, were more occupied with worldly than religious matters and in some cases their natural inclinations were anything but pious. It would be a mistake to think that their reading—done in Latin with the ease that comes of long habit— was exclusively edifying. Hence such Latin books as the *De Nugis Curialium,* the *Speculum Stultorum,* the *Otia Imperialia,* and the mass of light, satirical, and scurrilous verse that we know as Goliardic poetry.

Since the Latin language was international, the Latin writings of any *Twelfth-* particular country are also a measure of the extent to which that country *Century* participates in the general progress that is being made. There was a time, *Renais-* in the eighth century, when England led the world in learning, when at *sance* the beginning Bede was writing and at the end Charlemagne was forced to bring Alcuin from York to direct the intellectual reforms which he was bent on in France. And there was also a time a century later when King Alfred could lament that "there were very few on this side of the Humber who could ... translate a letter from Latin into English." Fortunately the Benedictine Reform [1] and the Norman Conquest had brought improvement. However limited were the Conqueror's own bookish interests, he had a re- spect for learning and filled the English churches and monasteries with learned bishops and abbots and monks. As a result, a generation later Eng- land was ready to participate in the general awakening that was taking place in Europe. The twelfth century is one of those periods in history in which many things have their beginnings and in which there is both sub- stantial achievement and promise of greater achievement to come. It was

---

[1] See above, p. 100.

the century in which the great cathedrals of Europe were begun. It was the century of the troubadours and of Chrétien de Troyes. It witnessed the rapid development of scholastic philosophy with William of Champeaux, Abelard, and Peter Lombard, preparing the way for the great Schoolmen of the thirteenth century, Albertus Magnus, Thomas Aquinas, and Duns Scotus. And it saw the founding of the universities, above all of Paris, but also of Bologna and Oxford and, towards the end of the century, Cambridge. What the University of Paris alone meant to the intellectual life of the Middle Ages can hardly be estimated. Everywhere there are signs of quickened intellect and new life. It is not without reason that we have come to speak of a Twelfth-Century Renaissance,[2] and in the Latin literature and learning of this century England has a full share.

John of Salisbury

From the large number of Latin writers of England in the twelfth and thirteenth centuries a few names stand out in bold relief. Of these the earliest is that of John of Salisbury. His experience is typical of many for whom a career in the Church was equivalent to a position in public life, whether assumed willingly or, as in his case, against inclination. He was born about 1120, and studied for twelve years in Paris and at Chartres under such teachers as Abelard and William of Conches. Chartres was a center of literary and humanistic studies, and John of Salisbury owes his wide acquaintance with classical poets to the tradition which the famous Bernard established there. On his return to England in 1154, after some years in the service of the Pope, he became secretary to the Archbishop of Canterbury, Theobald, and later held the same office under Becket, whose cause he supported and whose exile he shared. The last four years of his life he spent as Bishop of Chartres, where he died in 1180. His two principal works are the *Policraticus* and the *Metalogicon*,[3] both finished in 1159 and dedicated to Thomas à Becket, then chancellor to Henry II. The latter is a defense of logic and apart from an interesting section on the author's student years in France is of value chiefly for its account of scholastic studies in his day. The *Policraticus* is of wider interest.

The Policraticus

The *Policraticus* (Statesman's Book), whether conceived as a whole from the beginning or growing under the author's hand, is the embodiment of a large purpose which must have been in his mind whether he had formulated it consciously or not. For the work is nothing less than a treatise on the good life, which, since we live in an organized society, involves a consideration of the welfare of the State. With all its essay-like informality in the individual chapters, it hangs together in a fairly logical way. While John addresses

---

[2] C. H. Haskins, *The Renaissance of the Twelfth Century* (Cambridge, Mass., 1927); G. M. Paré, *et. al.*, *La Renaissance du XIIe siècle: les écoles et l'enseignement* (Paris, 1933).
    [3] Critical editions of the *Policraticus* and the *Metalogicon* have been published by C. C. J. Webb (Oxford, 1909 and 1929). The *Policraticus* can now all be read in translation, part of it in John Dickinson, *The Statesman's Book of John of Salisbury* (1927), the remainder in Joseph B. Pike, *Frivolities of Courtiers and Footprints of Philosophers* (Minneapolis, 1938). C. C. J. Webb's *John of Salisbury* (1932) is popular but authoritative. Good brief accounts will be found in Helen Waddell, "John of Salisbury," *E&S*, XIII (1928). 28-51, and R. L. Poole, *Illustrations of Medieval Thought* (2ed., 1920), ch. VII.

himself to the chancellor of England, he has in mind the whole governing class as well as that intangible entity, posterity. He begins by attempting to clear away the habits and practices which he considers unworthy, or foolish, or actually immoral, and which are not always recognized as such, particularly when they occur where they do the most harm—at the court and in high places. And so he condemns hunting, gaming, actors and mimics, magic and astrology, and the things inimical to the public welfare—pride, concupiscence, flattery, especially as a vicious means of advancement. All this occupies the first three books. In the next three he considers the proper functioning of the State—the character and conduct of the prince and his relation to the law, the commonwealth and its members, the administration of justice, the behavior of its armed forces, the cohesion of its parts. And in the concluding books he turns successively to the things which his own studies have shown to be important, first to the intellectual and ethical principles "which have in view the health of body and soul," and hence to the efforts of philosophers to attain wisdom and truth; and lastly to those private virtues on which all happiness ultimately depends—modesty, moderation, sobriety, and the like—all of which leads to the conclusion that the happy man is he who fears God and frames his life accordingly. There are sometimes long digressions which tend to obscure the plan, but it is impossible not to sense the larger purpose which throughout animates this really lengthy work.

John of Salisbury is not a profound or original thinker, a philosopher *His* who builds a new system or tears down old ones. He is content not to be *Character* dogmatic on matters about which a wise man may well confess doubt, and he specifically disclaims originality. But he expresses his convictions boldly, even to justifying the putting to death of tyrants, and he quotes a conversation which he had with Pope Adrian IV in which he assuredly did not mince words on the corruption of Rome and the papal court. His weakness is the result of the very circumstance to which he owes much of his strength —the twelve years which he spent in study at Paris and Chartres. He has read everything and he quotes endlessly—Horace and Virgil, Juvenal, Ovid, Terence, and the whole range of Latin writers, pagan and Christian, until at times present reality is lost in the wealth of historical example. There is enough of himself on every page, however, to dominate the thought, so that interest does not flag. Student and moralist, he has been forced to spend his life with kings and chancellors, archbishops and popes. He has seen the shortcomings not so much of Church and State as of prelates and statesmen, and being a man of convictions he sets down his philosophy of life for the benefit of those among whom it may do some good.

Walter Map (*c.* 1140-*c.* 1209) needed a Boswell. Like Johnson he was a *Walter* greater talker than writer; he was noted for his witty conversation and his *Map* good stories. His life would have made a fascinating biography, beginning with his student years in Paris and continuing with his experiences as a clerk in the king's household and as an itinerant justice, and ending with his death as Archdeacon of Oxford. He was a favorite of Henry II, traveled with him, met scores of interesting people, and saw Rome as a delegate to the third Lateran Council. He passed in the Middle Ages as the author of some of the most famous of the Goliardic poems; he may have written verses of this sort in his early days. A persistent and early tradition credits him with the authorship of the prose *Lancelot* and other Arthurian romances, a tradition that cannot be accepted in any literal sense. His one extant book, *De Nugis Curialium* [4] ("Courtiers' Trifles"), passed completely unnoticed in the Middle Ages and survives in a single manuscript copied two hundred years after it was written. It is a collection of stories, historical anecdotes, scraps of folklore, witty remarks and amusing incidents, occasionally bits of satire and denunciation, without order or plan, written down between 1181 and 1193.[5] A somewhat comparable book is the *Otia Imperialia* of Gervase of Tilbury, who chose England for his birth and death but lived most of his life abroad. It is a veritable Book of Knowledge into which the author put all the interesting things he knew about the earth and its history, with a collection of wonders thrown in for good measure. It was written in 1211 for the entertainment and (we may suspect) the edification of the Emperor Otto IV.

Gervase of Tilbury

Giraldus Cambrensis

Another interesting personality of Henry II's reign, Giraldus Cambrensis,[6] was like his friend Walter Map a Welshman and a cleric, but there the resemblance ends. For whereas Map was possessed of an amiable indolence and acquired numerous preferments, Giraldus had the zeal of a reformer, loved a fight, and was always willing to excommunicate his opponent. He spent the best years of his life in an unsuccessful effort to become Bishop of St. David's and raise the see to metropolitan rank in Wales, the equal of Canterbury and York. He is commonly classed as an historian and indeed he wrote a *Topography of Ireland,* the *Conquest of Ireland,* an *Itinerary of Wales,* based on his journey through Wales with Archbishop Baldwin to preach the Third Crusade, a *Description of Wales,*[7] and other more strictly historical works. For he was a voluminous writer, whose extant writings fill eight volumes in the Rolls Series. But among them are a number of pieces of a more general character, including two which are in the

[4] Edited by M. R. James (Oxford, 1914) and earlier by Thomas Wright for the Camden Soc. (1850); trans. by F. Tupper and M. B. Ogle (1924) and by M. R. James (1923; *Cymmrodorion Record Ser.,* No. IX).

[5] James Hinton, "Walter Map's *De Nugis Curialium*: Its Plan and Composition," *PMLA,* XXXII (1917). 81-132.

[6] Also known as Gerald de Barri. His dates are *c.* 1146-1220. He spent, as he tells us himself, three periods of several years in study at Paris and shows wide acquaintance with classical literature. He served as archdeacon of Mynyw (St. David's) and in other ecclesiastical capacities. He was elected Bishop of St. David's in 1198, but in spite of three trips to Rome could not overcome the influence of the Archbishop of Canterbury and the King's natural fears. The election was not confirmed, and he retired gracefully from the field. For an excellent treatment of Gerald see the lecture of F. M. Powicke, "Gerald of Wales," *Bull. John Rylands Library,* XII (1928). 389-410, reprinted in *Christian Life in the Middle Ages and Other Essays* (Oxford, 1935).

[7] A translation of these four works is in the Bohn library, *The Historical Works of Giraldus Cambrensis,* ed. Thomas Wright, and the two on Wales are available in the Everyman's Library.

nature of an autobiography,[8] and even in the works which have an importance for the historian there is so much incidental anecdote and observation, popular tradition, legend, and folklore that they have considerable appeal to the general reader. His narrative is always swift and vigorous, full of the unexpected, lively, never hampered by moderation or restraint. Even his outrageous egotism is so frank as to disarm criticism.

The name of one other Welshman should be found with those of Walter *Geoffrey* Map and Giraldus Cambrensis in this place, that of Geoffrey of Monmouth. *of* But since his *History of the Kings of Britain* (1137) and his verse life of *Monmouth* Merlin (*Vita Merlini*) owe their interest chiefly to their connection with Arthurian romance, consideration of them will be postponed until chapter VIII, where they may be given their proper place in the development of the Arthurian legend.

We have already seen in the preceding chapter how widespread was the *Chroniclers* interest in history among the new rulers of England after the Norman Conquest and how that interest was satisfied by Anglo-Norman poets for those who could not read Latin. The same interest gives us a long series of chronicles and histories in Latin unequaled in any other country of Europe. We cannot speak here of the many monastic annals compiled at religious houses and concerned mainly with local affairs. These belong with a few notable exceptions to the middle and south of England and tend to disappear after 1300. The more ambitious chronicle commonly begins with the Anglo-Saxons, or at times with the creation of the world, and comes down to the writer's own day. Thus Simeon of Durham [9] covers the period from 616 to 1130, and Florence of Worcester, whose *Chronicon ex Chronicis* is a rather bare record of events, begins with the time of Julius Caesar and continues to within a year or so of his own death in 1118. Ordericus Vitalis, the son of a Norman father and an English mother, compiled between 1130 and 1141 an *Historia Ecclesiastica* from Creation to the time of writing, an interesting and valuable source for the period beginning with the Norman Conquest. Two writers stand out for their literary interest. William of Malmesbury, whose *Gesta Regum Anglorum* (449-1128) is the most ambitious of his several undertakings, treats the writing of history as an art. He is careful to differentiate his work from that of the mere chronicler, and justifies an occasional digression on the score of variety and interest. Henry of Huntingdon, whose value to the historian is rather slight, inserts in the form of

---

[8] *De Rebus a se Gestis* and *De Jure et Statu Meneuensis Ecclesiae* (Vols. I and III of the edition in the Rolls Series). These have been translated by H. E. Butler, *The Autobiography of Giraldus Cambrensis* (1937), except for a portion of the latter which has no autobiographical interest. The *Speculum Ecclesiae*, one of the pieces of more general character referred to in the text, has not been translated. It is a collection of satirical and often scurrilous sketches of unworthy clerics.

[9] All of the works mentioned will be found edited in the Rolls Series. For a full list of the English chroniclers and an appraisal of their historical importance see Charles Gross, *Sources and Literature of English History . . . to . . . 1485* (2ed., 1915), pp. 326-399. English translations of the more important are included in the Bohn Library, the Church Historians of England, the Everyman's Library, etc. On the origins of the medieval chronicle see R. L. Poole, *Chronicles and Annals: A Brief Outline of Their Origin and Growth* (1926).

Latin translation many ballads and popular traditions which he heard among the people, and these do much to make up for his rather brief and matter-of-fact style. Of special importance for the reign of Henry II are William of Newburgh's *Historia Rerum Anglicarum* (to 1197), the work of a careful student with many of the ideals of the modern scholar, the *Gesta Regis Henrici Secundi* ascribed to Benedict of Peterborough and possibly the work of Richard Fitz-Neal, author of the famous *Dialogus de Scaccario* ("Dialogue of the Exchequer"), and the *Chronica* of Roger Hoveden whose work is of greatest value for the closing decade of the twelfth century. It may be said of all these writers that for the past they merely compile or slavishly copy from earlier sources and that they become interesting and assume importance when they reach the period of which they have personal knowledge.

St. Albans In the thirteenth century one school of historians stands out above all others, the chroniclers who wrote at the great monastery of St. Albans. Situated only twenty miles from London on one of the main highways, the abbey was a convenient stopping place for travelers the first night out of the city, and frequently had as guests the king and other magnates of the realm. In the days when most current events were known by direct report this gave the abbey a unique advantage in the gathering of historical material. The greatest of the St. Albans chroniclers was Matthew Paris, who *Matthew* seems to have been as gifted as an illuminator and worker in gold and silver *Paris* as he was as an historian. His principal work, the *Chronica Majora*,[10] incorporates that of his predecessors John of Cella and Roger of Wendover and continues to the year 1259. It is a vivid and colorful narrative. His history was continued by a fellow monk, William Rishanger (to 1306), and by others down to Thomas Walsingham, who closes the series in 1422. In the first half of the fourteenth century a monk of Chester abbey, Ranulf Higden, compiled a universal history called the *Polychronicon,* extending from the beginning of the world to 1327, which was continued by others to 1357 and enjoyed an enormous popularity in the century following. It would not be possible to omit mention of the "Chronicle" of Jocelyn de *Jocelyn de* Brakelond,[11] though it is not a chronicle in the usual sense. It is really a *Brakelond* life of the abbot Samson and an account of his efforts to restore discipline and a business-like conduct of affairs in the great Benedictine monastery of Bury St. Edmunds. It is charming in its frankness, sincerity, and occasional touches of shrewd humor. Its picture of laxity, petty politics, the self-seeking of unscrupulous monks, and the sympathetic portrait of abbot Samson leave with one an indelible impression of what sometimes went on in a great monastic house. The story is familiar to all readers of Carlyle's *Past and Present.*

[10] Edited in the Rolls Series (1872-83). His *Historia Minor* is an abridgment with additions (1067-1253). He is also the author of *Vitae Abbatum S. Albani,* various saints' lives, etc.
[11] Edited by J. G. Rokewode (1840; Camden Soc., Vol. 13). It may be read in English in the translation of L. C. Jane *The Chronicle of Jocelin of Brakelond* (1907). It was written in 1202 and covers the years 1173-1202.

In the Latin literature of England in the Middle Ages the prose is of *Latin* much greater significance than the verse. Nevertheless a good bit of verse *Verse* was written, ranging from the serious epic to the light, the satirical, and at times the highly indecorous. Joseph of Exeter, who accompanied Archbishop Baldwin on the Third Crusade,[12] composed an epic in six books known as the *De Bello Trojano* (c. 1184) in the manner of Virgil. It is a more than respectable performance, but unfortunately, so far as modern readers are concerned, has run into fatal competition since the Renaissance with a certain Greek poem. If Joseph of Exeter falls somewhat short of his model, Virgil, it is a still farther cry from Horace to the *Nova Poetria* [13] of Geoffrey de Vinsauf, an interesting mixture of classical precept and medieval practice. A delightfully amusing satire on ambitious monks is Nigel Wireker's *Speculum Stultorum* [14] (c. 1180), a mirror in which fools may see themselves as the ass Burnellus, who thought his tail was too short. His adventures with the doctors of Salerno, his years of study at the University of Paris, at the end of which he is still only able to say *ya,* his determination to found a new kind of monastery where every monk may have a mistress, are related with much more than mere humor. Finally, there is the large body of strongly rhythmical verse, by turns trivial, amorous, scurrilous, and coarse, written by university students sowing their wild oats or by *scholares vagantes* who have quit the academic life permanently or temporarily and taken to the road. Although we must discard the attribution of much of this verse to Walter Map, Englishmen seem to have had a share in its pro- *Goliardic* duction.[15] It is the poetry of the bohemian life and the tavern. It shows no *Verse* respect for rank or authority, makes light of death, has no concern for the future either in this world or the next. It is the flaunted gaiety of the socially declassed, the voice of defiant nonchalance in rags.

[12] He celebrated the expedition in a Latin poem called the *Antiocheis,* of which only a few lines remain.

[13] Text in E. Faral, *Les Arts poétiques du XII° et du XIII° siècle* (1923).

[14] In Thomas Wright, *Anglo-Latin Satirical Poets* (2v, 1872; Rolls Ser.). On Wireker see the articles of John H. Mozley: "On the Text of the *Speculum Stultorum,*" *Speculum,* IV (1929). 430-442; V (1930). 251-263; "The Unprinted Poems of Nigel Wireker," *Speculum,* VII (1932). 398-423; "Nigel Wireker or Wetekre," *MLR,* XXVII (1932). 314-317. As an example of the occasional poet, who in this case was not English but spent a number of years in England and wrote much for English patrons, see J. C. Russell, "Master Henry of Avranches as an International Poet," *Speculum,* III (1928). 34-63. For the large body of Latin political verse consult the collections of Thomas Wright noted on p. 222.

[15] Such verse is known as Goliardic poetry from the fact that a certain Golias, called *episcopus* or *pontifex,* who has numerous children or disciples, is frequently mentioned as the author and progenitor of it. The authorship of some of the poems is concealed under the names Primas and Archipoeta. An Englishman credited with others, Serlo of Wilton, is mentioned among the acquaintances of both Walter Map and Giraldus Cambrensis. A number of texts are printed in Thomas Wright, *The Latin Poems Commonly Attributed to Walter Mapes* (1841; Camden Soc., Vol. 16). Further references will be found, together with a valuable introduction summarizing the results of modern scholarship, in Olga Dobiache-Rojdestvensky, *Les Poésies des goliards* (1931). See also Helen Waddell, *The Wandering Scholars* (1927), P. S. Allen, *The Romanesque Lyric* (1928), the same author's *Medieval Latin Lyrics* (1931), and F. J. E. Raby, *A History of Secular Latin Poetry* (2v, Oxford, 1934). Howard Mumford Jones contributed translations to Allen's earlier volume; other translations will be found in John Addington Symonds, *Wine, Women, and Song: Medieval Latin Students' Songs* (1884) and Helen Waddell, *Mediæval Lyrics* (1929).

Variety of
the Latin
Literature

Space forbids the proper consideration of much more that is important in the Latin literature of England. We can only hint at its variety. Scientific interests are represented by Alexander Neckham (1157-1217), whose *De Naturis Rerum*,[16] like Bartholomeus Anglicus's *De Proprietatibus Rerum* (*c.* 1230-50), ranges over the whole field of physical and natural science. Not content with Western scholarship, Adelard of Bath [17] traveled to Greece and Asia Minor in search of Arabic learning, and Daniel Morley went from Paris to Toledo gathering Arabic teachings on earthly and heavenly bodies (*De Naturis Inferiorum et Superiorum*). One of the greatest of medieval scientists, Roger Bacon (*c.* 1214-1294), who is also one of the few Englishmen who knew Greek in his century, covered in his *Opus Majus* not only mathematics and the sciences, but grammar, logic, and moral philosophy, experimenting with the microscope and pointing the way to the inductive methods of modern research.[18]

In the Middle Ages as now, each man wrote about the thing that interested him. Ralph de Glanville, appointed Chief Justiciar of England in 1180, produced a treatise invaluable for the historian, *De Legibus et Consuetudinibus Regni Angliae*. Osbern (fl., 1090), a monk of Christ Church, Canterbury, was given to translating saints' lives from Old English. Ailred of Rievaulx (*c.* 1109-1166), abbot of the Cistercian monastery of that name in Yorkshire, composed a rule for recluses and a number of works on religious and historical subjects. The great Bishop of Lincoln, Robert Grosseteste (*c.* 1175-1253) translated Aristotle's *Ethics* and wrote so extensively on science, mathematics, religion, etc. that the list of his works fills twenty-five closely printed pages.[19] An Englishman of the thirteenth century is supposed to have compiled that widespread collection of stories with a moral, the *Gesta Romanorum*,[20] at the same time that Odo of Cheriton (1247) was producing his Latin fables and his sermons on the Sunday gospels. In the fourteenth century Richard of Bury, Bishop of Durham (1287-1345), an indefatigable if sometimes unscrupulous book collector, expressed his love of books in a delightful treatise, the *Philobiblon*.[21] And, lest the preachers should be entirely neglected, room may be found for the mention of the *Summa Praedicantium* of John Bromyard (*c.* 1390), full of good stories and apposite illustrations.

[16] Edited by Thomas Wright for the Rolls Series (1863). On the general subject of medieval science see Lynn Thorndike, *A History of Magic and Experimental Science* (6v, 1923-41), and C. H. Haskins, *Studies in the History of Mediæval Science* (Cambridge, Mass., 1924).

[17] His *De Eodem et Diverso* was written about 1116. His other writings include *Questiones Naturales* and treatises on the abacus and the astrolabe.

[18] The *Opus Majus* has been translated by Robert B. Burke (2v, Philadelphia, 1928). His other writings include the *Opus Minus, Opus Tertium*, a *Compendium Philosophiae*, a Greek grammar, works on alchemy, etc.

[19] See F. S. Stevenson, *Robert Grosseteste* (1899) and S. Harrison Thomson, *The Writings of Robert Grosseteste, Bishop of Lincoln, 1235-1253* (Cambridge, 1940).

[20] An English translation is available in the Bohn Library (1877).

[21] Text and translation by E. C. Thomas (1888); translation separately (1902) in the King's Classics and now in the Medieval Library. In a number of MSS the work is attributed to Thomas Holkot.

An adequate survey of the medieval Latin literature of England would require a large volume. It is the purpose of the present chapter merely to suggest its wealth and variety and thus reveal the more intellectual side of English culture in the Middle Ages.[22]

[22] The student who wishes to pursue the subject further may consult the monumental work of Max Manitius, *Geschichte der lateinischen Literatur des Mittelalters* (3v, 1911-31), which unfortunately only reaches to the end of the twelfth century; Adolf Ebert, *Histoire générale de la littérature du moyen âge en occident,* trans. by J. Aymeric and J. Condamin (3v, 1883-89, superior to the German edition); F. J. E. Raby, *A History of Christian-Latin Poetry* (Oxford, 1927) and *A History of Secular Latin Poetry* (2ed, 2v, Oxford, 1957).

VI

Wit and Wisdom

In two previous chapters [1] we traced the survival of the Old English literary tradition in its most prevalent form, religious pieces in prose and verse. It is now necessary to note its appearance also in three works not of a religious nature, the *Proverbs of Alfred, The Owl and the Nightingale,* and Layamon's *Brut.* The first two of these we shall consider in the present chapter. Layamon's *Brut* we shall merely recognize as belonging with them in time and secular character, but we shall postpone the further consideration of it until chapter VIII, where we can better indicate its place in the development of the Arthurian legend. There is the more reason for this since in spite of being written in English and being in verse and style the heir of Old English poetry, it derives its subject matter from a French source.

Proverbs
of Alfred

The *Proverbs of Alfred* belongs to a very old type of didactic literature. There seems to be something perennial in the desire to hear universal truths even when they are so obvious as to be truisms. Nowadays the proverb is generally short and pithy, "the wisdom of many and the wit of one," as Lord Russell expressed it, and is thus justified by its cleverness and quotable quality. But there is apparently an equal disposition to treasure bits of homely wisdom distilled from experience, especially when clothed with authority, associated with the name of one who is reputed wise. It is this that accounts for the popularity of the sayings of "Poor Richard" in colonial America. In literature the proverb may also be a short discourse offering moral guidance or practical advice as in the Proverbs of Solomon, and it is this form which the *Proverbs of Alfred* takes. There is no reason to suppose that King Alfred is in any way responsible for the observations here attributed to him, but his reputation for wisdom was traditional and his name, like that of King Solomon, carried conviction to the average Englishman in the centuries following his death.

Their
Character

Bad luck has pursued this interesting Middle English text. What appears to have been the oldest and best MS [2] was mostly consumed in the fire that destroyed a part of the Cotton collection and damaged the Beowulf codex. Our next oldest text is also fragmentary [3] and a third MS was lost for thirty years. In its fullest form the *Proverbs of Alfred* consists of about thirty-five

---

[1] Chs. II and III.

[2] Brief extracts are preserved and recently three leaves have been identified and printed by N. R. Ker in *MA*, v (1936). 115-120.

[3] Discovered and published by Carleton Brown in *MLR*, xxi (1926). 250-260.

sayings amounting to a little more than 600 lines.[4] The precepts fall into three easily distinguished groups. In the initial group, consisting of the first eleven sayings, the advice is general or concerned with matters of public interest: a king should be learned and wise; earl and atheling should rule justly; wealth without wisdom is of little value; it is transitory and often the cause of a man's undoing; life itself is uncertain. In the middle group (sayings 12-29), the largest and most interesting section, the precepts concern personal conduct. There is advice on choosing a wife: choose her not for her face or her possessions—you may regret your choice the rest of your life. There are rather cynical warnings against failing to rule one's wife firmly, listening to her counsel, telling her too much of your business— "woman is word-mad." Other teachings concern friendship, sparing the rod, excessive drinking, misplaced confidence—believe not every man, confide not too much in others; a fair apple is often bitter inside. The suggestions are sometimes picturesquely and effectively expressed. Instead of telling every one of your sorrow

> Seie it þine sadel boȝe
> & rid te singinde

—tell it to thy saddle-bow and ride singing away. Much of this section and the next anticipates the advice of Polonius to Laertes. The last group of precepts is addressed to "my son so dear," resembling in this respect some of the proverbs of Solomon, and is of the familiar type of parental advice. It has to do chiefly with choosing one's companions, especially whom to avoid. Give the drunken man the road, cherish the old man's counsel, and the like. There is at the end a curious warning not to choose for a companion the little man, the "long" man, or the red-haired man.

The reputation of Alfred's proverbial sayings was already well established in the twelfth century. They are referred to in the twelfth-century part of the *Annals of Winchester* and mentioned by Ailred of Rievaulx, who died in 1166. But we cannot be sure that these allusions are to the *Proverbs* in written form, since in all likelihood such sayings circulated freely in oral tradition. In *The Owl and the Nightingale,* discussed below, in which *Dissemina-* proverbs are often quoted, eleven are specifically attributed to Alfred, but *tion* only three of these are found in the existing collection. Nevertheless it is almost certain that the literary form in which we have them goes back to

[4] The most recent edition is that of Helen P. South, *The Proverbs of Alfred Studied in the Light of the Recently Discovered Maidstone Manuscript* (1931). Valuable also is the edition of E. Borgström (Lund, 1908) for its complete texts of the Trinity and Jesus MSS and its critical apparatus. For a detailed study of the various versions and their relation see O. S. A. Arngart, *The Proverbs of Alfred:* I. *A Study of the Texts* (Lund, 1942). A slightly later collection is known as the *Proverbs of Hendyng.* Editions from different MSS will be found in Thomas Wright and J. O. Halliwell, *Reliquiae Antiquae* (1841-43), I. 109-116; K. Böddeker, *Altenglische Dichtungen des MS Harl. 2253* (Berlin, 1878), pp. 285-300; H. Varnhagen, in *Anglia,* IV (1881). 182-200; G. Schleich, "Die Sprichwörter Hendings und die Proverbis of Wisdom," *Anglia,* LI (1927). 220-277 (a critical text). S. Singer, "Die Sprichwörter Hendings," *Studia Neophil.,* XIV (1942), 31-52, offers a commentary and a reconsideration of the manuscripts. Modern renderings of both collections are in Jessie L. Weston, *The Chief Middle-English Poets* (Boston, 1914). For the gnomic poems of Old English see above, p. 43.

the twelfth century. The Cotton MS was written early in the thirteenth century and it is not the parent version. The language is more easily thought of as that of the twelfth than of the thirteenth century. The metrical form is essentially that of the Old English alliterative verse, much relaxed and threatening at any moment to break into three-stress lines, occasionally bound together into pairs by rime. The collection was probably put together in Sussex. As a work of literature the *Proverbs of Alfred* is interesting not only in its own right, but as an example of popular English tradition more secular than religious in its content.

The existence of such a work in the twelfth century causes no surprise. Though not religious, except incidentally, it has its roots in folk wisdom and it traces its authority to an Old English king. But *The Owl and the Nightingale* [5] is another story. Written not far from the year 1200, it is a truly amazing phenomenon in Middle English literature.

The Owl and the Nightingale

It is cast in the form of a debate, a heated argument between the two birds. The literary debate, very popular in the Middle Ages, is a form that is likely to flourish in a period of intellectual immaturity. It represents argument for the sake of argument, disagreement not through conviction but for the sake of matching wits. It is as though the individual has just discovered that he has a mind and enjoys the exercise of his new-found capacity. As we grow older and more polite we avoid arguments, and since nations and civilizations are somewhat like individuals, the artificial disputation has largely disappeared from our literature. The origin of the form has been traced back to the classical eclogue of Theocritus and Virgil,[6] which sometimes portrays a contest of skill between two shepherds. In the Middle Ages there are well-known examples as early as the eighth century. A *Conflictus Veris et Hiemis* is attributed to Alcuin and in the ninth century Sedulius Scotus composed *De Rosae Liliique Certamine.* Thereafter examples multiply and we get disputes between water and wine, the heart and the eye, youth and age, Phillis and Flora, Ganymede and Helen— academic, moral, witty, sometimes obscene. One of the most famous English examples is the *Debate between the Body and the Soul,* which will be discussed in the next chapter. The conventions of the type can be seen through the variety of subject matter and treatment. There is generally an opening describing the setting and the occasion for the debate or the circumstances under which the poet witnesses or overhears it. The debate itself follows in the form of actual dialogue, and a decision may or may not be rendered at the end. Often, as in *The Owl and the Nightingale,* the poet professes to be ignorant of the result.

Literary Debate

In the present instance the author comes upon the two birds in a secluded

---

[5] The best-known editions are those of J. E. Wells (1907, revised 1909; *Belles Lettres Ser.*), W. Gadow (1909; *Palaestra,* LXV), J. W. H. Atkins, with translation (1922), and J. H. G. Grattan and G. F. H. Sykes (1935; *EETSES,* 119).

[6] Cf. J. H. Hanford, "Classical Eclogue and Mediæval Debate," *Romanic Rev.,* II (1911). 16-31, 129-143.

spot in an unnamed valley. The Nightingale is perched in a thick hedge, safe from her opponent's claws, while the Owl occupies an old tree-stump. The Nightingale is the aggressor and provokes the argument by open insults. "Monster," she says, "fly away! I am the worse for seeing thee. Thy ugliness spoils my song. When I hear thy foul howling I would rather spit than sing!" The Owl waits until evening to reply, and although she is ready to burst with rage, she controls herself very well. The Nightingale, she says, wrongs her time and again. If once she would come out into the open, she would sing another tune. This, of course, the Nightingale declines to do, and instead continues to revile her opponent. "Thou art loathsome to behold.... Thy body is short, thy neck is small, thy head is greater than all the rest of thee." In this vein she accuses the Owl of unclean habits, raising a filthy brood that defiles its own nest, and being in general a symbol of all that is worthless, after which she breaks out into melodious song. The Owl listens perforce, puffed out and swollen "as if she had swallowed a frog." After a while the Nightingale, quite unreasonably, proposes that they stop their useless squabbling and proceed in a decent and orderly manner to argue their case before a suitable judge. The Owl agrees, but the Nightingale's tone does not undergo any noticeable change. The dispute turns upon the respective merits of their singing, but breaks over constantly into personalities and mutual abuse. Neither can see that the other serves any useful purpose. The Owl accuses the Nightingale of singing amatory songs and of enticing men and women to sin. The Nightingale retorts that the Owl is a bird of ill omen, whose song is ever of sorrow and misfortune. In the end the birds set out to lay their case before the judge—the Owl says she can repeat every word from beginning to end—but the poet disclaims knowledge of the outcome.

It would seem that so delightful and lively a poem might be allowed to stand as an example of the bird fable, as a story told for its own sake, without our seeking to find in it a hidden meaning which isn't there. But the *Not an Allegory* impulse to read allegorical significance into early works of literature, from which even the *Beowulf* has not escaped, has been at work also on *The Owl and the Nightingale*. The poem has been interpreted as symbolizing the antagonism between pleasure and asceticism, gaiety and gravity, art and philosophy, the minstrel and the preacher. Most recently it has been viewed as a conflict between the ideals of the newer love poetry of courtly origin and the religious, didactic poetry so prominent in medieval verse. A plausible case can be made out for all these interpretations and it is a pleasant exercise for one's ingenuity, but there is no necessity for seeing in the poem anything more than a lively altercation between two birds, with the poet's skill sufficiently revealed in the matching of wits, the thrust and parry of the opponents, the shrewd observation and homely wisdom for which the argument gives constant occasion. Its popularity is not easy to estimate. It survives in only two manuscripts, but there is record of a third and possibly also of a version in French which belonged in the fourteenth century to the abbey of Titchfield in Hampshire.[7] This is not far from the region in which, on the evidence of dialect and allusions, the poem was probably written. It is interesting to note that the two MSS in which it is preserved today are those in which many of the religious poems discussed above [8] as evidence of the survival of the native tradition have likewise come down to us. That the poem is of English inspiration appears likely not only from the general tone and the frequent citation of English proverbs, many of them attributed to Alfred, but from the fact that no source has been found for the debate as a whole. The author was familiar with the matter found in books on natural history, but the theme and conduct of the poem seem to have been largely his own invention.

Date

It seems rather likely that the poem was written during the twelfth century, although the attempt to fix upon a more precise date has led to sharp differences of opinion. The earlier of the two MSS in which it exists is assigned on paleographical grounds to the first half of the thirteenth century. It contains an Anglo-Norman chronicle which stops at 1216 and the rest of the page is left blank, contrary to the usual practice of the scribe, as if with an eye to its possible continuation.[9] The MS was most likely written at about this time. The extant texts of *The Owl and the Nightingale,* however, go back to an earlier copy, which was itself not the author's original. Allowing for a reasonable time to permit of these stages in its transmission, we may venture to assign the poem to a date before 1200. More precise dating depends upon the interpretation placed upon certain allusions in the text. Near the middle of the poem there is reference to an incident that happened in the time of King Henry, and the mention of the king prompts the poet to say "Jesus his soule do merci!" The king alluded to can hardly be other than Henry II, who died in 1189, and if the natural interpretation is placed upon these words and we infer that the king is dead, we must date the poem after, but perhaps not long after 1189.[10] A seemingly pregnant allusion to "this peace" has been connected with a proclamation of 1195.[11] An allusion to a papal mission to the north is less clear, and has been interpreted in various ways. On the whole, a date in the closing years of the

---

[7] See R. M. Wilson, "More Lost Literature, II," *Leeds Studies,* VI. 31-32.

[8] Ch. II.

[9] Although, as J. E. Wells has pointed out (*MLN,* XLVIII. 515-519), the blank half page comes at the end of a gathering, this is still the most natural interpretation.

[10] Some scholars who interpret other allusions as referring to an earlier date seek to show that the expression might have been used of a living person. See, for example, Henry B. Hinckley, "The Date, Author, and Sources of the *Owl and the Nightingale,*" *PMLA,* XLIV (1929). 329-359, and Kathryn Huganir, *The Owl and the Nightingale: Sources, Date, Author* (Philadelphia, 1931). Arguments against such an interpretation are presented by Frederick Tupper, "The Date and Historical Background of *The Owl and the Nightingale,*" *PMLA,* XLIX (1934). 406-427, and J. W. H. Atkins, "A Note on the Owl and the Nightingale," *MLR,* XXXV (1940). 55-56. For additional discussion by these and other scholars see the bibliographies mentioned on p. 109.

[11] J. Hall, *Selections from Early Middle English,* II. 566, notes the peace maintained by the Justiciar Hubert Walter during Richard I's absence in 1194-98, and Frederick Tupper, in the article referred to above, calls attention to the *Edictum Regium* of 1195 "requiring every man above the age of fifteen years to take an oath that he would do all that in him lay for the preservation of the King's Peace."

twelfth century would seem to agree best with the present state of our knowledge.

Naturally the authorship of such a poem is a matter of considerable in- *Authorship* terest. Near the beginning of the debate the birds agree to refer their differences to "Master Nicholas of Guildford," who is praised by the Nightingale as wise and prudent and an enemy of vice, one who has moreover insight in matters of song. The Owl remarks that he was rather passionate in days gone by and fond of the nightingales, but his ardor is now cooled and she will trust his judgment. Again at the very end of the poem his name is introduced with obvious explicitness and his place of residence is carefully specified as at Portisham, in Dorsetshire. He is shamefully neglected by the bishops, who bestow livings on their own kin, even on children, while passing him by. He has but one dwelling, whereas it would be for their own good if he were always at their service with livings in several places. He delivers many right judgments and much wisdom "through his mouth and through his hand," whereby things are better even as far away as Scotland. The most natural explanation of these passages is that the author was taking the opportunity to call attention to himself, and we should therefore seek to identify this Nicholas of Guildford. Various persons have been proposed, but none of them possesses all the qualifications for a completely satisfactory identification.[12] Whoever he was, he was a man of considerable learning, of an age to have left the wildness of youth behind him, a cleric living at the time he wrote the poem in the Dorset town of Portisham.[13]

The Owl and the Nightingale would have been a remarkable poem at any date, even in the time of Chaucer. It would cause perhaps less surprise about the year 1200 if it had been written in French. But the only thing French about it is the four-stress couplet in which it is cast. For a poem of 1704 lines to be written at this date in English on a secular theme, when almost everything that we have in English verse is either religious or didactic, is what seems so extraordinary. One remembers as comparable only occasional passages in Layamon's *Brut*. Its charm lies in its naturalness and freshness, the frankness with which the birds bring their accusations against each other, the liveliness and skill with which they meet each charge. They are very human in their emotions and their reasoning, but they never cease to be birds, each revealing the characteristics which are associated with its species in the popular mind. The poem is without a dull moment; it is a superb *jeu d'esprit,* the clearest proof that the English poetic impulse, in districts sufficiently removed from the court, survived the Norman Conquest.

[12] Gadow equates him with one of that name found in documents of the diocese of Salisbury in 1209 and 1220, but there is nothing to connect this man with Portisham. Miss Huganir suggests a certain Nicholas, son of Thorwald, who served as an itinerant judge in certain counties between 1179 and 1182. Nothing connects him, however, with either Guildford or Portisham.

[13] A note in the MS indicates that a song once in the volume was the work of a *John* of Guildford, but it is not necessary to believe that he was therefore the author of the present poem.

VII
For Their Soul's Need

In the period before 1250, when the popular literature intended for the upper class was almost certain to be in French, there is no more typical example of the writing produced for the religious instruction and moral guidance of the mass of the people than the *Ormulum*. Some of the most interesting and characteristic works of the period to be written in English were composed, as the author of this long poem tells us, to be read to the folk "for their soul's need."

The
Ormulum

The *Ormulum* [1] is a poem which, if it had been preserved in its entirety, would have reached the amazing length of 150,000 lines. We have, however, only about an eighth of it, some 20,000 short verses. As the author tells us in his preface,

> Þiss boc iss nemmnedd Orrmulum
> Forrþi þatt Orrm itt wrohhte,
> & itt is wrohht off quaþþrigan,
> Off Goddspellbokess fowwre. [2]

It would seem that Orm combined the ending of the Latin word *speculum*, so familiar in titles of medieval books (*Speculum Historiale, Speculum Vitae,* etc.), with his own name. It is possible that he was conscious of the diminutive force of the ending and was suggesting modestly that his effort should be thought of as "the little book of Orm." If so, it is the only evidence in the entire work that he had a sense of humor, for it would have filled ten volumes of modern print.

The name Orm (or Ormin) is Scandinavian. In the dedication addressed to Walter, his brother, Orm says that they were both members of the same religious order, the order of Augustinian canons. Attempts to identify him have not been successful, [3] but from his dialect it would seem that he lived in the northeast Midlands, possibly in northern Lincolnshire, and wrote about the year 1200. His laborious task was carried out at his brother's bidding and now that he has finished it he asks him to examine every verse and see that it contains nothing contrary to true belief. Conscious of his

---

[1] Ed. R. M. White (2v, Oxford, 1852) and Robert Holt (2v, Oxford, 1878).

[2] This book is named *Ormulum*
Because Orm wrought it,
And it is wrought of the *quadriga*
Of the four books of the gospel.

[3] For conjectures see Henry Bradley, "Where Was the *Ormulum* Written?" *Athenaeum,* May 19, 1906, p. 609, and James Wilson, *ibid.,* July 28, 1906, p. 104.

own rectitude he scorns detractors and rests confident that he will have earned his reward in Heaven.

What is the *Ormulum?* The author tells us that he has attempted with the little wit that the Lord has lent him—unfortunately not an understatement—to explain to ignorant folk most of the gospels that are read in the Mass throughout the year. From the list of Latin texts drawn up at the beginning as a kind of table of contents it is apparent that he went beyond the gospels and included also a number of excerpts from the Acts of the Apostles. His method is to begin with a paraphrase of the biblical passage and then to explain it in an extended exposition: *Its Purpose*

> Icc hafe sammnedd o þiss boc
> Þa Goddspelless neh alle,
> Þatt sinndenn o þe messeboc
> Inn all þe ʒer att messe.
> ⁊ aʒʒ affterr þe Goddspell stannt
> Þatt tatt te Goddspell meneþþ,
> Þatt mann birrþ spellenn to þe follc
> Off þeʒʒre sawle nede.

From this statement it might be inferred that the poet follows the missal and explains the gospel narratives as they occur day by day. This, however, is not what he does. He has reassembled the texts in a chronological arrangement, giving us the life of Christ in a series of episodes with homiletic interpolations. He has at times supplied links implying that his work was to be read consecutively and not in sections according to the gospel of the day. Where he found the materials for his explanations is still largely an unsolved problem.[4]

It must be admitted that in literary value the *Ormulum* approaches what the physicist calls the absolute zero. It is very tedious. Orm was careful not to overestimate the intelligence of his hearers, and he explains the obvious at painful length. He is a master of the art of writing without making the thought advance. He repeats himself shamelessly without so much as varying the phrase. He would have made a good pedagogue. Yet, paradoxically, the *Ormulum* is not without interest. In the first place, as a document in English cultural history it shows with what plain fare any literary taste of the humble classes might have to be satisfied when they were dependent for their books on the benevolent zeal of the pious. One can only hope that an abundant oral literature, though unrecorded, supplied what was missing from a well-balanced diet. In the second place, the *Ormulum* is not without interest as a revelation of human personality, for there *is* a personality be- *Its Value*

[4] The latest attempt at a solution is in H. C. Matthes, *Die Einheitlichkeit des Ormulum* (Heidelberg, 1933), where it is suggested that Orm used a *Biblia cum Glossis*, i.e., a text of the Bible provided with the interlinear gloss of Anselm of Laon (or more probably Peter Lombard) and the marginal commentary or *Glossa Ordinaria* commonly attributed to Walafrid Strabo. The present writer's objections to this theory are stated in *JEGP*, xxxvi (1937). 263-268. Cf. also Matthes' supplementary discussion, "Quellenauswertung und Quellenberufung im *Orrmulum*," *Anglia*, LIX (1935). 303-318.

hind it. It comes out most clearly in the dedication and the preface, but is apparent throughout the work. It is that of a completely serious nature, pursuing its laborious task with unswerving devotion and entire conviction. Orm is never in doubt about the importance of his mission. His zeal never flags. He is meticulous about little things, determined to be clear even to the dullest mind, for souls are at stake. He devises a new system of spelling,[5] thereby becoming our first spelling reformer, and admonishes future copyists always to write consonants twice where they are doubled in his copy: "otherwise they may not write rightly the word." He was obviously a "fussy" person, one that we might not enjoy living with, but distinctive. We would be touched by his piety and unselfishness, wearied by his prolixity, irritated by his insistence upon little things of no importance, but we would remember him. The reward which he deserved and confidently looked forward to in the next world is doubtless his, but the hope that his book would be often copied and widely read was never realized. What survives is apparently a fragment of his own holograph manuscript.

Vices and
Virtues

At about the same date as the *Ormulum* an anonymous treatise in prose was written in the East Midland area, probably in Essex. It has been given the name *Vices and Virtues,*[6] since the beginning is a soul's confession of its sins and the remainder an extended discourse by Reason on a wide variety of virtues. The treatise is cast in a slight framework of dialogue which amounts to little more than an occasional request by the soul for further instruction from Reason. Each vice or virtue is treated as a separate item without much attempt at continuity or strict sequence. Yet the occasional instances in which the preacher passes from the general to concrete and particular illustrations of his teaching, or drops a remark which hints at contemporary conditions, save the work from the dullness to which its commonplace matter and workaday style would predispose it. Once in a long while the author surprises us with a striking thought or picturesque phrase, as when he remarks that it is "a great wrath of God that man is so blind that he goes to Hell laughing." But in general he presents his matter plainly and soberly, in a manner consistent with his aim, expressed at the close through the mouth of Reason: "Dear soul, I have made this little writ with sore toil ... in order to instruct thee, to warn thee, and to help thee and to save thee."

Genesis
and
Exodus

Serving the soul's need in another way is the biblical paraphrase of *Genesis and Exodus*[7] written in its present form about 1250 in Norfolk, although probably originating somewhat farther north. It consists of slightly more than 4000 lines in fairly regular four-stress couplets. The author has great faith in human nature:

---

[5] The *Ormulum* is of the greatest value to the Middle English philologist in indicating for us the quantity of the vowels in the many words which it contains.

[6] Ed. F. Holthausen (London, 1888-1921; EETS, 89 and 159).

[7] Ed. Richard Morris (London, 1865; EETS, 7). The suggestion of Ten Brink that the *Exodus* might be by a different author is disposed of by A. Fritzsche, "Ist die altenglische *Story of Genesis and Exodus* das Werk eines Verfassers?" *Anglia,* v (1882). 43-90.

Cristene men ogen ben so fagen
So fueles arn quan he it sen dagen,
Ðan man hem telled soðe tale
Wid londes speche and wordes smale
Of blisses dune, of sorwes dale.[8]

And so he begins to tell the story of Genesis with many an interesting detail. The Devil was created on Sunday and "fell out" on Monday. Adam was made "in Damascus field." While God created woman Adam slept and saw in a dream much that should be hereafter. The woman's first name was Issa; after she brought us to woe Adam named her Eve. Abel was a hundred years old when Cain slew him. Such legendary matter is most prevalent in the first five hundred lines. The *Exodus* is more selective and considerably shorter than the *Genesis*. It is concerned mainly with the life of Moses. "Out of Latin," says the poet, "this song is drawn," and it is clear that he drew upon more than the Bible. He certainly used the *Historia Scholastica* of Peter Comestor and we may feel fairly sure that he used it at first hand.[9] It is equally certain that in the earlier pages he had other sources as well, possibly one of the biblical paraphrases in French verse. *Genesis and Exodus* lacks the poetical quality, the richness of phrase and emotional force, of the Old English *Genesis* and other Old English biblical poetry, but it tells its story clearly and easily, and by a judicious selection of incidents offers a pleasantly versified survey of early Old Testament history.

Written in the same dialect and at about the same time is the Middle English representative of a popular medieval type, the *Bestiary*.[10] The poem, some 800 short lines, is made up of descriptions more or less fabulous of the lion, eagle, serpent, ant, hart, fox, spider, whale, mermaid, elephant, turtle-dove, panther, and the culver or dove, followed in each case by a Christian application or moral. The *Bestiary* is associated in our minds with popular science, and doubtless it was for its natural history that it enjoyed its great popularity. But in plan and intention it was a work of religious and moral edification and should be so thought of. The fictitious natural history is adopted for the sake of the moral.

The Bestiary

Cethegrandë [whale] is a fiś [fish]
Ðe moste ðat in water is.

When the sea is stormy it comes to the surface. Sailors, thinking it is an island, take refuge on its back and build a fire. When the whale eventually feels the heat, it dives to the bottom, carrying all its too trusting victims

[8] Christian men ought to be as fain
As birds are when they see it become day,
When man tells them a true tale
With native speech and words small,
Of bliss's down [upland], of sorrow's dale.

[9] Cf. Fritzsche, *op. cit.,* p. 48.

[10] Edited several times but most accessible in Richard Morris, *An Old English Miscellany* (London, 1872; EETS, 49) and Joseph Hall, *Selections from Early Middle English* (Oxford, 1920). See also above, p. 136.

to destruction. It symbolizes the devil and his wiles. The serpent when old fasts until its skin grows loose about it; then it strips off its covering by crawling through a stone with a hole in it. Man by fasting and penance should in like manner free himself from the sins in which he has become enveloped. The elephant is made to illustrate all Christian history. It falls, like man, because of a tree; it cannot be raised by its fellows until one young elephant (like Christ) effects its release. The English poem is a free rendering of the Latin *Physiologus* of Theobaldus, an eleventh-century abbot, it is thought, of Monte Cassino. But all medieval bestiaries go back ultimately to a Greek text of the fourth century written in Alexandria, or, more probably, in Caesarea in Palestine,[11] and translated into Syriac, Armenian, and most of the European languages. The influence of the *Physiologus* on medieval art was widespread, and allusions to bestiary material are frequent in literature down to the Age of Elizabeth, when Lyly made unnatural natural history a feature of Euphuistic style.[12]

A religious theme which enjoyed equal popularity throughout Europe in the Middle Ages was the story of Christ's descent into Hell to release the souls of those who had lived worthily and died before His coming. The *Harrowing of Hell*[13] in Middle English verse was written about 1250. It is based on the apocryphal *Gospel of Nicodemus*,[14] which contributed not only this striking episode to literature but is largely responsible for the popularity of such legends as that of Longinus, who pierced Christ's side with his spear and was cured of blindness by the blood which fell on his eyes, of St. Veronica and her handkerchief, of Seth's mission to Paradise for the oil of mercy, of Antichrist, and other characters and incidents. The framework of the *Harrowing of Hell* is narrative, but after a forty-line introduction the account proceeds entirely by means of dialogue in which Adam and Eve, Abraham, David, John the Baptist, and Moses call confidently upon Christ and in each case have their claims acknowledged. The form of the text renders it suitable for dramatic presentation, but there is no evidence that it was ever so produced.

The Harrowing of Hell

The Body and Soul

The liveliest of the early religious and admonitory works considered in this chapter is a spirited debate known as the *Disputisoun between the Body and the Soul*.[15] The poet, lying in bed on a winter night, sees a mar-

---

[11] See Max Wellmann, *Der Physiologus* (Leipzig, 1930). The standard earlier authority is Fr. Lauchert, *Geschichte des Physiologus* (Strassburg, 1889); Lauchert is also the author of the article in the *Catholic Encyclopedia*.

[12] Cf. John Lyly, *Works*, ed. R. W. Bond (3v, Oxford, 1902), intro., I. 131-134.

[13] The text is edited from all MSS by William H. Hulme, *The Middle-English Harrowing of Hell and Gospel of Nicodemus* (London, 1907; *EETSES*, 100). For the development of the legend see Hulme's introduction and J. Monnier, *La Descente aux Enfers* (Paris, 1905). On the popularity of the theme in drama see Karl Young, *The Drama of the Medieval Church* (Oxford, 1933), I. 149-177, and the works mentioned on p. 561.

[14] The Latin *Gospel of Nicodemus* consists of two parts, the *Acta Pilati* (fourth century) and the *Descensus Christi ad Inferos* (second or third century). The text is in C. Tischendorf, *Evangelia Apocrypha* (Leipzig, 1876), English translation in M. R. James, *The Apocryphal New Testament* (Oxford, 1924). Versions in Middle English verse (c. 1300-1325) and prose exist, the verse texts being edited by Hulme, as above.

[15] Four of the seven manuscripts of the text are printed by W. Linow, *Þe Desputisoun bitwen þe Bodi and þe Soule* (Erlangen, 1889; *Erlanger Beiträge*, 1).

velous vision—the body of a proud knight lying on a bier. As the soul of the dead man is about to depart, it pauses and beholds the body from which it has just come. "Woe worth thy flesh, thy foul blood!" it says, and proceeds to taunt the Body truculently. Where now are its castles and towers, its rich clothes, its fine horses, its cunning cooks, through whose skill it made its foul flesh to swell? Now both Body and Soul shall suffer the pains of Hell. The Body retorts that it was the Soul's business to keep it from evil. But this simple exculpation does not suffice. "Body, be still!" says the Soul. "Who taught thee all this wit?" Both of us shall answer for our misspent life at Doomsday. Thou hast paid no heed to God. Now thou art loathsome to see: no lady would kiss thee: thy friends would flee if they saw thee coming down the street. The Body's rejoinder is that it did nothing without the Soul, that it would have been better off without a soul, like a dumb beast conscious of no hereafter. The Soul denies that it had any influence over the Body after its childhood, and the Body argues that more strict discipline in youth would have saved it. After this the Soul weeps and reiterates its charges of the Body's wilful ways. Finally the Body laments its past life, but as the Soul says, it is too late. Repentance is futile after death. And now the Soul may linger no longer. The fiends of Hell are heard crying exultantly as they come to fetch it away. There is a terrifying description of the tortures inflicted by the devils as they fall upon the unhappy Soul, and the dreamer awakes in a cold sweat because of the scene which he has witnessed.

The origin of this lively conception has been traced back to the Eastern *Its* church,[16] to a sermon, or sermons, of the *memento mori* type in which a *Origin* reminder of death is used as an inducement to virtue, and the admonition is pointed by an *exemplum* portraying the death of a sinful man amid the reproaches of the departing soul. There were apparently two types of this sermon: one a fairly common type in which only the soul speaks, and the other a type of which the only example yet known consists of some fragments embedded in an Irish homily of the *Leabhar Breac,* in which the body speaks in reply. The first may be considered the prototype of those Body and Soul texts in which the Soul addresses the Body, but the Body does not reply.[17] The second type is presumably the ancestor of the debates between the Body and Soul. The earliest literary treatment of the debate type is a long Latin poem of the twelfth century, the importance of which has only recently been demonstrated.[18] It is the source of a number of subsequent treatments in Latin, French, Spanish, etc. In spite of considerable merit, the poem is lacking in that lively interchange of accusation and rejoinder necessary to the true debate. This defect was supplied by a thirteenth-

---

[16] On the beginnings of the legend see Th. Batiouchkof, "Le Débat de l'ame et du corps," *Romania,* xx (1891). 1-55; 513-578, and Louise Dudley, · *The Egyptian Elements in the Legend of the Body and Soul* (Baltimore, 1911).

[17] Such as the Old English *Address of the Soul to the Body* (see above, p. 81) and the early Middle English text preserved in the *Worcester Fragments* (see p. 82).

[18] Eleanor Kellogg Heningham. *An Early Latin Debate of the Body and Soul* (1939).

century poem, the *Conflictus Corporis et Animae,* which may well have been the work of Bishop Grosseteste.[19] In this Latin form the Body and Soul theme attained its widest circulation,[20] and it is from this text that the Middle English poem derives.

Nearly all these works of religious edification or moral exhortation of the thirteenth century may be considered as patterns for later writings of a similar kind. The *Ormulum,* for example, may be compared with the *Northern Homily Cycle* (p. 205), the *Genesis and Exodus* with the earlier part of the *Cursor Mundi* (p. 206), the *Vices and Virtues* with *Handlyng Synne* (p. 204) or the *Parson's Tale.* Occasionally they inspired direct imitation as when an unknown poet modeled after the debate of the *Body and Soul* a similar dialogue between the *Body and the Worms.*[21] Always the motive is the same: each poet is writing for the people something "for their soul's need."

[19] See Hans Walther, *Das Streitgedicht in der lateinischen Literatur des Mittelalters* (Munich, 1920), pp. 70 ff.

[20] There are 132 MSS extant. The poem is often called the *Visio Philiberti.* Entering into the Body and Soul poems and many other religious works involving legends of Heaven and Hell are elements which received wide circulation in the Middle Ages through the apocryphal *Visio Pauli.* On this important text see Theodore Silverstein, *Visio Sancti Pauli: The History of the Apocalypse in Latin together with Nine Texts* (London, 1935; *Studies and Documents,* ed. K. and S. Lake, Vol. IV).

[21] Edited by Karl Brunner, *Archiv,* CLXVII (1935). 29-35.

VIII

The Arthurian Legend to Layamon

The most popular theme which later English poetry derived from medieval *The*
legend is the story of King Arthur, his wife, Guinevere, and the celebrated *Arthurian*
knights—Lancelot, Gawain, Perceval of Grail fame, and many others— *Legend*
associated with his court.[1] The origin of many of the stories which came
eventually to make up this complex body of material is obscure and we
cannot even be certain that an historical figure lies behind the character of
Arthur himself. In the present chapter we shall consider the development
of the legend up to Layamon, the point at which it first makes its appearance in English, reserving our treatment of the romances concerned with
this matter for a later chapter.

It is universally acknowledged that the story of Arthur belongs to Celtic *Of Celtic*
tradition and that it originated with the particular branch of the Celts settled *Origin*
in Wales and Cornwall. It seems to have remained largely a matter of local
interest until the twelfth, or as some believe, the eleventh century. It
achieved European circulation and renown with the publication of the
Historia Regum Britanniae (1137) of Geoffrey of Monmouth and the
Arthurian romances of the greatest of French writers of romance, Chrétien
de Troyes (fl. 1160-90).[2] On these simple facts there is general agreement,

---

[1] The first comprehensive work on the Arthurian legend was J. D. Bruce, *The Evolution of
Arthurian Romance . . . to . . . 1300* (2v, Baltimore and Göttingen, 1923; rptd. with supplement
to bibliography by A. Hilka, 1928; *Hesperia*, Ergänzungsreihe, VIII-IX). The subsequent
bibliography may be found in *Arthurian Bibliography*, Vol. I (1922-29), Vol. II (1930-35)
compiled by John J. Parry and Margaret Schlauch for the MLA (1931, 1936), and continued
for subsequent years in *MLQ*. E. K. Chambers, *Arthur of Britain* (1927) is a brief but stimulating treatment. For the earliest materials see Robert H. Fletcher, *The Arthurian Material in
the Chronicles* (1906; *Harvard Studies & Notes in Phil. & Lit.*, x). Edmund Faral's discussion
of this material, *La Légende Arthurienne* (3v, Paris, 1929), has a strong anti-Celtic bias. On
the French Arthurian romances the article of Gaston Paris, "Romans en vers du cycle de la
Table Ronde," *Hist. Litt. de la France*, XXX (1888), 1-270, is indispensable.

[2] Chrétien de Troyes is the author of the earliest Arthurian romances that have come down
to us: *Erec et Enide, Cligés, Lancelot* (or *Le Conte de la Charette*), *Yvain*, and *Perceval*, or
Le Conte du Graal. In addition, he mentions a poem on King Marc and Iseult which has not
survived but which must have been concerned with at least a part of the Tristan and Iseult
story. The extant romances of Chrétien were written in the order named, but they cannot be
dated more precisely than *c.* 1160-1190. (For an attempt to push the earlier date forward
somewhat, see F. E. Guyer, in *MP*, XXVI (1929). 257-277.) The standard editions of *Erec,
Cligés, Lancelot,* and *Yvain* are those of Wendelin Foerster (Halle, 1884-). These romances
have been translated into English by W. W. Comfort for the Everyman's Library (1913). The
Conte du Graal was left unfinished at Chrétien's death (about 10,000 lines) and continued
by a succession of continuators to a length of 60,000 lines. The text of Chrétien's portion is
now available in Alfons Hilka, *Der Percevalroman* (Halle, 1932), replacing the very scarce
edition of C. Potvin (6v, Mons, 1865-71). For a bibliography of Chrétien scholarship see John
R. Reinhard, "Chrétien de Troyes: A Bibliographical Essay," *Essays and Studies in English
and Compar. Lit.* (Ann Arbor, Mich., 1932), pp. 195-231, and Wilhelm Kellermann, "Wege

but on a number of other important questions scholarly opinion is sharply divided. How fully developed were Arthurian stories in Celtic literature? How much did Chrétien and other French poets owe to Celtic sources? Were there Arthurian romances in French before Chrétien? Was Arthur an historical figure? Did Geoffrey of Monmouth have an ancient book in the British tongue, as he maintained, even though his own work is demonstrably more than a translation of such a volume?

Celticists and Inventionists

On the first three of these questions scholars split sharply into two schools, the Celticists and the inventionists. The former are strongly impressed by the many parallels between the romances of Chrétien and of other medieval poets on the one hand and Celtic stories, folk-tales, and popular traditions on the other.[3] They believe that the writers of French romances derived an important part of their material from Welsh and Breton tradition, either written or oral. The opponents of this view, however, feel that the indebtedness of French authors to Celtic sources has been overstressed. They insist that Chrétien and his contemporaries were not folklorists but poets possessed with creative imagination, and that they enjoyed the same privilege of inventing their stories as do modern poets. It may be questioned whether what we know of the ways of medieval poets in other fields than Arthurian legend justifies the belief that they habitually exercised this privilege, but at least the position of the inventionists has the virtue of simplicity: what cannot be traced to a source fairly close at hand can be credited to the invention of the poet.

Scarcity of Welsh Texts

It must be admitted that the Celticists have sometimes pushed their quest for parallels pretty far, but the proper presentation of their point of view is rendered difficult by the paucity of Welsh and Breton literature that has come down to us from early times. For Brittany there are no literary texts from the Middle Ages. What survives from the Welsh literature of this period is mainly contained in four manuscripts that fill two moderate-sized volumes of modern print.[4] If the surviving Welsh literature were in any way comparable in richness to that of Ireland, where geographical and political separation permitted an unbroken continuity of language and literary tradition, many problems of Arthurian origins which must continue to trouble us would be readily settled. As it is, recourse must be had constantly to Irish literature. Since the Welsh and the Irish are merely different branches of the same ethnic and linguistic stock, it is to be assumed that they preserved many traditions in common and may well have influenced each other. Although Irish literature does not know Arthur, we find many parallels in incident and motif with Arthurian romance, which give us some

---

und Ziele der neuen Chrestien de Troyes-Forschung," *Germ-Rom. Monatsschrift*, xxiii (1935). 204-228.

[3] For examples of this view see the studies of Arthur C. L. Brown, particularly *Iwain: A Study in the Origins of Arthurian Romance* (Boston, 1903; *Harvard Studies & Notes in Phil. & Lit.*, viii.) and "The Round Table before Wace," *ibid.*, vii (1900). 183-205. A more extreme position is taken by Roger S. Loomis, *Celtic Myth and Arthurian Romance* (1927).

[4] W. F. Skene, *Four Ancient Books of Wales* (2v, Edinburgh, 1868).

idea of what we might expect in Welsh literature if it had been preserved in equal fullness. However, the existence among the *Mabinogion* [5] of a Welsh story like *Kulhwch and Olwen* with its obviously primitive features is an indication that a well-developed body of Arthurian narrative existed among the Welsh before such stories appear in French literature in the work of Chrétien de Troyes.

The Mabinogion

With the poems of Chrétien French romances of Arthurian theme reached their highest perfection in the Middle Ages. But these poems are also the earliest Arthurian romances that have come down to us, and therefore some students are disposed to credit Chrétien with the creation of the type. This is somewhat as if the author of *Hamlet* had been the inventor of English tragedy, or at least of the revenge play It is not usual for new literary types to spring fully formed from the heac of Jove, and such a method of accounting for *Hamlet* would not carry full conviction even if we could not trace the development of English drama back through the *Spanish Tragedy* and *Gorboduc* to the *Quem quaeritis* (see chapter xix). It is some such difficulty as this that many scholars find with the view that Chrétien was the creator of Arthurian romance. And, indeed, there is some evidence at least that Arthurian stories that could not have come from Geoffrey of Monmouth were known on the Continent at least by the time Chrétien was writing and probably as early as the close of the previous century. This is not the place to go into the evidence, which Pio Rajna called attention to,[6] of Italians who had been named after Arthur and Gawain before 1100, or the implications of the Arthurian sculpture on the cathedral at Modena in northern Italy, which some scholars date 1099-1106 and others put after the middle of the twelfth century.[7] It is enough for us here to recognize that there are many uncertainties in the early history of the Arthurian legend, many questions on which it is ill-advised to be too dogmatic.

Were There Arthurian Romances before Chrétien?

If Arthur played a part in actual history, it was as a leader of the Celts in their resistance to the Teutonic invaders at the beginning of the sixth century. The name is Roman (*Artorius*) and suggests a Roman family settled in Britain. We know of a Roman military man who held a high com-

Arthur

---

[5] The *Mabinogion* has become almost an English classic in the translation of Lady Charlotte Guest, which has often been reprinted. A critical edition of the Welsh text with scholarly apparatus and a more literal, French translation will be found in J. Loth, *Les Mabinogion* (2ed., 2v, Paris, 1913).

[6] Pio Rajna, "Gli eroi brettoni nell' onomastica italiana del secolo xii," *Romania*, xvii (1888). 161-185, 355-365.

[7] The bibliography of this controversy has become too extensive to record here. The arguments for an early date are presented (with excellent plates) by Roger S. Loomis in "The Date, Source, and Subject of the Arthurian Sculpture at Modena," *Medieval Studies in Memory of Gertrude Schoepperle Loomis* (Paris, 1927), pp. 209-228, and "La Légende archéologique à la cathédrale de Modène," *Gaz. des Beaux-Arts*, xviii (1928). 109-122. The most recent attacks on an early date are Leonardo Olschki, "La Cattedrale di Modena e il suo rilievo Arturiano," *Archivum Romanicum*, xix (1935). 145-182, and G. H. Gerould, "Arthurian Romance and the Date of the Relief at Modena," *Speculum*, x (1935). 355-376, to which Professor Loomis has replied in "The Modena Sculpture and Arthurian Romance," *Studi Medievali*, n.s. ix (1936). 1-17, and "Geoffrey of Monmouth and the Modena Archivolt," *Speculum*, xiii (1938). 221-231. From these articles the previous scholarship on the question can be assembled.

mand in the island in the third century,[8] and who might have left numerous descendants in a profession which was traditional in Roman families. There is no mention of Arthur in any contemporary record, and we cannot but consider it strange that Gildas,[9] who mentions the battle of Mount Badon—in later accounts Arthur's most famous battle—makes no mention of Arthur, but names Ambrosius Aurelianus as the distinguished Roman leader of the Celtic forces. The earliest explicit mention of the Arthur of later romance is

Nennius

in a compilation of around 800 known as the *Historia Brittonum,* by Nennius.[10] Here Arthur receives a paragraph and is said to have been twelve times chosen as the leader of the Celts and to have been victorious in twelve great battles. In the last of these, the battle of Mount Badon, he is credited with killing 960 of the enemy single-handed. It is clear that in Nennius Arthur has already become the object of legendary exaggeration, but it is interesting to observe that Nennius describes him as *dux bellorum,* not as a king, and explicitly says that there were many more noble in rank than he. This seems to ring true, and in spite of the lack of trustworthy evidence, most scholars are disposed to agree with Oman when he says, "I . . . incline to think that a real figure lurks beneath the tale of the *Historia Brittonum.*"

It would be interesting to pause over the bits of Arthurian material in the *Annales Cambriae* (c. 954),[11] in the *Chronicle of Mont St. Michel* (after 1056) in which Arthur is called "Rex Britannorum," in the lives of certain Welsh saints,[12] the miracle reported by Herman of Tournai some time after 1113,[13] and the testimony of William of Malmesbury to the existence of popular traditions concerning Arthur in his *Gesta Regum Anglorum* (1125) since this is the work of an Englishman. None of these texts throw any light on the historical character of Arthur, but they would bear witness to his growing popularity and the existence of numerous legends about him as well as about Gawain, Kai, Bedevere, and others associated with him. We must, however, turn at once to the most important work in the earlier history of this legend.

Geoffrey of Monmouth

Geoffrey of Monmouth (c. 1100-c. 1155) was born and reared in Wales, though possibly of Breton stock,[14] and, like Sir Walter Scott later, must have been saturated from childhood with the folk tales and traditions of the story-

[8] Cf. the art. "Artorius" in Pauly-Wissowa, *Real-Encyclopädie,* Charles Oman, *Englana before the Norman Conquest* (1910), p. 211, Kemp Malone, "Artorius," *MP.* xxii (1925). 367-374, and R. G. Collingwood and J. N. L. Myres, *Roman Britain and the English Settlements* (Oxford, 1936), pp. 320-324.

[9] The *De Excidio et Conquestu Britanniae* (written about 545) gives after a fashion an account of the history of Britain (first twenty-six chapters) but the greater part of the treatise is an attack upon certain rulers in Gildas's own day, the policy of forming an alliance with the Teutons, and the vices of the British people which have brought their present misfortunes upon them. He also makes no mention of Constantine, Germanus, Hengist, and others whom he might be expected to refer to. The standard edition is that of Mommsen in the *Mon. Germ. Hist.* (1898). There is a translation in John A. Giles, *Six Old English Chronicles* (1848).

[10] The standard editions are those of Mommsen, *op. cit.,* and Ferdinand Lot, *Nennius et l'Historia Brittonum* (Paris, 1934). Translation also in Giles.

[11] On these matters see Bruce, and other works mentioned in the footnote on p. 165.

[12] Cf. the most recent examination of these texts by J. S. P. Tatlock, "The Dates of the Arthurian Saints' Legends," *Speculum,* xiv (1939). 345-365.

[13] See E. Faral, "Un des plus anciens textes relatifs à Arthur," *Arthuriana,* i (1929). 21-29.

[14] See Sir John Edward Lloyd, "Geoffrey of Monmouth," *EHR,* lvii (1942). 460-468.

loving Celts. From the age of about thirty he was living as a canon at Oxford, and, having friends like Walter the Archdeacon and Robert de Chesney, must have looked forward in like manner to a career in the Church. Whether obeying an innate urge or acting with an eye to promotion, he produced a book ostensibly recording the early history of Britain, the *Historia Regum Britanniae* (1137).[15] It is full of legendary matter that has found its way into later English literature—stories of Locrine, Lear, Gorboduc, Cymbeline, and the like. What is more important, it reaches by the middle of Book VI the figures of Uther Pendragon and Merlin, and continues with Arthurian matters to the end of the work. In all about two-fifths of a sizable volume are devoted to the doings of King Arthur.[16] We get the story of his birth and Merlin's share in the affair between Uther and Ygerne. Upon Uther's death, Arthur becomes king, subdues the Picts and Scots, conquers Ireland, Iceland, Norway, Dacia, Aquitaine, and Gaul, with of course the help of Gawain and other loyal supporters. There is an excellent account of his single combat with Frollo, governor of Gaul. He celebrates his victories with a magnificent court and coronation ceremony attended by princes from all over western Europe. In the midst of the revelry Rome demands tribute of the Britons, a demand which is not only scornfully rejected but which leads Arthur to determine on the conquest of the imperial city. He commits the government and Queen Guanhumara to his nephew Mordred and sails for the Continent, only to be recalled by his nephew's treason and his wife's disloyalty. There is an account of Guinevere's flight to a nunnery, the defeat of Mordred, and the carrying of the mortally wounded Arthur to Avalon. Here is the full framework of the story so well known to us in later times. In it Arthur occupies the center of the stage and has not yet been thrust into the background by the adventures of his famous followers. He is represented as a great warrior, conquering all the better known parts of the world, rather than as a fairy king holding sway over a realm not too clearly defined.

In the dedication and in three other places in the volume Geoffrey claims *His* as his authority a certain ancient book in the British tongue—that is, in *Avowed* Welsh or Breton—which he was given by his friend Walter, Archdeacon of *Source* Oxford. This book, he says, related in due sequence and in stories of exceeding beauty the whole history of the island from Brutus, the first king of the Britains, down to Cadwallader, the son of Cadwallo. All he has had to do is to turn it into simple and unadorned Latin. This modest avowal is not to be taken too seriously. No such book is known and in his later references to it the author, it strikes us, "doth protest too much." It is hard to reconcile his close paraphrases and direct borrowings from Gildas, Nennius, Bede, Livy, and even Virgil, with the idea of a simple translation of a Celtic book, to say nothing of the appearance, thinly disguised, of numerous incidents

---

[15] The text is conveniently available in Acton Griscom, *The Historia Regum Britanniae of Geoffrey of Monmouth* (London, 1929) and Edmond Faral, *La Légende Arthurienne* (3v, Paris, 1929).

[16] Geoffrey of Monmouth is possibly the author also of a Latin poem of 1529 lines on the life of Merlin. Text and translation will be found in J. J. Parry, *The Vita Merlini* (Urbana, 1925).

in recent history transferred to ancient times. Geoffrey's *Historia* is a mixture of matter drawn from previous books, the products of his own free invention, and probably a large element of legendary lore. It would not have done to admit that what purported to be a serious history was partly fiction and partly a synthesis of old wives' tales.[17]

The popularity of Geoffrey's history, whatever some of his contemporaries thought of its validity, was very great,[18] but its enjoyment was naturally limited to those who could read Latin. For a large number of men and women at the court it would have remained a closed book if it had not been translated. Several translations, indeed, soon appeared in French verse, among them one by Geoffrey Gaimar, another by Wace. Gaimar's version is lost,[19] no doubt a victim of neglect after the appearance of Wace's more bril-

Wace

liant rendering, the *Roman de Brut* (1155).[20] Wace was a Norman poet (*c.* 1100-*c.* 1175) who wrote under English patronage.[21] In his 15,000 lines he converted Geoffrey's dignified prose narrative into a lively and vigorous story. Geoffrey was ostensibly writing history; Wace was writing a poem. He paints vivid pictures, dramatizes important incidents, gives expression to his personal feelings, and never seems to forget the audience he is aiming to please. He makes a few interesting additions to his source, and mentions three times the Round Table in a manner which suggests that it was already familiar to his audience. Yet these are the earliest references to it in literature. It is apparent that he was familiar with Arthurian traditions apart from what he found in Geoffrey of Monmouth.[22]

Layamon's
Brut

The Arthurian story makes its first appearance in English in the work of a humble priest living on the banks of the Severn in Worcestershire. As he tells us in the preface to his work, his name was Layamon [23] and he was attached to the church at Ernley (Arley Regis), near Radstone. While enjoying this quiet life of a clerk, he says, it came into his mind to write about

[17] On Geoffrey of Monmouth's literary practices see Vol. II of Faral, who minimizes, however, the elements that may have come from popular tradition.

[18] This is evident from the more than 200 manuscripts still extant. Alfred of Beverley, writing about 1150, says it was such a common subject of conversation that any one who did not know its stories was considered a fool. A part of its popularity may have been due to the satisfaction it gave the Anglo-French court to point to something in the past history of Britain comparable to Charlemagne and his peers in France. See G. H. Gerould, "King Arthur and Politics," *Speculum*, II (1927). 33-51.

[19] On Gaimar see above, p. 138. A text known as the Münchener *Brut* has sometimes been thought a fragment of Gaimar's version, but there are objections to this view. See the discussion by Alexander Bell, "The Munich *Brut* and the *Estoire des Bretuns*," *MLR*, XXXIV (1939). 321-354.

[20] Edited by Le Roux de Lincy (2v, Rouen, 1836-38). A new edition has now appeared in the *SATF*, edited by Ivor Arnold (2v, Paris, 1938-40).

[21] Layamon tells us that Wace dedicated the *Roman de Brut* to Eleanor of Aquitaine, and it was for her husband, Henry II, that he began a poem of similar character on the history of Normandy, the *Roman de Rou* (Rollo). See above, p. 138.

[22] See also Margaret Houck, *The Sources of the Roman de Brut of Wace* (Berkeley, 1941; *Univ. of Calif. Pub. in English*, Vol. V, No. 2).

[23] Properly Laȝamon. The spelling *Layamon* is a concession to printers' fonts sanctioned by usage. The guttural spirant was vocalized in the twelfth century to form a diphthong *au*, often written *aw*. Consequently some scholars prefer the modernization Lawman. The only edition of Layamon's *Brut* is that of Sir Frederic Madden (3v, 1847), where the two texts are printed in parallel. See also N. Bøgholm, *The Layamon Texts: A Linguistical Investigation* (Copenhagen, 1944; *Travaux du cercle linguistique de Copenhague*, III).

the noble deeds of the English, and with this purpose in view he traveled about in search of books on the subject. The three that he acquired were Bede's *Ecclesiastical History* in the Old English translation inspired by King Alfred; the Latin text of this, which he does not seem to have fully recognized; and the work of a French clerk named Wace ("how he could write!"). He set out to condense these three works into a single narrative, but it is clear that he soon found himself so completely under the spell of Wace that he put the other two aside and devoted himself to turning the *Roman de Brut* into English. Allusions in his poem show that he was writing after the death of Henry II (1189) and probably just before King John forbade the payment of Peter's pence in May, 1206. It is customary, therefore, to assign Layamon's *Brut* to the year 1205.

The English poem is twice the length of the French. The difference is due mainly to a certain leisurely manner that seems to characterize Layamon. *Layamon's Additions* He adds to an idea already adequately expressed a line of explanation or supplement; he sometimes repeats himself in only slightly different words. He did not aim at terseness or compression. To a slight extent the difference in length is due to new materials which he introduced. These are not numerous but have a certain significance. They include such things as the gifts which the elves conferred upon Arthur at birth, the description of his armor—its magic properties or fabrication by supernatural smiths—the dream in which he received warning of Mordred's treason, and added circumstances in the account of the passing of Arthur. But the longest and most interesting addition which Layamon makes is the story of the creation of the Round Table—describing the fighting that broke out at a Christmas feast over precedence at table, and telling how some time later when the king was journeying in Cornwall a skilful craftsman in wood offered to fashion him a table at which sixteen hundred or more could sit without discrimination yet which could be folded up and carried about from place to place. An attempt has often been made in the past to account for these additional features by suggesting that Layamon may have had a version of the *Roman de Brut* fuller in certain respects than that available in the edition of Le Roux de Lincy—in other words, an expanded Wace. But the recent publication of a new text based upon all the extant manuscripts does not support this view, and we must continue to suppose that Layamon, like Wace, was familiar with Arthurian traditions, oral or written, not found in his immediate source.

In spite of the fact that he was translating from a French source Layamon *Its English Character* is a thoroughly English poet. He had apparently been brought up on the Old English alliterative verse and his own lines are so clearly in this tradition that about half of them can be scanned by Old English standards. He makes frequent use of rime, however, as an additional ornament. The tradition which he represents is apparently a late one which has left behind some of the older practices and acquired certain new habits in their place.[24]

---

[24] See J. S. P. Tatlock. "Laȝamon's Poetic Style and Its Relations," *Manly Anniversary Studies* (Chicago, 1923), pp. 3-11.

Nevertheless it is still English. His vocabulary is remarkable for the small number of French words in it, particularly in view of the fact that he was translating from a French poem. But it is in those less tangible qualities of tone and spirit that he is perhaps most English of all.[25] In scores of little touches he adds to or alters a scene, an image, or an idea, until it appears something quite different from what it was in Wace. He has an eye for nature and outdoor life, the sea and the sky. Arrows fly as thick as hail; a cornered warrior is compared to a wild boar at bay; Childeric pursued by Arthur is likened to a fox with the dogs following close on his trail, seeking his hole only to be trapped. These are images drawn from his own observation, but he seems to be equally at home, at least in imagination, in describing animated scenes of feasting and revelry in hall and palace or the very different activities of war and the battlefield. Layamon is more than a translator; he is a poet and his effects are the effects of conscious art.

Layamon the Poet

This is the first and also for quite a while the last appearance of King Arthur in English. When he again returns to the island of his birth it will be after a considerable sojourn in France, a sojourn which has profoundly altered his character.

---

[25] See Henry Cecil Wyld, "Laȝamon as an English Poet," *RES*, VI (1930). 1-30.

IX
The Romance: I

To most people today the word *romance* [1] suggests a love story, and be- *Definition* cause some medieval romances involve famous love stories—such as those of Lancelot and Guinevere, Tristan and Iseult, Floris and Blancheflour— they assume that a love interest is a necessary ingredient in the romance of the Middle Ages. This is not strictly true. One has only to think of the romances of Alexander, Richard the Lion-Hearted, and many lesser figures to realize that medieval romance could get along very well with little or no love element. The basic material is knightly activity and adventure, and we may best put the emphasis in the right place if we define the medieval romances as a story of adventure—fictitious and frequently marvelous or supernatural—in verse or prose. Except for the few romances in which a love story is the main feature,[2] love, if it enters into the narrative at all, is either subordinated to the adventure (*Erec, Yvain*), or is incidental, as when a Saracen princess conceives a desperate passion for the hero (*Bevis of Hampton*), or is used as a motivating force, an excuse for the adventures of the hero (*Guy of Warwick*). It may be added that the earlier romances are in verse; those in prose are generally late. The former ordinarily range in length from one thousand to six thousand lines, with occasional productions running to nearly double this limit. The commonest metres are the eight-syllable couplet and a variety of tail-rime stanzas (*aabccb, aaabcccb*, and twelve-line stanzas of more elaborate pattern).

The romance in verse, in so far as it tends to be a narrative of heroic *Character-* adventure, has some things in common with the epic.[3] But it has less unity of *istics* action and the characters are not so well defined. Although occasional romances have a simple and skilfully managed plot, many are little more than

---

[1] The word *romance* comes from a Latin adverb *romanice*, meaning "in the Roman manner" (*loqui romanice*, to speak in the Roman manner, i.e., speak colloquial Latin). In time, with the change of Vulgar Latin into the various Romance languages, it came to mean more particularly French, and then something written in French, especially something translated from Latin. Samson de Nanteuil calls his metrical translation of the *Proverbs of Solomon* a romance. As was natural, however, the word came gradually to designate the most popular type of French poem and hence a poem of this type in any language. See Reinald Hoops, *Der Begriff 'Romance' in der mittelenglischen und frühneuenglischen Literatur* (Heidelberg, 1929; *Anglistische Forschungen*, No. 68).

[2] The type is better represented in France, where courtly love enjoyed greater vogue. For a treatment of these see Sarah F. Barrow, *The Medieval Society Romances* (1924; *Columbia Univ. Studies in English and Compar. Lit.*, No. 34).

[3] For an interesting paper suggesting that romance is transplanted epic, which has undergone a kind of sea-change in the passage, see N. E. Griffin, "The Definition of Romance," *PMLA*, xxxviii (1923). 50-70. For a stimulating discussion of the whole subject see W. P. Ker, *Epic and Romance* (2ed., 1908).

a loose succession of incidents strung on a biographical thread. The characters of medieval romance are poorly differentiated. They are types rather than individuals. The hero conforms to a pattern, that of the ideal knight, and within the pattern there is little room for individual variation. Lancelot, Tristan, Gawain—they are hardly distinguishable, although we can occasionally recognize Lancelot by catching a glimpse of Guinevere in the background, or Tristan if he is contriving a secret meeting with Iseult. Since the romance deals for the most part with types and the hero is himself an idealized type, the action likewise does not admit of great variety. There is only one way in which a knight may prove himself worthy to be the hero of the story and that is by showing himself superior to other knights. Now the ways in which one may dispose of an opponent in tournament or battle are limited, and it is therefore not surprising that the poet occasionally foists in a giant or a dragon to lend variety to his hero's adventures. Yet in spite of the obvious weaknesses of the genre—weakness in plot, faintness of characterization, sameness of incident—it is surprising how interesting the individual romance, taken by itself, contrives to be.[4]

An Aristocratic Genre

The romance in its beginning was an aristocratic type appealing to the tastes of the upper class. As long as French remained the normal language of the English ruling classes the romances that circulated in England were French and those written in England were written in French. This means that romances in English are not to be expected until English begins to displace French as the language of polite society, that is, until the middle of the thirteenth century. There is only one English romance that can be dated with certainty earlier than 1250. Unfortunately by this time the romance in France, and indeed in Europe generally, had passed its prime. The great

English Romances Late

creative period of medieval romance was the twelfth century,[5] and the beginning of the thirteenth. By the end of the latter century the type begins to deteriorate. Poets, chewing over the old straw, are driven to desperate measures to make it seem more palatable. Overstraining after effect replaces the easy confidence of a Chrétien de Troyes or Gottfried von Strassburg. Most of our English romances belong to the fourteenth century and nearly all of them are translations or adaptations from French originals. Yet while they seldom come up to the level of medieval romance at its best, it must not be thought that they are quite what readers of Chaucer might infer from *Sir Thopas*.

The "Matters" of Medieval Romance

While medieval romance was at the height of its popularity a Continental poet, Jean Bodel, wrote in his *Chanson des Saisnes*:

N'en sont que trois materes a nul home entendant
De France, et de Bretaigne, et de Rome la grant.

---

[4] Years from now any one curious about our current mystery stories will probably find in them a similar tendency to run to type, yet the individual story manages to be interesting.

[5] The romance is a product of the twelfth century, along with the troubadour lyric, the great cathedrals, scholastic philosophy, and other evidences of the creative mind at work in this renaissance period. See Haskins, as above.

It has been customary ever since to speak of medieval romance under these headings—the Matter of Rome, by which is meant romances based on classical history and legend, the Matter of France, meaning stories of Charlemagne and his peers, and the Matter of Britain or the Arthurian cycle. This is a fairly adequate statement of aristocratic taste on the Continent, but it needs to be supplemented in one direction for England. It leaves out of account a group of romances of great interest. These are the romances concerned with native English heroes or with a figure like Havelok the Dane, whose fortunes are tied up with England and whose principal adventures take place in the island. Later it would have been necessary for a comprehensive classification to take cognizance of many romances of Eastern and other exotic themes.

i. *The Matter of England*

It is possible to suppose that when the English language spread to the upper class it was adopted first by those whose interests were less closely bound up with the Continent and who were more ready to identify themselves with the people among whom they lived. And it may equally well be that having come to look upon England as their country of first allegiance they were interested in stories about English worthies. At all events, we cannot help noticing that most of the romances, and certainly the most popular, written in English before 1300 were concerned with English subjects and that only after 1300 do we find stories of the Charlemagne and Arthurian cycles or of classical legend being adapted for a public that now preferred its entertainment in English rather than in French.[6]

The two earliest of these romances, it would seem, are *King Horn* and *Havelok the Dane*. The former has often been placed as far back as 1225, but the basis for so early a date is very questionable. We must distinguish here, as in the case of *Havelok,* between the underlying legend and the romance in its English form. A more conservative date about 1250 for the English versions of both stories seems safer. *King Horn*[7] relates the adventures of a prince who is driven out of his country by pagan invaders, but in the end wins back his possessions and throne—the so-called exile and return motif. During the hero's youth his father's kingdom of Suddene (in southwestern Scotland) is invaded by people called Saracens in the poem, but apparently Scandinavians. With a dozen companions he is set adrift in a boat which carries him to the Mull of Galloway.[8] Here he is loved by

King Horn

---

[6] The only exceptions to this generalization are *Floris and Blancheflour*, of the first half of the thirteenth century, and *Arthur and Merlin* and *King Alisaunder*, which may have been written shortly before 1300.

[7] Editions by J. Hall (Oxford, 1901), G. H. McKnight (1901; *EETS*, 14), and T. Wissmann (Strassburg, 1881; *Quellen u. Forschungen*, XLV). The text of this and a number of other romances discussed in the present chapter can be read conveniently in W. H. French and C. B. Hale, *Middle English Metrical Romances* (1930). For an excellent discussion of the date, versions, etc., of *King Horn* see Laura Hibbard, *Mediæval Romance in England* (1924), pp. 83-102. See also W. H. French, *Essays on King Horn* (Ithaca, 1940).

[8] The most convincing attempt to explain the hitherto baffling geography of the romance is that of Walter Oliver, "*King Horn* and Suddene," *PMLA*, XLVI (1931). 102-114. In this con-

the king's daughter Rimenhild, but he is forced through the treachery of a companion to leave the country. After the lovers have sworn to remain faithful for the usual seven years he goes to Ireland. He fights valiantly for the Irish king and remains in his service until recalled by a message from Rimenhild. With the help of Irish soldiers he returns in time to prevent her marriage to an unwelcome suitor. The same warriors help him to regain his own kingdom, whereupon he comes back and marries the much harassed but faithful and romantically patient lady. This simple action is built up with enough good fighting, dangers, narrow escapes for Rimenhild, and conduct worthy of both hero and heroine to make it a lively and satisfying tale.[9]

Havelok

The romance of *Havelok* [10] has a somewhat more artfully constructed plot. The heroine is an English princess named Goldborough, left an orphan at the tender age of two. While she is growing up, the country is ruled by a regent named Godrich, who has promised her father not only to preserve the kingdom for her but to marry her to the best, fairest, and strongest man living. Instead he shuts her up in Dover Castle. This constitutes the first part of the story. In part two we make the acquaintance of Havelok, who is in somewhat like fashion the victim of treachery. When his father, the King of Denmark, dies the boy is given over to a trusted councilor named Godard, who rewards the confidence placed in him by arranging with a fisherman named Grim to have Havelok drowned. A luminous mark on the boy's shoulder and a bright light which issues from his mouth, however, tell Grim as plainly as words that he is the royal heir. So the fisherman flees with his family and Havelok to England and settles near the mouth of the Humber at a place afterwards called Grimsby. There with his sons he pursues his occupation of fishing, and Havelok sells his basket of fish like the rest. In time the lad grows big and very strong. When a famine occurs he is unwilling to be a burden on Grim and seeks employment in Lincoln, the nearest large city. He gets a job with the Earl of Lincoln's cook and is a great favorite with everyone.

It is necessary now for the poet to find some way of bringing the hero and

---

nection cf. the resemblances to the legend of St. Cuthbert pointed out by Irene P. McKeehan, "The Book of the Nativity of St. Cuthbert," *PMLA*, xlviii (1933). 981-999.

[9] The story is treated in a later English version, *Horn Childe and Maiden Rimnild*, found in the Auchinleck MS (printed in an appendix in Hall and by Caro, below), and in ballads telling the episode of Horn's return to save Rimenhild (*Hind Horn*, Child, No. 17). It was adapted in French by Geoffrey de la Tour Landri and in this form was turned into English prose in the fifteenth-century *King Ponthus and the Fair Sidone* (ed. F. J. Mather, Jr., *PMLA*, xii (1897). 1-150). The origin of the legend and the relation of the versions, English and French, are much disputed questions. In addition to the references given in a previous note see especially T. Wissmann, *King Horn: Untersuchungen* ... (Strassburg, 1876; *Quellen u. Forschungen*, xvi); J. Caro, "Kleine Publikationen aus der Auchinleck-Hs: Horn Childe and Maiden Rimnild," *ESt*, xii (1889). 323-366 (text and study); O. Hartenstein, *Studien zur Hornsage* (Heidelberg, 1902; *Kieler Studien*, iv); W. H. Schofield, "The Story of Horn and Rimenhild," *PMLA*, xviii (1903). 1-83; Paul Leidig, *Studien zu King Horn* (Borna-Leipzig, 1927); Leslie G. Burgevin, "The Origin and Development of the Saga of King Horn," *Harvard Univ. ... Summaries of Theses, 1931*, pp. 212-215.

[10] Edited by W. W. Skeat (revised by K. Sisam, Oxford, 1915), and by F. Holthausen 3ed., Heidelberg, 1928); earlier ed. by Skeat in *EETSES*, 4 (1868).

heroine together. A parliament which Earl Godrich convenes at Lincoln offers a convenient excuse. In the festivities called forth by the occasion Havelok wins a prize and much local fame by putting the stone twelve feet farther than any other man. When Godrich hears of this record-breaking achievement he has an idea. He has sworn to marry Goldborough to the best, fairest, and strongest man in England. He will marry her to Havelok, the kitchen knave! Goldborough is forced to submit to the marriage, outrageous as it seems to her. However, one night as she lies beside Havelok, bewildered and somewhat resentful, she sees the luminous mark on his shoulder and is told by an angel that she is married to a king's son. Filled with joy, she kisses him. This unexpected attention wakes him up from a dream in which he has seen all Denmark and England subject to him. With the help of Grim's three sons he invades Denmark and wins the support of a Danish noble named Ubbe, especially when Ubbe discovers the great light that issues from Havelok's mouth as he sleeps. It is of 107 candlepower. Havelok regains his kingdom, conquers England, and rewards all who have been good to him, especially the Earl of Lincoln's cook. He and Goldborough live a hundred years and have many children. As a final word the poet begs his hearers "to say a paternoster for him that hath made the rime and therefore sat up many nights."

It has seemed well to tell the story of *Havelok* at some length to show that English romances are not all formless and that authors of medieval romance could occasionally construct a good plot. Notwithstanding its naïve elements suggestive of the fairy tale *Havelok the Dane* is a well-planned story. As in *King Horn*, the emphasis is on the adventure. Neither romance has much of the glamour or sophistication of courtly society. In fact *Havelok* is almost democratic in tone. There is respect for honest labor, the hero is associated most of the time with common people, and such people and their activities play a large part in the story. His great triumph is not in knightly competition but in putting the stone. The charm of his character is not revealed in courtly graces, but in homely and natural virtues—a cheerful, sunny disposition which makes the children and the cook like him, a readiness to accept without question his humble lot as a fisher boy and scullery knave. Though both *King Horn* and *Havelok* are based on earlier French narratives,[11] they seem to reflect the spirit of the English middle class, or to be the work of minstrels little acquainted with the ways of the court.[12] It is among such that we might well look for the authors of romances at a time when the upper class was just beginning to adopt English in numbers. While dating these two romances *c.* 1250, we must allow for minor revisions at least in *Havelok* shortly after 1300.[13]

Bourgeois Elements

[11] For the French versions see above, pp. 138, 141.

[12] Defects in one of the MSS show that both romances were copied from an original with only twenty lines to a page. Such a book, if 3½x4 inches in size and composed of 120 leaves, would have held *Horn* and *Havelok* and been very convenient for a minstrel.

[13] England is twice described as extending from Roxburgh to Dover, which could hardly be said until Roxburgh became a border fortress in 1296 (J. W. Hales, *Folia Litteraria,* pp.

Guy of
Warwick

Enjoying the widest popularity and longest life accorded to any English romances were two stories written about 1300, *Guy of Warwick* and *Bevis of Hampton*. The former has been preserved in four versions ranging in length from seven to twelve thousand lines.[14] It is very typical of romances in which everything is subordinated to adventure. It consists of the individual encounters of the hero with an endless succession of adversaries. The excuse is love. Felice, daughter of the Earl of Warwick, will not consider marriage with the hero, who is only the son of her father's steward, until he proves his worth in the field. After many victories Guy returns hopefully, only to be told by his sweetheart that she will marry a mere knight only if he is the best knight in the world. Guy's mingled disappointment and unquenchable hope are the incentive for a wide variety of additional combats and adventures, after which the rather difficult mistress is satisfied and the marriage takes place. Here the romance would have had to end and perhaps originally did end. But an excuse was found for continuing it. After a few months of married life Guy's conscience hurts. All his achievements have been for a selfish end, to win the love of Felice. He feels that he should do something for God, fight against the infidel in the cause of the true faith. Accordingly with Felice's consent he sets out on a third series of adventures, and when he returns he has little more than time to withdraw from the world and compose his soul for death. This part of the romance is reminiscent of the crusades, and the spirit of renunciation and humility in which he spends his last days in his lonely cell almost suggests the possibility of a monkish hand in this part of the story.

Its
Popularity

By the year 1410 the fame of *Guy of Warwick* had spread even to the Holy Land where the Sultan's lieutenant remarked that they had the story in books in their own language. In England it was published by the earliest English printers and in the Elizabethan period was made into ballads and plays. In the seventeenth century it was told in poems of epic proportions and was also adapted to the tastes and purses of the plebeian citizenry in the form of chapbooks that lasted on into the eighteenth century, when it became the object of antiquarian interest.[15] Such popularity was no doubt due in part to the belief that the romance had an historical foundation. The story is laid in the reign of Athelstan (925-940), the grandson of King Alfred. In the romance Guy returns to England in time to take a leading part in Athelstan's fight with the Danes. Guy's fight in single combat with Colbrand, the Danish champion, was accepted as fact for a long time and was told in a number of chronicles as sober truth—so well did the storyteller

---

30-39). The only Parliament held at Lincoln was in 1300. Such details suggest that the story was brought up to date shortly after the turn of the century.

[14] A French romance of *Gui de Warewic*, earlier than the English, exists in thirteen MSS (ed. Alfred Ewert, 2v, Paris, 1932-33; *CFMA*, 74-75). The English romance, in various versions, is edited by J. Zupitza (1875-91; *EETSES*, 25, 26, 42, 49, 59).

[15] See Ronald S. Crane, "The Vogue of *Guy of Warwick* from the Close of the Middle Ages to the Romantic Revival," *PMLA*, xxx (1915). 125-194. The larger aspects of the survival of medieval romance are studied in the same author's dissertation (Univ. of Pennsylvania), on which the above article is in part based.

do his work. Patriotism thus combined with interest in the story to keep the romance alive long after better romances were forgotten.

Equally famous were the adventures of Bevis of Southampton. We have romances, often in several versions, from France, Italy, Scandinavia, and the Netherlands, to say nothing of two in Celtic and several in Slavonic. The story begins with a variant of the Hamlet theme. Bevis's mother plots her husband's death and afterwards marries the murderer. Bevis is sold to foreign merchants, and in time is taken into the service of Ermin, King of the Saracens. Ermin's daughter Josian falls in love with him and most of his adventures grow out of his efforts to maintain his reputation as a Christian knight amidst pagan envy and treachery, or else to defend Josian against her Saracen suitor. In the end marriage and the recovery of his inheritance give him twenty years of happiness before he dies. *Bevis of Hampton* is not a remarkable example of medieval romance. It is made up of stock motifs and episodes—the January and May marriage of Bevis's parents, the child ordered to be put to death but spared through the pity of the servant, the hero sold to heathen merchants, the ubiquitous Saracen princess, fights with giants, wild boars, dragons, the wicked steward who tries to steal the credit for the hero's exploit, as in *Tristan and Iseult,* etc. The articulation of the episodes is loose and inexpert. What gives the romance its chief distinction is its exuberance, its racy, buoyant style, and the spirit of broad humor in which it is written. A thirty-foot giant whom Bevis fights was among his own people so small that everybody picked on him. They called him the dwarf and he was forced to run away. When Bevis fells him and is on the point of cutting off his head, Josian suggests sparing him that he may be her page. When Josian is baptized they decide to baptize the giant too. A special font is constructed, but when the bishop attempts to push him in he leaps out and cries, "Priest, wilt thou drown me? ... I am too big to be Christian." The author wrote with evident gusto, which has not always been appreciated. His learned German editor says, "The strain in which this work is written is serious, even severe." [16]

Richard Cœur de Lion [17] is one instance in which history really furnished a hero and a series of adventures adequate and ready to the poet's hand for the purposes of romance. Richard I as a ruler would not have inspired much enthusiasm among the English. He looked upon his office as a means to an end, and spent only six months of his ten-year reign in England. But his adventurous nature, his daring exploits and personal triumphs as the leader of the Third Crusade, his captivity in Germany, the picturesque circumstances of his death, and the magnanimity with which he treated the fanatical warrior whose bolt had struck him were a source of patriotic pride and popular admiration which increased as reality passed into legend. The author of the romance has a general idea of the facts in Richard's life, but

Bevis of Hampton

Richard Cœur de Lion

[16] Ed. E. Kölbing (1885-94; *EETSES,* 46, 48, 65). For the Anglo-Norman version see above, p. 142.
[17] Edited from all the MSS by Karl Brunner, *Der mittelenglische Versroman über Richard Löwenherz* (Vienna, 1913; *Wiener Beiträge,* XLII).

he does not hesitate to alter history to suit his purpose. He has Richard's captivity precede the crusade and in order to explain it, has Richard journey as a pilgrim to the Holy Land first. It would seem that his knowledge of history was somewhat sketchy and confused, but he was a storyteller and not a historian, and did not feel called upon to aim at scholarly accuracy. Moreover he introduced legendary elements freely and these are at times the most interesting part of his narrative. Such an element is the episode during Richard's captivity in which his captors try to bring about his death by admitting a lion to his cell. He meets the lion with a tremendous kick and as the animal opens its jaws wide in a howl of pain Richard thrusts his arm down the lion's throat, tearing out its heart and various other organs, in fact "all that he found," says the storyteller. Then taking the heart still warm, he goes into the hall, dips it into the salt and eats it before the astonished court. Thus the poet accounts for his nickname, Lion-Hearted. It is a romance of adventure, historical and pseudo-historical. The author refers to his source as French, but the strong English bias and open scorn expressed for the French king put its English origin beyond any doubt. It dates from about 1300.

Athelston

What *Richard Cœur de Lion* does on a large scale the romance of *Athelston* [18] does on a small. In some 800 lines a poet of about 1350 has constructed a purely fictitious story about a king who bore a name famous in Old English history.[19] He has used scraps of history, legend, folklore, and commonplaces of romance. How he has woven together this heterogeneous assortment of ideas will be seen from the footnote below.[20] It will suffice here to remark that by a shameless disregard for historical truth he has devised a well-knit and highly effective plot. The romance has many qualities of the ballad—tags, and repetitions, and commonplaces, to say nothing of the opening in which the four messengers meet on the edge of a wood and with-

---

[18] Ed. A. M. Trounce, *Athelston: A Middle English Romance* (1933; also 1951; EETS, 224).

[19] See the account of the *Battle of Brunanburh*, above, p. 56.

[20] Athelston meets three other messengers and swears blood-brotherhood with them. On this motif see G. H. Gerould, "Social and Historical Reminiscences in the Middle English *Athelston*," *ESt*, xxxvi (1906). 193-208. Upon becoming king he makes his companions respectively, Archbishop of Canterbury, the Earl of Dover, and the Earl of Stane, giving also to the last named his sister in marriage. Believing the jealous representations of Dover, he sends for the Earl of Stane and his family, ostensibly to confer knighthood on the two sons. Instead he throws them into prison, and when the Queen begs him on her knees to give them a hearing he becomes enraged and kicks her, killing his unborn heir. On the kicked Queen see A. C. Baugh, "A Source for the Middle English Romance, *Athelston*," *PMLA*, XLIV (1929). 377-382. The Queen appeals to the Archbishop, who similarly incurs Athelston's anger. But the Archbishop excommunicates the King and puts all England under an interdict. This incident recalls the story of Thomas Becket; see Gerould, as above, and Paul Brown, *The Development of the Legend of Thomas Becket* (Philadelphia, 1930). The King agrees to permit the accused noble and his family to have a trial by ordeal. They must walk over nine red-hot stones. This is the story of Queen Emma and the plow-shares; see L. A. Hibbard, "*Athelston*, a Westminster Legend," *PMLA*, xxxvi (1921). 223-244. As the countess successfully completes her part of the ordeal, she is seized with the pains of childbirth and is delivered of a son. The King, now fully convinced and penitent, adopts the child in place of the heir which his wicked rage had destroyed. The child is said to be Saint Edmund, king and martyr. This last touch is a perversion of history amounting to genius. Athelston, the hero of Brunanburh, was succeeded by Edmund. Edmund was a younger brother, however, not a nephew, and Edmund Martyr lived a century before!

out explanation proceed to swear blood-brotherhood with one another. It is probably the work of a minstrel, but the humiliation of the king by the power of the Church and the prominence given to moral issues has been cited as evidence that the story was written under ecclesiastical influence.[21]

All these romances, it will be seen, capitalize upon the interest in native figures, real or imaginary. By the time most of them were written the habit of writing romances in English was thoroughly established, and poets were ready to go outside the English circle for their themes.

ii. *The Matter of Rome*

Medieval romances based on classical stories generally had to do with one of four subjects: Alexander the Great, the Trojan war, the siege of Thebes, and the adventures of Æneas. All four were made into long French romances in the twelfth century, and all four had English offspring, but only two enjoyed genuine popularity in England. These were the stories of Alexander and of Troy, with Alexander well out in front.

All popular medieval treatments of Alexander [22] go back ultimately to a *The* romantic biography in Greek prose, written at Alexandria some time before *Legend of* 200 A.D.[23] The author, who is known to modern scholarship as pseudo- *Alexander* Callisthenes, doubtless embodied in his account current legends concerning Alexander's birth designed to make the founder of his native city an Egyptian. This amazing story is one of the two features that insured the popularity of the work in later times. The other is the extended treatment of Alexander's travels, especially in India, with its multitude of strange sights, marvels of nature, and wonderful experiences.[24] Pseudo-Callisthenes was translated into Latin *c.* 300 A.D. by Julius Valerius,[25] and in an abridgement of the ninth century circulated widely.[26] Finally, about 950, the Greek was again translated into Latin by one Leo, Archpresbyter of Naples. This version, generally known as the *Historia de Preliis* [27] (i.e., the wars of Alexander), enjoyed still greater popularity. From one or another of these Latin derivatives of pseudo-Callisthenes a great number of accounts in the vernaculars of western Europe was composed. The oldest is a Provençal poem of the eleventh century by Alberic of Pisançon, of which only a fragment is preserved. It was, however, adapted in French about 1160 in lines of ten syllables, and altered and continued toward the end of the century in twelve-

[21] Wells, p. 25.

[22] The most extended treatment of the Alexander legend, Paul Meyer, *Alexandre le Grand dans la littérature française du moyen âge* (Paris, 1886), is now somewhat antiquated. For an excellent brief discussion see the introduction to F. P. Magoun, Jr., *The Gests of King Alexander of Macedon* (Cambridge, Mass., 1929).

[23] Edited (one recension) by W. Kroll, *Historia Alexandri Magni* (Berlin, 1926).

[24] This feature of the story was already known in England in Old English times. See above, p. 104 for a mention of the *Letter of Alexander to Aristotle* and the *Wonders of the East*.

[25] *Res Gestae Alexandri Macedonis,* ed. B. Kübler (Leipzig, 1888).

[26] It is often called the *Zacher Epitome* because it was edited by J. Zacher (Halle, 1867). It was incorporated in condensed form by Vincent of Beauvais in his *Speculum Historiale* (c. 1250).

[27] Ed. F. Pfister, *Der Alexanderroman des Archipresbyters Leo* (Heidelberg, 1913). It is translated in English (omitting Book II) in Margaret Schlauch, *Medieval Narrative* (1928).

syllable verses. This later *Roman d'Alexandre* [28] was the standard form in which the story circulated in French. There was, however, another French poem written in England (*c.* 1280) by Thomas of Kent. It was based on the *Zacher Epitome* and is known as the *Roman de Toute Chevalerie.*[29] From it is derived the best known English romance on the subject, *King Alisaunder.*[30]

King
Alisaunder

King Alisaunder runs to 8000 lines (in four-stress couplets). Since it is found in a manuscript of 1330-40 it cannot be later than this and is probably to be dated *c.* 1300. It is divided by the author into two parts. The first tells the story of Nectanebus, the Egyptian king who exercises his magic on Olympias, the wife of Philip of Macedon, and becomes the father of her child, Alexander. It also relates at length Alexander's military exploits, treating with especial fullness his triumph over Darius. The second part deals with Alexander's conquest of India and the multitude of fabulous creatures and terrifying experiences which he met with in the course of his extensive travels. While the romance is clearly intended for oral delivery, as numerous remarks indicate, it is the work of a bookish man. He frequently appeals for authority to his sources. On one occasion, he declines to relate an incident which he finds in his French "geste" because it is contradicted by the scholarship (*lettrure*) on the subject.[31] In another place he supplies a gap in his French source from another work in Latin,[32] and once he speaks of the strange people in Egypt "in *oure* bokes as we findith," where he seems to identify himself with those who have and use books—clerks. Alexander romances in general descend by a literary rather than a popular tradition, and nowhere is this better illustrated than in the English *King Alisaunder.*

Alexander
A *and* B

The same thing is true of the two fragments of a romance in alliterative verse known as *Alexander A* and *Alexander B.*[33] In the former the author is clearly not dependent upon any previous romance in French. He tells of the ancestry and conquests of Philip of Macedon through 450 lines taken from the Latin of Orosius because, as he remarks, he could not find any book when he began to write that told of Alexander's birth. But apparently he later got hold of a copy of the *Historia de Preliis* and so he plunges at once into the story of Nectanebus. He has hardly described the youthful feats of Alexander when the fragment breaks off. Practically the whole of *Alexander B* (1139 lines) is given over to the exchange of letters between Alexander and Dindimus discussing the Brahmin way of life. The author

[28] Ed. H. Michelant (Stuttgart, 1846) and E. C. Armstrong, *et. al.* (Princeton, 1937; *Elliott Monographs*, Vols. 36 and 37). The popularity of this version is responsible for our still calling the twelve-syllable line an Alexandrine.

[29] Still unpublished. See above, p. 141.

[30] In H. Weber, *Metrical Romances of the Thirteenth, Fourteenth, and Fifteenth Centuries* (Edinburgh, 1810), Vol. 1, superseded by ed. of G. V. Smithers (2v, 1952-7; *EETS*, 227, 237).

[31] Cf. lines 3511-21.

[32] This batail destuted [lacking] is,
In the French, wel y-wis,
Therefore Y have, it to colour,
Borowed of the Latyn autour. (lines 2199-2202.)

[33] The best edition is that of F. P. Magoun, Jr., *The Gests of King Alexander of Macedon* (Cambridge, Mass., 1929), who believes that *B* is a continuation rather than a part of *A.*

handles the alliterative line with apparent ease, drops into dialogue when necessary, and tells his story fluently. He wrote in the West Midlands and, as nearly as we can judge, in the middle third of the fourteenth century.[34]

Next to the story of Alexander the most popular subject for romances of classical theme was the fall of Troy, and this in spite of the fact that Homer was completely unknown to western Europe in the Middle Ages. The Middle Ages derived their knowledge of the Troy story from two short prose accounts translated from late Greek. These went under the names of Dares and Dictys respectively.[35] The two accounts are usually found together in medieval manuscripts and although involving some duplication each includes matter not found in the other. The combination gave a fairly complete, if wholly prosaic, account of events from the story of Jason and the Golden Fleece through the particulars of the siege to the return of the Greeks and the death of Ulysses at the hands of his son Telegonus. The first vernacular treatment of this material was the work of a Norman-French poet, Benoît de Sainte-More, whose *Roman de Troie* [36] runs to 30,000 verses. *The Roman de Troie* It is a spirited and effective narrative, but not a little of its fame today is due to the elaborate treatment of an episode that here makes its first appearance in literature—the Troilus and Briseida (Cressida) story.[37] A century later Benoît's verse was turned into Latin prose by a Sicilian judge, Guido della Colonna, as the *Historia Destructionis Troiae* (1287).[38] In these two forms the story had a wide circulation and passed into later vernacular versions.

The earliest Troy romance in English is the *Seege of Troye,* a poem of *Seege of Troye* about two thousand lines.[39] There is frequent appeal to the "lordings" to listen and it is obviously intended for minstrel production. It was designed to be recited or read in two installments, for the minstrel pauses just half

[34] Other Alexander romances survive. One in alliterative verse of the early fifteenth century is known as *Alexander C.* It runs to nearly 5700 lines and lacks a few leaves at the end. Another preserved in a Cambridge MS is in stanzas of alternate rime (ed. Rosskopf, Erlangen, 1911). A prose romance running to about 100 pages is in the Thornton MS, 1430-40. Two long Scottish poems, written in the fifteenth century are mentioned below (p. 300).

[35] Dares Phrygius, *De Excidio Trojae Historia* (sixth century), and Dictys Cretensis, *Ephemeris de Historia Belli Trojani* (fourth century). Dares and Dictys represent themselves as having fought in their respective armies, Dares on the side of the Trojans and Dictys on the side of the Greeks. Both claims, of course, are fraudulent. They were made to give the authority of eye-witnesses to works written centuries later. See N. E. Griffin, *Dares and Dictys: An Introduction to the Study of Medieval Versions of the Story of Troy* (Baltimore, 1907).

[36] It was written in the second half of the twelfth century, possibly about 1155-60, and dedicated to the English queen, Eleanor of Aquitaine. This is the date arrived at by its modern editor, L. Constans, *Le Roman de Troie, par Benoît de Sainte-Maure* (6v, Paris, 1904-12; *SATF*). For a slightly later date (after 1184) see the argument of F. E. Guyer, "The Chronology of the Earliest French Romances," *MP,* xxvi (1929). 257-277.

[37] The love story begins at line 13, 261 and accompanies the main narrative at intervals to the death of Troilus (lines 21, 397 ff). It serves to fill in the uneventful periods of truce and adds an important element of variety to the narrative. It is not thought that Benoît invented this love story, but if he followed an expanded Dares, as some believe, his source has disappeared.

[38] Ed. N. E. Griffin, *Guido de Columnis: Historia Destructionis Troiae* (Cambridge, Mass., 1936).

[39] Mary E. Barnicle, *The Seege or Batayle of Troye* (London, 1927; *EETS,* 172). See the valuable study by G. Hofstrand, *The Seege of Troye* (Lund, 1936), and C. H. A. Wager, *The Seege of Troy* (1899), which is still important.

way through for an intermission—"Rest we now a litel pece"—and suggests that the company "fyl þe cuppe and mak ous glad." The original poem from which the existing manuscripts descend was written in the northeast Midlands at the beginning of the fourteenth century and follows the plan of Dares with additions from Benoît and commonplaces of classical tradition. But in order to cover the ground from the adventures of Jason and the Golden Fleece to the destruction of Troy and the triumphant return of the Greeks, it is necessary for the poet to hurry from episode to episode without time to pause for those particulars and details that lend

Other Treatments

interest to a story. Very different is the *Laud Troy Book*,[40] which covers the same ground but was written to be read. Apparently the work of a cleric, it fills more than 18,000 verses of considerable fluency. It is somewhat older than the existing MS and dates from about 1400. To the latter half of the fourteenth century belongs also the *Gest Historiale of the Destruction of Troy*, a poem in 14,000 alliterative verses.[41] It is a product of the Alliterative Revival in the north. The Troy story seems to have enjoyed considerable popularity in Scotland. Extensive fragments of a version attributed to the Scottish poet Barbour have been preserved, imbedded in MSS of Lydgate's *Troy Book*.[42]

Thebes and Æneas

Classical times and the Middle Ages took a strange interest in the unnatural story of Œdipus and his marriage to his own mother. When his sons quarreled over the right to rule Thebes and the party of Polynices laid siege to the city, the opportunity existed for an epic narrative, comparable to that which described the siege of Troy. The Virgilian epic, the *Thebaid*, by Statius, a Roman poet of the Silver Age, gave western Europe such a treatment. Either the *Thebaid* or an epitome of it was made into a French poem in the twelfth century called the *Roman de Thèbes*, and this in turn became the basis of other romances. The only English poem on the subject was Lydgate's *Siege of Thebes*, discussed below.[43] The story of Æneas is practically unrepresented in English [44] until Caxton translated a French prose romance in his *Eneydos* (1490), although it was available to the English upper classes in the French *Roman d'Eneas*. It is apparent, therefore, that the stories of Alexander and of Troy were the only themes in the Matter of Rome that showed any real vitality in medieval England.

[40] So called because the unique MS in which it is preserved was once in the possession of Archbishop Laud. Edited by J. E. Wülfing (1902-3; *EETS*, 121-122).
[41] *EETS*, 39 and 56 (1869-74).
[42] For Lydgate, see below, p. 296. For treatments in prose see p. 301.
[43] Chaucer's *Knight's Tale* treats an episode loosely attached to the Thebes story. So too are the Anglo-Norman romances *Ipomedon* and *Prothesilaus* mentioned on p. 141.
[44] Chaucer tells the story of Dido in the *House of Fame* and more briefly in the *Legend of Good Women*.

X

The Romance: II

iii. *The Matter of France*

When we turn to the Matter of France we are met by a slight anomaly. Considering the Continental possessions and the long and close association of the English nobility with France, one might expect considerable interest in a body of legends centering in the French court and in important Carolingian families. Instead we find only limited representation of this great collection of stories, and those which are found in English versions seem to be written without special enthusiasm. It would appear that the political rivalry between the two countries which had developed by the time romances in any number were being written in English had dampened the interest in material which centered in the doings of French personages. In any case the national appeal which such stories had in France was lacking in England.

The French *chansons de geste,* which included more than one hundred poems, were recognized not long after 1200 as falling into three general groups.[1] The most famous is the *geste du roi,* the epics more or less directly connected with Charlemagne, in many of which he appears as the champion of Christendom in wars against the infidel. Of these the best known is the *Chanson de Roland.* A second group is concerned with his struggles with his vassals. The epics of this group constitute the *geste de Doon de Mayence,* so called from the supposed ancestor of the rebels. The third concerns the adventures and conquests of William of Orange and members of his family. This group likewise takes its name from the legendary progenitor of the family and is known as the *geste de Garin de Monglane.* While each of these branches of the French epic has many points of interest, not all are represented in English. Indeed the only Charlemagne romances that have come to us in English verse belong to the cycle of the king, the *geste du roi.*[2]

Chanson de Geste

---

[1] The classification is that of Bertran de Bar-sur-Aube, the author of two such poems, *Girart de Vienne* and *Aymeri de Narbonne.* In the former (after 1205) he says:

> N'ot que trois gestes en France la garnie . . .
> Du roy de France est la plus seignorie,
> Et l'autre apres, bien est droiz qui jeu die,
> Fu de Doon a la barbe florie,
> Cil de Maience qui molt ot baronnie . . .
> La tierce geste, qui molt fist a prisier,
> Fu de Garin de Monglenne au vis fier. (lines 11-47.)

[2] This is not the place to enter into the vexed question of the origin of the French epic. The most popular explanation in recent years is that of Joseph Bédier, *Les Légendes épiques*

Song of
Roland

Among these the Middle English *Song of Roland*[3] stands somewhat apart. Preserved in a single MS, it tells the famous story of Roland's last stand in 1049 four-stress lines rimed in couplets. When it breaks off Roland is just about to blow the blast on his horn that will summon Charlemagne. In spite of its rough versification and many careless rimes it manages a monotonous succession of individual combats with vigor and considerable variety. The poem naturally suffers by comparison with the great French epic on which it is based, but it does not entirely deserve the harsh words which it usually receives. Except for the late *Rauf Coilyear* ("Ralph the Collier"),[4] in which Charlemagne *incognito* is entertained by a peasant, with humorous consequences, the remaining Charlemagne romances fall into two classes, a Ferumbras group and an Otuel group.

The
Ferumbras
Group

The Ferumbras group treats the incidents found in two French *chansons de geste*, the *Destruction de Rome* and *Fierabras*, which in versions differing but slightly from those that are preserved seem to be the direct sources of the English romances. *The Sowdone* [i.e., Sultan] *of Babylone*[5] tells first how Laban (usually Balan) with the help of his son Ferumbras, sacks Rome, gets possession of the cross, the crown of thorns, and the nails of the Crucifixion, and sends them to Spain. The second part covers rapidly the incidents more fully treated in *Sir Ferumbras*.[6] Here Charlemagne's army, having come to Spain to punish the Saracens and recover the sacred relics, is met by Ferumbras, a formidable knight twenty feet tall. He is conquered in single combat by Oliver and becomes Christian, thereafter fighting on the Christian side. Oliver, on his way back to camp, is taken captive by a

(4v, Paris, 1908-13; 2ed., 1914-21). Recognizing in many of the *chansons de geste* the prominent notice taken of churches and monasteries along the great pilgrim routes of the Middle Ages, he suggested that these churches furnished the jongleurs with historical facts and traditions to be worked up into poems. In this way any claim to prominence which a church had because of the historic importance of its founder, the possession of the tomb or relics of a heroic figure, or the like, would be enhanced and more widely disseminated. The acceptance of this theory as a comprehensive explanation of the origin of the *chanson de geste* is not unattended by difficulties, although as a method of accounting for individual poems it is at times very convincing. Various critiques and correctives of Bédier's views are contained in the articles of F. Lot. For a bibliography and summary of Lot's position see E. J. Healy, "The Views of Ferdinand Lot on the Origins of the Old French Epic," *SP*, XXXVI (1939). 433-465. The older work of Léon Gautier, *Les Épopées françaises* (4v, 2ed, Paris, 1878-82) is still of value as a descriptive survey. For an excellent brief account of the many theories of the origin of the Old French epic see K. Voretzsch, *Introduction to the Study of Old French Literature* (Eng. trans., 1931), pp. 89-99.

[3] Edited by S. J. Herrtage (1880; *EETSES*, 35).

[4] Written in Scotland *c.* 1475 or slightly before. Edited by S. J. Herrtage (1882; *EETSES*, 39); William H. Browne (Baltimore, 1903). See also H. M. Smyser, "*The Taill of Rauf Coilyear* and Its Sources," *Harvard Studies & Notes in Phil. & Lit.*, XIV (1932). 135-150.

[5] Edited by Emil Hausknecht (1881; *EETSES*, 38). It is in quatrains of alternate three- and four-stress verses. For a discussion of its source see the careful study of H. M. Smyser, "The Sowdon of Babylon and Its Author," *Harvard Studies & Notes in Phil. & Lit.*, XIII (1931). 185-218, supplemented and corrected by the same author's "A New Manuscript of the *Destruction de Rome* and *Fierabras*," *ibid.*, XIV (1932). 339-349.

[6] Known as the Ashmole version to distinguish it from that in the Fillingham MS. The edition in *EETSES*, 34 is printed in long lines which disguise its true metrical form. It is really in 10,540 verses, of which the first 6820 are in quatrains (*abab*), the last 3720 in romance sixes (*aab ccb*). Fragments of the author's original draft are preserved, written on the back of two documents belonging to the diocese of Exeter at the end of the fourteenth century. The romance was apparently composed at about the same time and place.

Saracen force, and the greater part of the story grows out of his capture and the circumstance that the Sultan's beautiful daughter, Floripas, is in love with another of Charlemagne's knights, Guy of Burgundy. Her determined and resourceful personality plays a large part in the ultimate victory of the Christians and the recovery of the relics. Needless to say, she receives her reward in marriage to Guy, after being duly baptized. It is a pity that the unique manuscript in which *Sir Ferumbras* is preserved has lost a leaf or two at the beginning and end, for it is much the best of the English Charlemagne romances. The author was a conscious artist and took obvious pains with his work. It is full of effective scenes and nice touches. Incidentally it is almost the only case in which any part of an English romance has come down in the author's autograph. By comparison the recently recovered Fillingham *Firumbras*[7] seems lacking in distinction. The same incidents are treated more briefly by one who seems to be telling a story without being a storyteller.

The Otuel group consists of five romances. *Roland and Vernagu*,[8] in *The Otuel Group* tail-rime stanzas, is full of wild statements and childish exaggeration. The earliest part relates the circumstances under which Charlemagne comes to the aid of the Patriarch of Jerusalem and receives the crown of thorns, the arm of St. Simeon, Our Lady's smock, and many other relics. His invasion of Spain is like a triumphal march, after his prayers have caused the walls of one or two stubborn cities to fall. The romance takes its name from the latter part in which his douzepers are challenged by a forty-foot Saracen named Vernagu. After Ogier and several other paladins who undertake to fight him are picked up by Vernagu and carried off under his arm to prison, Roland disposes of him although he barely escapes the same ignominious treatment. The romance is incomplete, and as it breaks off amid the general rejoicing, it seems to be about to proceed to the story of Otuel which we have in other Middle English versions. *The Sege of Melayne*[9] (Milan) may have been intended to form another introduction to the Otuel story, although nothing corresponding to it in French literature is known. It relates a very unhistorical incident but tells its story well. Its most significant feature is the character of Archbishop Turpin, who abandons his priestly robes and conducts himself with great credit on the battlefield.

Three romances tell the story of Otuel proper. His reason for challenging Roland is partly the fact that Vernagu, whom Roland had killed, was his uncle. They all tell the same story with slight variations. Otuel in the midst of his single combat with Roland is converted to Christianity when the

---

[7] So called from the owner of the MS at the beginning of the nineteenth century. Lost for a hundred years, it was acquired by the British Museum in 1907 (Add. MS 37, 492). Edited by Mary I. O'Sullivan (1935; *EETS*, 198).

[8] *EETSES*, 39. See Ronald N. Walpole, *Charlemagne and Roland: A Study of the Source of Two Middle English Metrical Romances*, Roland and Vernagu *and* Otuel and Roland (Berkeley and Los Angeles, 1944; *Univ. of Calif. Pub. in Mod. Phil.*, xxi, No. 6).

[9] *EETSES*, 35. It is in twelve-line tail-rime stanzas of the late fourteenth century. The dialect of the original was northern, though it is preserved in a Midland copy.

Holy Ghost descends in the form of a dove and settles on his helmet. King Charles welcomes him to his company and promises him the hand of his daughter, Belesant. After he has accompanied Charlemagne on his expedition to Spain and contributed his share to the victory of the Christians, he marries Belesant and becomes lord of Lombardy. The oldest version in English is the *Otuel* in four-stress couplets preserved in the Auchinleck MS.[10] It is without much merit. Somewhat better is the *Duke Rowland and Sir Otuell of Spayne* [11] preserved in the same manuscript as the *Sege of Melayne*. It has more minstrel vigor. Like the *Sege of Melayne* it is in tail-rime stanzas and was composed in the north. The third romance, the Fillingham *Otuel and Roland*,[12] is probably a continuation of *Roland and Vernagu* and differs from the other Otuel romances in carrying on the story for another thousand lines with material drawn from Pseudo-Turpin.[13] In brief form the addition recounts Charlemagne's victories over the Saracen Ebrahim and the King of Navarre and concludes with Roland's death at Roncevaux. All three Otuel romances have a number of peculiar features in common and even individual lines or short passages. Although they diverge widely enough to preclude the possibility of mutual dependence, they are probably all based ultimately upon an English romance now lost.

Religious Interest in Charlemagne Romances

The interest in the Charlemagne romance in England seems to have been mainly pietistic—the glorification of the Christian faith. The Fillingham *Otuel* opens with a demand for attention "in the worchype of ihesu cryst," and the *Ferumbras* in the same manuscript ends with a promise of one hundred days' pardon to all who listen to the story "with gode devocyoun." *The Sowdone of Babylone* begins with a homiletic opening, and the rough draft of *Sir Ferumbras* was begun on the back of two ecclesiastical documents. Both Ferumbras and Otuel, the two chief Saracen champions, are converted, and there are many cases of divine intervention. In the *Sege of Melayne* the militant bishop Turpin, although somewhat melodramatic and blustering, is a truly heroic figure and certainly the main character. The subject of the Sultan of Babylon-Ferumbras romances is the loss and recovery of the Crown of Thorns and other sacred relics, supposedly given by Charlemagne to the church of St. Denis. Indeed these romances constitute a kind of Carlovingian counterpart of the Grail theme in Arthurian romance, with Roland and Oliver answering to Perceval and Gawain in Chrétien. Judged by both choice of subject and treatment the English Charlemagne

---

[10] *EETSES,* 39.

[11] *EETSES,* 35.

[12] Ed. Mary I. O'Sullivan, *Firumbras and Otuel and Roland* (as above, note 7). The *Roland and Vernagu* and the *Otuel and Roland* are often given the group title *Charlemagne and Roland.* See the important studies of Ronald N. Walpole, *Charlemagne and Roland: A Study of the Sources of Two Middle English Romances,* Roland and Vernagu *and* Otuel and Rolnad (Berkeley and Los Angeles, 1944; *Univ. of Calif. Pub. in Mod. Phil.,* Vol. XXI, No. 6, pp. 385-452), and H. M. Smyser, *"Charlemagne and Roland* and the Auchinleck MS," *Speculum,* XXI (1946). 275-288.

[13] A spurious *Historia Caroli Magni et Rotholandi,* written in the twelfth century and fathered on Archbishop Turpin. The latest edition is that of H. M. Smyser, *The Pseudo-Turpin* (Cambridge, Mass., 1937).

romances seem, with one or two exceptions, to be a group in which the missionary spirit is made to work through minstrel recitation.

iv. *The Matter of Britain*

The development of the Arthurian legend up to its first appearance in English in Layamon's *Brut,* while encumbered with numerous vexed questions, is not without a recognizable continuity.[14] Now, so far as England is concerned, that continuity is broken, for English romances on Arthurian subjects do not begin to appear until about 1300 and in spite of the interval of but a century that divided them from Layamon, they seem to be separated, generally speaking, by a much wider gulf. The reason is not far to seek. Arthurian romance enjoyed its great creative period in the latter part of the twelfth century and the beginning of the thirteenth, particularly in France and Germany. It was the period of Chrétien de Troyes, Wolfram von Eschenbach, Gottfried von Strassburg, and others only less great. As the thirteenth century wore on, the impulse lost some of its force. The English Arthurian romances follow later and, since their sources are nearly all French, reflect this earlier development. But to read them without knowing their French background is like seeing a play in which we have missed the second act.[15] It might seem reasonable to expect that the English romances, built on so solid a French foundation, would reach an equally high level. Unfortunately, the great days of medieval romance were past, and English poets, with a few notable exceptions, were unable to recapture the spontaneity and fire of their Continental predecessors.

English Arthurian Romances Late and Derivative

It is one of the distinctions of Chrétien that he got away from the biographical or compendious type of romance found, for example, in the *Roman d'Alexandre* or *Bevis of Hampton* and confined himself to a single episode or closely related group of episodes in his hero's career. Later Arthurian romance generally follows this pattern.[16] There are accordingly almost no English romances which attempt to cover the whole life of Arthur. There is a short poem of 642 lines, probably written in the second half of the fourteenth century, to which the name *Arthur*[17] has been given. It is of slight value and would scarcely deserve mention if it were not the only example of this inclusive type. Elsewhere we have only romances on certain aspects of Arthur's career, or on the adventures of individual knights of the Round Table, or on themes such as the history of the Holy Grail.

Romances of Arthur

[14] See ch. VIII. It should be remembered that Layamon's *Brut* is a translation of Wace and therefore represents the state of Arthurian development prior to Chrétien.

[15] For the linguistic conditions that account for the lateness of English romance see above, p. 111.

[16] In thirteenth-century France the separate stories were again combined into long composites, this time intended for reading rather than recitation. These were in prose. The best known is the Vulgate Cycle generally attributed in the manuscripts, though quite falsely, to Walter Map. Malory's *Morte Darthur* is an example of such a composite in English.

[17] *EETS*, 2. It is incorporated in a Latin chronicle of the kings of Britain. It traces briefly Arthur's life from birth to death. From the circumstance that the narrator pauses every hundred lines and bids the listener to say a paternoster one must assume a clerical origin.

and Merlin   The early life of Arthur is intimately associated with the figure of Merlin. It was through Merlin's magic that Uther Pendragon gained access to Ygerne the night Arthur was begotten. His advice and supernatural powers are helpful to Arthur on many occasions from the time the young prince pulls the sword from the stone and becomes king until he has emerged successfully from his contests with the rebels at home and his enemies abroad. This phase of Arthurian story is told in a romance of nearly ten thousand lines, called *Arthur and Merlin,* written about 1300.[18] It is not an inspired production; indeed it becomes rather tedious with its endless detail of battles and combats and its particularity concerning the numbers in each army and division and petty band. It is evidently based on a French source—variously referred to as the *Brut,* "the romance," or simply "the book"—apparently in verse and similar in content to the French prose *Merlins.*

Gawain   Gawain's early adventures, largely military, constitute a major element in the romance just spoken of. His various exploits were destined to become the most popular of the subjects from which English poets chose their themes. A dozen romances, many of them short and rather late, attest his continued popularity. The greatest, of course, is *Sir Gawain and the Green Knight,* more fully discussed among the works of the *Pearl* poet.[19] Admirably smooth in style and narrative technique is *Ywain and Gawain* [20] (*c.* 1350), in which Gawain and the hero fight a drawn battle, each ignorant of the other's identity. It is an adaptation of Chrétien's *Yvain* slightly condensed. Further evidence of Gawain's preëminence in popular favor is the fact that his son is made the hero of a romance, *Libeaus Desconus* (The Fair Unknown).[21] In this story Gingelein, the unknown and untried knight, undertakes to free the Queen of Sinadoun from captivity and enchantment. He succeeds, after preliminary encounters with sundry knights and giants, and in the end weds the lady.[22]

Lancelot   Lancelot is the subject of only one English romance, the late-fifteenth-century *Lancelot of the Laik.*[23] It tells of his part in the war between Arthur

[18] Eugen Kölbing, *Arthour and Merlin, nach der Auchinleck-HS, nebst zwei Beilagen* (Leipzig, 1890; *Altenglische Bibliothek,* iv).

[19] See below, pp. 236.

[20] Ed. Gustav Schleich, *Ywain and Gawain* (Oppeln, 1887).

[21] Ed. Max Kaluza (Leipzig, 1890; *Altenglische Bibliothek,* v). The source is a French romance closely resembling *Le Bel Inconnu* (ed. G. P. Williams, Paris, 1929; *CFMA,* 38). See further Wm. Schofield, *Studies on the Libeaus Desconus* (Boston, 1895); *Harvard Studies & Notes in Phil. & Lit.,* iv.).

[22] Most of the Gawain romances can be found in Sir Frederic Madden, *Syr Gawayne* (London, 1839; *Bannatyne Club,* LXI). For other editions see Wells and the *CHEL.* These include *The Green Knight,* a fifteenth-century retelling of *Sir Gawain and the Green Knight; The Turk and Gawain,* in which a more primitive form of the same story can be recognized; *Sir Gawain and the Carl of Carlisle* which treats the temptation part of the story in a variant form. *The Wedding of Sir Gawain and Dame Ragnell*—there is a modernization by George Brandon Saul (1934)—is a version of the story, so beautifully told by the Wife of Bath, of the knight and the loathly lady. In the *Geste of Sir Gawain* the hero, surprised in his love-making, is forced to fight the lady's father and brothers. His reputation for valor and fine courtesy is maintained in *Golagrus and Gawain,* involving an expedition to the Holy Land; his generosity is featured in *The Awntyrs (Adventures) of Arthur,* where an adventure of Gawain is loosely combined with a religious theme better known in *The Trental of St. Gregory.*

[23] There are several editions, the most useful being that of W. W. Skeat (1865; *EETS,* 6).

and Galiot (Galehault), following the French prose *Lancelot,* and doubtless
ended with Guinevere's acceptance of him as her lover, although this part
of the text is missing. In spite of some vigorous battle scenes, in which both
Gawain and Lancelot distinguish themselves, it is a bookish production with
a tedious prologue which is not fully redeemed by some interesting Chaucerian echoes, and the story pauses in the middle while Arthur receives
with more patience than the reader a seven-hundred-line sermon on the
duties of kingship.[24] The author was a Scot who affected certain dialectal
traits of Southern English. While this is our sole Lancelot romance so far
as title goes, the stanzaic *Morte Arthur* [25] (*c.* 1400) is really concerned chiefly Morte
with Lancelot's adventures, his love for the queen, their final parting, and Arthur
his death. It takes its name from the latter half when the lovers are betrayed
by Agravain and Arthur makes war on Lancelot. It is in the midst of this
struggle that Arthur is forced by Mordred's treason to return home and
later receives his death wound. The narrative is terse and the action rapid.
The *Morte Arthur* is the most ballad-like of the longer English romances.
It is to be sharply distinguished from the romance of similar title, the alliterative *Morte Arthure* (*c.* 1360).[26] The latter is the story of Arthur's
Roman campaign, which in this romance is interrupted by Mordred's treason.
Unlike the stanzaic tale, the alliterative *Morte Arthure* makes no mention
of Arthur's being carried off by boat to be healed of his wounds. He here
dies a mortal's death and is buried at Glastonbury. The romance is found
in a MS copied by Robert Thornton *c.* 1430-40, but recent discoveries make
it clear that in Thornton's text the original has been altered and shortened.[27]
That original was undoubtedly Malory's source for the episode in the *Morte
Darthur* (Book v), paraphrased and severely condensed. The alliterative
Morte Arthure is remarkable for its careful workmanship and artistic
elaboration. On various occasions the author lets his pen flow—the farewell
scene between Arthur and Guinevere, Arthur's banquet, his fight with the
giant, his dream, his final battle—and the result is a fullness of treatment
and richness of detail rare in the romances of England. The narrative is that
of a vigorous and genuinely gifted poet.

Two of the most popular subjects of the Arthurian cycle in the Middle *Perceval*
Ages, the Perceval-Grail theme and the Tristan story, receive but little

---

[24] On the basis of this passage a date after 1482 has been suggested. See Bertram Vogel,
"Secular Politics and the Date of *Lancelot of the Laik,*" *SP,* XL (1943). 1-13.

[25] The most accessible editions are those of J. Douglas Bruce (1903; *EETSES,* 88) and
Samuel B. Hemingway (Boston, 1912). On the interesting question of the relation of this
poem to Books XX and XXI of Malory, see Bruce, "The Middle English Metrical Romance *Le
Morte Arthur* (Harleian MS 2252): Its Sources and the Relation to Sir Thomas Malory's
Morte Darthur," *Anglia,* XXIII (1900). 67-100.

[26] The best editions are those of E. Brock (1871, *EETS,* 8), Mary M. Banks (1900), and
Erik Björkman (Heidelberg, 1915). S. O. Andrew, "The Dialect of *Morte Arthure,*" *RES,* IV
(1928). 418-423, argues convincingly that the original dialect was Northwest Midland. On
the sources see R. H. Griffith, "Malory, Morte Arthure, and Fierabras," *Anglia,* XXXII (1909).
389-398, and Tania Vorontzoff, "Malory's Story of Arthur's Roman Campaign," *MA,* VI
(1937). 99-121. The latter is a corrective to P. Branscheid, "Über die Quellen des stabreimenden
Morte Arthure," *Anglia Anzeiger,* VIII (1885). 179-236, meritorious for its day and still useful.

[27] E. V. Gordon and E. Vinaver, "New Light on the Text of the Alliterative *Morte
Arthure,*" *MA,* VI (1937). 81-98.

attention from English poets. *Sir Perceval of Gales (Wales)*,[28] in sixteen-line stanzas linked by conscious repetition, tells a part of the story found in Chrétien's *Perceval*. Perceval, reared in the forest in ignorance of knighthood, is here even more the rustic than usual, but shows his ability by killing the Red Knight and other opponents, rescues the Lady Lufamour from her Saracen suitor, and marries her. In the end he is happily reunited with his mother. There is no Grail quest; the Grail is not even mentioned. The English romance preserves the Perceval story in a distinctly primitive form, and although the question has been much discussed, it is doubtful if the poem owes anything to Chrétien's romance or its continuations.[29] The

The Holy Grail quest of the Holy Grail is not treated in any Middle English romance outside of Malory. But quite early an attempt was made to account for the Grail and its mystical history. This appears in Robert de Boron's *Joseph d'Arimathie* (see p. 141) and in greatly expanded form in the Vulgate *Estoire del Saint Graal*.[30] A brief English romance in 709 alliterative lines, *Joseph of Arimathie*[31] (*c.* 1350), tells the early part of the story, and a century later a London skinner, Henry Lovelich, told it at great length in a poem which goes by the name of *The History of the Holy Grail*.[32] The story of Tristan and Iseult comes off still worse at the hands of English poets. The only separate treatment of the theme (i.e., outside of Malory) is

Tristan a northern poem of about 1300 called *Sir Tristrem*.[33] It is written in a curious eleven-line stanza in which most lines have three stresses. The effect of the verse is quite staccato and the narrative is equally so. Although the poet contrives to tell the story in most of its incidents—from the birth of the hero, his adventures at the court of King Mark and in Ireland, his mission to conduct Iseult to be the bride of his uncle, the drinking of the fateful love potion, the many adventures which his clandestine meetings with Iseult lead to, down to the final episode in which he dies—the narrative is generally so abrupt and condensed that without previous knowledge of the story it would in some places hardly be understood and in others would seem poorly motivated. It is seemingly the work of a minstrel telling a tale already familiar to his audience.

[28] J. Campion and F. Holthausen, *Sir Perceval of Gales* (Heidelberg, 1913; *Alt-und Mittelenglische Texte*, No. 5). There is an earlier edition by J. O. Halliwell (1844; *Camden Soc.*). The poem was written in the north Midlands about 1350.

[29] The literature is too extensive to be listed here. The student may consult Reginald H. Griffith, *Sir Perceval of Galles: A Study of the Sources of the Legend* (Chicago, 1911) and a series of articles by Arthur C. L. Brown called "The Grail and the English *Sir Perceval*" in *MP*, XVI-XXII (1919-24); opposed by Bruce (I. 309-312) and others.

[30] For a discussion of this part of the Vulgate cycle, see Bruce, I. 374-394.

[31] W. W. Skeat, *Joseph of Arimathie* (1871; *EETS*, 44).

[32] See p. 300.

[33] Edited by E. Kölbing, *Die nordische u. die englische Version der Tristansage* (2v, Heilbronn, 1878-82) and by George P. McNeill, *Sir Tristrem* (Edinburgh, 1886; *Scottish Text Soc.*, VIII). Bertram Vogel, "The Dialect of Sir Tristrem," *JEGP*, XL (1941). 538-544, shows that the dialect of the Auchinleck text is prevailingly that of London or the southeast Midlands and not Northern, and suggests that the author was a Londoner who had spent part of his youth in the north. It seems simplest, however, to believe that the numerous instances of *a* for Old English *ā* and occasionally other Northern features are inherited from a Northern original.

English romance contrives to treat most of the major figures and famous themes of Arthurian legend—Merlin and the early life of Arthur, Lancelot, Gawain, the morte d'Arthur, Perceval, the Grail history, Tristan and Iseult. Only the Grail quest is lacking. Nevertheless what remains seems like the chance survival of a few romances, and not always the best, from a much larger number that either died on the lips of the minstrels who chanted them or have perished in the precarious course of manuscript transmission.

v. Non-cycle Romances

There were many romances outside the three "matters" noted by Jean Bodel and the group which we have called the Matter of England. Among them is one of the earliest to be written in English, *Floris and Blaunche-*   Floris and *flour*,[34] probably dating from somewhat before 1250. It is an Eastern story   Blaunche- with analogues in the *Arabian Nights*. It concerns a king's son who refuses to   flour give up the girl he loves, even after she has been sold to merchants and carried overseas, who finds her in Babylon among the maidens of the Sultan, and eventually is united to her. Although somewhat too brief and condensed in style, it is a charming little love story. *Ipomedon*[35] is an artfully contrived   Ipomedon variation of the Guy of Warwick theme—the hero must establish his reputation for prowess before winning his lady's hand. In *The Squire of Low Degree*[36] a simple squire is in love with the King of Hungary's daughter.   The The lady in this case is favorable to him. She is also faithful to the point   Squire of of keeping what she supposes is his dead body in her room for seven years.   Low When he reappears alive and suitable explanations have been made the   Degree lovers are married with the full approval of the King. *Eger and Grime*,[37] in which the lady will wed only a knight who has never been conquered, won the commendation of even so unpartisan a critic as Lowell. A somewhat different theme appears in *Amis and Amiloun*,[38] the devoted friendship of two men, which does not stop for leprosy or the slaying of the one's children when the other's life is at stake.

A group of romances, often in the twelve-line tail-rime stanza popular in the north,[39] concerns the patiently suffering wife, plotted against, exiled, deprived of her children, but eventually restored to happiness. Such is the matter of *Sir Eglamour*[40] and *Torrent of Portingale,* which closely resemble   Sir each other. In *Sir Isumbras*, the husband suffers as well. Sometimes, as in *Oc-*   Eglamour *tavian,* a wicked mother-in-law brings about the wife's persecution, some-

---

[34] Most recent edition by A. B. Taylor (Oxford, 1927). The reader will be reminded of the charming French chante-fable, *Aucassin et Nicolete,* of the thirteenth century.

[35] E. Kölbing, *Ipomedon, in drei englischen Bearbeitungen* (Breslau, 1889).

[36] Ed. W. E. Mead (Boston, 1904).

[37] Ed. J. R. Caldwell (Cambridge, Mass., 1933; *Harvard Studies in Compar. Lit.,* IX).

[38] Ed. MacEdward Leach (1937; *EETS,* 203).

[39] A score of romances in this stanza form indicate its vogue at one time. An attempt has been made by A. M. Trounce, "The English Tail-Rhyme Romances," *MA,* I (1932). 87-108, 168-182; II (1933). 34-57, 189-198; III (1934). 30-50, to show that these romances have their source in East Anglia, but the conclusion cannot be accepted.

[40] For editions of the romances mentioned in this section see Wells' *Manual* and Laura A. Hibbard, *The Mediæval Romance in England.*

times a treacherous steward, as in *Sir Triamour*. In *Le Bon Florence of Rome* treachery is manifold and knows no bounds.

William of Palerne   The supernatural enters incidentally into many romances, but in certain stories it is fundamental. *William of Palerne* tells the story of a prince of Spain who has been turned into a werewolf by his stepmother. The werewolf carries off William, the King of Apulia's son, who, when found and brought up by the Emperor, falls in love with the Emperor's daughter. After many adventures William's identity is revealed, the wicked stepmother is forced to return the werewolf to his rightful form, and the story ends in marriages all around.[41] The twelve-thousand line *Partonope of Blois*[42] is a fairy-mistress story in which Partonope's love for the mysterious Melior is twice interrupted when he disobeys her instructions and breaks the spell, but in which of course he eventually marries her. In the romance of *Partenay*[43] (or *Melusine*) the hero is not so fortunate. He marries a fairy of great beauty, promising not to disturb her on Saturdays, and is supremely happy until one Saturday he spies on her and finds that on this day she is a serpent from the waist down. He is forgiven the first time but when he repeats his offense he loses her forever. The brief alliterative romance, the *Chevelere Assigne*,[44] less than four hundred lines long, is the only treatment of the swan-knight story in English verse.

Minor Romances   A few minor romances are interesting for special reasons. The *Tale of Gamelin* is found in a number of manuscripts of the *Canterbury Tales*, generally assigned to the Cook, and was probably among Chaucer's papers waiting to be worked up for one of the pilgrims. It is the story of the ill-treated younger brother which was to find its way into *As You Like It*. *Sir Degrevant* concerns a vassal wronged by his overlord, who marries the daughter and not only recovers his own but inherits his overlord's lands. It suggests the usurer plot in Elizabethan drama. *Generides*, of which we have a version in couplets and a second in rime royal, is an interesting compound of stock features—wicked steward, exiled king, faithless wife, lovers separated and estranged. In the end Clarionas comes like Iseult to cure Generides and the lovers are married.[45]

Romances of Didactic Intent   Certain romances, finally, seem to have been composed with a clearly didactic intent. *Sir Amadas* exemplifies courtesy, generosity, pledges kept at great sacrifice, and the like. *Sir Amadas* has exhausted his estate in entertainment and liberality, even giving his last forty pounds to pay off the debts of a dead knight and permit the burial of the body. When he later marries a princess and regains his former prosperity it is through the help of the soul of the grateful dead. *Sir Cleges* turns on a familiar folk motif.

---

[41] For an interesting discussion of the story's reflection of actual people see Irene P. McKeehan, "*Guillaume de Palerne*: A Medieval 'Best Seller'," *PMLA*, XLI (1926). 785-809.

[42] Ed. A. T. Bödtker (1912; *EETSES*, 109).

[43] Ed. W. W. Skeat (1866; *EETS*, 22).

[44] Ed. Henry H. Gibbs (1868; *EETSES*, 6).

[45] Sometimes classed with the romance is *The Seven Sages of Rome*, known in the East as the *Book of Sindibad*. It is a collection of framed tales and exists in three different Middle English versions. Ed. Killis Campbell (Boston, 1907); Karl Brunner (1933; *EETS*, 191).

The hero, forced to share any reward he receives with grasping officials, asks for twelve strokes.[46] A didactic purpose is obvious in *The King of Tars*. A Christian princess married to a heathen sultan gives birth to a formless lump of flesh. After the heathen gods have proved powerless, baptism changes the monstrosity to a handsome boy.[47] In *Titus and Vespasian* [48] (*c.* 1400) we have a thoroughly religious romance with its stories of the life of Christ, Pilate, Judas, and others woven into the miraculous cure of Vespasian from leprosy through the agency of St. Veronica's handkerchief and his own belief in Christ. The shorter and perhaps slightly earlier *Siege of Jerusalem*,[49] in alliterative verse, is similar in matter, but the poet's main interest is in the description of the battle. In stories such as these two it is difficult to say where romance ends and religious legend begins.[50]

vi. *The Breton Lay and the Fabliau*

Most medieval romances were too long to be recited at one sitting and some of them are furnished with convenient stopping points at intervals in the story. It is obvious, however, that short narratives suitable for a brief recitation, capable like the modern short story of being read or heard in complete form at one time, would be composed. Certain romances just considered, such as *Sir Cleges* and *Sir Eglamour,* are of suitable length for a single recitation and do not differ in subject matter and treatment from some of the stories discussed in the present section. They could well be included here. But it has become customary to segregate a small number of such short pieces and give them, with not too much warrant, the distinctive name of *Breton lays*.

The Breton Lay

It would seem that at one time the Bretons had a reputation for storytelling, a reputation which may owe much of its currency in the later Middle Ages to Marie de France. It is conceivable that their shorter tales were distinguished by a particular musical form, that they showed a predilection for love and the supernatural in subject matter, and that many of them had their setting in Brittany. But by the time such tales were written in English, that is, in the fourteenth century, references to the lays of the Bretons seem to be a mere convention. They are always spoken of as belonging to the rather distant past. Thus, when Chaucer's Franklin begins to tell one of them he says:

[46] See John R. Reinhard, "Strokes Shared," *Jour. Amer. Folk-Lore*, xxxvi (1923). 380-400.
[47] See Lillian H. Hornstein, "A Folklore Theme in *The King of Tars*," *PQ*, xx (1941). 82-87; "The Historical Background of *The King of Tars*," *Speculum*, xvi (1941). 404-414; "New Analogues to the *King of Tars*," *MLR*, xxxvi (1941). 433-442. The valuable discussion of Robert J. Geist, "On the Genesis of *The King of Tars*," *JEGP*, xlii (1943). 260-268, should also be consulted.
[48] Ed. J. A. Herbert (1905; *Roxburghe Club*).
[49] Ed. G. Steffler (Emden, 1891), and E. Kölbing and Mabel Day (1932; *EETS*, 188).
[50] On the relation between saint's legend and romance see Irene P. McKeehan, "Some Relationships between the Legends of British Saints and Medieval Romance," [Univ. of Chicago] *Abstracts of Theses*, Humanistic Ser., ii (1926). 383-391, and the portion printed in full as "St. Edmund of East Anglia: The Development of a Romantic Legend," *Univ. of Colorado Studies*, xv (1925). 13-74.

> Thise olde gentil Britouns in hir dayes
> Of diverse adventures maden layes,
> Rymeyed in hir firste Briton tonge;
> Whiche layes with hir instrumentz they songe,
> Or elles redden hem for hir plesaunce. . . .

This is similar to the opening lines of *Sir Orfeo,* a passage which is also found at the beginning of the *Lay le Freine,* where we are told:

> In Brytayn þis layes arne y-wryte,
> Furst y-founde and forþe y-gete. . . .
>
> When þey myght owher [anywhere] heryn
> Of adventurës þat þer weryn,
> Þey toke her harpys wiþ game,
> Maden layes and ȝaf it name.

The same passage tells us that Breton lays may treat of almost any subject—weal or woe, joy and mirth, treachery and guile, even jests and ribaldry; some, it says, are of faëry, but most are about love. Certainly there is nothing distinctive in the subject or treatment of the so-called Breton lays in English, and whether a given short romance is classed as a Breton lay or not depends mainly on whether it says it is one (e.g., *The Earl of Toulouse, Sir Orfeo, Lay le Freine*), or has its scene laid in Brittany (*Sir Degarë*), or contains a passing reference to Brittany (*Sir Launfal*), or tells a story found among the *lais* of Marie de France. Doubtless reference to the Bretons was often no more than a trick of the poet to lend authority or the charm of age to his story.

Emare

We can but glance in passing at the delightful little English poems which constitute the group. *Emare* [51] is a supreme instance of a story made up of the commonplaces of romance. There is not a novel character or situation in it. To list its episodes is to begin a motif-index of medieval romance—the emperor who wishes to marry his own daughter, the heroine set adrift in a boat, in this case twice, the wicked mother-in-law who not only opposes her son's marriage but by a substitution of letters brings about the unhappy bride's exile, pilgrimages to Rome with their chain of coincidences bringing about final recognition and reunion. It must not be supposed, however, that the story is without charm. Emare herself is very beautiful, and bears her sufferings with so much sweetness and patience that she wins our hearts. The king, her husband, loves her so loyally and behaves so honorably that we rejoice with him when his wife and child are at long last restored. *Emare*

Sir
Degare

is classed as a Breton lay because the poet says it is one. Chaucer's Constance story told by the Man of Law, which is very similar, is not. *Sir Degarë* [52] is also made up of familiar features—the king who will marry his daughter

---

[51] Ed. A. B. Gough (Heidelberg, 1901), Edith Rickert (1908; *EETSES,* 99), and in French and Hale's *Middle English Metrical Romances.*

[52] Ed. David Laing (1849; *Abbotsford Club*), and in French and Hale, *op. cit.* A later text is in Hales and Furnivall's edition of the Percy Folio, Vol. III. See also George P. Faust, *Sir Degare: A Study of the Texts and Narrative Structure* (1935; *Princeton Studies in English,* 11).

only to one who overcomes him in battle, the daughter forced to yield to an unknown knight in the forest, the child left on a hermit's step, the youth who nearly marries his own mother but recognizes her through a pair of gloves that will fit no one else, the son who discovers his father through a sword with a missing piece. The scene is Little Britain, but this is the only thing that makes it a Breton lay.

Two of the English lays derive ultimately from *lais* of Marie de France. Le Freine The *Lay le Freine*,[53] so named, as the English poet tells us, because *freine* in French means ash-tree, tells the story of an infant abandoned in a hollow ash, who later wins a husband and her parents back through one turn of Fortune's wheel. *Sir Landeval* [54] is about a knight who enjoys the love of a Sir fairy mistress as long as he refrains from any mention of her, who breaks Landeval the covenant and loses her, but, since there are extenuating circumstances, recovers her favor. *Sir Landeval* was elaborated by Thomas of Chester in his *Sir Launfal*,[55] without always being improved in the process. *Sir Orfeo* [56] *Other* retells the classical story of Orpheus and Eurydice with medieval modifica- *Lays* tions. *Sir Gowther*,[57] telling the legend of Robert the Devil, is not without its didactic intent; indeed one manuscript ends with the words, "Explicit Vita Sancti." *The Earl of Toulouse* [58] is the story of a vassal persecuted by the Emperor; in the end he not only wins justice but marries the Emperor's beautiful widow. It resembles in a number of ways the story of *Sir Degrevant* (see above), but because the author of *The Earl of Toulouse* says he got · it from "a lay of Bretayn" the latter is included among Breton lays.

The edifying element found in some of the lays becomes the chief feature *Miracles* of another type of short narrative, the miracle of the Virgin. The miracle *of the* of the Virgin is a kind of *conte dévot* or pious tale in which devotion to *Virgin* the Virgin wins her intercession. Thus, the nun who has run away from her convent and has returned repentant after a period of worldly life finds her absence unnoticed. Because she had venerated the Virgin from the days when she was a young novice, her place has been supplied and her duties have been performed by the Mother of Christ. Readers are familiar with the story in John Davidson's *Ballad of a Nun* and in the dramatic production *The Miracle,* in which Lady Diana Manners appeared in the rôle of the Virgin. In another widely distributed example a harlot is induced to pray. She prays in a chapel dedicated to the Virgin and at her death is assured of salvation. The tale told by Chaucer's Prioress is another well-known example of the type. A small collection of these stories is found in the *South English Legendary.* A more important group of forty-two apparently once formed part of the famous Vernon manuscript, but in the present mutilated condition of the codex only nine are preserved. Finally, not to mention

[53] Ed. H. Weber, *Metrical Romances*, Vol. I, and H. Varnhagen, *Anglia*, III (1880), 415-423.
[54] Ed. G. L. Kittredge, *Amer. Jour. Phil.*, x (1889). 1-33, and Rudolf Zimmermann (Köningsberg, 1900).
[55] Most conveniently available in French and Hale, *op. cit.*
[56] In French and Hale, *op. cit.*
[57] Ed. Karl Breul (Oppeln, 1886).
[58] In French and Hale, *op. cit.*

scattered examples, there is a collection of eighteen in a Phillipps manu‚ script now in the British Museum. These collections, which are all in verse, extend from the thirteenth to the fifteenth century, but the type is dateless and examples in English may well have existed as early as the twelfth century.[59]

The Fabliau

One other form of narrative poem in Middle English must be mentioned here, and its aim was simply to entertain. The fabliau, like the lay and the miracle of the Virgin, is short, but there the resemblance stops. It is a humorous story, generally ribald or at least unconventional, told in verse with conscious literary art. In the Middle Ages it enjoyed its greatest vogue in France,[60] but turned into prose it forms an important element in such collections of tales as we have in Boccaccio's *Decameron* and their derivatives in all the languages of Europe. It is in no sense biographical and seeks its effect in the rapid succession of events forming a single episode. Its humor is not that of the jest, nor does it depend on a play on words, but is the humor of situation, rooted in human nature. It has a special fondness for wives who trick their husbands, and individuals whose greed or gullibility makes them fair game for the cleverness of rogues.

Examples in Chaucer

In English the type is best represented by a half dozen stories in Chaucer's *Canterbury Tales,* those told by the Miller, the Reeve, the Friar, the Summoner, the Merchant, and the Shipman. The Cook's tale would undoubtedly have been of the type if he had gone on. That Chaucer was aware of the effect which such of his tales would have upon some readers is evident in his warning just before beginning the *Miller's Tale:*

> And therefore, whoso list it nat yheere,
> Turne over the leef and ches another tale.

Dame Sirith

Before Chaucer the only true fabliau in English is *Dame Sirith* [61] (*c.* 1250), turning on a trick by which Dame Sirith, a hypocritical bawd, succeeds in terrifying a young wife named Margeri into accepting as a lover the clerk Wilekin. The plot outrages probability, but the tale is skilfully told with much natural dialogue. There are a few post-Chaucerian pieces such as *The*

---

[59] The basic work on the miracles of the Virgin is A. Mussafia, *Studien zu den mittelalterlichen Marienlegenden* (5 parts, Vienna, 1887-98; *Sitzungsberichte der kgl. Akad. der Wissenchaften,* Philos.-hist. Classe, CXIII-CXXXIX). Much important material on collections in Latin, French, and English will be found in H. L. D. Ward, *Catalogue of Romances . . . in the British Museum,* II (1893). 586-740. A list of Latin miracles running to nearly 1800 items has been published by Father Poncelet in *Analecta Bollandiana,* XXI (1902). 241-360. One of the best known collections in the Middle Ages was that of Johannes Herolt, which can be read in the translation of C. C. S. Bland (1928), with an excellent short Introduction by Eileen Power. G. G. Coulton, *Five Centuries of Religion,* I (Cambridge, 1923). 501-516, offers a brief discussion with examples. Ruth W. Tryon, "Miracles of Our Lady in Middle English Verse," *PMLA,* XXXVIII (1923). 308-388, publishes a number of hitherto unprinted texts.
[60] The standard work on the subject is J. Bédier, *Les Fabliaux* (4ed., Paris, 1925). For the fabliau in English see the introduction to George H. McKnight, *Middle English Humorous Tales in Verse* (Boston, 1913), H. S. Canby, "The English Fabliau," *PMLA,* XXI (1906). 200-214, and W. M. Hart, "The Fabliau and Popular Literature," *PMLA,* XXIII (1908). 329-374.
[61] In McKnight, as above, and for discussion see Edward Schröder, "*Dame Sirith,*" *Nachrichten aus der neueren Philologie und Literaturgeschichte,* I (1937). 179-202 (*Gesellschaft der Wissenschaften zu Göttingen*).

Wright's Chaste Wife [62] and *The Prioress and Her Three Suitors*,[63] but they do not merit treatment here. When we consider that nearly one hundred and fifty specimens of the fabliau are found in Old French, we can only believe that these realistic episodes from everyday life ran counter to the more puritan spirit in England and were less often committed to writing than allowed to die on the lips of minstrels and other purveyors of backstairs entertainment.[64]

[62] Edited by Furnivall, *EETS*, 12.

[63] Ed. Johannes Prinz, *A Tale of a Prioress and Her Three Wooers* (Berlin, 1911; *Literarhistorische Forschungen*, 47), and J. O. Halliwell, *Minor Poems of . . . Lydgate* (1840; *Percy Soc.*, 11), pp. 107-117.

[64] A number of stories found in the French fabliaux occur in the English ballads.

XI

The Omnibus of Religion

Ignorance among the Lower Clergy

In 1222 the Bishop of Salisbury ordered an examination of the priests in seventeen of his parishes. The examination was a simple one, based on the words, *Te igitur clementissime Pater ... rogamus* ("we therefore beseech thee, most merciful Father"). These words open the first prayer in the Canon of the Mass, the most solemn and at the same time an invariable part of the service. Five could not tell the case of *te* or identify the governing verb. Some of the others refused to answer. The incident is unfortunately not an isolated case. The ignorance of parish priests was frequently appalling, especially in country parishes remote from towns and larger centers. In the register of William of Wykeham, Bishop of Winchester, it is more than once recorded that a priest was made to take oath that within one year he would learn the Creed, the Ten Commandments, the Seven Deadly Sins, etc. under penalty of being fined forty shillings. In the light of such cases we need not be surprised at frequent complaints that the simplest spiritual needs of the people were not being cared for.[1]

The Coming of the Friars

When an evil is clearly recognized the remedy is often not far off. At the beginning of the thirteenth century St. Francis and St. Dominic conceived almost at the same time the idea of carrying religion directly to the people, without the organization of churches and religious houses. St. Francis was filled with the need for embracing poverty and ministering to the poor, St. Dominic with the necessity of combating heresy. With incredible rapidity they gained followers and soon the Friars Minor and the Friars Preachers had spread over many parts of Europe. The Dominicans reached England in 1221 and the Franciscans in 1224. Though learning was in the beginning more necessary to the Preachers than to the Minorites, both orders soon found it necessary to the successful prosecution of their work. The friars were in time to become famous for learning and for works in which that learning was adapted to the spiritual needs of the people.

Their Emphasis on Preaching

While the activities of the friars were greatest among the depressed classes in the poorer quarters and on the edges of large cities, there were few localities that did not come under their influence. So great was the stress which they laid upon preaching that they even curtailed the rest of the service to save more time for the sermon. It was their method of bringing home the teachings of Christ and enforcing his precepts with the vividness of direct speech. Some friars traveled from place to place, preaching in parish

[1] For a brief statement of the facts see G. G. Coulton, *Medieval Panorama* (1938), pp. 156-160, or Margaret Deanesly, *The Lollard Bible* (1920), pp. 193-195.

churches, the churchyard, the market-place, and the crossroads; others preached regularly in their own churches—which in the course of time they established—on Sundays and festivals and on rainy days, when, as Pecock tells us, great numbers were wont to come to the friars' churches.[2] One reason for their popularity was their concern with basic social and moral questions. Another was undoubtedly the skill with which they adapted themselves to their audience, generously sprinkling their discourse with anecdote and illustration and even adopting devices learned from the minstrels. There is little doubt that they sometimes preached in verse. Wyclif accuses them of corrupting the word of God, "some by riming and others by preaching poems and fables." [3]

The success of the friars was naturally a shock to the regular clergy, *Their* arousing bitterness in some but warm admiration in others. It is not necessary *Influence* to suppose that nothing would ever have been done for the people without the stimulus of the mendicants,[4] but the action soon to be taken may well have owed something to the example of the friars. Robert Grosseteste, lecturer to the Franciscans at Oxford and one who, though not belonging to the order himself, expressed the desire to have about him at all times members of the order, issued a set of Constitutions shortly after he became Bishop of Lincoln, requiring the clergy in his diocese to know and to teach the people in their mother tongue the Decalogue, the Seven Deadly Sins, the Seven Sacraments, and the Creed. A few years later his example was followed by the Bishop of Worcester,[5] while in 1246 the Bishop of Chichester set up a similar though simpler requirement that the laity be taught the Paternoster, Creed, and Ave. These efforts toward reform were inspired by the activities of Innocent III and the decrees of the fourth Lateran Council (1215-16), soon reaffirmed by the Council of Oxford called by Stephen Langton in 1222. But the injunctions of individual bishops were of direct force only in their own dioceses. In 1281 a regulation of national scope was

---

[2] See A. G. Little, "Popular Preaching," in *Studies in English Franciscan History* (Manchester, 1917), and the two books of G. R. Owst, *Preaching in Medieval England* (Cambridge, 1926) and *Literature and Pulpit in Medieval England* (Cambridge, 1933). On the friars' sermons see Horace G. Pfander, *The Popular Sermon of the Medieval Friar in England* (1937).

[3] See the references gathered by Deanesly, *Lollard Bible*, p. 148n.

[4] Edmund Rich, Archbishop of Canterbury (1234-40) in the *Merure de Seinte Eglise* (*Speculum Ecclesiae*), written toward the end of his life, discusses the Seven Deadly Sins, Seven Virtues, Seven Gifts of the Holy Ghost, Ten Commandments, Twelve Articles of the Faith, Seven Sacraments, Seven Works of Mercy, and the Seven Petitions of the Pater Noster. This is the standard list of subjects for popular instruction, but there is no indication that it was intended for the people. The Latin text can be had only in early editions. The French text has been edited by Harry W. Robbins (Lewisburg, Pa., 1925). A Middle English translation is printed in C. Horstman, *Yorkshire Writers*, 1 (1895), and a modernized version has been published by Francesca M. Steele (1905).

[5] C. R. Cheney, *English Synodalia of the Thirteenth Century* (Oxford, 1941), proposes a date for Grosseteste's statutes after the synod held at Worcester, but the evidence is not convincing. Grosseteste's *Templum Domini,* a treatise on the Virtues and Vices, Articles of the Faith, Ten Commandments, and Sacraments, exists in more than sixty manuscripts but has not been printed. An English poem of the same name has been published by Roberta D. Cornelius, *The Figurative Castle* (Bryn Mawr, 1930), pp. 91-112. It shows some resemblance to the first half of Grosseteste's treatise, but the indebtedness has been questioned. For Grosseteste's *Château d'Amour,* which includes brief treatments of the Ten Commandments, Creed, Seven Sacraments, Seven Gifts of the Holy Ghost, etc., see above p. 139.

Archbishop Peckham's Constitutions (1281)

adopted. John Peckham, a Franciscan friar, almost immediately upon becoming Archbishop of Canterbury called a general council at Lambeth and issued the famous Constitutions of Lambeth. They begin with a preamble which asserts that "the ignorance of priests casts the people into the pit of error" and then proceeds:

> As a remedy for this peril we expressly command that four times a year, that is, once in each quarter of the year, upon one or more holy days each priest having charge of the people, either personally or through some one else, shall explain to the people in their mother tongue, without any fantastic subtlety, the fourteen articles of the faith, the ten commandments of the decalogue, the two precepts of the gospels [love of God and love of man], the seven works of mercy, the seven deadly sins with their offspring, the seven cardinal virtues, and the seven sacraments of grace. And lest any one on account of ignorance excuse himself from the aforesaid things, which all ministers of the church are bound to know, we touch upon them here in a brief summary.

A series of paragraphs on the topics mentioned carries out the promise of the last sentence. Peckham's Constitutions were constantly referred to for upwards of two hundred years and were followed by a succession of pronouncements from bishops in various parts of England reaffirming them in spirit and often in identical words.[6] They remained the authoritative outline of doctrine upon which the people were supposed to be instructed until the end of the Middle Ages.

Manuals and Treatises in Latin and French

This basic body of theological teaching was already old long before Peckham's time, but now that he had provided for its regular presentation to the people it was soon embodied in a number of works intended for the common people or for those priests who were in need of simple manuals or ready-made discourses suitable for oral presentation. Authoritative sources upon which the authors of such popular treatises could draw were not lacking. There were especially two great works which became the parents of a numerous offspring, the huge compilation of Raymond of Pennafort called the *Summa Casuum Poenitentiae* (c. 1235) and the twin treatises of Guillaume de Perrault, the *Summa de Vitiis* and *Summa de Virtutibus* (before 1261). From these and other sources Friar Lorens, the confessor of Philip the Third, compiled in 1279 a treatise called the *Somme des Vices et Vertus,* commonly known as the *Somme le Roi,* which circulated widely. An analogous work, and in parts identical, went by the name of *Miroir du Monde.* Both the *Somme le Roi* and the *Miroir du Monde* became in turn the parents of numerous works in French and English. The interdependence of the many treatises in which the Ten Commandments, the Twelve Articles of the Faith (Apostles' Creed), the Seven Deadly Sins,

---

[6] See J. L. Peckham, *Archbishop Peckham as a Religious Educator* (1934; *Yale Stud. in Religion,* No. 7), pp. 83-96. The movement for the reformation of the clergy and for the instruction of the people in essential doctrine is traced in ch. 1 of E. J. Arnould, *Le Manual des Péchés: Étude de littérature religieuse anglo-normande* (XIIIᵉ siècle) (Paris, 1940), which appeared during the Second World War and reached this country too late to be utilized in the writing of this chapter.

the Four Cardinal and Three Theological Virtues, the Seven Sacraments, the Paternoster, the Seven Gifts of the Holy Ghost, and often other doctrinal matters were covered makes it difficult and often impossible to tell where a given English work owes its chief debt. Chaucer's *Parson's Tale* is an excellent case in point.

The English works[7] range all the way from simple and unpretentious *In English* manuals to highly ingenious and sometimes quite fanciful allegories. The earlier ones are often in verse. Thus, when John Thoresby, Archbishop of York, published in 1357 an explanation in Latin of the points prescribed by Peckham, known in modern times as the *Lay Folks' Catechism*,[8] he issued at the same time a somewhat expanded version in English. The crude verse of the English was the work of John Gaytryge, a monk of St. Mary's abbey, York; it is commonly known as *Dan John Gaytryge's Sermon*. A little later *John* a still longer version, likewise in verse, was prepared by John Wyclif or one *Gaytryge* of his followers.[9] At the beginning of the fifteen century a canon regular of Lilleshall in Shropshire, John Mirk by name, wrote a manual of *Instructions for Parish Priests*.[10] He likens many priests to the blind leading the blind,

> Wharefore þou preste curatoure . . .
> ʒef thou be not grete clerk,
> Loke thow most on thys werk.

He includes some general instructions on the duties of a parish priest, with specific directions on the form of baptism, the method of hearing confession, and the like, but parts of his text were intended to be taught to the people, and this doubtless was one reason for his writing the whole in verse. For priests who could manage the Latin a much fuller treatment was provided in the *Speculum Christiani* (c. 1360). It is the work of an Englishman and *Speculum* covers the usual topics. At least sixty-five extant manuscripts testify to its *Christiani* popularity. It is mentioned here because the whole work was translated into English by a Lollard, doubtless, as the editor notes, for the benefit of the many unlearned Lollard preachers and possibly to provide a manual of devotion for laymen.[11] As an example of the elaborate allegorical method we may cite *Jacob's Well*, a collection of ninety-five sermons or discourses de- *Jacob's* livered to some audience at intervals of a few days (c. 1425). Man is likened *Well* to a well which must be cleansed with the implements used in cleaning wells, protected against pollution through the springs of the senses, etc. It

---

[7] See on the general subject H. G. Pfander, "Some Medieval Manuals of Religious Instruction in England and Observations on Chaucer's Parson's Tale," *JEGP*, xxxv (1936). 243-258.

[8] An explanation of the Mass and directions for hearing it were provided in English verse about 1300; see *The Lay Folks Mass Book* (1879; EETS, 71). In the following century appeared a book for private devotions known as the *Primer*; see *The Primer or Lay Folks' Prayer Book* (1895; EETS, 105).

[9] All three texts are printed in *EETS*, 118.

[10] Ed. Edward Peacock (1868, rev. ed. 1902; EETS, 31). Most of Mirk's treatise is translated from the second part of William de Pagula's (or Page's) *Oculus Sacerdotis*, one of a number of Latin texts called forth by the same need. Space does not permit the discussion of these here.

[11] Ed. Gustaf Holmstedt (1933; EETS. 182).

is in prose; the preacher must have been able to count on the attention—and the endurance—of his audience. Although each discourse fills only about thirty minutes and for the sake of interest closes with one or two illustrative stories, it is one of the most voluminous treatises of the kind that we have.[12]

Virtue and vice in the abstract are likely to be dull subjects. How interesting a treatise on the Ten Commandments, the Deadly Sins, and the Sacraments can be when these things are brought realistically into relation with **Handlyng Synne** life is seen in the *Handlyng Synne* (1303) of Robert of Brunne.[13] Based on the Anglo-Norman *Manuel des Péchés* of William of Wadington(?),[14] with many omissions and additions, it is in reality a collection of tales and anecdotes and concrete instances illustrating the vices and weaknesses of man. Holidays are holy days, not to be spent in dancing, wrestling, crowning a beauty queen, haunting taverns, or playing chess when one should be in church. Women should not be proud of their hair, use powder "or other flour to make them whiter of color," or borrow clothes to go to the dance. Miracle plays are forbidden, but one may play the Resurrection in church. Minstrels get their clothes, and their meat and drink, through folly.... Seldom do we get such a picture of the details of medieval life. There is not a dull page in the 12,630 lines of the *Handlyng Synne*.

Ayenbite of Inwit More simply doctrinal are the translations into English of Friar Lorens's *Somme*. The best known of these today is the *Ayenbite of Inwit* ("Remorse of Conscience")[15] translated in 1340 by Dan Michel of Northgate, who tells us that the manuscript was written with his own hand and belonged to the library of St. Augustine's, Canterbury. As a specimen of the Kentish dialect it is important, but it seems to have had no circulation. Other translations of the *Somme* were made in the course of the next hundred years, and one of these, *The Book of Vices and Virtues,* in the East Midland dialect enjoyed greater popularity, since it has come down to us in several manuscripts.[16] Preserved in more than thirty copies is an adaptation of the *Somme* **Speculum Vitae** in verse by William of Nassyngton which went by the name of *Speculum Vitae*. Using the Paternoster as the point of departure, it presents the whole body of doctrinal and ethical teaching necessary for laymen in a lively, realistic style which marks the author as a person of considerable literary gifts.[17]

[12] Only the first half has been published, edited by Arthur Brandeis (1900; *EETS*, 115). An edition of the rest is promised by G. R. Owst.

[13] I.e., manual of sins. Ed. F. J. Furnivall, with the *Manuel des Péchés* in parallel (1901-3; *EETS*, 119, 123). The author's full name was Robert Mannyng, of Brunne or Bourne (Lincs.). He belonged to the Gilbertine priory at Sempringham, but he was for a time at another Gilbertine house at Sixhills and at Cambridge. His literary activity falls between 1303, when he began the *Handlyng Synne*, and 1338, when he finished a translation of Langtoft's *Chronicle*. The latter forms the second part of his *Story of England*; the first part is based on Wace's *Roman de Brut*. The two parts are edited respectively in the Rolls Ser. (1889) and by T. Hearne (2v, Oxford, 1725). The latest examination of the facts of Robert's life is by Ruth Crosby, "Robert Mannyng of Brunne: A New Biography," *PMLA*, LVII (1942). 15-28.

[14] See p. 140.

[15] Ed. Richard Morris (1866; *EETS*, 23).

[16] Ed. W. Nelson Francis (1942; *EETS*, 217).

[17] An adequate account must await the publication of this important text. Only the first 370 lines have been printed (*ESt*, VII. 468-72). The best discussion is that of Hope Emily

Standing somewhat apart from those works which embody in one way or another Peckham's program is a poem which was intended nevertheless to act as a spur to righteousness. It is difficult now to see in its 9624 pedestrian lines how it could ever have become the most popular work of the fourteenth century, but more than a hundred extant manuscripts show that in this re- spect the *Prick of Conscience* surpassed the *Canterbury Tales, Piers Plow- man,* and every other Middle English poem. In a prologue and seven parts it tells of the wretched nature of man, the unstableness of the world, and of death which is inevitable, thus building up to the last four parts which treat of Purgatory, Doomsday, the pains of Hell, and the joys of Heaven. It was long attributed to Richard Rolle, but there is neither external nor internal evidence to justify our continuing to do so.[18]

The Prick of Conscience

Although none of the manuals for priests recommend including the Sun- day gospel as part of the sermon, the practice was certainly contemplated as early as Orm, and indeed most medieval books of sermons were made up of homilies on the Sunday gospel or epistle. With the spread of popular preaching vernacular collections of such homilies in verse were prepared for delivery either by the author or by others lacking in cunning or industry. They may have been intended for private reading as well. One such col- lection, the *Northern Homily Cycle* (*c.* 1300), provides sermons for the Sundays and certain festivals throughout the year, many of them furnished with appropriate exempla. The latest student of this cycle believes it to be the work of a Dominican.[19] Prose collections of similar scope, almost cer- tainly intended to provide ready materials for unlearned priests, are found in the *Festial*[20] of John Mirk, whom we have already mentioned as the author of *Instructions for Parish Priests,* and in an anonymous compilation, also of the fifteenth century, known as the *Speculum Sacerdotale.*[21]

Northern Homily Cycle

Allen, *Radcliffe Coll. Monographs,* No. 15, pp. 169 ff, and her *"Speculum Vitae:* Addendum," *PMLA,* xxxii (1917). 133-162. We cannot feel sure of the date, the identity of the author, or the immediate source of the poem. The author says he has translated from the Latin of John de Waldeby, but Miss Allen has shown that Waldeby's treatise on the Paternoster is not the source. In our present state of knowledge the closest connection seems to be with Friar Lorens and an English prose *Myrour to Lewde Men and Wymmen,* similar in content and often verbally identical. The *Speculum Vitae* is also one of the sources of *Jacob's Well.*

[18] See Hope Emily Allen, "The Authorship of the *Prick of Conscience," Radcliffe Coll. Monographs,* No. 15, pp. 115-170, and the references under Rolle in ch. xiii. The only edition is that of Richard Morris for the *Philological Society* (1863).

[19] James E. Carver, *The Northern Homily Cycle* (1941), abstract of his N. Y. Univ. diss. He believes it was written between 1295 and 1306, probably before October, 1303. (For his evidence see *MLN,* liii (1938). 258-261). Only fragmentary texts have been published by John Small, *English Metrical Homilies from Manuscripts of the Fourteenth Century* (Edin- burgh, 1862), and C. Horstmann, *Altenglische Legenden* (Heilbronn, 1881), pp. 1-188. A new edition is in preparation by Carver. The sources of the exempla are studied in Gordon H. Gerould, *The North-English Homily Collection: A Study of the Manuscript Relations and of the Sources of the Tales* (1902). The suggestion (*MLN,* xxii. 95-96) that the work was based on Robert of Gretham's *Miroir* has not been substantiated.

[20] Ed. Theodor Erbe (1905; *EETSES,* 96).

[21] Ed. Edward H. Weatherly (1936; *EETS,* 200). Space does not permit a discussion of the large body of sermon literature that has been preserved from the fourteenth and fifteenth centuries. For this the reader must be referred to the two books of G. R. Owst mentioned above. A collection of sermons formed at Oxford in the first half of the fifteenth century is edited by Woodburn O. Ross, *Middle English Sermons* (1940; *EETS,* 209). Although preaching in Latin was confined to sermons for monks and the clergy and scholarly audiences, many

Life of
Christ

In a day when the Bible was not a familiar book to the layman some form of gospel harmony presenting the life of Christ was an appropriate substitute. The *Stanzaic Life of Christ* is a long fourteenth-century poem, probably by a monk of St. Werburgh's abbey in Chester, who drew his material not from the Bible but from Higden's *Polychronicon* and the *Legenda Aurea*. Apart from exemplifying a type of religious omnibus it derives a certain interest from having been used in the composition of the *Chester Plays*.[22] Even more popular were treatments of the Passion, of which two in Middle English have come down to us. The *Northern Passion*[23] is much superior to the *Southern Passion,* and is found also in Midland and Southern manuscripts. It is based upon an Old French *Passion,* and in an expanded form is sometimes incorporated in the *Northern Homily Cycle*. It was used in certain episodes of both the *York* and the *Towneley Plays*. The *Southern Passion*[24] is always found as part of the *South English Legendary* (discussed below) and seems to have been written for this collection.

The
Passion

Cursor
Mundi

An attempt to cover the outstanding events of the Old as well as the New Testament is the northern poem called the *Cursor Mundi,*[25] because, as the author explains, it runs over the whole world. It is one of the longest of the omnibus poems, filling nearly 24,000 lines, with additional pieces at the end. After a prologue in which the author explains his plan and his intention of writing in English for the common people he divides his story into seven ages, beginning with Creation and ending with the Last Judgment. He has drawn his material from various sources, about a fifth from Herman of Valenciennes' *Bible,*[26] other parts from Grosseteste's *Château d'Amour*, Methodius, an Old French legend of the Holy Rood, and the Assumption of the Virgin from a Southern English poem on the subject. What cannot be otherwise accounted for is usually attributed to Peter Comestor (whom he names), but we shall probably find some day other more immediate sources for some of this matter. The work belongs to the last part of the thirteenth century or early in the next.

South
English
Legendary

What goes by the name of the *South English Legendary*[27] could almost be described as a group of similar works having certain parts in common. It is obviously a matter of gradual growth, undergoing modifications and accretions for upwards of a hundred years. Like the *Legenda Aurea*, to which it bears an obvious family likeness,[28] it consists not only of saints'

---

sermons preached in the vernacular are preserved only in Latin. A famous example is John Bromyard's *Summa Predicantium* of the middle of the fourteenth century.

[22] See the edition of Frances A. Foster (1926; EETS, 166).

[23] Ed. Frances A. Foster (1913-16; EETS, 145 and 147).

[24] Ed. Beatrice Daw Brown (1927; EETS, 169).

[25] Ed. Richard Morris (1874-78; EETS, 57, 59, 62, 66, 68).

[26] Lois Borland, "Herman's *Bible* and the *Cursor Mundi*," SP, xxx (1933). 427-444.

[27] One manuscript that has been printed in full is Laud 108, dating 1280-90. It is edited by C. Horstmann (1887; EETS, 87).

[28] For a discussion of the possible influence of the *Legenda Aurea* on the English collection see Minnie E. Wells, "The *South English Legendary* in Its Relation to the *Legenda Aurea*," *PMLA*, li (1936). 337-360.

legends but narratives for important seasons in the ecclesiastical year. The many manuscripts in which it was copied differ greatly in the number, choice, and arrangement of items, but it is possible to see, along with the addition of new legends, a gradual expansion of the biblical and apocryphal matter until, in one of its later forms, the whole is divided into a Temporale and a Sanctorale and arranged approximately in accordance with the calendar. Although the earliest manuscript belongs to the end of the thirteenth century, the collection can hardly have been begun before about 1275. There is reason to think that it originally took shape in or near the abbey of Gloucester, and that the original compilation was the work of a Franciscan.[29] Probably many groups and individuals, however, had a hand in it in the course of its development.

It is interesting to note how many of the works discussed in this chapter belong to the north. The *Cursor Mundi,* the *Northern Homily Cycle,* and the *Northern Passion* come to mind immediately. Thoresby was Archbishop of York and John Gaytryge, who translated his *Catechism,* was a monk there. While we no longer need to think of the *Prick of Conscience* as associated with Rolle and Yorkshire, it is nevertheless a northern poem, and the Nassyngton who wrote the *Speculum Vitae* was most likely an advocate in the ecclesiastical court at York. The *Stanzaic Life of Christ* was probably written at Chester, and the *Handlyng Synne* certainly in Lincolnshire. In this list the northeast is especially prominent. We must recognize an active religious ferment in any region which in addition could give birth to Wyclif and the Lollard movement, call forth the great mystics, and produce the most ambitious cycles of biblical plays.[30]

Prominence of the North

[29] See Minnie E. Wells, as above, and her later article, "The Structural Development of the South English Legendary," *JEGP,* XLI (1942). 320-344.

[30] Space does not permit discussion of the collections of exempla for the use of preachers, such as the Latin *Liber Exemplorum* (c. 1275), ed. A. G. Little (1908), *Speculum Laicorum* (c. 1285), ed. J. T. Welter (Paris, 1914), and *Fasciculus Morum* (c. 1320?), still unpublished, or of collections translated in the fifteenth century into English, like the *Gesta Romanorum* (*EETSES,* 33) and the *Alphabet of Tales* (*EETS,* 126-127). See T. F. Crane, introduction to *The Exempla ... of Jacques de Vitry* (1890; *Folk-Lore Soc. Pub.,* XXVI) and "Mediæval Sermon-Books and Stories and Their Study since 1883," *Proc. Amer. Philos. Soc.,* LVI (1917). 369-402; J. T. Welter, *L'Exemplum dans la littérature religieuse et didactique du moyen âge* (Paris, 1927); and J. H. Mosher, *The Exemplum in the Early Religious and Didactic Literature of England* (1911).

XII

The Lyric[1]

*Lyric Not
Common
in Old
English*   It is a commonplace of literary history that there is little or no lyric in the poetry of the Anglo-Saxons. Such dramatic pieces as the *Seafarer,* the *Husband's Message,* or the *Wife's Lament,* or such elegiac reflections as the *Ruin* are lyrical rather than lyrics. Cædmon's *Hymn, Eadwacer,* and *Deor,* the last so fine in its simple unity and directness, come closest perhaps to the lyric in expressing the personal emotion of the poet.[2] But it is evident that Old English poetry found its most natural expression in the epic and in other types of narrative verse.

*or in
Anglo-
Norman
Poetry*   Likewise the Normans seem to have been without a lyrical bent. If we are to accept Gaston Paris's analysis of the Norman character,[3] the Norman was practical and business-like, earnest rather than gay. At all events, in the lyric of northern France, that is, in the poetry of the trouvères, the Normans seem to have played a very minor part. The same observation holds true for England. In the very considerable body of Anglo-Norman poetry there are few secular lyrics,[4] and it does not seem that Continental specimens were often copied in manuscripts written in England. During the period when French was the predominant language of the upper class it would be useless to look for lyrics of the French courtly type in English. The few lyrical fragments older than the thirteenth century, such as *St. Godric's Hymns* and *Cnut's Song,*[5] are of liturgical and clerical inspiration. When, therefore, English secular lyrics begin to appear about 1250, it is a little difficult to say precisely what are their antecedents.

---

[1] A convenient introduction to the Middle English lyric is the little volume of *Early English Lyrics* edited by E. K. Chambers and F. Sidgwick (1907) with an essay by Chambers on "Some Aspects of the Mediæval Lyric" and a list of important manuscripts in which the lyrics are found. Carleton Brown's three volumes, *English Lyrics of the XIII*th *Century* (Oxford, 1932), *Religious Lyrics of the XIV*th *Century* (Oxford, 1924), and *Religious Lyrics of the XV*th *Century* (Oxford, 1939), are indispensable collections of texts, as is Richard L. Greene's *The Early English Carols* (1935). Richard Morris, *An Old English Miscellany* (1872; EETS, 49) prints many of the older lyrics, and Thomas Wright and J. O. Halliwell, *Reliquiae Antiquae* (1841-3) includes many isolated texts. Böddeker's edition of poems in MS Harl. 2253 is mentioned below; W. Heuser's *Die-Kildare-Gedichte* (Bonn, 1904; *Bonner Beiträge zur Anglistik,* xiv) and *The Minor Poems of the Vernon MS,* ed. C. Horstmann and F. J. Furnivall (2v, 1892-1901; EETS, 98 and 117) should be noted. On special aspects of the Middle English lyric consult Otto Heider, *Untersuchungen zur mittelenglischen erotischen Lyrik (1250-1300)* (Halle, 1905), Alex. Müller, *Mittelenglische geistliche u. weltliche Lyrik des XIII. Jahrhunderts . . . nach Motiven u. Formen* (Halle, 1910), and the works mentioned in subsequent notes to this chapter.

[2] On all of these pieces see Part I, above.

[3] Gaston Paris, *La Littérature normande avant l'annexion (912-1204)* (Paris, 1899); see especially pp. 19-20 and 39-40.

[4] If the court referred to by Denis Piramus can be assumed to be the English court (see p. 137), there may have been more Anglo-Norman secular lyrics than we know about.

[5] See above, pp. 119-120.

In considering the origins of the Middle English lyric we must of course *Genesis* distinguish between religious and secular types. The religious lyric belongs *of the* to an ecclesiastica! and literary tradition which knows no national bound- *Middle* aries. It is as wide as the Christian faith itself. The secular lyric, on the *English* other hand, could conceivably have roots in the native soil, or in Continental *Lyric* poetry—French or Provençal—or in the secular Latin lyric which is con- veniently, if somewhat loosely, characterized by the term Goliardic.

In view of the scarcity just remarked of lyrics in Old English, any *Popular* native impulses that lie behind the Middle English lyric should presumably *Song* be sought in folk and minstrel song. That popular songs, often accom- panied by dancing, were sung, especially by women, is sufficiently clear, although specimens of the songs themselves are wholly lacking. The twelfth-century chronicler of the deeds of Hereward the Exile tells us that women and girls sang of him in their ring-dances.[6] While this would suggest a ballad rather than a lyric, a love song is unmistakably referred to in the story told in the same century by Giraldus Cambrensis.[7] A parish priest in Worcestershire, he says, had been kept awake all night by dancers in the churchyard so that in the service the next morning he sang the refrain

Swete lamman dhin are!

(Sweet leman, thy favor!) instead of *Dominus vobiscum.* Such references to popular songs become more numerous in succeeding centuries.

There is no evidence of the direct influence of Provençal poetry upon the *Provençal* English lyric, and little to make such influence probable.[8] But the troubadour *Influence* lyric was widely imitated in northern France and certain conventions which *Negligible* make a sporadic appearance in the English lyric could have reached England by way of French poets. Possible Provençal influence is therefore part of a larger question—how much does the English lyric of the Middle Ages owe to the lyric poetry of France?

To answer this question it is necessary to recall briefly the principal *Old French* types and general characteristics of the Old French lyric.[9] It is customary *Types*

---

[6] *De Gestis Herwardi* (ed. S. H. Miller, Peterborough, 1895, p. 12; *Lestorie des Engles* (1888; Rolls Ser.), II. 344): Mulieres ac puellae de eo in choris canebant.

[7] *Gemma Ecclesiastica* (*Opera*, Rolls Ser., II. 120).

[8] See H. J. Chaytor, *The Troubadours and England* (Cambridge, 1923), especially pp. 20-23 and ch. III. J. Audiau, *Les Troubadours et l'Angleterre* (2ed., 1927), while disposed to believe in the direct imitation of the troubadours in England, admits that "elle se cache le plus souvent sous des réminiscences vagues et presque insaississables" (p. 35). The resemblances pointed out by Elinor Rees, "Provençal Elements in the English Vernacular Lyrics of Manuscript Harley 2253," *Stanford Studies in Lang. and Lit.* (1941), pp. 81-95, are often commonplaces and are found equally in the poetry of the trouvères.

[9] The student should consult Alfred Jeanroy's *Les Origines de la poésie lyrique en France au moyen âge* (3ed., 1925) and the same author's chapter in L. Petit de Julleville, *Histoire de la langue et de la littérature française*, I. 345-404; Gaston Paris, "Les Origines de la poésie lyrique en France au moyen âge," *Jour. des Savants*, 1891-92 (pub. separately, 1892); and the histories of Old French literature mentioned on p. 110. A recent study is Guido Errante, *Lirica romanza del primo secolo: un saggio d'interpretazione* (1943; Columbia Univ. diss.) On the Provençal lyric see A. Jeanroy, *La Poésie lyrique des troubadours* (2v, 1934) or the shorter treatments in H. J. Chaytor, *The Troubadours* (1912) and J. Anglade, *Les Troubadours: leurs vies, leurs œuvres, leur influence* (1908).

to distinguish two groups, the popular and the courtly.[10] The former includes certain of the more objective forms. The *chanson de toile* (also called
Popular *chanson d'histoire* or *romance*) tells a story, generally of a young girl having
Types a love affair frowned upon by her parents, languishing for a distant lover,
deserted by one to whom she has given her love, etc. We should have to
look for analogous themes in English among the ballads, which the *chanson
de toile* resembles in the directness and economy with which it tells its story.
In the *chanson de la mal mariée* the poet observes a woman rebellious
against marriage or lamenting her bondage to a husband she does not love.
It is a highly conventional type and is not found in the English lyric. The
aube (Prov. *alba*) is a lyric in which two lovers who have spent the night
in each other's arms are forced to part by the coming of dawn, evident in
the growing light, the song of the lark, or the announcement of the watch.
They try to explain away the unwelcome signs and voice their annoyance
over the interruption of their love. The situation occurs in Chaucer's
Troilus[11] and is familiar to everyone in *Romeo and Juliet*, in Juliet's

> Wilt thou be gone? It is not yet near day.
> It was the nightingale, and not the lark....[12]

Popular in southern France, the *aube* is scarcely found in the north and is
quite unknown to the English lyric. Finally, there is the *pastourelle*,[13] a
very distinctive type, and in this case one that was more popular among
the trouvères than with the troubadours. The poet, usually represented as
a knight, comes upon a shepherdess tending her flock in the fields and makes
love to her. There is always verbal fencing, ending either in easy success or
in disappointment which the poet turns off with cavalier grace. Not more
than three specimens have been found in England before 1500, none of them
really close to the French type. Thus, so far as the "popular" types of French
lyric are concerned, French influence upon the English lyric appears to be
negligible.

Courtly   Among the courtly types of French lyric there are numerous minor varie-
Types ties, which can be passed over quickly. The *rondet* or dance song, not found
in English, follows the form of the modern triolet, and the *ballette*, ancestor
of the ballade, does not appear in English until Chaucer introduced it under
the influence of fourteenth-century French poets (Machaut, Deschamps,

---

[10] It may be questioned whether the distinction is well founded. Some scholars hold, however, that the so-called popular types are not dependent on Provençal models. One of the oldest
of these, the *rotrouenge*, is omitted from consideration here because there is not sufficient
evidence to justify a definition. The term is thought to be used in Old French for any song
with a refrain (P. Meyer, *Romania*, xix. 102; Jeanroy, *ibid.*, xxx. 424). In like manner the
reverdie must be rejected as a distinctive type, although the celebration of the return of spring
could well have formed the subject of lyrics in itself besides being the introductory setting for
the pastourelle and other forms.

[11] III. 1415-1533 and 1695-1712.

[12] On poems distantly related to the *aube* found in later English literature see Charles R.
Baskervill, "English Songs on the Night Visit," *PMLA*, xxxvi (1921). 565-614.

[13] W. Powell Jones, *The Pastourelle, A Study of the Origins and Tradition of a Lyric Type*
(Cambridge. Mass., 1931).

etc.). The *estampie*,[14] *lai, descort*,[15] and *motet* [16] are forms scarcely to be identified in Middle English. The debate types—*tenson* and *jeu parti*—and the personal or political *serventois* (Prov. *sirventes*) can be paralleled, but the poetical debate and the political poem are such natural forms and are found so early in the Latin poetry of the Middle Ages that it is doubtful whether we should credit the English examples to French inspiration. All these types, however, are of secondary importance. The courtly form par excellence of the French lyric was the love song or *chanson d'amour,* the equivalent of the Provençal *canso.*

More than half of all the Old French secular lyrics that have been pre- *The* served are *chansons.* The *chanson* consists generally of five stanzas and an *Chanson* envoy,[17] and the theme is always love. The universality of love as a subject *Courtoise* for poetry would suggest that here, if anywhere, the influence of France on the English lyric could be exerted. The difference, however, between the French and the English love-songs is more basic than the similarity. This difference begins with the very conception of love itself that is revealed in the lyrics of the two countries. The love of the *chanson courtoise* is courtly *and* love, the devotion of the poet to a married woman. The relation is that of *English* vassal and overlord. The lover is enlisted in the service of love. He expects *Love-Songs* the lady to be haughty and capricious; he endures any hardship and suffers all in the desire to make himself worthy of her. Love is for him a cult, and he expresses his devotion in extolling the physical charms, the goodness, and the spiritual excellences of the woman who is to him its major divinity. One would expect this poetry to be full of fire and emotion. It is not. It is cold.[18] The poet analyzes his emotions, theorizes about the cause and effect of love, and finds enjoyment even in the suffering which he endures. The monotony with which the *chansons courtoises* repeat this conventional attitude is the fault with which they are most often charged, and to pass to the English love-lyric is like stepping from make-believe into the real world. Here we have no *Frauendienst* of the knightly class, but feelings natural to two young people between whom there is no social gulf. The English lyric is frank and outspoken. It looks forward to marriage or the intimacies of possession:

> He myhte sayen þat Crist hym seʒe,   regarded
> Þat myhte nyhtes neh hyre leʒe,
> hevene he hevede here.

The poet's affection is for a *burde* "maiden" *in bower,* a *may,* or a *maide,* or his *make.* She is his *sweet leman* or his *sweeting:*

[14] W. O. Streng-Renkonen, *Les Estampies françaises* (Paris, 1931; *CFMA,* 65). Lloyd Hibberd, "Estampie and Stantipes," *Speculum,* XIX (1944). 222-249, is primarily concerned with the music.

[15] A. Jeanroy, L. Brandin, and P. Aubry, *Lais et descorts français du XIIIe siècle* (1901).

[16] Originally a musical term, designating a song for several voices with different words for each. See J. B. Beck, *La Musique des troubadours* (1910).

[17] Sometimes six or seven stanzas. The number of lines in the stanza varies greatly.

[18] Jeanroy in L. Petit de Julleville, *Histoire de la langue et de la littérature française,* I. 372.

> Blow, northerne wynd,
> Sent þou me my suetyng!
> Blow, norþerne wynd,
> Blou! blou! blou!

He has no reason to conceal her identity: she is Annot, or Alysoun, or "woneþ by west."

Few Early
Secular
Lyrics

In English secular lyrics that have been preserved are not numerous.[19] One of the most lilting of English songs is that in which the poet rejoices over the good fortune that has let him fall in love with Alysoun:

Bytuenë Mersh and Averil,	
When spray biginneþ to springe,	
Þe lutel foul haþ hire wyl	little bird
On hyre lud to synge	voice
Ich libbe in love-longinge	
For semlokest of alle þinge;	seemliest
He may me blisse bringe,	She
Ich am in hire bandoun.	at her disposition
An hendy hap ichabbe y-hent	fortunate chance I have got
Ichot from heuene it is me sent:	I know
From alle wymmen mi love is lent	departed
And lyht on Alysoun.	alighted

Alysoun

He describes her fair hair, brown eyes, her "middel smal"; no man can tell all her goodness. His only fear is lest someone else should take her from him:

Icham for wowyng al forwake,	
Wery so water in wore,	pond (weir)
Lest eny reve me my make.	deprive . . . of
Ychabbe y-ʒerned ʒore.	for a long time
Better is þolien whyle sore	to suffer
Þen mournen evermore.	
Geynest under gore,	most gracious
Herkne to my roun.	song
An hendy hap ichabbe y-hent,	
Ichot from hevene it is me sent:	
From alle wymmen mi love is lent	
And lyht on Alysoun.	

Love
Themes

A favorite occupation of the love poet in all times and places is to dwell on his lady's graces. Besides entering incidentally into a number of lyrics, such description makes up the whole of two early lyrics. In one the poet boasts "Ichot a burde in a bour ase beryl so bright" and in five stanzas he compares her successively to gems, flowers, various birds, and even to herbs

---

[19] That more of the secular lyric has possibly been lost than is preserved is suggested by the so-called Rawlinson fragments. These are opening lines and stanzas (possibly in some cases complete little poems) preserved in a single leaf of the early fourteenth century from what may well have been some minstrel's notebook. They are edited by W. Heuser, "Fragmente von unbekannten Spielmannsliedern des 14. Jahrhunderts, aus MS Rawl. D. 913," *Anglia*, xxx (1907). 173-179.

medicinal to the body as she is medicine to his soul. In the other he describes her eyes, her merry mouth, her teeth, in fact her whole appearance. She has lovely "rede lippes ... romaunz forto rede" and even "hire neose ys set as hit wel semeþ." One must not think, however, that medieval poets did not also experience the sorrows of love. In a little thirteenth-century piece despair is expressed in what must be close to the ultimate in condensation:

> Foweles in þe frith   woods
> Þe fisses in þe flod.   fishes
> And I mon waxe wod.   mad
> Mulch sorw I walk with   much sorrow
> For beste of bon and blod.

In a lyric in the famous Harleian manuscript,[20] from which some of the above examples have been taken and which preserves most of the small number of pre-Chaucerian love lyrics that have come down to us, the poet complains:

> Wiþ longyng y am lad,
> On molde y waxe mad,   earth
> A maide marreþ me.

He protests that he loves her faithfully and will die before his time if she does not show pity:

> Levedi, wiþ al my miht
> My love is on þe liht,
> To menske when y may,   honor
> Þou rew & red me ryht!
> To deþe þou havest me diht:
> Y deȝe longe er my day,
> Þou leve upon my lay   believe
> Treuþe ichave þe plyht
> To don þat ich have hyht   promised
> Whil mi lif leste may.

The sentiments expressed in these poems are those of lovers everywhere; neither in thought or tone are we reminded of the French lyric. A common French convention, however, represents the poet as wandering by the way and coming unexpectedly upon a love adventure,[21] and this convention is reflected in one thirteenth-century lyric in another manuscript:

> *Nou sprinkes the sprai:*   springs
> *Al for love icche am so seeke*
> *That slepen I ne mai.*

[20] Harl. 2253, a collection of pieces in French and English, of quite varied character, gathered together about 1340, with greatest probability somewhere in Herefordshire. The English lyrics are all in K. Böddeker, *Altenglische Dichtungen des MS Harl. 2253* (Berlin, 1878). A number of graceful little love poems are found in the works of Chaucer, but they follow a later convention.

[21] For the French type as imitated in English, often at a very great distance, see the excellent study of Helen E. Sandison, *The "Chanson d'Aventure" in Middle English* (Bryn Mawr, 1913).

Als I me rode this endre dai   other day
   O mi pleyinge
Seih I hwar a litel mai   saw
   Bigan to singge:
   "The clot him clingge!
Wai es him i lovve-longinge   in
   Sal libben ai,"   shall live
      Nou sprinkes, etc.

Son icche herde that mirie note
   Þider I drogh;   drew
I fonde hire in an herber swot   sweet
   Under a bogh
   With joie inogh.
Son I asked, "Thou mirie mai
   Hwi sinkes-tou ai?"   singest thou
      Nou sprinkes the sprai, etc.

Than answerde that maiden swote,
   Midde wordes fewe:
"Mi lemman me haves bi-hot   promised
   Of lovve trewe;
   He chaunges a newe.
ȝiif I mae, it shal him rewe
   Bi this dai!"
      Nou sprinkes, etc.

The Cuckoo Song

The association of love with spring is older than the Middle Ages, but seems to have had less meaning in classical times in the climate of the Mediterranean. In the poetry of more northern countries, however, the return of warm weather was greeted with an enthusiasm which is not always appreciated by the modern reader, who controls his comfort with a thermostat. What is perhaps the best-known lyric in Middle English, the famous *Cuckoo Song* (*c.* 1300), is a simple outburst of joy at the return of Spring:

Sumer is i-cumen in,
   Lhude sing, cuccu!
Groweth sed and bloweth med
   And springth the wde nu.   woods
      Sing, cuccu!
Awe bleteth after lomb,   ewe
Lhouth after calve cu,   cow
bulluc sterteth, bucke verteth;   leaps up
   Murie sing, cuccu,
      Cuccu, cuccu!
   Wel singes thu, cuccu,
   Ne swik thu naver nu!

This delightful song, with all the freshness of popular poetry, is set to music of an elaborate kind [22] with Latin directions for singing by several voices (as a round). As spring brought enjoyment of the out of doors, so winter aroused very different emotions. In the opening stanza of a lyric, of which unfortunately the rest has been cut away in the manuscript, the season is made to symbolize the poet's sorrowful mood over some wrong which he has suffered:

> Mirie it is while sumer ilast
>   With fugheles song,
> Oc nu necheth windes blast   *but now nigheth*
>   And weder strong.
> Ej! ej! what this nicht is long,   *how . . . long*
>   And ich wid wel michel wrong
> Soregh and murne and fast.   *sorrow and mourn*

The Religious Lyric

It is to be regretted that we have relatively few secular lyrics preserved. The great bulk of the Middle English lyric—and its bulk is great—is religious or moral. We should hasten to add, however, that the religious lyrics are almost always touching in their sincerity, often imaginative in conception, and occasionally startle us by their sheer beauty. In spite of the fact that most of them involve some form of appeal to Christ or the Virgin Mary for salvation or intercession, they take a great variety of shapes.[23] If they suffer somewhat from the uniformity of their devotional appeal, we must remember that the piety and religious fervor which produced them are the guarantee of their emotional validity.

Lyrics Addressed to the Virgin

The simplest form of lyric addressed to the Virgin is that in which the poet sings her praises. She is most often described as the mild mother, Queen of Heaven, angels' bliss.[24] She has come of high kin and is without spot or blemish. Sometimes we hear echoes of the secular love poem: she is "flower of all" and "brightest in bower." "Thy love is ever alike new." Often praise is mingled with prayer as in the charming poem which begins

---

[22] See the account by Dom Anselm Hughes in Grove's *Dictionary of Music and Musicians* (3ed.), where it is described as the oldest known canon, the oldest known six-part composition, etc. A facsimile of the manuscript is reproduced as the frontispiece of Vol. v. The date usually given (c. 1240) rests on an untenable inference. Manfred F. Bukofzer, *"Sumer Is Icumen In": A Revision* (Berkeley, 1944; *Univ. of Calif. Pub. in Music*, Vol. ii, No. 2), offers strong arguments against so early a date for the music, which he puts about 1310. This seems a little late linguistically for the lyric. See also Carleton Brown, *English Lyrics of the XIII*[th] *Century*, pp. xv ff., for the testimony of Giraldus Cambrensis as to the existence of counterpoint in Wales and Yorkshire c. 1190.

[23] Consult F. A. Patterson, *The Middle English Penitential Lyric: A Study and Collection of Early Religious Verse* (1911), Heinrich Corsdress, *Die Motive der mittelenglischen geistlichen Lyrik . . . und ihr Verhältnis zur lateinischen Hymnologie des Mittelalters* (Weimar, 1913), and Samuel Singer, *Die religiöse Lyrik des Mittelalters* (Bern, 1933).

[24] Among the poems, mostly doctrinal, of William of Shoreham, vicar of Chart-Sutton in Kent (c. 1325) is a graceful little hymn to the Virgin, there attributed to Robert Grosseteste, in which the Virgin is described as the dove of Noah that brought back the olive branch, the bush of Sinai, the temple of Solomon, etc. Shoreham's poems were edited by Thomas Wright for the Percy Soc. (1849) and more recently by M. Konrath (1902; *EETSES*, 86).

Of on that is so fayr and briȝt
velud maris stella
Briȝter than the day is liȝt,
parens et puella,
Ic crie to the, thou se to me,
Levedy, preye thi sone for me
tam pia,
That ic mote come to the,
Maria.

Underlying all such appeals is the thought of the Virgin as the link between
God and mankind, a thought which occasionally takes a novel turn:

Thou my sister and mother
And thy son my brother—
Who should then drede?
Who-so haveth the king to brother
And eke the queen to mother
Well ought for to spede.[25]

The Virgin as Subject   Almost all the circumstances of the Virgin's life were the subject of
poems. There are poetical accounts of the Annunciation, like the blind John
Audelay's [26]

The angel to the vergyn said,
Entreng into here boure,
Fore drede of quakyng of this mayd,
He said, "haile!" with gret honour,
"Haile! be thou quene of maidyns mo,
Lord of heven and erth also. . . ."

Among numerous poems on the Five Joys, one in the Harleian manuscript
is interesting for its use of the conventional French opening already illustrated in the secular lyric and now become a matter of meaningless habit:

Ase y me rod this ender day
By grenë wode to sechë play,
Mid herte y thohte al on a may,
Suetest of allë thinge.
Lythe *&* ichou tellë may   listen
Al of that swetë thinge.

"With al mi lif y love that may," the poet says and proceeds to comment
on the Annunciation, the Birth of Christ, the Resurrection, the Ascension,
and the Virgin's own Assumption into heaven as the moments of greatest
joy in her life.

[25] In quoting from lyrics, especially of the fifteenth century, I have sometimes slightly
modernized the spelling where no harm is done to the metre or rime.
[26] John Audelay (*c.* 1425) was a monk of Haghmond Abbey, near Shrewsbury. He is the
author of fifty-five didactic and devotional poems. The best edition is that of Ella K. Whiting,
The Poems of John Audelay (1931; *EETS,* 184).

Some of the most effective lyrics, both of the Virgin and of Christ, are *Dramatic* those in which the mood is portrayed dramatically, in monologue or dialogue *Lyrics* form. There is a charming dialogue between the Virgin and her Child, beginning

> As I lay upon a night
>   Alone in my longing,
> Methought I saw a wonder sight,
>   A maiden child rocking.
>
> The maiden would withouten song
>   Hir child o sleep bring;
> The child thought she did him wrong,
>   And bade his moder sing.
>
> "Sing now, moder," said that child,
>   "What me shall befall
> Here-after when I come to eld—
>   So don modres all.
>
> "Each a moder truly
>   That kan her cradle keep
> Is wont to lullen lovëly
>   & singen her child o sleep.
>
> "Swetë moder, fair & fre,
>   Sithen that it is so,
> I prayë the that thou lulle me
>   & sing somewhat there-to."

In response to this request Mary relates the events from the Annunciation to the birth of the Christ-child, and he continues prophetically with an out-line of his own life, ending in his death and resurrection. In the final stanza the poet tells us that the vision came to him on Christmas day:

> Certainly this sight I say,   saw
>   This song i herdë sing,
> As I lay this Yules-day
>   Alone in my longing.

One of the most beautiful of Middle English lyrics, certainly of those con-cerning the Virgin, begins:

> Suddenly afraid,
>   Half waking, half sleeping,
> And greatly dismayed,
>   A woman sat weeping.

It is the Virgin, weeping over the body of Christ:

> With favor in her face far passing my reason,
> And of her sore weeping this was the encheson   cause
> Her son in her lap lay, she said, slain by treason.
> If weeping might ripe be, it seemed then in season.

> "Jhesu!" so she sobbed;
> So her Son was bobbed   beaten
> And of his life robbed,
> Saying these words, as I say thee:
> "Who cannot weep, come learn of me."

Three more stanzas reveal the Virgin's grief, partly in dialogue with the poet, each rising to the same thought—Who cannot weep, come learn of me.[27]

Lyrics to Christ   As with lyrics of the Virgin, so in poems addressed to Christ we have songs of simple praise. A poem taking its theme from the well-known hymn long attributed to St. Bernard, the *Jesu Dulcis Memoria,* begins:

> Ihesu, swete is the love of thee,
> Noon othir thing so swete may be;
> No thing that men may heere *&* see
> Hath no swetnesse aʒens thee.

and continues as a rosary of fifty stanzas. It is an example of devotion put in the form of meditation. Another lyric of similar intent may have been written by a woman:

> Now I see blostme spring   blossom
> I herde a fuheles song;   bird's
> A swete longing
> Myn herte throughout sprong
> That is of love newe
> That is so swete and trewe
> It gladdeth all my song . . .

The song is of Christ; alas, that I cannot turn all my thought to him and make him my leman! It is an expression of spiritual yearning, and the prayer in the closing stanza begins with the words

> Iesu, leman sweet,
> I send thee this song.

Christ as lover is the theme of the Franciscan Thomas of Hales' *Love Rune* mentioned above (p. 123). Among simple appeals to Christ for help and salvation Richard Caister's *Ihesu, lord, þat madist me* at the beginning of the fifteenth century was deservedly popular, as seventeen manuscripts show.[28]

The most beautiful of the religious lyrics is the *Quia amore langueo,* beginning:

---

[27] On laments of the Virgin see H. Thien, *Über die englischen Marienklagen* (Kiel, 1906) and for their Continental background E. Wechssler, *Die romanischen Marienklagen* (Halle, 1893).

[28] On the author see the Rev. Dundas Harford, "Richard of Caister, and his Metrical Prayer," *Norfolk Archæology,* XVII (1910). 221-244.

In a valey of this restles minde   Quia
    I soughte in mounteine and in mede,   Amore
Trusting a trewe love for to finde.   Langueo
    Upon an hill than I took hede;
    A voice I herde, and neer I yede,
In huge dolour complaininge tho,
    "See, dere soule, how my sides blede,
Quia amore langueo."

The poet comes upon a man wounded and sitting under a tree. It is Christ
—"true love that fals was nevere"—suing for man's soul. She has left him
and is hard to woo, but—

    I wole abide till sche be redy;
        I wole her sue if sche seie nay;

The poem parallels the secular love complaints:

    Fair love, lete us go pleye!
        Apples ben ripe in my gardaine.
    I schal thee clothe in a newe aray;
        Thy mete schall be milk, hony, and wine.
    Fair love, let us go digne!   dine
    Thy sustenaunce is in my crippe, lo!   scrip
        Tarie thou not, my faire spouse mine,
    Quia amore langueo.

He will care for her always:

    Mine owne wife, go not me fro!
        Thy meede is marked whan thou art mort,   dead
    Quia amore langueo.

It is but a step from the devotional lyric to poems of moral reflection and *Reflective*
admonition. Many of these spring from the thought, sometimes used as a *and*
refrain, *Timor mortis conturbat me.* They stress the transitoriness of worldly *Admoni-*
pleasures: *tory Poems*

    Wynter wakeneth al my care,
    Nou this levës waxeth bare;
    Ofte y sike *&* mournë sare   sigh
        When hit cometh in my thoht
        Of this worldes joie—how hit geth al to noht.

Man is but dust. Why should he be proud? This is the theme of the famous
Earth upon Earth, which was often copied and exists in many forms: [29]

    Erthe upon erthe is wonderly wrought
    Erthe upon erthe hath worship of nought
    Erthe upon erthe hath set all his thought
    How erthe upon erthe might be high brought.

[29] Hilda M. R. Murray, *The Middle English Poem, Erthe upon Erthe, printed from Twenty-four Manuscripts* (1911; *EETS*, 141).

Similar is the reflection *Ubi sunt qui ante nos fuerunt:*

> Where beth they biforen us weren
> Houndës ladden and havckës beren   led . . . hawks bore
> And hadden feld and wode?

Where are those rich ladies in their bower, wearing gold in their hair?
They ate and drank and made merry, but in the twinkling of an eye their
souls were lost. Where now is that laughter and song?

Lyrics in which the poet reflects on the Passion and Resurrection, and
dwells on the sacrifice Christ has made for man are very numerous. Particularly melodious is one beginning:

> Somer is comen *&* winter gon
>   This day biginnith to longe,
> *&* this foulës everichon
>   Joye hem wit songe.
> So stronge kare me bint,   binds
> Al wit joye that is funde
>   In londe,
> Al for a child
> That is so milde
>   Of honde.

Christ is often represented as appealing to man, complaining that man has
rejected him, and offering mercy freely to those who will accept it. One
such dramatic lyric begins:

> Undo thi dore, my spouse dere,
> Allas! wy stond I loken out here?   locked
>   Fre am I thi make.
> Loke mi lokkes *&* ek my heved
> *&* al my bodi with blod beweved   enveloped
>   For thi sake.
>
> Allas! allas! hevel have I sped   sin
> For senne Iesu is fro me fled,   evil
>   Mi trewe fere.   companion
> With-outen my gate he stant alone,
> Sorfuliche he maket his mone
>   On his manere.

Reflections such as this led one poet to contemplate a baby crying in its
crib, sorrowfully:

> Lollai, lollai, litil child, whi wepistou so sore?
> Nedis mostou wepe, hit was iȝarkid the ȝore   prepared for
> Ever to lib in sorow, and sich and mourne evere,   sigh
> As thin eldren did er this, whil hi alives were.   they
>   Lollai, lollai, litil child, child lolai, lullow,
>   Into uncuth world icommen so ertow.   unknown

Beasts and birds and fishes in the flood are fortunate when they come into the world, but man is born to sorrow. After five stanzas the poet concludes:

Child, thou nert a pilgrim bot an uncuthe gist	unknown guest
Thi dawes beth itold, thi jurneis beth icast;	days are numbered
Whoder thou salt wend north other est	whether
Deth the sal betide with bitter bale in brest.	shall
Lollai, lollai, litil child, this wo Adam the wroȝt,	
Whan he of the appil ete, and Eve hit him betacht.	handed

A more cheerful note is brought into the fifteenth century by the rapid *The Carol* rise to popularity of the carol [30] associated with Christmas and Epiphany. It is a time of rejoicing:

> Now may we singen as it is
> *Quod puer natus est nobis.*

Often the theme is the simple story of Christ's birth:

> *Make we mery in hall & bowr,*
> *Thys tyme was born owr Savyowr.*
>
> In this tyme God hath sent
> Hys own Son, to be present,
> To dwell with us in verament,
>   God that ys owr Savyowr.
>
> In this tyme that ys be-fall,
> A child was born in an ox stall
> & after he dyed for us all,
>   God that ys owr Savyowr.
>
> In this tyme an angell bryght
> Mete III shepherdis upon a nyght,
> He bade them go anon ryght
>   To God that ys owr Saviowr.
>
> In thys tyme now pray we
> To hym that dyed for us on tre,
> On us all to have pytee,
>   God that ys owr Saviowr.

But we have also carols celebrating merely the joyful spirit of the season:

> *Make we mery, bothe more & lasse*
> *For now ys the tyme of Crystymas.*
>
> Lett no man cum in to this hall,
> Grome, page, nor yet marshall,
> But that sum sport he bryng with-all,
>   For now ys the tyme of Cristemas.

---

[30] For an interesting theory concerning the origin of the word see Margit Sahlin, *Étude sur la carole médiévale: l'origine du mot et ses rapports avec l'église* (Uppsala, 1940).

> If that he say he can not syng,
> Some oder sport then lett hym bryng,
> That it may please at this festing,
>   For now is the time of Cristemas.
>
> If he say he can nowght do,
> Then for my love aske him no mo,
> But to the stokkes then let hym go,
>   For now is the time of Cristemas.

Political, Satirical, and Convivial Songs

Space does not permit more than a passing reference to the political poems which offer editorial comment on current events,[31] or to those comments, often satirical, upon abuses of the time and the weaknesses of an erring humanity.[32] Nor is there need to speak of the shorter poems of Chaucer, whose more important work is treated elsewhere, or of Lydgate who is likewise discussed in another place.[33] It would be pleasant to touch on the small number of humorous, satirical, and convivial songs which appear toward the end of the Middle English period. One answers the question "when to trust a woman" by suggesting, "when nettles in winter bear roses red, and thorns bear figs by nature," when laurels bear cherries, when sparrows build churches, when wrens carry sacks to the mill, and other possibilities equally likely. There is the lament of the man married to a shrewish wife:

> All that I may swink or swete,
>   My wife it will both drink and ete...

and the warning to young men not to marry.
A drinking song such as

> Tapster, fille another ale.
> Anonne have I do.
> God sende us good sale;
>   Avale the stake, avale!   drink down the pledge(?)

---

[31] An example is the *Song of Lewes* written by a sympathizer with Simon de Montfort after his victory in the battle of Lewes (1264). It is directed at the King's brother, Richard, Earl of Cornwall, each stanza ending:

> Richard, thah thou be ever trichard [traitor]
> Tricchen shalt thou nevermore!

See the edition of C. L. Kingsford (Oxford, 1890). Many political songs have a narrative base, as, for example, those of Laurence Minot concerning incidents between 1333 and 1352. Minot's poems have been often edited; the best edition is that of Joseph Hall (Oxford, 1897). For collections of political songs, in Latin, French, and English, see Thomas Wright, *The Political Songs of England, from the Reign of John to that of Edward II* (1839; *Camden Soc.*, VI); Thomas Wright, *Political Poems and Songs relating to English History ... from the Accession of Edw. III. to that of Ric. II* (2v, 1859-61; Rolls Ser.); cf. also Livingston Corson, *A Finding List of Political Poems Referring to English Affairs of the XIII and XIV Centuries* (n.d.; Univ. of Penna. diss.).

[32] See for examples the poems in Carleton Brown, *Religious Lyrics of the XIVth Century*, pp. 152 ff., one of which expresses the idea that the world is run by flattery and dissembling, another speaks with mild bitterness of fair-weather friends, etc.

[33] For Richard Rolle, who wrote a small number of lyrics, see ch. XIII. A conscientious but uninspired versifier, James Ryman (c. 1490) has left a large number of devotional poems, which are edited by Zupitza in *Archiv*, LXXXIX (1892). 167-338.

> Here is good ale ifounde.
> Drinke to me,
> And I to thee,
> And lette the cuppe go rounde—

reminds us that conviviality has expressed itself in song in practically all periods of literature.

Most of our early lyrics are anonymous. Some show the same kind of *Authorship* variations between texts as we find in the ballads and these variants have apparently arisen in the course of oral transmission.[34] It is natural to attribute most of the religious pieces to clerkly authorship,[35] but it is not impossible that some of the secular love songs, too, were written in the shadow of the church. Jolly Absolon had many brothers, and the spirit of the English secular lyric finds its closest parallel in the Latin love songs of the *scholares vagantes*.[36] The earlier Middle English lyrics were intended for the ear rather than the eye. Many of them are accompanied in the manuscripts by music,[37] and we should make liberal allowance for the loss which they suffer in being deprived of their melody. Few popular songs of our own day, similarly stripped, would stand up so well.

In the later fourteenth century and certainly in the fifteenth the lyric becomes increasingly literary.[38] From the village green and the great hall it *Late* passes to the study. Spontaneity at times gives way to the gracefully turned *Tendencies* conceit. At times the imaginative quality becomes genuinely arresting. The fifteenth-century poet was unwittingly looking forward to Alan Seeger's *I Have a Rendezvous with Death* when he wrote:

> Farewell, this world! I take my leave forever!
> I am arrested to appear at Goddës face. . . .[39]

Philosophy takes its place beside religion; the poet is as likely to address Fortune as God:

> A! Mercy, Fortune, have pitee on me,
> And thynke that thu hast done gretely amysse
> To parte asondre them which ought to be
> Alwey in one; why hast thu doo thus?
> Have I offendyd the? I, nay ywysse!
> Then torne thy whele and be my frende agayn,
> And send me joy where I am nowe in payn.

---

[34] See the various texts of the *Alma Redemptoris Mater*, beginning "As I lay upon a night," in Greene, pp. 166-7.

[35] For the importance of the Franciscans as authors of the religious lyric see Rossell H. Robbins, "The Authors of the Middle English Religious Lyrics," *JEGP*, xxxix (1940). 230-238, and "The Earliest Carols and the Franciscans," *MLN*, liii (1938). 239-245.

[36] For references see p. 149, note 15.

[37] An important collection of facsimiles with transcriptions is in Sir John Stainer's *Early Bodleian Music* (2v, 1901).

[38] Extensive collections of fifteenth-century lyrics are edited to Bernhard Fehr in *Archiv*, cvi, cvii, and cix.

[39] Brown, *Religious Lyrics of the XVᵗʰ Century*, p. 236.

And thynke what sorowe is the departyng
Of two trewe hertis lovyng feithfully,
For partyng is the most soroughfull thynge,
To myn entent, that ever yet knewe I.
Therefore, I pray to the right hertely
To turne thy whele and be my frende agayn,
And send me joy where I am now in payn. . . .[40]

With such a lyric as this we look forward to the poetry of the Renaissance.

[40] *Ibid.*, p. 262.

XIII
Richard Rolle and Other Mystics

Mysticism [1] is the most intense form of personal religious experience. In *Definition* Christian mysticism the individual seeks through solitary contemplation to enter into direct communion with God or to attain spiritual union with God. In such union, with its accompanying illumination, the will seems temporarily in abeyance and the individual is in a state of complete though receptive passivity. The experience is by nature transient, and above all, it is ineffable: it cannot be expressed in words or conveyed from one person to another.

The mystic state is not an experience into which one can enter at will. *The Three* When St. Paul said that he was *caught up* to the third heaven, he meant, as *Stages* St. Bernard observed, that he could not have attained such rapture by any strength or toil of his own. One must hear the call of God, after which grace supplies the strength that is lacking in the individual. Once the awakening has taken place, there are three stages, generally speaking, through which the soul must pass. The first is Purgation. "Pure truth is seen only with a pure heart." By sanctity of life, sincere repentance, and an intense desire for holiness the obstacles are removed which stand in the way of the soul's progress. The second stage, known as Illumination, is that in which the mind detaches itself from outer sensations and yields in complete surrender to the will of God. The soul prepares itself, as it were, for union with the Divine Presence. Meditation is the basis of mystical detachment and one who hopes to attain to the highest of the mystical states should, in the words of Rolle, "accustom himself to meditation and devout prayer before he reaches out to the contemplation of heavenly joys." For Rolle, meditation on the Passion seemed the most fitting form which such devotion could take. The final stage, known as Contemplation, is that in which the soul is brought into the presence of God and becomes one with God. It is a state of ecstasy or vision, incapable of being described in words, generally one of the purest and intensest joy. It is in this stage that the individual sometimes sees visions, hears voices, and experiences "those ab-

[1] The student of English mysticism can begin with two small but excellent books: Dom David Knowles, *The English Mystics* (1927) and Evelyn Underhill, *The Mystics of the Church* (n.d.). Dom Cuthbert Butler's *Western Mysticism* (1922) contains liberal extracts from St. Augustine, St. Gregory the Great, and St. Bernard. More extended discussions of mysticism are Evelyn Underhill, *Mysticism* (1911), and W. R. Inge, *Christian Mysticism* (1899). See also William James, *The Varieties of Religious Experience* (1902), Lectures XVI and XVII, and Arthur Devine, *A Manual of Mystical Theology* (1903). Francis D. S. Darwin, *The English Medieval Recluse* (1944), gives a general picture of the recluse in a brief and popular form.

normal psychic phenomena which appear so persistently in the history of the mystics." [2] For the mystical experience also yields knowledge and comprehension of spiritual things, truth intuitively perceived. Truth is revealed to the contemplative soul as material things are visible to the bodily eye. The mystic reward is thus not only the personal joy felt in being present in spirit with God, but at times the deeper understanding of spiritual truth.

Necessarily Personal   As we have already observed, mysticism is in the highest degree personal. The contemplative experience must come from within and is a manifestation of divine grace. It is not communicable. One might suppose, therefore, that since mystic exaltation begins and ends with the individual, there would be no occasion for putting it into words. There are several reasons why this is not so. In the first place, the inner light that the mystic attains is felt to be authoritative, and we can understand the impulse to share his insight with others and perhaps lead others to a similar desire for inner illumination. Again, the mystic in the light of his experience may feel that he is in a position to instruct others in the way to contemplative joy. And finally, the mystic is not unlike the poet in his wish to give permanence to the things that he has felt deeply and to give vent to his joy in the outpouring of his emotion. Hence the very considerable body of mystical writing—autobiographical, didactic, lyrical.

The Fourteenth Century   The fourteenth century is the great age of mysticism, not only in England but in other parts of Europe as well. [3] Whether, as has been suggested, it was a reaction against the extremes of scholasticism or a part of the general religious awakening discussed in a previous chapter, it reflects the mystics' dissatisfaction with casual observances and the ordinary forms of worship—"any long psalter unmindfully mumbled in the teeth," as the *Cloud of Unknowing* puts it. Rolle contrasts the fervor of the contemplative with the lukewarm devotion of the monks. Mysticism reflects the craving for a more eager, personal spirituality having its source in the individual. It must not be thought, however, that the flowering of mysticism in the fourteenth century is a sudden phenomenon. Its roots reach back to apostolic times, and the mystical tradition in the west descends from St. Augustine and (Pseudo) Dionysius the Areopagite to the great triumvirate, St. Bernard, Richard of St. Victor, and St. Bonaventura. [4]

[2] Evelyn Underhill, *Mysticism,* p. 319.

[3] In Germany there were Meister Eckhard (d. 1327), John Tauler (d. 1361), and Henry Suso (d. 1365), to mention only the greatest. In Flanders Jan Ruysbroek died in 1381, and in Italy we have Jacopone dà Todi (d. 1306), who belongs mostly to the preceding century, and St. Catherine of Siena, who died in 1380.

[4] The mysticism of St. Bernard is found chiefly in his *Sermons on the Canticles* (Eng. trans., 2v, Dublin, 1920), in which the fifteenth sermon is particularly significant; in *The Love of God* (trans. Edmund G. Gardner, 1916; T. L. Connolly, 1937); and in *The Steps of Humility* (ed. and trans. by Geo. B. Burch, Cambridge, Mass., 1940). Richard of St. Victor's masterpiece is the *De Gratia Contemplationis,* commonly known as *Benjamin Major,* in five books. *Benjamin Minor,* a shorter treatise, serves as a kind of introduction to the larger. An English version of the *Benjamin Minor,* dating from the middle of the fourteenth century, is printed in Horstman, *Yorkshire Writers,* I. 162-172. A later version can also be had in Edmund G. Gardner, *The Cell of Self Knowledge* (1910). The *Four Degrees of Burning Love* has not been translated. Mystical writings form but a small part of St. Bonaventura's works. Most important is the *De Triplici Via,* sometimes known as the *Incendium Amoris* (in Vol. VIII

English mysticism finds its first formal expression in the writings of *Richard*
Richard Rolle, hermit of Hampole.[5] The account of his awakening some *Rolle*
time in early manhood is best quoted in his own words:

I was sitting forsooth in a chapel and whilst I was delighting in the sweetness
of prayer or meditation, suddenly I felt a merry and unknown heat in me. At
first I was uncertain, doubting from whom it should be. After a long time I
became convinced that it was not of a creature but of my Maker, for more hot
and gladder I found it. . . .

Whilst truly I sat in the same chapel and sang psalms as I might in the
evening before supper, I perceived, as it were, the sounds of readers or rather
singers above me. Whilst also I took heed, praying to heaven with all desire,
suddenly, in what manner I know not, I felt in me the noise of song and was
aware of the most pleasing heavenly melody, which dwelt with me in my mind.
Forsooth my thought was changed to continual mirth of sound and thenceforth
for fullness of inward sweetness I burst out singing what before I said—forsooth
privily and only before my Maker. . . .

Wherefore from the beginning of my changed soul unto the high degree of
Christ's love which, God granting, I was able to attain, in which degree I might
sing the love of God with joyful song, was four years and about three months.[6]

From this time on, his life was spent in the exercise of piety—meditation,
prayer, writing, and giving spiritual comfort to others.

Rolle's more important mystical writings are in Latin.[7] One of the most *Latin*
significant, the *Melos Amoris,* often called *Melum Contemplativorum* and *Writings*
also known as the *Book of the Glory and Perfection of the Saints,* has only
lately been published (see Supplement). It is an extensive account of his
mystical joy, written in a highly mannered prose hard to reconcile with the
genuineness and intensity of feeling which it expresses. There are autobiographical passages indicating that his mode of life was not free from

---

of the standard edition, *Opera Omnia,* Quaracchi, 1882-1902). A work commonly attributed
to him in the Middle Ages, the *Meditationes Vitae Christi,* but not his, had great influence.
A brief section (chs. 74-92) was turned into English by an anonymous follower of Rolle as
The Privity of the Passion (Horstman, I. 198-218), modernized in Geraldine E. Hodgson,
Some Minor Works of Richard Rolle with The Privity of the Passion (1923), and large
portions were Englished by Nicholas Love before 1410 as *The Mirrour of the Blessed Lyf of
Jesu Christ* (ed. Lawrence F. Powell, 1908).

[5] What we know of Rolle's life, apart from autobiographical allusions in his writings, comes
from the *Office of St. Richard Hermit* compiled in hope of his canonization at the end of the
fourteenth century. It is supposed that he was born about 1300 at Thornton Dale, some forty
miles from York. He was for a time at Oxford, but returned home at eighteen for religious
reasons. Improvising a hermit's dress from his father's rain hood and two of his sister's
kirtles, he went off by himself, leaving his sister convinced that he was mad. He was taken
in by a family named Dalton, where he was given a solitary cell or room, and there composed
some of his earlier works. After he left the Daltons his movements cannot be traced very
definitely, but we may be sure that he pursued a solitary life most of the time. He lived for
a while in the archdeaconry of Richmondshire, but at the end of his life he was at Hampole,
in southwest Yorkshire. It is supposed that his death in September, 1349, was due to the
plague. For a translation of the *Office* see F. M. M. Comper, *The Fire of Love* (1914), pp.
xlv-lviii.

[6] *Incendium Amoris,* ch. xv, adapted from the translation made by Richard Misyn (1435).

[7] The definitive study of the Rolle canon is Hope Emily Allen, *Writings Ascribed to Richard
Rolle, Hermit of Hampole, and Materials for His Biography* (1927; MLA Monograph Ser.,
III). For a briefer account see the same author's intro. to *English Writings of Richard Rolle,
Hermit of Hampole* (1931) and Frances M. M. Comper, *Life of Richard Rolle* (1929).

criticism and attack. His best known works are the *Incendium Amoris,* written in middle life, and the somewhat later *Emendatio Vitae.*[8] It is from the former of these that we have quoted the account of his initiation into the mystical experience. The *Mending of Life* offers practical advice on the means to grace, through despising the world, embracing poverty, cultivating humility, and the like. The last chapter treats the joys of the contemplative life.

Rolle seems to have acquired disciples and he became in time the spiritual adviser to certain holy women—a nun of Yedingham, one of Hampole, and a recluse named Margaret Kirkby. For them he wrote his three English epistles on the love of God and its attainment through contemplation—*Ego Dormio, Commandment of the Love of God,* and the *Form of Living.* They are among his latest works, and the *Form of Living,* written for Margaret Kirkby, is of the three the most orderly and mature exposition of his views.[9]

Calor, Canor, Dulcor

For Rolle "joy in þe life of Jhesu" is the keynote of his mysticism, in which the loving contemplation of the Holy Name of Jesus has its part. The tokens of his mystical union were *Calor, Canor,* and *Dulcor*—Heat, which signifies not merely burning love but the physical sensation of warmth; Song, which means that his soul was filled with heavenly music and he responded in spiritual melody; Sweetness, which means a sense of inexpressible joy felt in the soul. The sensuous character of Rolle's contemplative experience together with the fact that it seems to have been present not intermittently but more or less constantly has led some to question his place in the inner circle of mystics. Nevertheless his reputation for piety and the character and extent of his writings make him a figure of the greatest importance in the spiritual revival of the fourteenth century. This is not the same as saying that he occupies a place of equal importance in English literature. His literary reputation until recently has rested in no small measure on a work, the *Prick of Conscience,* which he did not write. His few lyrics have in them more piety than poetry, and his English treatises, though written in competent prose, are less important than his Latin writings. Though his *Meditations on the Passion* has passages of deep feeling expressed with simple fervor, and his translation of the Psalter with its accompanying commentary was widely read until the time of the Reformation, we must conclude that his importance lies mainly in his influence on later mystics and on subsequent religious thought. We miss in his work those personal qualities that endear the author of the *Ancrene Riwle* to us. Great

[8] These two works are available in English versions, *The Fire of Love . . . and The Mending of Life,* ed. Frances M. M. Comper (1914). Several other modern versions of the *Mending of Life* have been published. G. C. Heseltine, *Selected Works of Richard Rolle, Hermit* (1930), is useful. Most of the texts in Geraldine E. Hodgson's *Some Minor Works of Richard Rolle* (1923) are no longer thought to be by Rolle, but are useful as illustrating English mysticism in the fourteenth century.

[9] All three epistles are printed in H. E. Allen, *English Writings of Richard Rolle,* and in Horstman, *Yorkshire Writers,* I. 3-71. *The Form of Living* has been published in modernized form by G. E. Hodgson (1910).

as was his piety and admirable his devotion to an ideal, Rolle's personality as it emerges from his writings was too severe and uncompromising to leave with the reader the pleasing sense of grace or charm.

Uncompromising in a different way is the unknown author of the *Cloud of Unknowing*,[10] one of the most spiritual of the mystical treatises of the fourteenth century. He is firm in his aloofness, writing not for all and sundry but for the chosen few who have an inclination towards the contemplative life and have even made some progress towards it. Specifically he addresses a young man of twenty-four. He rules out "worldly praters, open praisers or blamers of themselves or of any other, ... and all manner of carpers: cared I never that they saw this book. For mine intent was never to write such thing unto them." His single theme is the love of God and the perception of the Divine Presence through a quiet spirituality. Our own ignorance and God's incomprehensibility are like a great cloud (the *cloud of unknowing*), which is between God and the soul, which the soul beats upon in its yearning for God, and through which God may at times send a gleam into the heart. He is scornful of those who "stare as though they were mad, ... hang their heads on one side, as if a worm were in their ears, ... gape with their mouths ... or row with their arms in the time of their speaking, as though they needed to swim over a great water." Such physical manifestations are mere hypocrisy. The true contemplative is unostentatious, "with a soft and demure behavior as well in body as in soul." We are completely at a loss to identify this remarkable author, although he has also left us a half dozen shorter treatises including a translation of the *Mystica Theologia* of Pseudo-Dionysius and an *Epistle of Privy Counsel* which in some ways is finer than his major work.[11] It is supposed that he wrote about 1350 although a fairly clear allusion to the Lollards in the *Cloud of Unknowing* has not been accounted for in an entirely satisfactory way.

Writing somewhat later in the century, Walter Hilton, an Augustinian canon of Thurgarton (Notts.) who died in 1396, produced the *Scale* (or *Ladder*) *of Perfection* and a number of shorter works.[12] Hilton writes for a nun who had become a recluse, although he also had a larger audience in mind. The whole spirit and approach make the *Scale of Perfection* strikingly different from the *Cloud of Unknowing*.[13] Where the author of the latter

The Cloud of Unknowing

Walter Hilton: The Scale of Perfection

[10] The Middle English text is edited by Phyllis Hodgson, *The Cloud of Unknowing and The Book of Privy Counselling* (1944; *EETS*, 218). For modernization see the following note.

[11] These three works are all included in Dom Justin McCann's modernized edition of *The Cloud of Unknowing* (1924). The other four short pieces are in Edmund G. Gardner's *The Cell of Self-Knowledge* (1910). The *Cloud* has also been published in modernized versions by Father Henry Collins (1871) and by Evelyn Underhill (1912).

[12] The *Scale of Perfection* has been edited by Dom Ephrem Guy (1869), J. B. Dalgairns (1870), and Evelyn Underhill (1923), and in a French translation with valuable notes by Dom Noetinger and Dom Bouvet (1923). Hilton's *Letter to a Devout Man of Secular Estate*, a treatise on the mixed life, is included in the English editions of the *Scale* above. The only other work of Hilton's that has been printed is the *Song of Angels*, included in Gardner's *Cell of Self-Knowledge*, as above.

[13] Although an early tradition attributes the *Cloud of Unknowing* to Hilton, it is inconceivable to the present writer that he could have written it.

is aloof and self-contained Hilton is solicitous and humble. As he says, "a man that would climb upon a ladder that is high, and setteth his foot upon the lowest stave, can [not] at the next step get up to the highest, but must go by degrees from one to another," and so he spends much time on elementary directions for piety, discussing at length the Deadly Sins, and the need for surmounting them. Indeed so constantly is he preoccupied with the weaknesses of the flesh and with matters proper to the preacher rather than the mystic that one is frequently led to doubt his place among true mystics. Ecstasy for him is a quiet glow, but the soul is nevertheless detached from worldly concerns and "through grace it is drawn into the privy-chamber, into sight of our Lord Jesus, and heareth his privy counsel, and is wonderfully comforted in the hearing." Hilton is not a great original thinker; he has absorbed what suits him from earlier mystics—particularly Rolle and the author of the *Cloud*. He supports his exposition constantly by quotation from biblical and other authorities and respects learning in its proper place. The *Scale of Perfection* is carefully planned and wrought out with painstaking consideration. Its devotional matter and attention to what may be called the first steps in spirituality won for it widespread and lasting popularity.

Julian of Norwich

The autobiographical type of mystical treatise is best represented in English by the record of two women who saw visions and, being themselves simple and unlettered, had their experiences committed to writing through the good offices of another. Julian (or Juliana) of Norwich, born about 1342 and still alive in 1416, was a recluse in a cell attached to the church of St. Julian at Norwich. In her thirty-first year (1373) she fell desperately ill and for a week was not expected to live. When the crisis had passed she experienced in rapid succession sixteen revelations or "shewings," mostly of Christ's sufferings in the Crucifixion. Twenty years later she received certain "teaching inwardly" by which she came to understand more fully the previous "shewings." It is often difficult to know where revelation ends and subsequent reflection begins, but her *Revelations* exist in two forms, a shorter and a fuller version, and it is supposed that the shorter form records more nearly her original visions.[14]

Margery Kempe

Very different in personality was Margery Kempe of Lynn. Until recently all that was known of her was the little eight-page quarto printed about 1501 by Wynkyn de Worde. But in 1934 a manuscript in the possession of Colonel William Butler-Bowden was identified by Miss Hope Emily Allen as a complete copy of Margery's book.[15] Margery Kempe was born about 1373, the daughter of a former mayor of Lynn. She was married to John Kempe, "worshipful burgess" of Lynn, to whom she bore fourteen children

[14] The earlier version was edited by Dundas Harford, *Comfortable Words for Christ's Lovers* (1911). The most available editions of the fuller *Revelations of Divine Love* are those of Grace Warrack (1901) and Dom Roger Hudleston (1927). A French translation by Dom Mennier (Tours, 1900) has a valuable introduction.

[15] The identification was announced in the London *Times*, Dec. 27, 1934. A modernized version was published by the owner (1936) and the original text by Sanford B. Meech (1940; EETS, 212) with preliminary notes and observations by Hope Emily Allen. Miss Allen is at work on a full discussion and commentary which will appear as Vol. II of this edition. *The Book of Margery Kempe* was put into final shape between 1436 and 1438.

before they agreed to a life of continence. For six months after the birth of her first child she was out of her mind, but one day Christ appeared to her and spoke to her and her reason was miraculously restored. It was some time, however, before she abandoned her pride of dress, envy of her neighbors, and other sinful ways. Gradually she began to see visions and to receive other evidences of God's favor.

The spiritual change wrought in her showed itself, after her pilgrimage to Jerusalem, in frequent and abundant weeping. The sight of the crucifix, a good sermon, the taking of communion would cause her to break into tears and utter loud cries, and sometimes writhe on the ground, frequently to the great annoyance of those present. On Corpus Christi day, as the priests bore the sacrament about the town in solemn procession, "she cried, 'I die, I die,' and roared so wonderfully, that people wondered upon her." She takes obvious satisfaction in her wonderful "cryings," noting that on one day she had fourteen. She seems to attach importance to their loudness. She tells us that on one occasion when receiving the sacrament "she cried so loud that it could be heard all about the church, and outside the church," and she records with distressing frequency the occasions on which "she cried and roared," and "wept full boisterously."

Margery Kempe was no recluse. She traveled to London and Canterbury, to Norwich, Lincoln, and York, to Rome and Jerusalem, and Compostella, and, at the age of sixty, to Danzig, Aachen, and other places on the Continent. Nor was she one to hide her light under a bushel. She confessed her sins from childhood to several different confessors and "shewed her manner of living to many a worthy clerk, to worshipful doctors of divinity, both religious men and others of secular habit." She insisted on wearing white, even though it made her conspicuous, and notes without reticence that on one occasion in a church at Leicester "there was so much people that they stood upon stools for to behold her."

Of the quiet sense of oneness with God experienced by other mystics Margery Kempe says little. Instead, she reports at length many conversations with Christ, and mentions other occasions on which she was spoken to by the Virgin Mary, St. Peter, St. Paul, St. Katherine, "or whatever saint in heaven she had devotion to." She appears to have been quite susceptible to the power of suggestion and her experiences often recall those of Rolle, Julian of Norwich, and other mystics whose writings had been read to her, but for valid comparisons one must look to certain women on the Continent, and especially in Germany, at about the same period. Each reader will form his own opinion of Margery's neurotic temperament and of the extent to which her eccentricities and hysterical outbursts were the result of genuine religious feeling. Certainly her boisterous weeping and sobbing, her "roaring" and writhings would not have found favor with the deeply spiritual, albeit outspoken, author of the *Cloud of Unknowing*. But as a human document and for its many glimpses of medieval life the *Book of Margery Kempe* has great interest, and as time goes on will reach a widening circle of readers.

XIV

The Alliterative Revival

In the last few chapters—on the romance, the religious omnibus, the lyric, and the writings of the mystics—we have become increasingly aware of the intense literary activity that marks the whole fourteenth century, an activity that reaches its culmination for most readers today in the great narrative poetry of Chaucer. It is an activity that extends from one end of England to the other, an activity in which London and the court participate to no overwhelming extent but rather share along with many other sections of the country. The widespread distribution of the ferment that was at work is indicated perhaps nowhere more plainly than in the emergence about 1350 of the Old English alliterative tradition after it had lain hidden for nearly two hundred years.

Alliterative Verse

Roughly between the years 1350 and 1400 there appeared a score of poems, ranging from a few hundred lines to several thousand, in a metre which had clearly evolved in an unbroken development from the old four-beat alliterative measure of *Beowulf* and Cynewulf. It is not an antiquarian revival, but the reappearance of a metrical pattern which has undergone considerable change. The line has become in most cases the unit of thought, and the alliteration is therefore not so much structural as decorative. With some poets hunting the letter becomes a passion, and the alliteration falls on three syllables in a half-line or is carried through several consecutive lines. Verse of this sort was obviously associated in Chaucer's mind with the north, as is indicated by the well-known words of the Parson:

Associated with the North and West

> But trusteth wel, I am a Southern man,
> I can not geste—rum, ram, ruf—by lettre.

And most of the poems in the alliterative revival belong to the north and to the northwest Midlands. While one of the most important—*Piers Plowman*—has its origin in the west Midlands, we may think of the alliterative revival as occurring in the north and more particularly the northwest of England.

Three of the earliest poems in the revival, *Alexander A, Alexander B,* and *William of Palerne,* have already been discussed in the chapters on the romance. There we have likewise treated other later romances in alliterative verse, such as *The Wars of Alexander, The Destruction of Troy,* the *Morte Arthure,* and the religious romance *The Destruction of Jerusalem.* It is not practicable to include them again here, where as part of the alliterative

232

movement they would be fully entitled to a place.[1] We shall have to be content with this brief reference, and confine ourselves in this and the following chapter to the other classes of alliterative poetry. In the present chapter we shall treat the works of the *Pearl* poet and one or two poems in some ways *The* Pearl related to his. In the chapter which follows we shall consider a group of *Poet* poems concerned with social and ethical questions, of which the most important is the great social document *Piers Plowman*.

Of the many unique manuscripts gathered together in the seventeenth century by the famous antiquary Sir Robert Cotton, among which are the *Beowulf* codex, the two texts of Layamon's *Brut,* the *Ludus Coventriae,* and others only less famous, one is a modest quarto volume known as Nero A x.[2] The contents consist of four alliterative poems in a hand of the end of the fourteenth century. Accompanying the text are twelve illustrations of quite crude workmanship depicting episodes in some of the poems. None of the texts is accompanied by any title, but they have been named, in the order of their occurrence in the manuscript, the *Pearl, Purity* (or *Cleanness*), *Patience,* and *Sir Gawain and the Green Knight*.

The *Pearl* [3] is not only first in the manuscript but shares with the *Gawain* Pearl the first place in the interest of modern readers. In a hundred stanzas of twelve lines each,[4] ingeniously linked in groups of five by repetition and a refrain, the poet tells how a lovely pearl, smooth and white, slipped from his hands into the grass and was lost in the ground. In his grief he often visits the spot which covers his pearl, and one August day, lulled by the fragrance of herbs and flowers, he falls asleep on the little mound. There as he slumbers he dreams that he is in another world, a world of crystal cliffs, bright woods, and strands pebbled with precious stones. Such sights make him forget his grief, and he wanders about in sheer delight. Finally he comes upon a stream, clear and sparkling, beyond which he thinks must be Paradise. It is backed by a crystal cliff, at the foot of which sits a child—

> A gracious maiden full debonaire;
> Glistening white was her robe:
> I knew her well; I had seen her before.

The longer he looks at her the better he knows her. He has an impulse to call her, but seeing her in so strange a place deters him. She is spotless, and her dress is trimmed profusely with pearls. She wears a crown, from beneath which her hair falls loosely on her shoulders. No tongue could fittingly describe the sight:

---

[1] See above, pp. 182 ff. On the later alliterative movement in Scotland see Sir William Craigie, "The Scottish Alliterative Poems," *Proc. Brit. Acad.,* xxviii (1942). 217-236.

[2] It is reproduced in facsimile in *EETS*, 162.

[3] Edited by Richard Morris (2ed., 1869; *EETS*, 1), Sir Israel Gollancz (1891; 1921), and Charles G. Osgood (1906; *Belles-Lettres Ser.*). A translation is included in Gollancz's edition, and there are modern renderings by G. G. Coulton (1907), Osgood (1907), Sophie Jewett (1908), and Stanley P. Chase (1932).

[4] The rime scheme is *ababababab bcbc*. There are 101 stanzas, but one is considered spurious or was canceled by the author.

So clean was it and clear and pure,
That precious pearl where it was set.

Thus arrayed she comes down to the brink. She was nearer to me, he says, than aunt or niece. Finally she speaks to him and he then addresses her:

O Pearl, quoth I, in pearls bedight,
Art thou my pearl that I have 'plain'd,
Regretted when all alone at night?
Much longing for thee have I restrained
Since into the grass thou didst from me glide.

Grown in stature and in wisdom, she reveals to him her life as spouse of the Heavenly Bridegroom. The dreamer's pearl was not lost when it was put in a coffer so comely as is this gracious garden. Along with thousands of others she shares a most happy lot. When the poet objects that she did nothing to deserve so great a reward, since she "lived not two years in our land" and knew neither her Paternoster nor Creed, she enters upon an elaborate discourse on the part played by merit and grace in salvation and the equality of the saved before God,[5] illustrating her views at length by biblical parables. The poet is finally granted a view of her abode—the New Jerusalem—vividly adapted from the Apocalypse. His effort in trying to cross the stream and reach the heavenly city wakens him from his dream, and he rises from the mound on which he had slumbered, filled with a new spiritual strength.

The Allegory This beautiful and seemingly transparent allegory has been interpreted in various ways and has led to considerable controversy. The traditional view sees in the poem an elegy in which the poet grieves for the death of a two-year-old daughter and is consoled by her in a vision of a common medieval type. This view was challenged by Schofield in 1904, who denied the autobiographical interpretation and suggested that the poet was merely upholding the virtue of purity under the symbolism of a pearl, with appropriate personification.[6] While his view has not found much favor [7] his example has led others to attempt new explanations and various modifications of the original interpretation. The *Pearl* has been taken as symbolizing the Eucharist [8] and more recently as recording a state of "spiritual dryness" experienced by the poet and not unknown to religious and to mystics.[9] Still

[5] The orthodoxy of the poet's views was questioned by Carleton F. Brown, "The Author of *The Pearl* Considered in the Light of His Theological Opinions," *PMLA*, xix (1904). 115-153, and defended by James Sledd, *MLN*, lv (1940). 381. While his attitude toward grace has been shown to be good doctrine, equality of reward appears to be stressed beyond medieval orthodoxy.
[6] W. H. Schofield, "The Nature and Fabric of *The Pearl*," *PMLA*, xix (1904). 154-215; "Symbolism, Allegory, and Autobiography in *The Pearl*," *PMLA*, xxiv (1909). 585-675.
[7] Schofield's interpretation was opposed by Osgood (*ed. cit.*) and his objections to an autobiographical interpretation were disposed of by Coulton in *MLR*, ii (1907). 39-43.
[8] R. M. Garrett, *The Pearl—An Interpretation* (Seattle, 1918; *Univ. of Wash. Pub. in English*, Vol. iv, No. 1).
[9] Sister M. Madeleva, *Pearl: A Study in Spiritual Dryness* (1925).

others have sought to reconcile the elegiacal and symbolical interpretations.[10] There is symbolism, to be sure, in incidental ways in the poem, and the problems of divine grace and the equality of heavenly rewards constitute the major theme for discussion, but there are too many features which are meaningless on any other assumption than that the poet mourns the loss of a real child.[11] The poem treats certain aspects of salvation in the *A Personal* framework of a personal elegy, employing the medieval conventions of *Elegy* vision and debate.

Viewed as a personal elegy the *Pearl* is a poem of deep feeling, the poet's grief yielding gradually to resignation and spiritual reconciliation. In its sensuous beauty, its artistic restraint, its skilful manipulation of a complex and difficult metrical pattern, and its imaginatively beautiful descriptions of the garden, the pearl-maiden, and the New Jerusalem, it is in its best parts unsurpassed by anything in Middle English poetry.

In two respects *Purity*,[12] the second poem in the manuscript, resembles *Purity* the *Pearl*—in its preoccupation with an ethical question and in its predilection for extended paraphrases of biblical incident. For here we have a discourse on purity, showing how impossible it is for one who is unclean to approach God's pure presence, and enforcing the point by the parable of the man without a wedding garment. This and other episodes such as the Fall of Lucifer and the Expulsion from Paradise are merely preliminary, however, to the main purpose, which is to tell the stories of the Flood, the Destruction of Sodom and Gomorrah, and the profanation of the holy vessels in Belshazzar's Feast. The homiletic purpose is plain, and at the end the poet not only reminds us that "upon þrynne wyses" he has showed the sorrow that uncleanness causes our Lord but he closes with a prayer for grace. The stories are vividly told, but the poem suffers by comparison with the *Pearl* through the lack of any framework or artistic motivation.

This is also true of its companion piece, *Patience*,[13] which devotes all *Patience* but the first sixty of its 531 lines to the story of Jonah and the whale. But concentration upon a single subject gives greater unity to the piece, and the poet has allowed his imagination freer rein in embellishing his theme. He shows us the activity in getting under sail, describes vividly the storm at sea, pictures with realistic detail the slimy insides of the whale, and reports dramatically Jonah's conversations with God. God's rebuke of Jonah for his impatience leads the poet to his closing reflection. He who is too hasty in tearing his clothes will often sit sewing them up. Even poverty must be borne with patience, which "is a noble point, though it displease

[10] Jefferson B. Fletcher, "The Allegory of the *Pearl*," *JEGP*, xx (1921). 1-21, and René Wellek, "*The Pearl*: An Interpretation of the Middle-English Poem," *Studies in English* (Charles Univ., Prague), IV (1933). 1-33. Both these papers stress the complex character of the symbolism.

[11] For an attempt to identify the child see Oscar Cargill and Margaret Schlauch, "*The Pearl* and Its Jeweler," *PMLA*, XLIII (1928). 105-123.

[12] Edited by Richard Morris (2ed., 1869; *EETS*, 1), Robert J. Menner (1920; *Yale Stud. in English*, 61), and Sir Israel Gollancz (1921).

[13] Edited by Richard Morris (as above), Hartley Bateson (Manchester, 1912; 2ed., 1918), and Israel Gollancz (1913).

oft." In both *Purity* and *Patience* the poet's principal indebtedness is to the Bible, and the *Pearl* not only draws its parables from the same source but derives its description of the New Jerusalem from the Apocalypse. Other sources in Tertullian, an eclogue of Boccaccio, and even the *Book of the Knight of La Tour Landry* have been suggested but with the possible exception of Boccaccio's eclogue, must be described as very doubtful. The poet refers once to Jean de Meun and his part of the *Roman de la Rose,* and he has drawn scattered details in *Purity* from Mandeville's *Travels* in their French form. But while the author of these poems was apparently well read, we have not been very successful in tracking down the sources of his inspiration outside of the Scriptures.

There seems to be no reason to doubt that the three poems the *Pearl, Purity,* and *Patience* are the work of one man. The fourth poem in the manuscript is of such a different kind that if it were not found in association with the others we might well hesitate to attribute it to the same authorship, in spite of obvious stylistic resemblances.[14] *Sir Gawain and the Green Knight* [15] is a courtly romance, the finest Arthurian romance in English. Though it exemplifies the knightly virtues of courage and truth, it is in no sense a story told to enforce a moral. It is quite in the spirit of French romance, told for its own sake.

Sir Gawain and the Green Knight

The plot itself is so well known as to need no retelling. The main adventure is the challenge, which Gawain accepts, of an exchange of blows with the Green Knight, in which he beheads the challenger but must submit to the same hazard a year later. With this is combined the adventure at Bercilak's castle, in which Gawain is tempted on three successive mornings by his host's wife and in which his only fault is in concealing the magic girdle which she gives him. Both of these stories are found separately either in Celtic or in Old French romances.[16] They are first found combined in the English poem,[17] and whether we owe the combination to the English poet

Subject Matter and Treatment

[14] Apart from the stylistic features common to all four poems, there are noteworthy parallels between *Sir Gawain and the Green Knight* and *Purity.* It should be remembered, however, that the romance also shows many striking parallels in phrases and lines with the *Wars of Alexander.*

[15] There are older editions by Sir Frederic Madden for the Bannatyne Club (1839) and Richard Morris (1864; *EETS,* 4); revised by I. Gollancz (1897 and 1912), but the romance is best studied in the edition of J. R. R. Tolkien and E. V. Gordon (1925) or the new edition of Sir Israel Gollancz with introductory essays by Mabel Day and Mary S. Serjeantson (1940; *EETS,* 210). Modern renderings by Jessie L. Weston (1898), often reprinted, T. H. Banks (1929), G. H. Gerould (1934), etc. are available separately or in anthologies.

[16] The fullest study of the sources of the romance is George L. Kittredge, *A Study of Gawain and the Green Knight* (Cambridge, Mass., 1916). The challenge or beheading game is found in an episode known as *The Champion's Bargain* which closes the Irish romance (at least as old as the eleventh century) of *Fled Bricrend,* or *Bricriu's Feast.* From there it passed into French, where it was embodied independently into four separate romances (the *Livre de Caradoc,* incorporated in the first continuation of Chrétien's *Perceval,* the short thirteenth-century romance *La Mule sanz Frain,* the prose Grail romance known as the *Perlesvaus* in which the adventure is attributed to Lancelot, and another thirteenth-century romance entitled *Gawain et Humbaut* in which the ending has been completely changed). Parallels to the temptation motif are not so close, but in one form or another it is found in the Old French *Ider,* in the late English *Carl of Carlisle,* and elsewhere.

[17] There are many theories accounting for the combination. Kittredge believed that *Sir Gawain and the Green Knight* was based on a lost French romance in which the adventures

or to his source we must grant that it was a happy inspiration which tied the three temptations to the three blows offered Gawain at the Green Chapel and made the wound received from the third blow the result of his concealing the girdle. Accepting the supernatural as a prerogative of medieval story, we have a skilfully contrived plot,[18] a feature always worthy of remark in medieval romance. But it is only one, and that perhaps the least, of the qualities which give this remarkable poem its high place among English romances. From the beginning almost to the end it proceeds by a succession of scenes and situations full of color and movement and vivid detail. We begin with the New Year's feast, the guests exchanging greetings and gifts, the maidens laughing and making mirth till it is time to eat, then washing and seating themselves at tables. Just as the music ceases and the first course has been served the Green Knight enters. He is fully described— stature, appearance, dress, armor, horse, trappings—as he rides straight up to the daïs. And so it goes from episode to episode like a succession of tapestries or medieval illuminations. The descriptions of the seasons as they mark the passing of the year and bring Gawain to the time when he must set out to keep his pledge are no mere literary exercises, and the hunting scenes have all the excitement and lifelikeness of first-hand experience or observation. Striking, too, is the poet's mastery of dialogue, always easy and natural, but particularly skilful in the extended conversations between Gawain and the lady of the castle, as she seeks an opening and he adroitly evades and parries each thrust. Finally, one should remark the dexterous way in which the poet keeps the various actions moving forward simultaneously, passing from the dalliance of the lady to the husband's adventures in the chase and back again to the bed chamber until all parties are brought together naturally at the end of each day. But there is no end of things to exclaim over and we can only hint at the enjoyment to be had from reading and rereading this fine romance.[19]

---

were combined. J. R. Hulbert, "Syr Gawayn and the Grene Knyʒt," *MP*, xiii (1915-16). 433-462, 689-730, believes they were originally joined in a Fairy Mistress story as the conditions which the hero must fulfill. Else von Schaubert, "Der englische Ursprung von *Syr Gawayn and the Grene Knyʒt*," *ESt*, lvii (1923). 330-446, maintains that they were first combined by the English poet. This is also the view of Miss Day in the essay noted above. O. Löhmann, *Die Sage von Gawain und dem grünen Ritter* (Königsberg, 1938), likewise believes in the English origin of the romance, but argues that a Fairy Mistress story has been changed into a test of the hero.

[18] The idea that *Sir Gawain and the Green Knight* is connected in some way with the Order of the Garter is most fully advocated in Isaac Jackson, "*Sir Gawain and the Green Knight* considered as a 'Garter' Poem," *Anglia*, xxxvii (1913). 393-423, and opposed by J. R. Hulbert in the article already referred to (*MP*, xiii, especially pp. 710 ff.).

[19] In the absence of any objective evidence for determining the order of composition it has seemed best to treat the poems in the order in which they occur in the manuscript. *Patience* and *Purity* probably belong together, and since *Purity* has a number of parallels with the *Gawain*, it probably stands closer to the latter. On artistic grounds the *Pearl* and *Gawain* should follow the homiletic pieces, though this is not a safe criterion for pieces unlike in kind. One could argue for an order which would put the *Gawain* first, followed by the *Pearl*, the bereavement in which led the poet to the moral concerns of *Purity* and *Patience*. Such an order would have the advantage of putting *Patience* after *Purity*, to which it is superior in structure and unity.

All that we know about the author of these four poems is what can be cautiously inferred from his work, and all attempts to identify him with Huchown, Strode, or any other individual have failed. The dialect of the manuscript, which there is no reason to think differs essentially from that of the author, would indicate that he belonged to the northwest Midlands, probably south Lancashire, and this general locality is supported by the landscape and local allusions in the poems. He need not have been a priest in spite of his preoccupation with theological and moral questions, though a position as chaplain in some nobleman's household would make such an interest natural and account for his familiarity with the ways of courtly life. Naturally, however, such knowledge could be otherwise accounted for. His vocabulary contains a large French element which might result from his social status or his acquaintance with French literature. This was certainly considerable. He impresses us as a man of cosmopolitan taste whose horizon was not bounded by the limits of a provincial neighborhood. That he was at once observant and imaginative is apparent. His literary activity coincides roughly with the earlier part of Chaucer's career, and in the absence of more precise information we cannot do better than to date his work c. 1375.

Various other alliterative poems have from time to time been attributed to the *Pearl* poet. Among them the one that has found most supporters is

St. Erkenwald[20] which attributes to the Old English bishop of this name a miracle not otherwise recorded. When St. Paul's in London was being rebuilt a tomb was uncovered in which was the body of a pagan judge. Since he had always been just in his awards, his body and clothing were still as fresh as at the time of his death. At Erkenwald's bidding the corpse reveals its identity, whereupon the bishop's tears fall on the body, constituting baptism and releasing the soul. Bodily decay at once sets in. The story is told in 352 clear and straightforward verses, but the present writer at least cannot accept the attribution to the *Pearl* poet.

Associated with the poems previously discussed is a short piece of twenty-eight tail-rime stanzas, each with thirteen alliterative lines, called the *Pistel*

of Swete Susan.[21] It tells the story of Susanna and the Elders from the thirteenth chapter of Daniel (in the Vulgate), with the description of the garden embellished with details drawn from the *Roman de la Rose*. It is told simply and effectively, at times with the deft touches of an artist. When Susanna, allowed to speak to her husband, has avowed her innocence and fidelity to him,

> Ðei toke þe feteres of hire feete,
> And evere he kyssed þat swete:
> "In other world schal we mete."
> Seide he no mare. (lines 257-60)

[20] Edited by Horstmann, *Altenglische Legenden* (1881), Gollancz (1922), and Henry L. Savage (1926; *Yale Stud. in English*, 72).
[21] Edited by Hans Köster, *Huchown's Pistel of Swete Susan* (Strassburg, 1895; *Quellen und Forschungen*, LXXVI).

A passage in Wyntoun's *Orygynale Cronykil* (*c.* 1420) asserts that the author was Huchown of the Awle Ryale (Royal Court), who is there credited also with the *Gret Gest off Arthure* and the *Awyntyre off Gawane*.[22] The attribution cannot be accepted, but the passage has led some to believe that Huchown was not only the *Pearl* poet but the author of most of the poems in the alliterative revival.[23] Naturally such extravagant claims have not met with much favor. While the six poems discussed in the present chapter are linked together by certain features of subject matter and treatment it seems best to hold to the conservative view which limits the work of the *Pearl* poet to the poems preserved in the famous Cotton manuscript.

[22] He made the *Gret Gest off Arthure*
And the *Awyntyre off Gawane*
The Pystyll als *off Swete Swsane*. . . .

The *Gret Gest off Arthure* is believed to be the alliterative *Morte Arthure*, presumably in its fuller form (see ch. x, above). The *Awyntyre off Gawane* is identified by those who believe Huchown to be the *Pearl* poet with *Sir Gawain and the Green Knight*, by others with the *Awntyrs of Arthur* (see p. 190, note 22).

[23] George Neilson, '*Huchown of the Awle Ryale*', *the Alliterative Poet* (Glasgow, 1902), who argues that Huchown is to be identified with the "gude Sir Hew of Eglintoun" mentioned by Dunbar in his *Lament for the Makaris*. In spite of the extravagance of his thesis Neilson's book contains much interesting matter.

XV

Piers Plowman and Other Alliterative Poems

Poems of Social Protest

It is a noteworthy feature of the alliterative revival in the second half of the fourteenth century that a number of poems in the older measure, and among them some of the most important, are poems of social and moral protest.[1] This should not cause surprise when we remember that the period was ushered in by the Black Death with its grave economic and political consequences, that it saw the Peasants' Revolt in 1381, and that Wyclif and the Lollard movement are only another manifestation of the general upheaval which unsettled so many established conditions and beliefs. Nor should it seem altogether strange that much of this social criticism should appear in alliterative verse rather than in the more conventional measure of the court. The criticism is directed at the government which tolerated so many abuses, and like most forms of political opposition came from those outside the group in power. The poems which we shall consider in the present chapter all express the point of view of the common man. They are like voices crying in the wilderness, denouncing evils without seeming so much as to hope for their redress.

Wynnere and Wastoure

The earliest, apparently, is *Wynnere and Wastoure*,[2] dating from about 1352. Allusions in the prologue indicate that it is by a "western man" and in all probability a professional minstrel of the old school, since he complains that the minstrel's calling is not what it once was but is filled with beardless youths who "jangle als a jaye and japes telle." In some five hundred lines the poem presents a dispute between thrift (Winner), representing the merchants, lawyers, the Pope, the four orders of friars[3]—all men of property—and waste represented by a gay young spendthrift who neglects his lands and dovecotes, sells his holdings, and squanders his money on revelry and proud clothes for himself and his wife. In the third and pre-

---

[1] Social complaint is not unknown to English verse before the period of which we speak, but it is for the most part brief and sporadic. *When Holy Church Is under Foot* has been mentioned above (see p. 123). Two poems in MS Harl. 2253 offer respectively *A Satire on the Consistory Courts* and a *Song of the Husbandman,* the latter a husbandman's complaint that he is taxed and fleeced until he has nothing left. A poem in the Auchinleck MS on *The Evil Times of Edward II* (476 lines) parallels more closely some of the poems discussed in the present chapter, at least in the abuses which it describes. The late fourteenth-century *Sir Penny* treats a theme—money can do anything—found also in Latin and French. Most of these poems are printed in Thomas Wright's *Political Songs of England* (1839; *Camden Soc.*).

[2] Edited by Sir Israel Gollancz (1920, 1931), and previously for the Roxburghe Club (1897). For further evidence bearing on the date see J. R. Hulbert, "The Problems of Authorship and Date of *Wynnere and Wastoure*," MP, XVIII (1920). 31-40; J. M. Steadman, Jr., "The Date of *Winnere and Wastoure*," MP, XIX (1921). 211-219; Gardiner Stillwell, "*Wynnere and Wastoure* and the Hundred Years' War," ELH, VIII (1941). 241-247.

[3] The meaning of the two hosts and their constituents is not very clear.

sumably last "fitt" the King (Edward III) gives the disputants the surprising advice to go each his own way—Winner to the Pope at Rome, Waster to Cheapside—each to live "in a land where he is loved most." The conclusion of the poem is missing, so that the final attitude of the author is unknown, but he seems to be trying to please both sides and therefore presents his ideas in the familiar debate form.

Less unified is the *Parlement of the Thre Ages*.[4] Not capable of being exactly dated, it has been associated on rather slight grounds with *Wynnere and Wastoure* and attributed to the same author. This at least is quite doubtful.[5] The *Parlement* in general plan reminds us of *Purity* and *Patience*: the poet puts forward a proposition which offers the excuse for a long narrative illustration. In this case, after a prologue of 103 lines telling how he shot, dressed, and concealed a hart (i.e., he was poaching[6]), he falls asleep. In his dream he sees three men—Youth, aged thirty, gaily dressed in green; Middle Age, sixty years old, in sober gray; and Old Age, in black, described as a decrepit old man of a hundred, mumbling his Creed. In the *parlement* (talk, discussion) which follows each explains his philosophy of life. The young man speaks of his leman, of dancing, chess, hawking by the river. Middle Age deprecates Youth's expensive clothes, the price of which would purchase lands. Old Age assures them they are both foolish. He was once just like them. Now death has stolen upon him, as it has on many another great and proud. This gives the poet his opportunity to relate the experience of some of these, and in the remainder of the poem, more than half of its 665 lines, he gives accounts of each of the Nine Worthies, next of the "wights that were wisest"—Aristotle, Virgil, Solomon, and Merlin—and finally of "the proudest in press that paramours loved"—Amadas and Ydoine, Samson and Delilah, Tristan and Iseult, and others. All these prove that nothing avails against death; and Old Age, urging his companions to confess their sins, goes off with the words, "Death dings on my door; I dare no longer abide." The theme is naturally perennial and such social criticism as occurs in the poem is purely incidental.

The greatest of all the alliterative poems of social protest is *Piers Plowman*, or more properly *The Vision of William concerning Piers the Plowman*. Even this longer title is inadequate to describe the poem in its fullest form, for it has come down to us in three very different states.[7] The earliest or *A*-text is rather short (2579 lines) and consists of a prologue and eleven

Marginal notes: Parlement of the Thre Ages   Piers Plowman

---

[4] Edited by Israel Gollancz (1915) and earlier for the Roxburghe Club (1897).

[5] Gollancz's theory of common authorship is opposed by Hulbert (*MP*, XVIII. 31-34) and Steadman (*MP*, XXI. 7-13).

[6] See H. L. Savage, "Notes on the Prologue of the *Parlement of the Thre Ages*" (*JEGP*, XXIX (1930). 74-82), who here and elsewhere has shown how exact was the poet's knowledge of deer hunting and outdoor life.

[7] The three versions were edited separately by W. W. Skeat for the *EETS* (1867-84; texts in Vols. 28, 38, 54, notes and glossary in Vols. 67, 81) and later *en regard* (2v, Oxford, 1886). No one should ever belittle the work of Skeat, who through his tireless labors as an editor did an incalculable service to Middle English scholarship. Nevertheless, more critical editions of all three texts are badly needed, and are in preparation.

Three
Texts

cantos or *passus*.[8] The second or *B*-text is a revision of the first and a continuation amounting to the prologue and twenty passus (7241 lines). The third or *C*-text represents a further revision, sometimes slight but sometimes considerable. It is of about the same length as the *B*-text (it is 7353 lines [9]) but is divided into twenty-three passus. Such repeated revisions of the poem are evidence of its continued popularity, a popularity which is confirmed by the existence today of more than fifty manuscripts. It is therefore worth while to consider in some detail the contents of this remarkable work.

The First
Vision

In its earliest form the poem consists of three successive visions, two of them intimately connected, the third rather incoherent. As the poem opens, the author clad as a hermit is wandering one May morning on the Malvern hills, falls asleep on the bank of a brook, and dreams a marvelous dream. In a wilderness, he knows not where, but doubtless the neighborhood in which he has been wandering, he sees off to the east a tower on a high hill, down in the valley below a dungeon, and in between a "field full of folk"— some plowing, some wearing fine clothes, business men, beggars, pilgrims, hermits, friars of the four orders preaching and often covetous, parish priests hurrying to London, lawyers, bishops, and tradesmen of all kinds. Soon a lady named Holy Church comes down from the cliff and chides the dreamer for sleeping. Doesn't he see all these people so busy in their various ways? Somewhat afraid, he asks her to explain what the scene before him means. She tells him that Truth, who is God, dwells in the tower and that the Father of Falseness (the Devil) inhabits the dungeon. He asks her to teach him how to save his soul. Truth is best, she says, and charity, and especially love of the poor. But he wishes to know more, how he can recognize and thus avoid Falseness. She bids him look on his left. There he sees a woman, richly clad in a scarlet robe and many jewels, the equal of a queen. She is Lady Meed, the symbol both of just reward and of bribery, more often the latter. She is about to be married to False, with the assistance of Guile, Simony, Liar, and other evil characters, until Theology protests. The King thereupon proposes to marry her to Conscience, but Conscience refuses, pointing out many evil practices which Lady Meed is responsible for. Unable to reconcile the two, for bribery and conscience are naturally irreconcilable, the King appeals to Reason, who consents to serve the King if Conscience will be their counselor. At this point the dreamer awakes and the first Vision ends.

Second
Vision

But before he has walked a furlong drowsiness overtakes him and he again dreams. In his second vision, the vision of the Seven Deadly Sins and the search for Truth, he is back with his field full of folk, to whom Conscience is about to preach a sermon. Conscience alludes to the recent pestilences and the destructive wind of Saturday [January 15, 1362], evidences of God's anger at the sins of the people. He calls upon sundry classes and individuals to repent—wasters, Pernel the Courtesan, priests, prelates, etc.

---

[8] A portion of a twelfth passus with a conclusion by John But is found in one MS.
[9] These figures are based upon Skeat's texts. Manly gives *B* as 7242 and *C* as 7357 (*CHEL*, II. 3).

His words have the effect of making the various sinners confess their evil ways, repent, and even set out to seek St. Truth. A Palmer whom they meet and whose life has been spent visiting holy places seems a natural person to direct them in their quest. But he fails them miserably, admitting that he never knew a palmer to seek such a saint! It is at this point that a simple plowman named Peter puts forth his head and says he knows the saint very well. Common sense and a clean conscience have acquainted him with St. Truth and he has served him for the last fifteen years. No man is better pay. The way to his court is through Meekness to Conscience and thus on through the Ten Commandments. Grace is warden of the gate. If Grace permits them to enter, they shall see Truth himself in their hearts.

This is another way of saying that to attain to God man must "do well," must lead a worthy life. But what does the poet consider a worthy life? A concrete instance makes it fairly clear: Piers tells the company that before he can go with them and show them the way to Truth he has a half-acre to plow. It is an interesting picture. Some help him to plow, but others sit and drink or pretend to be sick and won't work until Hunger compels them. The whole episode suggests that man should do the task that falls to his lot. The names of Piers' wife and children imply further that the ordinary man at least, besides working in season, should keep out of mischief and mind his own business.

In the eighth passus Truth gives Piers a pardon which is found to contain only two lines

> Et qui bona egerunt, ibunt in vitam eternam;
> Qui vero mala, in ignem eternam.

A priest sniffs at such a pardon, but as the dreamer wakes and reflects on his dream he is convinced that Do-well is worth more at Doomsday than all the pardons of St. Peter's church. The passus concludes with the words *Explicit hic Visio Wilhelmi de Petro de Plowzman. Eciam incipit Vita de Do-well, Do-bet, et Do-best secundum wyt et resoun.*

The ninth passus accordingly marks a new departure in the poem. The poet, taking up Piers' quest, roams about a whole summer in search of Do-well. Two Franciscan friars tell him that Do-well dwells with them, but he disputes their claim and continues his search. As he rests beside a wood, he again falls asleep and dreams. He soon meets Thought, who is described as a large man like himself. Thought explains that Do-well is when a man is mild of speech, true of tongue, and fair in his dealings. Do-bet, besides practising these virtues, gives to the poor. Do-best bears a bishop's cross. For further information they go to Wit, whose wife is Dame Study, and who sends Piers to her cousin Clergy (learning) and his wife Scripture (book-knowledge). There is much rambling observation and moralizing in these episodes, so that when the dreamer says he is none the nearer for all his walking to knowing what Do-well is, we can only agree

Third Vision

with him. As the text breaks off he has asked Scripture to direct him to Kind Wit (Common Sense).

Continua-
tion in the
B-text

It is impossible to continue our analysis of the poem as it proceeds in the B-text, partly because the larger plan, the quest of Do-well, Do-bet, and Do-best, is vague and at times completely obscured, partly because the constant digressions, parenthetical discussions, and breaks in continuity show that the author was powerless to resist the impulse to pursue any idea suggested by another idea or even by a word that he happens to use. Mention of the cardinal virtues leads him into a digression on cardinals from Rome. He simply cannot make his thought hew to the line. As a result this part of the poem consists of many dialogues and discourses on truth, poverty, learning, charity, and the like, exemplified in the conduct of figures like Faith and Hope contrasted with Samaritan, or in the friar Flattery, or Haukyn the Active Man. There are some memorable scenes such as the dinner at which a friar, a "doctor on the high daïs," ate his food and drank wine with gluttonous delight, while not four days past he had preached before the Dean of St. Paul's on hunger endured as a penance. There are narratives of the Annunciation, episodes in the life of Christ, visions of the Resurrection and the Harrowing of Hell, which are vigorously related, and there is many a vivid flash of satirical observation which dies away before we have quite discerned what it was meant to illuminate. Read for the individual visions and scenes the poem is genuinely absorbing, but it is the despair of anyone who seeks in it a completely orderly plan or logical development from episode to episode.

Date

When and by whom was this long and intensely earnest poem written? Neither of these questions is easily answered, but a number of topical allusions in the three texts offer a basis for inference concerning the date. The A-text makes reference to a "Southwestern wind on a Saturday at even" (v. 14) which has long been recognized as an allusion to a severe windstorm mentioned in the chronicles as occurring on Saturday, Jan. 15, 1362. This and other allusions to events of the year or two previous have led to a fairly general acceptance of 1362 as the date of the first version. Some allusions can be interpreted, however, as referring to events in the later 'sixties [10] and the composition of the poem may have extended over several years. The B-text likewise presents somewhat conflicting evidence, but a date not long after 1377 seems best to fit the facts. The revision may likewise have extended over a considerable time.[11] The C-text has usually been dated 1393,

[10] Oscar Cargill, "The Date of the A-text of Piers Ploughman," *PMLA*, XLVII (1932). 354-362, argues for 1376, which seems too late; Bernard F. Huppé, *"Piers Plowman* and the Norman Wars," *PMLA*, LIV (1939). 37-64, suggests 1370-76, probably after 1373; J. A. W. Bennett, "The Date of the A-text of *Piers Plowman," PMLA*, LVIII (1943). 566-572, while dissenting from some of the views expressed in these articles, argues that certain lines in Passus IV must have been written after October, 1367, and before September, 1370.

[11] Bernard F. Huppé, "The Date of the B-text of *Piers Plowman," SP*, XXXVIII (1941). 33-44, argues from a passage in Passus XIX that the poem was not completed until after the autumn of 1378. On the other hand, Miss Mildred E. Marcett's strong case for identifying the "doctour on the heigh dese" with the friar William Jordan (*Uhtred de Boldon, Friar William Jordan, and Piers Plowman,* 1938) suggests a date around 1370 or even slightly earlier for this episode,

as Skeat thought, or 1398, as Jusserand argued. But it has been shown that a date not later than 1387 is suggested by a number of considerations,[12] and we may tentatively accept this year as the *terminus ad quem* for the final form of the poem.

One of the most remarkable things about this series of poems is the *Authorship* mystery that surrounds their authorship. We are accustomed to anonymity in works of medieval literature, especially in the romance, where stories were told and retold, and in religious poems where personal reputation was not the author's main object. It is also true that practically all the poems that make up the alliterative revival are by poets whose names we do not know. Nevertheless it is surprising that in *Piers Plowman,* the three texts of which contain so many seemingly personal revelations, the poet has so completely concealed his identity. For all the poem's popularity, no contemporary reference to the author has come down to us. Even the John But who wrote a conclusion to the *A*-text that is preserved in one manuscript seems not to have known the name of its author, and his statement that "When this work was wrought .... Death dealt him a dint" may be only an inference from the poem's unfinished appearance. Two fifteenth-century notes in manuscripts of the poem [13] are the sole clue to the author's name, and on the strength of their testimony *Piers Plowman* has generally been attributed to William Langland.

On the basis of these notes and of allusions scattered through the three *Hypo-* texts of the poem a hypothetical biography would run somewhat as follows. *thetical* Born about 1332 at Ledbury in Shropshire, the son (possibly illegitimate) of *Biography* Eustace de la Rokayle, the author was sent to school, perhaps at the priory of Great Malvern, by his father and his friends, and took minor orders. At the age of about thirty he began the first version of *Piers Plowman*. In the course of the work he moved to London, where he lived in Cornhill with his wife Kitte and his daughter Calote, a kind of clerical vagabond earning his bread by means of the *Paternoster, Placebo, Dirige,* the Psalter, and the Seven Penitential Psalms, which he sang for the souls of those who contributed to his support. In the *B*-text he mentions his age as forty-five. The

---

and Father A. Gwynn, "The Date of the *B*-text of *Piers Plowman,*" *RES,* XIX (1943). 1-24, has gathered other evidence for a date *c.* 1370-72 for Passus XIII-XX, while recognizing that the revision of Passus I-VIII must have taken place as late as 1376-7. J. A. W. Bennett, "The Date of the *B*-text of Piers Plowman," *MA,* XII (1943). 55-64, interprets certain passages as evidence that work on parts of the *B*-text was going on as late as 1377 and possibly in 1379 or even later. Work on the *B*-text extending over ten years need cause no great surprise.

[12] Sister Mary Aquinas Devlin, "The Date of the *C* Version of Piers the Plowman," [Univ. of Chicago] *Abstracts of Theses,* Humanistic Ser., IV (1928). 317-320.

[13] Ashburnham MS 130, now in the Huntington Library, says simply "Robert or William langland made pers ploughman." The other, Trin. Coll. Dublin MS D. 4. 1, makes an important additional assertion: "Memorandum quod Stacy de Rokayle pater Willielmi de Langlond, qui Stacius fuit generosus, et morabatur in Schypton vnder Whicwode, tenens domini le Spenser in comitatu Oxon, qui predictus Willielmus fecit librum qui vocatur Perys ploughman." In 1559 John Bale in his *Scriptorum Illustrium Maioris Britanniae Catalogus* stated that Langland was born at Cleobury Mortymer in Shropshire. It has been plausibly suggested that this is a scribal error for Ledbury, in which case Langland's birthplace would be the same as that of John Masefield. See Allan H. Bright, *New Light on 'Piers Plowman'* (Oxford, 1928).

C-text would thus belong toward the end of his life. Most of the allusions on which this inferential biography is based are found only in the *C*-text.

Single or Multiple Authorship

It is obvious that the picture here sketched assumes that all three versions of *Piers Plowman* are the work of one man. This assumption was questioned as long ago as 1856, and in 1906 John M. Manly [14] brought the issue clearly to the fore in an article which not only argued that the three texts were by different poets but that the *A*-text itself was not a unit. The prologue and first eight passus, he maintained, were by one man and the remainder of the *A*-text by another, to which John But added a conclusion. According to this hypothesis five different authors had a hand in the poems which go by the name of *Piers Plowman*. Manly's opinion was based upon what he felt to be "differences in language, differences in versification, differences in the use and in the kind of figurative language, and above all by such striking differences in the mental powers and qualities of the authors as make it highly improbable that they can be one and the same person." He further supported his view by the famous theory of a "lost leaf." [15] Manly's theory was at once attacked by Jusserand and others, and the controversy over single or multiple authorship has not yet ended. We cannot follow the course of this controversy here.[16] But however opinion may vary as to the justice of Manly's contention, it cannot be denied that it has enormously stimulated the study of the poem and led to a much better understanding of it. It is hazardous to attempt a statement of present scholarly opinion since it is still strongly divided.[17] It may be said, however, that Manly's belief in differences in language and versification has not been confirmed, and that the treatment of allegorical characters and the use of the Bible are noticeably alike in the three versions.[18] To the present writer it seems that separate authorship for the *A* and *B* texts has not been proved, but that in the *C*-text the attitude towards the poor, the treatment of ecclesiastics, the preoccupation with theological matters,[19] numerous changes for the

---

[14] "The Lost Leaf of *Piers the Plowman*," *MP*, III (1906). 359-366. Manly presented his views more fully in "*Piers the Plowman* and its Sequence," *CHEL*, II. 1-48.

[15] In Passus v of the *A*-text Conscience preaches a sermon which leads to confessions by the Seven Deadly Sins. In this series of confessions the sin of Wrath is left out, and between lines 235 and 236 there is a dislocation of sense, the confession of Sloth suddenly changing to that of Robert the Robber. The loss of a leaf at this point would explain the abrupt ending of the confession of Sloth and the absence of a suitable introduction to the character of Robert the Robber. By assuming a manuscript with 30-40 lines to the page Manly shows that this lost leaf could have belonged to the sheet next to the inner sheet of a gathering and that its counterfoil would come where the confession of Wrath should occur, i.e., after the confession of Envy. The confession of Envy, as has often been noticed, closes abruptly. The significance of this demonstration for Manly's theory of multiple authorship lies in the fact that the author of the *B*-text in revising this portion of the poem did not deal with these defects adequately and therefore could not have been the original poet.

[16] The earlier articles in the controversy are reprinted in *EETS*, 139. For subsequent bibliography see Wells' *Manual* and its supplements, and Morton W. Bloomfield, "Present State of *Piers Plowman* Studies," *Speculum*, XIV (1939). 215-232.

[17] The best statement of the argument for single authorship is that of R. W. Chambers in his preface to Bright's book noted above.

[18] Dorothy L. Owen, *Piers Plowman: A Comparison with Some Earlier and Contemporary French Allegories* (1912); M. R. Adams, "The Use of the Vulgate in *Piers Plowman*," *SP*, XXIV (1927). 556-566.

[19] See George Sanderlin. "The Character of 'Liberum Arbitrium' in the *C*-text of *Piers Plowman*." *MLN*, LVI (1941). 449-453.

worse in the text,[20] and other considerations raise serious doubts about the authorship of this version.[21] Even in the B-text it cannot be denied that the poet is incapable of steering a straight course, possibly because he has become more deeply involved in his allegory. But until Manly's theory of a lost leaf is more satisfactorily disposed of, his claim for separate authorship of the A, B, and C texts cannot be dismissed.

The greatness of the poem is due almost entirely to the A and B versions. *The* Whatever its shortcomings in design—and these are most apparent in the B *Poem's* continuation—we are in the presence throughout of a powerful imagination, *Greatness* wayward and rhapsodic though it is in the B-text. In the vivid delineation of scenes and the realistic painting of character the poem bears comparison with the best of medieval allegories, with the *Roman de la Rose* or the *Divine Comedy*. Its distinguishing characteristic is its trenchant satire, both in sidelong glance and direct attack. And permeating the whole is the evident sincerity of the author or authors, the deep moral earnestness which compels us to read every line with close attention while insuring our interest up to the very end.

So popular a poem was naturally not without imitators. A Wyclifite at- Pierce the tack on the friars was given the name *Pierce the Ploughman's Creed*[22] (*c.* Plough- 1394). The author goes to each of the four orders looking for some one to man's teach him the Creed, but a Minorite runs down the Carmelites, the Do- Creed minicans abuse the Austin friars, and so on. A poor plowman named Piers abuses them all in a long and general condemnation, finally explaining the Creed himself. The poem, which was apparently written in London, is interesting mainly for its outspoken criticism of the mendicant orders.

Another alliterative poem, once attributed to the author of *Piers Plow-* Richard *man,* was published many years ago under the title *Richard the Redeless.*[23] the Written after Richard II had been taken prisoner (September, 1399), the Redeless poem offers belated advice to the King. It criticizes him for surrounding himself with young and inexperienced advisers who squandered his money and thought only of fashionable clothes, and for filling the country with retainers who wore his livery and oppressed the people. It breaks off, shortly after the beginning of Passus IV, in the midst of an attack on the Parliament of 1398 and its indifference to the public welfare. The poem was known to Nicholas Brigham, a sixteenth-century antiquary, by the title *Mum, Sothsegger* (Hush, Truth-teller). The identification is certain because Mum and he quoted the first two lines (in a Latin paraphrase). When accordingly a the Soth- manuscript turned up in 1928 containing some 1750 lines of a poem made segger up throughout of a dialogue between Mum and Sothsegger it seemed reason-

[20] See T. D. Hall, "Was 'Langland' the Author of the C-text of *The Vision of Piers Plowman?*" *MLR*, IV (1908). 1-13.

[21] Even Chambers admits that "C is probably much interpolated" (*op. cit.,* p. 23).

[22] Edited by W. W. Skeat (1867, 1895; *EETS,* 30) and in a convenient small edition (Oxford, 1906).

[23] Edited originally by Thomas Wright (1838; *Camden Soc.*) and more recently by W. W. Skeat (1873; *EETS,* 54). It is also included in his edition of *Piers Plowman* (2v, Oxford, 1886). But see the following note.

able to assume that the two somehow belonged together. They have now been so published under the title *Mum and the Sothsegger*.[24] An interval must have separated the writing of the two parts since allusions in the new fragment to contemporary events indicate a date for it *c.* 1403-6. The poet suggests that the most valuable member of Henry's household would be a Truth-teller. He fears that the King may be led by selfish counselors. Mum bids him keep quiet. Truth-tellers get no thanks. And he finds out to his sorrow that most of the world follows Mum's policy. Finally a gardener tending his bee-hives encourages him to go on and he will find Truth-teller in man's heart. He is advised to write his book and give a copy to the King, whereupon he launches into his account of the many evils which beset the country. We are conscious of a considerable change of style as we pass from *Richard the Redeless* to the later fragment and there are other difficulties which prevent us from being sure that we are dealing with two parts of the same work, but on any other assumption it is difficult to account for the association of the unusual names Mum and Sothsegger with both poems.

Death and Life

Related more closely to *Wynnere and Wastoure* and to *The Parlement of the Thre Ages* is a poem dating from the end of the fourteenth century but preserved only in a seventeenth-century transcript in the Percy Folio. *Death and Life* [25] relates a vision in which Lady Life, described as very beautiful, disputes with Death, a woman of horrible appearance. Recalling the theme of Old Age's discourse in the *Parlement,* Death boasts of those whom she has struck down from Adam to Lancelot and Gawain and Galahad. But Life tells how Death herself was vanquished, recounting the Resurrection and the Harrowing of Hell, and finally in the character of Eternal Life assures her followers that through baptism and the Creed they need have no fear of Death. There are beautiful passages in the poem testifying to the continuance of the poetical impulse in the north well after the productions of the *Pearl* poet.

The alliterative poems which we have considered in this chapter have much in common. Of them *Piers Plowman* would alone be sufficient to guarantee the major importance of the group. Taken together they are the most significant vernacular expression of English social thought in the Middle Ages.

[24] Ed. Mabel Day and Robert Steele (1936; *EETS,* 199).

[25] The text is in Vol. III of *Bishop Percy's Folio Manuscript,* ed. Hales and Furnivall, but there are more recent editions by James H. Hanford and John M. Steadman, Jr. in *SP,* xv (1918). 221-294, and by Sir Israel Gollancz (1930). See also Edith Scamman, "The Alliterative Poem: *Death and Life,*" *Radcliffe Coll. Monographs,* No. 15 (1910). 95-113.

XVI

Chaucer: I

Geoffrey Chaucer,[1] the only known son of John Chaucer, a vintner of *Chaucer's*
London, was born about 1340.[2] Of his early life and education we know *Life*
nothing.[3] The earliest biographical fact of which we are sure is that in
April, 1357, he was a page in the household of the Countess of Ulster, wife
of the King's son Lionel. The Countess spent the following Christmas at
Hatfield in Yorkshire, and at this time Chaucer probably made the acquaintance of John of Gaunt, his lifelong patron and friend, who was among the
guests. In 1359 he went to France with the army, where he was taken pris-

---

[1] The most valuable book for the student to have is *The Complete Works of Geoffrey Chaucer*, ed. F. N. Robinson (Boston, 1933), with its scholarly and bibliographical apparatus. *The Complete Works of Geoffrey Chaucer*, ed. Walter W. Skeat (7v, Oxford, 1894-97) is still of value for its notes and glossary; it is often cited as the *Oxford Chaucer*. The one-volume abridgment (Oxford, 1897) and the Globe Chaucer, ed. Alfred W. Pollard, *et al.* (1898) are not, or but slightly, annotated. The volume of selections from the *Canterbury Tales* edited by John M. Manly (1928) contains an admirable introduction. Special bibliographies are E. P. Hammond, *Chaucer: A Bibliographical Manual* (1908), D. D. Griffith, *A Bibliography of Chaucer, 1908-1924* (Seattle, 1928), W. E. Martin, *A Chaucer Bibliography, 1925-1933* (Durham, N. C., 1935), and Wells' *Manual* with its supplements. For a comprehensive survey of Chaucer's work the following can be recommended: R. K. Root, *The Poetry of Chaucer* (2ed., 1922), R. D. French, *A Chaucer Handbook* (2ed., 1947), and G. L. Kittredge, *Chaucer and His Poetry* (1915). Of interest in various ways are Émile Legouis, *Geoffrey Chaucer* (Paris, 1910; English trans., 1913), A. Brusendorff, *The Chaucer Tradition* (1925), T. R. Lounsbury, *Studies in Chaucer* (3v, 1892), J. L. Lowes, *Geoffrey Chaucer and the Development of His Genius* (1934), J. M. Manly, *Some New Light on Chaucer* (1926), H. R. Patch, *On Rereading Chaucer* (1939), Percy V. D. Shelly, *The Living Chaucer* (Philadelphia, 1940). Among special studies Walter C. Curry, *Chaucer and the Mediæval Sciences* (1926) and Edgar F. Shannon, *Chaucer and the Roman Poets* (Cambridge, Mass., 1929; *Harvard Stud. in Compar. Lit.*, VII) may be mentioned for their wide scope. The publications of the Chaucer Society contain texts, monographs, the *Life Records* compiled by W. D. Selby, F. J. Furnivall, E. A. Bond, and R. E. G. Kirk (index by E. P. Kuhl in *MP*, x. 527-552), and source material. There is a concordance by J. S. P. Tatlock and A. G. Kennedy (Washington, 1927). The allusions to Chaucer are gathered together in C. F. E. Spurgeon, *Five Hundred Years of Chaucer Criticism and Allusion, 1357-1900* (7 parts, 1914-24; *Chaucer Soc.;* also 3v, Cambridge, 1925). — The chronology of Chaucer's writings has been worked out by a long succession of scholars, so that today we may feel that the main lines have been laid down. Of major importance in this work are F. J. Furnivall, *Trial-Forewords* (1871; *Chaucer Soc.*, 2nd Ser., 6) John Koch, *The Chronology of Chaucer's Writings* (1890; *Chaucer Soc.*, 2nd Ser., 27), J. S. P. Tatlock, *The Development and Chronology of Chaucer's Works* (1907; *Chaucer Soc.*, 2nd Ser., 37), and the two articles of J. L. Lowes in *PMLA*, xix (1904). 593-683 and xx (1905). 749-864. For other contributions to the subject the reader must be referred to the bibliographies mentioned earlier in this note.

[2] In 1386 Chaucer testified in the Scrope-Grosvenor trial, a suit over a disputed coat of arms, and gave his age as "forty years and upwards." In the absence of any more precise indication, it seems best to hold to a round number, although some are disposed to put the date a few years later. On the Chaucer family see Alfred A. Kern, *The Ancestry of Chaucer* (Baltimore, 1906).

[3] It has been suggested that he may have gone to school at St. Paul's, but the suggestion rests on nothing more than the fact that in 1358 the schoolmaster bequeathed nearly a hundred books to the school and the collection included many titles which Chaucer was later acquainted with. Cf. Edith Rickert, "Chaucer at School," *MP*, xxix (1932). 257-274.

oner, for in March, 1360, Edward III contributed £16 towards his ransom. After October we know nothing about his life for the next six years, although subsequent events make it likely that at some time during this period he was taken into the King's service. In any case, by 1366 he is already married to a Philippa, one of the damoiselles in the Queen's service, who seems to have been the daughter of Sir Payne Roet and sister of Katherine de Swynford, mistress and later wife of John of Gaunt.[4] In 1367 Chaucer appears as a valet in the King's household and the next year as an esquire. As such he begins to be employed on small missions and from then on his name occurs pretty constantly in the records. Chaucer's early history, as thus seen, is quite normal for one whose parents were able to secure a place for their son in the household of some noble. He was more fortunate than many, however, in being taken into the service of a member of the royal family.

Public Service   From this time on his life is a record of employment in one form or another of public service, rewarded by pensions, grants, and special payments. He is sent abroad frequently on the King's business, sometimes on "secret negotiations," once as a member of the group which tried in 1381 to arrange a marriage between Richard II and the daughter of the King of France. Most of these journeys were to France and the Low Countries, but at least two were to Italy. These are of special importance since they gave him an opportunity to become acquainted with Italian literature, especially with the work of Dante and Boccaccio. The first Italian journey which we can be sure of was in 1372, when he went to Genoa to negotiate a commercial treaty. His business also took him to Florence and from an allusion in the *Clerk's Tale* it is conjectured that he may have been in Padua and met Petrarch.[5] He was gone about six months. The second Italian mission was in 1378. This time he was gone only four months and his business brought him in contact with Barnabo Visconti, lord of Milan, whose death is the subject of a stanza in the *Monk's Tale*.

In 1374 Chaucer received the first of several appointments in the civil service. He was made Controller of the Customs and Subsidy on Wool, Skins, and Hides in the port of London, with the usual provision that he should keep the records with his own hand. He was now freed from his attendance upon the King, and went to housekeeping in an apartment above Aldgate. During this period he seems to have enjoyed considerable prosperity, receiving in addition to his salary and the annuities which he and Philippa had, certain wardships and a fine which brought him in sums as

---

[4] The relationship is not entirely clear. Katherine was the sole heir of Sir Payne Roet. Moreover Chaucer's relation to John of Gaunt does not seem to have been that of a brother-in-law. Philippa may have been Katherine's sister-in-law, in which case she would have been a Swynford. On the other hand, Thomas Chaucer, who was almost certainly the poet's son, has the Roet arms on his tomb. Philippa seems to have had social connections since she receives a number of grants and honors, in some of which her husband did not share.
[5] The argument for the affirmative is presented by J. J. Jusserand, "Did Chaucer Meet Petrarch?" *Nineteenth Century*, xxxix (1896). 993-1005. On this general aspect of Chaucer's life see James R. Hulbert, *Chaucer's Official Life* (Menasha, 1912).

large as £104, the equivalent of twenty or more times that amount today. In 1382 he received the additional appointment of Controller of the Petty Customs with permission to exercise the office by deputy. These positions he resigned or lost in 1386. At this time he gave up his apartment over Aldgate, and perhaps was already living in Kent, for he was appointed a justice of the peace there in 1385 and the next year represented Kent in Parliament.[6] On this occasion he had the uncomfortable experience of seeing his friend John of Gaunt stripped of most of his power. In June of the following year Philippa received the last payment of her pension and it is assumed that shortly after that she died.

In the last dozen years of his life Chaucer's position and financial status fluctuated. In 1388 he sold his annuity, apparently through necessity. However, the next year, when Richard asserted his royal prerogative, Chaucer was appointed Clerk of the King's Works, in charge of the repairs and upkeep of the royal residences and other properties. It was a fairly lucrative position and in addition he was given special commissions of a similar nature the following year. In September, 1390, he was robbed three times, twice on the same day, of money belonging to the King. The thieves were caught and Chaucer was forgiven the loss of the money. His loss of the clerkship nine months later does not seem to be connected with the robberies. Although the King gave him a reward of £10 in 1393 and granted him an annuity of £20 the next year, he was apparently in financial difficulty, since he was forced to borrow small sums and in 1398 was sued for debt. From about 1395 he seems to have been attached in some capacity to John of Gaunt's son, Henry of Lancaster, and when Henry was declared king on September 30, 1399, Chaucer sent the well-known *Complaint to his Empty Purse*. Four days later Henry IV responded with an annuity of 40 marks. The poet promptly leased a house in Westminster, but lived to enjoy his new security only a few months. According to a late inscription on his tomb in Westminster abbey, he died October 25, 1400.[7] *Later Years*

From this brief sketch of Chaucer's life we may make certain observations which will be helpful in understanding his character as a poet. In the first place he was an active man of affairs and must have had a highly developed practical side. Poetry was for him not a vocation but an avocation. As the eagle says in the *Hous of Fame,* *His Literary Affiliations*

> For when thy labour doon al ys,
> And hast mad alle thy rekenynges,
> In stede of reste and newe thynges,
> Thou goost hom to thy hous anoon;
> And, also domb as any stoon,

---

[6] On this period of his life see an illuminating paper by Margaret Galway, "Geoffrey Chaucer, J. P. and M. P.," *MLR*, xxxvi (1941). 1-36.

[7] Lewis, for whom he wrote the *Astrolabe*, and Thomas Chaucer, a prominent member of the government in the early part of the fifteenth century, were probably the poet's children. On the latter see Martin B. Ruud, *Thomas Chaucer* (Minneapolis, 1926) and A. C. Baugh, "Kirk's Life Records of Thomas Chaucer," *PMLA*, xlvii (1932). 461-515.

Thou sittest at another book
Tyl fully daswed ys thy look.... (lines 652-8)

He read and he wrote because he wanted to, because there was something within him, as in every true poet, that impelled him to write. But since writing was a pastime he did not always take it too seriously. In the second place, all his life was spent in association with people at the court and in government circles, people for whom French had been not so long ago more familiar than English and whose tastes were formed on things French. Such an environment is sufficient to account for the fact that Chaucer is completely Continental in his literary affiliations. He is remarkably indifferent to English writings, but the *Roman de la Rose* and the poems of Machaut are his missal and breviary; in Latin Ovid is his bible. His indebtedness to recent and contemporary French poets, including Deschamps and Froissart, and to certain classical authors at either first or second hand is the most noticeable characteristic of his early work and has often led to the designation of it as his French period. With his two journeys to Italy he comes under the influence of Italian poetry, the *Divine Comedy* to some extent but more especially certain poems of Boccaccio. With the *Hous of Fame* begins what is often called his Italian period. He never deserts his first love, French poetry, so full of allegorical love visions and their conventions, but he builds on the old framework with new matter from Italy. It is only relatively late—in certain aspects of the *Troilus* and chiefly in the *Canterbury Tales*—that having learned all he could from his teachers and having won the complete mastery of his art, he dares to strike out on his own with confidence and ease. This phase of his career can only be described as his English period.

The Romance of the Rose

The *Roman de la Rose* was the most popular and influential of all French poems in the Middle Ages, and set a fashion in courtly poetry for two centuries in western Europe.[8] This poem Chaucer tells us he translated, and it is altogether likely that it is one of the ways in which he served his apprenticeship in poetry. The version which has come down to us covers only a part of the original, and though generally printed in editions of Chaucer, is probably not all his work. But there are passages from the *Roman* scattered through his poetry as late as the *Canterbury Tales*.

Book of the Duchess

The earliest of Chaucer's original poems of any length is the *Book of the Duchess*. It is an elegy recording in an unusually graceful way the loss which John of Gaunt suffered in 1369 in the death of his first wife, Blanche. After relating a story which he has been reading, the tragic story of Ceys and Alcyone, the poet falls asleep and dreams that he comes upon a knight dressed in black, sitting sorrowfully beneath a tree in the woods. The

[8] It was begun about 1225 by Guillaume de Lorris as a vision picturing in allegorical form the quest of a lover for his ideal, symbolized by a rose. It ran to only about 4000 lines. Some forty years later it was continued by Jean de Meun in a more realistic and satirical vein, with not a little that is frankly didactic, until it reached a length of 18,000 lines. The standard edition of the French text is by E. Langlois (5v, 1914-24; *SATF*). There is a verse translation in English by F. S. Ellis in the Temple Classics.

stranger recognizes his solicitude and tells him the cause of his grief: he has played a game of chess with Fortune and the goddess has taken his queen. The poet seems not to understand quite what he means and he tells him in detail the story of his love—how he met one day a lady, whom he describes: her beauty, accomplishments, gentle ways, soft speech, goodness. Her name was White. He finally persuaded her to accept his heart and they lived in perfect bliss full many a year. All this he relates sadly and at length. Now he has lost her.

> "Allas, sir, how? what may that be?"
> "She ys ded!" "Nay!" "Yis, be my trouthe!"
> "Is that youre los? Be God, hyt ys routhe!"

The simplicity and restraint of this close, the absence of strained sentiment, show the delicate instinct of the artist. The poem is greatly indebted to Machaut, Froissart, Ovid, and other poets, in fact is a mosaic of passages borrowed or remembered, but the concept and, what is more important, the tone and treatment are Chaucer's own.

It is apparently ten years before we get another long poem from his pen, although we can hardly believe that he wrote nothing in all this time. However, he had been to Italy and he had read Dante's great vision of a journey to the Inferno, to Purgatory, and to Paradise. Such earnestness and tragic grandeur were beyond his power of emulation, but the idea of a journey to regions unknown was one which he could turn to his own purposes. The *Hous of Fame,* generally dated about 1379, is a badly proportioned, *The* Hous incomplete, and utterly delightful poem. It is in three books, with all the of Fame epic machinery of invocations, proems, apostrophes, and the like. In the first book the poet dreams that he is in the temple of Venus, where he reads on the wall and tells at length the story of Dido and Æneas. The episode is pleasantly related but is a digression and is artistically one of the blemishes in the poem. At the end he steps out of doors and sees flying toward him an eagle of great size and shining so brightly that it appears to be of gold. It is obviously of the same family as Dante's eagle in the ninth book of the *Purgatorio.* The eagle seizes him in its claws and immediately soars aloft with him, telling him that Jove means to reward him for his long service to Venus and Cupid by taking him to the house of Fame where he will hear abundant tidings of Love's folk. The second book is wholly taken up with the eagle's flight and is one of the most delightfully humorous episodes in literature, what with the eagle's friendliness and loquacity, and the poet's utter terror. The contrast between the eagle's talkativeness and familiarity— he calls him Geoffrey—and the speechless fright of the poet, who can answer only in monosyllables, "Yes" and "Well" and "Nay", is high comedy. Unfortunately the third book, which describes what the poet saw when the eagle set him down outside of Fame's house, carries us to the point where he is about to hear an announcement from "a man of greet auctoritee" and leaves us still waiting for the expected news. For at this point the poem breaks off. Scholars have interpreted the poem in different ways and taken it perhaps too seriously. Some have seen in it an allegory of the poet's life,[9] others a conventional love vision of a kind for which French literature furnished many models,[10] and still others have tried to solve the mystery of the news which the poet is about to hear. One explanation [11] holds that Chaucer's purpose was to introduce a series of stories as in the *Legend of Good Women* and the *Canterbury Tales*. But it seems likely from an allusion at the beginning of Book Three to "this lytel laste bok" that the poem as we have it is nearly complete and that the announcement was something which Chaucer decided not to write or perhaps later suppressed.

If the *Hous of Fame* was left unfinished, it would be far from the only work which Chaucer began and did not complete. At about this time he apparently started what was to be a considerable poem of *Anelida and Arcite,* but after some three hundred lines he abandoned the project. It is a pity that it remains such a fragment, if for no other reason than that it keeps from the full recognition of its worth the beautiful "Complaint" of Anelida, which with its perfect balance of strophe and antistrophe is one of the most finished and charming examples of the type in medieval literature. To this period may also belong some of the shorter pieces such as the *Complaint unto Pity* and *A Complaint to his Lady*.

Anelida and Arcite

The *Parlement of Foules* is clearly an occasional poem, but the occasion for which it was written is not so clear. It takes its theme from the popular belief that on St. Valentine's day the birds choose their mates, and it accordingly represents a gathering of birds for that purpose. Dame Nature holds on her hand a formel or female eagle of great beauty and goodness, for whom three royal and noble eagles make their respective pleas. Although Nature advises in favor of the royal suitor, the formel asks and is granted a year in which to make her choice. There is much amusing by-play over the impatience of the lesser birds and the varied opinions that they express, but one cannot escape the thought that the essence of the poem is the competition of the three noble eagles for the hand of the worthy formel. The most commonly accepted interpretation is that the poem celebrates the betrothal of Richard II to Anne of Bohemia, whom he married in January, 1382. The rival suitors according to this theory were Friedrich of Meissen and Charles VI of France.[12] Other interpretations have been suggested,[13]

Parlement of Foules

[9] Sandras, Ten Brink, and early scholars quite generally.

[10] W. O. Sypherd, *Studies in Chaucer's Hous of Fame* (1907; *Chaucer Soc.*, 2nd Ser., 39).

[11] J. M. Manly, "What Is Chaucer's *Hous of Fame?*" *Kittredge Anniversary Papers* (Boston, 1913), pp. 73-81.

[12] The interpretation was proposed by Koch in 1877 and modified by O. F. Emerson, "The Suitors in Chaucer's *Parlement of Foules*," *MP*, VIII (1910-11). 45-62; reprinted in *Chaucer Essays and Studies* (Cleveland, 1929). The objections to it were summed up by J. M. Manly, "What Is the *Parlement of Foules?*" *Festschrift für Lorenz Morsbach* (Halle, 1913; *Studien zur englischen Phil.*, 50), pp. 279-290.

[13] Edith Rickert, "A New Interpretation of the *Parlement of Foules*," *MP*, XVIII (1920). 1-29, identified the formel eagle with Philippa, a daughter of John of Gaunt. More recently Haldeen Braddy, in *"The Parlement of Foules:* A New Proposal," *PMLA*, XLVI (1931). 1007-1019, and in subsequent papers, has suggested a connection with negotiations in 1377 for the marriage of Richard with the princess Marie of France. For parallels to the general situation see Willard E. Farnham, "The Contending Lovers," *PMLA*, XXXV (1920). 247-323.

and if none of them carries complete conviction, the fact need not detract from our enjoyment of the poem as one of Chaucer's smaller but most finished productions.

At about this time, somewhere in the early eighties, Chaucer translated *Boethius* the *Consolation of Philosophy* of Boethius,[14] if we may judge by the fact that its influence is very noticeable in such poems as *Palamon and Arcite* (included in the *Canterbury Tales* as the *Knight's Tale*) and *Troilus and Criseyde,* which were written, it would seem, between 1382 and 1385-6. It is significant as an indication of the range of Chaucer's interests, but as a translation it leaves much to be desired. Chaucer's prose both here and in the *Astrolabe* (1391), and in the prose tales included in the *Canterbury Tales* as well, is formless and undistinguished.

Troilus and Criseyde[15] is at once Chaucer's longest complete poem and *Troilus* his greatest artistic achievement. In some 8000 lines, in stanzas of rime *and* royal, it tells a tragic love story from the time Troilus first sees Criseyde, a *Criseyde* young and beautiful widow whose father, Calchas, has abandoned Troy and gone over to the Greek side, until she proves unfaithful to him, and death puts an end to his suffering. For three skilfully ordered books the story rises steadily to a climax when Troilus, with the aid of Pandarus, his friend and the uncle of Criseyde, having overcome her natural caution and conventional reserve, finally possesses her completely, both body and soul. For three years they are united in a mutual love that could not be more complete. Then in the last two books events move inevitably toward their tragic conclusion. Through an exchange of prisoners Criseyde must go to her father in the Greek camp. She leaves, swearing undying love and fidelity and promising to find some way of returning before ten days are past. But by the time the ten days are up her handsome Greek escort, Diomede, has caused her to change her mind, and within a few months she has given him the brooch which had been Troilus's parting gift to her when she left.

The main features of the story Chaucer took from a poem by Boccaccio called the *Filostrato.*[16] Boccaccio had found the latter part of it in Benoît

---

[14] Boethius illustrates the medieval conception of tragedy, the fall of a great man from his high estate. In the innermost counsels of the emperor Theodoric, he was accused of disloyalty, thrown into prison, and eventually (524) put to death. The *Consolation of Philosophy* was written in prison, and was so in harmony with Christian teaching on the questions which it discusses that it became one of the most widely read books of the Middle Ages. For the earlier translation due to King Alfred, see above, p. 99. It was later translated by Queen Elizabeth. See Howard R. Patch, *The Tradition of Boethius: A Study of His Importance in Medieval Culture* (1935).

[15] The definitive edition of the poem is that of R. K. Root (Princeton, 1926). Professor Root has settled a long controversy over the date of the poem by identifying a rare astronomical phenomenon mentioned in Book III, which shows that it could not have been finished before May, 1385. Cf. R. K. Root and H. N. Russell, "A Planetary Date for Chaucer's *Troilus*," *PMLA*, xxxix (1924). 48-63. See also Thomas A. Kirby, *Chaucer's Troilus: A Study in Courtly Love* (University, La., 1940; *Louisiana State Univ. Stud.*, No. 39).

[16] As is well known, the story of the Trojan war was familiar to the Middle Ages not through Homer but in two late accounts by Dares Phrygius and Dictys Cretensis. These were made the basis, about 1155, of the French poem by Benoît mentioned in the text. An account in Latin prose, the *Historia Trojana*, was taken from Benoît's poem about 1287 by Guido della Colonna (ed. N. E. Griffin. Cambridge, Mass., 1936; *Mediaeval Acad. of Amer.*, Pub.

Relation to Boccaccio's Filostrato

de Sainte-More, who had hit upon the idea of filling out with a love story the lagging intervals between periods of fighting in his *Roman de Troie.* All that part of the story which precedes Criseyde's departure for the Greek camp is due to Boccaccio, and he also created the character of Pandarus. But while Chaucer's indebtedness to the Italian poem is very great, his own contribution is still greater. He has basically altered the character of Pandarus and he has added complexity and mystery to Criseyde until she is much more than Troilus's mistress. Without losing its essential qualities of medieval romance or abandoning the conventions of courtly love, *Troilus and Criseyde* has taken on many of the characteristics of the psychological novel. It should be remembered that less than 2600 lines in Chaucer's poem have their counterparts in Boccaccio.

The Character of Criseyde

What gives the story its chief interest and acts as a constant challenge to understanding is the character of Criseyde. She combines the qualities that will always appeal in woman, beauty and mystery. Her behavior is never transparent and we try without complete success to penetrate the mingling of impulses and the complex workings of her mind. In her early defensive attitude toward the advances of Troilus there is probably a mixture of caution and the courtly love tradition which expected the woman to be difficult to approach. She is more interested in her reputation than her virtue. Her ultimate surrender is brought about partly by circumstance, but when she yields it is because she has made her own decision. How much of her emotion is the womanly love of being loved we cannot say, but during the three years that she gives herself to Troilus her affection is genuine and complete. When finally as a result of separation she abandons him for Diomede she reproaches herself, but her love is not the kind that is proof against every storm. Her father was a traitor and an opportunist; she was of a yielding disposition, "slydynge of corage." When in the end she gives Diomede gifts which Troilus had given her, we cannot but admit that she was without depth of feeling. And yet withal, her faults spring from weakness rather than baseness of character, and the poet in pleading that we judge her not too harshly says, "I would excuse her if I could."

The Legend of Good Women

The *Legend of Good Women* was begun, according to the prologue, as a penance imposed by Queen Alceste for his offenses against the God of Love in writing the *Troilus* and the *Romance of the Rose,* which speak slightingly of women. Chaucer refers to the work elsewhere as the *Seintes Legende of Cupide,* and it was to be a collection of nineteen stories about women famous for their faithfulness in love. A twentieth and longer legend of Alceste would doubtless have completed the whole. The most interesting part of the poem is the long Prologue, with its frank enjoyment of nature

---

No. 26). Boccaccio adopted from Benoît the love story, keeping only as much of the war and the fighting as he needed for background to the Troilus and Criseyde story. The *Filostrato* can be had most conveniently with an English translation in *The Filostrato of Giovanni Boccaccio,* by N. E. Griffin and A. B. Myrick (Philadelphia, 1929), with an excellent introduction on the development of the story. See also Karl Young, *The Origin and Development of the Story of Troilus and Criseyde* (Chaucer Soc., 1908).

and the spring, its amusing picture of the God of Love's anger at the poet, the Queen's generous intercession, the partly gratuitous enumeration of his works, and the penance that is imposed upon him. Some of the legends had been written earlier, but even so, the poem as it has come down to us is unfinished, breaking off in the midst of the ninth legend. It has been suggested that Chaucer found the idea too monotonous. If the suggestion recently made [17] that he was writing the poem for Joan, the widow of the Black Prince, is accepted, we might assume that her death in August, 1385, removed the immediate occasion for writing it. It does not make any easier our understanding the fact that he subjected the Prologue to a very careful revision in 1394; one does not ordinarily devote so much time and labor to the preliminary part of an unfinished work. In any case, if he abandoned the project originally to devote himself to the *Canterbury Tales,* we cannot feel regret, and to this, his last and best-known work, we turn in the next chapter.

[17] Margaret Galway, "Chaucer's Sovereign Lady: A Study of the Prologue to the *Legend* and Related Poems," *MLR,* xxxiii (1938). 145-199. Objection to so early a date, based on Chaucer's supposed use of Deschamps' *Lai de Franchise,* has little force. See Marian Lossing, "The Prologue to the Legend of Good Women and the *Lai de Franchise,*" *SP,* xxxix (1942). 15-35.

XVII
Chaucer: II

The Canterbury Tales

If Chaucer had never written anything more than the works considered in the preceding chapter, he would have been recognized as a great poet, but he would not have been so popular a poet since his popularity today rests in large measure upon the *Canterbury Tales*.[1] Any one who knows anything about Chaucer knows the *Canterbury Tales*. He knows the General Prologue with its wonderful portrait gallery of pilgrims, and he knows at least some of the tales. And he would be willing to admit perhaps that such a work deserves closer acquaintance.

The Framed Tale

It would seem that about 1387 Chaucer, having finished or laid aside the *Legend of Good Women,* conceived the idea of writing a collection of stories of more varied character. He doubtless had on hand some material suitable for his purpose, such as the *Palamon and Arcite,* which in the Prologue to the *Legend of Good Women* he had said was little known, and "the lyf also of Seynt Cecile," mentioned in the same place. The idea of binding a collection of stories together in a framework is a familiar one in literature. It extends from ancient India to Uncle Remus. Chaucer's plan was to relate 120 stories and have them told by a group of pilgrims, thirty in number, journeying from London to Canterbury. Each pilgrim agrees to tell two tales each way. Harry Bailey, the Host of the Tabard Inn, where Chaucer and the other travelers assemble, agrees to go along and act as master of ceremonies. It was an admirable method for bringing together people of various types and different social classes. The group includes a knight and an esquire, his son, professional men like the doctor and the lawyer, a merchant, a shipman, various representatives of the religious orders such as the prioress, the monk, the honest parson, and the friar, a substantial farmer, a miller, a reeve, a London cook, and several craftsmen, not to attempt a complete list. Nearly all are described with such particularity as to suggest that in some cases at least Chaucer was drawing his portraits from individuals in real life.[2] How the suggestion for such a plan came to him, if not from experience, we cannot say. Boccaccio had used a somewhat

---

[1] Full critical apparatus is provided for the study of the *Canterbury Tales* in J. M. Manly and Edith Rickert, *The Text of the Canterbury Tales* (8v, Chicago, 1940). A new collection of *Sources and Analogues of Chaucer's Canterbury Tales* has been prepared by a group of scholars under the editorship of W. F. Bryan and Germaine Dempster (Chicago, 1941).

[2] For one or two plausible identifications and a number of interesting speculations see J. M. Manly, *Some New Light on Chaucer* (1926).

analogous idea in the *Decameron,* a collection of a hundred stories told by *Earlier*
ten people of the gentle class who have retired within a palace to escape the *Examples*
plague. It is unlikely that Chaucer knew the *Decameron,* since if he had
known it he would certainly have made use of it. In any case, Chaucer's
plan admits of greater discrepancies among the pilgrims, greater variety in
the stories they can appropriately tell, and greater opportunity for incidental
adventure. A closer analogy is found in the *Novelle* [3] of Giovanni Sercambi,
written about 1374. Here we have actually the device of a pilgrimage, with
a leader and by-play among the pilgrims, but the stories are all told by the
author. It is unlikely that Chaucer was acquainted with this collection for
the same reason as that which we have alleged in the case of the *Decameron.*
At present we can best believe that Chaucer's plan for the *Canterbury Tales*
was a happy idea of his own.

The plan laid down in the General Prologue was only partially carried *The*
out. There are but twenty-four tales, and of these, two are interrupted before *Unfinished*
the end and two break off shortly after they get under way. Even before *Character*
Chaucer laid aside the work, possibly about 1395, there are indications that *of the*
he had altered his original intention. At the beginning of the *Parson's Tale* *Work*
the Host says, "Now lakketh us no tales mo than oon," showing that
Chaucer then had in mind only one tale from each pilgrim. There are many
marks of the unfinished state in which he left the work. In putting his life
of St. Cecilia in the mouth of the Second Nun he neglected to make the
necessary revision and she accordingly refers to herself as an unworthy *son*
of Eve. The Man of Law says he will speak in prose, but instead he tells
the story of Constance in well-turned stanzas. The *Shipman's Tale* was apparently written for the Wife of Bath, with the result that this "good felawe"
whose beard had been shaken by many a tempest alludes to himself as
a woman; and some students have seen equally clear evidence that the *Merchant's Tale* was originally intended for one of the religious pilgrims.[4]
Small matters like this are not serious. What is much more troublesome is
the fact that we cannot now tell in what order the tales would have ultimately been arranged.

The beginning is clear enough. When the party has ridden a short dis- *The*
tance out of town Harry Bailey bids them draw lots and by good luck or *"Groups"*
manipulation the lot falls to the Knight to tell the first tale. He relates the
story of the love of two friends, Palamon and Arcite, for the same lady.
When he finishes, the pilgrims all express enthusiastic approval and the
Host, pleased at so good a start, calls upon the Monk to tell the next tale.
But the Miller is drunk and unruly and insists on telling his story in spite
of all entreaty. His indecent tale is about a carpenter, and when he finishes,
the Reeve, who "was of carpenteris craft," takes offense and tells an equally

[3] Karl Young, "The Plan of the Canterbury Tales," *Kittredge Anniv. Papers* (Boston, 1913),
pp. 405-417, and Robert A. Pratt and Karl Young in *Sources and Analogues,* pp. 1-81.
[4] The present writer believes that the evidence clearly points to the Friar ("The Original
Teller of the *Merchant's Tale,*" MP, xxxv (1937). 15-26); for a dissenting opinion see Germaine
Dempster, *ibid.,* xxxvi (1938). 1-8.

vulgar story about a miller. Chaucer has evidently an eye to contrast and means to offset the seriousness of the Knight's story with these two in a lighter vein. The Cook next exclaims with glee over the Reeve's story and offers to tell a joke about an apprentice in the city. But Chaucer must have felt that three humorous stories in a row would be too many and stopped after fifty lines. Up to this point the sequence of tales is clear; the incompleteness of the *Cook's Tale,* however, leaves us with no hint as to what was to follow. Other stories are bound together into groups in a similar way, but the arrangement of the groups is not indicated. In some of the stories and links there· are occasional allusions to the time of day and to places along the way. These apparently guided scribes or editors, as we should say, of manuscripts, but there is great variation among the early texts. Modern editions usually follow the arrangement of the Ellesmere manuscript or adopt an arrangement of the groups that does least violence to the local allusions. The precise order of all the tales is something which at his death Chaucer himself had not settled.

Dramatic The *Canterbury Tales* is more than a collection of stories. It is a pageant
Character of fourteenth-century life, a *comédie humaine,* in which a group of thirty people of various classes act their parts on this mundane stage in such a way as to reveal their private lives and habits, their changing moods as well as their prevailing dispositions, their qualities good and bad. Much of this life is revealed not by the stories they tell but by their behavior along the road and their remarks by the way. Chaucer never lets us forget that the stories in his collection are part of a pilgrimage, incidental to it in fact, and in the links between the tales he accomplishes his end in a variety of ways. Most important is the part played by Harry Bailey, the hearty, boisterous Host, with his frankness, his rough humor, his unconscious profanity which so shocks the Parson, and his good sense. He twits the pilgrims, draws the shy ones out, shows a clumsy deference to those entitled to it, smooths over differences, and keeps the company generally in good spirits. There are, of course, quarrels, and these are used most effectively to introduce some of the stories. The Reeve's resentment of the Miller's tale has been mentioned. A similar feud breaks out later between the Friar and the Summoner and results in the telling by each of them of a story defaming the other's calling. A humorous and realistic touch is given when some story proves tiresome and the speaker is cut short. The effect is particularly ironic when it is Chaucer's own story that the Host objects to, but it is a useful device, too, when the lugubrious tragedies of the Monk threaten to weary the reader as well as the original company. One of the most realistic incidents is that in which the pilgrims are overtaken at Boughton-under-Blee by a Canon and his Yeoman. The Yeoman talks too freely about his master's private affairs and the Canon rides off "for verray sorwe and shame." Whether the Yeoman tells a story because Chaucer noticed that his pilgrims were short one of their thirty or because he saw an opportunity of using in this way his knowledge of the frauds practised by alchemists we shall never

know. In any case, the incident contributes much to our feeling that a minor drama is being unfolded all along the route.

A lesser unity is achieved at least once within the whole by the concentration in a fairly close sequence of several stories which deal in one way or another with the problem of marriage. The question is opened by the Wife of Bath, whose philosophy of life is distinctly earthy. She has had five husbands and is not unwilling to take a sixth. She openly renounces the idea that virginity is to be preferred by all to matrimony. But she is equally frank in describing her former husbands and in telling how she maintained the upper hand over all of them. Her theory, confirmed by practice, has been that happiness in marriage depends on the acceptance of the wife's mastery, and the story she tells of the knight and the loathly lady is meant to illustrate and enforce this view. Any debate that might have been provoked by a doctrine so contrary to medieval notions is prevented by the quarrel between the Friar and the Summoner, which bursts into flame as soon as she has finished, but when each has told his story and cooled his wrath the Host calls on the Clerk for a tale. The tale which he tells is one of a woman's submission to her husband, the story of Patient Griselda, whose patience was finally rewarded with happiness. There is sharp contrast at least between the Wife's and the Clerk's stories. The Merchant next tells the story of January and May, a fabliau about an old man who marries a young wife and is shamefully tricked by her. It introduces a somewhat different marriage problem. The *Squire's Tale* which follows is a fragment of Eastern romance and has nothing to do with marriage, nor has the *Franklin's Tale,* which is a story of generosity and honor put to a severe test. But in the story told by the Franklin the married life of Arviragus and Dorigen is so harmonious and happy, and their relations are governed by such mutual tolerance and forbearance as well as confidence and love, that it is easy to see in it the ideal solution of the marriage relationship. Their vows express this forbearance and in a long aside the Franklin voices the conviction that

The So-Called Marriage Group

> Love wol not been constreynëd by maistrye.
> Whan maistrie comth, the God of Love anon
> Beteth his wynges, and farewel, he is gon!

The "Marriage Group," as the sequence here surveyed is called, is brought to a close with the *Franklin's Tale* and it is thus natural to suppose that the views of the Franklin were those of Chaucer himself.[5]

[5] The existence of a Marriage Group was first suggested by Miss Hammond (*Manual*, p. 256), but the full exposition of the idea is due to Professor Kittredge, in an article called "Chaucer's Discussion of Marriage," *MP*, IX (1912). 435-467. A number of scholars deny a conscious intention on Chaucer's part to present a marriage "group," and point out that various aspects of marriage and "maistrie" in marriage are presented in several other tales as well. Full reference to the scholarly literature on the question will be found in the bibliographies mentioned on p. 249.

*An
Anthology
of
Medieval
Literature*

Viewed merely as a collection of separate pieces, the *Canterbury Tales* in its extent and variety offers a remarkable anthology of medieval literature. The courtly romance is represented well enough by the *Knight's Tale* or the story of Constance told by the Man of Law, not to mention the fragmentary *Squire's Tale,* while we have in *Sir Thopas* a parody of the more popular type of romance, such as *Guy of Warwick* and *Bevis of Hampton.* The *Franklin's Tale* is a Breton lay, with its setting in Brittany, its fidelity of true lovers, and its element of the supernatural or marvelous. The *Physician's Tale* of Virginius and his daughter, whom he kills to save her honor, is the retelling of a classical legend, like many examples in Old French literature and like Chaucer's own "Ceys and Alcyone" in the *Book of the Duchess.* The *Wife of Bath's Tale* is a folk-tale which was often given literary form. The coarser type of story is represented by a quarter of the collection, by the fabliaux of the Miller, Reeve, Merchant, and others. Two widespread religious types appear in the saint's legend (St. Cecilia) told by the Second Nun and in the miracle of the Virgin related so beautifully by the Prioress. The Monk's numerous examples of great men who have fallen from their high estate to misery and death are tragedies, as the Middle Ages understood the word, while the story of the three rogues told by the Pardoner is an exemplum, one of thousands of such stories with which preachers adorned their sermons and pointed a moral. The sermon or didactic treatise, though hardly to be considered a tale in the most liberal sense of the word, is represented by the *Parson's Tale* and by Chaucer's own second attempt, the *Melibeus.* Finally, we have a truly magnificent example of the beast fable, familiar to every one in the Middle Ages through *Reynard the Fox,* in the story of Chauntecleer and Dame Pertelot which the Nun's Priest tells. Without forcing matters we might note that there are even examples of the short lyric in the "Envoy" to the *Clerk's Tale* and the "Invocation to Mary" at the beginning of the *Second Nun's Tale.* The *Canterbury Tales* is a miniature five-foot shelf of medieval literature.

*Chaucer's
Character
as a Poet*

When we look at Chaucer's poetry as a whole and try to comprehend its character in its larger aspects, we must recognize that this character was due partly to his environment, partly to himself—the mysterious combination of hereditary qualities that made him the kind of person he was. Environment made him a court poet. He wrote for the circle in which he lived; therefore we see him as a graceful occasional poet and a teller of tales. The tastes of the court, as we have said, had been formed on French literature [6] and as his environment determined his education and literary background, so he was attracted by, and his literary tastes were almost wholly formed upon, the literature of France and Rome and later of medieval Italy. He scarcely refers to English writings, and when he does it is to parody the romances or to refer somewhat humorously to riming rum-ram-ruf. Of course he was the heir of previous centuries of English civilization and of a language adequate for his purpose, but what he owes to previous English

---

[6] Cf. the note on Richard II's books on p. 142.

writers is slight in comparison with his debt to French and Latin and Italian books. Others had translated and adapted French works before, but nobody else, either in his own day or before or after his day, so completely transferred to English the whole spirit of polite literature in Europe. This much of his poetic character comes from the accident of environment; the rest comes from himself. Environment could not make him the incomparable storyteller that he was. And environment alone will not account for the largeness and sanity of his mind. It may have taught him to keep his own counsel on political and public questions or to keep his opinions on such matters out of his poetry. But it may be that he was not easily wrought up over issues which at times provoke the quiet laughter of the gods. He was by nature tolerant, gentle, whimsical, good-humored, at all events in his poetry. And he had an incomparable sense of humor. His humor is all-pervasive. It flickers and glows and occasionally flashes like lightning in a summer sky. At times he seems unable to repress it, as when in the *Book of the Duchess,* a poem upon a sad occasion, he offers the God of Sleep the best gift he can think of, a feather bed, if he will make him sleep like Alcyone. But this is only at times. When the occasion really calls for it he can be serious, and he is capable of deep pathos.

Chaucer is sometimes denied the rank of a great poet on the ground that he lacked the higher seriousness, that his poetry is without great themes nobly conceived. It is true that he is not given to lofty and impassioned sentiments. His *Paradise Lost* is but the earthly paradise that Troilus lost, and his *Purgatorio* is generally such as lovers and lesser mortals experience in this life. But no one can deny the dignity and seriousness of the *Troilus* at certain great moments in the poem. We know that he was capable of moral earnestness and deep feeling, and if he chose more often to be cheerful and in general to devote himself to lighter themes, there are some students of medieval literature—and not the least devoted among them—who rest content with his choice.

XVIII

Other Contemporaries of Chaucer

*The
"Moral"
Gower*

When Chaucer at the close of *Troilus and Criseyde* addressed his book to a fellow poet with the salutation "O moral Gower," he was paying his friend a sincere compliment, little supposing that the adjective would in time acquire a connotation anything but helpful to John Gower's reputation with modern readers. But we have become suspicious of literature aimed at our improvement, and are prepared to be bored by anything to which a moral, or the word *moral,* is attached. Gower is the victim of this prejudice. But it must also be admitted that he suffers by comparison with his greater contemporary. Although the names of Chaucer and Gower were constantly coupled together with equal respect throughout the fifteenth and sixteenth centuries, nowadays we rightly prefer Chaucer's humanity and humor to the unrelieved earnestness of Gower's larger works. Yet modern criticism has sometimes gone too far in dismissing this dignified figure with an impatient shrug.

His Life

It is surprising how little we know about a man who was personally known to both Richard II and Henry IV and who has left us a body of poetry that fills four large volumes. He was of a Kentish family, and had considerable wealth, which it is conjectured he made in trade. But if we decline to identify with the poet a John Gower who was connected with some questionable transactions in land, we know him only for his friendship with Chaucer, later strained, as the owner of certain manors in Norfolk and Suffolk, and as a liberal benefactor in his will of churches in Southwark.[1] In his later years he had an apartment in the priory of St. Mary Overy, in Southwark. Late in life (1398) he married Agnes Groundolf, perhaps his second wife. No children are mentioned in his will, which was probated Oct. 24, 1408. He died presumably in that month and was buried in the priory church, now St. Saviour's, where his tomb can still be seen.

The effigy on Gower's tomb shows the poet's head resting on three folio volumes bearing the titles *Speculum Meditantis, Vox Clamantis,* and *Confessio Amantis.* These are his three principal works.[2] Though their titles are

---

[1] In 1393 as an esquire in the service of Henry Earl of Derby he was given a collar. Two months after the Earl became Henry IV he granted (Nov. 21, 1399) "for life to the king's esquire John Gower two pipes of wine of Gascony yearly." *CPR, 1399-1401,* p. 128 and *CCR, 1399-1402,* p. 78. On Dec. 11, 1397 Thomas Caudre, canon in the priory of St. Mary Overy in Southwerke was bound to do or procure no hurt or harm to John Gower; *CCR, 1396-99,* p. 238. Cf. also *CCR, 1402-5,* p. 484.

[2] *The Complete Works of John Gower,* ed. G. C. Macaulay (4v, Oxford, 1899-1902). Cf. George R. Coffman, "John Gower in His Most Significant Role," *Univ. of Colorado Stud.,* Ser. B, Vol. ʜ, No. 4 (1945). 52-61.

in Latin the poems are in French, Latin, and English respectively. The first, also known as *Speculum Hominis* or *Mirour de l'Omme* (before 1381), consists of some 30,000 lines of French verse. It treats in great detail the Seven Deadly Sins and their "daughters," then in equal fullness the corresponding Virtues, and shows the effects of the conflict between the two groups in all classes of society from Pope and cardinals down to craftsmen and laborers, concluding with a long tribute to the Virgin. The work is carefully planned and in spite of its great length is no more tedious than other works of its kind. It shows general resemblances to treatises like the *Somme le Roi* and the *Miroir du Monde,* but no immediate source has been found.[3] The *Vox Clamantis,* a Latin poem of 10,000 lines, was written shortly after the Peasants' Revolt in 1381, of which the first third of the poem gives a vivid account. This part may have been a later addition, for the major theme of the poem is a representation, like that in the *Mirour de l'Omme,* of the evils of society—clergy, knighthood, peasantry—and of man as a microcosm in which the sins of the world are abundantly exhibited. Gower has borrowed extensively from previous Latin poets, classical and medieval, but he obviously handles his Latin fluently and forcefully. The *Confessio Amantis* is the work of Gower's later years, when he had come to realize that a didactic intent unrelieved by entertaining features does not win many readers:

Mirour de l'Omme

Vox Clamantis

Confessio Amantis

> Bot for men sein, and soth it is,
> That who that al of wisdom writ
> It dulleth ofte a mannes wit
> To him that schal it aldai rede,
> For thilke cause, if that ye rede,
> I wolde go the middel weie
> And wryte a bok betwen the tweie,
> Somwhat of lust, somwhat of lore. . . .

He will therefore write of Love. He is himself one of Love's unrewarded servants. Venus hears his complaints and bids him confess to her priest, Genius. But a priest hears confessions of sin, and so the scheme of the poem is the Seven Deadly Sins, expounded by the priest, and applied, not always very easily, to the lover's problems. Stories illustrate the various points as they arise. It is obvious that as a framework for a collection of tales, Gower's plan is much inferior to Chaucer's. But to criticize it on this score is quite unfair. It assumes that the framework is an excuse for telling a series of stories, whereas in Gower's case the stories are secondary, a concession to his public. He is still the moralist and preacher; he has not abandoned the didactic purpose, but is attempting to make his teaching more palatable by a liberal use of tales and anecdotes. Under the circumstances it is surprising how well he can tell a story. He is neither dramatic nor humorous

---

[3] See above, p. 202, and cf. R. Elfreda Fowler, *Une Source française des poèmes de Gower* (Macon, 1905).

His nature was essentially sober, but his narrative is always fluent, generally rapid, and at times marked by genuine grace of both language and metre. The popularity of the *Confessio Amantis* is attested by more than forty extant manuscripts.[4]

Gower as Poet

Gower is not a great poet. He is an earnest man with a message for his times. He is alarmed at the way the world is going. He exhorts the King, preaches to the public. He is for reform within the established order. He is opposed to Lollardry, and the Peasants' Revolt fills him with horror. What more can the serious and thoughtful layman do than try to arouse his contemporaries to action?

Barbour's Bruce

If we look to the north, to Scotland, we meet at this time, in addition to some of the poems in the alliterative revival, the famous work of John Barbour called *The Bruce* (1376),[5] relating in more than 13,000 lines the guerilla warfare between Robert Bruce and the English. The poet is equally stirred by the deeds of Douglas, Bruce's loyal supporter, and indeed closes his poem with Douglas's adventures in Spain, in which he met his death. Barbour was Archdeacon of Aberdeen and died in 1395. He calls his poem a romance, and the style and spirit of the narrative partly justify the designation, but this should not blind us to the fact that Barbour was of a studious nature and a man of wide reading. He meant his work to be taken as history, and in many places his narrative is believed to embody authentic tradition.[6] Barbour's younger contemporary, Andrew of Wyntoun, held *The Bruce* in

Andrew of Wyntoun

such regard that he incorporated a portion of it in his *Original Chronicle*.[7] This, in its 30,000 lines of eight-syllable verse, covers the period from the origin of the world (whence its name) down to the year 1408. In form and matter it belongs with *The Bruce,* although chronologically it falls in the fifteenth century. It was completed shortly after 1420.

Increasing Use of Prose

It is worth a moment's reflection that none of Chaucer's writings in verse leave us with the feeling that they could just as well have been in prose. This is not true of all his contemporaries. The *Mirour de l'Omme* and the *Vox Clamantis* deal largely with subjects for which prose would be appropriate, and the same may be said of Wyntoun's *Chronicle*. As the fourteenth century wears on we notice the greater use of prose, for reasons which become more influential in the fifteenth century and which will be discussed

---

[4] Gower is the author of a series of *Cinkante Balades* of love and a *Traitié* consisting of eighteen additional balades in French for married lovers. Both sequences are among the most graceful of his poems. He also composed other short pieces and a *Chronica Tripertita* in Latin, begun in 1387 and continued at intervals, dealing with events in the later years of Richard's reign.

[5] Edited by W. W. Skeat (4v, 1870-89; *EETSES*, 11, 21, 29, 55; reprinted in 1894 for the *STS*, 31-33). On the Scottish literature of the period see T. F. Henderson, *Scottish Vernacular Literature* (3ed., Edinburgh, 1910) and Friedrich Brie, *Die Nationale Literatur Schottlands von den Anfängen bis zur Renaissance* (Halle, 1937).

[6] The contention of J. T. T. Brown, *The Wallace and the Bruce Restudied* (Bonn, 1900; *Bonner Beiträge zur Anglistik*, VI), that the text as we have it was seriously tampered with by John Ramsay, the copyist, at the end of the fifteenth century, has been resented but not disproved, and has something to recommend it.

[7] The best edition is that of F. J. Amours (6v, Edinburgh, 1903-14; *STS*, 50, 53, 54, 56 57, 63).

in the next chapter. Here we are concerned chiefly with the writings of three men, Mandeville, Trevisa, and Wycliť.

The *Travels of Sir John Mandeville* is one of the best-known books of the Middle Ages. Everyone knows about the incredible things he pretends to have seen: the gigantic race with one eye in the middle of the forehead, people with no heads but with eyes in their shoulders, others with great ears hanging to their knees, snails so great that many persons may lodge in their shells, and scores of other marvels. Setting out to write merely a guide-book for those who might be making a pilgrimage to Jerusalem, he gives the usual account of routes, and towns, and places of interest at the more important points. But when this part of his plan is finished he continues with his travels in Egypt, Asia Minor, Persia, India, Cathay or China, and many other places. He professes to have been born at St. Albans, to have left England in 1322, and, after spending years on his vast journey, to have arrived at Liége, where he was persuaded to write down his experiences.[8] The original, composed apparently between 1366 and 1371,[9] was in French, but it was soon translated into Latin and English. There are at least two translations into English, one from the Latin and one from the French original.[10] The earliest English manuscripts are of the beginning of the fifteenth century, but it cannot be doubted that the translations were made soon after the original appeared.

In the last fifty years the sources of Mandeville's *Travels* have been minutely traced, and it is now known that the whole work is a compilation which could have been written without the author's venturing a foot from home. What is more, it has even been thought the work of a Liége physician generally known as John of Burgundy or John with the beard (*ad Barbam*), the author of other works including medical treatises and a lapidary.[11] The

---

[8] References to thirty-four different John Mandevilles in medieval England are gathered together by K. W. Cameron, "A Discovery in *John de Mandevilles*," *Speculum*, XI (1936). 351-359.

[9] Arpad Steiner, "The Date of Composition of *Mandeville's Travels*," *Speculum*, IX (1934). 144-147.

[10] The version translated from the French is edited from a Cotton MS by P. Hamelius (2v, 1919-23; *EETS*, 153-154). Previous printed editions of Mandeville are all incomplete until that of A. W. Pollard (in modern spelling, 1900). The Egerton MS, edited by Sir George Warner for the Roxburghe Club (1889) with valuable apparatus, contains a composite text derived in part from one of the versions from French and in part from the version based on the Latin translation. The original French is available only in the Roxburghe volume noted above.

[11] In the fourth part (now lost) of Jean d'Outremeuse's *Myreur des Histoires* a note recorded that on Nov. 12, 1372 there died at Liége a man of distinguished birth who was content to be known as Jean de Bourgogne, called "with the beard." On his deathbed he revealed himself to Jean d'Outremeuse and made him his executor. In his will he called himself John de Mandeville, knight, count of Montfort in England and lord of the Isle of Campdi and of the castle Pérouse. However, having had the misfortune in his country to kill a count who is not named, he undertook to traverse the three parts of the world, coming to Liége in 1343. Having sprung from the nobility, he preferred to keep himself hidden. He was moreover a great naturalist, profound philosopher and astrologer, adding to this an unusual knowledge of physic, seldom being mistaken in a diagnosis. He was buried with the Guillemins. Now, as a fact, there existed down to the French Revolution a tomb in the church of the Guillemins with an epitaph several times independently copied down: Hic iacet nobilis Dominus Joannes de Montevilla Miles, alias dictus ad Barbam. . . . etc., recording that he was born in England, was of the medical profession, and died Feb. 7, 1372. For other considerations complicating the

theory of Hamelius [12] that the author was the Liége poet and chronicler Jean d'Outremeuse rests on rather slender grounds and as yet has not found many adherents.

Trevisa

Less romantic but no less important is the work of John Trevisa. Born in Cornwall, he entered Oxford in 1362, became a fellow of Queen's College, and for more than forty years was vicar of Berkeley and chaplain to three of the Lords Berkeley. His most important translations were made at the command of Thomas, Lord Berkeley, a true patron of learning. Trevisa died in 1402.[13] Apart from his having translated the Bible, a matter still in dispute, his most important works are his translations of Higden's *Polychronicon*,[14] which he finished in 1387, and of the *De Proprietatibus Rerum* of Bartholomew Anglicus,[15] completed in 1398. He is to be credited with the translation of a rule of princes, *De Regimine Principum*, found in a single MS. Among his shorter renderings are the *Gospel of Nicodemus*, the *Dialogus inter Militem et Clericum*, a discussion of the secular power of the Church, and the *Defensio Curatorum*, translated from a sermon of Richard FitzRalph, Archbishop of Armagh, against the friars.[16] Not the least interesting of Trevisa's works are two short, original essays on translation prefixed to the *Polychronicon*, the first justifying translations into the vernacular, the second explaining his method.[17] Trevisa has been accused of wordiness, but his aim was above all to be clear. His prose shows care and a certain amount of conscious artistry, looking forward at times to the balance and alliteration of Euphuism.

Thomas Usk's *Testament of Love* [18] is better known than it deserves to be, because borrowings from *Piers Plowman* and Chaucer's *Troilus* make it

---

problem the reader must be referred to E. B. Nicholson, "John of Burgundy, *alias* Sir John Mandeville," *Academy*, xxv (1884). 261-2; the article of Nicholson and Sir Henry Yule in the *Encyclopaedia Britannica*, eleventh ed.; G. F. Warner in the *DNB*, and the discussions listed in the next note.

[12] P. Hamelius, "The Travels of Sir John Mandeville," *Quar. Rev.*, ccxxvii (1917). 331-352, and the introduction to the *EETS* edition noted above.

[13] The best account of Trevisa's life is in Aaron J. Perry's introduction to three of Trevisa's shorter pieces edited for the *EETS*, 167 (1925). See also the same author's "John Trevisa: A Fourteenth Century Translator," *Manitoba Essays* (1937), pp. 277-289.

[14] See above, p. 148. Trevisa's translation is edited in the Rolls Ser. (9v, 1865-86).

[15] See above, p. 150. Trevisa's translation has not been printed since 1582, but selections (modernized) can be had in Robert Steele, *Mediæval Lore from Bartholomew Anglicus* (1893, and later reprints).

[16] The last two works and a doubtful translation from Methodius are edited by Perry, *op. cit.* A translation of the *De Re Militari* of Vegetius, often attributed to Trevisa, must be given up. Cf. Perry, p. xcvii (and see below, p. 301).

[17] Conveniently reprinted in Alfred W. Pollard, *Fifteenth Century Prose and Verse* (1903) pp. 201-210.

[18] Edited by W. W. Skeat, *Chaucerian and Other Pieces* (Oxford, 1897; *Oxford Chaucer*, Vol. vii). Usk was executed in 1388 after a checkered and seemingly none too honorable political career. Ramona Bressie, "The Date of Thomas Usk's *Testament of Love*," MP, xxvi (1928). 17-29, attributes the allegory to a period of imprisonment covering roughly the first six months of 1385. This seems a little early to allow for the borrowings from *Troilus and Criseyde*. See also the same author's "A Study of Thomas Usk's *Testament of Love* as an Autobiography," [Univ. of Chicago] *Abstracts of Theses*, Humanistic Ser., vii. 517-521. The third book has been traced to St. Anselm's *De Concordia Praescientiae et Praedestinationis*, of which it is in part a translation. See George Sanderlin, "Usk's *Testament of Love* and St. Anselm," *Speculum*, xvii (1942). 69-73.

useful in fixing the dates of these poems. It is a political allegory in prose, *Thomas* written while the author was in prison. In it he treats the cause of his im- *Usk:* prisonment, justifies his conduct, and indicates that he should be released and *Testament* restored to favor. The allegory is full of obscurities which we can hardly *of Love* hope to clear up, but even if we could, no great service would be done to English literature.

The most famous writer of English prose at the end of the fourteenth *Wyclif* century was John Wyclif,[19] but it must be confessed that his importance rests more upon his efforts toward social and ecclesiastical reform than on his contributions to literature. Now that we believe he had very little hand in the translation of the Bible that goes by his name, his position in the history of English prose must be judged by his sermons and a number of tracts, expository and controversial, the canon of which is not easy to determine.

Born, as is now thought, about 1328 at Wycliffe in the North Riding of *His Life* Yorkshire, he proceeded to Oxford about 1345 and gradually distinguished himself so that by 1360 he had become Master of Balliol College. During these years he received the usual strict training in scholasticism with its basis in grammar and logic and its emphasis on Aristotle. After further years spent in the study of theology he lectured on the Bible and the *Sentences* of Peter Lombard, a standard textbook of the day. In 1361 he was appointed rector of Fillingham, but resigned his charge in 1368 to accept one nearer Oxford, at Ludgershall. Although he was given leaves to pursue his theological studies, his academic career was prolonged and he did not receive his degree as Doctor of Theology until 1372.

About this time he appears in the service of the king and we may think of him as entering upon the second stage of his career. His opposition to the papal claims on the Crown [20] recommended him to the government, and in 1374 he was rewarded with the rectory of Lutterworth, in Leicestershire, which he held until his death. In this year he was sent to Bruges as a member of a commission to negotiate with representatives of the pope. During the next few years he stated his position at length in two Latin treatises, the *De Dominio Divino* and *De Civili Dominio,* laying down the principle that all temporal lordship is under the overlordship of God, that the condition on which it may be exercised is righteousness, and that if this condition is violated the unrighteous may be deprived of their property. He maintains that the Church has no concern with temporal matters, that the clergy has no right to hold property, and in any case that the civil authority may deprive it of its property if unworthy of the trust. Such views, however acceptable to the State, were bound to bring him into conflict with the rulers of the Church.

As long as Wyclif's departures from orthodoxy were largely confined to

[19] The best biography is Herbert B. Workman, *John Wyclif: A Study of the English Medieval Church* (2v, Oxford, 1926).

[20] In 1374 Gregory XI demanded the payment granted by King John in 1213 together with all arrears.

temporal matters he seems not only to have escaped official censure but to have enjoyed a measure of political support. On occasion he was consulted by the king. John of Gaunt, seeing that he might be useful, enlisted him in his service. Consequently when Wyclif was attacked in 1377 by the Church and arraigned before Courtenay, Bishop of London, and when Gregory XI denounced his views and ordered his arrest, he was supported by John of Gaunt and other members of the royal family and suffered only minor inconveniences. But when he began about 1379 to attack such basic beliefs of the Church as the doctrine of transubstantiation he alienated many of his previous supporters, including John of Gaunt. In 1380 he was publicly condemned by a committee of twelve Oxford scholars, and shortly afterwards he left Oxford for good.

His Con-
demnation

The rest of his life, which may be thought of as the third and last phase of his career, was spent at his parish in Lutterworth. There, impaired in health, he continued to defend his views while he gathered together and edited his sermons, organized his writings into an elaborate *Summa,* and directed the flock of "poor priests" who were spreading his ideas over many parts of England. In 1382 Courtenay, now archbishop, called a council of forty-four bishops, doctors of theology, and others on whose support he could count—the Blackfriars Synod—and obtained a sweeping condemnation of Wyclifite views. But though Wyclif's followers were hunted down, punished, and forced to recant, Wyclif remained unmolested in his Lutterworth parsonage. Courtenay evidently knew when to stop. During his two remaining years Wyclif suffered a partial paralysis, the result of a stroke. His death occurred on the last day of the year 1384.

The "Poor
Priests"

It is not a part of our purpose to discuss here in detail Wyclif's views as set forth most fully in his many Latin writings. Such a discussion belongs to political and social history rather than to literature. We have already mentioned his theory of "dominion" as presented in two basic works about 1375-6.[21] Equally basic is his insistence on the absolute authority of the Bible.[22] Gregory XI's condemnation led him to an examination of the constitution and claims of the Church,[23] which he followed with a similar consideration of the office of the king [24] and the authority of the pope.[25] He felt that material possessions had made the Church worldly. He there-

His
Views

[21] The *De Dominio Divino* and *De Civili Dominio*, like most of Wyclif's Latin writings, have been published by the Wyclif Society.

[22] *De Veritate Sacrae Scripturae* (1378).

[23] *De Ecclesia* (finished late in 1378) asserts that the exercise of religious functions by ecclesiastics depends on their worthiness. He condemns indulgences by the pope, trentals, prayers for the dead, and the like, rejects the cult of the saints, and opposes (more mildly than in his later writings) relics and pilgrimages.

[24] *De Officio Regis* (1378) really concerns the question of Church and State. The king is God's vicar and therefore must rule wisely and justly. He has jurisdiction over the clergy, should see that the clergy perform their functions in a worthy manner, and he is not bound to obey the pope.

[25] *De Potestate Papae* (1379) asserts that the primacy of the pope depends upon character (sanctity) and that he is not necessarily St. Peter's successor. It questions the right of the Romans to determine the succession. The *De Ordine Christiano* is a brief statement of the same position.

fore urged the king to take back the endowments of the Church and restore the clergy to their original poverty. He opposed both the employment
of ecclesiastics in secular office and the life of monastic retirement which
too often fell away from the spiritual ideal. The function of the clergy, in
his opinion, was to minister to the people. For this reason he was at the
beginning more sympathetic to the friars, but in the end he found them
wanting and attacked them bitterly.

Wyclif's English writings are not always easy to separate from those of *His*
his followers.[26] His sermons, which fill two volumes, are for the most part *English*
to be accepted as his, but they are generally only two or three pages long *Writings*
and were probably prepared for the guidance of his poor priests. Many of
his English treatises represent translations and abridgments of his Latin
works, and some of these may have been prepared by his followers. Among
those that can be attributed to Wyclif himself, some are treatments such
as we find elsewhere of the Ten Commandments, The Seven Deadly Sins,
and the Seven Works of Mercy. More interesting are the *De Papa* and
The Church and Her Members in which he puts into English the views
already put forward in Latin concerning the authority of the pope, the objection to monastic orders, the lapses of the friars, disendowment, and the
like. Two of his English treatises are especially interesting because they deal
with social questions and are not adaptations of Latin works. *Of Servants
and Lords* was inspired by the Peasants' Revolt. It is a very moderate treatment, insisting on the duty servants owe to their lord as well as the obligation of lords, but discussing in plain terms the many ways in which the
poor are wronged. *Wedded Men and Wives* offers wholesome advice on
marriage and the rearing of children. Virginity is a higher state than matrimony, but matrimony is holy. He is not at all sure that celibacy is a wise
requirement for the priesthood. The whole treatise is a compound of biblical
precept and good common sense.

The so-called Wyclif Bible [27] appears to owe little more to Wyclif than *The*
the impulse behind it. It was apparently the work of his companions and *Wyclif*
helpers. Nicholas of Hereford translated about three-fourths of the Old *Bible*
Testament, as we learn from a note in one of the manuscripts. The style is
awkward and anything but idiomatic and does not agree with any of the
translations which Wyclif gives in his sermons. Apparently it was early felt
to be unsatisfactory, and perhaps even before Wyclif's death a revision was
undertaken by John Purvey,[28] who assisted Wyclif in his last days at Lutterworth. Although Purvey was aided, as he says, by "many good fellows and
cunning," his revision was not completed until about 1395. It is in every
way superior to the early version. Not a little of the sentence structure and

[26] The principal collections are Thomas Arnold, *Select English Works of John Wyclif* (3v,
Oxford, 1869-71), which contains many pieces now rejected from the Wyclif canon, and F. D.
Matthew, *The English Works of Wyclif Hitherto Unprinted* (1880; EETS, 74), which like-
wise includes some doubtful works. A convenient small volume is Herbert E. Winn, *Wyclif:
Select English Writings* (1929).

[27] Edited by J. Forshall and Sir F. Madden (4v, Oxford, 1850).

[28] Purvey's part in the translation rests on strong evidence, just short of proof.

an occasional fine phrase have been carried over into the Authorized Version of 1611.

Even though Wyclif may have had no part at all in the actual work of translation, the important step of putting the whole Bible into English for the first time was the result of his attitude toward the Scriptures as the ultimate authority in all questions concerning man's moral and spiritual life. He believed it was the right of simple men to turn to the Bible for "the points that be most needful to salvation." Simple piety was worth more than forms and ritual. His poor priests resembled the early friars in seeking to bring religion home to the common man. Coming from the north where we have seen that so many of the religious movements of the fourteenth century had their beginning, Wyclif sought in a different way what Rolle and the mystics were seeking—to bring a more direct and personal meaning into religious life.[29]

[29] Exemplifying Wyclif's purpose to bring religious instruction to the poor is an anonymous treatise of the late fourteenth century called *Pore Caitiff*. It is found in a large number of MSS, but has been printed only in modernized form and in selections. In addition to treatments of the Paternoster, Creed, etc., it discusses patience, temptation, and other subjects for poor men's spiritual profit. Extracts have been printed in R. Vaughan's *Life of Wycliffe* (1852), pp. 382 ff. See also M. T. Brady, *"The Pore Caitif: An Introductory Study," Traditio,* x (1954). 529-548.

XIX
The Beginnings of the Drama

Mimicry and make-believe are well nigh universal human impulses and drama has therefore developed independently at various times and places in the world's history. Among the Greeks it attained high distinction. Among the Romans it was less popular. Conditions in the Roman Empire were politically disturbed, and the populace preferred to shout and cheer at the chariot races and gladiatorial combats of the circus and amphitheatre rather than quietly watch a play. The theatre apparently did not attract the best literary talents in Italy. Plautus and Terence are not comparable to Virgil, Horace, or Livy in other forms of literature, and Seneca's tragedies were closet dramas. The most popular theatrical entertainments were the performances of mimes [1] in which coarse humor and indecency combined to secure at times the attention of the vulgar. The hordes of barbarians pouring into Rome did not help matters. Drama had apparently never developed among the Teutons, and witty dialogue was wasted on the speakers of an unfamiliar tongue. With the rise of Christianity the theatre ran into other difficulties. The Church objected to its associations with paganism, to the fact that in its lower forms it often ridiculed the new religion, and perhaps most of all to the immorality of both performances and performers. With the fall of the Empire, Roman drama disappeared, and for five hundred years only a faint dramatic tradition may have survived, passed on from the mimes to the medieval minstrel. *Disappearance of Roman Drama*

It is ironical that the Church, the force that had done most to drive Roman drama out of existence, should have been the institution in which modern drama was to take its rise. For the drama of the Middle Ages is not a continuation of Roman drama but a development from entirely new beginnings in the services of the Church,[2] first in the more solemn service of the Mass and later in the less rigid office of Matins. Theoretically no departure from the text of the missal was permitted in the celebration of Mass, but actually intrusions crept in, at first in the form of musical embellishments at the end of the gradual, to which words were in time added,[3] *Beginnings of Modern Drama in the Church*

[1] See H. Reich, *Der Mimus* (2v, Berlin, 1903).

[2] The authoritative work on the liturgical drama is Karl Young, *The Drama of the Medieval Church* (2v, Oxford, 1933), where full references to previous literature are given. For the background of the drama in folk custom and a general survey of dramatic developments see E. K. Chambers, *The Medieval Stage* (2v, Oxford, 1903).

[3] The *gradual* is a chant sung after the epistle of the day, and closes with *alleluia*. The name *sequence* was at first applied to the melody in which the final *a* of *alleluia* was prolonged. Later words were fitted to such melodies and the term *sequence* designated both the words and music. Additions to other parts of the service are called tropes. For the distinction

and later through amplifications woven into various other chants. The latter are called *tropes,* and it is with a trope in the Mass of Easter that we are most concerned.

The Quem quaeritis

The Introit or opening chant began with the words *Resurrexi et adhuc tecum sum.* At about the year 900 we find it prefaced by a trope which the following slightly normalized text exemplifies in its simplest form:

> Quem quaeritis in sepulchro, o Christicolae?
> Jesum Nazarenum crucifixum, o caelicolae.
> Non est hic; surrexit sicut praedixerat;
> ite, nuntiate quia surrexit de sepulchro.[4]

These lines are a paraphrase of the dialogue between the angel and the Marys at the tomb of Christ as implied in the Gospel of St. Matthew. As sung antiphonally—i.e., alternately by the two halves of the choir—they constitute merely a dialogued chant. They never became much more as long as they were attached to the Mass. But they are of great importance, for they are the germ out of which modern drama grew.

Development of the Trope

The development of this trope in the Mass never went far enough to be embarrassing to the service, and indeed it could not have grown much without becoming so. The words, however, were equally appropriate to the office of Matins a little earlier in the day, a service with which the *Elevatio Crucis* was in many places associated. When transferred to the end of this office the *Quem quaeritis* underwent a gradual change. Two members of the choir, robed in white to suggest angels, took positions beside the altar, while three others in black represented the Marys. This simple but momentous change[5] introduced the element of impersonation and the result was a miniature opera. Slowly other lines were added. *Who will roll away for us the stone?* the Marys ask, approaching the supposed sepulcher. The angels, after announcing the Resurrection, invite the Marys to *Come and see the place where the Lord was laid,* which they do, and then hold up the linens with suitable words. When the angels bid them carry the news to the disciples they do so, and in some places Peter and John race to the sepulcher (cf. John, 20:4). In certain texts the episode in which Christ appears to Mary Magdalene (cf. John, 20:11-18) occurs. When all of these amplifications are present we have a sizable and highly dramatic ceremony.

So successful an innovation was soon imitated, and a similar ceremony was introduced at Christmas. By a slight change in wording the dialogue be-

---

and for the development of tropes see C. Blume, introduction to *Analecta Hymnica,* LIII, and L. Gautier, *Histoire de la poésie liturgique au moyen âge: les tropes* (Paris, 1886).

[4] Whom seek ye in the sepulchre, O Christians?
Jesus of Nazareth who was crucified, O angels.
He is not here; he has arisen as he foretold;
go, announce that he has arisen from the grave.

The fullest collection of *Quem quaeritis* texts is in Carl Lange, *Die lateinischen Osterfeiern* (Munich, 1887).

[5] It occurs in a few texts of the Introit trope. In time temporary or permanent structures known as Easter sepulchers were constructed for the ceremony.

tween the angels and the Marys could be adapted to the shepherds who Officium
came to adore the Christ-child. *Obstetrices* or midwives replace the angels Pastorum
as interlocutors, and the result is:

> Quem quaeritis in praesepe, o pastores, dicite.
> Salvatorem Christum Dominum, infantem pannis
> involutum, secundum sermonem angelicum.
> Adest hic parvulus cum Maria matre sua....
> Et nunc euntes dicite quia natus est.[6]

Such a conversation though plausible, is lacking in any biblical authority, differing in this respect from the words spoken at the tomb. It is quite obviously an imitation of the Easter trope, and is known as the *Officium Pastorum*.

The simple little act of worship performed by the shepherds offered only Officium
limited possibilities for dramatic development. More productive were cer- Stellae
tain other ceremonies of the Christmas season. On Twelfth Day was celebrated the coming of the Magi, not only to adore but to bring rich gifts. As
kings they were impressive in their costumes of Oriental splendor, but more
important was the fact that they had to pass through the kingdom of Herod
and be questioned concerning the new-born king whom they were seeking.
Herod soon becomes the central figure in the action. Surrounded by a considerable retinue of courtiers, scribes, messengers, and soldiers, he symbolizes
the tyrant's power jealous of any threat to its supremacy. He dislikes what
the Magi tell him, sends for his learned men, is unwillingly convinced that
their book contains disturbing prophecies, and in one text throws the book
down in a rage. We have thus early the model for the ranting Herod of
later drama.[7] From the fact that a star suspended from the roof of the
church guided the Magi on their journey the ceremony here described is
known as the *Officium Stellae*, the Office of the Star.[8]

Two other developments took place at the Christmas season. One was a Ordo
natural extension of the *Stella*, showing the slaughter of the innocents by Rachelis
Herod's soldiers. The children are slain and Rachel, representative of the *and*
grieving mothers of Israel, sings her lament in a little duet with conventional Ordo
consolatrices. From the latter circumstance the episode is known as the Prophe-
Ordo Rachelis. The other was the *Ordo Prophetarum*, a ceremony of some tarum
interest since it originated not in a chant of the choir but in a sermon.[9] In

---

[6] Whom seek ye in the manger, O shepherds, tell us.
Christ our Lord the Savior, an infant wrapped in
swaddling clothes, as the angels say.
Here is the little one with Mary, his mother....
And now go and say that he is born.

[7] Cf. *Hamlet*, III. ii. 16.

[8] In addition to Karl Young, as above, see Heinrich Anz, *Die lateinischen Magierspiele* (Leipzig, 1905).

[9] The development from sermon to dramatic ceremony was first studied by M. Sepet, *Les Prophètes du Christ* (Paris, 1878; also published in installments scattered through the *Bibliothèque de l'Ecole des Chartres*, Vols. XXVIII, XXIX, and XXXVIII), the basic treatment. Karl Young corrects Sepet in detail and adds important texts in his "Ordo Prophetarum," *Trans. Wisconsin Acad.*, XX (1921). 1-82, and in his *Drama of the Medieval Church*, ch. XXI. A translation of

the Middle Ages an attempt to convince unbelievers out of their own mouths, wrongly attributed to St. Augustine and entitled *Contra Judaeos, Paganos, et Arianos,* was frequently read as a *lectio* in the Christmas··Matins. In one section of this sermon various Old Testament prophets—Isaiah, Jeremiah, Daniel, etc.—are called upon by the preacher to testify to the coming of Christ. When their words are not merely reported but delivered by separate personages appropriately costumed the sermon becomes elementary drama. In time episodes connected with some of the prophets, such as Nebuchadnezzar and Balaam, were represented. It has been claimed that from such episodes sprang the treatment of Old Testament subjects in medieval drama. While this may be doubted, it is apparent that once the impulse towards dramatic representation was abroad, a sermon or any other suitable material could become the stuff out of which drama was made.

From Church to Craft

The amalgamation and elaboration of such dramatic ceremonies within the church in time put a strain upon the services. And what is more, additional episodes tended to develop, if not actually in the office, at least in a transitional stage ending in separation from the church. The birth of Christ, for example, called for some explanation. If Adam and Eve had not fallen, man would not have been in need of redemption. A scene was needed showing the temptation of Eve by Satan in the Garden of Eden. But why did Satan tempt Eve? Out of malice for having been driven out of Heaven. Why was he driven out of Heaven? That also must be told. Finally, the evil brought to the world by man's disobedience can be symbolized by the slaying of Abel by Cain. Such an extension of theme is illustrated in the twelfth-century Anglo-Norman *Adam,* which consists of a long episode, running to nearly 600 lines, on the Fall and Expulsion from Paradise, a shorter treatment of Cain and Abel, and a Prophets play, incomplete.[10] The same episodes sometimes served as an equally suitable introduction to the drama of Easter. Not only would such an extensive action take up much time and interfere with the service proper, but it would tax the resources of the clergy. In some places it was necessary to call in outsiders of good and discreet character to assist in the performance. Realistic elements verging on the humorous crept in. Balaam delivered his prophecy after a little by-play in which he beat his ass and the faithful beast brayed touchingly. In one text Mary Magdalene is shown with her lover, singing a profane song and buying aids to her complexion, before being converted and exchanging the cosmetics for ointment. Such incidents are inappropriate to the solemn ritual of the church. Adequate space for settings and accommo-

Realism and Humor

---

the pertinent portions of the sermon has been published by Edward N. Stone in the *Univ. of Wash. Pub. in Lang. and Lit.,* Vol. iv, No. 3 (1928).

[10] The play is mostly in French with a few liturgical elements in Latin. The stage directions, also in Latin, are remarkably detailed with respect to action, costume, and setting. The most satisfactory edition is that of Paul C. Studer (Manchester, 1918). The play has been twice translated into English: (1) by Sarah F. Barrow and Wm. H. Hulme in *Western Reserve Univ. Bull.,* Vol. xxviii, No. 8 (1925); (2) by Edward N. Stone in *Univ. of Wash. Pub. in Lang. and Lit.,* iv (1926). 159-193.

dation for the crowds that would want to witness the performances raised other difficulties. And so from choir to nave, and nave to church-porch were natural steps on the way to the public square. Once outside the church the performances gradually broke their liturgical bonds. Latin, the liturgical language, gave way to the vernacular.[11] At the same time the musical rendering yielded to the more realistic spoken word. We must suppose that the laity now participated to an increasing extent while the clergy more and more withdrew until the plays ended up entirely in the hands of the people.

The transition here sketched may be accepted with some confidence in its main outlines, but it must be admitted that we are far from clear about many of its details. While the drama is growing up within the church we can trace its development with fair continuity, although we would gladly know more about the genesis of some of its later and more elaborate texts. *Mystery* When we turn to the large vernacular cycles it is as though something in *Cycles* between had dropped out. For example, we can observe the tendency, already described, for the episodes of liturgical drama to collect in sequences, but there is no sequence of episodes in liturgical drama comparable in scope to the great mystery cycles. At one stage we see the drama in the process of passing out of the church and the control of the clergy. We next see it in the hands of the craft guilds or mysteries and in the control of the civic authorities. The intermediate steps are missing. A factor of considerable importance was probably the establishment in England of the festival of Corpus Christi, but its influence has yet to be defined.[12] We know that Corpus Christi day[13] was generally observed in England from 1318 on, *Corpus* and that by papal decree a procession with five (nondramatic) pageants *Christi* constituted a major feature of the observance. The pageants or tableaux *Day* suggested the need for Corpus Christi by portraying the Fall of Man, then the prophecies, the coming, and the death of Christ, and finally the triumph of Corpus Christi in the Judgment Day. With many additional details this constitutes the subject matter of the mystery cycles, and since Corpus Christi day came to be the most popular date in England for the performance of mystery cycles, it is likely that in scope, time of performance, and the use of movable pageant wagons the mystery cycles owe something to the Corpus Christi procession. One may put it another way by saying that the religious plays emerging from the church took the form in which we know them under the inspiration of the Corpus Christi festival. It is perhaps significant

[11] The transition can be seen in certain texts from England, France, and Germany in which the words of a speech are first sung in Latin and then spoken in the vernacular. In England this stage is illustrated by the Shrewsbury fragments, conveniently available in Adams, *Chief Pre-Shakespearean Dramas* (Boston, 1924), pp. 73-78.

[12] For a discussion of the problem see Hardin Craig, "The Corpus Christi Procession and the Corpus Christi Play," *JEGP*, XIII (1914). 589-602, and M. Pierson, "The Relation of the Corpus Christi Procession to the Corpus Christi Play in England," *Trans. Wisc. Acad.*, XVIII (1915). 110-165.

[13] Corpus Christi day is the Thursday following Trinity Sunday, i.e., a little more than eight weeks after Easter. It falls generally at the end of May or early in June, an ideal time for outdoor performances.

that the second quarter of the fourteenth century seems to have been the period in which they were taking shape.

In spite of their religious content and their association with the festival of Corpus Christi it is important to stress the civic character of the English religious cycles. Where the cycles attained significant size and were performed regularly every year it was because the governing body of the city considered them an asset to be maintained and promoted, just as countless chambers of commerce today seek conventions and promote fairs or other activities that attract visitors and augment local prestige. In the beginning the various pageants must have been distributed to the guilds by mutual agreement or on the decision of the central authority; otherwise it is unlikely that we should find so many crafts giving plays especially appropriate to them.[14] As we read the records of a city like York [15] we see the city council regulating the performances, settling disputes between guilds, imposing fines, reassigning plays, and exercising many other sorts of control. At first the attitude of the guilds is one of pride in performance, and there is rivalry in getting possession of a pageant. Later the plays become a duty, often burdensome upon crafts whose prosperity had declined. But while the burden is sometimes shifted or shared by another guild, the attitude of the city fathers is always that the plays must go on.

Cycles of mystery plays [16] seem to have been a regular feature only in some of the larger towns. Other places were content with an occasional episode, a saint's play, or a performance by a visiting troupe. The evidence for the existence of a cycle is clear for only about a dozen places in England. Of these, London alone is in the south and the few mentions of its plays suggest occasional performances by the parish clerks and not the guilds. The important centers were in the north and the Midlands—York, Wakefield, Beverley, Newcastle-upon-Tyne, Norwich, Coventry, and Chester. The performance was not in all cases on Corpus Christi day, but this was the most usual practice. Naturally the size and scope of the cycles varied greatly in different localities and sometimes at different dates. The York cycle at the height of its development contained as many as fifty-seven pageants. At the other end of the scale stood Worcester, which never seems to have had more than five. Of all this religious drama we are fortunate in having a considerable part preserved. It is rather remarkable that the only important cycle of which no fragment remains seems to be that of Beverley, which contained thirty-eight plays. We have two of the Coventry plays and one each from Norwich and Newcastle; all three of these cycles originally consisted of about a dozen plays.[17] We also have preserved two isolated plays

14 At Newcastle the Noah play was assigned to the shipwrights and other watermen, the Magi to the goldsmiths, the Disputation in the Temple to the lawyers, the Flight into Egypt to the stable keepers, the Last Supper to the bakers, etc. It was so elsewhere.

15 For example, the *York Memorandum Book,* ed. Maude Sellers (2v, Durham, 1912-15; Surtees Soc., 120, 125).

16 On the English cycles see E. K. Chambers, as above, and Charles M. Gayley, *Plays of Our Forefathers* (1907).

17 Newcastle may have been slightly larger, but the evidence is not unequivocal. The Coventry cycle almost certainly contained ten plays. The best edition of the extant Coventry

of *Abraham and Isaac* which we cannot localize. They may be fragments of otherwise lost cycles or they may always have been independent. The same may be said of three items in the Digby MS. Of the cycles preserved in full, those of York, Wakefield, and Chester, and the misnamed *Ludus Coventriae,* we shall speak more at length. When we consider that we have a cycle in Cornish which we can use for purposes of comparison we must conclude that time has dealt rather gently with us in the matter of the old English mystery plays, and avoid the mistake of supposing that much of major importance has disappeared without leaving some trace behind.

The most extensive English cycle of which we know was that of York.[18] *The* York In the form in which it has come down to us it consists of forty-eight Plays plays, but the MS dates from about 1475 and the cycle was at one time longer. The plays are first referred to in 1378 and then they are spoken of as "of old time." They cover very fully the whole of biblical history. They begin with the creation of the world and pass successively through the expulsion from Paradise, the killing of Abel, the story of Noah and the flood, of Abraham and Isaac, and of the Israelites in Egypt. In all, eleven plays are devoted to Old Testament matter. Then come the Annunciation and visit to Elizabeth, and the birth of Jesus with the familiar episodes of the shepherds and the Magi up to the slaughter of the innocents. With Play xx we take up the life of Christ—his dispute with the doctors in the temple, his Baptism, Temptation, Transfiguration, encounter with the woman taken in adultery, his raising of Lazarus, and finally his entry into Jerusalem. With the events leading to the Crucifixion the treatment becomes unusually full. Sixteen plays tell the story from the conspiracy to take Jesus, the Last Supper through the accusation and trial, the Crucifixion, the Resurrection, on to the journey to Emmaus and the incredulity of Thomas. The last few pageants portray Christ's Ascension, the death of Mary, her appearance to Thomas, and her Assumption. The whole concludes with the Judgment Day. Allowing for individual omissions and modifications, this may be taken as typical of the scope of the English cycles. It must not be supposed that the York plays reached such a degree of elaboration in one creative effort. It is likely that the original cycle was much smaller. There are evidences that it underwent major revision at two different times, and it is likely that subdivision, amalgamation, and alteration frequently occurred in individual plays as occasion arose. The cycle was not static, but subject to improvement and frequent modification to adapt it to changing conditions among the crafts that produced it. This will account for the great variations in tone, effectiveness, versification, and humor in its different parts.

On the whole it is a dignified and impressive production. Only rarely, as in the case of the *Annunciation,* is the action undramatic, and in certain

---

plays is that of Hardin Craig, *Two Coventry Corpus Christi Plays* (London, 1902; *EETSES,* 87). The Norwich and Newcastle fragments will be found in O. Waterhouse, *The Non-Cycle Mystery Plays* (London, 1909; *EETSES,* 104). The Digby Plays were edited by F. J. Furnivall (London, 1896; *EETSES,* 70).

18 *York Plays,* ed. Lucy Toulmin Smith (Oxford, 1885).

episodes it is highly realistic and vigorous. Homely humor enlivens the play of Noah and the flood, in which Noah's wife demurs about entering the ark and prefers to go to town. When she finally yields to persuasion she saves face by complaining that Noah might have told her earlier of his plans, and she expresses her annoyance by giving him a clout over the head. In the play of the shepherds there is much excitement over the appearance of the star, voiced in exclamations of "Wow!" and "Golly!" There is an attempt to differentiate the shepherds. The Second Shepherd thinks the others have something to eat and comes up eagerly. Their gifts are not without a suggestion of amusing simplicity. The First Shepherd presents a brooch hung with a little tin bell and the Second offers two cobb-nuts on a ribbon. Both, simple souls that they were, naïvely express the wish that the new-born King will remember them when he comes into power. The Third Shepherd, on the other hand, offers somewhat apologetically a horn spoon that holds forty peas, and in his simple piety asks no reward. Realism of another kind accompanies the Crucifixion. The four soldiers, as they nail Jesus to the cross, find the cross too large and while they pull and stretch they make comments that are almost too realistic. Again, as they carry the cross up the hill they make much of its weight. One of them must set it down or his back will break; another is out of breath. Finally they set the cross in the mortise and accompany the driving in of the wedges with taunting remarks. While in such scenes we may question the dramatists' taste, we cannot deny them vigor and a lively dramatic sense.

The Towneley Plays

Some forty miles southwest of York lies the town of Wakefield, to which with most probability the cycle known as the *Towneley Plays* [19] is to be assigned. Originally rather small, Wakefield experienced rapid growth in the fifteenth century when heavy taxes in York drove many engaged in the woolen industry to other nearby centers.[20] This circumstance may account for the close relation of the Towneley cycle with the *York Plays* which we shall notice shortly. The cycle is only slightly shorter than that of York. The extant MS, which has lost at least two plays, contains thirty-two pageants treating a range of subjects similar to that indicated in the description of the York cycle. It is even more composite. Three stages are recognized by which it attained its present form. Beginning as a group of plays of simple religious tone, it took over early in the fifteenth century five plays,

[19] So called from the circumstance that the MS (dated *c.* 1460) was long preserved at Towneley Hall in Lancashire. It is now in the Huntington Library in California. The latest edition is that of George England and Alfred W. Pollard (London, 1897; *EETSES*, 71).

[20] See Herbert Heaton, *The Yorkshire Woollen and Worsted Industries* (Oxford, 1920). There is some doubt whether Wakefield had a sufficient number of guilds to produce a cycle as extensive as the *Towneley Plays*. Unfortunately medieval records of Wakefield have almost completely disappeared. It has recently been shown, however, that there were Corpus Christi plays there in 1533 (*LTLS*, March 5, 1925, p. 156). It would seem that Wakefield reached its height as a woolen center some time in the first half of the fifteenth century, after which its woolen trade was on the decline. This would correspond with the period at which on other grounds we know that the Towneley cycle was being expanded and revised. The association of the cycle with Wakefield rests upon a number of clear local allusions in some of the plays.

and possibly more, from the York cycle.[21] Other plays showing York influence were conceivably revised or composed at the same time. Finally in
the reign of Henry VI [22] and probably in the second quarter of the fifteenth
century a writer of great dramatic gifts contributed a number of plays,
mostly in a distinctive nine-line stanza, and touched up several others. It is
the work of this man that gives the *Towneley Plays* their special distinction
in early English drama, and in our ignorance of his name and identity we
refer to him justly as "the Wakefield master."

The work of the Wakefield master is unique in medieval drama. Nowhere *The*
else do we find such a combination of what we call nowadays "good *Wakefield*
theatre" with boisterous humor and exuberance of spirit. Satirical sallies *Master*
and farcical situations burst forth without regard to propriety or convention.
In the *Murder of Abel* this medieval Aristophanes introduces a scene of
rough humor in which Cain and Garcio abuse each other, and he makes
Cain boldly rebellious toward God, who, he says, has given him only sorrow
and woe. To so solemn a play as the *Doomsday* he contributes two broadly
humorous scenes. The devils carry on a lively dialogue alluding to the
unusual amount of evidence they have against women and remark that if
the Judgment Day had not come when it did they would have had to make
Hell larger. Nowhere does his ability appear, however, to better effect than
in the *Second Shepherds' Play.*[23] As a prelude to the adoration he tells the
story of Mak, a notorious sheep-stealer, and his attempt to steal a sheep
from the shepherds by concealing it in a cradle and pretending that it is a
baby to which his wife has just given birth. The theme is a folk-tale [24]
worked up through successive moments of dramatic suspense to a climax
in which the culprit's guilt is dramatically revealed. There is humor of
situation and humor of dialogue and incidental allusion—jibes at shrewish
wives and crying children, taxes and the poor man's lot. The length of the
Mak episode is hopelessly out of proportion to the proper matter of the
play. The *Second Shepherds' Play* as a shepherds' play is an artistic ab-
surdity; as a farce of Mak the sheep-stealer it is the masterpiece of the English religious drama.[25]

Not so much can be said for the third great English cycle which we can *The*
definitely localize. The *Chester Plays* [26] are rather lacking in dramatic *Chester*
Plays

[21] Miss Marie C. Lyle has argued that these plays are the residue of a parent cycle from
which both York and Towneley descend. Cf. *The Original Identity of the York and Towneley
Cycles* (Minneapolis, 1919; *Research Pub. of the Univ. of Minn.* Vol. VIII, No. 3).
[22] See Mendal G. Frampton, "The Date of the Flourishing of the Wakefield Master," *PMLA*,
L (1935). 631-660.
[23] There are two (alternate) plays of the shepherds in the cycle, both by the Wakefield
genius. The first, however, is overshadowed by the second.
[24] See A. S. Cook, "Another Parallel to the Mak Story," *MP*, XIV (1916). 11-15; A. C.
Baugh, "The Mak Story," *MP*, XV (1918). 729-734; B. J. Whiting, "An Analogue to the Mak
Story," *Speculum*, VII (1932). 552; Robert C. Cosbey, "The Mak Story and Its Folklore Analogues," *Speculum*, XX (1945). 310-317.
[25] On the work of the Wakefield master see Millicent Carey, *The Wakefield Group in the
Towneley Cycle* (Baltimore and Göttingen, 1930; *Hesperia, Ergänzungsreihe*, XI).
[26] Ed. Hermann Deimling and Dr. Matthews (2v, 1893-1916; *EETSES*, 62, 115).

quality. As a cycle they are much more of one texture than the York or Towneley plays and that texture is narrative rather than dramatic. This uniformity is the more remarkable when we consider that the plays were performed occasionally as late as 1575.[27] In the sixteenth century they had become the object of antiquarian interest: no less than four extant MSS were copied out between 1591 and 1607, and various traditions concerning their origin were recorded. One of these traditions credits the composition of the cycle to Ranulf Higden in 1328. Higden was a monk of Chester abbey, well known as the author of the *Polychronicon* (cf. p. 148). There is nothing improbable in this attribution. The character of the plays is quite in keeping with what we might expect from such an author. Whoever wrote them originally was a man of cosmopolitan taste, learned but not deep, scholarly rather than popular, with little or no humor and slight ability to project himself into his characters. He may have been familiar with the way similar religious cycles were drawn up in France, for in the curtailed character of the Old Testament matter and in certain features of the treatment the *Chester Plays* resemble the French *mystères* rather than the other English cycles.[28]

The Ludus Coventriae

The last of the four extant cycles presents a number of problems. In the seventeenth century it was wrongly identified with the plays for which Coventry was famous, and the name then attached to the MS has caused it ever since to be known as the *Ludus Coventriae*.[29] The one thing that we can be surest of about this collection is that it has nothing to do with Coventry. Apart from the fact that the two genuine Coventry plays that have been preserved show no resemblance to the corresponding episodes in the *Ludus Coventriae*, we know that the Coventry plays were given on Corpus Christi day (a Thursday) whereas the *Ludus Coventriae*, as we learn from the Banns or Proclamation, was performed on Sunday. From allusions in the text we also know that the plays were given in installments, successive groups being given in successive years. Finally the Proclamation, in advertising the performance, announces that it will be given in "N. towne." This was formerly taken to designate some town whose name began with *N*, but the *N* is more likely to stand for the Latin word *nomen* and to indicate performance by a traveling company which would thus be free to insert any desired name in the announcement at this point. The *Ludus Coventriae* is interesting in many ways, but it is less significant dramatically than the other cycles.

Except for the *Ludus Coventriae* the extant English cycles seem all to

[27] On the development of the cycle see a valuable study by F. M. Salter, "The Banns of the Chester Plays," *RES*, xv (1939). 432-457; xvi (1940). 1-17, 137-148, and the joint publication of Salter and W. W. Greg, *The Trial & Flagellation with Other Studies in the Chester Cycle* (1935; *Malone Soc. Studies*).

[28] Albert C. Baugh, "The Chester Plays and French Influence," *Schelling Anniversary Papers* (1923), pp. 35-63.

[29] *Ludus Coventriae*, ed. K. S. Block (1922; *EETSES*, 120). See also a brilliant essay by W. W. Greg in his *Bibliographical and Textual Problems of the English Miracle Cycles* (1914), pp. 108-143.

have been given in a manner peculiar to England.[30] Each episode was per- *Method of* formed on a separate stage set on wheels so that it could be drawn from *Perform-* point to point in the city. The stations were designated in advance. At one *ance* time there were as many as fourteen in York and each episode in the cycle had to be repeated fourteen times. Fortunately for the actors, a smaller number generally sufficed. Where the entire cycle was given in one day it was necessary to begin early—at six o'clock in the morning or even earlier. But the crowd was in a holiday mood, pageant wagons and streets were gay with flags and bunting, and the occasion must have been one of the memorable events of the year for many a citizen who lived within reach of a town that boasted of a cycle of Corpus Christi plays.

It must not be supposed that communities less fortunate were without any *Non-Cycle* form of dramatic entertainment. Isolated plays are common enough in the *Plays* fourteenth and fifteenth centuries, though in most cases only the records of their performance have survived. Popular Bible stories such as that of Noah or of Abraham and Isaac were sometimes given by themselves, and many a saint was celebrated in a dramatic representation of his life or martyrdom. Indeed, once the drama is established as a literary form, almost any subject of religious or doctrinal significance might be made into a play. We have a play of *Mary Magdalene,* in which elements of the morality play, which we shall turn to in a moment, are combined with the miracle of her conversion. The Croxton *Play of the Sacrament* dramatizes a widespread story of the torture of the sacred Host by Jews. At York as early as 1378 there was a *Paternoster Play,* and in the fifteenth century a *Creed Play* was sometimes performed in place of the Corpus Christi cycle. The last two have not come down to us. We would gladly know more about them since they may well have been transitional types to the morality play. Clearly there is a tendency to go outside the range of Bible story in the search for variety, and such a search finds its most characteristic expression in the type just mentioned and to which we now turn.

It is not easy to define simply the morality play. From the point of view *The* of the dramatis personae the morality differs from previous drama in dealing *Morality* with personifications of abstract qualities such as Beauty, Strength, Gluttony, *Play* and Peace, or with generalized classes such as Everyman, King, and Bishop. But not all plays concerning such characters are morality plays. In its true form the morality is distinguished by certain characteristic themes treated allegorically. These include such subjects as the summons of Death, the conflict of vices and virtues for supremacy in man's life, and the question of his ultimate fate as debated by the Four Daughters of God. They all seem to center in the problem of man's salvation and the conduct of life as it affects his salvation. The morality is also characterized by a definite purpose or object which it seeks to promote. Whereas the mystery plays were to bring the important facts of the Bible vividly home to the average

[30] Much useful information on the method of performance is gathered together in M. Lyle Spencer, *Corpus Christi Pageants in England* (1911).

man, the morality teaches a lesson about right living—preaches a sermon in dramatic form. We may combine these considerations into a definition by saying that the morality play presents allegorically some object lesson or warning by means of abstract characters or generalized types for man's spiritual good.

Its
Origin

The origins of the type are not easily traced. When it appears in our first text it is already fully formed. Earlier possible examples such as the *Paternoster* and *Creed* plays are, as we have seen, lost. The elements which enter into it are common in medieval literature. The allegorical method and admonitory purpose are everywhere in the Middle Ages and its main themes are known in various forms. Thus, the conflict of personified vices and virtues forms the subject of a long Latin poem by the fourth-century poet Prudentius.[31] The summons of Death, bringing home the warning that death strikes often when least expected and is no respecter of persons, was present in the medieval treatments of the Dance of Death, although more familiar to us in Holbein's famous series of woodcuts. The argument of the Four Daughters of God, Mercy and Peace pleading for man's salvation and Righteousness and Truth for his eternal punishment, was a widespread motif, and we have already discussed the *Debate between the Body and Soul* in its Middle English form. But these things represent the ultimate, not the immediate, sources of the morality play. It has been suggested that the medieval sermon was often rather dramatic in character and by others that allegorical figures occasionally occur in the mystery plays. By what process of synthesis, however, these various elements of theme and method were gradually or suddenly combined into the morality play we cannot say.

The Pride
of Life

The earliest play of this type that has come down to us, *The Pride of Life*,[32] dates from about 1400. It is unfortunately incomplete, but a long prologue tells us what to expect and the five hundred lines that we have are more than half of the play and enable us to judge adequately of its character and quality. A King shows by his boastful speech that he fears nothing—not even Death—and his knights, Fortitude (or Strength) and Sanitas (or Health), assure him that with their help he will live forever. The Queen is not so sure. She reminds him that all men die and that Holy Church bids him think of his end. Her words have little effect and she sends for the Bishop. Although the Bishop preaches a long sermon on the evils of the times—wit is now treachery, love is now lechery, rich men are ruthless, etc.—and urges the King to mend his ways, the King is defiant.

[31] The *Psychomachia*, of which the best edition is that of Joannes Bergman (Vienna, 1926; *Corpus Scriptorum Ecclesiasticorum Latinorum*, LXI); English trans. by Mary L. Porter (Raleigh, N. C., 1929; *Meredith College, Raleigh, Quar. Bull.*, Ser. 23, No. 1). On the subject in general see E. N. S. Thompson, *The English Moral Plays* (New Haven, 1910; *Trans. Conn. Acad.*, xiv. 291-414), and W. Roy Mackenzie, *The English Moralities from the Point of View of Allegory* (Boston, 1914).

[32] The text of many of the early moralities may be found in A. Brandl, *Quellen des weltlichen Dramas in England vor Shakespeare* (Strassburg, 1898), J. M. Manly, *Specimens of the Pre-Shakespearian Drama* (2v, Boston, 1897), and J. Q. Adams, *Chief Pre-Shakespearean Dramas* (Boston, 1924).

He will try conclusions with Death and sends his messenger, Mirth, to seek him out. The text breaks off in the midst of Mirth's proclamation, but from the prologue we know that Death fought with the King and slew him. Although the arrangement of the dialogue is rather mechanical—in the beginning all speeches are three quatrains long—there are vigorous passages, and the author was not unskilful in the management of the action.

It is interesting that this, the earliest of the English moralities of which any part has come down to us, should have as its theme the summons of Death, the theme of the last and greatest of the medieval moralities, *Everyman*. The fact that its characters are for the most part not abstractions but individuals generalized to represent a class may suggest that we have in *The Pride of Life* something like a transition stage to the more fully developed, abstract type. In subject and treatment its closest affinity is to the scene depicting the death of Herod in the *Ludus Coventriae*, to which the resemblance is rather striking. Like the mystery plays *The Pride of Life* was performed outdoors, as the opening lines with a reference to the weather show, and the audience was a fairly mixed one.

The longest and most comprehensive of the English moralities of the **The** fifteenth century is *The Castle of Perseverance*.[33] It contains over 3600 lines **Castle of** and tells the story of man's career from birth to death and final judgment. **Persever-** We see him, alternately persuaded by his good and bad angels, yielding to **ance** the delights of the World. Even after he has been rescued and brought to the Castle of Perseverance with the Seven Virtues as defenders against the forces of the World, the Flesh, and the Devil, he is lured again into sin. We witness his death, the bitter chiding of the Body by the Soul, and his final trial, with the Four Daughters of God arrayed on opposite sides, pleading respectively for mercy and strict justice. Like the *Pride of Life* it was given outdoors and an interesting diagram in the MS shows the arrangement of the playing space. Of very different character is the morality of *Wisdom,* **Wisdom** also known as *Mind, Will, and Understanding*.[34] It requires a large cast and calls for elaborate and expensive costuming. The Devil entices Mind, Will, and Understanding from what appears to be the monastic life, but in the end they are recalled and brought to repentance by Wisdom, who is Christ. It can hardly have been intended for a popular audience, and it has been suggested that its purpose was to combat the growing tendency of monks to desert their monasteries.[35] We cannot at present date the play more closely than c. 1460. A still stranger production is the play known as *Mankind*.[36] Here we have the framework of the morality adapted to the **Mankind**

[33] The text is edited by F. J. Furnivall and A. W. Pollard in *The Macro Plays* (1904; *EETSES,* 91). A facsimile of the MS is included in J. S. Farmer's *Student's Facsimile Series.* For discussion see Walter K. Smart "The *Castle of Perseverance:* Place, Date, and a Source," *Manly Anniversary Studies* (Chicago, 1923), pp. 42-53, where reasons are advanced for assigning the play to Lincolnshire, c. 1405.

[34] Also edited in *The Macro Plays,* as above.

[35] See the valuable monograph of Walter K. Smart, *Some English and Latin Sources and Parallels for the Morality of Wisdom* (Menasha, 1912).

[36] Printed among *The Macro Plays,* as above, and in Manly, Adams, etc. For date and locality see W. K. Smart, "Some Notes on *Mankind,*" *MP,* xiv (1916). 45-58; 293-313.

purposes of low comedy. It was performed in an inn-yard and a collection was taken from the spectators at a certain point in the performance. So far as the play has a morality motive at all it is to be found in the character of Mercy who in the beginning urges gratitude to God for man's redemption and stresses his own large part in it, and at the end chides Mankind for paying so little heed to his words. But most of the play is given over to horse-play and coarse humor. Some of the lines are unprintable. As a morality play it is so debased as to be rather a contradiction of the type, but it is valuable as showing the step that had been taken by about 1471 towards the popular stage.

Everyman

Somewhat later, probably around the turn of the century, we get the classic of the English morality plays, *Everyman*.[37] With a fine sense of unity the play avoids any direct representation of Everyman's heedless life and confines itself to the hour in which he receives the summons of Death. Told by the messenger that he must go on a long journey, he pleads in vain for a delay and has only the consolation of knowing that he can ask his more intimate friends to accompany him. But he finds that Fellowship, Kindred, Cousin, and Worldly Goods cannot or will not go with him into the next world. Good Deeds, with whom he has had all too little to do in his lifetime, alone stands by him and descends with him finally into the grave. In its 900 lines *Everyman* conveys its lesson with a simple effectiveness that has been more than once demonstrated by revivals on the modern stage.[38]

The morality play represents a collateral line in the descent of English drama. From the Mak episode to the *Four P's* to *Gammer Gurton's Needle* we perceive a continuity in which the morality forms no essential link and into which it can hardly be fitted. Its place is off to one side. At a point in the development of the drama (about the beginning of the fifteenth century) when the mystery cycles are approaching maturity, it appears as a type of play which does not concern Bible story and which suggests the homily in dramatized form. While it must be considered somehow an offshoot from the main dramatic stem, its origin is far from clear. After a brief career it loses its distinctive character and in the sixteenth century lives only, in much altered form, in the didactic interlude such as *Wealth and Health,* or the moral interlude such as *The Nice Wanton,* or as the medium of religious controversy. Its elements occasionally appear

[37] Often edited; an excellent text by W. W. Greg in *Materialien zur Kunde des älteren englischen Dramas,* IV (Louvain, 1904); modernized in Clarence G. Child, *The Second Shepherd's Play, Everyman, and Other Early Plays* (Boston, 1910).

[38] It is a disputed question whether *Everyman* or its exact counterpart, the Dutch play *Elckerlijc,* is the original, but it is almost certain now that the Dutch play is the earlier. The more important discussions of the subject are K. H. De Raaf, *Den Spyeghel der Salicheyt van Elckerlijc* (Groningen, 1897); H. Logeman, *Elckerlijc-Everyman, de Vraag naar de Prioriteit opnieuw onderzocht* (Gand, 1902); J. M. Manly, "Elckerlijc-Everyman: The Question of Priority," *MP,* VIII (1910-11). 269-277; F. A. Wood, "Elckerlijc-Everyman: The Question of Priority," *MP,* VIII (1910-11). 279-302; E. R. Tigg, "Is *Elckerlijc* prior to *Everyman?*" *JEGP,* XXXVIII (1939). 568-596. All except De Raaf (supported by Creizenach, *CHEL,* v. 59n, English ed., p. 53n) argue for the priority of the Dutch play.

in Elizabethan chronicle play, comedy, and tragedy, but otherwise by the time of Shakespeare it drops out of sight until the performance of *Everyman* inspired in the twentieth century a temporary revival in such plays as *The Passing of the Third Floor Back* and *The Servant in the House*.[39]

[39] This revival is treated in Joseph W. Barley, *The Morality Motive in Contemporary English Drama* (Univ. of Penna. diss., Mexico, Mo., 1912).

XX

Ebb Tide

*The
Fifteenth
Century*

The fifteenth century is commonly dismissed as a dreary and barren waste in the history of English literature. Such a judgment is severe, and results in part from the reader's disappointment when he finds that the high level reached at the end of the fourteenth century in the *Pearl, Sir Gawain and the Green Knight, Piers Plowman,* and the poetry of Chaucer is not maintained in the work of Lydgate, Hoccleve, and their contemporaries. Moreover, the fifteenth century has little new to offer. In many respects it continues the fourteenth, rather than breaking new ground. Its poets appear as followers of Chaucer and Gower, and later of Lydgate, rather than as leaders pointing new directions. It continues to treat the themes and types already current. Thus it shows an unbroken continuity with the past, and for this reason we have considered some of the works of this century along with those of earlier periods, especially in the chapters on the romance, the lyric, and the drama. However, in the drama and in English prose the fifteenth century made significant contributions. We should not forget that it was the century which produced Malory and the *Second Shepherds' Play.*[1]

*Continuing
Tradition*

Nowhere is the fifteenth century more plainly the child of the fourteenth than in its religious writings. Many of these works, except for the tyranny of dates, could be thought of as products of the earlier period. At the beginning of the century two of the three parts of Deguilleville's trilogy [2] were rendered into English. Lydgate made a verse translation of the first in his *Pilgrimage of the Life of Man,*[3] while an anonymous translator turned it into excellent prose.[4] There were still other translations, including one by Skelton now lost. An English prose version of the second, known as *Grace Dieu, or The Pilgrimage of the Soul,* made in 1413, has survived in at least

---

[1] The literary history of the fifteenth century remains to be written, although there are useful chapters in Vol. II of the *CHEL.* In the absence of Professor Wells' long promised bibliography we are dependent upon the *CBEL* and Lena L. Tucker and Allen R. Benham, *A Bibliography of Fifteenth Century Literature* (Seattle, 1928; *Univ. of Wash. Pub. in Lang. and Lit.,* Vol. II, No. 3). F. J. Snell's *The Age of Transition: 1400-1580* (2v, 1905) covers the period rather superficially. G. Gregory Smith, *The Transition Period* (1900; *Periods of European Literature,* ed. Geo. Saintsbury, Vol. IV) gives the European background. Eleanor P. Hammond, *English Verse between Chaucer and Surrey* (Durham, N. C., 1927), offers a selection from the poetry with valuable commentary. W. A. Neilson and K. G. T. Webster, *Chief British Poets of the Fourteenth and Fifteenth Centuries* (Boston, 1916) is a volume of modernizations.

[2] *Le Pèlerinage de la Vie Humaine* (1330-31, revised 1355), *Le Pèlerinage de l'Ame* (between 1330 and 1358), *Le Pèlerinage de Jhesucrist* (1358). All three poems have been edited by J. J. Stürzinger for the Roxburghe Club (1893-97).

[3] See the discussion of Lydgate below.

[4] *The Pilgrimage of the Lyf of the Manhode,* ed. Wm. A. Wright (1869; *Roxburghe Club*).

eight manuscripts,[5] and was printed by Caxton in 1483. These two poems of Deguilleville obviously stem from the *Roman de la Rose* and look forward to Bunyan. *Dives and Pauper* (1405-10) is a long prose treatise in dialogue form. It is a treatment of the Ten Commandments with an extended prologue on poverty and is still unedited.[6] Touching the mystical tradition at one or more removes is Nicholas Love's *Mirrour of the Blessed Lyf of Jesu Christ* (c. 1410),[7] a free translation of parts of the *Meditationes Vitae Christi* doubtfully attributed to St. Bonaventura, from which Rolle had previously drawn. The *Orologium Sapientiae, or The Seven Points of True Wisdom*[8] was translated from the German mystic, Henry Suso, by an unknown chaplain for an unknown "moste worschipful lady." *The Revelations of St. Birgitta*[9] was naturally inspired by the establishment of the Bridgettine order in England in 1415. Legends of the saints continued to be written, although this type of narrative was soon to disappear from English poetry. Osbern Bokenham, "a suffolke man, frere Austyn of the convent of Stokclare" (Stoke Clare), composed a collection of thirteen *Legendys of Hooly Wummen*[10] (c. 1445) running to more than 10,000 lines. *Bokenham* It may be compared with legends in the *South English Legendary*, manuscripts of which continued to be copied throughout the fifteenth century. Into one of them was inserted a new version of the Theophilus legend, the story of the clerk who, like Faustus, sold his soul to the devil, in this case for worldly goods. But unlike Faustus he was saved from carrying out his compact when the Virgin went to Hell and forced Satan to return the charter. This version[11] is in lively six-line stanzas (romance sixes) and with its free use of dialogue reminds us of some of the shorter romances.

We may note also as growing out of the fourteenth century the efforts to *The* defend or expound the doctrines of Wyclif. Best known of these is the *Lollards Apology for Lollard Doctrines*, a lengthy tract at one time attributed to Wyclif himself.[12] In it the author takes up, one by one, thirty points of Lollard belief, which he apparently has been accused of holding, and de-

---

[5] Cf. Ward, *Cat. of Romances*, II. 580-585, and Victor H. Paltsits, "The Petworth Manuscript of *Grace Dieu*...," *Bull. N. Y. Pub. Library*, XXII (1928). 715-720. The Caxton text (with some omissions) will be found in Katherine I. Cust, *The Booke of the Pylgremage of the Sowle* (1859).

[6] There are six MSS and three early printed editions. See H. G. Richardson, "Dives and Pauper," *N&Q*, 11 Ser., IV (1911). 321-323; H. G. Pfander, "Dives et Pauper," *Library*, 4 Ser., XIV (1933). 299-312; H. G. Richardson, "Dives and Pauper," *ibid.*, XV (1934). 31-37. The Seven Deadly Sins and their contrasting virtues are worked into a fanciful allegory in the *Speculum Misericordiae*, printed by Rossell H. Robbins, *PMLA*, LIV (1939). 935-966.

[7] Ed. Lawrence F. Powell (1908). Twenty-three manuscripts attest its popularity, besides the fact that it was printed by Caxton, Pynson, and Wynkyn de Worde (twice).

[8] Ed. K. Horstmann, *Anglia*, X (1888). 323-389.

[9] Ed. W. P. Cumming (1929; *EETS*, 178). To the second quarter of the century is to be assigned the verse translation of the *Revelations* of Methodius (ed. Charlotte D'Evelyn, *PMLA*, XXXIII. 135-203).

[10] Ed. Mary S. Serjeanston (1938: *EETS*, 206). Sister Mary Jeremy, "The English Prose-Translation of *Legenda Aurea*," *MLN*, LIX (1944). 181-183, has revived the suggestion that Bokenham may have been the translator of the prose version preserved in a number of manuscripts and used by Caxton along with other sources.

[11] Ed. W. Heuser, *ESt*, XXXII (1903). 1-23.

[12] As by its editor, J. H. Todd (1842; *Camden Soc.*, XX).

fends his views: the pope is not Christ's vicar on earth, it is wrong to sell indulgences, to excommunicate, to encourage the worship of images, etc. Another defense of basic Wyclif doctrines, *The Lanterne of Liȝt* [13] (*c.* 1410), discusses such matters as the supreme authority of the Bible, the primary importance of preaching, the evil of clerical endowments, and the authority of the pope, considered to be Antichrist. On the whole, the tone of both these tracts is moderate. Certainly they are less belligerent than the *Remonstrance against Romish Corruptions in the Church,* [14] by Wyclif's friend and disciple John Purvey, at the close of the previous century (1395).

Secular Works   When we turn to secular writings we find the fifteenth century likewise carrying on the conventions and traditions of the fourteenth. The use of allegory and the dream-vision as a framework for popular didacticism, a device with a long and distinguished history extending from Martianus Capella and Boethius down, is seen in *The Court of Sapience* [15] (*c.* 1465). In this poem of some 2300 lines in rime royal we have first a debate between the Four Daughters of God, carried on at length, and then we are taken with the author on a dream journey to the Court of Sapience, where the Seven Liberal Arts are expounded. Thus theological and secular instruction is fitted into a slight allegorical framework. Something like the same purpose lies behind *The Assembly of Gods,* [16] formerly attributed, like the *Court of Sapience,* to Lydgate. Here a dispute among the Gods is followed by a battle between the Seven Deadly Sins and their corresponding virtues, recalling the *Psychomachia* of Prudentius, and leading to an explanation by Doctrine and others of the gradual progress from idolatry to "reconciliation" in New Testament times. The many personages which are introduced do not make easier the task of following the complicated allegory. *Sidrac and Boctus,* by Hugh of Campedene, [17] is a verse translation in over 12,000 lines of the *Fontaine de Toutes Sciences,* [18] offering instruction on a variety of topics—theological, cosmological, sociological, moral, and others—in a dialogue between the sage Sidrac and King Boctus of Bactria. More frankly practical are George Ripley's *Compend of Alchemy* [19] (1471) and the anonymous *Libell (Little Book) of Englische Policye* [20] (*c.* 1436), which put into verse quite mundane matters. The former explains the pseudo-science

[13] Ed. Lilian M. Swinburn (1917; *EETS,* 151).

[14] Ed. J. Forshall (London, 1851).

[15] Ed. Robert Spindler (Leipzig, 1927; *Beiträge zur engl. Phil.,* VI). On the sources see Curt F. Bühler, *The Sources of the Court of Sapience* (Leipzig, 1932) in the same series.

[16] Ed. Oscar L. Triggs (1896; *EETSES,* 69). The movement of the lines, each hurrying on to the end, is utterly unlike Lydgate, who loves a caesura, and as Miss Hammond remarks, seems to think in half-lines. The piece has been dated 1403 and 1420-22. I should put it on stylistic grounds not much earlier than the earliest manuscript, which is not older than 1468.

[17] See K. Bülbring, "Sidrac in England," *Festschrift für Wendelin Foerster* (Halle, 1902), pp. 443-478. There was also a translation in prose, of which a fragment is preserved.

[18] See *Hist. Litt.,* XXXI (1893). 285-318.

[19] Last printed in Elias Ashmole, *Theatrum Chemicum Britannicum* (1652); extract in Hammond, *op. cit.* Ripley wrote much on scientific subjects in Latin (see Tanner, *op. cit.*).

[20] Ed. Thomas Wright, *Political Poems* (1859-61), Wilhelm Hertzberg (Leipzig, 1878), and Sir George Warner (Oxford, 1926). Selections in Hammond, *op. cit.* Abridged and modernized text in W. H. Dunham, Jr. and Stanley Pargellis, *Complaint and Reform in England, 1436-1714* (1938), pp. 3-30.

of alchemy to Edward IV in rime royal; the latter deals with foreign trade and what ought to be England's commercial policy.

Social satire of the *Piers Plowman* type is skilfully presented in the little ballad known as *London Lickpenny*.[21] The poet's experiences in London, where he is unable to get any attention at the King's Bench, Common Pleas, or Chancery, and succeeds only in being robbed of his hood, are told in sixteen eight-line stanzas, most of which end in the refrain, "For lacke of money, I may not spede." The Scottish tradition of Barbour is continued in the work of Blind Harry the minstrel, who presents something of a problem. Toward the end of the fifteenth century he appears in the records as receiving small gifts from the king, and ever since this time he has been remembered as the author of the most popular poem in Scotland down to the eighteenth century. The poem, *The Wallace*[22] (*c.* 1475), is an epic of some 11,000 lines recounting the heroic deeds of the Scottish patriot Sir William Wallace, who was finally captured and executed by the English in 1305. The humble origin of Blind Harry and his blindness from birth are facts incompatible with the literary character of the poem, its aureate vocabulary,[23] the extensive topographical knowledge displayed, which is detailed and exact, and above all the many borrowings from other works of English and French literature. It is likely that the poem in its present form owes much to another hand.[24] About 1450 Richard Holland, a priest and follower of the Douglases, wrote *The Buke of the Howlat* (Owl).[25] It is the familiar story of the bird that became overproud of its borrowed plumage, with nice satirical implications in the parts assigned to the various other birds. Any general political allegory, however, which the poem may have had was probably slight and has now lost its meaning.

London Lickpenny

The Wallace

Throughout the fifteenth century the authority of Chaucer was paramount, although Gower is mentioned with almost equal respect. Lydgate pays tribute to him on numerous occasions, always in the same tone, as

> The noble poete of Breteyne,
> My mayster Chaucer.

The Chaucerians

Hoccleve, whose affection seems to have sprung from personal acquaintance, calls him "maister deere and fadir reverent." That he felt Chaucer's death deeply is apparent from the frequency with which he alludes to it:

> Death, by thi deth, hath harm irreparable
> Unto us doon;

[21] Printed in Hammond, pp. 238-239.

[22] Edited by John Jamieson (2v, Edinburgh, 1820) and James Moir (1889; *STS*, 6-7,17); facsimile, ed. Sir William Craigie (1939). On the writers mentioned in this paragraph see William Geddie, *A Bibliography of Middle Scots Poets* (Edinburgh, 1912; *STS*, 61); T. F. Henderson, *Scottish Vernacular Literature* (3ed., Edinburgh, 1910).

[23] The excessive use of Latin derivatives, often slightly assimilated. See John C. Mendenhall, *Aureate Terms: A Study in the Literary Diction of the Fifteenth Century* (Lancaster, Pa., 1919).

[24] See the exhaustive examination of the problem by J. T. T. Brown, *The Wallace and The Bruce Restudied* (Bonn, 1900; *Bonner Beiträge zur Anglistik*, vi), where an interesting case is made out for John Ramsay, known to Dunbar as Sir John the Ross. The identification, however, is disputed.

[25] The best edition is in F. J. Amours, *Scottish Alliterative Poems* (1897; *STS*, 27), pp. 47-81.

and he had his portrait painted in his *Regiment of Princes* "to puïte othir men in remembraunce of his persone." Many other writers pay Chaucer lip service [26] or follow his example, albeit at long remove. For the qualities that make Chaucer great are those incapable of imitation. As Lydgate says:

> We may assay forto countrefete
> His gay style but it wyl not be.

Additional Canterbury Tales

It is not easy to follow the Chaucer tradition in the fifteenth century since it takes a variety of forms and ranges from close dependence, in poets like Hoccleve and Henryson, to occasional verbal echoes which merely indicate familiarity with Chaucer's works. Some go so far as to include among the "Chaucerians" any one who wrote in Chaucer's better-known metres, such as the *Troilus* stanza (rime royal). But such influence is doubtless in many cases at second or third hand. In the anonymous *Plowman's Tale* [27] we have a very un-Chaucerian piece arbitrarily attached to the *Canterbury Tales*. It is a Lollard tract in verse form, in which, under the guise of a conversation between a griffon and a pelican, the author launches into a long denunciation of the pope and the clergy—their pride, luxury, greed and the evil practices resulting therefrom, and many other abuses within the Church. Almost every idea expressed can be paralleled in the writings of Wyclif and his followers, but it is not without interest as a tract for the times and its irony is sometimes telling. More successfully fitted to the *Canterbury Tales* is the *Tale of Beryn* [28] with its Prologue detailing the doings of the pilgrims in the cathedral town and especially the ill-starred attempt of the Pardoner to spend the night with Kit the bar-maid. The Prologue has some of Chaucer's realistic vigor, but none at all of his sly humor or happy turn of phrase. The tale is rather long-drawn-out. Besides these attempts to continue the *Canterbury Tales* we should note that Lydgate's *Siege of Thebes,* discussed below, is fitted with a prologue likewise linking it with the return journey.

In the early editions of Chaucer a number of poems by other poets were commonly included. Some of these were considered genuine, others included because they were in Chaucer's manner. Apart from pieces by poets like Lydgate and Hoccleve and Henryson, who will be discussed later, a little sheaf of poems deserves mention. *La Belle Dame sans Mercy* [29] is a translation in 856 lines from Alain Chartier. The translator's preface and the opening of the poem proper, with its garden and gentlefolk and the approach to the conversation between the lover and his lady, are such as Chaucer might have devised, but he never could have carried on the tiresome and long-winded debate in which the lover pleads and the lady repels all his

[26] Caroline F. E. Spurgeon, *Five Hundred Years of Chaucer Criticism and Allusion, 1357-1900* (3v, Cambridge, 1925).

[27] Printed by Skeat in the *Oxford Chaucer*, VII. 147-190. From an allusion in the poem and from other considerations it is apparent that it was written by the author of *Pierce the Ploughman's Creed.*

[28] Ed. F. J. Furnivall and W. G. Stone (1909; *EETSES*, 105).

[29] All the pieces mentioned in this paragraph are printed in Vol. VII of the *Oxford Chaucer.*

pleas for mercy. The author, Sir Richard Ros, about whom little is known
except his parentage, does not have much to recommend him but a certain
metrical skill. *The Flower and the Leaf* is somewhat lacking in substance. The
It is little more than a tableau gracefully described,[30] in which one company Flower
of knights and ladies representing the Flower gets drenched in a shower and the
and is hospitably given shelter by another company representing the Leaf. Leaf
The author alludes to herself as a woman, and since this is true also of
another poem, *The Assembly of Ladies,* it has been suggested that they are
both by the same writer. But since the former is thought to date from about
1450 [31] and the latter shows a much later treatment of the final *e,* this is
at least doubtful. *The Assembly of Ladies* is not very logically planned. In The
the usual dream convention the author, along with her four companions Assembly
and many others, is peremptorily summoned to appear before a lady named of Ladies
Loyaltè, merely to allow each one to present a "bill" complaining of broken
promises, disappointment in love, and the like. The poem owes something
to Lydgate's *Temple of Glas.* In tone and phrasing the most Chaucerian of
all these apocryphal pieces is a little poem of 290 lines called *The Cuckoo
and the Nightingale.* In the manuscripts it is just as fittingly called *The* The
Book of Cupid, God of Love, for it explains that the God of Love has great Cuckoo
power over folk, even over the poet, who is "old and unlusty." The body and the
of the poem is a dispute between the two birds over the joys and sorrows of Nightingale
love, recalling at times in setting and circumstances the altercation in the
Owl and the Nightingale. On the basis of an "Explicit Clanvowe" in the
Cambridge MS it has been attributed to Sir Thomas Clanvowe, a friend of
Chaucer's friend, Lewis Clifford, and quite possibly known to Chaucer
himself.[32] But whatever its authorship the piece has quite enough charm
to account for its influence on Milton in his sonnet "To the Nightingale" and
for the modernization found among Wordsworth's poems.

In many ways the Scottish Chaucerians were more successful in their *Scottish*
efforts than their English contemporaries. In 1406, at the age of eleven, the *Chaucerians*
young King James I of Scotland was captured by the English and for
eighteen years was a prisoner in England. He does not seem to have been
badly treated and had plenty of leisure in which to acquire the intimate
knowledge of Chaucer's poetry which he shows. Upon his release in 1424
he was married to Joan Beaufort, the niece of two of the most powerful
magnates in England. The story of his capture and imprisonment, his
falling in love at first sight when, like Palamon in the *Knight's Tale,* he
caught a glimpse of a surpassingly beautiful lady in the garden below his
prison window, and the dream in which he is carried aloft, like Chaucer
in the *Hous of Fame,* to the palace of Venus and later is advised by Minerva

---

[30] Dryden, who translated it in his *Fables Ancient and Modern,* thought it was by Chaucer
and says, "I was so particularly pleased, both for the invention and the moral, that I cannot
hinder myself from recommending it to the reader."

[31] It must be admitted that the dates of these poems are highly conjectural.

[32] Kittredge (*MP,* I. 13-18) argued for Sir John Clanvowe, who died in 1391. Although
Skeat's dating of the poem after 1402 is none too secure, Thomas seems the better candidate.

The Kingis
Quair

—such incidents form the subject of *The Kingis Quair* ("King's Book").[33] Written apparently just before his release, in a language the Chaucerian character of which has been somewhat obscured by Scottish copyists,[34] it makes a very pleasing little romantic story out of facts which are in part at least autobiographical. As its 197 stanzas are those of Chaucer's *Troilus* the form has generally been known since as "rime royal." Later in the century another Scottish poet, Robert Henryson, schoolmaster of Dunfermline, caught some of the spirit of Chaucer in his *Fables*,[35] where he told such stories as "The Cock and the Fox" and "The Town Mouse and the Country Mouse," adding to each, however, a rather un-Chaucerian "moral." He turned the tale of Orpheus and Eurydice into rime royal and wrote a number of shorter moralizing pieces. His ballad of *Robene and Makyne* has been admired as an early pastoral and considered superior to the *Nut Brown Maid,* a judgment with which many will agree. But the poem which attaches itself most closely to Chaucer is *The Testament of Cresseid.* In this piece Cresseid, deserted by Diomede, curses the gods and is punished by leprosy. Ashamed to be seen by her friends, she goes to the spittel-house to live among the lepers. The crowning torture which she endures is to be given alms, as one of the beggars, by Troilus, whom Henryson represents as still living and who happens to pass by in a company of knights. Neither recognizes the other at the time, although Troilus is disturbed by a puzzling resemblance to Cresseid and she afterwards learns who he was. In a closing lament Cresseid blames her own unfaithfulness on "lustis lecherous," crying

Robert
Henryson

The
Testament
of
Cresseid

> Fy! fals Cresseid! O, trew knight Troilus!

The poem presents a grim incident with moving pathos, and shows how a less tolerant poet would have concluded Chaucer's great poem.

Charles
d'Orléans

Although the English translations of the poems of Charles d'Orléans [36] contain occasional echoes of Chaucer, he may be mentioned here not so much because he shows the influence of Chaucer as because he is the heir to the French tradition of Deschamps and Froissart which so greatly influenced Chaucer. In the case of Charles d'Orléans this tradition expressed itself wholly in the conventional chanson and ballade of love. In spite of an occasional sentiment or graceful phrase that recaptures one's attention, the poems tend to become tiresome in their repetition of a few stock themes— praise of the lady, appeals for pity, avowal of lifelong service, conventional despair, and the like. Such poetry is something of an anachronism in the second quarter of the fifteenth century.

[33] The most recent editions are those of Alex. Lawson (1910), W. W. Skeat (1911; *STS*, n.s. 1), and W. Mackay Mackenzie (1939). The date and authorship of the poem have been questioned, but without much success. The most authoritative biography of James I is that of E. W. M. Balfour-Melville (1936).

[34] Sir William Craigie, "The Language of the *Kingis Quair*," *E&S*, xxv (1940). 22-38.

[35] The works of Henryson have been edited by G. Gregory Smith (3v, 1906-14; *STS*, 55, 58, 64), and in one volume by H. Harvey Wood (2ed, Edinburgh, 1958).

[36] Ed. Robert Steele (1941; *EETS*, 215; notes by Robert Steele and Mabel Day, 1946, *EETS*, 220).

It has been said that John Lydgate lived thirty years too long for the *Lydgate*
good of his literary reputation. Be this as it may, it is certain that to the
last half of his life belong most of the incredibly voluminous writings which
students of literary history know, if only by name, today. He was born in
Lydgate, in Suffolk, probably around 1370, and at the age of about fifteen
was admitted to the nearby abbey of Bury St. Edmunds. It is suspected that
he was sent to study for a time at one of the universities. In any case he was
ordained a priest in 1397, after which we know nothing more about him
for nearly twenty years. In 1423 he was elected prior of Hatfield Broadoak,
in Essex. He soon relinquished the office, certainly by 1430 [37] and possibly
in 1425, for about 1426 he was in Paris, and probably remained long enough
to have translated a poetical pedigree for the Earl of Warwick, written
the *Dance of Macabre,* and begun his translation of Deguilleville, this last
at the command of the Earl of Salisbury. From 1434 until he died Lydgate
was back at Bury St. Edmunds. The date of his death is uncertain, but it
probably occurred in the year 1449.[38]

Among Lydgate's poems, which run to well over 100,000 lines, there are *His*
many unsolved problems of chronology, but fortunately his longer pieces *Volumi-*
can all be dated with some approximation to definiteness. His selection *nous*
from Aesop's fables and *The Churl and the Bird* [39] were probably written *Production*
toward the close of the fourteenth century. To the period just after 1400
belong certain pieces in which the influence of Chaucer is very evident—
the *Floure of Curtesy,*[40] a valentine poem praising his lady in the courtly
love manner, the *Complaint of the Black Knight,*[41] which echoes the situation in Chaucer's *Book of the Duchess,* and the *Temple of Glas,*[42] in
which a surpassingly beautiful lady complains to Venus of being separated
from her knight, the knight reveals his love sickness, and the lovers are
happily united through the favor of the goddess. The last employs the
familiar convention of the imaginary dream. Between these poems and the
beginning of the *Troy Book* in 1412 stands *Reason and Sensuality,* after
the *Troy Book* the *Life of Our Lady. Reason and Sensuality* [43] (*c.* 1408), in
spite of its 7000 lines, still makes rather pleasant reading with its allegory
of the poet's meeting with Venus and the journey to the Garden of Pleasure
which Guillaume de Lorris had acquainted us with in the *Roman de la Rose.*
The Life of Our Lady [44] (nearly 6000 lines in rime royal) is now edited.

Lydgate's later years were occupied by a series of enormous translations

[37] See Georg Fiedler, "Zum Leben Lydgate's," *Anglia,* xv (1893). 389-395.

[38] The best account of his life is that of J. Schick in his edition of the *Temple of Glas*
(1891; *EETSES,* 60), followed not too cautiously by the *DNB.*

[39] Both in *The Minor Poems of John Lydgate,* ed. Henry N. MacCracken, Vol. ii (1934;
EETS, 192).

[40] *Minor Poems,* ii. 410-418.

[41] *Minor Poems,* ii. 382-410.

[42] Ed. Schick, as above.

[43] Ed. Ernst Sieper (1901-3; *EETSES,* 84, 89).

[44] Ed. Joseph A. Lauritis, Ralph A. Klinefelter, and Vernon F. Gallagher (Pittsburgh, 1961;
Duquesne Univ. Stud., Philol. Ser., No. 2).

*His
Transla-
tions*

of well-known works. The *Troy Book* [45] (30,117 lines in decasyllabic couplets), rendered from the Latin prose of Guido della Colonna, occupied most of his time from 1412 to 1420. This was followed by the *Siege of Thebes* [46] (1420-22), based on a French prose condensation of the *Roman de Thèbes*. It is provided, as already noted, with a prologue attaching it to the homeward journey of Chaucer's Canterbury pilgrims, and serves as a companion piece to the *Knight's Tale* on the outward journey. Although only 4716 lines, it is still too long for such an occasion. *The Pilgrimage of the Life of Man* [47] (1426-30) fills nearly 24,000 lines in octosyllabic couplets. It renders the first of Deguilleville's three *Pèlerinages* (see p. 288). Finally, the longest of all his works, *The Fall of Princes* (1431-38), is also the most tedious. One can hardly appreciate the taste of an age which endured more than 26,000 lines detailing the tragedies which have befallen the great. [48] It is based on the French prose *Des Cas des Nobles Hommes et Femmes* of Laurent de Premierfait, itself an expansion of Boccaccio's *De Casibus Virorum Illustrium.* At the time of his death Lydgate was at work on the *Secrees of Old Philisoffres,* a translation of the *Secreta Secretorum* attributed in the Middle Ages to Aristotle. It was finished by a disciple, possibly Benedict Burgh. [49]

*Shorter
Pieces*

In addition to his longer works Lydgate's shorter pieces fill two volumes in modern print. [50] He was evidently known as a ready versifier, able to turn out a poem suitable for any occasion, and therefore during most of his life was at the call of any one who chose to command his services. He wrote poems on the occasion of Henry VI's coronation, on Gloucester's marriage, on a royal entry into London, the departure of Thomas Chaucer for the Continent, etc. He composed verses for mummings at Bishopswood, Eltham, Hartford, London, Windsor, and for the mercers and the goldsmiths of London. [51] His lyrics and shorter poems likewise show a certain un-monastic variety. There are, of course, many religious lyrics of the types familiar to us elsewhere—hymns and prayers to the Virgin and Christ, translations of Latin hymns, little sermons in verse, and all varieties of hortatory and devotional poems. They are marked by sincerity, smoothness of metre, and an occasional happy image. Some, like the *God Is Myn Helpere* and *An Holy Medytacion,* are among the best things he wrote. There are

[45] Ed. Henry Bergen (1906-35; *EETSES,* 97, 103, 106, 126). On Lydgate's sources see, in addition to Bergen, E. Bagby Atwood, "Some Minor Sources of Lydgate's *Troy Book,*" *SP,* xxxv (1938). 25-42.

[46] Ed. Axel Erdmann and Eilert Ekwall (1911-30; *EETSES,* 108, 125).

[47] Ed. F. J. Furnivall and Katharine B. Locock (1899-1904; *EETSES,* 77, 83, 92).

[48] Ed. Henry Bergen (1924-27; *EETSES,* 121-124). He well characterizes it as "a collection gathered throughout the centuries describing the most memorable and crushing blows dealt by fate to the illustrious personages of mythology and history, and written, as the author himself said, with the object of teaching princes the virtue of wisdom and moderation by holding up to them the example of misfortunes provoked by egotism, pride and inordinate ambition."

[49] Ed. Robert Steele (1894; *EETSES,* 66). Other fifteenth-century translations in prose are edited by Steele (1898; *EETSES,* 74). On Benedict Burgh see below, p. 302.

[50] Henry N. MacCracken, *The Minor Poems of John Lydgate* (1911-34; *EETSES,* 107 and *EETS,* 192). The first volume contains a discussion of the Lydgate canon.

[51] These are all printed by MacCracken, as above. On the general type see Robert Withington, *English Pageantry: An Historical Outline* (2v, Cambridge, Mass., 1918-20).

didactic and moralizing pieces ranging from *A Dietary,* giving simple rules for good health, or *Stans Puer ad Mensam,* teaching the rules of courtesy and conduct, to his own *Testament,* which combines moral reflection with interesting autobiographical allusions. Of similar utilitarian aim are admonitory pieces like the *Dance of Macabre* or fables like *The Churl and the Bird* and *Horse, Goose, and Sheep,* with its refrain advising man "For no prerogatif his neyghburghe to dispise." The good monk saw nothing inappropriate in composing an occasional love poem in the courtly tradition, such as *My Lady Dere* or *A Lover's New Year's Gift,* and his muse occasionally takes a humorous and satirical turn as in *Bycorne and Chychevache* and *The Order of Fools. Bycorne and Chychevache* presents an amusing picture of a fat and a lean beast, who feed only on patient husbands and wives respectively. Chychevache is distressingly thin; she complains that it is a "dear year" in patient wives. The *Order of Fools* describes a new mendicant order which is made up of all sorts from the sacrilegious and adulterous to the credulous and those who marry an old woman for money. It is not right to think of all these shorter pieces as the work of Lydgate's early years, but it is true that his standing as a poet would have been higher if he had written only these and had not made the interminable translations which constitute the great bulk of his writings.

Some blame for the latter, however, must be shared by the numerous *Poetry* patrons who requested him to make them. The *Life of Our Lady* and the *to Order* *Troy Book* were written at the command of Prince Hal, while the *Fall of Princes* was translated at the desire of Humphrey, Duke of Gloucester, uncle and regent of Henry VI. The Deguilleville was for Thomas de Montacute, Earl of Salisbury. When Henry VI visited the shrine of St. Edmund at Christmas in 1422 Lydgate's abbot commanded him to write the *Legend of St. Edmund and Fremund,* and when the abbot of St. Albans wished his house to be honored in a similar way he turned to the monk of Bury for the *Life of Albon and Amphabel.* Many other shorter pieces were written upon request, such as the mummings, already mentioned, for the mercers and the goldsmiths of London. Lydgate was the most competent literary handy-man available, and we should be expecting too much to hope that all his odd jobs should have been done and his extensive commissions executed with the inspiration of high art.

Strictly contemporary with Lydgate and an even more devoted admirer *Hoccleve* of Chaucer was Thomas Hoccleve (*c.* 1369-*c.* 1450). From the age of nineteen or twenty he spent the better part of forty years as a clerk in the Privy Seal Office. Fortunately he is one of the most autobiographical of English poets. He was given an annuity of £10 in 1399, and on various occasions when it was in arrears (as it often was) he appealed in ballades to those who might expedite its payment. Whatever he received he spent on a merry life, eating and drinking to excess, haunting the tavern, kissing the girls and paying for their refreshment, riding on the river and paying the boatmen lavishly, for the pleasure of being called "master." All this he tells us in *La Male Regle de T. Hoccleve* (*c.* 1406). He promises there to amend his ways. In any case, a few years later he married. For a period of five years he suffered from a nervous breakdown (*c.* 1415-20) and, as he says, was mad. In the *Complaint* and *Dialogue with a Friend,* which really form a single poem of some 800 lines (*c.* 1421-2), he writes at length about his illness and his difficulty in convincing others of his recovery. About 1425 he seems to have been retired on a corrody at the priory of Southwick in Hampshire. He was apparently alive in 1448, but died probably a year or two later.

The Regiment of Princes
The bulk of Hoccleve's verse is not large, and the range is limited.[52] A few autobiographical pieces, a dozen occasional poems, mostly short, an equal number of lyrics to the Virgin and Christ, some of them translations, a couple of tales from the *Gesta Romanorum,* two short translations (*The Letter of Cupid, Learn to Die*), and the *Regiment of Princes* make up his work. Of these the longest (5463 lines) is the *Regiment of Princes* (1412), written for the young prince who was about to become Henry V. It is the usual advice on how to live and rule, put together from the *De Ludo Scachorum* of Jacobus de Cessolis, the *Secreta Secretorum,* and the *De Regimine Principum* of Egidio Colonna, with a long prefatory section (2000 lines) full of personal allusion. Hoccleve does not have Lydgate's fatal fluency, or Gower's social and moral urge. He does not write for the sheer love of writing, and he seldom rises to the level of poetry. Yet his complete frankness, his many personal revelations, and his frequent references to current events make his verse almost always interesting. In poets of the fifteenth century, or indeed of later centuries, this is no small merit.

The Amateurs
About the middle of the century we can distinguish a number of amateurs who hazarded an occasional venture in verse. George Ashby, who lived to be nearly eighty, and who was for "full fourty yere" a clerk of the Signet, left behind him three poems.[53] *A Prisoner's Reflections,* written during an imprisonment in 1463 in the Fleet, is a modest consolation of philosophy in 350 lines of rime royal. His other poems are *The Active Policy of a Prince* (918 lines), written for Edward, Prince of Wales, and a paraphrase of some extracts from the *Liber Philosophorum Moralium Antiquorum.*[54] John Shirley,[55] who died in 1456 at about the age of ninety, is chiefly remembered as the copyist of a number of manuscripts containing the works of Chaucer and Lydgate, but wrote two prologues in verse for books which he compiled. In one of Shirley's manuscripts is preserved the only copy of a poem of 172 lines called *Evidence to Beware and Good Counsel* by "that honurable squier," Richard Sellyng.[56] Two stanzas attributed in manuscripts

---

[52] It is all printed in *Hoccleve's Works* (EETSES, 61, 72, 73).

[53] *George Ashby's Poems,* ed. Mary Bateson (1899; EETSES, 76).

[54] For other translations of the *Dicts and Sayings of the Philosophers* see below, p. 302.

[55] See Otto Gaertner, *John Shirley: Sein Leben und Wirken* (Halle, 1904) and Hammond, *op. cit.* Miss Hammond conjectures that he may have run a bookshop and lending library in London.

[56] See "Richard Sellyng," by the present writer, in *Essays and Studies in Honor of Carleton Brown* (1940), pp. 167-181.

to "Halsham Esquier" have been referred to John Halsham, who died in or before 1415 owning lands in Sussex, Kent, Norfolk and Wilts.[57] None of these poems is intrinsically important, but they are interesting as suggesting the extension of literary activity among those not of the literary profession or the Church.

[57] Helen P. South, "The Question of Halsam," *PMLA*, L (1935). 362-371.

XXI

Looking Forward

Growth of a Reading Public   All through the fifteenth century there is growing evidence of the extension of the reading public.[1] That works were being written to be read through the eye rather than taken in through the ear is apparent not only from the frequency with which reference is made to reading, but from the length of such poems as Lydgate's *Troy Book* and the *Fall of Princes,* which could not conceivably have been intended for minstrel recitation. The industrial development at this period and the growth of a landed gentry were accompanied by more widespread education and the leisure to enjoy it. The new reading public is nowhere more plainly indicated than in the production of certain late romances very different in length and character from those of an earlier period. We have already spoken of the *Gest Historiale of the Destruction of Troy* with its 14,000 long alliterative lines.[2] More extreme cases are the two Gargantuan poems of the London skinner, Henry Lovelich. Written about 1425, the *Merlin*[3] reaches a total of 27,852 four-stress lines when the manuscript breaks off, and the *History of the Holy Grail*[4] runs to nearly 24,000 lines, with an additional section of several thousand missing in the beginning. On a similar scale two treatments of the Alexander legend were written in Scotland—one an anonymous poem completed in 1428 in 11,000 lines,[5] the other a narrative of about 20,000 verses written by Sir Gilbert Hay towards the end of the century.[6]

Prose Romances   Growth of the reading public is also shown by the use of prose for works which would earlier have been written in verse. In this century we witness the beginning of the prose romance.[7] What is apparently the earliest is a prose *Alexander* in the Thornton MS (1430-40),[8] but from about the middle

---

[1] On this general subject see the articles of H. S. Bennett, "The Author and His Public in the Fourteenth and Fifteenth Centuries," *E&S*, XXIII (1938). 7-24; "Caxton and His Public," *RES*, XIX (1943). 113-119; "Science and Information in English Writings of the Fifteenth Century," *MLR*, XXXIX (1944). 1-8; J. W. Adamson, "The Extent of Literacy in England in the Fifteenth and Sixteenth Centuries: Notes and Conjectures," *Library*, 4 Ser., x 1929). 163-193; C. L. Kingsford, *English Historical Literature in the Fifteenth Century* (1913), and the same author's *Prejudice and Promise in Fifteenth Century England* (1925).

[2] See above, p. 184.

[3] Ed. Ernst A. Kock (1904-32; *EETSES*, 93, 112; *EETS*, 185).

[4] Ed. F. J. Furnivall (1874-78; *EETSES*, 20, 24, 28, 30).

[5] Ed. R. L. Graeme Ritchie (4v, 1921-29; *STS*, n.s. 12, 17, 21, 25). On the controversy over the authorship that has raged for fifty years see Ritchie's intro., where the presentation of the case for Barbour is no more conclusive than previous attempts.

[6] Only selections have been printed; see A. Hermann, *The Forraye of Gadderis; The Vowis* (Berlin, 1900).

[7] Prose romance might have developed from stories like the Old English *Apollonius* (see p. 104), but any such development was cut short by the Norman Conquest.

[8] Ed. J. S. Westlake (1913; *EETS*, 143).

of the century date *Pontus and Sidone* [9] and a very long prose *Merlin*.[10] Of about the same date are prose condensations of the Troy and Thebes stories in a Rawlinson MS.[11] With the introduction of printing a number of new prose romances were produced, all of them taken from French originals. Caxton translated (1469-71) and printed at Bruges in 1474 or 1475 his *Recuyell of the Historyes of Troye*.[12] In England he made and printed translations of *Godeffroy of Boloyne* [13] (1481), the story of the siege of Jerusalem in the first crusade, deriving ultimately from William of Tyre and familiar later in Tasso's *Gerusalemme Liberata;* the excellent story of *Paris and Vienne* (1485); *Charles the Great* [14] (1485), from the French prose *Fierabras; The Foure Sonnes of Aymon* [15] (c. 1489), recounting Charlemagne's struggle with these valiant nobles; *Blanchardyn and Eglantine* [16] (c. 1489), a pleasing story reminiscent, in its earlier part, of the Perceval and involving in the remainder the hero's rescue of his lady from the usual unwelcome suitor. His *Eneydos* (1490) has been mentioned in a previous chapter. Malory's great work, which Caxton printed, will be discussed later. Caxton's practice was followed by his successor Wynkyn de Worde, who set his apprentice Henry Watson to translating books from the French. One such is the romance of *Valentine and Orson* [17] printed by him soon after the turn of the century. Nor did the fashion die with the fifteenth century. About 1525, Sir John Bourchier, Lord Berners, best known for his translation of Froissart, occupied his leisure at Calais by turning into English the story of *Huon of Bordeaux*,[18] loosely connected with the Charlemagne cycle. Many of these prose romances enjoyed considerable popularity throughout the sixteenth century, were frequently reprinted, exerted their influence on Spenser and others, and even furnished material for the Elizabethan drama.

The prose romance, however, is only one type in which the translators *Other* were busy. Translation from the French was, of course, characteristic of the *Prose* whole Middle English period, at least from the time of Layamon, and we have already mentioned a number of works turned into English verse in the fifteenth century, notably in Lydgate's longer poems. At this time several lesser men were contributing individual pieces to the growing body of popular books available in the native tongue. John Walton, a canon of Osney, seems to have succeeded Trevisa as literary purveyor to the Berkeley family. To him has plausibly been attributed the translation of Vegetius' *De Re Militari* made in 1408 for Lord Thomas Berkeley, Trevisa's former

[9] Ed. F. J. Mather, Jr., *PMLA*, XII (1897), pp. l-lxvii, 1-150.
[10] Ed. Henry B. Wheatley (1865-69; *EETS*, 10, 21, 36) with an introduction by Wm. E. Mead (1899; *EETS*, 112).
[11] The *Sege of Troy* is edited by N. E. Griffin, *PMLA*, XXII (1907). 157-200; both are printed by Friedrich Brie, "Zwei mittelenglische Prosaromane: The Sege of Thebes und The Sege of Troy," *Archiv*, CXXX (1913). 40-52, 269-285.
[12] Ed. H. Oskar Sommer (2v, 1894).
[13] Ed. Mary N. Colvin (1893; *EETSES*, 64).
[14] Ed. Sidney J. H. Herrtage (2v, 1880-81; *EETSES*, 36-37).
[15] Ed. Octavia Richardson (2v, 1884-85; *EETSES*, 44-45).
[16] Ed. Leon Kellner (1890; *EETSES*, 58).
[17] Ed. Arthur Dickson (1937; *EETS*, 204).
[18] Ed. S. L. Lee (4v, 1882-87; *EETSES*, 40, 41, 43, 50).

patron,[19] and in 1410 he certainly translated for Berkeley's daughter Elizabeth, who was later to marry the Earl of Warwick, Boethius' *Consolation
of Philosophy* [20] into eight-line stanzas and rime royal, with much indebtedness to Chaucer's prose version. Sometime in the earlier part of the century
an anonymous translator turned *Palladius on Husbandry* [21] also into rime
royal.

*East
Anglian
Patronage*

Scrope

But in some ways the most interesting group of poet-translators was that
which wrote for a little coterie of East Anglian patrons around the middle
of the century.[22] Stephen Scrope (*c.* 1396-1472) translated and presented to
his stepfather, Sir John Fastolf, a version in prose of *The Dicts and Sayings
of the Philosophers* [23] from the French of Tignonville. There were other
translations of the *Dicts,* the best known of which was that of Anthony
Wydeville, Earl Rivers (after 1473), printed by Caxton. Scrope also translated from Christine de Pisan *The Epistle of Othea to Hector,* [24] a variety
of courtesy book offering instruction to a prince in the form of a hundred
stories with spiritual and chivalric applications. Later in the century a second
translation was made by Anthony Babyngton.[25] Scrope may have done the
translations of *Tulle of Old Age* printed by Caxton [26] and the *Boke of
Noblesse,* [27] more often attributed to William Worcester, Fastolf's secretary,
who is known to have made a revision of Scrope's *Dicts and Sayings.* An-

Metham

other Norfolk author, John Metham, in addition to treatises on palmistry
and physiognomy, wrote in 1448-9 for Sir Miles Stapleton and his wife a
poem of 2200 lines in rime royal called *Amoryus and Cleopes,* [28] a variant
of the Pyramus and Thisbe theme loosely associated with the story of
Alexander the Great. Stapleton, prominent in Norfolk affairs, was a friend
and neighbor of Fastolf. Most of the legends of Osbern Bokenham, already
discussed,[29] were written for various ladies in Suffolk, including Katherine
Howard, great-grandmother of Henry Howard, Earl of Surrey, and Lady
Isabel, wife of Henry Bourchier, later Earl of Essex. For the latter's son

Burgh

Benedict Burgh, mentioned above as the possible continuator of Lydgate's
Secrees of Old Philisoffres, wrote a verse paraphrase of the *Distichs of
Cato,* [30] a miscellaneous body of aphorisms on conduct and morals. Finally

[19] See Mark Science, as below, pp. xlviii-xlix.
[20] Ed. Mark Science (1927; *EETS,* 170).
[21] Ed. Rev. Barton Lodge (1873-79; *EETS,* 52, 72).
[22] See Samuel Moore, "Patrons of Letters in Norfolk and Suffolk, *c.* 1450," *PMLA,* xxvii
(1912). 188-207; xxviii (1913). 79-105.
[23] Ed. Margaret E. Schofield (Phila., 1936), with an introduction containing the best
account of Scrope's life, and Curt F. Bühler (1941; *EETS,* 211), who prints also an anonymous
translation and modifications of Scrope's translation.
[24] Ed. G. F. Warner (1904; *Roxburghe Club*).
[25] Ed. James D. Gordon (Phila., 1942).
[26] Ed. Heinz Susebach (Halle, 1933; *Studien zur englischen Philologie,* 75).
[27] Ed. J. Gough Nichols (1860; *Roxburghe Club*).
[28] *The Works of John Metham,* ed. Hardin Craig (1916; *EETS,* 132).
[29] See p. 289. To Norfolk apparently belongs the translation of Methodius mentioned above,
p. 289.
[30] The best edition is that of Max Förster, "Die Burghsche Cato-Paraphrase," *Archiv,* cxv
(1905). 298-323. For Burgh's other works see Max Förster, "Über Benedict Burghs Leben und
Werke," *Archiv,* ci (1898). 29-64.

we may note that William de la Pole, Duke of Suffolk, husband of Alice Chaucer and friend of Charles d'Orléans, besides being a literary patron wrote ballades in French and, if the attribution is sound, a small group of poems in English.[31] The various persons who thus appear as patrons of letters in Norfolk and Suffolk were all well known to the Pastons. Many of them appear in the *Paston Letters,*[32] a collection of letters by and to members of this well-known Norfolk family over a period of three generations (1422-1509), which, if not literature, are fascinating for the pictures they give us of life in fifteenth-century England.[33]

Paston Letters

The inference lies close at hand that the growth of a landed gentry and the rising fortunes of the middle class were having a stimulating effect on certain types of writing. This inference is borne out by a succession of courtesy books intended for just such classes.[34] There are works belonging to the type known as parental advice, such as Peter Idley's *Instructions to His Son,*[35] the anonymous Scottish *Ratis Raving,*[36] both in verse, and the *Book of the Knight of La Tour-Landry,* written by the French author (1371-72) for his daughters, and twice rendered into English, once about 1450[37] and again by Caxton in 1484. The contemporary *Babees Book*[38] offers more limited instructions on social amenities and the behavior of young people, while John Russell's *Boke of Nurture,* the work of Humphrey, Duke of Gloucester's marshal, deals comprehensively with the whole training for service with a nobleman. Even such a collection as the volume commonly known as the *Book of St. Albans,* containing treatises on hawking and heraldry, and one on hunting by Dame Julians Barnes,[39] shows by its frequent reference to "gentill men" the class to whose interests it appealed.

Courtesy Literature

English prose in the fifteenth century found its most voluminous expres-

[31] See Henry N. MacCracken, "An English Friend of Charles of Orléans," *PMLA*, xxvi (1911). 142-180.

[32] Ed. James Gairdner (6v, 1904).

[33] Although he was not a part of the Norfolk group, mention should be made of John Tiptoft, Earl of Worcester, whose translation of Cicero's *De Amicitia* and Buonaccorso's *De Honestate* were printed by Caxton, and to whom other translations are questionably attributed. He was an enthusiast for the new learning, traveled in Italy buying books, and generously assisted Italian and English scholars. See R. J. Mitchell, *John Tiptoft, 1427-1470* (1938), and H. B. Lathrop, "The Translations of John Tiptoft," *MLN*, xli (1926). 496-501. It would be pleasant to pause over the early humanists—Grey, Gunthorpe, Flemming, and John Free. They are a part of English cultural history, but the importance of humanism for literature came later. See George R. Stephens, *The Knowledge of Greek in England in the Middle Ages* (Phila., 1933), W. F. Schirmer, *Der englische Frühhumanismus* (Leipzig, 1931), and R. Weiss, *Humanism in England during the Fifteenth Century* (Oxford, 1941).

[34] For the different types and a brief sketch of early courtesy literature see ch. 1 of John E. Mason, *Gentlefolk in the Making* (Phila., 1935).

[35] Ed. Charlotte D'Evelyn (1935; *MLA Monograph Ser.,* vi).

[36] Ed. J. R. Lumby (1870; *EETS,* 43), and, more recently, R. Girvan (1939; *STS,* 3rd ser., Vol. xi). The title is supposed to mean Rate's raving.

[37] Ed. Thomas Wright (1868, revised 1906; *EETS,* 33).

[38] This and other early courtesy books, including Russell's *Boke of Nurture* are ed. by F. J. Furnivall (1868; *EETS,* 32).

[39] Julians' Barnes was the name of a messuage near St. Albans. Dame Julians was presumably the wife or widow of the country gentleman who owned it. The familiar designation Dame Juliana Berners is an invention of eighteenth-century antiquarians, as is the legend that she was abbess of Sopwell priory. See the introduction to William Blades' edition (1901) and the communications of W. W. Skeat in the *Academy,* lxxv (1908). 87-88, 110-111. Much of the *Book* is based on Twici's *Treatise on Hunting* and other earlier works.

Pecock

sion in the work of Reginald Pecock (*c.* 1395-*c.* 1460). A brilliant career at Oxford recommended him to Humphrey, Duke of Gloucester, who brought him to court and later secured for him the bishopric of St. Asaph. His active and original mind was soon employed on numerous expository and controversial works. *The Reule of Crysten Religioun* [40] (1443) has been well described as "the first book of a *summa theologica.*" The *Donet,*[41] which followed soon afterwards, serves as an introduction to it and, at the same time, a more general guide to the Christian life. The *Poore Mennes Myrrour* is an extract from the first part of the *Donet* prepared for the "persone poorist in haver (possessions) and in witt." His most famous work is a systematic attempt to refute by reason, rather than authority, the views of the Lollards. It is known as the *Repressor of Over Much Blaming of the Clergy* [42] (*c.* 1450). Two other treatises remain, the *Folewer of the Donet* [43] (before 1454), which supplements the *Donet* with an exposition of the more intellectual virtues residing in the reason rather than the will, and *The Book of Faith* [44] (*c.* 1456), which defends the authority of the Church even if it be admitted that she can err. While Pecock's position was, generally speaking, orthodox enough, his daring and often tactless statements played into the hands of his enemies, and he had a genius for alienating even those who might have admired his ability and sympathized with his views. In the end his independence and self-confidence gave his opponents their opportunity and brought about his condemnation. He was forced to recant, or go to the stake, and he spent his closing years confined in Thorney abbey without books or writing materials. Though he escaped the flames, his works nevertheless were burnt, and all six that survive exist in unique manuscripts. Of late his prose style has come in for enthusiastic praise, but sober judgment can hardly acquiesce in too high an estimate of his purely literary importance.

Religious and Secular Works

Pecock's contemporary, William Lichfield, who was associated with him on several occasions, was parson of All Hallows the Great in Thames Street. He was famous as a preacher and left at his death in 1448, as we learn from a contemporary record, 3083 sermons. They have not come down to us, but we have from his hand an interesting version of a portion of the *Ancrene Riwle.*[45] Other writers at the same time were using prose for secular subjects. John Capgrave, an Austin friar of Lynn, when he died in 1464 was at work on a *Chronicle of England,*[46] which reaches the year 1417. That

[40] Ed. Wm. Cabell Greet (1927; *EETS,* 171). On Pecock see V. H. H. Green, *Bishop Reginald Pecock: A Study in Ecclesiastical History and Thought* (Cambridge, 1945).

[41] Ed. Elsie V. Hitchcock (1921; *EETS,* 156). The name of Donatus, author of the little catechism of Latin grammar (the *Ars Minor*) with which everybody began his study of Latin in the Middle Ages, came to designate a primer or elementary book on any subject.

[42] Ed. C. Babington (2v, 1860; Rolls Ser.).

[43] Ed. Elsie V. Hitchcock (1924; *EETS,* 164).

[44] Ed. J. L. Morison (Glasgow, 1909), with an excellent essay on Pecock's relation to fifteenth-century thought.

[45] He wrote also a poem called *The Complaint of God to Sinful Man* (*EETS,* xv. 198-232), preserved in more than a dozen manuscripts.

[46] Ed. F. C. Hingeston (1858; Rolls Ser.). He also wrote in Latin the *Nova Legenda Angliae,* ed. C. Horstmann (2v, Oxford, 1901), and, in English, lives of St. Augustine and Gilbert of Sempringham.

verse, however, was not completely discarded for such purposes is shown by the *Chronicle* of John Hardyng,[47] whose experience in the battle of Agincourt unfortunately did not improve his metrical aim. And we may note that while his best-known work, the *De Laudibus Legum Angliae* (1471), is in Latin, Sir John Fortescue, Chief Justice of the King's Bench, wrote in English *On the Governance of England,*[48] the first work in English on constitutional history, and other shorter pieces.

Of all the books of English fifteenth-century literature the best known is Malory's *Morte Darthur,* not only because it is still often read in its own right but because it has furnished the inspiration for the *Idylls of the King* and numerous other modern treatments of Arthurian story. Gathering together, as it does, the main body of Arthurian legends into one comprehensive narrative, it has enjoyed, except for a brief period in the days of Dryden and Pope, an almost unbroken popularity down to our own time. It is a work which obviously required much leisure to produce. Therefore, the author's closing request to his readers, "Pray for me, while I am on live that God send me good deliverance," is not without meaning when properly understood. For the book, as we now know, was written in prison, where Malory spent the major part of the last twenty years of his life. *Malory: Morte Darthur*

It is only in recent years that we have learned the full story of Sir Thomas Malory.[49] The date of his birth is unknown, but he was the son of a Warwickshire gentleman who died in 1433-34. Entering the service of Richard Beauchamp, Earl of Warwick, he was with the "Father of Courtesy" at Calais possibly in 1436. He was knighted before 1442 and served in the Parliament of 1445. By this time he had begun taking the law into his own hands, after the turbulent manner of his day, and was soon launched on a career of violence which led to a variety of felonies and misdemeanors, including assault, extortion, jail breaking, poaching, and a cattle raid. The two most serious offenses of which he was accused were lying in ambush with an armed band to murder Humphrey, Duke of Buckingham, and two attacks on Coombe abbey, in which with a hundred followers he broke down doors, terrorized the monks, and plundered the abbot's chests. For his various offenses he was kept in fairly continuous confinement from about 1451 on, and died, presumably in prison, on March 12, 1471. He was buried near Newgate, in a chapel at the Grey Friars. In view of his life it *Malory's Life*

[47] Ed. Henry Ellis (1812). On Hardyng, see C. L. Kingsford, *English Historical Literature in the Fifteenth Century* (Oxford, 1913), ch. vi.

[48] Ed. Charles Plummer (Oxford, 1885). See his *Works,* ed. Lord Clermont (2v, 1869).

[49] Our knowledge goes back to an identification made in 1894 by G. L. Kittredge, most fully presented in "Who Was Sir Thomas Malory?" *Harvard Studies & Notes in Phil. & Lit.,* v (1896). 85-166. A few details were added in 1922 by E. K. Chambers in his *Sir Thomas Malory* (*English Association Pamphlet,* No. 51). These two discussions led to the discovery of four documents, including a very important King's Bench indictment, which became the basis of Edward Hicks, *Sir Thomas Malory, His Turbulent Career* (Cambridge, Mass., 1928). A score of additional records were printed by the present writer in "Documenting Sir Thomas Malory," *Speculum,* VIII (1933). 3-29. A summary of our knowledge up to 1929 is given in an appendix to Eugène Vinaver, *Malory* (Oxford, 1929). See also George L. Kittredge, *Sir Thomas Malory* (Barnstable, privately printed, 1925).

is interesting to contemplate the profession at the close of the *Morte Darthur,* that he was "the servant of Jesu both day and night."

His
Sources

It is possible that the nearby house of the Grey Friars, which possessed a considerable library in Malory's day, supplied him with the books which he needed to solace his dreary hours in Newgate. For the *Morte Darthur* these books need not have been many. The thirteenth century had seen the compilation in France of long prose versions of the Arthurian stories, such as the prose *Tristan* and the cycle known as the Vulgate, or ordinary, version (made up of the *Estoire del Saint Graal,* a *Merlin* and its continuation,[50] an enormous *Lancelot,* a *Queste del Saint Graal,* and the *Morte Artu*) or its derivative, the Pseudo-Robert de Boron cycle. Such a collection, perhaps in three or four volumes, was Malory's principal source, although the precise combination of versions which he based his work on is not found in any surviving manuscript.[51] It is so, too, with his French *Tristan,* which must be reconstructed from the characteristics of three different manuscripts among those we know.[52] Malory made use of the alliterative *Morte Arthure* in English [53] and possibly of the stanzaic *Morte Arthur.* In general, his method was to abridge and condense his sources severely, especially by omitting minor episodes and digressions. The result is a much less discursive narrative, though it must be admitted that he sometimes left out important incidents and introduced unnecessary obscurities into his text.

The *Morte Darthur* was printed in 1485 by Caxton, with some misgivings about its credibility, and all subsequent editions have been hitherto derived from his.[54] One of the most interesting discoveries of recent years, however, is that of a manuscript in the Fellows' Library of Winchester College,[55] which is independent of Caxton's text and closer to Malory's original. It furnishes further proof of Malory's identity with the Warwickshire knight, renders more certain his use of the alliterative *Morte Arthure,* and makes it clear that Caxton condensed his text in many places. One may confidently expect that its publication will give us Malory's work in a still more acceptable form.

In spite of obvious defects the *Morte Darthur* is a great book. The older

50 Known as the *Suite de Merlin* or *Livre d'Artus.*

51 Malory's *Merlin,* for example, was in part similar to the Huth *Merlin,* edited by Gaston Paris and J. Ulrich (2v, 1886; *SATF*).

52 On this subject see Eugène Vinaver, *Le Roman de Tristan et Iseut dans l'œuvre de Thomas Malory* (Paris, 1925), and the same author's *Malory,* pp. 128-154. The latter is the best general discussion of Malory's sources, replacing that of H. Oskar Sommer in Vol. III of his edition of the *Morte Darthur* (1891) and Vida D. Scudder, *Le Morte Darthur of Sir Thomas Malory & Its Sources* (1917).

53 See above, p. 191.

54 The most scholarly edition, but still rather inaccurate, is that of H. Oskar Sommer (3v, 1889-91). An excellent text in modernized spelling is that of A. W. Pollard (2v, 1900). That in the Everyman's Library (2v, 1906) is also a good modernized reprint of Caxton's text, and there are of course many other editions and abridgments.

55 See the communications of W. F. Oakeshott to the London *Times,* Aug. 25, 1934 and to the *LTLS,* Sept. 27, 1934. The manuscript is more fully discussed by Eugène Vinaver, "Malory's *Morte Darthur* in the Light of a Recent Discovery," *Bull. of the John Rylands Library,* XIX (1935). 438-457. A new text of Malory based on this manuscript and Caxton, edited by Professor Vinaver, appeared in 1947 under the title *The Works of Sir Thomas Malory* (2ed, 3v, Oxford, 1963).

spirit of courtly love was something Malory either did not understand or *Style* found uncongenial. The romantic charm of his original was partly lost on *and* the blunt practical nature which our knowledge of his life suggests. But *Spirit* he had a genuine admiration for knighthood and chivalry, and would have endorsed the words of Caxton in his preface, that the book was offered "to the intent that noble men may see and learn the noble acts of chivalry, the gentle and virtuous deeds that some knights used in those days, by which they came to honor, and how they that were vicious were punished and oft put to shame and rebuke." Malory was himself a man of action and dispatch, and his style suggests such a man. He converted the long and involved periods of his French originals into simple, idiomatic prose. Where his original is diffuse, Malory is terse and forthright. Yet his short, firm sentences, while they give an impression of intentional economy, are seldom abrupt, but flow in a naturally modulated prose rhythm. The style of the *Morte Darthur,* when all is said and done, is Malory's greatest distinction, and it is wholly his own. But he has also preserved for subsequent generations a matchless body of romantic stories which might otherwise have remained the property of the Middle Ages, forgotten by modern poets and readers in the English-speaking world, as they have been forgotten in France.

As a symbol of the spread of English prose in the fifteenth century there is nothing more indicative than the enormous bulk of William Caxton's [56] many translations. A number of these have already been mentioned, but in addition to turning French romances into English he translated, generally from the French, such major works as the *Mirrour of the World* (1481), *Caxton* *The Golden Legend* [57] (1483), *The Royal Book* (1488), besides many titles only less well known.[58] But it is impossible to think of Caxton apart from his services as England's first printer, as the man who in 1476 set up the first printing press in England, who gave the world the *Morte Darthur* and put in print the *Canterbury Tales.* It is as a printer rather than as a writer that he is primarily remembered. He was a business man who, after a successful career in the commercial world, turned to the new method of producing books, and he remains a business man to the end. It is not to

[56] Born about 1422 in Kent, he was apprenticed in 1438 to Robert Lange, a London mercer who became Lord Mayor the following year. Caxton was later admitted to the Mercers' Company in 1453. About 1445 (possibly in 1441) he went abroad and lived for thirty years "in the contres of Braband and Flanders, Holland and Zeland." He became in time governor of the Merchant Adventurers at Bruges. In the early seventies he learned the art of printing at Cologne, and printed three books abroad. He seems to have returned to England towards the close of 1476 and set up his press at Westminster. His publishing (and writing) was done in the last twenty years of his life. His death occurred sometime in the year 1491. The best recent account of Caxton's life, with new documents, is that of W. J. B. Crotch in the Introduction to his edition of *The Prologues and Epilogues of William Caxton* (1928; *EETS,* 176). William Blades' *Life and Typography of William Caxton* (2v, 2ed., 1882) is a classic work. See also Seymour de Ricci, *A Census of Caxtons* (1909; *Bibl. Soc., Illustrated Monographs,* No. xv), E. Gordon Duff, *William Caxton* (1905) and, for a popular treatment, Nellie S. Aurner, *Caxton, Mirror of Fifteenth-Century Letters* (1926).

[57] On Caxton's sources see Pierce Butler, *Legenda Aurea—Légende Dorée—Golden Legend* (Baltimore, 1899), and p. 289, note 10.

[58] See A. T. Byles, "William Caxton as a Man of Letters," *Library,* 4 Ser., xv (1934). 1-25.

be doubted that he was genuinely fond of reading, but as a publisher his approach to literature was practical, and his style has the journeyman quality of one working at his job. He did not have a natural and instinctive sense of form. He seems never to have grasped the function of the sentence as a unit of thought. His ideas, unless controlled by his original, are joined one to another in a loose and at times unending chain, often without logical or syntactical cohesion. Compared with Trevisa, or Malory, or even Pecock, he cannot be said to have advanced the art of English prose. But for making available to English readers the most popular and useful books of his day— a truly noble five-foot shelf—his service to English culture is inestimable.

Popular Literature   In the preceding pages we have been surveying the writings of the fifteenth century which circulated in manuscripts and printed books. It remains to say something of the considerable body of popular literature which existed for the most part only in the memory of the people and which was passed on from generation to generation by word of mouth. We shall never know how much of this traditional literature there was, for most of the tales and folk songs are probably lost. But there is one type of folk song, the popular ballad, which lived on, and indeed still lives on in Britain and America, and which has been recorded in modern times to the extent of some three hundred examples.[59] One of the ballads is as old as the thirteenth century and some originated as late as the seventeenth, but they were clearly flourishing by the close of the Middle English period and it has become customary in literary histories to treat them there. They may not unfittingly close our discussion of the Middle Ages and serve as one of a number of links establishing continuity with modern times.

The Ballad   The popular ballad is one type of narrative song with certain clearly marked characteristics which distinguish it from other kinds of poetry. It is composed in simple stanzas, generally of two or four lines, suitable to a recurrent tune. Most commonly the stanza consists of alternate four and three stress lines riming on the second and fourth, as in the opening verse of *Sir Patrick Spens:*

> The king sits in Dumferling toune,
> Drinking the blude-red wine:
> "O whar will I get a guid sailor,
> To sail this ship of mine?"

The story is usually a single episode, the climax of events only briefly sketched or hinted at. "It begins," as Gray said of *Child Maurice,* "in the

[59] The great collection of British ballads is that of F. J. Child, *English and Scottish Popular Ballads* (5v, Boston, 1882-98). An excellent one-volume abridgment is H. C. Sargent and G. L. Kittredge, *English and Scottish Popular Ballads, edited from the Collection of Francis James Child* (Boston, 1904), with an introduction by Kittredge. Among the best discussions of the ballad are F. B. Gummere, *The Popular Ballad* (1907), Gordon H. Gerould, *The Ballad of Tradition* (1932), and, from the Scandinavian point of view, J. C. H. R. Steenstrup, *The Medieval Popular Ballad* (Eng. trans., 1914). Of wider scope and great value is W. J. Entwistle, *European Balladry* (1939). On the folk tale see Stith Thompson, *The Folktale* (1946).

fifth act of the play." Sometimes the story is revealed in a succession of brief scenes. The presentation is thus to a high degree dramatic, and the effect is one of condensation and severe economy. Ballad art is always objective, with no marks of personal authorship and no attempt to analyze or interpret the action or the characters of the story. In many ballads there is a refrain, and a frequent characteristic is the habit of repeating a stanza with slight modifications that advance the story, a device Gummere aptly called incremental repetition. In general the ballad reflects the simple direct approach to a story characteristic of unlettered people, the people who through the centuries have made the ballads what they are when they become known to us.

Most readers of this book will be familiar with some ballads, such as *Edward* and *Barbara Allen,* and will recognize in them the characteristic tendency to tragedy which the ballads as a whole show. A simple dénouement often serves the purpose of such a theme, as when in two stanzas the ladies in *Sir Patrick Spens* sit hopelessly *Tendency to Tragedy*

> Waiting for thair ain deir lords,
> For they'll se thame na mair—

or when we are told of *Bonnie James Campbell:*

> Saddled and briddled
> and booted rade he;
> Toom hame cam the saddle,
> but never cam he.

Many of the ballads, like *Edward* mentioned above, concern domestic tragedies of one sort or another. In *Babylon* two out of three sisters are killed by a young outlaw before he learns from the third that he is their brother. *Twa Sisters* is the age-old tragedy of the younger sister preferred to the elder, while *Lord Thomas and Fair Annet* tells the equally old story of the rivalry between wealthy bride and lowly sweetheart. *Child Maurice* is doubly tragic in that the husband, thinking to kill his wife's lover, learns that he has slain her only son. The situation was dramatic enough to be made in the eighteenth century into Home's tragedy of *Douglas.* Outraged propriety leads "the cruel brother" in the ballad of that name to revenge himself on his sister on her marriage day, because she forgot to ask his consent to the marriage:

> She leand her oer the saddle-bow,
> To give him a kiss ere she did go.

> He has taen a knife, baith long and sharp,
> And stabbd that bonny bride to the heart.

Love naturally occupies a prominent place in the ballads, and more often than not it is the sorrow and tragedy of love rather than the happy fulfill- *Love* ment of young hope. Remorse over deserting a sweetheart leads the ballad of *Fair Margaret and Sweet William* to a simple, if obvious, conclusion:

> Fair Margaret dy'd today, today,
>   Sweet William he dy'd the morrow;
> Fair Margaret dy'd for pure true love,
>   Sweet William he dy'd for sorrow.

The lady in *Fair Janet* must be separated from her lover, to whom she had borne a son:

> "O we maun part this love, Willie,
>   That has been lang between;
> There's a French lord coming oer the sea,
>   To wed me wi a ring."

There is a touch of melodrama in the close, when she gets up from child-bed to go through with the wedding but falls dead while dancing with her true love. One of the finest examples of the ballad way of telling a story is *Lord Randal*. Each stanza follows the same formula:

> "O where ha you been, Lord Randal, my son?
> And where ha you been, my handsome young man?"
> "I ha been at the greenwood; mother, mak my bed soon:
> For I'm wearied wi hunting, and fain wad lie down."

Slowly, in spite of his evasive answers, the mother learns that her son has been poisoned by the girl he loves. Jealousy and revenge motivate the tragedy in *Young Waters* and in *Young Hunting*. Not all the love stories, however, end tragically. The daring and loyalty of the lady are sometimes rewarded, as in *Young Beichan* or *The Gay Goshawk*. Even seduction, though sometimes successfully resisted, when carried out does not always end unhappily for either the seducer or the seduced. A third of all the ballads deal with love, and naturally not many of the familiar situations fail of treatment.

Outlaw Life and Other Themes   The ballads reflect, of course, the social conditions of the period and the region that produced many of them. Border feuds find expression in the fine ballad of *Captain Car* and in *Kinmont Willie*, while two of the most famous ballads, *The Battle of Otterburn* and *The Hunting of the Cheviot*, tell in different ways the fight between Percy and Douglas which in one version or the other moved Sir Philip Sidney's heart "more than with a trumpet." There are ballads, too, of outlaw life such as *Johnny Armstrong* and *Adam Bell, Clim of the Clough, and William of Cloudesly*, besides the group concerned with the more famous Robin Hood. The supernatural enters into such ballads as *Thomas Rymer* and *Clerk Colvin*, whose adventure with a mermaid proves his undoing.[60] Sometimes the ballad turns journalistic and reports a local event as in *Bessie Bell and Mary Gray*, or the sixteenth-century *Mary Hamilton*, which records the punishment meted out for a case of child-murder at the court of Mary Queen of Scots. On

---

[60] See Lowry C. Wimberly, *Folklore in the English & Scottish Ballads* (Chicago, 1928).

rare occasions the theme is a humorous incident, such as the delightful revelation of human nature in *Get Up and Bar the Door*.

Best known probably of all the ballad subjects are Robin Hood and his *Robin* carefree yeomen and their varied adventures in the "merry greenwood." *Hood* His fame was known to the author of *Piers Plowman,* but how much earlier we cannot say. He is the people's counterpart of aristocratic heroes like Sir Gawain. Courteous, ever ready for an adventure, and with a rough and ready sense of humor, he is the champion of the weak and the friend of honest poverty. As an outlaw he is free from the ordinary restraints of law. Though loyal to the king, he helps himself freely to the king's deer, and levies with a clear conscience on knights and barons, bishops and abbots, the silver which he bestows with equal readiness on those who need it. He takes the law into his own hand and deals out rough justice on the spot, as when in *Robin Hood and Allen a Dale* he not only prevents the marriage of Allen's sweetheart to an old man but unites the lovers in a very unecclesiastical ceremony. He has, of course, the physical virtues which befit the yeoman ideal, such as uncanny skill with the bow and the long staff, though he often meets his match and generously acknowledges the superior strength or craft of his opponent. His life is marked by frequent encounters with the sheriff of Nottingham, and if he generally comes off from them successfully, not the least reason is his sincere and unfailing devotion to Our Lady. More than thirty ballads, some early and some late, recount his lively adventures. By about 1500, and perhaps earlier, a number of episodes were woven together into a miniature epic printed as *A Gest of Robyn Hode*.[61]

The origin of the ballad is a question on which opinion has gradually *Ballad* shifted.[62] The concept of the folk forming a homogeneous community, *Origins* with a common fund of experience and common responses to whatever affects the community, expressing as a group the emotion felt by all, not only in rhythmic movement and dance, but in words which result in a record of the event celebrated, was widely held a generation ago. *Das Volk dichtet,* it was said, and with certain modern instances of group composition which could be pointed to in the Faroe islands, among Negroes in the southern part of the United States, and elsewhere, it was possible to erect a communal theory for the origin of the ballad. The refrain, which was considered a primitive and essential feature of the earliest ballads, could be sung by the group, while a leader and a few of the more inventive, or more vocal, contributed most of the verses. Although it would be rash to deny the possibility that a few of our ballads originated in this way, it cannot be proved, and such an origin is unlikely in the case of most of the English ballads that have been preserved. While ballads are doubtless older than our earliest

---

61 For the literature of the subject see J. Harris Gable, *Bibliography of Robin Hood* (Lincoln, Neb., 1939; *Univ. of Nebraska Stud. in Lang., Lit., and Crit.,* No. 17).

62 For the older view see the discussions of Kittredge and Gummere, as above, and F. B. Gummere, "The Ballad and Communal Poetry," *Harvard Studies & Notes in Phil. & Lit.,* v (1896). 41-56, and *The Beginnings of Poetry* (1901). For the argument against the communal theory see Louise Pound, *Poetic Origins and the Ballad* (1921).

recorded specimen, the *Judas* found in a late thirteenth-century manuscript, the English ballads do not reflect so simple a social structure as the communal theory necessarily assumes.

Effects of Oral Transmission

But if the ballads were not written by the people acting as a group, they have certainly been rewritten by them, if we may use the word of people who had seldom learned the use of a pen. In the process of oral transmission over the centuries the ballads that lived in the memories and on the lips of the people have been slowly transformed. The numerous versions that have been collected of some of the more popular ballads show that this transformation has not always been for the better. But there can be little doubt that in other cases the selective memory of the people has sifted the matter of a ballad, dropping out non-essentials and leaving the main features of the incident or story in greater relief. If the ballad is not communal in origin, it is, as has been well said, communal in transmission,[63] and owes some of its most distinctive qualities to the genius of the folk.

Ballad Tunes

No one who has not heard ballads sung can have a just appreciation of their effectiveness. Ballad melodies,[64] as traditional as the words, not only contribute greatly to their appeal but by their slow tempo and leisurely movement allow each stanza to work its influence on the listener. Ballads were never meant to be scanned quickly with the eye. When printed in books they are like museum specimens, interesting and often beautiful, but revealing only a small part of their true character and charm.[65]

[63] See the discussion of G. H. Gerould, "The Making of Ballads," *MP*, xxi (1923). 15-28.

[64] Sigurd B. Hustvedt, *A Melodic Index of Child's Ballad Tunes* (Berkeley, 1936; *Pub. Univ. of Calif. at Los Angeles in Lang. and Lit.*, Vol. i, No. 2), and the music included in many of the works mentioned in the following note.

[65] British ballads are still being sung in America, particularly in communities more or less isolated, by the descendants of English and Scotch-Irish settlers who brought them to this country in the eighteenth century. An excellent collection of such versions, with the music, will be found in Cecil J. Sharp, *English Folk-Songs from the Southern Appalachians* (2ed., 2v, 1932). Arthur K. Davis, Jr., *Traditional Ballads of Virginia* (Cambridge, Mass., 1929), contains 51 ballads in 650 versions. A similar collection is Phillips Barry, Fannie H. Eckstorm, and Mary W. Smyth, *British Ballads from Maine* (New Haven, 1929). Many versions of British and American ballads may be found in Reed Smith, *South Carolina Ballads* (Cambridge, Mass., 1928), with interesting evidence of the communal process, John H. Cox, *Folk-Songs of the South* (Cambridge, Mass., 1925), Arthur P. Hudson, *Folksongs of Mississippi and Their Background* (Chapel Hill, 1936), W. Roy Mackenzie, *The Quest of the Ballad* (Princeton, 1919) and *Ballads and Sea Songs from Nova Scotia* (Cambridge, Mass., 1928), Emelyn E. Gardner and Geraldine J. Chickering, *Ballads and Songs of Southern Michigan* (Ann Arbor, 1939). The student interested in American folk poetry should consult Louise Pound, *American Ballads and Songs* (1922), John A. Lomax, *Cowboy Songs and Other Frontier Ballads* (1910; new ed., 1938), John A. and Alan Lomax, *American Ballads and Folk Songs* (1934) and *Our Singing Country* (1941), Carl Sandburg, *The American Songbag* (1927), Roland P. Gray, *Songs and Ballads of the Maine Lumber Jacks, with Other Songs from Maine* (Cambridge, Mass., 1924), Earl C. Beck, *Songs of the Michigan Lumberjacks* (Ann Arbor, 1941), the delightful volumes of Dorothy Scarborough, *On the Trail of Negro Folk-Song* (1925), and *A Song Catcher in Southern Mountains* (1937), and Newman I. White, *American Negro Folk-Songs* (Cambridge, Mass., 1928). For further references see Alan Lomax and Sidney R. Cowell, *American Folk Song and Folk Lore: A Regional Bibliography* (1942).

BIBLIOGRAPHICAL
SUPPLEMENT

Boldface numbers refer to pages in text

BOOK I: THE MIDDLE AGES
Part I. The Old English Period (to 1100)
I. Folk, State, and Speech

3 At this writing the latest book-length survey of the Old English period is S. B. Greenfield's *Critical History of Old English Literature* (1965), with generous bibliographical footnotes. See also his bibliography of Old English in D. M. Zenser, *Guide to English Literature* . . . (1961). W. Bonser's *Anglo-Saxon and Celtic Bibliography 450-1087* (Oxford, 1957) excludes "all material dealing with literature and linguistics as such" (viii). A second ed. of Stenton's *Anglo-Saxon England* came out in 1947. See also P. H. Blair, *An Introduction to Anglo-Saxon England* (Cambridge, 1956); D. Whitelock, *The Beginnings of English Society* (1952); N. R. Ker, *Catalogue of MSS Containing Anglo-Saxon* (Oxford, 1957); P. Clemoes (ed.), *The Anglo-Saxons* (1959); and K. Sisam, *Studies in the History of Old English Literature* (Oxford, 1953). K. Jackson's *Language and History in Early Britain* (Cambridge, Mass., 1953) deals chiefly with Celtic matters, as do, in part, C. Fox and B. Dickins (eds.), *The Early Cultures of Northwest Europe* (1950). On the Sutton Hoo archeological finds see C. Green, *Sutton Hoo* (1963) and the writings listed by F. P. Magoun and J. B. Bessinger in *Speculum,* xxix (1954). 116-124 and xxxiii (1958). 515-522 respectively.

4 See also J. Godfrey, *The Church in Anglo-Saxon England* (Cambridge, 1962).

5 A short Old English grammar, with special attention to syntax, is that of R. Quirk and C. L. Wrenn (1955; 2ed, 1958). A longer one, for more advanced students, is that of A. Campbell (Oxford, 1959).

11 A fuller sketch of Old English times is that of K. Malone, *Emory University Quar.,* v (1949). 129-148.

II. Anglo-Latin Writings

12 M. L. W. Laistner's *Thought and Letters in Western Europe A.D. 500-900* (2ed., 1957) throws light on Anglo-Latin writers and their sources of information.

13 On Aldhelm see also E. R. Curtius, *Europäische Literatur und Lateinisches Mittelalter* (Bern, 1958), pp. 53-54, 454-455.

15 Two MSS of Bede's *Historia* . . . are now available in the series *Early*

English MSS in Facsimile: the Leningrad MS, ed. O. Arngart, and the Moore MS, ed. P. H. Blair (Copenhagen, 1952 and 1959). On Bede see also Curtius, *op. cit.,* pp. 54-55. Bede's *Opera de Temporibus* have been edited by C. W. Jones (Cambridge, Mass., 1943). For Bede studies in recent years see W. F. Bolton, "A Bede Bibliography," *Traditio,* xviii (1962). 436-445.

16 Bede's metrical life of Cuthbert has been edited by W. Jaager (Leipzig, 1935); his prose life, with the anonymous life, by B. Colgrave (Cambridge, 1940). The Whitby life of Pope Gregory has been translated by C. W. Jones, *Saints' Lives and Chronicles in Early England* (Ithaca, N.Y. 1947), pp. 95-121.

18 Eadmer's life of Anselm is now to be had in a separate edition by R. W. Southern (1963); see also Southern's *St Anselm and His Biographer* (1963). The following recent editions are noteworthy: F. Barlow, *Vita Ædwardi Regis* (1962) and A. Campbell, *Chronicon Æthelweardi* (1962).

III. The Old Tradition: Poetic Form

20 For the Germanic background see also J. de Vries, *Die geistige Welt der Germanen,* (2ed., Hall/Saale, 1945). On speakings, see also H. M. Chadwick, *The Heroic Age* (Cambridge, 1912), of which *The Growth of Literature* is an expansion. The studies of Mr and Mrs Chadwick were carried further by Milman Parry in his papers on Homer (see *Harvard Stud. in Classical Phil.,* xli. 73-147 and xliii. 1-50 and *Trans. Amer. Phil. Assoc.,* lxiv. 179-197) and by Parry's disciple A. B. Lord in *The Singer of Tales* (Cambridge, Mass., 1960), a work which, like the Chadwicks' book (ii. 299-456) and Parry's papers, leans heavily on Yugoslavic speakings. Parry's method in isolating the set phrases ("formulas") of Homeric diction has been applied to Old English poetry by F. P. Magoun and others, with results still in the stage of learned debate. See Magoun's paper in *Speculum,* xxviii (1953). 446-467 and R. Quirk's critique in *Early English and Norse Studies presented to Hugh Smith in Honour of his sixtieth Birthday* (1963), pp. 150-171. The Chadwicks summed things up as follows (iii. 753): "The diction of heroic narrative poetry tends everywhere to abound in static epithets, descriptive circumlocutions, kennings, repetitions and recurrent formulae." This statement of the case will doubtless be generally accepted. And Cædmon, the earliest English poet known to us by name, was an illiterate singer as Bede tells the tale. But it need not follow that all or even many of the Old English poems committed to writing were composed by such singers. Cædmon's was a special case: his songs were written down (from dictation) because thought to be divinely inspired, but speakings as a rule did not win written record. Indeed, why should they? The clerical poets made free use, naturally enough, of the conventional poetic diction familiar to them from childhood. In so doing they were following in the steps of Cædmon, who had turned the native English way of versifying into a tool for God's service; see p. 60. But their compositions, made to be read aloud, were writings, not speakings.

On the runes see R. W. V. Elliott, *Runes: An Introduction* (Manchester, 1959); K. Schneider, *Die germanischen Runennamen* (Meisenheim, 1956); and R. Derolez, *Runica Manuscripta* (Bruges, 1954).

21 The Franks Casket is better dated in the sixth century. See K. Schneider in *Festschrift für Walther Fischer* (Heidelberg, 1959), pp. 4-20.

23 A more recent metrical study is that of A. J. Bliss, *The Metre of Beowulf* (Oxford, 1958); reviewed by W. P. Lehmann in *JEGP*, LIX (1960). 137-142, by G. Storms in *ES*, XLVI (1965). 418-422.

29 See H. Marquart, *Die altenglischen Kenningar* (Halle/Saale, 1938); reviewed in *JEGP*, XXXVIII (1939). 282-285 and *MLN*, LV (1940). 73-74.

30 On the supposed Old English poetic *koiné* see F. Klaeber, *Beowulf* (3ed, Boston, 1936). lxxxviii and K. Malone in *Revue belge de Philologie et d'Histoire*, XLII (1964). 155-156.

IV. The Old Tradition: Popular Poetry

32 A second ed. of K. Malone's *Widsith* is now in print (Copenhagen, 1962).

34 On the Runic Poem see K. Schneider, *Die germanischen Runennamen* (Meisenheim, 1956), *passim*.

35 Note also F. E. Harmer, *Anglo-Saxon Writs* (Manchester, 1952).

38 Grendon has been superseded by G. Storms, *Anglo-Saxon Magic* (The Hague, 1948). See also K. Schneider, *Festschrift . . . Spira* (Heidelberg, 1961), pp. 38-56.

41 K. Schneider takes *eorþan modor* (rightly, no doubt) for a compound word; see his *Runennamen* 605 top. One may compare the *fœmnanþegn* of *Beowulf* 2059.

43 On words of wisdom in *Beowulf* see K. Malone, *Humaniora, Essays honoring Archer Taylor* (Locust Valley, N.Y., 1960), pp. 180-194.

V. The Old Tradition: Courtly Poetry

45 A second ed. of K. Malone's *Widsith* has come out in the series *Anglistica* (XIII, Copenhagen, 1962). See also his papers in *Festschrift für L. L. Hammerich* (Copenhagen, 1962), pp. 161-167 and *Speculum*, XXXIX (1964). 35-44.

48 K. Malone's *Deor* is now in its fourth edition (1966). See also H. Hallmundsson, *American-Scandinavian Rev.*, L (1962). 267-271; M. W. Bloomfield, *PMLA*, LXXIX (1964). 534-541; and N. E. Eliason, *SP*, LXII (1965). 495-509.

50 From *Beowulf* 1125-1128 one gathers that the *wealaf* after swearing allegiance to Finn are released by him and take ship for Denmark, all but Hengest, whom Finn holds (as hostage?); see K. Malone, *Festschrift für Walther Fischer* (Heidelberg, 1959), pp. 1-3.

57 On *Maldon* see now *CL*, XIV (1962). 23-35 (by J. B. Bessinger) and 53-70 (by R. W. V. Elliott).

VI. Religious Poetry: Cædmon and his School

60 See C. L. Wrenn, *The Poetry of Cædmon* (1947) and the reviews in *MLR*, XLIII (1948). 250-252 and *MA*, XVII (1948). 56-57. On Bede's account of Cædmon see F. P. Magoun, *Speculum*, XXX (1955). 49-63 and K. Malone, *MLN*, LXXVI (1961). 193-195.

61 A later edition of the Old English *Exodus* is that of E. B. Irving (New Haven, 1953), reviewed by E. V. K. Dobbie in *JEGP*, LIII (1954). 229-231; by S. Potter in *MA*, XXV (1956). 30-33; and by C. L. Wrenn in *RES*, VI (1955). 184-189.

62 B. F. Huppé in his *Doctrine and Poetry: Augustine's Influence on Old English Poetry* (Albany, N.Y., 1959) includes a close study of *Genesis A*. On *Genesis* and *Exodus* see further *Anglia*, LXX (1952). 285-294; LXXV (1957). 1-34; LXXVII (1959). 1-11; and LXXX (1962). 363-378.

67 The latest editions of *Judith* are those of B. J. Timmer (1952) and E. V. K. Dobbie, in Krapp-Dobbie IV.

68 A tenth-century dating of *Judith* is now usual: see Timmer, ed., pp. 6-11, Dobbie, ed., p. lxiv, and H. M. Flasdieck, *Anglia*, LXIX (1950). 270. The poem as it has come down to us is in the West Saxon dialect, with some admixture of Anglian forms. These were formerly explained as relics of an Anglian original but are otherwise accounted for (not very convincingly) by F. Tupper and his followers; see *JEGP*, XI (1912). 82-89. The theory of a poetic *koiné* is likewise dubious; see F. Klaeber, *Beowulf* (3ed.), p. lxxxviii.

VII. Religious Poetry: Cynewulf and his School

70 On Cynewulf's poetry see also Marguerite-Marie Dubois, *Les Éléments Latins dans la Poésie Religieuse de Cynewulf* (Paris, 1943) and Claes Schaar, *Critical Studies in the Cynewulf Group* (Lund, 1949), with K. Malone's review of the latter in *Anglia*, LXX (1952). 444-450. Later editions: R. Woolf, *Juliana* (1955) and P. O. E. Gradon, *Cynewulf's Elene* (1958). *The Fates of the Apostles* follows *Andreas* in the Vercelli Book and the two poems are usually edited together, though they are otherwise unconnected.

74 On the runic passages of Cynewulf's poems see also R. W. V. Elliott's paper in *ES*, XXXIV (1953). 49-57 and K. Schneider, *Die germanischen Runennamen* (Meisenheim, 1956), pp. 548-557.

75 A recent ed. of *Andreas* and *Fates of the Apostles* is that of K. R. Brooks, reviewed by R. Willard in *MP*, LXII (1963). 45-51 and K. Malone, *Revue belge de Philologie et d'Histoire*, XLII (1964). 154-160. An important article by Hans Schabram, "*Andreas* und *Beowulf*," *Nachrichten der Giessener Hochschulgesellschaft*, XXXIV (1965). 201-218, attacks vigorously the view that the *Andreas* poet used *Beowulf*. For Felix's life of Guthlac see now the definitive ed. by B. Colgrave (Cambridge, 1956).

76 A recent ed. of *Phoenix* is that of N. F. Blake (Manchester, 1964); see also his paper in *Anglia*, LXXX (1962). 50-62.

VIII. Religious Poetry: Poems on Various Themes

78 The Dickins-Ross *Rood* is now in its fourth edition (1963).

79 The Advent poem has now been edited by J. J. Campbell with the title *The Advent Lyrics of the Exeter Book* (Princeton, 1959).

81 *Doomsday A* is to be dated early in the eleventh century according to Max

Förster, *Anglia*, LXXIII (1955). 7. F. Mossé, *Études Germaniques*, III (1948). 157-165, argues that *Doomsday C* had an Old Saxon original.

83 For the passages in *Solomon and Saturn* (first poem) that incorporate runes see K. Schneider, *op. cit.*, pp. 558-569. On *Gifts of Men* see J. E. Cross, *Neophilologus*, XLVI (1962). 66-70. *Falseness of Men* is called *Homiletic Fragment I* in Krapp-Dobbie II. 59 and *Admonition* is called *Homiletic Fragment II* in Krapp-Dobbie III. 224. For *Seafarer* see now the ed. of I. L. Gordon (1960). For editions of *Wanderer* and *Riming Poem* see Krapp-Dobbie III. 134-137 and 166-169. On *Wanderer* and *Seafarer* see also the following: D. Whitelock in the Chadwick Memorial Studies, *Early Cultures of N.W. Europe* (1950), pp. 259-272; R. M. Lumiansky, *Neophilologus*, XXXIV (1950). 104-112; S. B. Greenfield, *JEGP*, L (1951). 451-465; E. G. Stanley, *Anglia*, LXXIII (1955). 413-466; G. V. Smithers, *MA*, XXVI (1957). 137-153 and XXVIII (1959). 1-22; W. Erzgräber, *Festschrift . . . Spira* (1961), pp. 57-85; and A. A. Prins, *Neophilologus*, XLVIII (1964). 237-251.

85 It is now fashionable to date *Riming Poem, Wanderer,* and *Seafarer* late or latish and to doubt their Anglian origin; see esp. Mrs. Gordon's ed. *Seafarer*. But E. Ekwall, *Philologica: the Malone Anniversary Studies* (1949), p. 28, and H. M. Flasdieck, *Anglia*, LXIX (1950). 167-171, keep the older view and strengthen it with new evidence; see also G. V. Smithers, *English and Germanic Stud.*, IV (1951-1952). 84-85, who favors a latish date but a "Northern" origin for *Wanderer*. The Benedictine Office is now available in an edition by J. Ure; see Chapter x (Literary Prose) below. For the *Paris Psalter* see now B. Colgrave's edition in *Early English MSS in Facsimile*, VIII (Copenhagen, 1958).

IX. Secular Poetry

88 On the date of the *Durham Poem* see *JEGP*, LXI (1962). 591-594. *Ruin* is included in R. F. Leslie (ed.), *Three Old English Elegies* (Manchester, 1961). On the riddles, see the following: for text and notes, Krapp-Dobbie III; for text and translation, the *EETS* ed. of the Exeter Book; for the Leiden Riddle, R. W. Zandvoort, *English and Germanic Stud.*, III (1949-1950). 42-56; for other riddles, *Neophilologus*, XXX (1946). 126-127, XXXI (1947). 145-158; *PMLA*, LXI (1946). 620-623, 910-915, LXII (1947). 1-8, LXIII (1948). 3-6, LXIV (1949). 884 888; *MLN*, LXII (1947). 558-559, LXV (1950). 93-100; *Philologica: the Malone Anniversary Studies* (1949), pp. 1-19; *MA*, XXI (1952). 36-37; *SP*, XLIX (1952). 553-565; *ES*, XXXV (1954). 259-262; *RES*, IX (1958). 241-252; and *MS*, XX (1958). 93-97.

90 On *Eadwacer* and *Wife's Lament* as Old English representatives of the widespread *Frauenlied* genre see K. Malone, *CL*, XIV (1962). 106-117. *Wife's Lament* is included in R. F. Leslie (ed.), *Three Old English Elegies* (Manchester, 1961).

91 *Lover's* or *Husband's Message* is included in Leslie's book mentioned above. A. C. Bouman, *Patterns in Old English . . . Literature* (Leiden, 1962), tries to reconstruct a story pattern which, he thinks, underlies *Wife's Lament* and *Lover's* or *Husband's Message* but his pattern is not convincing, depending as it does on a reading in the latter poem which R. E. Kaske has shown to be highly unlikely; see *MA*, XXXIII (1964). 204-206. See also K. Malone, *ES*, XLVI (1965). 492-493. On the runes in *Lover's Message* see K. Schneider, *Die germanischen Runennamen* (Meisenheim, 1956), pp. 570-574.

92 A second ed. of Zupitza's *Beowulf* with new facsimile photographs and an introductory note (v-xvii) by Norman Davis is now available in the *EETS* series, No. 245 (1959). See also *Early English MSS in Facsimile*, I (1951) and XII (1963), both edited by K. Malone. Heyne-Schücking's *Beowulf* (ed. E. von Schaubert) is in its eighteenth edition (1963), and Chambers' *Beowulf, An Introduction* is in its third (1959), with a supplement by C. L. Wrenn, whose own *Beowulf* edition (1953) was issued in revised and enlarged form in 1958. A good prose translation is that of J. R. Clark Hall, as revised and annotated by C. L. Wrenn, with a Preface on words and meters by J. R. R. Tolkien (1940). Critical studies of *Beowulf* are too many to be listed here, but the following cannot go without mention: D. Whitelock, *The Audience of Beowulf* (Oxford, 1951); K. Sisam, *The Structure of Beowulf* (Oxford, 1965); and A. G. Brodeur, *The Art of Beowulf* (Berkeley, 1959), reviewed by J. C. Pope in *Speculum*, XXXVII (1962). 411-417, by Ad. Bonjour in *ES*, XLIII (1962). 501-504, and by K. Malone in *MLN*, LXXV (1960). 347-353. See also Bonjour's *Twelve 'Beowulf' Papers 1940-1960 . . .* (Geneva, 1962), Charles Donahue, "Beowulf and Christian Tradition," *Traditio*, XXI (1965). 55-116, and L. E. Nicholson (ed.), *An Anthology of Beowulf Criticism* (South Bend, Indiana, 1963), the last but not the least item of the list.

93 On the date of *Beowulf* see also G. Bond, *SP*, XL (1943). 481-493 and H. M. Flasdieck, *Anglia*, LXIX (1950). 135-171; Flasdieck concludes that "the date of the original MS of *Beowulf* cannot be later than c. 725 and, more probably, is between 675 and 700" (p. 171). But D. Whitelock, *op. cit.*, contends that the poem may have been composed as late as the latter half of the eighth century.

X. Literary Prose

96 On English prose before Alfred note R. J. Menner's dictum: "Prose must have been cultivated in the Anglian kingdoms before the time of Alfred, . . ." (*Philologica: the Malone Anniversary Studies*, p. 56). In the paper from which this dictum is taken Menner shows that the Blickling homilies were of Anglian origin (they have come down to us in a tenth-century Saxonized version) but he does not venture to date their composition. Flasdieck however sees no difficulty in setting this date "as early as the beginning of the 8th c." (*Anglia*, LXIX. 168).

97 Authoritative translations of the *Old English Annals* are those of G. N. Garmonsway, in Everyman's Library, No. 624 (1953) and of S. I. Tucker, edited by D. Whitelock with D. C. Douglas (1961). The editor's Introduction to the latter translation is the latest if not the last word on the origins and history of the versions. Miss Whitelock also gives us the most recent study of the Old English Bede, in *Proc. Brit. Acad.* XLVIII (1963 for 1962). 57-90. The Bodleian MS Hatton 20, with Alfred's translation of Gregory's *Regula Pastoralis*, has been published in the series *Early English MSS in Facsimile*, VI (Copenhagen, 1956), ed. N. R. Ker, and in the same series (III, 1953) we have the Tollemache Orosius (BM MS Add. 47967), ed. A. Campbell. This translation has been compared with the Latin text by S. Potter, *Anglia*, LXXI (1953). 385-437 and by J. Bately, *Classica et Mediaevalia*, XVII (1961). 69-105; the latter, who studied a large number of codices and established many variant readings hitherto unknown to Alfredian

scholarship, has shown that Alfred departed from his Latin text much less often than had previously been thought. On Alfred's *Blostman* see S. Potter in *Philologica: the Malone Anniversary Studies* (Baltimore, 1949), pp. 25-30. On the West Saxon prose translation of Psalms 1-50 see now J. I'a Bromwich, *The Early Cultures of Northwest Europe* (Cambridge, 1950), pp. 289-303; he tells us that "King Alfred has just as good a claim to the translation of the prose portion of the Paris Psalter as he has to the Cura Pastoralis and the Boethius" (103).

101 Ælfric's *De temporibus anni* (in English despite its title) is to be had in H. Henel's ed. of 1942; see C. L. Wrenn's review in *RES*, xx (1944). 232-234. On Ælfric's rhythmic alliterative prose see esp. O. Funke, *Anglia*, LXXX (1962). 9-36 and *ES*, XLIII (1962). 311-318. Marguerite-Marie Dubois's *Ælfric, Sermonnaire, Docteur et Grammairien* (Paris, 1943) is a full-scale study.

103 In recent years much work has been done on Wulfstan. See esp. D. Whitelock (ed.), *Sermo Lupi ad Anglos*, 3ed. (1963), with bibliography, which brings Wulfstan scholarship and criticism up to date in the form best suited to the student. Special mention, besides, must be made of the following: A. McIntosh, "Wulfstan's Prose," *Proc. Brit. Acad.*, XXXV (1949). 109-142; K. Jost, *Wulfstanstudien* (Bern, 1950); K. Jost (ed.), *Die 'Institutes of Polity, Civil and Ecclesiastical'* (Bern, 1959); D. Bethurum, *The Homilies of Wulfstan* (Oxford, 1957); J. Ure, *The Benedictine Office* . . . (Edinburgh, 1957); and P. Clemoes, "The Old English Benedictine Office . . ." in *Anglia*, LXXVIII (1960). 265-283. The *Blickling Homilies* MS (now owned by W. H. Scheide of Princeton, N.J.) is now to be had in facsimile: *Early English MSS in Facsimile*, x (Copenhagen, 1960), ed. R. Willard. On the dialect in which the homilies were composed see above (suppl. to p. 96).

104 A saint's life of some importance recently edited (though not for the first time) is that of St. Chad (Amsterdam, 1953), ed. R. Vleeskruyer; see A. Campbell's review in *MA*, XXIV (1955). 52-56. Of interest, too, is the first article of the Nowell codex, a fragment of a life of St. Christopher, ed. S. Rypins (1924; *EETS*, 161), pp. 68-76; see K. Sisam, *Studies in the History of Old English Literature* (Oxford, 1953), pp. 65-72 and K. Malone (ed.), *The Nowell Codex* (Copenhagen, 1963), pp. 114-115, 119. *Bald's Leech Book*, on which Cockayne drew for the second volume of his *Leechdoms* . . . , is now available in the series *Early English MSS in Facsimile*, v (Copenhagen, 1955), ed. C. E. Wright. The Old English *Apollonius* has been edited by J. Raith (Munich, 1956) and by P. Goolden (Oxford, 1958).

Part II. The Middle English Period (1100-1500)

I. General Characteristics of the Period

109 A new edition of Wells' *Manual* is in preparation under the general editorship of J. Burke Severs. There are new editions of Renwick and Orton (1952) and Loomis's *Reading List* (1948). To the Brown-Robbins *Index* there is now a Supplement by Rossell H. Robbins and John Cutler (Lexington, Ky.,

1965) as well as William Ringler, "A Bibliography and First-Line Index of English Verse Printed through 1500: A Supplement to Brown and Robbins' *Index of Middle English Verse*," *Papers of the Bibl. Soc. of America*, XLIX (1955). 153-180. The texts and editions cited in the *Middle English Dictionary* offer a very useful list, available separately: *A Bibliography of Middle English Texts*, by Margaret S. Ogden, Charles E. Palmer, and Richard L. McKelvey (Ann Arbor, 1956). The *Annual Bibliography of English Language and Literature*, published by the Modern Humanities Research Assoc., and the Annual Bibliography compiled by Paul A. Brown and numerous collaborators for *PMLA*, which since the issue for 1956 has been international in scope, are indispensable for all periods of English literature; the student will find convenient the surveys in *The Year's Work in English Studies*, issued annually since 1919 by the English Assoc., and *The Year's Work in Modern Language Studies*, since 1931, published by the M.H.R.A. The first issue of Rossell H. Robbins, "Middle English Research in Progress," appeared in *Neuphil. Mitteilungen*, LXV (1964). 360-366, with continuations appearing annually.

110   More recent general surveys of Middle English literature, at least in part, include H. S. Bennett, *Chaucer and the Fifteenth Century* (1947) and E. K. Chambers, *English Literature at the Close of the Fifteenth Century* (1946), both in the *Oxford History of English Literature;* George Kane, *Middle English Literature: A Critical Study of the Romances, the Religious Lyrics, 'Piers Plowman'* (1951); Margaret Schlauch, *English Medieval Literature and Its Social Foundations* (Warzawa, 1956); John Speirs, *Medieval English Poetry: The Non-Chaucerian Tradition* (1957); *The Pelican Guide to English Literature*, ed. Boris Ford: Vol. 1: *The Age of Chaucer* (1954, rev. 1963). The collected essays of Dorothy Everett, *Essays on Middle English Literature*, ed. Patricia Kean (Oxford, 1955), and of Laura Hibbard Loomis, *Adventures in the Middle Ages* (1962), gather together conveniently articles previously scattered. *Middle English Survey*, ed. Edward Vasta (Notre Dame, Ind., 1965) is an anthology of critical and interpretive articles.—For the Old French background Paul Zumthor, *Histoire littéraire de la France médiévale* (Paris, 1954), and Jessie Crosland, *Medieval French Literature* (Oxford, 1956), the latter often perceptive in its critical appraisals, may be consulted. R. Bossuat, *Manuel bibliographique de la littérature française du moyen âge* (Melun, 1951; two supplements, Paris, 1955, 1961) is indispensable in spite of many small inaccuracies. Ernst R. Curtius, *European Literature in the Latin Middle Ages*, trans. W. R. Trask (1953; German text, 1948), is broad in range and stimulating. W. T. H. Jackson, *The Literature of the Middle Ages* (1960), will help the student to see English literature in its European context.—The historical background has been enriched by several additional volumes in the *Oxford History of England:* Austin L. Poole, *From Domesday Book to Magna Carta, 1087-1216* (2ed, 1955), F. M. Powicke, *The Thirteenth Century, 1216-1307* (2ed, 1962), May McKisack, *The Fourteenth Century, 1307-1399* (1959), and E. F. Jacob, *The Fifteenth Century, 1399-1485* (1961). A revised and rewritten edition of *Medieval England* is ed. by A. L. Poole (2v, Oxford, 1958). Two excellent shorter treatments are Doris M. Stenton, *English Society in the Early Middle Ages, 1066-1307* (2ed, 1952), and A. R. Myers, *England in the Late Middle Ages, 1307-1536* (1952), both Pelican Books. *The Shorter Cambridge Medieval History*, ed. Philip Grierson (2v, 1952) is an abridgment of the

larger work. Indispensable for the background of much religious literature are Dom David Knowles, *The Monastic Order in England* (2ed, Cambridge, 1963), and *The Religious Orders in England* (3v, Cambridge, 1948-59).

II. The Survival of the Native Tradition

118 The items of R. M. Wilson in note 6 have been incorporated in *The Lost Literature of Medieval England* (1952). Cecilia Sisam, "The Scribal Tradition of the *Lambeth Homilies*," *RES*, n.s. II (1951). 105-113, is a valuable study leading to important general conclusions.

123 Betty Hill, "The 'Luue Ron' and Thomas de Hales," *MLR*, LIX (1964). 321-330, supplies important new data. Thomas of Hales wrote also in Latin and French. For an Anglo-Norman sermon by him see M. Dominica Legge, *Anglo-Norman Literature and Its Background* (Oxford, 1963). Of great interest for the Katherine Group is the *Facsimile of MS Bodley 34: St. Katherine, St. Margaret, St. Juliana, Hali Meiðhad, Sawles Warde,* ed. N. R. Ker (1960; *EETS*, 247).

125 The edition of the *St. Juliana* by Miss d'Ardenne mentioned in note 20 has been reprinted (1961; *EETS*, 248).

126 Additional evidence for Herefordshire is offered by Cecily Clark, "*Sawles Warde* and Herefordshire," *N&Q*, CXCIX (1954). 140.

III. The Ancrene Riwle

127 The intention of the *EETS* mentioned in note 1 is steadily being carried out. The following MSS have been printed: Cotton MS Nero A. XIV, ed. Mabel Day (1952; *EETS*, 225); Gonville and Caius College MS 234/120, ed. R. M. Wilson, 1954; *EETS*, 229); BM MS Royal 8 C.I., ed. Albert C. Baugh (1965; *EETS*, 232); Corpus Christi College, Cambridge MS 402 (*Ancrene Wisse*), ed. J. R. R. Tolkien (1962; *EETS*, 249); Cotton MS Titus D. XVIII, ed. Frances M. Mack (1963; *EETS*, 252); the second French version, from Trin. Coll., Cambridge MS R. 14. 7, etc., ed. W. H. Trethewey (1958; *EETS*, 240). See also W. H. Trethewey, "The Seven Deadly Sins and the Devil's Court in the Trinity College Cambridge French Text of the *Ancrene Riwle*," *PMLA*, LXV (1950). 1233-1246; John H. Fisher, "The French Versions of the *Ancrene Riwle*," *Middle Ages—Reformation—Volkskunde: Festschrift for John G. Kunstmann* (Chapel Hill, 1959; *Univ. of No. Carolina Stud. in the Germanic Lang. and Lit.*, No. 26), pp. 65-74; *The Ancrene Riwle: The Corpus MS. Ancrene Wisse*, trans. M. B. Salu (1955; *Orchard Books*); E. J. Dobson, "The Affiliations of the Manuscripts of *Ancrene Wisse*," *English and Medieval Studies Presented to J. R. R. Tolkien* (1962), pp. 128-163; Charlotte D'Evelyn, "Notes on Some Interrelations between the Latin and English Texts of the *Ancrene Riwle*," *PMLA*, LXIV (1949). 1164-1179.

128 That English was the original language of the *Ancrene Riwle* has become clear from Miss D'Evelyn's article just mentioned and especially from Hans Käsmann, "Zur Frage der ursprünglichen Fassung der *Ancrene Riwle*,"

Anglia, LXXV (1957). 134-156. *The Tretyse of Loue*, ed. John H. Fisher (1951; *EETS*, 223), derives in part from the *Ancrene Riwle*. See also John H. Fisher, "Continental Associations for the *Ancrene Riwle*," *PMLA*, LXIV (1949). 1180-1189.

133 C. H. Talbot, "Some Notes on the Dating of the *Ancrene Riwle*," *Neophilologus*, XL (1956). 38-50, offers important evidence for dating the work in the latter half of the twelfth century, possibly the closing years of the century. Peter Hackett, "The Anchoresses' Guide," *The Month*, n.s. XXIII (1960). 227-240, is a sensible survey.

134 *þe Wohunge of Ure Lauerd*, ed. W. Meredith Thompson (1958; *EETS*, 241).

IV. Anglo-Norman Literature

135 The best treatment of Anglo-Norman literature is now M. Dominica Legge, *Anglo-Norman Literature and its Background* (Oxford, 1963), to which may be added her earlier book, *Anglo-Norman in the Cloisters: The Influence of the Orders upon Anglo-Norman Literature* (Edinburgh, 1950; *Edinburgh Univ. Pub.: Lang. & Lit.*, No. 2). The *Dictionnaire des lettres françaises publié sous la direction du Cardinal Georges Grente. Le Moyen Age*, préparé par R. Bossuat, *et al.* (Paris, 1964), contains articles (of unequal value) on all the works mentioned in the present chapter. Much the best review of the current status of Anglo-Norman scholarship is K. V. Sinclair, "Anglo-Norman Studies: The Last Twenty Years," *Australian Jour. of French Stud.*, II (1965). 113-155, 225-278. Ruth J. Dean, "A Fair Field Needing Folk: Anglo-Norman," *PMLA*, LXIX (1954). 965-978, is useful.

136 On Eleanor of Aquitaine see E. R. Labande, "Pour une image véridique d'Aliénor d'Aquitaine," *Bull. Soc. des Antiquaires de l'Ouest*, 4th Ser., II (1953). 175-234; Rita Lejeune, "Rôle littéraire d'Aléanor d'Aquitaine et de sa famille," *Cultura Neolatina*, XLV (1954). 5-57, both being supplementary to the basic account in Alfred Richard, *Histoire des comtes de Poitou, 778-1204* (Paris, 1903), II. 54-457. The major part of W. F. Schirmer and U. Broich, *Studien zum literarischen Patronat im England des 12. Jahrhunderts* (Köln, 1962), is the discussion (by Broich) of Henry II as a literary patron. Florence McCulloch, *Medieval Latin and French Bestiaries* (Chapel Hill, 1960; *Univ. of No. Carolina Stud. in the Romance Lang. and Lit.*, No. 33), may be read in connection with the *Bestiaire* of Philippe de Thaün.

137 The Latin and Anglo-Norman lives of St. Edmund by Matthew Paris are discussed by C. H. Lawrence in *St. Edmund of Abingdon: A Study in Hagiography and History* (Oxford, 1960). Alexander Bell, "Notes on Two Anglo-Norman Saints' Lives," *PQ*, XXXV (1956). 48-59, discusses a *St. Osith* in the Welbeck Abbey MS and *La Passiun de Seint Edmund* in a Caius MS. *The Life of St. Catherine* by Clemence of Barking is edited by William Macbain (Oxford, 1964; *Anglo-Norman Text Soc.*, No. 18).

138 Alexander Bell (ed.), *L'Estoire des Engleis* by Geffrei Gaimar (Oxford, 1960; *Anglo-Norman Text Soc.*, Nos. 14-15) on which Ronald N. Walpole, "A

New Edition of Geffrei Gaimar's *L'Estoire des Engleis,*" *PQ,* XLI (1962). 373-385, is a critique.

139 Iain MacDonald, "The Chronicle of Jordan Fantosme: Manuscripts, Author, and Versification," *Studies in Medieval French Presented to Alfred Ewert* (Oxford, 1961), pp. 242-258. The *Chronicle* of the Dominican friar Nicholas Trevet (*c.* 1335) has not yet been edited. See, however, Ruth J. Dean, "The Manuscripts of Nicholas Trevet's Anglo-Norman *Chronicles,*" *Medievalia et Humanistica,* XIV (1962). 95-105. Also pertinent here are Isabel S. T. Aspin (ed.), *Anglo-Norman Political Songs* (Oxford, 1953; *Anglo-Norman Text Soc.,* No. 11) and Carl Selmer (ed.), *Navigatio Sancti Brendani Abbatis from Early Latin MSS* (Notre Dame, 1959). R. L. G. Ritchie, "The Date of the *Voyage of St. Brendan,*" *MA,* XIX (1950). 64-66, suggests that it was dedicated to Queen Maud and dates it before May 1, 1118, possibly *c.* 1106.

140 Sister Amelia Klenke has edited *Three Saints' Lives by Nicholas Bozon* (St. Bonaventure, N.Y., 1947; *Franciscan Inst. Pub., Hist. Ser.,* No. 1) and *Seven More Poems by Nicholas Bozon* (St. Bonaventure, N.Y., 1951; same ser., No. 2), the attribution of some of the latter being open to question. In "Nicholas Bozon," *MLN,* LXIX (1954). 256-260, she continues to argue that Bozon belonged to the diocese of York rather than Lincoln. New data on Peter of Peckham are given by M. Dominica Legge in "*La Lumiere as Lais*—a Postscript," *MLR,* XLVI (1951). 191-195, and *Anglo-Norman in the Cloisters,* pp. 63-68. For a summary of and selections (modernized) from the *Lumiere* see Charles V. Langlois, *La Vie en France au moyen âge* (4v, Paris, 1924-28), IV. 66-119. William of Wadington's authorship of the *Manuel des Péchés,* long considered doubtful, is now generally given up. The text is being edited for the Anglo-Norman Text Society by E. J. Arnould. See also Charlton Laird, "Character and Growth of the *Manuel des Pechiez,*" *Traditio,* IV (1946). 253-306. Though not mentioned in the text, worth noting is Henry of Lancaster's *Livre de Seyntz Medicines* (1352), ed. E. J. Arnould (Oxford, 1940; *Anglo-Norman Text Soc.,* No. 2). Cf. also the editor's study, *Étude sur le Livre des saintes medecines du duc Henri de Lancastre* (Paris, 1948), and R. W. Ackerman, "The Traditional Background of Lancaster's *Livre,*" *L'Esprit Créateur,* II (1962). 114-118.

141 On Robert de Boron see Mary E. Giffin, "A Reading of Robert de Boron," *PMLA,* LXXX (1965). 499-507. *The Romance of Horn by Thomas,* ed. Mildred K. Pope and T. B. W. Reid (2v, Oxford, 1955-64; *Anglo-Norman Text Soc.,* Nos. 9-10, 12-13). Brian Foster, "The *Roman de toute chevalerie:* Its date and author," *French Studies,* IX (1955). 154-158, assigns the romance to shortly after 1150. E. A. Francis, "The Background of 'Fulk FitzWarin,'" *Studies in Medieval French Presented to Alfred Ewert* (Oxford, 1961), pp. 322-327, may be mentioned.

V. Early Latin Writers

144 On John of Salisbury see Hans Liebeschütz, *Medieval Humanism in the Life and Writings of John of Salisbury* (1950; *Stud. of the Warburg Inst.,* 17), Georg Misch, *Studien zur Geschichte der Autobiographie,* V: *Johann von Salisbury und das Problem des mittelalterlichen Humanismus* (Göttingen, 1960;

Nachrichten der Akad. der Wissenschaften in Göttingen, 1960, No. 6), and *The Metalogicon of John of Salisbury, a Twelfth-Century Defense of the Verbal and Logical Arts of the Trivium,* trans. Daniel D. McGarry (Berkeley, 1955).

145 André Boutemy, *Gautier Map, conteur anglais* (Brussels, 1945).

146 H. G. Richardson, "Gervase of Tilbury," *History,* XLVI (1961). 102-114, is a good appraisal. For Giraldus Cambrensis should be noted *The First Version of the Topography of Ireland,* trans. John J. O'Meara (Dundalk, 1951), and Thomas Jones, *Gerald the Welshman's 'Itinerary through Wales' and 'Description of Wales': An Appreciation and Analysis* (Aberystwyth, 1950; also in *The National Library of Wales Jour.,* VI).

147 *The Historia Novella* by William of Malmesbury and the *Gesta Stephani* have both been edited by K. R. Potter (1955) for *Nelson's Medieval Classics.*

148 Richard Vaughan, *Matthew Paris* (Cambridge, 1958; *Cambridge Stud. in Medieval Life and Thought,* n.s., vol. 6) is excellent.

149 Geoffrey B. Riddehough, "A Forgotten Poet: Joseph of Exeter," *JEGP,* XLVI (1947). 254-259, and "Joseph of Exeter: The Cambridge Manuscript," *Speculum,* XXIV (1949). 389-396, should be noted. New translations of some Goliardic poems have been published by the translator, George F. Whicher, *The Goliardic Poets: Medieval Latin Songs and Satires* (n.p., 1949). On Serlo of Wilton see Albert C. Friend, "The Proverbs of Serlo of Wilton," *MS,* XVI (1954). 179-218, and *Serlon de Wilton: Poèmes latins, texte critique* . . . ed. Jan Öberg (Stockholm, 1965; *Acta Universitatis: Studia Latina,* XIV). The best treatment of Nigel Wireker (properly Nigel de Longchamps) is the introduction to A. Boutemy, *Nigellus de Longchamp, dit Wireker,* vol. 1 (Paris, 1959). The *Speculum Stultorum* has been edited by by J. H. Mozley and R. R. Raymo (Berkeley, 1960; *Calif. Stud. in English*) and there is now an excellent translation, *The Book of Daun Burnel the Ass,* trans. Graydon W. Regenos (Austin, Texas, 1959).

150 Theodore Silverstein, "Daniel of Morley, English Cosmogonist and Student," *MS,* X (1948). 179-196. E. Westacott, *Roger Bacon in Life and Legend* (1953), Theodore Crowley, *Roger Bacon: The Problem of the Soul in his Philosophical Writings* (Dublin, 1950), Stewart C. Easton, *Roger Bacon and His Search for a Universal Science: A Reconsideration of the Life and Work of Roger Bacon in the Light of His Own Stated Purposes* (Oxford, 1952), and Erich Heck, *Roger Bacon: Ein mittelalterlicher Versuch einer historischen und systematischen Religionswissenschaft* (Bonn, 1957, offset typescript) contribute, each by its own approach, to our understanding of Bacon. On Ailred of Rievaulx see Amédée Hallier, *Un éducateur monastique: Aelred de Rievaulx* (Paris, 1959); *The Life of Ailred of Rievaulx by Walter Daniel,* trans. F. M. Powicke (1950); and Carleton M. Sage, "The Manuscripts of St. Aelred," *Cath. Hist. Rev.,* XXXIV (1949). 437-445. We should now add to note 19 Sir Maurice Powicke, "Robert Grosseteste, Bishop of Lincoln," *Bull. John Rylands Library,* XXXV (1953). 482-507, and D. A. Callus (ed.), *Robert Grosseteste, Scholar and Bishop: Essays in Commemoration of the Seventh Century of His Death* (Oxford, 1955). Alfred C. Friend, "Master Odo of Cheriton," *Speculum,* XXIII (1948). 641-658, includes new biographical material and a consideration of the dates of his works. N. Denholm Young, "Richard de Bury (1287-1345)," *Trans. Royal Hist. Soc.,* 4th Ser., XX (1937), reprinted in his *Collected Papers on Mediaeval Subjects* (Oxford,

1946), pp. 1-25, makes significant additions to our knowledge, especially to the important articles of J. DeGhellinck, "Un évêque bibliophile au XIV⁰ siècle: Richard Aungerville de Bury (1345)," *Revue d'histoire ecclésiastique,* xviii (1922). 271-312, 482-508; xix (1923). 157-200. New evidence on the date of Bromyard's *Summa Predicantium* (earlier fourteenth century) is given in W. A. Pantin, *The English Church in the Fourteenth Century,* p. 147.

VI. Wit and Wisdom

153 The work of Arngart has been completed by a second volume (Lund, 1955), containing the texts.

154 Most important is N. R. Ker's *The Owl and the Nightingale, reproduced in facsimile from the surviving manuscripts, Jesus Coll. Oxford 29 and B. M. Cotton Caligula A. IX* (1963; *EETS,* 251). The Cotton MS has been edited by Eric G. Stanley (1960; *Nelson's Medieval and Renaissance Library*). There is a verse translation of the poem by Graydon Eggers (Durham, N. C., 1955). The following items deserve mention: Bertil Sundby, *The Dialect and Provenance of the Middle English Poem 'The Owl and the Nightingale': A Linguistic Study* (Lund, 1950; *Lund Stud. in English,* xviii), Robert M. Lumiansky, "Concerning *The Owl and the Nightingale,*" *PQ,* xxxii (1953). 411-417, and A. C. Cawley, "Astrology in *The Owl and the Nightingale,*" *MLR,* xlvi (1951). 161-174, the last discussing an astrological allusion possibly bearing on the date of the poem.

VII. For Their Soul's Need

158 J. E. Turville-Petre, "Studies on the *Ormulum* MS," *JEGP,* xlvi (1947). 1-27, R. W. Burchfield, "*Ormulum:* Words Copied by Jan Van Vliet from Parts Now Lost," *English and Medieval Studies Presented to J. R. R. Tolkien* (1962), pp. 94-111, and E. S. Olszewska, "Alliterative Phrases in the *Ormulum:* Some Norse Parallels," *ibid.,* pp. 112-127, are all useful.

162 Nita Scudder Baugh, *A Worcestershire Miscellany, Compiled by John Northwood, c. 1400, ed. from B. M. MS. Add. 37,787* (Philadelphia, 1956), prints the text of the *Body and Soul* and explains the hitherto puzzling disarrangement of the stanzas in this manuscript. Special aspects of the poem are discussed in Robert W. Ackerman, "*The Debate of the Body and the Soul* and Parochial Christianity," *Speculum,* xxxvii (1962). 541-565, and Sister M. Ursula Vogel, *Some Aspects of the Horse and Rider Analogy in* The Debate between the Body and the Soul (Washington, D.C., 1948).

VIII. The Arthurian Legend to Layamon

165 The work of Bruce, while still valuable, must now yield to *Arthurian Literature in the Middle Ages: A Collaborative History,* ed. Roger S. Loomis (Oxford, 1959). See also R. S. Loomis, *Arthurian Tradition and Chrétien de Troyes* (1949) and *The Development of Arthurian Romance* (1963); Jean Marx,

La légende arthurienne et le Graal (Paris, 1952) and *Nouvelles recherches sur la littérature arthurienne* (Paris, 1965). The annual bibliography in *MLQ,* begun by J. J. Parry and continued by Paul A. Brown was discontinued in 1963; the best current guide to Arthurian scholarship is the annual *Bulletin bibliographique de la Société Internationale Arthurienne* (Paris, in prog.). To note 2 should be added *The Continuations of the Old French* Perceval *of Chrétien de Troyes: The First Continuation,* ed. William Roach (3v in 4 to date, Philadelphia, 1949-55).

167   The *Mabinogion* should now be read in the scholarly translation of Gwyn and Thomas Jones (1950). On the historicity of Arthur and the beginnings see Thomas Jones, "The Early Evolution of the Legend of Arthur," *Nottingham Mediaeval Stud.,* VIII (1964). 4-21; John J. Parry, "The Historical Arthur," *JEGP,* LVIII (1959). 365-379, which makes some useful points; William A. Nitze, "Arthurian Names: *Arthur,*" *PMLA,* LXIV (1949). 585-596, 1235.

169   A *Variant Version* of the *Historia Regum Britanniae* was edited by Jacob Hammer (Cambridge, Mass., 1951). On the date of this version see Robert A. Caldwell, "Wace's *Roman de Brut* and the *Variant Version* of Geoffrey of Monmouth's *Historia Regum Britanniae,*" *Speculum,* XXXI (1956). 675-682. For a full discussion of Geoffrey of Monmouth see J. S. P. Tatlock, *The Legendary History of Britain: Geoffrey of Monmouth's Historia Regum Britanniae and Its Early Vernacular Version* (Berkeley, 1950).

170   On Wace see Michel de Roüard, "A propos des sources du *Roman de Rou,*" *Recueil de Travaux offert à M. Clovis Brunel* (2v, Paris, 1955), I. 178-182, Urban T. Holmes, Jr., "Norman Literature and Wace," in *Medieval Secular Literature: Four Essays,* ed. William Matthews (Berkeley, 1965), and Elspeth Yeo, "Wace's *Roman de Brut:* A Newly Discovered Fragment," *Manuscripta,* VIII (1964). 101-104. A new edition of Layamon's *Brut,* ed. G. L. Brook and R. F. Leslie, Vol. I [to line 8020] (1963; *EETS,* 250). See also W. J. Keith, "Laȝamon's *Brut:* The Literary Differences between between the Two Texts," *MA,* XXIX (1960). 161-172, and Herbert Pilch, *Laȝamons 'Brut': Eine literarische Studie* (Heidelberg, 1960; *Anglistische Forsch.,* 91).

IX. The Romance: I

173   The following items concern the Middle English romances generally: Karl Brunner, "Middle English Metrical Romances and Their Audience," *Studies in Medieval Literature,* ed. MacEdward Leach (Philadelphia, 1961), pp. 219-227 (inferences drawn from the character of the MSS) and "Die Überlieferungen der mittelenglischen Versromanzen," *Anglia,* LXXVI (1958). 64-73 (interesting statistics on the dates and the number of the MSS); Dieter Mehl, "Die kürzeren mittelenglischen 'Romanzen' und die Gattungsfrage," *Deutsche Vierteljahrsschrift für Litteraturwissenschaft und Geistesgeschichte,* XXXVIII (1964). 513-533; Albert C. Baugh, "The Authorship of the Middle English Romances," *Annual Bull. of the Modern Humanities Research Assoc.,* No. 22 (1950). 13-28 and "Improvisation in the Middle English Romance," *Proc. Amer. Philos. Soc.,* CIII (1959). 418-454; Gerald Bordman, *Motif-Index of the English Metrical Romances* (Helsinki, 1963; *FF Com.,* vol. 79, no. 190).

175 D. M. Hill, "An Interpretation of *King Horn*," *Anglia*, LXXV (1957). 157-172, finds symbolism in the poem; Charles W. Dunn, "Havelok and Anlaf Cuaran," *Franciplegius: Medieval and Linguistic Studies in Honor of Francis Peabody Magoun, Jr.* (1965), pp. 244-249.

181 On the legend of Alexander see George Cary, *The Medieval Alexander* (Cambridge, 1956).

X. The Romance: II

189 The English Arthurian romances in alliterative verse are discussed by J. L. N. O'Loughlin in *Arthurian Literature in the Middle Ages*, ed. Roger S. Loomis (Oxford, 1959), pp. 520-527, the others by Robert W. Ackerman, *ibid.*, pp. 480-519. Ackerman has also published a most useful *Index of the Arthurian Names in Middle English* (Stanford, 1952; *Stanford Univ. Pub., Univ. Ser., Lang. and Lit.*, x). On the short poem known as *Arthur* see J. Finlayson, "The Source of *Arthur*, an Early Fifteenth-Century Verse Chronicle," *N&Q*, CCV (1960). 46-47, who finds that the principal source is Wace.

190 *Ywain and Gawain* has been edited by A. B. Friedman and N. T. Harrington (1964; *EETS*, 254). *Sir Gawain and the Carl of Carlisle* has been twice edited: by Robert W. Ackerman (Ann Arbor, 1947; *Univ. of Michigan Contrib. in Mod. Phil.*, No. 8) and by Auvo Kurvinen (Helsinki, 1951; *Annales Academiae Scientiarum Fennicae*, Ser. B, vol. 71, pt. 2). M. Mills, "A Mediaeval Reviser at Work," *MA*, XXXII (1963). 11-23, concerns *Libeaus Desconus*.

191 William Matthews, *The Tragedy of Arthur: A Study of the Alliterative 'Morte Arthure'* (Berkeley, 1960); Angus McIntosh, "The Textual Transmission of the Alliterative *Morte Arthure*," *English and Medieval Studies Presented to J. R. R. Tolkien* (1962), pp. 231-240. William A. Nitze, *Perceval and the Holy Grail* (Berkeley, 1949; *Univ. of Calif. Pub. in Mod. Phil.*, vol. 28, no. 5).

192 Thomas C. Rumble, "The Middle English *Sir Tristrem*: Toward A Reappraisal," *Compar. Lit.*, XI (1959). 221-228.

193 Mabel VanDuzee, *A Medieval Romance of Friendship—Eger and Grime* (1963) is a study of the romance.

194 Charles W. Dunn, *The Foundling and the Werwolf: A Literary-Historical Study of 'Guillaume de Palerne'* (Toronto, 1960). L. F. Casson, *The Romance of Sir Degrevant: A Parallel-Text Edition* (1949; *EETS*, 221).

195 Robert J. Geist, "Notes on *The King of Tars*," *JEGP*, XLVII (1948). 173-178, studies the relationship of the MSS and the dialect. Thomas C. Rumble, *The Breton Lays in Middle English* (Detroit, 1965), is a welcome edition of the principal texts. G. V. Smithers, "Story-Patterns in Some Breton Lays," *MA*, XXII (1953). 61-92, is concerned especially with English examples.

196 William C. Stokoe, Jr., "The Double Problem of *Sir Degaré*," *PMLA*, LXX (1955). 518-534, corrects the views set forth by Faust and in the still earlier study of Clark H. Slover, *Sire Degarre: A Study of a Mediaeval Hack Writer's Methods* (Austin, Texas, 1931; *Univ. of Texas Stud. in English*, No. 11). Mention should be made of the edition of *Sir Degare* by Gustav Schliech (Heidelberg, 1929; *Englische Textbibliothek*, XIX), based on all the MSS. A. J. Bliss (ed.), *Sir Launfal* (1960; *Nelson's Medieval and Renaissance Library*) contains also *Sir Landevale* and Marie's *Lanval* in the Appendix. See also M. Mills, "The Composition and Style of the 'Southern' *Octavian, Sir Launfal* and *Libeaus Desconus*," *MA*, XXXI (1962). 88-109. On *Sir Orfeo* see the edition of A. J. Bliss (Oxford, 1954); J. Burke Severs, "The Antecedents of *Sir Orfeo*," *Studies in Medieval Literature*, ed. MacEdward Leach (Philadelphia, 1961), pp. 187-207; D. M. Hill, "The Structure of *Sir Orfeo*," *MS*, XXIII (1961). 136-153; Dorena Allen, "Orpheus and Orfeo: The Dead and the *Taken*," *MA*, XXXIII (1964). 102-111, an interesting theory that the romance represents the classical story as understood by a Celt and represents it in the light of Celtic popular beliefs; B. Mitchell, "The Faery World of *Sir Orfeo*," *Neophilologus*, XLVIII (1964). 155-159.

198 Beverly Boyd (ed.), *The Middle English Miracles of the Virgin* (San Marino, Calif., 1964; *Huntington Library Pub.*). See also R. W. Southern, "The English Origins of the 'Miracles of the Virgin,'" *Medieval and Renais. Stud.*, IV (1958). 176-216, and Harold F. Folland, "Our Lady and Her Miracles," *Western Humanities Rev.*, III (1949). 285-302. Two additional studies of the fabliau should now be consulted: Per Nykrog, *Les Fabliaux: Étude d'histoire littéraire et de stylistique médiévale* (Copenhagen, 1957), and Jean Rychner, *Contributions à l'étude des fabliaux: Variantes, remaniements, dégradations* (2v, Geneva, 1960).

XI. The Omnibus of Religion

200 A number of the works treated in this chapter are considered in W. A. Pantin, *The English Church in the Fourteenth Century* (Cambridge, 1955), chap. x: Religious and Moral Treatises in the Vernacular. See also Morton W. Bloomfield, *The Seven Deadly Sins: An Introduction to the History of a Religious Concept* (East Lansing, 1952).

202 On John Peckham and his Constitutions see Decima L. Douie, *Archbishop Pecham* (Oxford, 1952).

204 D. W. Robertson, Jr., "The Cultural Tradition of *Handlyng Synne*," *Speculum*, XXII (1947). 162-185.

206 Philip Buehler, "The *Cursor Mundi* and Herman's *Bible*—Some Additional Parallels," *SP*, LXI (1964). 485-499; Henning Larsen, "Origo Crucis," in *If by Your Art* (Hunt Festschrift, 1948), pp. 27-33; Paul E. Beichner, "The *Cursor Mundi* and Petrus Riga," *Speculum*, XXIV (1949). 239-250; J. J. Lamberts, "The Noah Story in Cursor Mundi (vv. 1625-1916)," *MS*, XXIV (1962), 217-232, is an attempt at a critical edition of this portion. An edition of *The South English Legendary* has been published by Charlotte D'Evelyn and Anna J. Mill (3v, 1956-9; *EETS*, 235, 236, 241). See also Beverly Boyd, "New Light on *The South English Legendary*," *Texas Stud. in English*, XXXVII (1958). 187-194, and Theodor Wolpers, *Die englische Heiligenlegende des Mittelalters: Eine Formgeschichte des Legendenerzählens von der spätantiken lateinischen Tradition bis zur Mitte des 16. Jahrhunderts* (Tübingen, 1964; *Anglia Beireihe*, 10). After a lapse of many years the edition of an early fifteenth-century Biblical paraphrase is being completed and deserves mention: *A Middle English Metrical Paraphrase of the Old*

Testament, ed. H. Kalen and U. Ohlander (Vols. i-iv, Göteborg, 1922-63; the last three volumes are in *Gothenburg Stud. in English*). See also Urban Ohlander, "Old French Parallels to a Middle English Metrical Paraphrase of the Old Testament," *Gothenburg Stud. in English,* xiv (1962). 203-224.

XII. The Lyric

208   The following discussions and editions may be noted: Arthur K. Moore, *The Secular Lyric in Middle English* (Lexington, Ky., 1951); Rossell H. Robbins (ed.), *Secular Lyrics of the XIVth and XVth Centuries* (2ed, Oxford, 1955); the same editor's *Historical Poems of the XIVth and XVth Centuries* (1959); Henry A. Person (ed.), *Cambridge Middle English Lyrics* (2ed, Seattle, 1962), seventy lyrics from MSS in Cambridge college libraries; R. T. Davies (ed.), *Medieval English Lyrics: A Critical Anthology* (1963); Nita Scudder Baugh (ed.), *A Worcestershire Miscellany Compiled by John Northwood, c. 1400, from B. M. Add. MS 37,787* (Philadelphia, 1956), a collection of religious pieces, mostly lyrical. See also Rossell H. Robbins, "Middle English Lyrics: Handlist of New Texts," *Anglia,* lxxxiii (1965). 35-47.

209   On the sources of the vernacular lyric see Peter Dronke, *Medieval Latin and the Rise of European Love-Lyric* (Cambridge, 1965).

211   For the student who wishes to explore further the convention of Courtly Love, the starting point is the treatise *De Amore* of Andreas Capellanus (*c.* 1185), ed. E. Trojel (Copenhagen, 1892), English translation by John J. Parry, *The Art of Courtly Love* (1941). See also Alexander J. Denomy. *The Heresy of Courtly Love* (1947), D. W. Robertson, Jr., "The Subject of the *De Amore* of Andreas Capellanus," *MP,* l (1953). 145-161, and Don K. Frank, "The Corporeal, the Derogatory and the Stress on Equality in Andreas' *De Amore,*" *Medievalia et Humanistica,* xvi (1964). 30-38. Courtly love, as implied in the text, is illicit, the devotion of the lover to a married woman, exemplified by the relations of Lancelot and Guinevere.

213   Most welcome is the *Facsimile of British Museum MS. Harley 2253,* with intro. by N. R. Ker (1965; *EETS,* 255). Also to be noted are G. D. Brook (ed.), *The Harley Lyrics: The Middle English Lyrics of MS. Harley 2253* (Manchester, 1948) and the important article of Theo. Stemmler, "Zur Datierung des MS. Harley 2253," *Anglia,* lxxx (1962). 111-118, which draws some of its best evidence from an unpublished M.A. thesis by J. A. Gibson (Univ. of London). Political and other allusions require a date about 1340. The Leominster origin rests on dubious evidence (see Ker).

215   Bukofzer's contention has been seriously challenged by B. Schofield, "The Provenance and Date of *Sumer is Icumen in,*" *Music Rev.,* ix (1948). 81-86. For the religious lyric see Stephen Manning, *Wisdom and Number: Toward a Critical Appraisal of the Middle English Religious Lyric* (Lincoln, Neb., 1962); Sister M. Aquinas Chester, "The Latin Hymn and the Middle English Lyric," *Papers of the Michigan Acad.,* xl (1954). 271-283; Ruth E. Messenger, *The Medieval Latin Hymn* (Washington, D.C., 1953); Theodor Wolpers, *Geschichte der englischen Marienlyrik im Mittelalter,*" *Anglia,* lxix (1950). 3-88.

221 On the carol: Richard L. Greene (ed.), *A Selection of English Carols* (Oxford, 1962); Rossell H. Robbins (ed.), *Early English Christmas Carols* (1961); "The Middle English Carol Corpus: Some Additions," *MLN*, LXXIV (1959). 198-208, and "Friar Herbert and the Carol," *Anglia*, LXXV (1957). 194-198; J. Copley, "The 15th Century Carol and Christmas," *N&Q*, CXCIX (1954). 242-243, and "John Audelay's Carols and Music," *ES*, XXXIX (1958). 207-212; and Richard L. Greene, "The Meaning of the Corpus Christi Carol," *MA*, XXIX (1960). 10-21.

XIII. Richard Rolle and Other Mystics

225 Hilda Graef, *The Light and the Rainbow* (1959) traces the history of mysticism from Old Testament times to the late Middle Ages. Shorter surveys are Gerard Sitwell, *Medieval Spiritual Writers* (1961) and Ray C. Petry, *Late Medieval Mysticism* (Philadelphia, 1957).

226 For English mysticism see David Knowles, *The English Mystical Tradition* (1961), Conrad Pepler, *The English Religious Heritage* (1958), Richard M. Wilson, "Three Middle English Mystics [Rolle, Julian of Norwich, Margery Kemp]," *E&S*, n.s. IX (1956). 87-112, and Eric Colledge, *The Medieval Mystics of England* (1962), the last a book of selections with short introductions.

227 An important Rolle text is now available for the first time, the *Melos Amoris*, ed. E. J. F. Arnould (Oxford, 1957). The editor's "Richard Rolle of Hampole," *The Month*, n.s. XXIII (1960). 13-25, is an excellent brief account.

228 The text of the *Incendium Amoris* is available in two editions: *The Incendium Amoris of Richard Rolle*, ed. Margaret Deanesly (Manchester, 1915; *Pub. of the Univ. of Manchester, Hist. Ser.*, No. XXVI) and Dom N. Noetinger, *Le Feu de l'Amour, le Modèle de la Vie Parfaite, le Pater, par Richard Rolle de Hampole* (Tours, 1928). The *De Emendatione Vitae* should be consulted in the edition of Leopold Denis, *Du Péché à l'amour divin ou l'Amendement du Pécheur* (Paris, 1926). See also Margery M. Morgan, "Versions of the Meditations on the Passion Ascribed to Richard Rolle," *MA*, XXII (1953). 93-103.

229 Two additional translations of *The Cloud of Unknowing* have appeared, one by Ira Progoff (1959), the other by Clifton Wolters (1961; *Penguin Books*). *Deonise Hid Diuinite and Other Treatises on Contemplative Prayer Related to 'The Cloud of Unknowing'*, ed. Phyllis Hodgson (1955; *EETS*, 231). Miss Hodgson in "Walter Hilton and *The Cloud of Unknowing*: A Problem of Authorship Reconsidered," *MLR*, L (1955). 395-406, concludes that the *Cloud* is not by Hilton. There are two additional translations of Hilton's principal work: *The Scale of Perfection*, trans. Gerard Sitwell (1953; *Orchard Books*), and *The Ladder of Perfection*, trans. Leo Sherley-Price (1957; *Penguin Books*). Cf. S. S. Hussey, "The Text of *The Scale of Perfection*, Book II," *Neuphil. Mitt.*, LXV (1964). 75-92. Attributed to Hilton is *The Goad of Love: An Unpublished Translation of the Stimulus Amoris formerly attributed to St. Bonaventura*, ed. Clare Kirchberger (1952).

230 For Julian of Norwich the following items should be noted: *The Revelations of Divine Love*, trans. James Walsh (1961; *Orchard Books*); *A Shewing* of God's Love: The Shorter Version of Sixteen Revelations, ed. Sister Anna M. Reynolds (modernized) (1958); P. Franklin Chambers, Juliana of Norwich: An Introductory Appreciation and an Interpretative Anthology (1955); Paul Molinari, Julian of Norwich: The Teaching of a 14th Century English Mystic (1958); Anna M. Reynolds, "Julian of Norwich," The Month, xxiv (1960). 133-144. Katharine Cholmley, Margery Kempe: Genius and Mystic (1947) may be added to the references in note 15.

XIV. The Alliterative Revival

233 On the Pearl poet the following should be noted: Henry L. Savage, The Gawain Poet: Studies in His Personality and Background (Chapel Hill, 1956); The Complete Works of the Gawain-Poet, in a Modern Version with a Critical Introduction, by John Gardner (Chicago, 1965); Coolidge O. Chapman, An Index of Names in Pearl, Purity, Patience, and Gawain (Ithaca, N.Y., 1951; Cornell Stud. in English, xxxviii). There is an edition of Pearl by E. V. Gordon (Oxford, 1953) and an edition with translation and interpretation by Sister M. Vincent Hillmann (Convent Station, N.J., 1961). Among many attempts at explanation and interpretation may be mentioned: Milton R. Stern, "An Approach to The Pearl," JEPG, liv (1955). 684-692; John Conley, "Pearl and a Lost Tradition," ibid., 332-347; Marie P. Hamilton, "The Meaning of the Middle English Pearl," PMLA, lxx (1955). 805-824; Stanton D. Hoffman, "The Pearl: Notes for an Interpretation," MP, lviii (1960). 73-80; F. E. Richardson, "The Pearl: A Poem and Its Audience," Neophilologus, xlvi (1962). 308-316; H. Pilch, "Das mittelenglische Perlengedicht," Neuphil. Mitt., lxv (1964). 427-446; Robert W. Ackerman, "The Pearl-Maiden and the Penny," Romance Phil., xvii (1964). 615-623; C. Carson, "Aspects of Elegy in the Middle English Pearl," SP, lxii (1965). 17-27; A. R. Heiseman, "The Plot of Pearl," PMLA, lxxx (1965). 164-171; P. M. Kean, "Numerical Composition in Pearl," N&Q, ccx (1965). 49-51, the last considering the problem of the extra stanza.

235 John W. Clark, "Observations on Certain Differences in Vocabulary between Cleanness and Sir Gawain and the Green Knight," PQ, xxviii (1949). 261-273. Charles Moorman, "The Role of Narrator in Patience," MP, lxi (1963). 90-95.

236 Much has been written in recent years about the "meaning" of Sir Gawain and the Green Knight, finding a particular allegory or symbolism by emphasizing one or another feature of the poem. Only a limited number of articles can be listed here: John Speirs, "Sir Gawain and the Green Knight," Scrutiny, xvi (1949). 274-300; D. E. Baughan, "The Role of Morgan le Fay . . . ," ELH, xvii (1950). 241-251; G. J. Englehardt, "The Predicament of Gawain," MLQ, xvi (1955). 218-225; Alan M. Markman, "The Meaning of Sir Gawain and the Green Knight," PMLA, lxxii (1957). 574-586; Laura H. Loomis's general survey in Arthurian Literature in the Middle Ages, ed. R. S. Loomis (Oxford, 1959), pp. 528-540; S. R. T. O. D'Ardenne, " 'The Green Count' and Sir Gawain and the Green Knight," RES, n.s. x (1959). 113-126, the Green Count being Amadeus VI, Count of Savoy (1334-83); Hans Schnyder, Sir Gawain and the Green Knight: An Essay in Interpretation (Bern, 1961), exemplifying the exegetical approach, to which M. Mills, "Christian Significance and Romance Tradition in *Sir Gawain and the Green Knight," MLR,* LX (1965) 483-493 is a useful caveat; Morton W. Bloomfield, "Sir Gawain and the Green Knight: An Appraisal," *PMLA,* LXXVI (1961). 7-19; Larry D. Benson, "The Source of the Beheading Episode in *Sir Gawain and the Green Knight," MP,* LIX (1961). 1-12; Marie Borroff, *Sir Gawain and the Green Knight: A Stylistic and Metrical Study* (New Haven, 1962; *Yale Stud. in English,* 152); G. V. Smithers, "What *Sir Gawain and the Green Knight* is about," *MA,* XXXII (1963). 171-189, with which may be read John Burrow, "The Two Confession Scenes in *Sir Gawain and the Green Knight," MP,* LVII (1959). 73-79; R. H. Bowers, "*Gawain and the Green Knight* as Entertainment," *MLQ,* XXIV (1963). 333-341; R. G. Cook, "The Play-Element in *Sir Gawain and the Green Knight," Tulane Stud. in English,* XIII (1963). 5-31; Mother Angela Carson, "The Green Chapel: Its Meaning and Its Function," *SP,* LX (1963). 598-605; David F. Hills, "Gawain's Fault in Sir Gawain and the Green Knight," *RES,* n.s. XIV (1963). 124-131; Stephen Manning, "A Psychological Interpretation of *Sir Gawain and the Green Knight," Criticism,* VI (1964). 165-177; Theodore Silverstein, "The Art of *Sir Gawain and the Green Knight," UTQ,* XXXIII (1964). 258-278; Larry D. Benson, *Art and Tradition in Sir Gawain and the Green Knight* (New Brunswick, N. J., 1965); T. McAlindon, "Magic, Fate, and Providence in Medieval Narrative and *Sir Gawain and the Green Knight," RES,* n.s. XVI (1965). 121-139, which relates the poem to the tradition of Christian hero and magical opposition. See also Larry D. Benson, "The Authorship of St. Erkenwald," *JEGP,* LXIV (1965). 393-405.

XV. Piers Plowman and Other Alliterative Poems

240 On the literature of social protest in general see John D. Peter, *Complaint and Satire in Early English Literature* (Oxford, 1956) and Rossell H. Robbins, "Middle English Poems of Protest," *Anglia,* LXXVIII (1960). 193-203. To note 1 should also be added T. W. Ross, "On the Evil Times of Edward II: A New Version from MS. Bodley 48," *Anglia,* LXXV (1957). 173-193. Jerry D. James, "The Undercutting of Conventions in *Wynnere and Wastoure," MLQ,* XXV (1964). 243-258, sees irony and humor as important stylistic features of the poem.

241 There is a new edition of *The Parlement of the Three Ages* by M. Y. Offord (1959; *EETS,* 246). Since note 7 was originally written two new editions of the A-text of *Piers Plowman* have appeared: *Piers the Plowman: A Critical Edition of the A-Version,* ed. Thomas A. Knott and David C. Fowler (Baltimore, 1952), and *Piers Plowman.* Vol. 1: *The A-version: Will's Visions of Piers Plowman and Do-Well. An edition in the form of Trinity College, Cambridge, MS. R. 3. 14 corrected from other manuscripts with variant readings,* by G. Kane (1960). The translation by Henry W. Wells has been reissued (1959) and a new translation by J. F. Goodridge has been published (1959; *Penguin Books*).

246 J. R. Hulbert, "*Piers the Plowman* after Forty Years," *MP,* XLV (1948). 215-225, challenges R. W. Chambers' arguments for unity of authorship. Other discussions of the three versions include: A. G. Mitchell and G. H. Russell, "The Three Texts of *Piers the Plowman," JEGP,* LII (1953). 445-456; B. F. Huppé, "The Authorship of the A and B Texts of *Piers Plowman," Speculum,* XXII (1947).

578-620; David C. Fowler, *Piers the Plowman: Literary Relations of the A and B Texts* (Seattle, 1961; *Univ. of Wash. Pub. in Lang. and Lit.*, 16); Gordon H. Gerould, "The Structural Integrity of Piers Plowman B," *SP*, XLV (1948). 60-75; T. P. Dunning, "The Structure of the B-Text of *Piers Plowman*," *RES*, n.s. VII (1956). 225-237; E. Talbot Donaldson, *Piers Plowman: The C-Text and its Poet* (New Haven, 1959; *Yale Stud. in English*, 113); and the same author's "Langland on the Incarnation," *ibid.*, n.s. XVI (1965). 349-363; Willi Erzgräber, *William Langlands 'Piers Plowman' (Eine Interpretation des C-Textes)* (Heidelberg, 1957; *Frankfurter Arbeiten aus dem Gebiete der Anglistik u. der Amerika-Studien*, 3); G. Kane, *Piers Plowman: The Evidence for Authorship* (1965).

247 Critical and interpretive studies: D. W. Robertson and Bernard F. Huppé, *Piers Plowman and Scriptural Tradition* (Princeton, 1951; *Princeton Stud. in English*, 31); S. S. Hussey, "Langland, Hilton, and the Three Lives," *RES*, n.s. VII (1956). 132-150; Robert W. Frank, Jr., *'Piers Plowman' and the Scheme of Salvation: An Interpretation of 'Dowel, Dobet, and Dobest'* (New Haven, 1957; *Yale Stud. in English*, 136); John Lawler, *Piers Plowman: An Essay in Criticism* (1962); Elizabeth Salter, *Piers Plowman: An Introduction* (Cambridge, Mass., 1962); Morton W. Bloomfield, *Piers Plowman as a Fourteenth-Century Apocalypse* (New Brunswick, N. J., 1962) and for a briefer statement an article with the same title in the *Centennial Review of Arts and Sciences* (Michigan State Univ.), V (1961). 281-295; Nevill Coghill, "God's Wenches and the Light That Spoke (Some notes on Langland's kind of poetry)," *English and Medieval Studies Presented to J. R. R. Tolkien* (1962), pp. 200-217; Hans Bruneder, *Personifikation und Symbol in William Langlands* Piers Plowman (Vienna, 1963); P. M. Kean, "Love, Law, and *Lewte* in *Piers Plowman*," *RES*, n.s. XV (1964). 241-261; Marshall Walker, "Piers Plowman's Pardon: A Note," *English Studies in Africa*, VIII (1965). 64-70. Because of an important allusion in the poem, mention may be made of *The Sermons of Thomas Brinton, Bishop of Rochester (1373-1389)*, ed. Sister M. Aquinas Devlin (2v, 1954; *Camden Soc.*, Third Ser., LXXXV-LXXXVI), and William J. Brandt, "Remarks on Bishop Thomas Brinton's Authorship of the Sermons in MS. Harley 3760," *MS*, XXI (1959). 291-296, the last a reply to a review in *Speculum*, XXX (1955). 267-271. Brinton, of course, is also known as Brunton.

248 Arthur B. Ferguson, "The Problem of Counsel in *Mum and the Soth-segger*," *SRen*, II (1955). 67-83.

XVI. Chaucer: I

249 The standard edition of Chaucer's works by F. N. Robinson appeared in a revised edition in 1957. *Chaucer's Major Poetry*, ed. Albert C. Baugh (1963) also offers a critical text of nearly all the poetry with extensive annotation. Dudley D. Griffith's *Bibliography of Chaucer, 1908-1953* (Seattle, 1955) supersedes his compilation of 1928. Albert C. Baugh's "Fifty Years of Chaucer Scholarship," *Speculum*, XXVI (1951). 659-672, may permit more recent work to be seen in perspective.

A number of overall treatments of the poet are to be noted, although they vary in character and value: Nevill Coghill, *The Poet Chaucer* (1949); J. S. P. Tatlock, *The Mind and Art of Chaucer* (Syracuse, 1950); Kemp Malone, *Chapters on Chaucer* (Baltimore, 1951); Gordon H. Gerould, *Chaucerian Essays* (Princeton, 1952); G. K. Chesterton, *Chaucer* (1956); Mary Giffin, *Studies on Chaucer and His Audience* (Quebec, 1956); Paull F. Baum, *Chaucer: A Critical Appreciation* (Durham, N.C., 1957); D. S. Brewer, *Chaucer* (2ed, 1960) and *Chaucer in His Time* (1963); Bertrand H. Bronson, *In Search of Chaucer* (Toronto, 1960); Marchette Chute, *Geoffrey Chaucer of England* (2ed, 1962); Edwin J. Howard, *Geoffrey Chaucer* (1964). Collections of reprinted articles and essays have been edited by Edward Wagenknecht (1959) and by Richard J. Schoeck and Jerome Taylor (2v, Notre Dame, 1960-1), both collections in inexpensive paperback form.

As this is being written a new edition of the *Chaucer Life Records,* ed. M. M. Crow and C. C. Olson, is announced as about to appear by the Oxford University Press. P. Godeile, "Chaucer en Espagne?", *Recueil de Travaux offert à M. Clovis Brunel* (2v, Paris, 1955), II. 9-13, calls attention to a document long in print but previously overlooked, indicating that Chaucer was in Spain in February, 1366, on an official mission. P. R. Watts, "The Strange Case of Geoffrey Chaucer and Cecilia Chaumpaigne," *Law Quar. Rev.,* LXIII (1947). 491-515, views the episode as a modern lawyer sees it, but cf. T. F. T. Plucknet, *ibid.,* LXIV, 33-36. Valuable background on life in Chaucer's day is provided in Edith Rickert, *Chaucer's World,* ed. C. C. Olson and M. M. Crow (1948), and, mainly in pictures, Roger S. Loomis, *A Mirror of Chaucer's World* (Princeton, 1965). There is a revised edition of Walter C. Curry, *Chaucer and the Medieval Sciences* (1960). An important article casting doubt on Chaucer's acquaintance at first hand with rhetorical treatises, as claimed by Manly in a widely accepted article, is James J. Murphy, "A New Look at Chaucer and the Rhetoricians," *RES,* n.s. xv (1964). 1-20, in connection with which may be noted the same author's "The Arts of Discourse, 1050-1400," *MS,* XXIII (1961). 194-205, and "The Medieval Arts of Discourse: An Introductory Bibliography," *Speech Monographs,* XXIX (1962). 71-78.

The interpretation of medieval poetry by methods familiar in early scriptural exegesis, with its emphasis on allegory and symbolism, is a subject on which scholars strongly disagree. Its current vogue and attendant reaction spring from two books: D. W. Robertson, Jr., *A Preface to Chaucer: Studies in Medieval Perspective* (Princeton, 1963) and D. W. Robertson, Jr. and Bernard F. Huppé, *Piers Plowman and Scriptural Tradition,* mentioned under the preceding chapter, together with earlier articles by the same authors. Among discussions of the method may be mentioned "Patristic Exegesis in the Criticism of Medieval Literature," *English Inst. Selected Papers, 1958-1959* (1960), a symposium participated in by E. T. Donaldson (The Opposition), R. E. Kaske (The Defense), and Charles Donahue (Summation); Morton W. Bloomfield, "Symbolism in Medieval Literature," *MP,* LVI (1958). 73-81; and R. E. Kaske, "Chaucer and Medieval Allegory," *ELH,* xxx (1963). 175-192, Francis L. Utley, "Robertsonianism Redivivus," *Romance Phil.,* xix (1965). 250-260, the last two review articles on Robertson's book.

251 On Thomas Chaucer's daughter, presumably the poet's granddaughter, see Marjorie Anderson, "Alice Chaucer and her Husbands," *PMLA,* LX (1945). 24-47. On Chaucer's French affiliations see Charles Muscatine, *Chaucer and the French Tradition: A Study in Style and Meaning* (Berkeley, 1957) and Haldeen

Braddy, *Chaucer and the French Poet Graunson* (Baton Rouge, 1947). A new text of the *Roman de la Rose* is being published by Felix Lecoy (vol. 1, Paris, 1965; *CFMA*, 92).

252-6 On the influence of Dante and Boccaccio see Howard Schless, "Chaucer and Dante," *English Inst. Selected Papers, 1958-1959* (1960), pp. 134-171, and Robert A. Pratt, "Chaucer's Use of the *Teseida*," *PMLA*, XLII (1947). 598-621. On the period of Chaucer's work discussed in the present chapter see Wolfgang Clemen, *Chaucer's Early Poetry*, trans. C. A. M. Sym (1964), a translation of *Chaucers frühe Dichtung* (Göttingen, 1963), itself a reworking of the author's earlier *Der junge Chaucer* (1938); Bernard F. Huppé and D. W. Robertson, Jr., *Fruyt and Chaf: Studies in Chaucer's Allegories* (Princeton, 1963), on *The Book of the Duchess* and *The Hous of Fame;* Georgia R. Crampton, "Transitions and Meaning in *The Book of the Duchess*," *JEGP*, LXII (1963). 486-500; *The Parlement of Foulys*, ed. D. S. Brewer (1960); J. A. W. Bennett, *The Parlement of Foules: An Interpretation* (Oxford, 1957); Charles O. McDonald, "An Interpretation of Chaucer's *Parlement of Foules*," *Speculum*, XXX (1955). 444-457; Sanford B. Meech, *Design in Chaucer's 'Troilus'* (Syracuse, N. Y., 1959); Robert A. Pratt, "Chaucer and *Le Roman de Troyle et de Criseida*," *SP*, LIII (1956). 509-539; John J. O'Connor, "The Astronomical Dating of Chaucer's *Troilus*," *JEGP*, LV (1956). 556-562. A second astronomical treatise which there is good reason to believe is by Chaucer has been discovered: *The Equatorie of the Planetis*, ed. from Peterhouse MS. 75. 1, by Derek J. Price (Cambridge, 1955).

XVII. Chaucer: II

258 A. C. Cawley (ed.), *Canterbury Tales* (1958; Everyman's Library, 307) reprints Robinson's text. The following books and articles deserve mention: Muriel Bowden, *A Commentary on the General Prologue to the Canterbury Tales* (1948); Robert M. Lumiansky, *Of Sundry Folk: The Dramatic Principle in the Canterbury Tales* (Austin, Texas, 1955); William W. Lawrence, *Chaucer and the Canterbury Tales* (1950); T. W. Craik, *The Comic Tales of Chaucer* (1964); Ralph Baldwin, *The Unity of the Canterbury Tales* (Copenhagen, 1955; *Anglistica*, V); Harold F. Brooks, *Chaucer's Pilgrims: The Artistic Order of the Portraits in the Prologue* (1962); C. Owen (ed.), *Discussions of the Canterbury Tales* (Boston, 1961); Robert A. Pratt, "The Order of the *Canterbury Tales*," *PMLA*, LXVI (1951). 1141-1167; Donald C. Baker, "The Bradshaw Order of *The Canterbury Tales*: A Dissent," *Neuphil. Mitt.*, LXIII (1962). 245-261; Bernard F. Huppé, *A Reading of the Canterbury Tales* (1964); Paul G. Ruggiers, *The Art of the Canterbury Tales* (Madison, 1965). It is impossible to list the many articles, critical and interpretive, of the individual tales and their tellers; for these the reader is referred to the annual bibliographies mentioned under chap. 1. Because of the interest in and importance of the Wife of Bath mention may be made of Robert A. Pratt, "The Development of the Wife of Bath," *Studies in Medieval Literature*, ed. MacEdward Leach (Philadelphia, 1961), pp. 45-79, and "Jankyn's Book of Wikked Wyves: Medieval Matrimonial Propaganda in the Universities," *Annuale Mediaevale*, III (1962). 5-27.

XVIII. Other Contemporaries of Chaucer

264   John H. Fisher, *John Gower: Moral Philosopher and Friend of Chaucer* (1964) is the first full length treatment of the poet. The same author has published "A Calendar of Documents Relating to the Life of John Gower the Poet," *JEGP*, LVIII (1959). 1-23. Other discussions include Gardiner Stillwell, "John Gower and the Last Years of Edward III," *SP*, XLV (1948). 454-471; Dorothea Siegmund-Schultze, "John Gower und seine Zeit," *Zs. für Anglistik u. Amerikanistik*, III (1955). 5-71; J. B. Dwyer, "Gower's *Mirour* and Its French Sources: A Reexamination of Evidence," *SP*, XLVIII (1951). 482-505; Lewis Thorpe, "A Source for the *Confessio Amantis*," *MLR*, XLIII (1948). 175-181.

267   Josephine W. Bennett, *The Rediscovery of Sir John Mandeville* (1954; *MLA Monograph Ser.*, XIX) must be given precedence over the references in note 11. Mrs. Bennett vigorously attacks the testimony of Jean d'Outremeuse, produces many additional John Mandevilles in England, including the region of St. Albans, and believes that some one of them was the probable author. She argues (less convincingly) for 1356 as the date of composition. Malcolm Letts, *Sir John Mandeville: The Man and His Book* (1949), retains more of the older views. Letts has also edited the French text (2v, 1953; *Hakluyt Soc.*). An abridged English version is edited by M. C. Seymour, *The Bodley Version of Mandeville's Travels . . . with Parallel Extracts from the Latin Text* (1963; EETS, 253) and has discussed "The Origin of the Egerton Version of *Mandeville's Travels*," *MA*, XXX (1961). 159-169. J. D. Thomas, "The Date of *Mandeville's Travels*," *MLN*, LXXII (1957). 165-169, dates the English translation between 1367 and 1370.

268   David C. Fowler throws "New Light on John of Trevisa," *Traditio*, XVIII (1962). 289-317. Two items on Usk deserve mention: Claes Schaar, *Notes on Thomas Usk's 'Testament of Love'* (Lund, 1950; *Acta Univ. Lundensis*, N. F. avd. 1, Bd. 46, pp. 1-46) and S. K. Heninger, Jr., "The Margarite-Pearl Allegory in Thomas Usk's *Testament of Love*," *Speculum*, XXXII (1957). 92-98.

270   There have been important developments in Wyclif studies, especially the Wyclifite Bible. To be noted are Joseph H. Dahmus, *The Prosecution of John Wyclyf* (New Haven, 1952); Kenneth B. McFarlane, *John Wycliffe and the Beginnings of English Nonconformity* (1952); Edward A. Block, *John Wyclif, Radical Dissenter* (San Diego, Calif., 1962; *San Diego State Coll., Humanities Monograph Ser.*, Vol. 1, No. 1); J. A. Robson, *Wyclif and the Oxford Schools: The Relation of the 'Summa de Ente' to Scholastic Debates at Oxford in the Later Fourteenth Century* (Cambridge, 1961; *Cambridge Stud. in Medieval Life and Thought*, n.s. VIII); Margaret W. Ransom, "The Chronology of Wyclif's English Sermons," *Research Stud. of the State College of Washington*, XVI (1948). 67-114. The most important contribution to our knowledge of the Wyclif Bible since the present chapter was written is Sven L. Fristedt, *The Wycliffe Bible*, Part I: *The Principal Problems connected with Forshall and Madden's Edition* (Stockholm, 1953; *Stockholm Stud. in English*, IV). Whether we accept his views as to Wyclif's more direct participation in the work of translation and revision, Fristedt's book must be the starting point for any future work in both text and authorship. See also the same author's "The Authorship of the Lollard

Bible: Summary and Amplification of the Wyclyffe Bible, Part I," *Studier i Modern Språkvetenskap* (Uppsala), xix (1956). 28-41, a necessary supplement to his book. Bodl. MS. 959, though not the original copy of the translator, as Forshall and Madden thought, is (the part from Genesis to Baruch 3:20) still the earliest and most important MS of the Early Version. This is being edited by Conrad Lindberg (3v, Stockholm, 1959-63; the last two volumes are in *Stockholm Stud. in English,* viii, x). See also Sven L. Fristedt, "The Dating of the Earliest Manuscript of the Wycliffite Bible," *Studier i Modern Språkvetenskap,* n.s. 1 (1956-9). 79-85. Mention may also be made of Henry Hargraves, "An Intermediate Version of the Wycliffite Old Testament," *Studia Neophil.,* xxviii (1956). 130-147, and David C. Fowler, "John Trevisa and the English Bible," *MP,* lviii (1960). 81-98, which claims a part for Trevisa in the work of translation.

XIX. The Beginnings of the Drama

273 Carl J. Stratman, *Bibliography of Medieval Drama* (Berkeley, 1954) is a convenient tool. Hardin Craig, *English Religious Drama of the Middle Ages* (Oxford, 1955) is a valuable contribution. Arnold Williams, *The Drama of Medieval England* (East Lansing, 1961) is a briefer treatment. O. B. Hardison, Jr., *Christian Rite and Christian Drama in the Middle Ages: Essays in the Origin and Early History of Modern Drama* (Baltimore, 1965), questions some of the traditional views. Useful for comparison with English developments is Grace Frank, *The Medieval French Drama* (Oxford, 1954).

276 *Le Mystère d'Adam* (*Ordo representacionis Ade*) has been edited by Paul Aebischer (Geneva, 1963).

277 The first volume of Glynne Wickham, *Early English Stages, 1300 to 1660* (1959) treats the period here discussed. On the English cycles in general see Eleanor Prosser, *Drama and Religion in the English Mystery Plays: A Re-evaluation* (Stanford, 1961; *Stanford Stud. in Lang. and Lit.,* xxiii) and Jerome Taylor, "The Dramatic Structure of the Middle English Corpus Christi, or Cycle Plays," in *Literature and Society,* ed. Bernice Slate (Lincoln, Neb., 1964), pp. 175-186.

279 A modernized version of the *York Plays* has been prepared by John S. Purvis (1957). See also J. W. Robinson, "The Art of the York Realist," *MP,* lx (1963). 241-251.

280 The translation of *The Wakefield Mystery Plays* by Martial Rose (1961) has a useful introduction. Other discussions of the Towneley cycle include: Arnold Williams, *The Characterization of Pilate in the Towneley Plays* (East Lansing, 1950); Martin Stevens, "The Composition of the Towneley *Talents* Play: A Linguistic Examination," *JEGP,* lviii (1959). 423-433; A. C. Cawley (ed.), *The Wakefield Pageants in the Towneley Cycle* (Manchester, 1958); John E. Bernbrock, "Notes on the Towneley Cycle *Slaying of Abel*," *JEGP,* lxii (1963). 317-322; Howard H. Schless, "The Comic Element in the Wakefield Noah," *Studies in Medieval Literature,* ed. MacEdward Leach (Philadelphia, 1961), pp. 229-243; Francis J. Thompson, "Unity in *The Second Shepherds' Play*," *MLN,* lxiv (1949). 302-306.

281 F. M. Salter, *Mediaeval Drama in Chester* (Toronto, 1955).

283 Arnold Williams, "The English Moral Play before 1500," *Annuale Mediaevale*, IV (1963). 5-22.

285 Jacob Bennett, "The *Castle of Perseverance*: Redactions, Place, and Date," *MS*, XXIV (1962). 141-152; Richard Southern, *The Medieval Theatre in the Round: A Study of the Staging of 'The Castle of Perseverance' and Related Matters* (1957); John J. Molloy, *A Theological Interpretation of the Moral Play, Wisdom, Who Is Christ* (Washington, D. C., 1952); Sister Mary P. Coogan, *An Interpretation of the Moral Play 'Mankind'* (Washington, D. C., 1947); Donald C. Baker, "The Date of *Mankind*," *PQ*, XLII (1963). 90-91, suggests 1464-69 on numismatic evidence.

286 Everyman has been edited by A. C. Cawley (Manchester, 1961). See also Henry de Vocht, *Everyman: A Comparative Study of Texts and Sources* (Louvain, 1947; *Materials for the Study of the Old English Drama*, n.s. xx); J. Van Mierlo, *De prioriteit van Elckerlyck tegenover Everyman gebandhaafd* (Antwerp, 1948; *Kon. VI. Acad. voor Taal en Letterkunde*, Reeks III, Nr. 27); R. W. Zandvoort, "Everyman—Elckerlijc," *Études Anglaises*, XI (1953). 1-15; Lawrence V. Ryan, "Doctrine and Dramatic Structure in *Everyman*," *Speculum*, XXXII (1957). 722-735.

XX. Ebb Tide

288 H. S. Bennett's *Chaucer and the Fifteenth Century* has been mentioned under Chap. I.

289 Elizabeth Zeeman, "Nicholas Love—a Fifteenth-Century Translator," *RES*, n.s. VI (1955) is a good treatment.

293 Ethel Seaton, *Sir Richard Roos, c. 1410-1482, Lancastrian Poet* (1961) identifies the poet (not the Richard Ros previously accepted), traces his family and his own career in detail, and claims on highly questionable grounds his authorship of a large corpus of English verse. There is an edition of *The Floure and the Leafe* and *The Assembly of Ladies* by D. A. Pearsall (1962). See also this editor's "*The Assembly of Ladies* and *Generydes*," *RES*, n.s. XII (1961). 229-237. The Scottish Chaucerians are discussed in A. M. Kinghorn, "The Mediaeval Makars," *Texas Stud. in Lit. and Lang.*, I (1959). 73-88, Kurt Wittig, *The Scottish Tradition in Literature* (Edinburgh, 1958), and James Kinsley (ed.), *Scottish Poetry: A Critical Survey* (1955), pp. 1-32 (by the editor).

294 There has been considerable interest in Henryson: Marshall W. Stearns, *Robert Henryson* (1949); Charles Elliott (ed.), *Robert Henryson: Poems Selected . . .* (Oxford, 1963; *Clarendon Medieval and Tudor Ser.*); Mary Rowlands, "The Fables of Robert Henryson," *Dalhousie Rev.*, XXXIX (1960). 491-502; Denton Fox, "Henryson's *Fables*," *ELH*, XXIX (1962). 337-356; David K. Crowne, "A Date for the Composition of Henryson's *Fables*," *JEGP*, LXI (1962). 583-590, suggesting a date not long after 1485 or 1486; Richard Bauman, "The Folktale and Oral Tradition in the Fables of Robert Henryson," *Fabula*, VI (1963). 108-124. On *The Testament of Cresseid* see excellent essay by E. M. W. Tillyard in *Five Poems, 1470-1870* (1948); A. C. Spearing, "*The Testament of Cresseid* and the 'High Concise Style'," *Speculum*, XXXVII (1962). 208-225; Douglas Duncan,

"Henryson's *Testament of Cresseid*," *EIC*, xi (1961). 128-135; Sydney Harth, "Henryson Reinterpreted," *ibid.*, 471-480 (a reply to the preceding item); Charles Elliott, "Two Notes on Henryson's *Testament of Cresseid*," *JEGP*, LIV (1955). 241-254. Charles d'Orléans' authorship of the English renderings of his poems has been denied. See Daniel Poirion, "Création poétique et composition romanesque dans les premiers poèmes de Charles d'Orléans," *Revue des sciences humaines*, n.s. fasc. 90 (1958). 185-211, and Sergio Cigada, *L'Opera poetica di Charles d'Orléans* (Milan, 1960). But see the vigorous rebuttal of John Fox, "Charles d'Orléans, poète anglais," *Romania*, LXXXVI (1965). 433-462. See also Harold Watson, "Charles d'Orléans: 1394-1465," *RR*, LVI (1965). 3-11.

295 W. F. Schirmer, *John Lydgate: A Study in the Culture of the XVth Century* (1961) is a translation by Ann E. Keep of the German original (Tübingen, 1952). Alain Renoir, "John Lydgate, Poet of the Transition," *English Miscellany*, XI (1960). 9-19, is a suggestive article, and see his *John Lydgate, Poet of Transition* (Cambridge, Mass., 1966).

296 See Alain Renoir, "The Immediate Source of Lydgate's *Siege of Thebes*," *Studia Neophil.*, XXXIII (1961). 86-95 and James M. Clark, "The Dance of Death in Medieval Literature: Some Recent Theories of Its Origin," *MLR*, XLV (1950). 336-345. The Pynson edition (1511) of *The Gouernaunce of Kynges and Prynces* is edited in facsimile by D. T. Starnes (Gainesville, Fla., 1957; *SF&R*).

297 There is an essay on Hoccleve in H. S. Bennett, *Six Medieval Men and Women* (Cambridge, 1955). The same author notes in "Thomas Hoccleve's Death," *LTLS*, Dec. 25, 1953, p. 833, that Hoccleve's corrody in the priory of Southwick was given to another on Aug. 18, 1437, which would normally imply his death, but so early a date would leave unexplained the *Balade to my gracious Lord of York* which has generally been dated *c.* 1448. See also H. C. Schulz, "Thomas Hoccleve, Scribe," *Speculum*, XII (1937). 71-81, which should have been mentioned in the original edition of this book, and Beverly Boyd, "Hoccleve's Miracle of the Virgin," *Univ. of Texas Stud. in English*, XXXV (1956). 116-122.

298 A. I. Doyle, "More Light on John Shirley," *MA*, XXX (1961). 93-101, offers new biographical matter including Shirley's will.

XXI. Looking Forward

300 Robert W. Ackerman, "Henry Lovelich's *Merlin*," *PMLA*, LXVII (1952). 473-484.

302 J. A. Mulders (ed.), *'The Cordyal' by Anthony Woodville, Earl Rivers* (Nijmegen, 1962). K. B. McFarlane, "William Worcester: A Preliminary Survey," *Studies Presented to Sir Hilary Jenkinson* (1957), pp. 196-221; Thomas D. Kendrick, "John Rous and William of Worcester," in his *British Antiquity* (1950), pp. 18-33.

303 *Paston Letters*, selected and ed. by Norman Davis (Oxford, 1958); Norman Davis, *The Language of the Pastons* (1955; *Sir Israel Gollancz Memorial Lecture*). There is a new edition (1957) of the book by R. Weiss mentioned in note 33.

304 Everett H. Emerson, "Reginald Pecock: Christian Rationalist," *Speculum,*
XXXI (1956). 235-242.

305 The discovery and publication of the Winchester MS has greatly stimulated the study of Malory. The text of Vinaver's edition without the commentary
is available in one volume (Oxford, 1954). Essays by several hands make up two
collective volumes: *Essays on Malory,* ed. J. A. W. Bennett (Oxford, 1963), and
Malory's Originality: A Critical Study of Le Morte Darthur, ed. (and partly
written by) Robert M. Lumiansky (Baltimore, 1964). One essay in the former
volume and all in the latter oppose Vinaver's contention that the *Morte Darthur*
is really eight separate tales rather than a unified work. The controversy has also
been carried on in articles in the learned journals. For these the student must be
referred to the annual bibliographies mentioned in this Supplement under p.
109. Of general interest is Arthur B. Ferguson, *The Indian Summer of English
Chivalry: Studies in the Decline and Transformation of Chivalric Idealism*
(Durham, N.C., 1960).

308 Two excellent collections of ballads are now available in Evelyn K. Wells,
*The Ballad Tree: British and American Ballads, Their Folklore, Verse, and
Music, together with Sixty Traditional Ballads and Their Tunes* (1950) and
MacEdward Leach, *The Ballad Book* (1951). Of first importance is Bertrand H.
Bronson, *The Traditional Tunes of the Child Ballads, with their Texts* (3v,
Princeton, 1959-65, in prog.). Two other books should be mentioned: Tristram
P. Coffin, *The British Traditional Ballad in North America* (Philadelphia, 1951;
Pub. Amer. Folklore Soc., Bibl. Ser., II) and MacEdward Leach and Tristram P.
Coffin (eds.), *The Critics and the Ballad* (Carbondale, Ill., 1961), selected essays.

Index

Raymond of Pennafort,
Summa Casuum Poenitentiae
_(c. 1235)_

Guillaume de Perrault,
Summa de Vitiis &
Summa de Virtutibus
(pre-1261)

Friar Lorens,
Somme des Vices et Vertus
(Somme le Roi)   (1279)

Miroir
du Monde

DATE DUE